Comparative Patterns of Economic Development, 1850-1914

THE JOHNS HOPKINS STUDIES IN DEVELOPMENT

Vernon W. Ruttan and T. Paul Schultz,
Consulting Editors

Comparative Patterns of Economic Development 1850–1914

Cynthia Taft Morris
Irma Adelman

The Johns Hopkins University Press
Baltimore and London

*Published with assistance from
the Karl and Edith Pribram Endowment*

The Johns Hopkins University Press
701 West 40th Street
Baltimore, Maryland 21211
The Johns Hopkins Press Ltd., London

The paper used in this publication meets the minimum requirements
of American National Standard for Information Sciences—
Permanence of Paper for Printed Library Materials, ANSI Z39.48-1984.

Library of Congress Cataloging-in-Publication Data

Morris, Cynthia Taft.
  Comparative patterns of economic development, 1850–1914.

  (Johns Hopkins studies in development)
  Bibliography: p.
  Includes index.
  1. Economic history—1750–1918.   2. Economic development—History.
I. Adelman, Irma.   II. Title.   III. Series.
HC51M645   1988   338.9′009   87-45480
ISBN 0-8018-3507-0 (alk. paper)

To our children and students, who bore with us,
and our husbands, who didn't

Contents

Preface:
Where Angels Fear to Tread

This book is the culmination of a project that began in the summer of 1965. With great optimism we set out to test propositions generated by *Society, Politics, and Economic Development* (Adelman and Morris 1967), by expanding our data set to include earlier development experience. It seemed to us a natural extension of our work to ask whether the hypotheses we had derived from our previous research were supported by the historical record.

The questions we ask here and our methodology are strongly influenced by our previous research on today's developing countries. This research was, and still is, controversial. Our friends gave us dire warnings about the likely even more skeptical reception of our historical endeavor. Historians would dislike our classificatory data and unconventional quantitative approach for doing violence to the complexity and detail of individual national histories. Quantitative economic historians would dislike them just as strongly for departing from accepted procedures of measurement and hypothesis testing. Economists would object to our use of soft data, lack of a priori model specification, and unfamiliar statistical techniques. Undeterred by these warnings and our initial ignorance of history, we were indeed the "fools" who stepped in "where angels fear to tread" (our original title for the book, which we reluctantly abandoned because it did not adequately describe our subject).

Our original intention to analyze contemporary and historical samples together proved infeasible. Our search for measurement procedures suitable to both samples posed intractable conceptual problems, and the technological contexts of growth differed too much between the two. In the present historical work, we focus on understanding better the reasons for the strikingly different paths of economic and institutional change that marked development experience during the nineteenth and early twentieth centuries, a period characterized by the dramatic spread of capitalism throughout the world. The broad hypotheses guiding us are that institutions played a major role in determining development performance, and that institutional and economic influences interacted very differently in countries at dissimilar levels of development and along diverse paths of economic growth.

We owe a major intellectual debt to our friends and critics. Our primary debt is to Svante Wold for the statistical technique and the computer program used to implement it. We are deeply indebted to Herman Wold, who has been a constant source of inspiration and encouragement. George Dalton and Jonathan Hughes warmly supported our endeavors from beginning to end; we had many stimulating discussions with them throughout the years. With comments that ranged from qualified approval to stinging critique, a long line of National Science Foundation reviewers prompted us to clarify our project. Among our most recent intellectual debts are those to a reviewer whose suggested revisions we spent a year accomplishing; another reviewer, whose critical insights greatly improved chapter two; and our friend and critic Jeffrey Williamson, whose well-honed judgments provoked us to sharpen our thinking about the course of poverty in the nineteenth century.

Our obligations to institutions are several. We thank the American University, the Giannini Foundation, the University of California at Berkeley, and Smith College for their support, direct and indirect, over the years. We are indebted to the Karl and Edith Pribram Fund for a very welcome publication subsidy. The National Science Foundation generously provided the American University with three grants covering nine years of our historical work (NSF Grants GS2275, GS3258, and SES79-14243). We particularly appreciate the final grant, which came in the face of continued controversy over our data and approach. Without that support, we would have had to rest with our published articles, and this book could not have been written.

Among those who made this project possible a few are so important that we doubt we could have completed it without them. Margaret and Albert Moe came first in time. Marge typed all the versions of the bibliography and data appendix through 1981 with unparalleled care, accuracy, devotion, and good will, in spite of deteriorating health. Al, refusing recompense other than the satisfaction of his passion for bibliographic work, checked over one hundred pages of references in the Library of Congress catalogs and stacks. The revisions he proposed enable the user to find the references much more easily.

Our debt to Frances Summe-Smith, American University graduate student and research assistant under our final NSF Grant, now a stockbroker, is enormous. She took complete charge of revising and bringing up-to-date the data and classifications for our quantitative economic and demographic indicators, preparing both the classification schemes and the numerous tables of underlying country data and sources. Without her persistence, good judgment, and detective work we could not have included foreign trade or wage variables in our data set. In the final months of data preparation she supervised the completion, correction, typing, and proofing of 250 pages of tables and organized eighteen years of research materials for shipment to Northampton, Massachusetts. We are deeply indebted to her for her intelligence, attention to detail, humor, patience, and friendship.

It is difficult to imagine the project's completion without Ellen Dibble of Smith College, for whose skillful typing, stylistic suggestions, and moral support we are very grateful. She typed many versions of the text, data appendix, and bibliography. She became an expert in style and format, expressing a keen interest in and being challenged by the numerous problems and complications we faced. With great capability and speed, she completed the final photoready appendix and bibliography, undaunted by hundreds of small changes.

We would also especially like to thank Carol Nuckton of the Giannini Foundation, who gave the entire manuscript a much-needed thorough editing, cutting, and simplification of language. We are also indebted to Eli and Gail Liss for an excellent index.

Many of our students have contributed to the project. Mary Phillipides Vlantikas, a top-notch student from American University of Beirut and now with the Federal Reserve of Boston, started the project off in the summer of 1965 with intensive work on social and political variables. Among American University Ph.D. students, Sue Headlee, now at Howard University, stands out for her extensive critique of chapter 1, excellent work on the wage variables, and keen interest in our approach. We value greatly her support and friendship over the past decade. Cindy Lamberts typed and retyped many tables and worked long and well on the foreign dependence variable, in spite of materials with imperialist viewpoints that greatly aggravated her. Henley Portner worked months on the government and transportation variables, and Debby Sandel worked on the political and economic institutional ones; both did an excellent job. At Smith College, Agnes Black undertook a massive consistency check between the bibliography and the appendix citations. Erica Massey spent one whole summer and close to one hundred hours during the final countdown in March 1987 resolving the inconsistencies thus uncovered with superb accuracy and dependability; she also proofed the entire camera-ready data appendix and bibliography. Lisa Genasci gave the manuscript its first skillful outside edit, suggesting many changes designed to help historians read it. Laurie James did a perfectionist job of proofing the text.

Finally, we would like particularly to thank Anders Richter of the Johns Hopkins University Press for his support and confidence from start to finish, and Penny James Moudrianakis for her patient and expert final editing of this and our first book (also published by Johns Hopkins).

We make no apologies for the twenty-one years this project lasted. Much of our work on contemporary development was published during those years. The demands of personal relationships and teaching frequently came first. While we would never have undertaken the project had we realized what it entailed, we have no regrets. Our intellectual journey has been an exciting one. As for the book's defects, we can only say with Cassius: "The fault, dear Brutus, lies not in our stars but in ourselves."

Comparative Patterns of Economic Development, 1850–1914

What our time needs most and lacks most is [an] understanding of the [economic] process, which people are passionately resolved to control. To supply this understanding is to implement that resolve and to rationalize it. This is the only service the scientific worker is, as such, qualified to render. As soon as it is rendered, everyone can draw for himself the practical conclusions appropriate to his individual interests.

—Schumpeter 1939

1 Economic Development and Institutional Change

The purpose of this research is to analyze the dynamics of societies during epochs of rapid economic growth. The study focuses on economic and institutional change in 23 countries during the nineteenth and early twentieth centuries. We investigate the nature and causes of the often striking differences in performance among groups of countries. We explore not only the reasons for successful development but also the causes for incomplete transformation and for failure.

Our central theses are: first, domestic institutional change was the most potent dynamic factor determining the pace and structure of economic development in the nineteenth century; second, initial institutions were more important than initial resources, capital, technology, demography, or markets in determining subsequent patterns of development; and third, there was no unique constellation of institutional prerequisites. We therefore investigate how different clusters of institutions interacted with economic conditions and policy to determine economic performance.

Our method is empirical and quantitative. We categorize the data according to economic and institutional influences and apply statistical techniques to analyze both the patterns of similarity within subsets of countries and the systematic differences between groups of countries.

Economic growth is a quantitative phenomenon. In the modern era it means that per capita GNP rises even as population grows and as human and other resources move out of agriculture into sectors of higher productivity (Kuznets 1968). Economic development involves quantitative changes in economic structure—changes in the distribution of labor and output between sectors, in sources of household income, and in the composition of consumption, savings, and investment. However, the essence of economic development is qualitative change: change in the relationships among individuals, classes, and political groups; and technological and institutional change in the ways that production, distribution, and consumption take place. Above all, development means dynamic evolution.

In Western Europe, the evolution of capitalism from the sixteenth and seventeenth centuries onward made possible the industrial revolutions of the nineteenth century. These two interrelated phenomena, capitalism and the industrial revolutions, generated unprecedented growth and development in Europe. Capitalist expansion permeated much of the world as Europeans sought raw materials, food, markets, and land. With European penetration, indigenous civilizations in Latin America were destroyed, while viable settlements in North America and in parts of Australasia were established. By the eve of World War I, Europe and the United States had been transformed into great industrial powers. Between the 1830s and the 1920s about fifty million Europeans migrated to the continents of North and South America until one-eleventh of the world's population consisted of Europeans living outside Europe (Thomas 1973, p. 244). European trade, investment, and settlement in Latin America, Southeast Asia, and, to a lesser extent, the rest of Asia led to a phenomenal expansion of food and raw material exports to Europe in exchange for manufactures. But only some of the affected non-European societies experienced export-based growth leading to domestic industrial expansion. Both the structure of growth and the dynamics of institutional change varied strikingly among the countries of the non-European world.

The study of history is indispensable for understanding the causes of today's underdevelopment. It is not so much that the roots of contemporary experience lie far in the past nor that any particular paths of economic change could be replicated. Rather, the usefulness of history lies in showing the wide range of experiences that account for the successes and failures of export-led growth in promoting domestic economic development. History enhances our understanding of the nature and importance of interconnections among economic, social, and political changes in a wide range of different institutional settings.

We study national units, even though variations within national boundaries often exceed "average" differences among countries. Although historical data really allow us no other alternative, our choice can be justified on other grounds. Institutional arrangements affecting property are fundamental to the processes of economic development, and national boundaries are indispensable to the evolution of these property institutions. Foreign trade, infrastructural investment, and relationships among advanced and dependent nations are all based on national units. Furthermore, the historical growth of the modern nation-state was closely tied to the expansion of capitalism so that its characteristics and policies need to be included in any historical study of growth and development.

In the remainder of this chapter, we review and evaluate the principal models of the dynamics of long-term structural change and institutional transformation. We use this literature to help specify variables for statistical analysis and define typologies for grouping countries by similarity of institutional transformations. Our main interest is in theories and theses that highlight causal mechanisms linking socioeconomic, economic, and political transformations during development, stagnation, or "underdevelopment." Why did the industrial revolution, which started in Great Britain, induce economic development in some countries, fail to induce development in others, and induce only limited development in still others?

In answering these questions we look for hypotheses about the characteristics and causes of nineteenth-century institutional transformations. Specifically, what do these models say about the types of institutional change that are most characteristic of expanding capitalism, the initial economic and institutional conditions that determine the character and extent of change, the dynamic forces that galvanize change, the agents of change and their motivations, and the consequences for economic well-being of different types of change?

We do not limit ourselves to theories that can be directly "tested" with our data, but we do restrict ourselves to theories that elucidate the structural and institutional changes represented by our data or illuminate the limitations of our undertaking. We attempt to illustrate major themes rather than to discuss the literature in detail.

The theories we review are drawn from development theory and economic history. Economic development theories provide diverse views about forces for institutional change in the nineteenth century. In classical and neoclassical theories, market opportunities and profit maximization are the great forces for economic and institutional change. Marx, Schumpeter, Gerschenkron, and Polanyi provide strikingly different visions of historical capitalist dynamics. Comparative historians incorporate a wide range of institutional forces in analyzing nineteenth-century industrial revolutions. Dependency theorists and other development pessimists studying underdeveloped countries stress negative institutional consequences of growth in very low income countries. Alternative positive views of nineteenth-century underdeveloped countries relate mainly to those with abundant agricultural resources.

CLASSICAL AND NEOCLASSICAL DEVELOPMENT OPTIMISTS

Development theorists in the classical and neoclassical traditions emphasize the historical force of expanding markets in inducing innovations and institutional changes favoring sustained economic growth. They assume a wide spread of benefits from growth in a world in which markets function reasonably well.

Classical Theories

In Adam Smith's theory of growth (1910), market opportunities and individual self-interest drive the institutional changes producing economic growth. Capital accumulation and innovation provide the internal dynamics while population growth provides the necessary labor. Capitalist transformations require two key institutional conditions: security of property and economic freedom. The impelling motives are the pursuit of private advantage, based on a human propensity to truck and barter, a preponderant interest in private frugality, and high rates of return. Extensions of navigation (e.g., opening up America and a passage to the East Indies) and growing towns instigate market extensions and thus institutional change. Markets attract private saving into capital accumulation and promote an increasing division of labor. In-

creased capital and specialization in turn stimulate the growth of urban manufacturing and agricultural improvements. Wider geographical markets and
increased division of labor lead to more capital accumulation and greater increases in national wealth. Higher wages follow and induce population
growth.

John Stuart Mill (1961) also underlines the importance of the security of
persons and property and positive attitudes toward work and saving. But in
addition he emphasizes the critical positive role of social arrangements that
"provide that the reward of everyone for his labour shall be proportioned as
much as possible to the benefit which it produces," and deplores laws and
usages that "chain up the efforts of any part of the community in pursuit of
their own good, or stand between these efforts and their natural fruits" (pp.
108–110). He lays great stress on the importance of knowledge and education.

In Mill's scheme, economic progress itself becomes a force for institutional
change, strengthening growth-promoting attitudes, contributing to greater
security of property, reducing uncertainty, and thereby further promoting
production and accumulation. Mill also stresses the dynamic benefits from
trade—particularly the spread of communication. The creation of new de-
sires with expanded trade "sometimes works a sort of industrial revolution in
a country whose resources were previously undeveloped for want of energy
and ambition in the people" (ibid., p. 581).

Classical authors hold diverse views on the welfare effects of sustained
growth and its associated institutional changes. Although Mill was an opti-
mist, he pointed to the possibility that the rich, the intermediate classes, and
many of the poor could grow richer, increasing national prosperity, "yet the
great class at the base of the whole might increase in numbers only, and not in
comfort nor in cultivation" (ibid., p. 699). Malthus (1914), while pessimistic
about population growth, gave great emphasis to the force of educational institutions in limiting population growth, arguing that such institutions induce
moral restraint among the poor. Ricardo (1911) assumed that landlords
would benefit most from long-term economic progress as an increasing scarcity of land raised the cost of feeding laborers and those who controlled the
land captured the gain. Because of England's expansion of food imports,
Ricardo's forecast failed, but his analysis of the consequences of sudden and
large changes in demand, technical methods, or economic policies remains
historically relevant. In his view, war or sudden demobilization or extensive
technological change cause rapid structural changes that increase unemployment and shift the distribution of income toward manufacturers as well as
landlords (ibid.).

In general, the contribution of the classical writers lay in their emphasis on
the *dynamic* institutional impacts of expanding markets, the positive role of
social arrangements conducive to innovations, the importance of stable political institutions to business investment incentives, and the differential impact
of economic growth on different classes of society.

Lewis's Classical Model of Dualistic Growth

In Lewis's two-sector model of dualistic growth (1954), the dynamic for institutional change is capital accumulation. He assumes that once a small capitalist class exists, capitalists save and plow back their profits into further expansion, leading to larger enterprises and a constantly rising capitalist surplus. Capitalist expansion depends on a labor surplus in agriculture that supplies the expanding industrial sector without lowering agricultural output. Social overhead capital can be created with very little capital by projects intensive in surplus labor. Communal family production on overly small holdings retains excess family workers by promoting the sharing of consumption goods, which enables workers with a negligible marginal product to obtain a subsistence. Other "surplus" workers with negligible marginal products sharing family consumption are excess casual urban wage laborers, petty retail traders making few sales, and unneeded domestic workers retained for social prestige. Capitalist expansion, mainly through industrialization, is slowed only when the sources of surplus labor dry up. (International migration from other labor-surplus countries may sustain the profitability of capitalist growth.)[1]

As for welfare effects, the Lewis model suggests how the persistence of precapitalist institutions sharply affects the structure, rate, and impact of economic expansion. All capitalists must pay a wage equal to at least the average product in agriculture. (In practice, they pay more to attract workers away from family production). One consequence is capitalist interest in keeping agricultural productivity low. Lewis points to colonial land and tax policies in Africa that forced labor into the capitalist sector by restricting real income in the subsistence sector. His model has frequently been applied to explain why capitalist expansion raises wages much more slowly than profits, thereby increasing inequality.

Trade Models with Institutional Change: Jones and Woolf

A few neoclassical trade models integrate trade theory with institutional analysis. Jones and Woolf (1969) attribute the success of industrial development in Western Europe and Japan to a rare conjunction of economic and institutional influences. In their view, a crucial aspect of gradually rising agricultural productivity from the sixteenth century onward was that numerous market-oriented farmers emerged from the disintegration of medieval farming. A slowing of population growth produced "breathing space," or a gap where

---

[1] Criticisms of the Lewis model question whether underemployed labor represents a true labor surplus. Since much surplus agricultural labor is needed at harvest time, its marginal product is positive, so that food output falls as labor shifts into manufacturing. This effect and increased food consumption by rural migrants to cities produce inflation. Then too, a labor surplus does not prevent severe bottlenecks for skilled labor (Higgins 1968, pp. 318ff.).

productivity gains exceeded population growth. This wide spread of surplus over subsistence generated a market for simple standardized manufacturing goods. Traders and entrepreneurs exploited regional differences in endowments, the temperate climate, and the availability of water transportation. Regional trade stimulated improvements in areas favorable to grain production, while pressuring farmers in areas with poorer soil to supplement their earnings with cottage industries. Rural manufacturing promoted population growth, denser settlement, and an increased supply of cheap labor with industrial skills. Urbanization favored the growth of merchandizing institutions, a middle class of small entrepreneurs, and a rising market for manufactured products as well as agricultural improvements.

Thus, the Jones and Woolf model combines classical trade mechanisms with the crucial role of rising classes of traders, entrepreneurs, and market-oriented farmers in bringing about both economic and institutional change. Expanding domestic markets emerge as the critical feature of interregional trade stimulating institutional change.

Neoclassical Institutional Models

Neoclassical studies of the early phases of development focus on institutional rearrangements that reduce the risk and transaction costs of market transactions or enable innovations to be made. Individuals motivated by the maximization of net private benefit join together or pressure governments for change. Basic economic and demographic developments cause disequilibria in markets, thereby leading individuals to demand institutional rearrangements necessary for the exploitation of profitable opportunities.

North and his colleagues (Davis and North 1971, pp. 6–7; North and Thomas 1970, p. 10) make a convenient distinction between (1) fundamental institutions that provide political, social, and legal ground rules for production, exchange, and distribution (e.g., laws or customs governing property rights, elections, and rights of contract); and (2) secondary institutional arrangements (involving individuals or the government or both) that govern how economic units can cooperate or compete. Neoclassical institutionalists for the most part analyze "secondary" institutional innovations, although they recognize that these can create pressures for fundamental changes.

The North and Thomas Model. According to North and Thomas (1970, 1973), a long series of institutional rearrangements facilitated the exploitation of profitable opportunities in Western Europe, establishing thereby the preconditions for nineteenth-century industrialization. Specifically, the expansion of population and settlement, and the consequent rise in land values, which started in the sixteenth century, caused increased exploitation of regional variations in resources, thereby expanding regional and international trade. Rising land values induced institutional rearrangements that commercialized private property and "freed" labor. But geographical expansion of trade was hampered by fragmentation of political authority and inadequate ground rules for profitable economic activity. Hence, pressures were exerted to enlarge political units and revise laws to reduce the high risk and cost of trade. The result was further institutional rearrangements such as the enforcement of private contracts and the establishment and spread of commercial and banking organizations, insurance companies, joint stock companies, and patent protection.

The accumulation of the varied rearrangements that reduced risks and costs promoted further market expansion, increased productivity, and further disintegrated restrictions on market activity. Eventually, a complete restructuring of legal ground rules for economic activity and the institutionalization of private property were achieved. Factors were rewarded according to their effort, which greatly increased the incentive for innovation, enterprise, and labor, leading finally to sustained economic growth. These institutional changes established the critical preconditions for sustained economic growth which led to industrialization.

Models of induced innovation.　Ruttan and his associates have supplemented the North and Thomas model with a demand model of induced institutional change which incorporates the public sector. Typically, changes in relative factor prices make profitable technical changes that can be implemented only by means of altered institutional arrangements. This creates public demand for these rearrangements. Population pressure in Japan, for example, caused a shortage of land that made existing voluntary arrangements for irrigation inadequate (Hayami and Ruttan 1971). Land values rose, creating profitable new opportunities that required changes in irrigation systems. Farmers pressed the public sector to research new methods and make new arrangements for irrigation. They pressed the private sector to supply additional power and plant nutrients. Since the social and political environments were favorable, a flow of innovations and institutional rearrangements resulted. These induced innovations supplemented those resulting from the general progress of science and technology.

Viewed broadly, the strength of the neoclassical approach to institutional change is its emphasis on the importance of incentives to the adoption of institutional restructuring. Its weakness is that many conditions and institutions must exist. For the North and Thomas model to work, favorable social and political conditions, together with effectively functioning markets, must be present. Market incentives are not sufficient to induce any given set of private or public sector institutional rearrangements. (See Olson 1982.) For the Hayami and Ruttan model to work, a country must have public research institutions or a responsive government, personnel capable of research, and private firms able to supply agricultural inputs.

De Janvry's work (1978) underlines the weakness of inducement mechanisms in neoclassical models. He combines the neoclassical theory of induced innovation with a class-power analysis of the politicobureaucratic process. He identifies neoclassical-type payoff matrices for alternative technologies, distinguishing among gains to different social groups. These payoffs identify the latent demands for particular institutional rearrangements. But effective demands are determined by the power of different socioeconomic groups over the politicobureaucratic structure and are "transformed into an actual supply of innovations by the innovation-producing institutions" (p. 303).

The neoclassical approach also commonly underrates the limitations that a lack of assets imposes on small cultivators. Risk and uncertainty also contribute to these cultivators' unresponsiveness to price changes when capital-intensive technologies are becoming more profitable. Fundamental institutions that weaken links between rewards and efforts have historically prevented the operation of the neoclassical mechanism of institutional change. Brenner (1976) points to the extremely different responses of Western and Eastern Europe to market opportunities for capitalist farming. In Western Europe, agricultural commercialization and increased use of wage labor proceeded steadily from the sixteenth century onward despite a slow pace and lags; the main Eastern European response was an increased "squeezing" of peasants because of the existence of institutions with a high potential for extracting a surplus.

ALTERNATIVE VISIONS OF NINETEENTH-CENTURY CAPITALIST DEVELOPMENT: MARX, SCHUMPETER, GERSCHENKRON, POLANYI

The visions of Marx, Schumpeter, Gerschenkron, and Polanyi of the institutional dynamics of capitalism contrast sharply with classical and neoclassical views. To Marx, the moving force for change was the capitalist search for ways to increase the surplus over wages by exploiting a system of "cooperative" wage labor. Schumpeter stressed innovations by creative entrepreneurs financed by banks. For Gerschenkron, dynamic nation-states seeking institutional substitutes for "prerequisites" for industrialization caused the institutional changes that promoted capitalism. Polanyi underlined basic human needs for status and the security of social relations as major causes of the institutional changes that disrupted the successful working of market systems.

Marx

Marx's vision of the internal dynamics of nineteenth-century industrial capitalism (1930) underlines class conflict and innovations as major causes of institutional change. According to Marx, the crucial institutional feature of capitalist expansion was the simultaneous creation of a class of propertyless wage workers obliged to sell their labor to subsist, and a class of capitalists owning the means of production and able to appropriate the excess product above the workers' subsistence (the surplus value). The causes of this transformation lay in the breakup of feudal society. The collapse of feudalism dispossessed the independent peasants, thereby creating a class of wage workers. Feudal magnates lost control over the sources of wealth, and the urban guilds lost control over industry regulations. The growth of production capacity through the actions of an expanding bourgeoisie caused class conflicts that resulted in a new set of class relationships based on capitalism. The transformation of cultivators into wage labor and the means of production into "capital" laid the necessary historical foundations for the capitalist form of production.

In Marx's model, how fast a country industrialized depended on the speed with which precapitalist institutional structures broke down and the rate at which technological innovation removed successive supply-side bottlenecks. Marx was the first to emphasize the close connection between institutions and types of production methods. In his view, the driving force for industrialization was the capitalist's search for ways to reduce costs by increasing the surplus above the wage bill. Technical revolutions in industry induced revolutions in transport and communications, which in turn required further technical change in the machinery industries and in the machines supplying power. These technical changes caused institutional changes as the process of cooperation became "a technical necessity dictated by the very nature of the means of labour" (ibid., bk. 1, p. 409). The development of the machinery industry led to the application of large-scale machinery to agriculture, and thus to the accelerated destruction of peasant holdings, to urbanization, and to a general increase in social mobility.

Brenner (1977), in amplifying Marx, sharply criticizes the classical and neoclassical theories that stress the growth-enhancing role of market forces for their failure to specify the institutional prerequisites. In Brenner's view, three conditions must be met before market expansion will induce continuous technical change and the growth of urban manufacturing. First, nothing must prevent workers from leaving agriculture when there are incentives to move into industry. Second, before division of labor can be accomplished there must first be a system of cooperative labor within a single workplace. Finally, workers, the "direct producers," must be without land for subsistence in order for the economic system to exert continuous pressure for technical change. Only under these three conditions can capitalists develop a technical capacity to produce more than the workers' subsistence and can the growth of markets and towns induce a continuous process of economic growth.

Schumpeter's Theory of Capitalist Dynamics

Schumpeter's theory (1939, 1950) is one of ongoing change and long cycles in nineteenth-century market economies. Creative entrepreneurs introduce major innovations that in turn cause both institutional change and economic progress. His fundamental proposition is that capitalist economic growth in the nineteenth and early twentieth centuries proceeded through crises caused by fluctuations in innovative activity. In Schumpeter's view, the major institutional features of economic forward surges and retardations involve the appearance of innovations in clusters. Entrepreneurs financed by banks provide the dynamics of innovational activity. Part of what entrepreneurs do is to initiate institutional changes that reorganize supply sources and products markets and introduce new organizational forms (Schumpeter 1950, p. 132).

Chandler's analysis of U.S. railroads in the nineteenth century ([United States] 1977)[2] illustrates how innovations caused constructive institutional change, while Coatsworth (1979) illustrates the negative institutional effects of railroads in Mexico. Railroads in the United States initiated managerial techniques for coordinating complex operations over wide geographical areas, the divorce of management from ownership, major changes in the financial and construction sectors (because they could not handle railroad demands), and the development of securities markets and modern accounting techniques. In contrast, railroads in Mexico were built to serve the export sector. By making large-scale landholding extremely profitable, they greatly accelerated the decline of small holdings, promoted a low-wage agricultural and industrial labor force, and increased the concentration of wealth.

Gerschenkron's Theory of Institutional Substitutions

Gerschenkron (1962) rejects the idea of a universal set of preconditions for industrialization, an idea implicit in both Marxian and neoclassical institutional analyses. He sees no absolutely necessary prerequisites for European industrialization. Rather, in his view, a series of institutional substitutions for missing prerequisites occurred, with "the degree of backwardness of the individual areas . . . [being] the dominant factor determining the nature of the substitutions" (1970, p. 103). The more backward a country was, the larger the scale of plants and enterprises, the more heavy rather than light industry, the greater the reliance on technological and financial borrowing from abroad, the greater the pressure on consumption levels, the greater the passivity of the agricultural sector, the greater the importance of national banks and state budgets, and the more virulent the ideologies under which industrialization proceeded. Gerschenkron sees the state playing a dynamic role in

---

[2]A country name before the date in a reference indicates that the full reference is located in that country's section in the bibliography.

fostering institutional change—less to increase private profits than to preserve elite power and position by forestalling detrimental change. He argues, for example, that in Russia state demand for capital goods substituted for the lack of peasant demand for manufactured goods; modern labor-saving technology substituted for the inadequacy of agricultural labor; imported technology and entrepreneurship substituted for domestic deficiencies; and government bureaucracy and large plants substituted for the lack of entrepreneurs (ibid.).

The number and intensity of institutional substitutions for these missing prerequisites "can be explained in terms of the rising degree of backwardness of the areas concerned":

> As we follow the course of the industrial spurt over time, we see how under the impact of diminishing backwardness also the pattern of substitutions begins to change and substitutions characteristic of a high degree of backwardness begin to be replaced by substitutions that have been used in areas of medium backwardness. In this fashion, temporally seen, the original morphology becomes more complex, is given a causal twist, and its organizing principle of the degree of backwardness becomes then a causal principle, explaining for us the nature of the processes of industrial change. (Ibid., p. 104)

Thus, a considerable variety of institutions can lead to a spirit of enterprise and perform the critical functions of saving, entrepreneurship, supplying labor, and innovation.

Some of Gerschenkron's specific propositions about the institutional substitutions typical of backward countries in Europe are not consistent with comparative evidence on countries outside Europe. Smith ([Japan] 1973) contrasts Japan with the West, pointing out that Japan concentrated on light rather than heavy industry. Smith shows that Japanese success lay rather in *rural* industry—its skill development, capital accumulation, and commercial practices—all of which occurred before foreign technology induced change to a new political leadership.

Institutional Theories of Growth and Retardation: Polanyi and Hughes

Among writers who stress institutional causes of long-term growth and retardation in nineteenth-century capitalist societies are Polanyi (1957) and Hughes (1977). Polanyi emphasizes the critical role of institutional changes that established labor, land, and money markets and assured the continuous availability of factors for long-term investment in complex specialized machines. In his view, the main institutional requirement for factor markets was the elimination of the customary regulatory and protective devices of medieval guilds, towns, and provinces as well as those of mercantilist states.

Polanyi disagrees with the Marxian thesis that nineteenth-century institutional changes served class interests and with the neoclassical proposition that they served to exploit profitable opportunities. Polanyi maintains that class interests "most directly refer to standing and rank, to status and security, that is, they are primarily not economic but social" (1957, p. 153). Most political interventions in the functioning of the market system "simply responded to the needs of an industrial civilization with which market methods were unable to cope" and had "no direct, and hardly more than an indirect, bearing on incomes" (p. 154).

Thus, according to Polanyi, the social history of the nineteenth century reflects a double movement: (1) the spectacular spread of market organization for commodities; and (2) a network of measures and policies designed to check the market with respect to labor, land, and money. This spontaneous institutional countermovement "was a reaction against a dislocation which attacked the fabric of society . . . and which would have destroyed the very organization of production that the market called into being" (ibid., p. 130). Institutional changes such as the growth of regulations regarding capital and land, and monopolistic combination among businesses and by labor unions, were part of this countermovement.

More recently, Hughes (1977) developed a similar thesis on the transformation of economic control in the United States: governmental controls over market activity were introduced not to promote profits but to constrain and offset the operation of the market (p. 6). He sees these nonmarket controls as a reaction to a long series of crises that led the government to take action to protect consumers, businessmen, or farmers from socially undesirable consequences of an unregulated private economy. He applies Polanyi's analysis to American economic history, suggesting that governments constantly "raised up barriers to the decisions of the markets in order to maintain at least a semblance of order which responds to other than purely economic stimuli" (1976, p. 49).

Hughes and Polanyi share with Adam Smith the view that regulations over economic activity in a market society retard economic growth. According to Polanyi, a wide range of public and private institutional changes disrupted market capitalist expansion. He maintains that the governmental and private measures of nineteenth-century societies to protect themselves from the drastic *social* consequences of market economies severely disorganized the dynamics of capitalist expansion and ultimately caused the collapse of market economies in the depression of the 1930s.

Taken together, the "grand" theorists add to classical and neoclassical schemes of capitalist change at two major points. First, they enrich our picture of historical agents of institutional change, adding the dynamic state (Gerschenkron), aggressive capitalists seeking ways to increase the surplus (Marx), individualistic creative innovators (Schumpeter), and individuals searching for institutional means to preserve social stability and mitigate the social consequences of unregulated capitalist expansion (Polanyi). Second, they enlarge our view of the core institutional changes involved in early capitalist expansion: the enlargement and transformation of the capitalist enterprise and concomitant shifts in the economic and political power of different classes (Marx); the invention of new organizational forms as a direct consequence of technical innovations (Schumpeter) or as a consequence of government drives for modernization (Gerschenkron); and the creation of institutions within capitalism, not to promote capitalist expansion, but to control and relieve its negative social impacts (Polanyi).

The grand theorists fail, as do classical and neoclassical historians, to explain why the structure and pace of early capitalist expansion varied so greatly across nations in the nineteenth century. (The exception is Gerschenkron, but he focused only on contrasts between the advanced and moderately backward countries of Europe.)

CONDITIONS FOR SUCCESSFUL NINETEENTH-CENTURY INDUSTRIALIZATION: THESES FROM COMPARATIVE ECONOMIC HISTORY

There is a common structure in much of the comparative analysis of nineteenth-century economies. Initial conditions or "forces promoting growth" provide the setting for an "industrial revolution," "takeoff," or accelerated economic expansion. One condition is of decisive importance, but which one is decisive varies among authors. A thesis about the source of institutional change follows: a sudden expansion of external markets, a revolutionary cost reduction in a leading sector, or an unexpected political, military, or technological challenge. Finally, the success or failure in making the transition to continuous economic development is attributed to various complex interactions among institutional and economic influences. The strength of these explanations lies in the multiplicity of the noneconomic institutional influences they incorporate. Their weakness is that they are not as explicit as the models discussed above.

Well-known "models" based on the experience of various countries are Rostow's stage theory of economic growth (1960), Black's "modernization" model (1966), Kuznets's theory of economic growth (1968), and Landes's explanatory scheme for the success of Western Europe (1969).

Rostow

Rostow stresses the historical role of economic, attitudinal, and institutional changes in creating the preconditions for a "take-off" in nineteenth- and twentieth-century societies. The necessary changes are increases in agricultural output to supply food, markets, and capital for the expansion of manufacturing and the building of social overhead capital; the replacement of traditional social attitudes and values by a belief in economic progress and a willingness to invest in new methods; a radical change to nationalistic political leaderships dedicated to economic modernization; and institutions for mobilizing domestic savings. Rostow views a change of leadership as the strongest institutional force for economic growth, and a rapidly growing leading manufacturing or transportation sector as the most effective economic stimulus.

Modernization Theorists

Elaborated in the 1950s and 1960s, "modernization" theory stresses multifaceted adaptations to "the unprecedented increase in man's knowledge, permitting control over his environment, that accompanied the scientific revolution" (Black 1966, p. 7). *Economic* modernization involves the rapidly expanded use of inanimate power and the increased specialization and integration of resources and people into well-knit economic systems with a greater capacity for assuring material welfare. *Social* modernization (or "mobilization") involves the transfer of commitments from local to national levels through the spread of literacy, communication, and urbanization. *Political* modernization involves the centralization and consolidation of national power, the differentiation of political structures, and the spread of political participation. The increasing application of science to new technologies, and the psychological adaptation of people to changing conditions and behavior, mark *intellectual* modernization (ibid., chap. 1).

Typically, the modernization process destabilizes the social and political order as some traditional groups are destroyed and other groups, old and new, become increasingly aware of their identity and interests (Huntington 1968). Severe conflicts result. Urbanization and the spread of education create aspirations that, if unsatisfied, galvanize groups into political action. Economic growth increases social frustrations not only among those whose income declines but also among those whose relative position is worsened (Huntington 1968; Olson 1963).

As for dynamic forces for change, the modernization literature is heterogeneous. Some theorists stress the primacy of noneconomic attitudinal forces: Hagen (1962) points to the emergence of a particular type of creative personality; McClelland (1961) underlines the proclivities of a society toward "achievement motivation"; Lerner and Pevsner (1958) emphasize the spread of literacy and mass communication; Black (1966) underscores the key role of scientific and technical innovations, while Adelman and Morris (1971b) emphasize the initiating role of market forces. But all treatments stress leadership in the early phase of change. In a historical study of nineteenth-century Japanese and Russian industrialization, Black et al. ([Japan] 1975) underline the crucial role in modernization of national leaderships driven by challenges from more advanced nations, capable of control and coordination, and willing to borrow methods and ideas from abroad.

The strength of the modernization approach lies in its stress on institutions and the breadth of the interconnections among socioeconomic, political, and attitudinal influences. Its weaknesses, however, are at least threefold: it implies a common path of change for all countries moving from "traditional" to "modern"; it fails to incorporate the impact of colonialism, imperialism, and international politics; and it provides no coherent theory of the mechanisms of change involved in moving from traditional to modern societies. One can say of modernization theory, as has been said of Rostow's stage theory, that it provides no consistent picture of "the mechanism of evolution which links the different stages" (Baran and Hobsbawm 1961, p. 236); it has the "logic of a stage theory without an endogenous propulsive force" (Fishlow 1965, p. 116).

Kuznets

Kuznets (1968, 1979) emphasizes the human dimension of new technology and knowledge. Historically, the essential capital investments were in human beings rather than "sticks, stones, and metals" (Kuznets 1968, p. 35), and these investments accounted for the greatly increased effectiveness of capital investment in raising output over the long term. In Kuznets's view, entrepreneurial action is the leading dynamic force in societal adaptations to opportunities for growth; its effectiveness in exploiting economic potential depended historically on both the institutional setting and the phase of economic growth.

Kuznets also underlines the failure of economic theory to incorporate institutions into the analysis of technological innovation (1979). He stresses the close interconnections between changes in production methods and institutions and attitudes. The mass application of major innovations requires "complementary" institutional changes: changes in the scale and organization of production, legal forms of ownership, prevailing work attitudes, power relations among production groups, and so forth. New methods cause "compensatory" institutional adaptations to disruptive effects such as the displacement of old technologies and skills, the depletion of resources, and the deterioration of the environment (ibid., pp. 67ff.).

Landes

Landes's model of European development (1969) incorporates complex causal interactions involving multiple economic changes and social and political institutional transformations. He explains the priority of Britain's industrial revolution by its many favorable initial conditions and a conjunction of dynamic influences. Britain's advantages over the Continent included lower transport costs, less fragmented markets, more favorable resources (especially coal), fewer legal impediments to the flow of goods and factors, and less inequality and poverty limiting the domestic market. The simultaneous expansion of foreign and domestic demand for textiles strained the rural cottage system of manufacturing and triggered an intense push for innovations. British skills and knowledge and an openness and flexibility of social structure together produced the strong economic response to dynamic stimuli marking Britain's industrial revolution.

According to Landes, British textiles posed a severe challenge as they flooded European markets, initiating industrialization there. But disadvantages in initial conditions accounted for a lag of more than a generation in Continental industrial revolutions. Chief among the Continental disadvantages were closed social structures and less favorable attitudes toward entrepreneurship.

The challenge-response mechanism for successful industrialization, stressed by Landes and others (e.g., Black 1966), has been criticized for its lack of precision. In reviewing Landes's *Unbound Prometheus,* Rosenberg writes: "[T]he industrial world is full of 'challenges,' and always has been. Why do some challenges in some places at certain times generate successful responses whereas other challenges elsewhere or at other times do not? Even Landes, for all his subtlety and resourcefulness, cannot really breathe interpretative life into so shapeless a form, although he tries valiantly to do so" (1971, p. 498). China and Japan, for example, both faced with the challenge of foreign penetration, responded differently—China by closing most of the country to change, and Japan by radically transforming political and economic structures. Scandinavia and Southeastern Europe were both faced with dramatic opportunities to sell primary products in Western Europe, but only the former used these to develop economically.

The strength of comparative history lies in its emphasis on institutions and its ability to incorporate the complexity of noneconomic and economic forces affecting the actual course of nineteenth-century economic development. Comparative historians analyze the institutional, attitudinal, and demographic conditions that contributed to Western European success. They stress human capital (skills, knowledge, and education); the role of diverse agents of change (entrepreneurs, merchants, states, innovators); and the sources and consequences of technical change.

Two weaknesses of most comparative treatments are the implicit use of Western Europe as a standard and the view of development as a series of phases through which most countries pass. Few well-developed theories explain contrasts among countries in the pace and structure of economic development. There is a tendency to catalog the multiple influences affecting the course of development without theorizing sufficiently about their interconnections and relative importance.

UNDERDEVELOPMENT: DEVELOPMENT PESSIMISTS ON ITS HISTORICAL CAUSES

It is now widely agreed that the Western European "model" of economic development is not applicable to underdeveloped countries. Most (but not all) models of nineteenth-century underdevelopment are found either in the diverse literature on dependency theory and the works of its critics or in the literature on staple export models—both of which are specifically targeted at underdevelopment. Since the nineteenth century was a period of phenomenal expansion of foreign trade, foreign investment, colonizing, and imperialism, this literature and its varied theses are important to the present study.

Development pessimists stress the negative impacts of economic growth on both institutions and the distribution of benefits from economic change. Dependency theorists focus on the mechanisms by which penetration of foreign capitalism has aggravated underdevelopment in peripheral nations. Neomarxists stress the force of capitalism ultimately to expand productive capacity and emphasize the ways in which domestic institutions within low-income countries have interacted with the forces of foreign penetration. In our work on poverty and income distribution in the early phases of growth (Adelman and Morris 1973, 1978a), we study how unfavorable initial domestic institutions and rapid structural change have contributed to poverty.

Theories of Dependent Growth

Dependency theory underlines politicoinstitutional changes caused by nineteenth- and twentieth-century foreign capitalist penetration. On the one hand, as argued by Baran (1968), European penetration of backward countries accelerated some of the preconditions for capitalist expansion. Expanding markets and contact with advanced technologies gave a powerful impetus to capitalism. European law and transportation systems accelerated production for the market in agriculture. When peasants became subject to price fluctuations and debt, even this favored capitalist expansion as peasant lands were seized, artisan industries were destroyed, and a pool of pauperized labor was created.

On the other hand, capitalist penetration fostered "a political and social coalition of wealthy compradors, powerful monopolists, and large landowners dedicated to the defense of the existing feudal-mercantile order" (ibid., p. 195). These alliances supporting expatriate export interests produced government policies that limited greatly the diffusion of growth in the nineteenth century. The result was a slowing and, indeed, preventing of a "transformation into industrial capitalism" (ibid., p. 194).

More recently, some dependency theorists (e.g., Cardoso and Faletto 1979) have distinguished different forms of dependency according to the type of class alliance supporting foreign interests. They differentiate, for example, between domestically controlled systems and enclave systems dominated by foreigners; or between primary-product specialization dependent on foreign inputs and reliance on domestic capital goods sectors. Differing forms of foreign-dominated economic structures are seen to produce diverse types of conflicts and alliances among indigenous classes which in turn produce varying types of political institutions (ibid.).

A core thesis of dependency theory is that the international division of labor between dependent areas specializing in primary products and "metropolitan" areas specializing in manufacturing is a major cause of poverty in the former. In dependent areas primary product exports and colonial tariffs combine to prevent diversification that would favor industrialization and development (Frank 1969). This thesis is most relevant to colonial and other politically dependent areas. However, Warren (1980) cites evidence of positive effects of primary product specialization in cases where backward countries are sufficiently independent politically to develop their own tariff policies.

Another mechanism for impoverishment stressed by dependency theorists is the transfer to Europe from the sixteenth century onward of the small economic surplus of peripheral countries, severely retarding indigenous capital formation (Frank 1969). Bagchi ([India] 1976) points to several means of draining off surplus from underdeveloped countries: direct charges for the "costs" of subjugation; interest payments on colonial public debts; and remitted profits from mines, plantation- and utility-product sales to advanced nations, and sales of imported manufactured goods in underdeveloped countries. Warren (1980) argues that for a drain of surplus to block economic development entirely, all the increased income generated by foreign investment must flow abroad. But there is little evidence that all the increased income flows abroad (ibid.). Foreign investment may increase exports enough so that earnings from exports offset negative effects on the capital account. Efforts to measure the drain founder on a lack of data and on disagreements about what might have happened without imperialist exploitation (Brewer 1980).

A great strength of dependency theory is the incorporation of the institutions of colonialism into the analysis of growth and institutional change in backward areas. These are an essential ingredient for explaining dualistic growth and failures to develop. A main weakness of dependency theory is that proponents of surplus drain and peripheralization theses cannot account analytically for strikingly diverse institutional and economic consequences of foreign capitalism in dependent areas, some of which managed a transition to quite widely spread growth.

Neomarxist Models of Dependency: De Janvry

Like Warren, de Janvry (1981) stresses the capacity of capitalism in peripheral nations to expand output greatly, while also underlining domestic institutional sources of dualistic growth and persistent poverty. In de Janvry's model, "social disarticulation" in peripheral nations results in no necessary connection between production and domestic consumption capacities. This contrasts with advanced nations with "socially articulated" economies where production and consumption capacities are closely connected. In advanced nations, capitalists reduce labor costs through innovations but permit wages to rise, with a lag, because they are an important source of demand for goods. Given the unplanned and class nature of capitalism, lagging wages produce underconsumption crises that lead capitalist nations to mold the peripheral nations they dominate to "create the external relations that are consistent with the necessities of the center" (ibid., p. 25).

In disarticulated economies, the final demand for capitalist production consists of export demand and luxury consumption demand determined by the capitalist surplus and rents. The driving force for institutional change is capital accumulation in the export and luxury goods sectors in response to the needs of capital accumulation at the center. High returns in the capitalist sector must provide for the repatriation of profits, luxury consumption, savings for reinvestment, and the costs of labor repression. As long as workers are supported by the subsistence economy and provide little demand for capitalist sector goods, the interest of capitalists is in keeping wages extremely low through policies of repression and cheap food imports. Limited market size, weak financing capacity, stagnation in food production, and deficits in the balance of payments create a persistent need for dependence on foreign capitalism. The domestic bourgeoisie typically remains dependent, trading or producing exportables and luxuries, thereby maintaining close ties with foreign capitalists (ibid.).

This model provides a better basis than dependency theory for differentiating paths of development by the nature of labor markets, characteristics of food-producing sectors, and the balance of political power between dependent and national bourgeoisie. In the model, over the long run capitalist competition with peasants for land leads to the dispossession of the latter and to reductions in the availability of below-subsistence labor. Where the pool of subsistence labor is substantially reduced and industrial wage labor is important, a "national" bourgeoisie that produces and trades mainly wage goods develops an interest in wages sufficiently high to provide a market for their production (ibid.).

Adelman and Morris on Poverty and Income Distribution

According to our study of poverty in the first half of the nineteenth century (Adelman and Morris 1978a), what mattered greatly to economic welfare was how fast capitalist institutions for accumulation and innovation spread, with rapid change worsening the position of the extremely poor in the short and even the medium run. In the early phases of commercialization and industrialization, new activities often did not expand in locations where old activities were displaced. When labor markets were very segmented and change was rapid, the numbers of extremely poor typically increased. The more dualistic capitalist expansion was (sectorally and geographically), the more it harmed the poor.

As for initial conditions, past rapid population growth where resources were limited and labor markets were segmented provided the least favorable demographic configuration, abundant unsettled lands the most favorable. Land institutions were crucial to the economic well-being of the poor: concentrated land distributions with cultivation by dependent tenants on small holdings were least favorable; widespread family farms large enough to produce a surplus were most favorable (ibid.).

Our studies of today's underdeveloped countries (Adelman and Morris 1973) give a pessimistic picture of remedies for poverty. Increases in productivity in very poor countries do not typically improve income distribution. Educational influences operate mainly to the benefit of middle-income groups. Government tax and financial policies on average improve the income distribution only where they are part of a market socialist package (Adelman and Robinson 1978) or a strategy for simultaneously providing the poor with access to technology, knowledge, and credit—a strategy seldom carried out.

Critics of our cross-sectional studies show the impacts of rapid growth on the very poor to be less systematically negative than we hypothesized (Paukert 1973; Ahluwalia 1976). However, other cross-sections include few of the countries at the low end of the spectrum of underdevelopment to which our most pessimistic generalizations apply. Our findings show favorable effects to be more likely at development levels that are intermediate or higher along the spectrum of underdevelopment.[3]

UNDERDEVELOPMENT: ABUNDANT AGRICULTURAL RESOURCES AND DEPENDENCY

Trade models that focus on lightly settled land-abundant areas in the nineteenth century are directly relevant to our study. "Vent-for-surplus" or "staple" models stress the role of resource-intensive staples in stimulating export expansion (Watkins [Canada] 1963; Marr and Paterson [Canada] 1980; Caves 1965). They stress the "linkages" or channels through which growth is transmitted. Together with nontrade linkage models, they provide insights into aspects of nineteenth-century institutional change that have not been incorporated into classical and neoclassical models: for example, the diverse institutional consequences of alternative export technologies (Baldwin 1971); and the impact of expatriate, fiscal, political, and distributional institutions on the transmission of growth (Hirschman 1958, 1977; Senghaas 1980, 1982).

---

[3]In chapter seven we will discuss further the literature on the historical course of poverty.

The Thomas model (1973) provides a complementary analysis of nineteenth-century international migration and investment.

Linkage Models

These models help explain contrasts in structural and institutional change among newly settled resource-abundant regions in the nineteenth century.

Early on, Baldwin (1971) analyzed the contrasting institutional consequences of different nineteenth-century agricultural export technologies. Here resources and technology determine the character of institutional change as well as the distribution of benefits from economic growth. Baldwin compared the favorable effects on domestic market growth from commodities like wheat where technology favored large family farms, with unfavorable effects from crops where technology favored large plantations. The fairly even distribution of the surplus in family farm operations on newly settled lands favored local industry and regional trading centers as well as "investments in homes, offices, warehouses, roads, schools, hospitals, etc." (ibid., pp. 474–475). In contrast, where technology favored large plantations, very poor workers, imported from older regions by wealthy investors, supplemented low incomes with home production on small plots of leased land. Since few made it into the planter class, market demand remained small and was largely for imported luxury goods. On the supply side in plantation economies, institutions slowed domestic expansion of manufacturing: planter dominated governments focused transportation on exports, planters showed little interest in improving worker education and skills, and planters sent savings abroad or reinvested them in exporting. Thus, in Baldwin's model, resource endowments determine products and technology that in turn determine the character of institutions.

Recent work reduces the importance of resources and technology, showing how in different institutional settings similar resources and techniques can lead to different development paths. Hirschman (1958) makes the concept of linkages the linchpin of a model of internal development in backward countries. He focuses on investment-generating forces set in motion by projects with strong linkages (backward, forward, final demand). In this model the critical resource is entrepreneurship, not natural resources. Projects with strong backward linkages are most likely to cause private entrepreneurs to respond to profitable opportunities for investments in complementary industries. Investment projects creating severe shortages of social overhead capital cause public authorities to act since "the desire for political survival is at least as strong a motive as the desire to realize a profit" (p. 64).

Hirschman's "generalized linkage approach" (1977) shows how institutional features of linkages limit positive spread effects from staple export expansion. Negative demand linkages arise when foreign imports destroy handicraft and artisan industries and thereby reduce domestic incomes. "Alien" linkages occur when sharp discontinuities in technology limit access to expatriates with knowledge and capital, cutting off small indigenous producers from unfamiliar capital-intensive techniques. Fiscal linkages operate through state taxation of the export sector and can be negative if tax revenues are spent unproductively. These various institutional and technological features of linkages and their interactions "constitute a structure that is capable of generating alternative paths toward development or underdevelopment for the different staple exporters" (p. 80).

Senghaas and Menzel (1979) also question the standard staple linkage approach in their investigation of the historical conditions in which primary export expansion leads to successful development. They define *successful autocentric development* (which is necessary to escape from "peripheral capitalism") as "increasing inter-linkages within and between sectors in terms of dense input-output interdependencies between agriculture, consumer goods industry, intermediate goods industry and producer goods industry" (p. 1). In case studies of pairs of countries sharing similar nineteenth-century initial economic conditions (Denmark and Uruguay, Sweden and Spain, Australia and Argentina), Senghaas (1980) finds that the strategic influences on the transmission of growth were not resources and technology but "sociostructural, institutional factors that in the critical initial development phase channeled political decision-making in different directions" (p. 47). Most important to successful early growth were (1) a shift of political power away from land-based oligarchies toward rising commercial and laboring classes and (2) greater equality in the distribution of property and resources in agriculture (ibid.). Where land-based oligarchies lost power to rising economic classes, the resultant policies favored wider growth. More equal distributions of land restricted oligarchic behavior and led to wider markets for manufactured goods.

The Thomas Model of International Trade, Migration, and Capital Flows

The Thomas model of the international economy focuses on long cycles in capital formation, migration, and institution building that marked the experience of land-abundant newly settled areas in the nineteenth century. In his classic work on the North Atlantic community, Thomas (1973) stresses the simultaneity between the long swings of capital formation in, and of migration to, the newly settled countries, particularly the United States, Canada, Australia, and Argentina. Depending upon past population structures and intervening balances of migration, population growth was cyclical. In the newly developing areas, population growth induced investment in infrastructure and institutions which generated export capacity with long gestation lags that contributed to long cycles in economic activity. The sensitivity of investment to monetary shocks aggravated instability from the "real" lagged relationships.

Thomas fits institutional structure and changes into this framework at several crucial points. First, investment in institutions such as educational systems, local government organizations, and hospitals increased dramatically as populations migrated to new geographic areas. Second, migration patterns were strongly affected by class structure. Emigration was caused in part by a lack of upward class mobility, which prevented the absorption of workers displaced by the changing structure of international trade. In the newly settled countries class mobility encouraged immigration until an eventual scarcity of land constrained wage earners to remain in the same class, thereby leading to pressures to restrict immigration. Third, the nature of Britain's monetary institutions and their gold standard aggravated investment cycles in both Britain and the periphery, leaving the major burden of Britain's balance-of-payments problems to the newly settled countries.

The Thomas model does not predict the striking differences stressed by Senghaas in international development experience arising from diverse political institutional conditions in dependent areas. The contrasting experiences of Australia and Argentina (both countries: Moran 1970; Ferrer and Wheelwright 1974) indicate that initial political structure and property institutions sharply affected the domestic consequences of long cycles in capital formation and migration, through their impact on public land, immigration, and education policies. These in turn affected distribution and thus the growth of domestic markets.

CONCLUSION

Tables 1-1 through 1-4 summarize leading theories of economic and institutional change relevant to nineteenth-century development experience. They show that no view of nineteenth-century economic history that proposes a single progression of economic and institutional changes for all countries can be correct. Each theory reviewed applies to a particular subset of countries: neoclassical institutionalists, Marx, Kuznets, and Rostow, for example, develop analytical schemes that assume success in establishing a favorable Western European–type institutional framework. Gerschenkron and modernization theorists analyze the nineteenth-century experience of moderately backward countries with governments capable of responding to political, economic, or technological imperatives originating in the prior advances of richer nations. Dependency and neomarxist institutionalists model very underdeveloped nations where foreign capitalism leads to sharply dualistic growth or failures to grow. Staple theorists and the Thomas model focus exclusively on dependent areas with great land abundance.

Taken together, these varied theories depict important nineteenth-century processes of economic and institutional change and their interconnections which our research design should incorporate. They also suggest strongly that these interconnections vary systematically across different sets of countries.

Table 1-1
Most Important Types or Processes of Institutional Change
Involved in Early Phases of Nineteenth-Century Economic Growth

Development Optimists

Classical	expansion of market institutions and of scale of enterprises accumulating capital through increased division of labor in production
Dual-sector models: Lewis	expansion of urban capitalist enterprises with reinvested profits and labor surplus from agricultural and informal sectors
Trade models with institutions: Jones and Woolf	expansion of regional and national trading institutions; growth of classes of traders, entrepreneurs, and market-oriented farmers
Neoclassical institutional	institutional rearrangements reducing risk and transaction costs of market transactions, thereby promoting growth of interregional and international trade

Alternative Visions of Nineteenth-Century Capitalism

Marx	breakdown of precapitalist institutions and rise of "machinofacture"; centralization and concentration of capital and proletarianization of labor force
Gerschenkron	state-promoted institutional changes in organization of labor markets, finance, and production that substitute for missing prerequisites for industrialization

Comparative Economic Historians

Rostow	radical changes in organization of production in one or more rapidly growing manufacturing sectors; spread of institutions for mobilizing savings
Modernization	economic specialization and integration, social mobilization, and political centralization and consolidation
Kuznets	growth in institutions raising stock of knowledge; institutional adaptations to technical innovations

Underdevelopment: Development Pessimists

Dependency	penetration of foreign capitalism impoverishing underdeveloped periphery by transfer of economic surplus abroad and destruction of artisan and peasant sectors through forced free trade and unequal exchange
Neomarxist institutional	penetration of foreign capitalism creating hegemonic alliances with landed elite and dependent bourgeoisie that expand production capacity while perpetuating semiproletarian peasant sector as source of food and cheap labor
Adelman and Morris	increasing economic specialization and integration; displacement and expansion as countries commercialize and

Table 1-1 (continued)

	industrialize, on balance increasing the numbers of extremely poor
Underdevelopment: Staple and Linkage Models	
Hirschman	proliferation of technico-institutional linkages generating institutional pressures for complementary investments through backward and forward linkages

Table 1-2
Most Influential Initial Institutional Conditions
Determining Path of Institutional Transformation

Development Optimists	
Classical	institutions providing security of property, economic freedom, and the linking of rewards to effort
Dual-sector models: Lewis	the beginnings of a capitalist sector; institutions retaining surplus labor through consumption sharing
Trade models with institutions: Jones and Woolf	market-oriented farms providing a widely distributed surplus above subsistence
Neoclassical institutional	social and political institutions favorable to the effective functioning of markets; the institutionalization of private property
Alternative Visions of Nineteenth-Century Capitalism	
Marx	creation of class of wage laborers without means of subsistence and class of capitalists owning means of production
Gerschenkron	level of backwardness of institutions supplying labor, capital, and final demand to industry; governments willing and able to develop institutions substituting for missing prerequisites
Comparative Economic Historians	
Rostow	political, social, and institutional framework for mobilizing domestic savings and investing them in modern sector; purposeful entrepreneurial elite and farmers responsive to expanding opportunities
Modernization	nation-state with educated elites capable of control and coordination and willing to borrow methods and ideas from abroad; relatively high level of precapitalist commercialization

Table 1-2 (continued)

Kuznets	inherited institutions and attitudes affecting spread of new knowledge and innovation; level of investment in human capital

Underdevelopment: Development Pessimists

Dependency	penetration of foreign capitalism and imperialist dominance of world trading system
Neomarxist institutional	geographical and sectoral penetration of foreign capital; strength of precapitalist social relations in agriculture; political strength of national versus dependent bourgeoisie
Adelman and Morris	character of land institutions and demographic influences affecting the size and distribution of economic surplus

Underdevelopment: Staple and Linkage Models

Hirschman	scarcity of entrepreneurial ability to make new investment decisions; no prerequisites other than entrepreneurship

Table 1-3
Most Important Dynamic Force For Institutional Change

Development Optimists

Classical	expanding urban and international markets
Dual-sector models: Lewis	expansion of urban capitalist manufacturing sector through reinvestment of profits
Trade models with institutions: Jones and Woolf	expanding interregional and international markets
Neoclassical institutional	population growth, market expansion, or technological innovation leading to changes in relative factor prices

Alternative Visions of Ninteenth-Century Capitalism

Marx	class conflicts within precapitalist institutions leading to the creation and expansion of wage-labor and capitalist classes, and the search by capitalists for ways to reduce costs by increasing surplus value
Gerschenkron	external politico-economic challenges to backward nations as advanced nations increase their lead over them, and domestic challenges to the survival of elites and their governments

Table 1-3 (continued)

Comparative Economic Historians

Rostow	sharp stimulus from domestic political revolution resulting in new modernizing leadership, or rapid expansion of foreign markets, or major innovation such as railroads
Modernization	political and economic challenge of expansionary policies of more advanced nations
Kuznets	additions to stock of knowledge the dominant factor in shaping course of growth; technological innovations have major role in transforming institutions and producing economic growth

Underdevelopment: Development Pessimists

Dependency	capital accumulation in center nations driving their investment in peripheral nations or colonies
Neomarxist institutional	capital accumulation in export and luxury goods sectors in response to needs of capital accumulation in center nations
Adelman and Morris	expansion of domestic and international market opportunities

Underdevelopment: Staple and Linkage Models

Hirschman	investment-generating forces set in motion by projects with strong backward and forward linkages

Table 1-4
Primary Agents of Institutional Change And Their Motivations

Development Optimists

Classical	individual self-interest of capitalists in increasing profits by expanding manufacturing
Dual-sector models: Lewis	urban capitalist drive to increase profits by reinvesting them in urban manufacturing
Trade models with institutions: Jones and Woolf	profit-maximization by entrepreneurs, traders, and market-oriented farmers
Neoclassical institutional	rational calculation by private enterprise of private profitability of institutional changes; governmental actions to promote changes enhancing private profits

Alternative Visions of Ninteenth-Century Capitalism

Marx	bourgeois capitalist drive to increase surplus over wage bill
Gerschenkron	drive of domestic elites and their governments in backward nations to preserve their positions of power and ways of life

Table 1-4 (continued)

	by institutional changes forestalling others detrimental to them; weighing by elites of advantages of economic progress over costs of requisite institutional and attitudinal changes

Comparative Economic Historians

Rostow	drive of modernizing leaderships to catch up with richer nations; response of profit-maximizing innovating entrepreneurs to expanding market opportunities
Modernization	drive of new national leaderships to promote political and economic modernization
Kuznets	entrepreneurs the energizing element in innovating and exploiting potential of increasing stock of knowledge

Underdevelopment: Development Pessimists

Dependency	drive of foreign capitalists to increase surplus over wage bill in center nations by draining surplus from investment in peripheral areas
Neomarxist institutional	drive (in peripheral nations) of state and foreign capitalists in alliance with dependent bourgeoisie and landed elite to increase surplus from capital accumulation
Adelman and Morris	utility-maximizing, profit-maximizing, or satisficing entrepreneurs, traders, and farmers

Underdevelopment: Staple and Linkage Models

Hirschman	drive of private entrepreneurs for profits and goal of political survival that induces government to invest in severely scarce social overhead capital

Theories of European Experience with Industrialization

Classical writers, neoclassical institutionalists, Marx, Schumpeter, and Gerschenkron portray a dynamic process of capitalist expansion in the nineteenth century in which innovations, capital accumulation, population growth, and expanding foreign demand and rising domestic incomes interacted to produce widespread industrialization. The agents were dynamic states in moderately backward nations seeking institutional substitutes for "missing prerequisites" for industrialization (Gerschenkron); and private entrepreneurs seen alternatively as profit-maximizers responding to market forces (classical, neoclassical), aggressive capitalists seeking to increase the surplus over wages (Marx), or creative innovating entrepreneurs (Schumpeter).

Crucial institutional changes reduced risks and transaction costs (neoclassical institutionalist); gave rise to innovative organizational forms (Schumpeter); expanded the middle class of farmers, traders, and entrepreneurs responsive to market opportunities (Jones and Woolf); transformed and enlarged the scale of business enterprise (classical, Marxist); and led to new growth-promoting attitudes and social rearrangements in agriculture that were conducive to productivity improvements (classical).

Important initial conditions were agricultural institutions providing incentives and means for the long, slow rise of productivity, creating the widely spread surplus above subsistence that was important to a domestic market (Jones and Woolf) and, with population growth, "freeing" a labor force for wage labor, an essential ingredient in capitalist organization (Marx). To these conditions, comparative historians add the important role of human capital, skills, and knowledge (Kuznets), flexible social structures (Landes), and leaderships dedicated to economic modernization (Rostow).

Theories of Underdevelopment and Dualistic Dependent Growth

Dependency theory contributes an essential ingredient to understanding dualistic development and failures to develop in the nineteenth century—the impacts of foreign dependency and imperialism on domestic social and economic institutions. Colonial domination accelerated legal and social changes that expanded markets in labor and land, and undermined the traditional institutions that protected individuals against economic ruin. Foreign-promoted export expansion created class alliances between landowners, mercantile groups, and foreign interests that in countries with weak initial market institutions limited the flow of capital and skills to nontrade sectors (Baran). Recently, neomarxists have explained the diversity of experience in dependent areas by focusing on production relations in agriculture (de Janvry) and widely varying power balances between dependent and "national" bourgeoisie, the latter promoting policies more favorable to domestic market expansion (Cardoso and Faletto).

"Staple" theories of export-based growth in resource-abundant areas contrast sharply with dependency theories. They analyze how massive nineteenth-century flows of European capital and migrants to lightly settled, richly endowed areas transmitted growth from export to domestic sectors. Earlier theorists stressed links between type of resources and technology and subsequent growth paths (Baldwin). More recent "linkage" approaches add crucial institutional dimensions, showing how similar resources and technology in different institutional settings led to diverse development paths (Hirschman, Senghaas).

Closing Comments

No one theory that we have examined handles well the diversity of nineteenth-century experience, even within the group of countries addressed. The literature is helpful indirectly in suggesting groups of countries that shared similar processes of change. But casual empiricism is the usual practice in delimiting the countries and periods to which each theory applies. Because of this, the literature is particularly weak on the diverse consequences of similar economic, demographic, and technological changes in different institutional settings. Following our research design, which is described in the next chapter, we will group countries by shared processes of change, allowing the structure of causation to vary at different levels and along different paths of development. By investigating the validity of conflicting hypotheses for different subsets of countries with both conventional and institutional variables, we will delimit more effectively than any previous quantitative study the domains to which familiar hypotheses apply.

2 The Research Design

Recalling several points made in chapter one, we focus on institutional change in the long-term evolution of societies in the modern epoch of rapid growth. We seek to understand why nineteenth-century paths of growth and development diverged so greatly among countries. Our thesis is that the contrasts in development paths may be explained by (1) institutional transformations governing the distribution, use, and transfer of property; (2) economic structure and change, including differences in resource endowments; and (3) the interactions between (1) and (2). The comparative approach allows us to apply statistical methods to the complex materials we use as data, and thus to gain a better understanding of the causal influences behind economic development.

We assume that theories about the development process are best based on studies of *groups* of countries with similar initial conditions and subsequent dynamics. We focus, as do Kuznets and Chenery, on the empirical features of the structural transformations necessary for sustained per capita income growth. Kuznets identifies a set of consistent changes in the composition of demand, production, trade, and employment typical of "modern economic growth." Chenery extends Kuznets's work significantly through statistical analysis of country deviations from Kuznets's uniformities. In Chenery's work, population size and trade orientation account for major divergences in the pattern and timing of structural transformations. Groupings of semi-industrialized countries by initial economic structures and trade policies provide further insights into causes of divergent development paths. We share Chenery's emphasis on the desirability of exploring more than one way of grouping countries to establish the "stylized facts" about the diversity of structural and institutional transformations.

Our work extends that of Kuznets and Chenery in several respects. First, we incorporate institutional changes directly into our statistical exploration of the transformations defining economic development, in contrast with Chenery, who in his statistical analyses treats them as peripheral. Second, with our measures of institutional influences, we are better able to explore alternative criteria for grouping countries. We incorporate both initial institutions and subsequent institutional dynamics into the criteria by which we group countries for statistical analysis of divergent country experiences.

Our study contrasts with, but in no way substitutes for, the detailed country and regional case studies that form the core of empirical work in economic history. Case studies seek to understand the individual particularities of the cumulative historical experience of a country. In contrast, our purpose is to understand the *systematic* features of the development experience of groups of countries with similar initial conditions and subsequent development dynamics. For the latter purpose, quantitative methods are most appropriate.

We apply a "social scientific" approach. Landes and Tilly (1971) define *social scientific history* as collective history "directly linking the recorded experiences of large numbers of persons or social units to patterns of behavior or change" (p. 71). Social scientific history uses explicit theoretical concepts, assumptions, and hypotheses and relies on systematic comparison "in order to develop and test general ideas of how these processes or phenomena work" (p. 73). Its hallmarks are "aggregation, marriage of theory and empiricism, and systematic comparison" (ibid.).

Social scientific history is not concerned with particular events carried out by particular people—the main subject of history. History per se treats the details of an individual country as a unique pattern in which specific sequences of events account for each country's experience. In contrast, social scientific history focuses on the relationships and processes that recur. Recurrent patterns in the nineteenth century suggest what happened "on the average" and suggest likely or "probabilistic" explanations of patterns of historical change (Tilly 1975, p. 16).

Our approach explicitly departs from that of conventional econometric hypothesis testing. Standard econometric approaches start with a formal model, specify a small subset of influences, estimate the model statistically, and examine how well the model fits the data. This approach is particularly useful when a well-established model fits reasonably well the institutional characteristics of a particular country and period—as, for example, in neoclassical modeling of economic structure and change in advanced competitive capitalist economies in the late nineteenth century. By contrast, we focus on institutional change in countries at widely different development levels with diverse socioeconomic and political institutions for which there are no generally agreed models. There is little agreement on either appropriate theories or choice of variables for modeling the patterns of development in these countries. We therefore take an empirical rather than a theoretical approach. We use statistical methods to study the salient configurations of economic and institutional change marking nineteenth-century national experience; we obtain empirical patterns grouping closely related variables for different country types and groups; we apply theory and a priori reasoning in interpreting the patterns; and we propose hypotheses for further study.

Although our statistical approach is empirical rather than theoretical, we use theory extensively in choosing variables, operationalizing them, developing criteria for dividing countries into subsamples, and interpreting our results. Thus, we apply theory to partially specify the economic and institutional dynamics of economic development. This mix of the theoretical and empirical, applied to a wide range of economic and noneconomic influences on development, provides a statistical counterpart to the work of such noneconometric economic historians as Gerschenkron (1962a, 1962b), Landes (1965a, 1965b), Rosovsky (1965), Hughes (1970), and Jones and Woolf (1969).

The approach we describe below is particularly useful for studying the interdependence between institutional and economic structure and change since appropriate numerical data are seldom obtainable, substantial multicollinearity renders conventional regression techniques of doubtful usefulness, and no widely accepted models are available for specifying the relevant institutional variables and relationships. It provides a fruitful variant to other econometric approaches through its use of classificatory data, a large set of potential variables, and a version of principal components analysis allowing for nonlinearity.

AN OVERVIEW OF THE RESEARCH DESIGN

Since our research design is complex, we summarize its structure before discussing our conceptual framework and the details of the design. The elements in our design form an interdependent whole. The questions we posed necessitated measures of institutional structure and change and a sample of countries at widely divergent development levels. The absence of accepted theories linking economic and institutional change led us to select an empirical over a theoretical statistical approach. Our joint use of economic and institutional measures contributed to a multicollinear data set that constrained our choice of statistical technique. Our premise that the causes of varying economic performance differ by development level and type of country required us to stratify our sample of 23 countries to gain insight into this complex structure of causation.

Our previous research on today's developing countries strongly influenced our choice of focus, variables, and techniques. *Society, Politics, and Economic Development* (Adelman and Morris 1971b) had taught us the critical importance of institutions to economic behavior and how greatly their role varied by development level. It also underlined the usefulness of factor analytic methods in studying the structure of development's causes across subsamples of underdeveloped countries. *Economic Growth and Social Equity in Developing Countries* (Adelman and Morris 1973) showed us that the correlates, economic as well as institutional, for the diffusion of benefits from growth were not the same as for growth rates and varied across different parts of our sample of today's developing countries. These two studies together determined the central focus of our historical investigation on the causes of the strikingly diverse responses of the European periphery and the non-European world to the challenges and opportunities created by the early industrial revolutions, especially Great Britain's.

In summary, we were faced in our historical research with the need to construct variables representing institutions and their change, form subsamples to study how the correlates of development performance varied across different parts of the sample, and select a technique suitable for use with intercorrelated variables.

The classificatory variables. Our historical data consist of 35 classificatory indicators. They differ from our contemporary data in that each country enters the statistical analysis three times: for its characteristics in 1850–1870, 1870–1890, and 1890–1914. Thus, the data form a pooled time-series cross-sectional set of observations. The variables represent diverse facets of economic, social, and political structure and institutions. They include indicators of economic development, initial economic and institutional constraints, socioeconomic and institutional changes, demographic patterns, and political systems.

The sample.   The full sample includes 23 countries of widely varying structures and development levels where *total* GNP (not necessarily per capita) probably increased substantially between 1850 and 1914. Since, as noted, each country enters the data set for three time periods, there are 69 observations in all.

The division of countries into subsamples.   We carry out five quantitative analyses, each involving a different division of the 23 countries into subsamples (chapters three through seven). Each sample division is designed to capture a particular aspect of national development processes. The five aspects we study are the evolution of market institutions, the pattern of industrialization, the character of agricultural development, the extent of foreign economic dependence, and the course of poverty. For each facet of development we construct a typology that defines the sample stratification appropriate for the study of that particular facet. The criterion for each sample stratification is similarity. The sample divisions are by countries, with the three observations for each country assigned to the same class (or subsample) in the typology to facilitate interpretation of the results in terms of national paths or strategies of development.[1]

The statistical technique.   Our statistical methodology is essentially the same as that used with considerable success in *Society, Politics, and Economic Development* (Adelman and Morris 1971b). Its use is particularly appropriate with a multicollinear data set. We use the more recently developed disjoint principal components method (S. Wold 1976) instead of separate factor analyses for each subsample for two related reasons: First, this method is particularly suitable when one is uncertain about which sample stratification best captures the varying structure of causation. Second, it provides a great deal of additional information not provided by conventional factor analysis: measures of the fit of individual observations to both their own and other subsample factor analytic models, the distance between subsamples, and the importance of each variable in discriminating between classes. Since the samples are not random (and thus are unsuited to conventional tests of sample

---

[1] By exception, the typology in chapter three follows a different procedure for stratification, as discussed below.

differences), the measures obtained are descriptive statistics indicating general orders of magnitude.

The synthesis of the five studies.   Our synthesis of the five quantitative studies (chapter eight) generalizes about institutional and economic causes of contrasting paths of economic change in the nineteenth century. It is a distillation of our statistical results consisting of hypotheses about the multifaceted structure of causation explaining the diversity of nineteenth-century development experience.[2]

THE CONCEPTUAL FRAMEWORK

This section summarizes our conceptual framework. It does not provide a theory of development but rather offers a research design for better understanding the diversity of historical experience from 1815 to 1914. Here we delineate the major types of nineteenth-century institutional change, specify their principal causes, and discuss agents of change and their motivations. Together these determine our selection and definition of variables, our choice of technique, and our division of countries into subsamples.

Types of Institutional Change

First, and fundamental to nineteenth-century capitalism, were changes in the laws defining property rights and their enforcement. As governments gradually strengthened exclusive ownership rights and property relations, capitalist expansion was facilitated and the evolution of land institutions was profoundly influenced.

Second, institutional rearrangements that reduced the cost of economic transactions were important. Governments eliminated legal and political barriers to trade among regions, introduced patent laws, limited individual liability for business debts, and provided public goods. Private groups organized insurance companies and developed trading institutions of wider geographic scope (see North and Thomas 1970). All such changes made it cheaper to exploit new economic opportunities.

Third, enlargements in institutional size made it possible to capture returns from economies of scale. Expansion of industrial and commercial private enterprises as well as public transportation services was a striking feature of the period.

Fourth, an increase in the preponderance of capitalist enterprises using wage labor and family enterprises producing for profit had profound consequences for economic development. In some regions at certain times, other

---

[2]No procedure exists for summarizing statistically the results in chapters three through seven.

market forms of property relations became important: large-scale tenancy using wage labor, plantation production using slaves for profit, and artisan and cottage production for long distance trade.

Fifth, particular socioeconomic groups created new organizations or transformed existing ones to protect themselves from unfavorable consequences of economic and technical change: falling prices and wages, competition from new technologies, or underselling by foreign competitors (Polanyi 1957). Unions and cartels protected their members from market competition, and business groups induced governments to take protective measures. (Some of these same organizations pressed governments to make the cost-reducing institutional changes discussed above.) Government agencies restricted market transactions, instituted zoning regulations, and provided social welfare.

Finally, governments explicitly used ideology to strengthen voluntary compliance with the existing property system and to persuade society of its legitimacy (North 1981). The spread of public educational systems served this purpose. Individual groups also used ideology to persuade diverse socioeconomic groups to cooperate in inducing governments to promote their interests.

The first four of these institutional changes describe the transformations from which capitalism grew. Individuals initiated and carried out these transformations through capitalist enterprises, profit-making commercial family enterprises, and the state. The last two institutional changes involved the political and organizational responses of particular socioeconomic groups as they were affected by the first four types of change. Ideology supported group coalitions, increasing their power within representative systems or directly influencing state economic policies. Political institutional responses significantly influenced the course of state economic policies.

What Galvanized Institutional Change?

We reviewed theories about the economic sources of institutional change in chapter one. Foremost in the discussions by neoclassical economic historians are geographical expansions of market demand, demographic changes, and technical improvements that changed relative factor prices. Price changes induced private groups and governments to alter institutions so that the new profitable opportunities could be exploited. Marxian analysis stresses the economic sources of changes in class structure, underlining ways in which technical advances created a new middle class, whose interests conflicted with those of landed proprietors and merchants, whose livelihood was closely tied to the land.

While these approaches are consistent with a wide range of institutional phenomena, they do not explain the timing of institutional change or its varied forms. Five types of events stand out in nineteenth-century economic history as important to the timing and extent of spread of capitalism and its benefits: increases in economic competition from other regions and nations, the acceleration of economic opportunities, political and military threats, colonial expansion, and demographic changes. Before their occurrence there was the long, slow expansion of economic opportunities preceding industrialization in Great Britain and other Western European countries. This accumulation of opportunities reached a threshold beyond which, given other favorable conditions, widespread spontaneous institutional responses occurred. (The character of this threshold is explored in chapter three.)

Both negative and positive effects of dramatic economic change helped induce institutional transformations. First, on the negative side, increased economic competition from other nations or regions threatened the survival of domestic enterprises in economically less advanced nations. For example, in continental Europe, expanded and cheaper transportation and other technical changes severely undercut domestic prices. Institutional responses varied according to whether a colonial or indigenous, landed or nonlanded, elite dominated state policies.

Second, on the positive side, the acceleration of economic opportunities also induced significant institutional transformations. Examples are many: agricultural nations experienced dramatic increases in British demand for their raw materials and food; the transportation revolution in the United States contributed to a striking increase in domestic demand for manufactures; the introduction of interchangeable parts led to a surge of technological possibilities in many countries.

Third, political and military events alternatively threatened or increased the economic or political power of certain nations. The loss of a major war— for example, Russia in the Crimean War—or the forced concession of rights to foreigners could galvanize an independent polity to change its institutions. The fourth type of event, colonial expansion, was a major source of institutional change for those colonized, since widespread implanted institutional changes promoted capitalism in these countries.

Finally, demographic change severely upset the existing balance between population and resources. There were complex interactions in an expanding "protoindustry" among population change, resources, expanding rural industry, and changes in land systems. Increases in population often caused increases in land prices, inducing a reorganization of agricultural property relations. But varying lags between demographic changes and their consequences render this source of change difficult to incorporate into a quantitative analysis of institutional change.

A grasp of the forces capable of galvanizing institutional responses promoting growth or development is a preliminary step, but it is not sufficient for understanding institutional transformations. For every historical case where one of these forces induced major institutional responses, there is another where it did not.

What Motivated Institutional Transformations?

A weakness in the historical literature on institutional transformations lies in the assumptions made about agents of change and their galvanizing motives. Neoclassical institutionalists emphasize an individual calculus of profit maximization. Schumpeter (1939) stresses the independent creative entrepreneur. North (1981) pictures a neoclassical state that changes institutions to maximize the revenues of rulers, subject to transaction and investment costs. This state uses ideology to induce compliance with the prevailing property system. Marx underlines the role of the bourgeois class in introducing technical changes that revolutionize institutions. The neomarxists view the state as "captured" by socioeconomic interest groups (de Janvry [Argentina] 1978). Only the last view allows for incorporating much socioeconomic diversity.

Our Assumptions

We cannot provide a well-articulated theory about institutional change. Nevertheless, several assumptions have influenced our research design and interpretations. We accept them as "maintained hypotheses."

First, we assume that the diversity of country experiences during the latter part of the nineteenth century and early years of the twentieth can be usefully represented by a small number of typologies. The process of change is neither universal nor unique.

Second, we assume that change occurs in interrelated clusters. Changes in market institutions reinforcing individual property rights influence industrialization processes, contribute to more rapid technical change, affect the distribution of the agricultural surplus, influence social relations in urban and rural areas, and affect and are affected by politically rising entrepreneurial groups. Industrialization entails a complex of interrelated structural, technological, institutional, and attitudinal change. Agricultural development and agrarian structure interact to affect possibilities for industrialization, the structure of foreign trade, the role of domestic demand in domestic growth, and the nature of political elites. Patterns of economic dependence affect the structure of trade and growth, set the parameters for local politics, and strongly influence domestic institutional development and government investment and trade policies. Finally, poverty is deeply embedded in the institutional and political structure of the country and is influenced by most aspects of government economic policy.

Third, we assume that political and institutional forces are important in setting the course of an economy. They interact with initial conditions to determine the outcome of accumulation patterns, the structure of economic activity, and the distribution of benefits from growth.

The Conceptual Basis for Our Division of Countries into Subsamples

Both our conceptual framework and our statistical technique require that we group countries according to the similarity of their paths of economic and institutional change. The appropriate sample division appears to us different for each aspect of the development process we study. The organizational typology defining each set of subsamples is derived from our view of the types, causes, and agents of nineteenth-century institutional transformations described above. We view the common model of change within each subsample as the typical path of transformation for that process and subsample.

The first typology of countries is based on the growth of market institutions; historically, their growth involved measures to strengthen individual property rights, reduce transaction costs, and reorganize to capture economies of scale. In chapter three we examine the growth of market institutions that provided supplies of labor, land, and capital on predictable terms to enterprises seeking profits from the sale of output. We focus on the contrasting ways in which market institutions interacted with other types of institutional change in different groups of countries. We begin here because of the presumed close connection in the nineteenth century between the growth of market institutions, the expansion of capitalism, and economic growth and development.

The second grouping divides countries by type of industrial expansion; industrialization caused a striking alteration in the preponderance of various forms of property relations and in the structure of the economy. In chapter four we focus on patterns of industrialization. The nineteenth-century change of greatest significance was the expansion of factory industry employing wage labor. We seek to establish the relative importance of broad classes of influences—market, resource, educational, land, institutional, technological, and demographic—in accounting for differences in the type and extent of industrialization.

The third typology defines subsamples by the response of agriculture to expanding economic opportunities. Institutional responses in agriculture also changed property relations, agricultural productivity, and interactions among agriculture, industry, and the world economy. Market development, patterns of industrial expansion, and institutional responses within agriculture to expanding economic opportunities were profoundly affected by economic relationships with other nations. In chapter five we group countries by interactions among agriculture, industry, and trade, focusing on institutional arrangements in the agricultural sector.

The fourth typology groups countries by the institutional character of their economic relations with other countries. Foreign economic dependence was related not only to international trade but also to the structure of political power. In chapter six we study the impact of dependency on export expansion, domestic growth, and institutional change. Under what differing circumstances did foreign economic relations sometimes promote growth and development, other times lead to uneven growth, and on occasion hamper growth altogether? We study how institutions and government policies helped determine the consequences of increasing foreign dependency.

The final typology groups countries by how change affected poverty, focusing on the consequences of the first four typologies for standards of living. In chapter seven we examine the course of poverty, considering the consequences for poverty of the expansion of market institutions, industrialization, technological advances in agriculture, and the increase of foreign trade and foreign dependence.

In sum, our view of the major kinds of institutional changes determining the course of long-term economic evolution in the nineteenth century played a key role in the construction of these typologies.

THE DATA

The Sample

In principle, we would have liked to include all countries where significant economic change occurred between 1850 and 1914. In practice, we were limited by the languages we could read and by what data we thought would be available to us.

The sample consists of 23 countries in which aggregate GNP increased substantially between 1850 and 1914. There are three observations on each country, one for each of the periods 1850–1870, 1870–1890, and 1890–1914. The indicators of levels and structure refer to the initial year of each period. For example, the data for the period 1850–1870 include various aspects of socioeconomic structure in 1850 (e.g., the level of per capita income, the literacy rate, the proportion of the population in agriculture). Measures of economic *change* (e.g., improvements in agricultural technology) or political characteristics (e.g., the stability of the political system) refer to the whole period 1850–1870. A few indicators refer to changes that occurred during the previous two-decade period. For example, a lagged indicator for the period 1850–1870 refers to 1830–1850.

The sample includes a wide range of countries, both currently developed and still underdeveloped. Western European countries in the sample are Great Britain, France, Germany, Belgium, the Netherlands, and Switzerland. Spain and Italy represent Southern Europe. Denmark, Sweden, and Norway represent Scandinavia. The sample includes land-abundant countries settled by Europeans: the United States, Canada, Australia, and New Zealand. Among developing countries, there are two Latin American nations, Argentina and Brazil. There are very poor countries where GNP per capita stagnated throughout the period: Burma, Egypt, India, and China. We also include Japan, a country in which initially slow transformations were followed by rapid growth. Thus, the sample includes countries at very different levels of development, with different regional characteristics, and with sharply contrasting experiences with economic development in the nineteenth century and beyond.[3]

The Variables

Our variables summarize diverse aspects of economic, social, political, and institutional structure and change. The influences represented come from the theories surveyed in chapter one and the literature on comparative economic history. We discuss briefly here the comparative literature relating to our economic, demographic, human resource, socioinstitutional, political, and market variables. The data appendix describes the principles used in constructing the variables, defines the principles of classification, and gives the assignments of countries to categories and the sources used for each assignment.

Economic influences. We include varied measures of the economic and technical achievements discussed in chapter one: levels and rates of improvement of per capita income and of industrial and agricultural technology, the rate of expansion of total exports, and changes in real wage levels. We also include the supply of agricultural resources, the importance of the agricultural labor force, and demographic and human resource features of the supply of labor. Lack of data forced us to omit the domestic supply of capital. (Foreign capital inflows are represented in the measure of foreign economic dependence.) Other omissions important to standard economic analysis are relative prices and the sectoral structure of export expansion. (We have only a crude indicator of shifts in export structure.)

Demographic variables. We include population size, the rate of growth of population, and international migration, but because of lack of data are not able to include domestic migration or fertility and mortality rates.

Comparative studies show complex relationships between population change and economic development. In Europe population growth contributed labor for industrial expansion where concentrations of population in rural areas of poor soil and small holdings attracted cottage industry. Population growth also supplied labor for industrialization. Where rural, and later factory, industry was established, broader employment possibilities lowered

---

[3]Some countries in our sample changed boundaries during the period of our study (France, for example). For the sake of consistency, we tried to use 1914 boundaries for the entire period, but we could not always do so. Some countries were not unified politically at the beginning of our period (Germany and Italy, for example). Thus we classified these countries by the characteristics of the geographical areas that later became these nations.

the age of marriage and increased the number of children per marriage. But responses of fertility to economic opportunities varied greatly across regions. Lee's study of the relationship between population growth and social change in preindustrial Bavaria ([Germany] 1977) shows that the character of land-holdings, the structure of families, the proximity to urban areas, social and cultural attitudes, and education and literacy all contributed to decisions by Bavarian families to limit their family size.

Population growth had other positive effects besides providing more labor. It accelerated economic expansion where productivity or land abundance yielded a sufficiently high living standard to expand the market for manufactured goods. Even where land was scarce, population growth had positive effects where it stimulated agricultural improvements (Boserup 1965; Mokyr [Belgium] 1976).

The Malthusian view emphasizes the negative side of population growth. Where land was scarce, population growth diminished its marginal productivity, raised the price of food, increased the cost of labor, diminished profits, and slowed capital accumulation. Population growth reduces capital per worker by requiring substantial funds for housing, education, and health (Easterlin 1967). Population growth also increases the burden of children's dependency.

Human capital.   Economists and comparative historians underline the importance of human capital. We include literacy to suggest the stock of human capital, and the spread of primary education (lagged) to represent investment in human capital. (We could not include the quality of education.)

Kuznets (1968), Cairncross (1962), and Hartwell (1965) stress the central role of increased knowledge in modern economic growth. For Cairncross, economic development is impossible without transformations in people's minds. Most important, he argues, are human attributes, whose causal significance we do not understand well: knowledge and experience, skill and self-discipline, the power to take a long view, respect for reasoning, and responsiveness to economic opportunities. Other economic historians stress the acquisition of specific skills. Schultz (1980), citing the case of U.S. agriculture, points to entrepreneurs' acquired abilities, which are enhanced by schooling, health, and, in particular, learning from experience. Smith ([Japan] 1973) emphasizes that specific skills, attitudes, roles, capital accumulations, and commercial practices contributed to Japan's dispersed premodern growth.

Socioinstitutional influences.   We incorporate a classification for the favorableness of attitudes to entrepreneurship and a measure of urbanization. Landes (1969) attributes Western European industrialization largely to social attitudes favorable to entrepreneurship and rational behavior. Hanley and Yamamura ([Japan] 1977) similarly underline the importance in preindustrial Japan of economic motives, foresight, rational fertility controls, and the responsiveness of peasants to economic opportunities that led to the long, slow rise in agricultural productivity. In contrast, Gerschenkron (1962a), writing on the Russian experience, plays down the importance of social attitudes, suggesting that only when unfavorable attitudes are crystallized in government action are they a barrier to industrialization.

Other economic historians take the view that social structure was more important than social attitudes in explaining Western European economic performance. According to Milward and Saul (1979), characteristics of social structure, determined by several centuries of history, explain why countries in Eastern Europe did not develop. As noted, Lee, studying population change and growth in Bavaria, emphasizes social structures such as village organization, the family, and religion ([Germany] 1977).

An unresolved question in the literature on social attitudes, education, skills, and social structure is that of causation between economic and social changes. Cairncross (1962) suggests that a change in social attitudes is more likely in response to changing economic conditions than the reverse scenario. Schultz (1968) proposes that economic growth raised the economic value of human agents, increasing their demand for education and for a variety of other institutions—for example, worker protection.

Agricultural institutions.   Three variables summarize land tenure and holding systems, land concentration, and the conduciveness of land institutions to productivity improvements. Historical case studies underline the importance of land tenure and size of holdings to efficiency, productivity increases, and income distribution. The relationships between land systems and productivity were complex: biological innovations often spread on small family holdings (Hayami and Ruttan 1971); mechanized techniques spread first to larger farms (Jensen [Denmark] 1937; Clapham [Germany] 1936). Independent family farms provided strong work incentives and cheap labor, but their limited assets made investment risky (Wright [United States] 1978). Larger-scale capitalist owners with wage labor could not always compete (Smith [Japan] 1959). However, in England, capitalist tenants with hired labor raised productivity significantly (Ernle [Great Britain] 1936). In contrast with these cases, large-scale estate owners with aristocratic values accumulated wealth in land and slaves and were slow to adopt new techniques (Dovring 1965).

Economic growth and market expansion transformed agricultural tenures and class relations. In densely settled countries, when poor peasants shifted to market production their indebtedness rose. Since their assets were often too few to survive cyclical price declines, many lost their land, with the result that land concentration increased. Legal changes undermined communal agricultural arrangements and "freed" workers to do wage labor (Sutch [New Zealand] 1969; Furnivall [Burma] 1931) or altered land relationships in other ways. Scott (1972) shows how colonial power helped local elites in Southeast Asia increase villagers' compulsory services, thereby transforming the relationship of landlord to community. Landlords who previously responded to community needs for stable incomes no longer did so when rising export demand and foreign marketing made communal production methods unprofitable.

Land systems and land abundance determined the amount and distribution of the agricultural surplus—that is, the excess of total food production over total food consumption by the agricultural population (Nicholls 1963). In poor land-scarce countries in Southeast Asia, investment to create a surplus was necessary to feed growing nonagricultural populations; scarce "slack" resources reduced the peasants' alternatives and independence (Scott 1972). In contrast, abundant land in the United States precluded dependent agrarian relations. In Australia, land was abundant but water was scarce; land concentration was promoted as "squatters" monopolized water supplies (Coghlan [Australia] 1918).

Political institutions.   We include six political variables. The strength of national representative political institutions and the extent of political stability describe key features of the political system stressed by classical economists. Indicators of the influence of new business and commercial classes in national leadership, the extent of the domestic economic role of the government, and the degree of foreign economic dependence help characterize the nature of national leadership. A measure of colonial status also is included. We were not able to incorporate indicators of local or regional political structures or of the effectiveness of governments. Nor could we include indicators of detailed characteristics of government policy such as trade policy, owing to a lack of consistent information.

As stressed in historical case studies, effective nation-states required "the creation of a standing bureaucracy administering a known corpus of law and separating the function and prerogative of office from personal interest" (Landes 1969, p. 123). An effective national government resulted in large free trade areas, unified transportation networks, and laws and regulations protecting private property and contracts (Hamerow [Germany] 1969; Black et al. [Japan] 1975; Seton-Watson [Italy] 1967). Political structures associated with rural societies had to be transformed into modern structures with leaderships that sought to promote capitalism (Black 1966; Black et al. [Japan] 1975). Governments willing to promote primary and advanced education, including technical education, played a vital role in European development (ibid.).

Theses about the relationship between socioeconomic and political change vary like the chicken-versus-egg debate. According to Anderson and Anderson (1967), industrialization and concomitant social changes in Europe induced political change. The growing middle class sought participation in political affairs, educational opportunities, and social advance for themselves and their children. Economic change required new laws, and population growth multiplied government functions. Deutsch (1953) argues that "social mobilization" (the breakdown of old commitments, making people available for new ones) pressured political practices and institutions to change.

In contrast, Black et al. ([Japan] 1975) remind us that in the traditional societies of Japan and Russia, which faced military and political challenges from more advanced societies, modernizing leaders took steps to reorganize social and political institutions. But it was a reorganization of an already existing, capable national bureaucracy.

Anderson (1974) emphasizes the importance to Europe of the feudal legacy of fragmented political authority. An estates system developed under feudalism, differentiating the nobility, clergy, and burghers as distinct orders within the feudal polity. This dispersal of sovereignty permitted a great diversity of populations and languages to persist. According to Anderson, a similar dispersion of absolute power within feudalism occurred in Japan, permitting autonomous urban enclaves within an overwhelmingly rural economy. The resulting urban vitality, found only in Europe and Japan, promoted a unique dynamic between town and country.

Moore (1966) and Warren (1980) accept Anderson's thesis (1974) that the feudal division of authority between the crown and nobility promoted, in Moore's words, a "vigorous and independent class of town dwellers" (Moore 1966, p. 418). Fragmented sovereignty enabled towns to realize their economic potential as they expanded long-distance trade and undermined the feudal character of the rural economy (Warren 1980). Vital were the immunity of certain groups and persons from the ruler's power, the concept of rightful resistance to unjust authority, and contracts of mutual engagement derived from feudal relations of vassalage. These also promoted the growth of parliamentary democracy (Moore 1966). Warren argues that once a certain threshold in the development of capitalism and political structure was reached, democracy became cumulative, accelerating urbanization and resulting in increased literacy, the development of a bourgeois ideology, a constantly changing, expanding economy, and the rising self-consciousness of the working class. Thus, democracy for the bourgeoisie led to democracy for other groups as well (Warren 1980).

Economic historians agree on the importance of government economic policies in the nineteenth century. Almost universally, national governments were involved in building railways and ports, either contributing funds or, in the more backward countries, actually constructing them. The construction of canals and roads was more a concern of local governments (Clough and Cole 1952). Public investment in education determined both the literacy of the population and the pool of talent from which technical and entrepreneurial skills were drawn (Levasseur 1897; Cipolla 1969). Governments were also behind the expansion and control of credit institutions, especially in the more backward countries (Cameron 1972).

The structure and extent of government-subsidized transportation and credit mattered. The transportation networks of Argentina, Italy, and Spain apparently served exports much better than internal trade, thereby slowing the growth of the latter (Scobie [Argentina] 1964b; Fenoaltea [Italy] 1968; Ringrose [Spain] 1970). Government credit policies also varied across countries. Some governments established rural credit institutions that promoted improved agricultural techniques and increased standards of living (Jensen [Denmark] 1937), while others—for example, Eastern European countries (Milward and Saul 1979)—neglected the agricultural sector. In colonial areas, agricultural credit institutions served mainly foreign exporters, while money was loaned to peasants at abnormally high interest rates (Furnivall [Burma] 1931; Owen [Egypt] 1969).

Tariff policies also affected the sectoral composition of development. In Europe, the political response to cheap grain imports in the late 1870s determined agricultural patterns there. For example, high tariffs in France slowed the transfer of resources to industry (Golob [France] 1944). In Great Britain, failure to protect agriculture accelerated the movement of resources out of agriculture (Orwin and Whetham [Great Britain] 1964). Low tariffs in Denmark, the Netherlands, and Switzerland induced a dramatic shift from grain production to specialized high-value agricultural exports (Jensen [Denmark] 1937; Brugmans [Netherlands] 1961; Gasser-Stäger [Switzerland] 1964).

But in underdeveloped countries without favorable initial conditions for nurturing industry, the lack of tariff protection destroyed handicraft industries without creating a substitute (Hlaing [Burma] 1964; Chaudhuri [India] 1968). In a colonial setting, there were other negative impacts of free trade on economic development and living standards, as is well documented in the literature. Legal "reforms" promoted commercial development and weakened protections against the loss of land, while government immigration policies kept wages low (Furnivall [Burma] 1931; Mukerji [India] 1972).

We noted the positive stimulus of inflows of immigrants and capital into unsettled lands in discussing Thomas's model (1973) in chapter one, but the ultimate impact of immigration depended on government economic policies. In Australia, for example, British purchases of consumption goods for convicts and colonial tariff protection helped Australian industry. Labor's political power there, increased by the heavy immigration to gold mines, broke the domination of large landholders. Family farmers were able to gain sufficient land to generate a surplus in food production. Conversely, in Argentina (Ferrer and Wheelwright 1974; McCarty 1973; Moran 1970), large landlords kept control and, with commercial and expatriate interests, succeeded in keeping wages low, thereby slowing domestic market growth.

The dependency theories discussed in chapter one emphasize the negative role of foreign domination. The features of foreign dependence discussed in chapter six were closely related to the structure of political power, especially government policies affecting trade and growth: tax, tariff, transportation, education, and immigration policies.

Market institutions.   We include three composite variables summarizing the level of development of the market system, its current speed of development, and its past rate of spread. We are not able to include our earlier disaggregated measures of factor market development (Adelman and Morris 1978b), because of statistical restrictions on the total number of variables imposed by sample size. (See the data appendix.)

In chapter one we discussed two models that place institutional conditions for the effective functioning of markets at the core of their models of capitalist development. North and Thomas (1973) stress the legal and economic institutional changes that reduce market transaction costs, while Polanyi (1957) underlines the drastic social changes required for markets to function. According to Anderson (1974), the revival of Roman law was another condition that encouraged industrialization in Europe. Islamic law was vague on matters of real estate; Chinese law was repressive, judging little on civil relations; Japanese law was rudimentary and fragmented. By contrast, Roman law provided a coherent systematic framework for the purchase, sale, lease, hire, loan, and willing of goods. This classical heritage of written civil law, unique in the nineteenth century, facilitated the passage to capitalism by providing for security of ownership, for fixity of contract, and for predictable economic transactions between individuals (ibid.). The transformation of conditional landownership into absolute private property was extremely important to European capitalism.

The range of the variables.   While we have included a wider range of institutional influences than any other statistical historical study to date, important omissions remain. As explained below, we offset these omissions to some extent with supplementary data on countries with high and low component scores in our statistical analyses. In this way, we incorporate a wider range of information in our interpretations than that directly represented by our indicators.

The included variables are listed below with the relevant appendix table numbers in parentheses and an indication of shortened titles used in the text tables:

Economic Variables
   Level of per capita income (table A1)
   Rate of change in per capita income (table A3)
   Level of development of techniques in industry (table A5)
   Rate of improvement in techniques in industry (table A6)
   Rate of improvement in techniques in industry, lagged (table A6)
   Level of development of techniques in agriculture (table A7)
   Improvements in techniques in agriculture (table A8)
   Improvements in techniques in agriculture, lagged (table A8)
   Percentage of labor force in agriculture (table A9)

Relative abundance of agricultural resources (table A14)[4]

Level of development of inland transportation (table A15)

Rate of improvement in inland transportation, lagged (table A16)

Rate of growth of total real exports (table A17), shortened in text tables to "Rate of growth of exports"

Degree of shift in structure of export sector (table A21), shortened in text tables to "Degree of shift in export structure"

Direction of change in average real wages in industry (table A22), shortened in text tables to "Change in real wages in industry"

Direction of change in average real wages or income of the employed agricultural poor (table A23), shortened in text tables to "Change in real wages in agriculture"

Demographic Variables

Total population (table A25)

Rate of population growth, lagged (table A30)

Net immigration (table A31)

Human Capital and Socioinstitutional Variables

Extent of adult illiteracy (table A35), shortened in text tables to "Extent of illiteracy"

Rate of spread of primary education, lagged (table A36)

Predominant form of land tenure and holding (table A37)

Concentration of landholdings (table A38)

Favorableness of land system to adoption of improvements (table A39), shortened in text tables to "Favorableness of land institutions to improvements"

Extent of urbanization (table A40)

Favorableness of attitudes toward entrepreneurship (table A41)

Politicoinstitutional Variables

Extent of domestic economic role of government (table A42)

Socioeconomic character of national political leadership (table A43), shortened in text tables to "Socioeconomic character of political leadership"

Strength of national representative institutions (table A44)

Extent of political stability (table A45)

Degree of foreign economic dependence (table A46)

Colonial status (table A47)

Market Institutional Variables

Component scores for composite indicator of level of development of market institutions (table A48), shortened in text tables to "Level of development of market system (composite)"

Component scores for composite indicator of rate of spread of market institutions (table A49), shortened in text tables to "Rate of spread of market system (composite)"

---

[4]Originally we defined this variable as a composite of abundance of land resources (measured by the availability of cultivable land per person) and institutional access to land (Adelman and Morris 1978b). The present variable is based only on estimates of cultivable land per person and is thus conceptually more precise.

Component scores for composite indicator of rate of spread of market institutions, lagged (table A50), shortened in text tables to "Rate of spread of market system, lagged (composite)"

Classification Schemes as a Form of Measurement

Our indicators are based on three kinds of information: (1) primarily quantitative data (e.g., illiteracy or the percentage of the labor force in agriculture), (2) a mix of statistical and qualitative information (e.g., foreign economic dependence or measures of technical change), and (3) primarily descriptive data (e.g., political stability or the character of national leadership). Variables are categorized even when the primary data are strictly quantitative, because data are rarely fully comparable across countries or periods. When point estimates are lacking, qualitative information and statistics on related characteristics are often sufficient to assign a country to a category defined by a range.

For each variable, category definitions based on explicit criteria are used to assign countries and periods to from one-out-of-four to one-out-of-eight ranked categories, and numerical scores are specified. The numbers themselves are arbitrary in the sense that they indicate rank order only.[5] It is important to note, however, that tests of the sensitivity of our results to reasonable alternative scoring specifications indicate the robustness of our results under alternative scoring schemes that maintain the same rankings.[6]

In recent years, a broadened concept of measurement has included not only cardinal but also ordinal and nominal scales (Adelman and Morris 1972). In the social sciences, ordinal measurement is the rule, not the exception. Although GNP is numerical, it is an ordinal measure of national economic welfare or national productive capacity. Indeed, as the literature of welfare economics makes clear, GNP may not yield an unambiguous ranking of welfare states. Similarly, while unemployment rates are numerical, they do not always provide a consistent ranking with regard to national output forgone. Hence the practice of calling economic indices "quantitative" because the primary data on which they are based are numerical is somewhat misleading.

Our classification scheme is similar to conventional economic indices in that it ranks observations ordinally. However, our data differ from conventional indices in several important respects. For one thing, the primary data

---

[5]Country assignments to lettered categories in the appendix tables are summarized in tables A51, A52, and A53. The scoring scheme for translating letters into numbers is given in table A54.

[6]We reran our statistical analyses using two alternative scoring schemes that preserved the ranking of countries and periods. Reruns with the squares, and reruns with the logarithms, of our numerical scores were substantially similar to the results given in this book. The relatively small number of differences usually involved shifts between primary and secondary loadings.

are often descriptive rather than numerical. For another, principles that are not widely accepted have been used to select and weight the components of the ranking schemes.

Economists, economic historians, and econometricians frequently oppose the use of "qualitative" measurement. First, economists criticize aggregations of ordinal or qualitative primary data as being neither as sensitive nor as reliable as measures composed from cardinal or at least quantitative primary data. But there is no real reason to suppose that composites of quantitative primary data provide more sensitive measures of the theoretical concepts they are supposed to represent than do reasonably well conceptualized composites of qualitative components. Further, most economists hold that composites of numerical data vary less with repeated sampling than composites of qualitative data, but certain historical numercial data—for example, quantity produced, population, or number of births—are frequently so inaccurate that they may actually vary more than qualitative rankings based on reasonably explicit criteria.

Second, economists and economic historians question the rules for aggregation of qualitative data, which are seldom based on theories as explicit as those for such measures as GNP, production, factor productivity, and cost of living. But a considerable number of indices widely used in econometric work are measures as ad hoc as those used in qualitative aggregation. Examples include the percentage of the population in cities of a given size as a measure of urbanization, the percentage of the labor force in agriculture, and various indices of economic concentration. The test of such measures is whether they show meaningful connections with other variables, not whether they have an explicit theoretical base. The same goes for useful qualitative measures.

Third, economists and economic historians point to difficulties in obtaining primary descriptive data. Because governments make a practice of collecting numerical or simple taxonomic data, such data are widely available, although of varying reliability. In contrast, there is no regular, systematic, or widespread collection of primary qualitative data. The collection of such data involves techniques with which few are familiar and for which economists have little taste.[7]

Method of Successive Definition

Many of our observations were ranked using concepts with neither accepted operational definitions nor agreed upon numerical measures. Since our main interest is in the institutional causes of strikingly divergent structures and rates of economic change in the nineteenth century, we had to develop measures of institutional influences. Our procedures for conceptualizing and de-

---

[7]See Lazarsfeld and Barton 1951 for a description of these methods.

fining these measures are well established in the history of scientific inquiry— in the physical as well as the social sciences. Kaplan (1964) discusses the importance of these procedures for the derivation of scientific concepts in the early stage of scientific inquiry in the physical sciences:

> In short, the process of specifying meaning is a part of the process of inquiry itself. In every context of inquiry we begin with terms that are undefined—not indefin- ables, but terms for which that context does not provide a specification. As we proceed, empirical findings are taken up into our conceptual structure by way of new specifications of meaning, and former indications and references in turn be- come matters of empirical fact. . . .
>
> What I have tried to sketch here is how such a process of "successive definition" can be understood so as to take account of the openness of meaning of scientific terms. *For the closure that strict definition consists in is not a precondition of sci- entific inquiry but its culmination.* To start with, we do not know just what we mean by our terms, much as we do not know just what to think about our subject- matter. We can, indeed, begin with precise meanings, as we choose: but so long as we are in ignorance, we cannot choose wisely. It is this ignorance that makes the closure premature. (Pp. 77-78, italics added)

Lazarsfeld and Barton (1951) describe this exploratory stage of data construc- tion in the social sciences:

> Where research contains exploratory elements, the researcher will be faced by an array of raw data for which readymade theoretical categories will not exist. He must formulate categories before he can do anything else. Probably the best way to start is with fairly concrete categories—the sort of categories which experienced policy-makers or participants in the situation use, worked out in as clear and logi- cal a form as possible. The job of figuring out what theoretical categories are appli- cable to the given field of behavior will involve switching back and forth between concrete categories closely adapted to the data themselves and general categories able to tie in with other fields of experience, until both concrete applicability and generality are obtained. The immediate problem is to get the raw data classified in some reasonable preliminary way, so that it can be communicated, cross-tabu- lated, and thought about. (P. 4)

In our case we began with a priori definitions based on our historical knowl- edge. Next, we studied descriptions of historical structure and change to see how well these fit our initial definition. The inadequacies of the initial fit were used to reformulate the concept.

Our choice of definition was constrained by a scarcity of data. It was also constrained because we chose to include countries at very low levels of devel- opment with poor data. Their inclusion was essential to avoid the usual bias of cross-sectional studies. However, it limited us to measurement by intervals sufficiently wide that we could use descriptive and judgmental information to make interval estimates when point estimates were unavailable.

Measurement by successive definition was used at the start of national income measurement. Inconsistencies between the initial definition and data on income and output stimulated reformulations of the definition of national income. Redefinitions were again tested for consistency with primary data. This process of redefinition is still continuing today. The parallel between national income measurement and our indicators does not mean that the latter are as reliable or as precise as measures of GNP in advanced countries.

The Construction of Institutional Indicators

Our indicator of the strength of national representative institutions illustrates our procedures. We sought an index that would rank countries by the development of their political institutions and their associated rising economic groups. We limited ourselves to national institutions because data on regional and local institutions were sparse, differences in the geographical scope of regional institutions were considerable, making comparisons difficult, and national institutions were most important for the formation of government economic policies.

In constructing the index, we selected various channels of influence on government policy used by rising new economic groups: the extent of legislative power of the parliament, the extent of popular suffrage, and the weight of opposition parties. Descriptive data were used to judge the relative position of each country in each period (1850–1870, 1870–1890, 1890–1914) with respect to each of these features of their respective legislative systems. We will discuss each channel briefly.

Most nineteenth-century countries made no clear distinction in lawmaking powers between the executive and the legislature; rather, the distinguishing characteristic among countries with parliaments was the precision of the division between the authority of ministers responsible to the parliament and that of the monarch. In countries with strong parliaments, the responsibilities of the legislature and cabinet were clearly defined and had been so for a considerable period of time. But in countries with weak national parliaments the separation of authority between the legislature and the monarch was ambiguous, thus leaving the lawmaking decisions to the play of personality.

Because the extent of popular suffrage was generally limited significantly by property qualifications in the nineteenth century, property qualifications together with fragmentary data on voting participation suggested the extent of popular participation. In countries with strong parliaments, franchise rights were extended to the majority of adult males, though usually minimum property requirements still applied. Countries with weak popular participation had extensive property qualifications limiting suffrage to a minority of the adult male population. Since women could not vote during most of the nineteenth century, their participation was not used in ranking the country observations.

Countries with strong representative institutions had no legal restrictions on opposition parties nor did they restrict the formation of such parties. But those with weaker systems forbade opposition parties or severely restricted their operation.

Using judgments about the strength or weakness of each country in each period with respect to legislative powers, suffrage, and opposition parties, we defined an overall classification system of four categories, allowing a certain amount of give and take to encompass the specifics of our data. In the top category we placed countries whose ranking was strong on all three dimensions and whose representative institutions had functioned sufficiently long to make the exercise of legislative power effective. In the second category we placed countries whose representative institutions were well established, with power shared between the monarch and the legislature. Those classed in the second category, however, either had limitations on the role of the legislature and its ministers or the franchise did not include a majority of adult males because of extensive property qualifications. Also, there were usually restrictions on the freedom of party opposition in the legislature.

The third category included countries judged to have only rudimentary national representative institutions because either the institutions had been established for less than a decade or the assignment of power to the legislature was unclear or very limited. This third category also included countries whose regional representative institutions were strong but whose general assembly or council at the national level was without major authority. Usually, the extent of suffrage in countries in this third category was very low. Then, in the fourth and lowest category were countries without national representative institutions constitutionally limiting the monarch. As can be seen in the full definitional scheme presented in the data appendix, various special combinations of characteristics led to assignments of plus and minus scores in each category of the scheme.

We illustrate the process of classification by showing how for 1850 to 1870 France was assigned to the second category, category B. France's national representative institutions were established in 1815 when constitutional government was introduced and an elected chamber was created (Anderson and Anderson 1967, p. 303). Thus, a fairly continuous national representative institution was present for more than twenty years before 1850. For most of the period 1850–1870, power was controlled by the monarch, whose ministers were directly responsible to him. However, the lack of a clear distinction between legislative and monarchial authority left lawmaking decisions to the play of personalities (ibid.). In general, therefore, it appears that the executive and the legislature shared power, but cabinet responsibility was not clearly established, a fact that kept France below the legislative-power criterion for category A.

Suffrage was quite limited in France until the constitutional law of 1875

(Act 1) granted universal suffrage in the election of the Chamber of Deputies (Anderson and Anderson 1967, p. 38). Before 1875, while suffrage was based on property qualifications and was not yet extended to a majority of adult males, it was not limited severely enough to rank France as a B⁻ for 1850–1870.

Freedom of political opposition in the French legislature was not yet in full effect. Although the republican constitution of 1848 stated that political associations must "respect the freedom of others and public security," this clause was capable of diverse interpretations. It was not until the law of syndicates of 1884 that real freedom of opposition was permitted in the political sphere (ibid., p. 302). The party opposition criterion, therefore, kept France back in category B status for 1850–1870.

In summary, France in 1850–1870 clearly could not be placed in category A. But neither would it fall into category C; national representative institutions had been established at least twenty years before 1850 and functioned quite effectively. But since cabinet responsibility had not yet been established, France would be ranked B rather than B⁺ for the period.

The illustration of France's classification for 1850–1870 shows how information and theory interacted in the derivation of indices for each of our variables. The information on the three main institutional dimensions helped us define the four categories and assign countries in time even when numerical estimates were sparse and descriptive information was limited. The procedure for defining the categories necessarily involved a back-and-forth analysis between descriptive characteristics of countries and periods and low-level theory. This combination allowed definitions to be meaningfully related to the concepts for ranking the countries.

THE STATISTICAL TECHNIQUE

There are two current ways of formulating models. One way selects some theoretically plausible model on the basis of its presumed applicability. The other studies in depth one or a few similar countries, then selects a model consistent with one's knowledge and intuition (as in models of protoindustrialization). The present technique provides a third approach. It predetermines a division of countries into classes by using criteria that are derived in part from theory and in part from hypotheses about the sources and consequences of a particular development process. It then uses only statistical constraints, rather than combinations of statistical constraints with constraints derived from theory, to estimate models of interactions among economic and institutional influences within each class of countries. The estimated models apply to the particular development process represented by a given sample stratification. We interpret the statistical results using theoretical reasoning based on the literature discussed in chapter one and in this chapter. Our interpretations suggest hypotheses for further study. Thus, the technique provides an unusual way to explore systematic variations in economic and institutional change.[8]

We chose an empirical approach to the statistical study of the interactions of social, political, and economic forces in economic development. This does not mean we consider this approach to be always desirable. Models with a priori specified functions can be very important in studying particular subsets of interactions about which a good deal is known. We maintain, however, that our empirical procedures are more suitable for the initial disentangling of those wider interactions crossing disciplinary lines about which much less is known.

In choosing a statistical technique, we faced multiple constraints. We required a method suitable to multicollinear variables and to studying interactions that varied not only by levels of development but also by type of country in ways not evident a priori. We rejected methods restricting variables to a small, statistically independent set because our earlier studies (Adelman and Morris 1971b, 1973) revealed little basis in accepted theory for selecting among the diverse forces impinging on the national capacity to generate widespread and continuous economic growth.

In our earlier work on today's developing countries, we used a variety of fairly powerful statistical techniques of the "analysis-of-variance" type to explore the structure of the complex phenomena involved in economic development. (See Adelman and Morris 1971a.) We used factor analysis to study the interactions of various types of economic, social, and political change in 74 underdeveloped noncommunist countries with a country's level of development and rate of economic growth (ibid.). We applied discriminant analysis to a grouping of the same countries by past growth and policy performance to forecast their development prospects (Adelman and Morris 1968). The canonical correlation technique enabled us to select subsets of closely associated targets and instruments from a set of national policy goals and a set of available policy instruments represented by our data, and to estimate the nature of the simultaneous relationships among the two subsets (Adelman et al. 1969). In studying income distribution patterns in 43 of today's underdeveloped countries, we employed hierarchical interactions analysis, a technique that uses an asymmetrical branching process to subdivide the original sample into a series of subgroups constructed so as to facilitate the prediction of the value of the dependent variable with the least degree of error (Adelman and Morris 1973). Each of these methods enabled us to explore in a flexible but orderly way the basic structure of data representing a wide range of country characteristics that were most likely to influence capacity for widely based, sustained economic growth.

---

[8]For a discussion of the implications of such approaches to modeling for the philosophy of science, see H. Wold 1975. Wold's method involves the use of causal models with blocks of latent variables. See also H. Wold 1976a and 1976b.

Here, we apply the technique of disjoint principal components models developed by S. Wold (1976) to the study of each of the five typologies used to divide the observations into subsamples.[9] The technique provides a novel approach to the early stage of modeling the determinants of contrasting economic change. The method of disjoint principal components models used here has several advantages over other methods. It is a principal components technique that permits the inclusion of variables that are significantly intercorrelated and it clusters widely ranging influences into separate statistical dimensions. But it is superior to conventional principal components or factor analytic techniques when studying groups of countries within which patterns of change are similar but across which they diverge. It constructs and compares a set of independent "models" of economic and institutional change, each appropriate to the historical processes typical of a particular class of countries. It thus elucidates differences among development processes by class of country as well as differences among classes in the consequences of similar processes.

Another advantage of the disjoint technique lies in its estimates of the degree of success of the sample division into types and the degree of separation between the models of change for each type. As noted above, the method measures the importance of individual variables in explaining both within- and between-sample variations. It also yields measures of individual observation fit to subsamples which are superior to conventional measures of distance from the boundary of a group. It replaces the concept of distance from a subsample boundary with that of the closeness of fit to its own principal components model. This procedure has an advantage similar to that of estimation based on structural relationships over that based on reduced-form or single-equation systems.

The disjoint principal components method starts with the principle that the observations in each of several classes are in some way similar. In botanical applications, for example, the observations could belong to several known species of a given plant, and the variables could be such traits as shape, length, or width of leaves. In our study of patterns of industrialization in chapter four, for example, the observations are assigned to four groups by type and extent of industrialization, while our variables represent varied economic and noneconomic country traits.

Given data describing traits of observations presumed on theoretical grounds to be relevant to the phenomenon studied, a model summarizing the behavior within each class is derived for that class by principal components analysis. One fits to each class the principal components model:

$$Y_{ij} = \alpha_i + \sum_{k=1}^{K} \beta_{ik} P_{kj} + \epsilon_{ij} \tag{1}$$

[9]We are indebted to H. Wold for calling this method to our attention.

where the Y_{ij} is the matrix of observations on variable i and object j, and where there are K principal components, P_{kj}, and a set of residuals ϵ_{ij}. (For simplicity of notation, the class index is omitted from all parameters of equation [1].) Once the set of disjoint models is obtained, one for each class, then the fit of the unclassified observations to each class model can be calculated and each unclassified observation can be assigned to the class for which its fit is closest. Similarly, an observation can, in principle, be reassigned from one class to another when its distance from its initial class model is great. In the present application, however, we rarely reassigned observations since the class definitions posed prior constraints on the assignment of observations. In addition, we avoided reassignments the only virtue of which would be to improve the statistical fit, because the meaningfulness of our interpretation depends on consistent principles of sample construction.

Once the principal components model has been estimated for each reference class, the method then calculates the distance of each observation from the model for each class in order to determine to which class the observation is closest.[10] This is done for each class model separately by treating the variable values for the observation (minus the mean for each variable) as the dependent variables in a linear regression in which the independent variables are the estimated components coefficients, β_{ik}, relating variables to components. One calculates, for each observation,

$$Y_{ij} - \alpha_i = \sum_{k=i}^{K} b_k \beta_{ik} + \epsilon_{ij}, \qquad (2)$$

where again the class index is omitted for the sake of notational simplicity. The result is a set of coefficients, b_k, relating the variable values for the observation to the variable loadings on the components, together with a set of residuals, ϵ_{ij}, indicating the deviations of the variable values for the observation from the estimated relationship. The variance of these residuals,

$$S_j^2 = \sum_{i=1}^{I} \epsilon_{ij}^2 / (I - K), \qquad (3)$$

standardized for degrees of freedom, indicates the distance of the observation from the model for the class. Calculation (2) is made separately for each class model, treating the observation as the dependent variable in regressions involving the principal components model for each class. In botanical applications, unclassified observations are then often assigned to the class for which their distance from the class model is the smallest, provided it is also less than, say, two standard deviations away from the class model. As noted, in our applications we rarely alter our initial classifications to obtain improved fits. We prefer to preserve the conceptual basis for each typology, treating deviations as the results of omitted influences.

[10]The possibility that the observation belongs to an unidentified class should be kept in mind.

A matrix of the degree of similarity between all pairs of classes is obtained by fitting the observations for a given class to the models for all other classes. The variance of the observations when fitted to class models other than their own is then compared to their variance when fitted to their own class model. If we let

$$S_{rq} = \sum_{j=1}^{Jr} S^2_{jq/Jr} \tag{4}$$

denote the value of the variance for all objects Jr in class r fitted to the model of class q, then the ratio

$$R = \frac{S_{rq}}{S_{rr}} \tag{5}$$

is the ratio of their variance when fitted to a given alternative class to their variance when fitted to their own class. The larger the R, the greater the distance between any two classes for a given set of observations and a given set of sample assignments.

If there are three or more variables, one can obtain a measure of the explanatory power of each variable. The combined variance of the residuals from all the class models for a given variable is compared with its total variance for the original data. The combined variance of the class residuals over all Q classes,

$$\sigma^2_{\epsilon i} = \sum_{q=1}^{Q} \sum_{j=1}^{J_q} \epsilon^2_{ij} / \Sigma \left(J_q - K_q - 1 \right), \tag{6}$$

represents the portion of the total sample variance for the given variable not explained by the class models. The explained portion is simply the difference between the total variance and the variance of the class residuals. The proportion of total variance of a given variable explained by the class models

$$\sigma^2_{\epsilon i} / \sigma^2_i \tag{7}$$

is thus a measure of its relevance to within-class variations.

One can also compute the importance of each variable in discriminating between classes. For a given variable one compares the variance of the class residuals when all observations are fitted to the classes to which they "belong" with the variance of the class residuals when all observations are fitted successively to the classes to which they do not "belong." It should be noted that the variances being compared cover different populations of observations. The variance with observations correctly classified counts each observation only once. The variance with observations incorrectly classified includes for each observation as many residuals as there are classes other than its own. The ratio of the variance with "incorrect" assignments divided by $(Q - 1)$ to the variance with "correct" assignments gives a measure of the discriminatory power of the variable. The higher the ratio, the greater the contribution of the variable to the correct assignment of individual observations.

Component scores may also be calculated for each observation within a class. They represent estimates of the values assumed by each of the unobserved components for each of the observations in a subsample. They can be thought of as observation scores on an unobserved indicator represented by the component index. Thus, component scores can be used to rank members of the sample with respect to each of the components in a set of class results. As in regression analysis, the score of an observation on a given variable is divisible into "explained" and "unexplained" parts. In principal components analysis the explained part shows how closely a particular indicator and the component index vary together. Country component scores are computed values indicating how each country and period "scores" on the unobserved component index.[11]

The method of disjoint principal components has the great advantage that it simultaneously derives models summarizing the behavior of observations within each set of classes and assigns unclassified observations on the basis of the structure and processes most characteristic of each class. This procedure contrasts with other methods (such as discriminant analysis or likelihood functions) that assign unclassified observations on the basis of estimated boundaries between classes. The advantage of this procedure over more conventional analysis-of-variance techniques is similar to the advantage of estimation procedures that use knowledge of the structural relationships among a set of interacting variables rather than rely on reduced-form or single-equation approaches. The method is flexible in permitting exploration of a phenomenon where a priori knowledge is limited with minimal specification of the relationships among the variables. It can be used for study of the nature of the structures and processes characteristic of each class, for the purpose of classifying observations of uncertain classification, or for both.

The typologies thus delineated in our analysis describe historical patterns of change, not the actual or potential changes that countries could have undergone in the nineteenth century. They by no means exhaust the patterns of change that countries could undergo. Neither do they produce random samples. Conceptually, they are closer to samples constrained by data availability from a population of nineteenth-century societies undergoing significant ag-

---

[11]Another piece of information supplementing that given by component scores is the residual standard deviation for individual country observations. With the inclusion of each successive component, the explained portion of the variable variance for a country observation typically increases, and the unexplained portion declines. Those country observations for which the decline in the unexplained variable variance is greatest may be viewed as those for which the process represented by the component is most relevant. Because the country observations with high component scores almost always showed the largest declines in unexplained variance, we decided not to clutter the text with references to both.

gregate economic change. Our statistical analysis, therefore, summarizes the average characteristic interactions within a specific data set. Conventional covariance analysis, with its stringent assumptions regarding random and independent samples, is clearly inappropriate for testing the significance of differences among the samples with which we work. Since these data represent an actual historical nonrandom sample, our testing procedures are based on nonparametric tests.

THE LIMITATIONS OF OUR APPROACH

The limitations of the present approach are several. First, the classificatory data are crude, discriminating only partially among observations, and serve only the purpose of studying interactions between quite broadly defined influences; this deficiency is inevitable in quantitative attempts that avoid the biases introduced in conventional quantitative work by the omission of complex institutional influences. Second, the study shares with others the disadvantages of treating national units as the appropriate focus of studies of industrialization. Third, the sample, while unusually large and varied, has been limited in size by data availability and language. Fourth, the statistical results provide not tested conclusions but hypotheses for further investigation.[12] Finally, although the study includes a wider range of potential influences than usual, important omissions remain.

---

[12]This feature contrasts less than might appear with the standard econometric approach, in which well-specified models are generally applied without testing the importance of omitted influences or of alternative models.

3 Patterns of Domestic Market Expansion

Polanyi (1957) argues that before modern times labor, land, and capital exchanges were never controlled, regulated, or directed by markets. Even by 1914, few countries had a fully developed market system through which (1) production decisions about the use of labor, land, resources, and capital were made by individuals or enterprises in response to price changes over which governments had no direct control and (2) incomes were derived primarily from selling products or services.

Both neoclassical institutional historians and Marxists emphasize the crucial role for capitalism played by the institutional changes that established individual property rights in land and made labor and capital responsive to changes in economic opportunities. For both groups, legal conditions for unhampered exchanges were prerequisites for capitalism: "freeing" labor from ties to the land; securing individual property rights and securing individual rights to purchase, sell, and use land for profit; and eliminating premodern legal restraints on capital and commodities.

Historical case studies suggest several other features of market systems in the nineteenth century. Formal, settled markets replaced migratory or occasional ones. Specialized institutions evolved for commodity exchange and for mobilizing labor, land, and capital—for example, staple goods exchanges, joint stock companies, and land mortgage and investment banks. Finally, market institutions expanded the geographical area of their activities, reaching nationwide scope in countries with more developed systems.

The spread of market institutions, while sometimes dramatic, was uneven outside Europe and the United States. In some areas, national institutions evolved for only a limited range of export or government-subsidized goods. In others, colonial powers dominated export marketing systems while domestic institutions for goods and factors remained rudimentary. Dualistic market expansion eventually gave way to a wider domestic market system in only a very few places.

On the basis of the literature surveyed in chapter one, we assume that the rate and structure of capitalist expansion depended significantly on institutions supplying land, labor, and capital, those affecting technical change, and those determining the nature of output demand. We expect that institutional changes reinforcing individual property rights, eliminating restrictions on market exchanges, and otherwise reducing the costs of economic transactions contributed significantly to expansions in output. Market growth changed property relations, linked rewards more closely to performance, and contributed to more rapid technical change. Governments established fundamental laws over property and transactions and evolved tariff, immigration, monetary, and transportation policies that directly affected market operations. All these institutional arrangements for marketing goods significantly influenced market demand and the size and distribution of the agricultural surplus.

In exploratory work the raw data must be reasonably classified before analysis can begin. Accordingly, operational definitions of market characteristics are needed for our analysis, but there are few, if any, precedents for measuring the extent of market system growth. Earlier we prepared twelve classificatory indicators of the level and spread of domestic market institutions which distinguished among commodity, land, labor, and capital markets (Adelman and Morris 1978b). We then constructed a typology of market development with which we here define four subsamples to represent contrasting paths of market institutional expansion.

THE MARKET INSTITUTIONAL VARIABLES

We began our study of each type of market by making rough judgments on four aspects of institutional growth: (1) the importance of market compared with nonmarket transactions, (2) the strength of medieval or mercantilist restrictions, (3) the importance of functionally specialized institutions, and (4) the geographical area over which institutions operated. Fragmentary data on price equalization or geographical mobility provided a cross-check. These aspects were used to group the countries and periods into four or more categories for commodity, land, labor, and capital markets.

The classification schemes covered development levels of market institutions in 1850, 1870, and 1890 and their speed of development during 1830–1850, 1850–1870, 1870–1890, and 1890–1914. The four dynamic classifications allowed us to enter them into the statistical analyses in both current and lagged forms.[1]

Descriptive information was, however, limited in several ways. In judging the importance of market restrictions, we could not assume that laws and regulations were enforced, so we relied on prevailing practice. Similarly, since we could not establish satisfactory equivalences between premodern and modern restrictions, we had to ignore the latter. Thus, our scheme for domestic commodity markets disregards the effects of oligopoly or cartelization in restricting the competitiveness of markets. In addition, we judged overall market development indirectly by assuming that a proliferation of specialized institutions signaled a strengthened national market system. For example, we

---

[1] In the early stage of our research we included all twelve market variables in the statistical analyses: four levels of development, four current dynamic classifications, and four lagged dynamic categories (see Adelman and Morris 1978b). As we expanded our data set, however, it became obvious that we did not have the necessary degrees of freedom to make such a detailed representation. Therefore, the twelve market variables were reduced to three composite measures before being introduced into the components analysis. Principal components analysis was applied to the four classifications by level of development of market institutions, and component scores on the first dimension were used to classify observations by overall level of market development. We formed a single composite from the four classifications by current rate of spread of development of market institutions and another composite from the classifications by past rates.

assumed that increases in the number and size of stock market exchanges, investment banks, and agricultural credit institutions furthered the overall development of domestic capital markets. Finally, we focused on *domestic* institutions; hence, we decided, *ceteris paribus,* to give lower rank to countries or periods in which foreigners dominated marketing networks.

Level of Development of Market Institutions

We illustrate our procedures by discussing land market development. In the nineteenth century, feudal claims exempting land from commerce and mortgage were liquidated and the legal and social relationships of people to land were transformed, but land markets remained rudimentary in most countries. The peculiarities of land as a commodity—its physical heterogeneity, the diversity of motives for its purchase, and the relatively small volume of transactions—hindered the development of land markets. Only in a few newly settled countries was the volume of land transactions sufficiently high to justify specialized institutions. Consequently, we based our classification scheme primarily on the extent of land commercialization and the existence of legal and social conditions for transforming land into a factor input and a source of profits.

Specifically, the major criteria used for judging land market development were (1) the extent of individualization of land ownership, (2) the extent of individual freedom to sell, mortgage, and exploit land, (3) the geographical extent of land commercialization, and (4) the spread of specialized agencies dealing in land (e.g., land mortgage and sales organizations). For each of these criteria, however, data permitted no more than broad judgments on whether or not a particular characteristic was "predominant" or "widespread." But a simple dichotomization of observations with respect to each of the four items permitted a fairly reliable four-category scheme.

Several conceptual problems arose in the course of classifying the countries in our sample. For example, the treatment of inheritance restrictions was not straightforward. We therefore used only those inheritance restrictions that limited land sales significantly—for example, the prevalence of entails or fixed legal limits on the size of farms. Lack of data precluded our treating the security of land titles. When the divergence between laws and practice posed a problem, we stressed practice. We did not, for example, weigh heavily the persistent yet disregarded feudal-type tithe laws.

Even our highest category of land market development represents only a rudimentary level of development. Countries in this category had institutional conditions for commercialization (e.g., land titles were individualized and landowners were free to sell, mortgage, and use land), land was widely used for commercial purposes, and there were institutions specializing in land mortgages. In countries at the second level, land market development was significantly held up by, for example, restrictive inheritance laws, quasi-feudal or communal land arrangements, and an important subsistence sector. At the third level were two groups of countries: (1) those without significant restrictions but in which subsistence was overwhelming—that is, local self-sufficiency was prevalent; and (2) those whose land was highly individualized but in which land use was restricted (e.g., by widespread joint cultivation by extended families or village control over agricultural practices). Lowest in the scheme were countries where most landownership was not individualized or where freedom of land transactions and use was severely constrained by feudal-type obligations.

Rate of Spread of Development of Market Institutions

Each classification scheme for the rate of spread of the development of market institutions over several two-decade periods distinguished among four categories, one of which was a residual. Data deficiencies permitted no more. We placed in the top category for each scheme those countries and years in which transaction monetization and institutional expansion were realized almost everywhere in the country. Next, we grouped countries where significant changes occurred but important regions or sectors were left unaffected. The bottom category was reserved for countries where relatively little change took place. Finally, we placed all remaining cases in a residual category that included a diversity of modest or moderate forms of expansion. The data appendix includes a description of each market institution scheme together with a description of the composite measures used in the statistical analyses.[2]

A Typology of Market Development and Spread

We next constructed a detailed typology of market development. Countries whose market institutions had evolved substantially over the nineteenth century were placed in different categories of market development for different periods. Because Scandinavian countries had continuing institutional restrictions on market development early on, they were placed in a low category. Later, they were assigned to the higher categories typical of the rest of Western Europe. Subsequently, we collapsed the detailed typology into four subsamples for our statistical analyses. The construction of these subsamples will be discussed in the next section.[3]

---

[2]Because our resources were limited, our data on market variables, first published in 1978 (Adelman and Morris 1978b) have been only slightly revised. When possible, we checked classifications against more recent general country histories (available for Sweden, Norway, France, Germany, and Great Britain). Only two scores were changed slightly as a result.

[3]In subsequent chapters, we form subsamples directly from country data, placing all three observations for each country in the same sample. Given this procedure, our dynamic interpretations of cross-sectional time-series results are closer to an intuitive view of a historical "path" of change than could be achieved with results based on the assignment of different time periods for

In constructing the detailed typology, we began with the degree to which transactions were marketized. Economies with widespread markets were distinguished from those with uneven regional and sectoral markets. These in turn were distinguished from subsistence economies. The strength of laws establishing individual property rights and facilitating market activity, as well as their success in reducing restrictions on markets, also were important in defining categories. In addition we discriminated between specialized institutions of wide geographical scope and regional or local arrangements such as migratory marketing (peddling or fairs). Developments within different market types proved interconnected. The growth of national goods markets coincided with widespread wage labor, specialized capital institutions, and monetized land transactions. The dualistic development of commodity markets was associated with dualistic factor market expansion.

Table 3-1 summarizes the final typology of twelve types of market structure and development.[4] At one end of the market development spectrum are the most industrialized countries of the 1890s, which had secure individual property rights, few restrictions, national markets for a wide range of commodities, diverse specialized regional capital institutions, and widespread commercialization of land and labor. At the other end are the subsistence economies of the 1850s and 1860s, which exhibited only peripheral market spread and considerable restrictions on labor and land. Intermediate along the spectrum are several types in which market development proceeded unevenly; these are listed principally by extent of market system development. Though the ordering of the extremes of development status is reliable, the difficulties encountered when comparing different paths of uneven market development make the exact ordering of countries in the middle range somewhat arbitrary.

Types A to D represent four phases of market development in the relatively advanced countries of Northwestern Europe, Scandinavia, and North America. In types A, B, and C, subsistence agriculture and premodern restrictions on commodity and factor flow had essentially disappeared by the nineteenth century. Their common dynamic characteristic was the presence of institutions for commodity exchange. National marketing had spread to many sectors in type A countries, to fewer in type B countries, and to still fewer in type C countries. But even in type C countries, home-produced manufactures had virtually disappeared and a market-oriented agriculture was prevalent. In all

---

a single country to different samples. Important to our decision to assign each observation for each country separately in this chapter was our desire to examine in detail the role of market institutional development as a prerequisite for industrial and agricultural change.

[4]See Adelman and Morris 1978b, tables A1 through A4 and B1 through B4, for the sources on which these classifications are based. In order to conserve space, the country classifications for the market variables, and the sources used in making them, have not been reprinted here.

Table 3-1
A Typology of the Structure and Spread of Domestic Markets[a]

Type	Description of Market		Country and Year
	Structure	Spread in Recent Past	
A	National markets for wide range of intermediate and consumers goods; wage labor widespread; specialized capital institutions mainly regional, some national; commercialization of land general; no significant premodern restrictions on markets.	Rapid spread of national marketing; rapid spread of wage labor in industry; rapid spread of limited liability, industrial securities, special capital institutions; spread of land-mortgage and land-sale institutions.	Belgium 1890 France 1890 Germany 1890 Great Britain 1890 Switzerland 1890 United States 1890
B	National markets for select staples and narrow range of manufactured goods; commercialization widespread; wage labor important but limited by prevalence of family enterprises; some specialized investment institutions, securities mainly railway and government; land commercialized but few specialized institutions; no significant premodern restrictions on markets.	First major spread of national forms of marketing; spread of wage labor in industry; spread of limited liability with beginnings of trading of industrial securities; development of land-mortgage and land-sale institutions in some countries.	Belgium 1870 France 1870 Great Britain 1870
C	National markets for a few exports only, regional markets with a wide range of manufactured goods, commercialization widespread; wage labor important in urban areas, mobility mainly short-distance rural–urban; limited mobility of capital with predominance of self-financing and securities limited to government and railway; land commercialized but usually no specialized institutions; no significant premodern restrictions on markets except moderate ones on limited liability in a few countries.	Rapid spread of commercialization of agriculture and specialized institutions for marketing, decline in migratory forms of marketing; moderate spread of wage labor and short-distance mobility; spread of banking finance of trade, spread of government and railway securities; rapid commercialization of land; restrictions on labor mobility removed in some countries.	Great Britain 1850 United States 1870 Netherlands 1870 Switzerland 1870 Denmark 1890 Sweden 1890 Netherlands 1890

D	Regional markets for agricultural produce supplying cities, local markets for artisan products; migratory forms of marketing and subsistence agriculture still important; wage labor of growing importance, some form of major barrier to interregional mobility (geographical, sociocultural); industry self-financed, banking finance of some trade, restrictions on limited liability; land markets undeveloped but without major restrictions; no important premodern restrictions on commodity and labor markets.	Rapid enlargement of area from which cities are supplied with food, elimination of legal restrictions or customs duties on trade in most countries; modest spread of wage labor in agriculture and industry; beginnings of banking system providing short-term credit; spread of commercialization of land transactions.	Belgium 1850 France 1850 Netherlands 1850 Switzerland 1850 United States 1850 Canada 1870 Denmark 1870 Sweden 1870 Germany 1870 Japan 1890[b]
E	Highly dualistic, land abundant: Foreign-dominated national marketing of staple exports with less developed domestic distribution; manufactured goods sold locally or imported; agriculture part commercialized and part subsistence, selling of a few products for cities; hired labor in plantation and pastoral enterprises and family labor in agriculture, severe rural labor scarcities with underemployment in cities; capital markets dualistic, with specialized foreign banking and marketing institutions financing exports and small industry being self-financed; land markets highly commercialized, with land in demand for productive and speculative purposes; in general, few restrictions on market development.	Extremely rapid expansion of pproduction staples for export, modest expansion of domestic manufactures, expansion of a few cash crops from subsistence sector; modest spread of non-seasonal wage labor, major increase in international and interregional migration of harvest labor; expansion of banking systems, but major increase in short-term credits provided by foreign-dominated staple producers, great increase in local indebtedness to buyers; rapid commercialization of land as government lands are sold, multiplication of land-mortgage companies, rampant land speculation.	Australia 1890 Argentina 1890 New Zealand 1890 Brazil 1890
F	Highly dualistic: national marketing of narrow range of intermediate goods to government or government-subsidized enterprises and of specialized	Rapid development of narrow range of intermediate goods primarily for the domestic market, spread of agricultural commercialization and	Italy 1890 Russia 1890 Spain 1890

Table 3-1 (continued)

Type	Description of Market		Country and Year
	Structure	Spread in Recent Past	
	agricultural or textile exports, local markets for artisan and shop products, subsistence agriculture important; close ties between agriculture and artisan industry limiting wage labor force; capital institutions dualistic, with foreign or government financing of nationally marketed goods and unorganized finance in rural areas; commercialization of land limited by social constraints on the supply of land. In general, few legal restrictions on markets.	small-scale industry serving local or regional markets, some regions with little if any market growth; modest spread of wage labor; limited spread of foreign- or government-dominated banking and joint stock companies; spread of commercialization of land in some areas, not in others.	
G	Highly dualistic peasant economies: foreign-dominated marketing of small number of staples, local markets for artisan goods and foodstuffs with peddlers to interior, important areas of self-sufficiency; wage labor in export sector and processing factories; capital institutions dualistic, with foreign banks and firms financing exports and with unorganized finance in villages (often foreign dominated as well); active demand for land by nonagriculturalists, widespread indebtedness by peasants contributing to large volume of land transactions. Few, if any, restrictions on markets.	Rapid expansion of cash cropping by peasants supplying export staples, increasingly centralized marketing of staples by foreign firms; spread of landless labor; rapid spread of moneylending in villages; rapid rise in indebtedness and loss of land, rapid increase in landownership among nonagriculturalists.	Burma 1890 Egypt 1890 India 1890
H	Subsistence agriculture important, but substantial commercialization of agriculture and artisan industry within framework of significant legal re-	Substantial enlargement of area of commercialized agriculture serving towns, expansion of artisan industry for local markets; modest expansion of	Germany 1850 Italy 1850 Japan 1870

Japan 1850
Spain 1850

wage labor force; establishment of a few banks; spread of monetization of land transactions.

strictions on internal trade and capital markets as well as some restrictions on labor and land markets; most products locally marketed, peddlers and fairs common; wage labor force small and mostly urban (except certain sectors of commercialized agriculture), ties between artisan industry and agriculture strong; few banks, and restrictions on joint stock companies, unorganized finance in rural areas. Restrictions on commercialization of land transactions in spite of considerable commercialization of agriculture.

Argentina 1870
Australia 1870
Canada 1850
New Zealand 1870

Rapid but irregular expansion of resource-intensive exports from very narrow base concentrated on waterways; minimal spread of wage labor, immigration insufficient to alleviate labor scarcity; some expansion of foreign-dominated banks and financing of exports; large blocks of land sold on market at terms determined by government, beginnings of specialized land companies.

I Overwhelmingly subsistence or pastoral economies with little industry and very small resource-intensive sector; small urban wage labor force with extreme scarcity of hired labor in rural areas; a few banks, financing of exports by merchants; supply of land dominated by government policies on sale of unsettled lands; few legal restrictions on markets but market development overwhelmingly constrained by transportation barriers.

Denmark 1850
Sweden 1850
India 1850
India 1870
Norway 1870

Some spread of commercialized agriculture and modest expansion of exports; expansion insufficient to absorb population growth; elimination of restrictions on terms of hire in several countries; establishment of a few banks insufficient to relieve capital shortage; modest increase in commercial land transactions.

J Overwhelmingly subsistence, farmed mainly by family units with a few exports exploiting natural resources, some but not major restrictions on the development of commodity markets; small urban wage labor force, underemployed labor in agriculture with hired labor usually having ties to land; few banks, with financing by storekeepers or foreign merchants; landownership individualized, small volume of land transactions limited by cus-

Table 3-1 (continued)

Type	Structure	Description of Market Spread in Recent Past	Country and Year
	tom and inheritance, restrictions on land sales eliminated over two decades earlier in all countries; no major restrictions on markets.		
K	Similar to (J) except that village or communal controls over the use of labor and land still important in major regions of the country.	Spread of commercialization in primary industries in some parts of the country on a limited scale.	Burma 1850 Burma 1870 New Zealand 1850 Norway 1850 Egypt 1870
L	Overwhelmingly subsistence, with major legal restrictions on all markets; legal, customary, or communal restrictions on internal trade; legal or strong customary constraints on mobility of labor; predominance of traditional finance by moneylenders, merchants, or landowners; restrictions on sale and mortgaging of land.	Little growth of markets except on a limited scale around towns and some limited growth of exports.	Egypt 1850 Brazil 1850 Brazil 1870 Russia 1850 Russia 1870 China 1850 China 1870 China 1890
Unclassified			Australia 1850 Argentina 1850 Italy 1870 Spain 1870 Canada 1890 Norway 1890

[a]For the classification schemes and sources on which the typology is based, see Adelman and Morris 1978b.
[b]See note c of table 3-2.

three types new factories, wage labor, and an increase in joint stock companies and in specialized financial and land-market institutions accompanied market expansion. In type D economies, subsistence agriculture and premodern forms of marketing were still important. Commercialization was weakening subsistence agriculture, however, and institutional barriers to domestic trade were being reduced or removed.

Types E, F, and G represent three distinct structures of dualistic market development, but all three had more segmented commodity and factor markets and greater regional contrasts than were found in types A to D. Production of a narrow range of goods for foreign or government markets had recently expanded, while marketing and finance remained rudimentary in the domestic food and artisan sectors. Wage labor had increased in both industry and agriculture. Specialized foreign-financed capital institutions served the expanding modern enclaves, while elsewhere finance was completely unorganized.

In other respects, type E, F, and G countries differed greatly. Type E countries were land abundant, and foreign-dominated export expansion led to massive immigration, rural labor scarcity, and widespread commercial land transactions there. Where export expansion involved highly profitable pastoral products, specialized land market institutions evolved. In type F countries domestic governments and internal markets played a much greater role. Type G countries were labor abundant, and export expansion and the freeing of land transactions from customary restrictions caused some peasants to lose their land or go into debt while others gained from the increased economic opportunities.

Toward the lower end of the spectrum, in type H countries, urban economies grew substantially in spite of continued legal trade restrictions. Below type H were subsistence economies where economic change was very slow, limited, or irregular. In some countries, foreign initiatives and finance stimulated resource-intensive exports, but they usually did little to widen market activity.

By 1890, few countries in our sample had achieved developed market systems and institutions. In most, labor migrated only short distances to new jobs, and land use was often determined by motives other than profit. In others, labor and capital were becoming somewhat mobile and land use was determined at least partly by profit motives, but resource and institutional constraints were still binding.

THE CONSTRUCTION OF SUBSAMPLES FOR STATISTICAL ANALYSIS

For statistical analysis the detailed typology was collapsed into four broad classes, each with roughly the same type of development of market institutions. Types A to D formed class 1, the development path typical of Northwestern Europe, but also including the United States. In class 2 the several phases of foreign exploitation of places with abundant land resources were combined (types I and E). Class 3 consisted of the densely populated subsistence economies suffering severe institutional constraints on their markets and dualistic foreign exploitation of their low-level labor-abundant resources (types J, K, L, and G). Types H and F composed the fourth class. In type H, substantial commercial development occurred despite significant legal restrictions on markets; in type F, national governments played an important role in establishing market institutions by purchasing selected commodities. Country observations yet unclassified were assigned to the groups to which they were statistically closest.[5] Table 3-2 presents the four subsamples and notes the assignment of each observation.

THE STATISTICAL ANALYSES

The statistical results consist of: (1) the principal components analyses (tables 3-3 to 3-6), (2) scores for each country observation on each component, (3) measures of statistical fit (tables 3-7 and 3-8), and (4) measures of the relevance of individual variables (table 3-9).

In our analysis we interpret the covariations of variables with "loadings" or weights of at least .17 in each component. We selected this cutoff on the basis of loadings with sensible interpretations across all findings of the research project.[6] In tables 3-3 to 3-6 the variables having their highest loading on component 1 are listed first and a box is drawn around these loadings. These are called *primary* high loadings. The boxes call attention, then, to the variables having the highest loadings reading across rows. *Secondary* high loadings include all others, rounding to at least .17, reading down component columns. These are marked with asterisks and also are important to the interpretation.[7] In the tables, we generally list the variables within each component in the order in which they are discussed in the text and footnotes.

We applied two criteria to selecting the number of components. We required (1) that the last component have at least five primary high loadings

[5]This procedure makes it difficult to give unambiguous definitions of subsample characteristics, but we use it in this chapter to preserve comparability with our earlier published study (Adelman and Morris 1978b). In subsequent chapters we do not alter initial classifications to improve statistical fit, preferring instead to preserve unambiguous class definitions.

[6]This cutoff is less restrictive than our earlier one, which was based on only a few sets of results (ibid.).

[7]We simplify the discussion in the text by not distinguishing between primary and secondary loadings. Comparison of the whole set of our earlier published results (Adelman and Morris 1978b, 1979, 1980, 1983) with our final set here indicates substantial stability in the composition of components (allowing for differences because of our new variables); however, the division of variables into primary and secondary high loadings is less stable.

Table 3-2
Patterns of Domestic Market Expansion:
Classes of Country Observations for Statistical Analysis

Country and Year	Type[a]	Country and Year	Type[a]
Class 1			
Belgium 1890	A	Canada 1890	U[b]
France 1890	A	Denmark 1890	C
Germany 1890	A	Netherlands 1890	C
Great Britain 1890	A	Norway 1890	U[b]
Switzerland 1890	A	Sweden 1890	C
United States 1890	A	Belgium 1850	D
Belgium 1870	B	France 1850	D
France 1870	B	Netherlands 1850	D
Great Britain 1870	B	Switzerland 1850	D
Great Britain 1850	C	United States 1850	D
Netherlands 1870	C	Canada 1870	D
Switzerland 1870	C	Denmark 1870	D
United States 1870	C	Germany 1870	D
		Sweden 1870	D
Class 2			
Australia 1890	E	Australia 1850	U[b]
Argentina 1890	E	Canada 1850	I
Brazil 1890	E	Argentina 1870	I
New Zealand 1890	E	Australia 1870	I
Argentina 1850	U[b]	New Zealand 1870	I
Class 3			
Burma 1890	G	Norway 1850	K
Egypt 1890	G	Burma 1870	K
India 1890	G	Egypt 1870	K
Denmark 1850	J	Egypt 1850	L
Sweden 1850	J	Brazil 1850	L
India 1850	J	China 1850	L
India 1870	J	Russia 1850	L
Norway 1870	J	China 1870	L
Burma 1850	K	Brazil 1870	L
New Zealand 1850	K	Russia 1870	L
		China 1890	L
Class 4			
Italy 1870	U[b]	Spain 1890	F
Spain 1870	U[b]	Germany 1850	H
Italy 1890	F	Italy 1850	H
Japan 1890	D[c]	Japan 1850	H
Russia 1890	F	Spain 1850	H
		Japan 1870	H

[a]See table 3-1 for definitions of the types.

[b] *U* indicates that the observation was initially unclassified. See table 3-1.

[c]Japan 1890 is the only instance of an observation that we reclassified. Initially it was classified with some hesitancy as type D. The first principal components analysis indicated that its distance from class 1 was much greater than its distance from class 4. Given our original hesitancy and the consistency between some of its leading characteristics and those of country observations in class 4, we decided to reclassify it as belonging to class 4.

and (2) that our interpretation of the processes represented by a component have wider relevance than the specific experience of a single country.

After describing the class characteristics, we describe the covariations summarized by each component and then identify the dynamic process we interpret the covariations to represent.[8] In interpreting a set of pooled cross-sectional and cross-temporal covariations as a "process" of change, we necessarily apply considerable outside theoretical and historical information. As we well know, there is no *statistical* justification for interpreting dynamically and causally the results of covariance analysis.

As noted in chapter two, the component scores for individual country observations can be thought of as scores on an unobserved indicator represented by the component index. As in regression analysis, the score of an observation on a given variable is divisible into "explained" and "unexplained" parts. In principal components analysis the explained part shows how closely a particular indicator and the component index vary together. Country component scores are computed values indicating how each country and period "scores" on the unobserved component index.[9]

We illustrate with component 1 in table 3-3 a component comprising the following variables with high primary loadings: improvements in techniques in agriculture, techniques in industry, and inland transportation (lagged); growth of exports and shift in export structure; changes in per capita income, real wages in industry, and real wages in agriculture; level of per capita income and of development of techniques in agriculture; predominant form of land tenure and holding, and favorableness of land institutions to improvements; socioeconomic character of political leadership, strength of national representative institutions, and extent of political stability; and favorableness of social attitudes toward entrepreneurship. A country with a high component score has proceeded farther than a country with a low one in a complex process involving multifaceted economic and political changes. Information about tariffs, taxes, and so on, in countries with high and low component scores can help explain the process summarized by the component. Using the statistical indication of variables with high loadings, the country component scores, and information on individual country characteristics, together with a priori theorizing, we interpret this component to represent successful industrialization.

Country scores on the second and third components refer to supplementary or alternative processes. For example, the variables with high loadings on

[8] In interpreting a component as a process of change, the signs may be reversed since only the relationships among the signs in a given index are important.

[9] The component scores should be carefully distinguished from the letter "grades" given each country and period in the 35 classification systems in the appendix. Tables A51 through A53 list these letter grades. The scoring scheme in table A54 assigns numbers to the grades that comprise the data for our statistical analyses.

Table 3-3
Patterns of Domestic Market Expansion:
Principal Components Analysis for Class 1
(Western European Path of Market Institutional Growth)[a]

Variable	Principal Component 1	Principal Component 2
Rate of improvement in techniques in agriculture	.18	−.02
Rate of improvement in techniques in industry	.21	.14
Rate of improvement in inland transportation (lagged)	.17	.10
Rate of growth of exports	.18	.03
Degree of shift in export structure	.17	−.12
Rate of change in per capita income	.17	−.16
Direction of change in real wages in industry	.23	−.08
Direction of change in real wages in agriculture	.20	−.01
Level of per capita income	.20	.13
Level of development of techniques in agriculture	.23	.09
Predominant form of land tenure and holding	.24	−.20*
Favorableness of land institutions to improvements	.22	−.09
Socioeconomic character of political leadership	.19	.08
Strength of national representative institutions	.20	−.04
Extent of political stability	.17	−.11
Favorableness of attitudes toward entrepreneurship	.21	−.00
Level of development of techniques in industry	.17*	.22
Rate of improvement in techniques in industry (lagged)	.20*	.21
Extent of urbanization	.16	.36
Percentage of labor force in agriculture	.14	−.29
Level of development of inland transportation	.20*	.40
Relative abundance of agricultural resources	.14	−.38
Colonial status	.08	−.24
Degree of foreign economic dependence	.07	−.32
Level of development of market system (composite)	.14	−.07
Rate of spread of market system (composite)	.13	−.02
Rate of spread of market system, lagged (composite)	.14	.07
Extent of domestic economic role of government	.14	−.02
Extent of illiteracy	.06	.07
Rate of spread of primary education (lagged)	.15	−.13
Rate of improvement in techniques in agriculture (lagged)	.14	−.01
Concentration of landholdings	.13	.01
Total population	.12	.13
Rate of population growth (lagged)	.14	−.10
Net immigration	.12	−.03

[a]See the introductory section to the statistical analysis in this chapter for a discussion of how to read the components results and of the way we interpret them. Variables are listed within components on which they have primary high loadings in the order in which they are discussed in the text. Variables with secondary high loadings (marked with asterisks) also are important to the interpretation.

the second component suggest the concomitants of strong agricultural improvements in a subset of industrializing countries. Country traits not measured by our variables for observations scoring high and low on this second component can help explain above-average agricultural performance.

Finally, the range of values of the included variables is useful in interpreting the results. Within a given subsample, values for a particular variable may vary only a little, including a small portion of the range of values in the full sample. In other subsamples, the values for the same variable may vary over the entire range of values in the full sample.

In discussing our statistical results we generally use the following conventions. First we characterize a component briefly at a higher level of abstraction and with a more dynamic interpretation than a mere listing of variables with high loadings would yield. Then we discuss the variables in the component in a more systematic way, taking slight stylistic liberties: subsuming a few variables under a single phrase, discussing some variables out of order, and referring to some secondary loadings in the discussion of primary loadings. (Variables with secondary loadings are marked with asterisks in the tables, as noted above.) When a large number of variables are subsumed in a single phrase, the individual variables are identified in a footnote. In our discussion of second and third components, which often represent processes that are most evident in only a few countries or periods, we identify country and period information reflecting these processes when to do so helps the interpretation. We hope these stylistic liberties do not make it difficult for our readers to follow the text discussion in the tables.

Class 1: Western European Path of Market Institutional Growth

This class was defined by its characteristics of market development. Premodern legal restrictions on factor and commodity markets were relatively modest; property rights and private contract obligations were in principle protected by law; feudal ties were virtually gone; and interest rate restrictions had almost disappeared. In addition, either independent ownership or tenancy with fixed cash rents prevailed and most landholdings were neither extremely large nor very small. The leading economic characteristics were widespread industrialization and comparatively high per capita income and agricultural productivity.[10] Common political characteristics included (1) national governments capable of organizing essential services and maintaining public order,[11] (2) at least the rudiments of "bourgeois" democracy, (3) limitations placed on the political power of landed elites by rising commercial and indus-

---

[10]Class 1 also includes countries that did not achieve widespread industrialization. Only Norway did not achieve a high score on agricultural productivity in the nineteenth century.

[11]The major exception was the United States during the Civil War.

trial groups, and (4) only modest arbitrary political interference with economic activities. Strong urban centers had considerable political influence.[12]

Indicators of level and pace of market institutional development are not significant in either of the two components in the pattern for this class of countries. This suggests that once a certain level of market, land, and political institutional development was reached (suggested by the common characteristics of the class), market institutions were, in general, no longer a constraint on industrialization.[13] This is not to say that market institutions were unimportant, but rather that they did not provide the dynamic for development once a market system was fully established.

The primary components pattern for this class (table 3-3) indicates that structural change in agriculture, industry, transport, and export expansion, and rising living standards all proceeded more rapidly where levels of economic achievement were higher and where independent family holdings predominated. With rapid economic change, rising business groups gained both more political power and greater social acceptance, and representative institutions were strengthened.[14]

Component 2 captures a pattern specific to the most advanced countries in the class, Great Britain and Belgium,[15] where national marketing, wage labor, and specialized capital and land market institutions were well developed. The component indicates that where the industrial revolution had recently proceeded furthest and fastest, population was more urban, railway networks were denser, agricultural resources were scarcer, and capitalist tenancy was more common.[16] In addition, colonial holdings were larger and net capital outflows were more important as capitalists sought higher returns in massive capital outflows to develop overseas colonies.[17]

Class 2: Land-Abundant Path of Dualistic Market Institutional Growth

Class 2 includes countries where land was abundant and there were only moderate restrictions on markets. European settlers came to exploit the rich agricultural resources. This class was defined by the government's role in freeing

---

[12]These generalizations are based on our data, the literature reviewed in chapter one, and country scores.

[13]Earlier runs in which the market variables were disaggregated by type of market suggest that the spread of wage labor and the introduction of specialized capital market institutions were the features of factor market development most closely associated with rapid industrialization. (See Adelman and Morris 1978b.)

[14]The interactions among these influences are discussed in more detail in chapter four.

[15]Great Britain in the 1870s and 1880s and Belgium after 1890 had the highest scores.

[16]In Belgium, market-oriented tenancy developed on a small scale; strictly speaking it was not capitalist since it did not entail permanent wage labor.

[17]The low scores on foreign dependence and colonial status together indicate important net capital outflows.

markets from institutional restrictions on export expansion. A second common feature was the dualistic structure of the early phases of export expansion. Argentina, Australia, Brazil (after 1890), and New Zealand (after 1870) are included in this class, as is Canada in the earliest decades of its export expansion. Despite great variation in tenure conditions, landholdings were concentrated.[18] Countries with important legal or customary restrictions are not included in the class. New Zealand is not included for 1850–1870 because Maori communal agriculture still predominated, and slavery excludes Brazil for the period 1850–1890.[19]

Among the included countries, political conditions ran the full range of scores on leadership character, the government's direct economic role, political stability, and national representative institutions. This wide variation reflected, in part, differences in foreign economic dependence, as will be discussed more fully in chapter six.

In the first component in table 3-4, the key dynamic process was the foreign exploitation and settlement of rich lands promoted by the removal of institutional restrictions on market systems as well as by the expansion of specialized institutions facilitating land transfers, capital flows, and commodity sales.[20] In this component, increased foreign and colonial dependence and more abundant land resources were associated with rapidly expanding exports, immigration, and population growth.[21] On the average, these processes were more rapid where legal conditions for market institutions had been established quickly, tenure systems had provided incentives for market production, and land holdings were very concentrated.[22] Change was faster where attitudes toward entrepreneurship were somewhat more favorable, parliamentary systems were stronger, and initial per capita income was higher.

The second component underlines the fact that indigenous political forces, not foreign-dominated market institutions, were foremost in significantly spreading economic growth—a spreading indicated by a shift of labor out of agriculture made possible by improvements in agricultural productivity. Where the political dominance of large landowners declined, governments invested in education and transportation and changed land policies to help

[18]The exception is Canada in 1850–1870. Canada after 1870 is not included in this class, because its growth pattern became less dualistic in that period.

[19]Despite its convict labor during part of the period, Australia in 1850–1870 was included because of its close statistical fit to the class. See note 5 above.

[20]The interaction between foreign penetration and market development is inferred from the associations in this component together with data on common class characteristics. The role of foreign penetration is discussed more fully in chapter six.

[21]The indicator of population growth is lagged. In this class, however, past and current rates of population growth are closely correlated.

[22]In several countries in this class, the state played a major role in distributing large tracts of land to individuals.

Table 3-4
Patterns of Domestic Market Expansion:
Principal Components Analysis for Class 2
(Land-Abundant Path of Dualistic Market Institutional Growth)[a]

Variable	Principal Component	
	1	2
Degree of foreign economic dependence	.21	−.16
Colonial status	.22	.09
Relative abundance of agricultural resources	.28	−.13
Rate of growth of exports	.24	−.14
Net immigration	.25	−.10
Rate of population growth (lagged)	.27	−.04
Rate of spread of market system, lagged (composite)	.27	−.18*
Predominant form of land tenure and holding	.18	.11
Concentration of landholdings	.26	−.12
Favorableness of attitudes toward entrepreneurship	.19	.18*
Socioeconomic character of political leadership	.16	.31
Extent of domestic economic role of government	.16	.18
Percentage of labor force in agriculture	.14	−.24
Rate of improvement in techniques in agriculture	.15	.23
Extent of illiteracy	.13	−.39
Rate of spread of primary education (lagged)	.16	.28
Rate of improvement in inland transportation (lagged)	.14	.23
Extent of urbanization	.15	.22
Level of per capita income	.19*	.21
Rate of change in per capita income	.14	−.22
Strength of national representative institutions	.20*	−.31
Level of development of market system (composite)	.15	.10
Rate of spread of market system (composite)	.08	.12
Favorableness of land institutions to improvements	.15	.03
Extent of political stability	.11	.01
Total population	.06	−.08
Level of development of techniques in industry	.08	.12
Level of development of techniques in agriculture	.11	.05
Level of development of inland transportation	.07	.11
Rate of improvement in techniques in industry	.15	.01
Rate of improvement in techniques in industry (lagged)	.12	.07
Rate of improvement in techniques in agriculture (lagged)	.07	.09
Degree of shift in export structure	.06	.02
Direction of change in real wages in industry	.12	−.06
Direction of change in real wages in agriculture	.08	.00

[a]See the introductory section to the statistical analysis in this chapter for a discussion of how to read the components results and of the way we interpret them. Variables are listed within components on which they have primary high loadings in the order in which they are discussed in the text. Variables with secondary high loadings (marked with asterisks) also are important to the interpretation.

smaller farmers serve growing cities.[23] Higher levels of per capita income and urbanization helped create markets for food. Australia scores high here, but its weight also explains the negative sign of economic growth rates—due to immigration so massive that it swamped striking increases in aggregate GNP.[24] Argentina and Brazil score low, both having experienced rapid per capita income increases promoted by economically and politically dominant large landowners, but both exhibiting highly dualistic growth.[25] Chapter six, on foreign dependence, will treat in more detail the respective roles of political and economic influences in widening domestic impacts of export-led growth.

Class 3: Uneven Market Institutional Growth in Agricultural Economies Severely Hampered by Restrictions

In the subsistence agricultural economies included in class 3, major legal, communal, or resource constraints restricted the operation of markets for land, labor, and capital, with the specific constraining factors varying greatly among countries. In some cases, village restrictions on labor and land slowed growth—for example, in Upper Burma, with its extended family agriculture,

[23] Australia's experience suggests the complexity of these interactions. A shift in political power led to land settlement laws that gave farmers greater access in the 1860s and 1870s. This, however, had little immediate effect in expanding small-scale wheat production, because the domestic market was so small. When ocean freight costs declined drastically in the last quarter of the century (an influence not covered by our variables), the changed settlement laws facilitated the expansion of wheat production for export. (Sinclair [(Australia) 1976, p. 103] makes the point about initial ineffectiveness; we infer the later influence from ibid., pp. 169ff.)

[24] In this class, the scores on national representative institutions are lower either because of authoritarian political institutions or because there were weak national institutions, although strong regional ones. The secondary high loading of national representative institutions in this component suggests greater political integration as well as somewhat greater national parliamentary democracy. This is the average relationship for class 2. The minus sign in component 2 reflects the weight of high-scoring Australia in that alternative pattern: in Australia the spread of growth was above average, but national parliamentary institutions were weak compared with regional ones.

[25] In the low-scoring country observations, the goverment's direct economic role was minimal, the national leadership was dominated by the landed elite, illiteracy was prevalent, and transportation was poor. Australia after 1890 had the highest score, almost double that of any other country in the sample. This suggests that the results reflect, in part, specific characteristics of the Australian pattern: the minus sign for changes in per capita income and that for the strength of national representative institutions. In terms of the first of these, the extremely fast development of aggregate national income in Australia in the second half of the nineteenth century was almost completely offset by an extremely high rate of immigration; per capita income hardly rose at all. The second result refers to Australia's regional representative institutions; because they were strong, the country's score on the indicator of *national* representative institutions was low. Australia was, however, far ahead of other countries in building feeder roads. The peculiarity of a slower lagged rate of market institutional development cannot be accounted for by the Australian experience recorded here.

and in New Zealand during the time of Maori communal agriculture. In China and India a combination of limited resources, a large population, and small peasant holdings prevented an effective market system. Slavery in Brazil, serfdom in Russia, and forced labor in Egypt limited labor mobility. In Scandinavia, too, in 1850, the geographical movement of labor was limited by severe overpopulation.[26]

In component 1 (table 3-5) foreign penetration and colonial dominance again led to the removal of institutional restrictions on markets and to dramatic export expansion. In contrast with class 2, however, the process went faster in countries that were more agricultural, heavily populated, and illiterate. The process was also fueled by faster population growth and modest net immigration.[27] Government actions reducing communal, slave, or serf forms of agricultural production accelerated these changes. The countries scoring high on the primary pattern (India and Egypt) were heavily dependent,[28] with only limited immigration associated with export expansion. Thus, population growth in this pattern reflects not the impact of immigration but probably the weakening of communal restraints on the birth rate as market opportunities increased. But nowhere in this component do we find increased positive long-term consequences, such as per capita income or wage benefits, associated with the pattern of dependent, export-oriented market development. Chapter seven, on poverty, will address the contrast between this pattern and that in class 2.

The secondary pattern summarizes an early Scandinavian dynamic: rising per capita income in small countries favored by socioeconomic and political conditions. Socioeconomic advantages included per capita income and agricultural productivity sufficient for a diffused surplus, high literacy for that time, and moderate land resources. Other advantages included lesser domination of policy by foreigners or large landowners and attitudes reasonably conducive to entrepreneurship. The high-scoring countries—Sweden in the 1850s and 1860s and Norway in the 1870s and 1880s—were facing severe overpopulation, which undoubtedly accounts for the lack of wage increases in the pattern. But other economic improvements suggest that overpopulation in Scandinavia was not a severe constraint on the development of market institutions. Nor does it appear to have spurred change.

China, where legal and customary restrictions on capitalism were important, scores the lowest on component 2. Little agricultural surplus, low per

---

[26] As noted later in this chapter, overpopulation was not as important a restriction on market institutional growth as the other restrictions in this class.

[27] Recall that variables with secondary high loadings also are important to the interpretation. In component 1 of table 3-5, these variables are illiteracy, land tenure, land concentration, spread of market institutions, export expansion, land abundance, and population.

[28] The low-scoring countries were China and Burma at midcentury; the inroads of marketization from exports had not begun. Customary restrictions on trade in China were extensive. In Burma, communal, extended-family agriculture was very important.

Table 3-5

Patterns of Domestic Market Expansion: Principal Components Analysis for Class 3 (Uneven Market Institutional Growth in Agricultural Economies Severely Hampered by Restrictions)[a]

Variable	Principal Component		
	1	2	3
Degree of foreign economic dependence	.29	−.17*	.11
Colonial status	.25	−.14	−.11
Rate of spread of market system, lagged (composite)	.21	.14	.03
Level of development of market system (composite)	.32	.08	.12
Percentage of labor force in agriculture	.33	−.04	−.05
Rate of population growth (lagged)	.20	−.00	.15
Net immigration	.20	−.13	.14
Rate of change in per capita income	.11	.21	.11
Level of development of techniques in agriculture	.10	.23	.03
Level of per capita income	.09	.18	.02
Extent of illiteracy	.29*	−.45	.07
Rate of spread of primary education (lagged)	.10	.43	−.14
Socioeconomic character of political leadership	.07	.17	.02
Favorableness of attitudes toward entrepreneurship	.10	.28	.03
Predominant form of land tenure and holding	.22*	.14	−.56
Concentration of landholdings	.19*	−.10	.35
Favorableness of land institutions to improvements	.13	.16	−.25
Rate of spread of market system (composite)	.21*	.03	.22
Rate of growth of exports	.17*	.13	.18
Direction of change in real wages in agriculture	.07	−.10	−.22
Relative abundance of agricultural resources	.21*	.18*	.22
Total population	.21*	−.31*	−.39
Level of development of techniques in industry	.08	.03	−.04
Level of development of inland transportation	.06	−.06	.00
Extent of urbanization	.06	.00	−.02
Rate of improvement in techniques in industry	.14	.02	−.05
Rate of improvement in techniques in industry (lagged)	.12	.05	−.07
Rate of improvement in techniques in agriculture	.08	.10	−.04
Rate of improvement in techniques in agriculture (lagged)	.06	.11	−.06
Rate of improvement in inland transportation (lagged)	.09	−.04	.03
Degree of shift in export structure	.06	.16	−.03
Direction of change in real wages in industry	.10	−.09	−.16
Extent of domestic economic role of government	.12	−.02	−.06
Extent of political stability	.08	.06	−.04
Strength of national representative institutions	.09	.02	−.04

[a]See the introductory section to the statistical analysis in this chapter for a discussion of how to read the components results and of the way we interpret them. Variables are listed within components on which they have primary high loadings in the order in which they are discussed in the text. Variables with secondary high loadings (marked with asterisks) also are important to the interpretation.

capita income, minimal investment in human capital, scarcity of land resources, and an indigenous leadership hostile to economic expansion help explain China's poor economic performance.

Component 3 documents a number of different ways that land institutions systematically constrained growth in very poor countries. On the one hand, in economies dominated by communal or servile land-labor systems (for example, Brazil and Egypt after midcentury), concentrated landownership caused rapid marketization and expanding primary exports to harm the agricultural poor, despite relative land abundance. On the other hand, in poor, very populous peasant economies (for example, India in the 1890s), export expansion was slower, but the establishment of individual property rights in land (hence the higher scores on land tenure) "freed" labor and land, increasing the breakup and loss of small holdings.[29] These and other influences on poverty will be considered more specifically in chapter seven.

Class 4: Government-Promoted Path of Dualistic Market Institutional Growth

In the agricultural economies of class 4, national governments promoted markets only in selected sectors. In the least developed countries of this class, both peasants and artisans increased production for the market in spite of restrictions on trade—for example, in Italy before unification, and in Japan and Spain at midcentury. In the more developed countries, governments responded to increased market sales by reducing barriers to free use of land and labor. Some also responded by directly promoting industry, but factories remained scarce and some sectors were left untouched by economic expansion, as in Italy, Spain, and Russia in the 1890s.[30] Class 4 differed from class 2 in its initial large population, which provided a potentially important domestic market; from both classes 2 and 3 in its moderate dependence on foreigners; and from class 3 in its considerable agricultural surplus. But it resembled class 2 in its narrow distribution of land and in the domination of its national leadership by landed elites.

In the primary pattern (table 3-6) commercial activity penetrated rapidly in overwhelmingly agricultural economies; institutional restrictions to markets rapidly broke down; mechanized industry spread in a few sectors, helped by domestic governments and foreign capital inflows; and exports of agricul-

---

[29]The positive covariation between agricultural wages and land systems in which the cultivator's independence was greater indicates that the negative effect of "freed" land was slightly offset by rising agricultural wages for the small wage-labor force. Egypt in 1850 was not yet faced with a scarcity of land, which accounts for that country's relatively high score on land abundance; in later decades, however, population growth created a scarcity of land.

[30]Germany is included in this class for 1850–1870 only, the period before political unification. Germany was more developed than the rest of class 4.

Table 3-6
Patterns of Domestic Market Expansion:
Principal Components Analysis for Class 4
(Government-Promoted Path of Dualistic Market Institutional Growth)[a]

Variable	Principal Component	
	1	2
Rate of spread of market system (composite)	.22	.05
Level of development of market system (composite)	.29	.08
Percentage of labor force in agriculture	.29	.11
Rate of improvement in techniques in industry	.18	−.09
Favorableness of land institutions to improvements	.20	−.08
Total population	.22	.05
Rate of growth of exports	.19*	−.21
Degree of shift in export structure	.19*	−.21
Rate of improvement in techniques in agriculture	.12	−.25
Rate of change in per capita income	.16	−.35
Level of development of techniques in agriculture	.17*	−.18
Predominant form of land tenure and holding	.18*	−.35
Concentration of landholdings	.22*	.30
Extent of domestic economic role of government	.19*	−.22
Degree of foreign economic dependence	.18*	.24
Extent of illiteracy	.22*	.35
Rate of spread of primary education (lagged)	.15	−.17
Level of per capita income	.15	.20
Relative abundance of agricultural resources	.15	.20
Rate of spread of market system, lagged (composite)	.15	−.02
Favorableness of attitudes toward entrepreneurship	.11	.05
Colonial status	.14	.08
Socioeconomic character of political leadership	.12	−.05
Strength of national representative institutions	.15	.15
Extent of political stability	.11	−.03
Rate of population growth (lagged)	.13	−.01
Net immigration	.11	.08
Extent of urbanization	.12	.10
Level of development of techniques in industry	.11	.03
Level of development of inland transportation	.12	−.15
Rate of improvement in techniques in industry (lagged)	.14	−.00
Rate of improvement in techniques in agriculture (lagged)	.08	−.13
Rate of improvement in inland transportation (lagged)	.15	−.07
Direction of change in real wages in industry	.15	.08
Direction of change in real wages in agriculture	.10	.09

[a]See the introductory section to the statistical analysis in this chapter for a discussion of how to read the components results and of the way we interpret them. Variables are listed within components on which they have primary high loadings in the order in which they are discussed in the text. Variables with secondary high loadings (marked with asterisks) also are important to the interpretation.

tural and manufactured products increased. Industrial expansion was faster where agricultural productivity was higher, and where land systems did not hamper, and large populations enhanced, internal markets.[31] We did *not,* however, find that reduced institutional barriers to trade, land transfers, and labor mobility led to rising agricultural productivity, wages, or per capita income. Rather, the main consequence was industrial expansion in a few sectors only. That is, the spread effects of institutional change and growth were much weaker here than in the class 1 countries.

In component 2, we see that above-average success in expanding and diversifying export capacity and in raising per capita income was closely associated with agricultural improvements. (We reverse the scores for ease of interpretation.) Higher agricultural productivity, made possible by land institutions that provided cultivator incentives for improvements with dispersed landownership, provided a significant diffused economic surplus. Domestic governments provided active support, by measures such as investment in education, rather than depending greatly on foreign capital and skills.[32] In Japan (the highest scorer), the government taxed agriculture to provide capital and expanded the educational system, increasing domestic skills. Educational investment was crucial because of scarce agricultural resources.

Measures of Statistical Fit

Table 3-7 indicates the degree of separation between the four components models. For each class it compares the own-class variance (the diagonal element in the table) with the variance when the country observations for that class are fitted to other class models. In each case, the own-class variance is

Table 3-7
Patterns of Domestic Market Expansion:
Cluster Distance Matrix for Principal Components Analyses

	Class 1	Class 2	Class 3	Class 4
Class 1	16.4	28.3	33.7	29.0
Class 2	30.1	14.4	26.2	30.4
Class 3	29.5	25.0	12.9	21.7
Class 4	25.5	26.3	21.0	16.2

NOTE: See text for explanation.

[31] More class 4 countries scored low on the composite indicator of land systems than class 1 countries did; thus, positive changes included the elimination of important restrictions on land use.

[32] Limited foreign dependence is implied by the negative association between export expansion and foreign dependence. As noted above, signs may be reversed for the sake of interpretation; only relationships among signs matter.

significantly lower than the other-class variance. We obtain the least difference when fitting class 4 to class 3 (31 percent). All other differences exceed
68 percent.

The statistical method calculates the distance of each country observation
from its own and all other class models (see table 3-8). In two instances an
observation was significantly closer to another class than to its own: Canada
at midcentury was closer to class 3, where market restrictions were severe,
than to its own relatively unrestricted class of land-abundant countries. At
the same time, Japan was closer to class 3 than to its own, where governments
played an active role in the economic arena. It was not until after 1870 that
the Japanese government really became active.[33] Two observations were borderline: Switzerland in 1850 and Russia in 1870. The other 65 observations
were correctly classified by the components models.

Importance of Variables to Between- and Within-Class Variations

Table 3-9 presents the statistical measures of the importance of individual
classification schemes in discriminating between classes and in "explaining"
within-class variations. Column 1 provides a measure of each indicator's contribution in discriminating among the four "types" of market expansion, *taking all classes together*. The measure compares the unexplained variance for
all observations when fitted to their "correct" class models with their unexplained variance when fitted to the "wrong" class models. The higher the
"incorrect" compared with the "correct" variance (adjusted to weight the
three incorrect fits and the one correct fit equally), the greater the variable's
contribution to explaining the correct assignments statistically.[34] Variables
with ratios over 5.0 are listed in order in column 1. Those with ratios below
5.0 are listed in order of their values in column 2.[35]

Fourteen variables have ratios of between-group relevance over 5.0. The
foremost importance of literacy underlines the crucial role of the diffusion of

---

The negative relationship between per capita income, on the one hand, and rates of growth of
exports, per capita income, and agricultural productivity, on the other, is a peculiarity. It may be
explained by the contrasting experiences of Japan (scoring high on this component), where dualistic growth in the latter nineteenth century was rapid, and Germany before 1870 (scoring lower
on this component), where growth was not yet effectively under way. Per capita income was lower
in Japan in 1890 than in Germany in 1850. (For the later, more successful decades, Germany is
not assigned to this class.)

[33] Note that all the misclassifications involve the earliest predominantly agricultural phase of
development. This is not surprising. The assignments to class 3 are based on severe *institutional*
restrictions. Canada faced severe geographic problems with transportation. Japan was borderline between classes 1 and 3 because the removal of restrictions came late in the period 1850–
1870.

[34] See equation (4) in chapter two.

[35] Those "important" in column 2 have values of "explained" variance over .50.

Table 3-8
Patterns of Domestic Market Expansion:
Degree of Fit for Principal Components Analyses
(Residual Standard Deviations for Three Classes Closest to Each Country Observation)

Country and Year	Assigned Class	Class to Which Closest	Residual S.D. – Closest Class	Class to Which 2d Closest	Residual S.D. – 2d Closest Class	Class to Which 3d Closest	Residual S.D. – 3d Closest Class
Belgium 1850	1	1	16	4	25	2	26
France 1850	1	1	17	4	25	2	29
Great Britain 1850	1	1	15	4	28	2	29
Netherlands 1850	1	1	19	4	21	2	23
Switzerland 1850	1	3	21	1	22	4	26
United States 1850	1	1	19	2	28	4	32
Belgium 1870	1	1	17	2	28	4	29
Canada 1870	1	1	17	2	22	3	23
Denmark 1870	1	1	13	4	23	3	24
France 1870	1	1	14	4	26	2	27
Germany 1870	1	1	18	4	30	2	32
Great Britain 1870	1	1	15	2	34	4	35
Netherlands 1870	1	1	17	4	25	2	25
Sweden 1870	1	1	13	3	21	4	23
Switzerland 1870	1	1	18	4	31	2	32
United States 1870	1	1	19	2	31	4	34
Belgium 1890	1	1	16	2	34	4	37
Canada 1890	1	1	17	2	22	4	30
Denmark 1890	1	1	16	2	27	4	28
France 1890	1	1	14	4	30	2	30
Germany 1890	1	1	20	4	32	2	36

Table 3-8 (continued)

Country and Year	Assigned Class	Class to Which Closest	Residual S.D.— Closest Class	Class to Which 2d Closest	Residual S.D.—2d Closest Class	Class to Which 3d Closest	Residual S.D.—3d Closest Class
Great Britain 1890	1	1	19	2	33	4	39
Netherlands 1890	1	1	14	2	25	4	29
Norway 1890	1	1	15	3	21	2	23
Sweden 1890	1	1	17	2	26	4	30
Switzerland 1890	1	1	17	2	31	4	35
United States 1890	1	1	19	4	33	2	35
Argentina 1850	2	2	13	3	21	4	26
Australia 1850	2	2	11	3	27	4	32
Canada 1850	2	3	19	2	23	1	25
Argentina 1870	2	2	11	3	20	4	26
Australia 1870	2	2	16	3	30	1	34
New Zealand 1870	2	2	17	3	24	1	27
Argentina 1890	2	2	11	1	32	3	33
Australia 1890	2	2	13	1	34	3	35
Brazil 1890	2	2	12	3	21	4	28
New Zealand 1890	2	2	15	1	26	3	34
Brazil 1850	3	3	9	2	19	4	23
Burma 1850	3	3	13	4	19	2	24
China 1850	3	3	12	4	22	2	27
Denmark 1850	3	3	15	4	22	1	22
Egypt 1850	3	3	12	4	23	2	26
India 1850	3	3	14	2	24	4	25
New Zealand 1850	3	3	20	2	23	4	29
Norway 1850	3	3	15	4	23	2	24

Russia 1850	3	11	3	4	18	2	23
Sweden 1850	3	14	3	4	21	1	24
Brazil 1870	3	10	3	4	18	2	20
Burma 1870	3	12	3	4	22	2	26
China 1870	3	12	3	4	23	2	30
Egypt 1870	3	10	3	4	20	2	29
India 1870	3	13	3	1	25	4	27
Norway 1870	3	12	3	3	23	2	24
Russia 1870	3	15	4	4	15	2	23
Burma 1890	3	9	3	4	21	2	27
China 1890	3	12	3	4	23	2	30
Egypt 1890	3	13	3	4	23	2	30
India 1890	3	12	3	1	25	3	31
Germany 1850	4	17	4	3	24	2	25
Italy 1850	4	14	4	4	16	2	24
Japan 1850	4	18	3	3	23	2	27
Spain 1850	4	9	4	3	16	1	22
Italy 1870	4	19	4	3	25	1	29
Japan 1870	4	18	4	3	22	2	26
Spain 1870	4	17	4	1	22	3	25
Italy 1890	4	18	4	3	23	1	28
Japan 1890	4	10	4	3	25	2	27
Russia 1890	4	21	4	3	21	2	25
Spain 1890	4	14	4	3	18	2	22

NOTE: The years 1850, 1870, and 1890 following country names in column 1 are shorthand for our three cross sections: 1850–1870, 1870–1890, and 1890–1914. As noted in chapter two and in appendix tables A51 through A53, some variables refer to the initial year of each period, some refer to the entire period, and a few lagged variables refer to the preceding period.

Table 3-9
Patterns of Domestic Market Expansion:
Importance of Classification Scheme to Between-Class and Within-Class
Variations, All Classes Together[a]

Variable	Between-Group Relevance	Within-Group Relevance
Extent of illiteracy	14.6	.79
Percentage of labor force in agriculture	10.9	.24
Direction of change in real wages in industry	8.0	.27
Total population	7.5	.60
Level of development of inland transportation	7.1	.59
Degree of foreign economic dependence	6.6	.47
Level of development of techniques in agriculture	6.5	.59
Strength of national representative institutions	5.9	.33
Level of development of market system (composite)	5.8	−.06
Level of development of techniques in industry	5.5	.49
Level of per capita income	5.4	.53
Favorableness of attitudes toward entrepreneurship	5.1	.55
Predominant form of land tenure and holding	5.0	.59
Relative abundance of agricultural resources	5.0	.58
Socioeconomic character of political leadership	4.4	.69
Rate of improvement in techniques in agriculture	3.4	.68
Rate of improvement in techniques in industry (lagged)	4.4	.53
Rate of spread of market system (composite)	4.2	.50
Rate of change in per capita income	1.8	.43
Rate of improvement in techniques in industry	4.8	.48
Rate of improvement in techniques in agriculture (lagged)	3.3	.43
Rate of improvement in inland transportation (lagged)	2.4	.35
Rate of population growth (lagged)	4.0	.23
Net immigration	2.6	.03
Concentration of landholdings	4.3	.26
Favorableness of land institutions to improvements	4.0	.25
Rate of spread of primary education (lagged)	2.2	.49
Extent of urbanization	3.6	.30
Colonial status	4.7	.34
Rate of growth of exports	1.4	.16
Degree of shift in export structure	4.2	.23
Extent of domestic economic role of government	1.8	.28
Extent of political stability	3.5	.48
Direction of change in real wages in agriculture	3.5	.28
Rate of spread of market system, lagged (composite)	2.5	.09

[a]Variables with between-group relevance over 5.0 are listed first, in descending order by that measure (column 1: 14.6–5.0). The remaining variables that have measures of within-group relevance over .50 are listed in descending order by the within-group measure (column 2: .69–.50).

entrepreneurial, technical, and other institution-building skills to all even moderately successful paths of development. Variables differentiating Northwestern Europe (with its developed market institutions), densely settled poor countries (with poorly developed market institutions), and the two other classes (with dualistic market structures) are: a greater shift of labor out of agriculture, rising industrial wages, higher development levels (in transport, technology, market institutions, and per capita income), less foreign dependence, better-developed parliamentary systems favoring rising entrepreneurial groups, favorable tenure arrangements, and better land resources. Large populations enhancing domestic market size distinguish the moderately backward European countries from more underdeveloped ones.

Column 2 of table 3-9 gives a measure of how well each variable explains statistically the variance *within* classes *for all classes together*. Twelve variables explain more than 50 percent of the within-class variance. Again, literacy explains more variance than any other variable, acting as a proxy in our results for skills, aptitudes, and attitudes critical to economic expansion. Then comes the structure of leadership power (how powerful rising economic groups were compared with landed elites). A vital agricultural sector, with rapidly improving agricultural productivity, is the next most important aspect of development determining how agriculture interacted with the rest of the economy. Our most direct measures of the size of the domestic market, population, and per capita income are among the remaining important variables, along with transportation networks and two indicators of the potential marketed supply of agricultural goods—agricultural productivity and agricultural resources. Institutional influences that crucially affected how well agriculturalists responded to market incentives are landholding and tenure systems and the speed of development of market institutions. The technological variables directly indicate the extent of profit-making responses to market expansion.

CONCLUSION

The results in this chapter suggest the following propositions.

1. Countries had to pass a threshold level of development of market institutions before successful capitalist industrialization could take place. The existence of this threshold is suggested by the Western European path of market institutional development (class 1). Only in this class do we find widespread industrialization. Initial conditions shared by all successful cases were well-established individual property rights, especially in land, and the removal of medieval as well as mercantilist restrictions on labor and capital mobility and land use.

2. Passing a threshold in market institutional development did not, however, assure industrialization. Although all countries in class 1 continued to expand their market systems, the pace of further market institution building

did not correlate with the speed of industrialization. Land institutions conducive to rising agricultural productivity, widespread transportation networks, political systems through which rising industrial interests could influence policy, and social attitudes favoring entrepreneurship were more important influences on industrialization in Western Europe than the speed of expansion of market institutions.

3. In moderately backward countries with administratively capable governments for that time (class 4), severe political, military, or economic challenges from Western Europe played a prominent role in inducing institutional changes that established market systems. Initial conditions were less favorable here than in class 1, but agricultural surpluses were considerable (however poorly distributed), and urban-rural trade networks were relatively well developed despite the lack of effective political and economic integration. Governments acted to eliminate market restrictions and, in contrast with class 1, their efforts were closely correlated with industrialization and export growth. But the spread of market institutions and industrial growth induced broad changes involving both agriculture and industry only when political and land institutions were favorable. A weakening of the control of landed elites over economic policies, domestic government actions taken in education and agriculture, and the provision of an adequate incentive structure by land institutions all contributed to the diffusion of growth.

4. In the most underdeveloped countries (classes 2 and 3) the strongest force for market institutional change was the intrusion of foreign economic interests. Our results show that in both land-abundant and densely settled countries, foreign economic penetration, the removal of market restrictions, and substantial export expansion occurred simultaneously. Colonial powers exerted their political dominion, formal or informal, to remove institutional barriers to the expansion of production for export. Here, our results suggest a sequence from economic opportunities to institutional change which is consistent with the neoclassical model of institutional change.

5. The consequences of foreign promotion of market institutional change in countries with poorly developed market systems varied significantly between land-abundant and densely populated poor countries. In the latter (class 3), our results show, foreign penetration under colonial domination and export expansion produced few local benefits. They induced investment in neither indigenous communities nor human capital. By contrast, in land-abundant countries, European immigrants settled, thereby encouraging investment in both construction and schooling for growing populations. This contributed to substantial domestic growth as long as political and land institutions were reasonably favorable. Most important, according to our results, was a reduction in the power of landed elites and a widening of land distribution. The latter was especially significant since land-abundant countries had concentrated land distributions.

Our results for land-abundant countries support the neoclassical model of induced institutional change for countries where foreigners responded to opportunities for profits by taking the initiative in developing overseas primary exports. Here, to grasp their opportunities, foreigners changed laws and undermined customary communal arrangements in order to build the institutions of a market system. But our results for moderately backward countries support the view of modernization theorists, which is that the major force for change was the response of national governments to the political threat of British economic and political preeminence. These governments eliminated market restrictions as a first step in rapidly expanding their economic potential and thus their political power.

4 Patterns of Industrialization

"Industrialization" relates to the spread of "mechanization" or "factory" industry. We share with Kuznets, Hughes, and others the view that widespread industrialization is best conceived of as a complex process of structural, technological, institutional, and attitudinal change, a key aspect of which is the application of scientific knowledge to most areas of economic life. Before 1914, however, in many countries increased mechanization did not lead to industrialization in this broader sense. Thus we focus here on the concrete institutional changes that accompanied the shift, however modest, from animate to inanimate power. The spread of factory organization, with its wage labor force and large amounts of fixed capital, was foremost among these changes and is usually viewed as the heart of the nineteenth-century industrial revolution.[1]

Here we explore further institutional influences on industrialization. We have already grouped countries by their market institutions and examined economic and institutional change within these groups. We found that the development of market institutions and industrialization did not consistently move together. Widespread industrialization occurred only where individual property rights were well established and institutional barriers to market expansion were few. But the reverse did not hold: Favorable market institutions did not necessarily lead to widespread industrialization with any predictable time lag.

We designed our typology of industrialization patterns to help explain the structure and extent of industrial expansion. Influences assumed to be crucial were initial resource and institutional conditions, transformations in social and political as well as market institutions, and dynamic external and internal forces. Our choice of variables reflects these assumptions.

Through our statistical analysis we seek to specify the ways in which social and political institutional influences help determine paths of industrial expansion. Formal historical models have for the most part been limited to variables stressed in standard economic theory.[2] Less well specified models incorporate a larger range of institutional influences; the models of Marx, Rostow, and Gerschenkron are perhaps the best known. (However, investigators "testing" these broad models disagree not only about their specification but even about the periods and geographic areas to which they apply.)[3]

---

[1] See Hughes 1970, p. xi; Kuznets 1958, pp. 141–142; and Deane (Great Britain) 1965, p. 84.

[2] The few quantitative studies of the process of industrialization using formal models include Fogel and Engerman 1971; Chenery 1960; Chenery, Shishido, and Watanabe 1962; Kelley and Williamson 1974; U.S. Department of Commerce, Bureau of Economic Analysis, 1972; and Williamson 1974. Kuznets (1971) provides well-known examples of a more inductive quantitative approach.

[3] See Rostow 1960, Gerschenkron 1962a, and Baran 1968. For case-study criticisms, see Rostow 1963. For a discussion of tests of Gerschenkronian hypotheses, see Sylla 1977, especially pp. 71ff. and the references cited therein. Siegenthaler (1972) makes an unusual attempt to in-

THE INDUSTRIALIZATION VARIABLES

Industrialization could not be measured directly. Two variables were needed: one to indicate the importance of "modern" or "factory" industry in 1850, 1870, and 1890, and the other to gauge the rate of expansion of factory industry during the periods 1830–1850, 1850–1870, 1870–1890, and 1890–1914. Since quantitative data on these variables were available for very few countries, diverse indirect indicators had to be used to classify countries into six or seven ranked categories. The full classification schemes, country assignments, and sources used for each country and period are given in the data appendix.

Variable 1: Level of Development of Techniques in Industry

This classification focuses on the importance of the substitution of factory production for preindustrial forms (artisan shops, cottage industry, home production)—a striking feature of nineteenth-century industrialization.

The proportion of the labor force in factories is a possible proxy for the extent of mechanization, but such data are rarely available, their quality varies greatly, and they offer only a general indicator of the importance of factory industry. "Factory" is sometimes defined as a manufacturing operation with more than 5 workers, sometimes with over 20 or 30. We therefore resorted to descriptive materials on the replacement of preindustrial methods by mechanized techniques. Various types of specific data were used: employment in factories, average employment in manufacturing enterprises, average horsepower in manufacturing, the size distribution of horsepower by enterprise, the value of output from factories, measures of the relative importance of manufacturing, and qualitative information on the spread of factories, among other pieces of information. For the post-1870 periods, it was sometimes possible to substitute data on factory employment for descriptive data on the importance of the factory sector. Other data—for example, output per worker, horsepower per worker, horsepower per enterprise, average size of enterprise, and the distribution of enterprises by size—helped determine whether factories or enterprises were large and employed high-horsepower machinery. Because inclusion of the metallurgical, construction, shipbuilding, and chemical industries would have greatly complicated intercountry comparisons, we concentrated instead on consumer goods and machinery production.

Up until the 1870s in Western Europe, the mechanization of consumer goods typically progressed from cotton spinning to weaving, followed by the

---

corporate directly institutional influences in testing the validity of Gerschenkron's broad hypotheses about backwardness and institutional change. He uses scalogram analysis to depict association patterns among institutional characteristics for twelve European countries.

spinning and weaving of other textiles, and then the mechanization of many other goods. But in countries that mechanized later, this progression was replaced by simultaneous mechanization in many industries. In the machinery industries, the progression of production techniques was from the handicraft fabrication of tools, to workshops where individuals used inanimate power to tool machines by hand, to more developed methods using interchangeable parts.

The level-of-technical-development indicator classified countries into seven categories stressing the following criteria: the extent of mechanization of textile production, the range of consumer goods produced mainly in factories, the extent of factory production of machinery, and the overall share of factory employment. The top three categories included countries where cotton spinning and weaving were largely mechanized: category 1 was marked by factory production of a wide range of consumer goods and well-developed machinery industries; category 2, by a narrower range of consumer goods but significant factory production of machines; and category 3, by mechanization confined mainly to textiles. The middle group, category 4, included countries where in 1850 only cotton spinning was fully mechanized but also those in which by 1870 or 1890 some factory production had occurred in several other industries. The bottom three categories were reserved for countries where hand methods prevailed: category 5 included countries where some domestic factories processed agricultural raw materials; category 6, countries where mechanized techniques prevailed only in a narrow expatriate export sector; and category 7, those where few if any factories existed.

Variable 2: Rate of Improvement in Techniques in Industry

This variable measures the rate of expansion of mechanized industry using inanimate power. Data on changes in value added by industry were used only to compare more advanced countries whose post-1830 additions to industrial output were produced mainly in factories. Value-added data were not used to compare countries from very dissimilar levels or with very different industrial structures, since a given percentage change would not mean the same thing for countries starting with a large industrial base as for those beginning from scratch. Industrialization from a substantial base ranked higher than more rapid industrial expansion from a narrow base. Both descriptive and numerical data on the spread of factories were used for countries just starting to build factory industry.

The classification scheme had seven categories. In categories 1 and 2 were countries starting the period with at least 20 percent of their GDP originating in industry and with significant mechanization as indicated by qualitative information. League of Nations data (1945) on rates of increase in manufacturing output distinguished between these two top categories. In categories 3 and 4 were countries that experienced a major spurt of industrial expansion from a narrow base; the two categories were distinguished by whether or not machinery production and consumer goods production increased significantly over time. In category 5 were countries whose factories almost exclusively processed primary products. Countries were assigned to categories 6 and 7 if their additions to industrial capacity were handicraft production or if the growth of industry was negligible.

THE TYPOLOGY

Our statistical method requires a sample stratification that groups countries by similarity of industrial development. This, in turn, entails developing a typology of industrialization. The criteria for dividing our sample by type of industrial development spring from Gerschenkron's typology of industrial development (1968).[4] Gerschenkron's hypothesis is that differences in economic development among European countries depended on their scores on a number of dichotomies in industrialization: whether or not industrialization was actively encouraged by governments; whether it was a gradual expansion or a widespread structural transformation; whether it was marked by a "takeoff" or exhibited continuous growth; whether it was dominated by producer or consumer goods production; and, finally, whether it led to stagnation or progress in agriculture. We follow Gerschenkron in several of these distinctions: whether industrialization was early and extensive, came late with a marked surge or spurt, or proceeded on its own or with direct government intervention; and whether or not agriculture progressed. We do not include the dichotomies of producer versus consumer goods, large versus small industrial plants, or strong versus weak banks.

We adopt Gerschenkron's organizing principle of economic development—that is, degree of backwardness—in distinguishing among European countries (and Japan). But our approach differs from his in the way we use statistical techniques to analyze our classificatory variables—the equivalent of his dichotomies or his "generalizable variabilities"—to obtain a well-articulated pattern that enhances their explanatory significance.

The typology (table 4-1) assigns each country to a given class on the basis of its industrial change over the entire period. Our criteria include the timing and pace of industrial expansion, the initial level of industrial development, the structure of expansion, and the importance of manufactured goods in exports. The top two classes include countries that experienced substantial industrialization, but differed in its structure and extent. For countries in class 1, industrialization came early and was extensive by the end of the nineteenth century; these countries became major exporters of manufactured goods. Less favorable initial conditions in class 2 countries and the challenge of in-

---

[4] Also relevant is Senghaas and Menzel's typology of industrializing "metropolitan" countries (1979).

Table 4-1
A Typology of Industrial Development in the Nineteenth and Early Twentieth Centuries

Class	Description of Class	Country	Principal Sources
1	Countries where most institutional restrictions to the growth of market systems were removed by the early nineteenth century; industrialization was under way before the middle of the century; widespread industrialization occurred in the latter part of the century primarily through the relatively autonomous growth of private enterprise; and the role of the government was mainly limited to social overhead capital and tariff policies. A key feature of industrialization in this class was the concurrent growth of markets for land, labor, and capital and expansion of domestic and foreign markets for manufactured goods.	Belgium France Great Britain Switzerland United States	Craeybeckx 1970; Van Houtte 1943, chap. 6 Roehl 1976; Fohlen 1970 Richardson 1965; Wilson 1965 Bürgin 1959, pp. 229–236; Kneschaurek 1964, pp. 133–149 North 1965
2	Countries that were moderately or severely backward in the first decade of the nineteenth century compared with the countries of class 1 but that subsequently industrialized rapidly. Institutional restrictions (including political ones) on factor markets persisted into the second half of the nineteenth century; governments played a more active role in industry than did class 1 governments, by direct subsidization or government purchases affecting the structure, though not necessarily the pace, of industrialization. A key feature of the industrialization of these countries was a more dualistic expansion than characterized the countries of class 1.	Germany Italy Japan Russia	Hoffmann 1963; Kindleberger 1975 Luzzatto 1969, pp. 221–223; Seton-Watson 1967, pp. 284–288; Gerschenkron 1962a Tsuru 1963, pp. 139–150; Landes 1965b, passim Portal 1965
3	Predominantly agricultural countries with reasonably abundant resources where modest industrial development directed toward domestic markets was associated with rapid primary export expansion and increases in per capita income late in the nineteenth or early in the	Argentina Australia	Díaz Alejandro 1970, chap. 4; Wythe 1949, pp. 83ff. Fitzpatrick 1949, pp. 181–183, 262–263

twentieth century. Their industrial development was marked by the expanded manufacture of consumer goods and construction materials for the domestic market as well as the growth of factories in selected sectors processing primary products for export.

	Brazil	Wythe et al. 1949, p. 160; Burns 1970, pp. 258–260
	Canada	Bertram 1963
	Denmark	Drachmann 1915, pp. 24–27; Glamann 1960
	New Zealand	Sutch 1969, pp. 98–101; Simkin 1951, pp. 61–64, 154–156, 178; Condliffe 1959, pp. 39–166, 247–250
	Norway	Lieberman 1970, chap. 5; Bull 1960, pp. 262–271
	Sweden	Jörberg 1961, chap. 2

4   Peasant economies at low levels of development where little if any mechanized industry developed before World War I. The mechanized industry was limited to some processing of exports, a handful of textile or steel factories, and some food, beverage, and construction industries on a minute scale. Export expansions that took place in the late nineteenth century, stimulated or directly promoted by foreign powers, did not lead to any significant mechanized industry serving domestic markets.

	Burma	Resnick 1970, pp. 57–58; Hlaing 1964, pp. 101–107, 136–137
	China	Eckstein et al. 1968, pp. 3–5; Allen 1965, pp. 900–908; Allen and Donnithorne 1954, pp. 168–179
	Egypt	Owen 1969, pp. 294–302; Issawi 1966a, p. 452
	India	Allen 1965, pp. 908–914; Gadgil 1942, chaps. 6 and 8; Buchanan 1934, chap. 7

Unclassified

	Netherlands	Brugmans 1969
	Spain	Vicens Vives and Nadal Oller 1969, pp. 668–678; Tortella 1971, pp. 93–95; Nadal 1973, pp. 532–620

dustrialization elsewhere resulted in more government intervention to remove market restrictions and promote industry; industrialization got started later and its structure was more dualistic. Among these countries, only Germany became a leading exporter of manufactured goods by 1914.

Class 3 uses Gerschenkron's dichotomy of whether or not industrial development was derived from trade expansion. Included countries were European or European settled, almost all with small populations, where more modest industrial growth came late in the nineteenth century. Industrialization resulted from the expansion of primary exports; higher incomes in the export sector induced considerable import substitution in consumer goods industries and led to increased processing in factories. Gerschenkron's categorization was also used for our class 4 countries, where export expansion took place under colonial domination, foreign trade growth did not stimulate factory industry significantly, and the few factories that existed were for processing exports.

Two countries were left unclassified because their paths of industrial expansion were dissimilar from the others in the sample: the Netherlands and Spain. From an early position of commercial power, the Netherlands stagnated economically until well into the latter half of the nineteenth century. Industrial development was delayed until the 1890s, when domestic markets began to grow and exports expanded modestly. Spain "failed" in early industrialization; the cotton industry, which had mechanized early on, stagnated in the second half of the nineteenth century. The loss of colonial power and domestic political instability slowed both export and domestic market expansion, and intermittent surges of primary exports after 1850 failed to induce much industrial growth.[5]

THE STATISTICAL ANALYSES

Since the statistical patterns relating to industrialization recur, we will describe the samples and results in some detail here, and refer back to them later. In the tables, the variables are listed within components on which they have primary high loadings in the order in which we discuss them in the text. As noted in chapter three, however, variables with secondary high loadings (marked with asterisks in the tables) also are important to the interpretation of components. The reader who has not read the book continuously is referred

[5]In the first run, the United States was left unclassified because special characteristics of its early industrialization were associated with the importance of primary exports. Since its statistical distance from class 1 was small and its later industrialization had many class 1 characteristics, we assigned it to that class in subsequent runs.

Spain was initially assigned to class 3, but descriptive studies later indicated that it would be more appropriate to treat it as an individual case of aborted industrialization than to place it in the class of late and limited industrial growth.

to the introductory sections of the statistical analyses in chapter three for a discussion of how to read the components results and of the way we interpret them.

Class 1: Substantial Early Industrialization through Autonomous Market System Growth

The countries that industrialized early include the early European industrializers (Great Britain, Belgium, France, and Switzerland) and the United States. By 1914, they had large industrial sectors exporting a wide range of factory products. Their "takeoffs," where identifiable, had occurred before 1850. Early in the century, all had the developed market institutions that defined the top-ranking class in chapter three. Even in Switzerland, where political unification had not been achieved, the principle of free internal commodity trade was established. For all class 1 countries, commercial capital and entrepreneurial skills had accumulated during the eighteenth century, substantial population growth had enlarged both the labor force and the market for wage goods, and the use of land for profit was common.

While governments played only a modest direct role in the industrialization of class 1 countries, governments were indirectly important in establishing a politicolegal framework for expanding market networks, developing transportation systems, and controlling tariff policies. Parliamentary systems with property restrictions on voting were the norm; the political influence of business and commercial classes was typically increasing. After midcentury, political climates were reasonably favorable to private entrepreneurial activity and industrial capital accumulation.

Though the timing, pace, and structure of industrialization varied considerably, by the first decades of the twentieth century all class 1 countries were major world producers and exporters of a diversity of industrial goods, including machinery. Great Britain, the earliest industrializer and the industrial world leader in the last quarter of the nineteenth century, had minimal government aid and few tariffs. France industrialized early but more gradually; the scarcity of mineral resources, greater government intervention, and high tariffs contributed to the slower growth of its manufacturing sector relative to Britain. Belgium, like Britain, was favored by coal deposits, but industrialization proceeded in spurts alternating with economic stagnation until strong international markets for industrial goods helped it overcome the constraints of a small internal market. In Switzerland, despite the lack of iron and coal and a small domestic market, textiles mechanized early; later, the industrial sector developed specialized exports intensive in skilled human inputs. In the United States, mechanization also began early, but primary products dominated exports until the last quarter of the nineteenth century, when extensive industrialization made the United States a major world exporter of a wide range of industrial products.

Table 4-2 presents the principal components analysis for class 1 countries. The first component summarizes familiar economic characteristics of early, fairly autonomous, and successful industrialization. Mechanization in industry interacted with expanding exports, new transportation networks, and agricultural progress in raising average wages in industry and agriculture. The higher the level of economic development, the faster the progress. Common economic characteristics of class 1 countries were a considerable initial surplus above subsistence in agriculture and a per capita income level significantly above that of today's underdeveloped countries.

Institutional changes, occurring simultaneously, affected economic expansion. Increasingly, stable representative systems permitted greater political power for new business, commercial, and, toward the end of the century, labor interests. Social attitudes and land tenure systems adapted to respond appropriately to new economic opportunities. Parliamentary systems were developing, political strife was moderate, rising business groups shared indirect political influence, and entrepreneurship was recognized to some extent. Land tenure favored agricultural improvements.

Component 2, where Great Britain scores high, indicates familiar causes slowing industrialization at high development levels.[6] The minus sign for the shift in export composition indicates failure to adapt to changes in international competition. The minus sign for agricultural wages (a secondary variable) shows the negative impact of international competition on agriculture. International migration is the other dynamic variable. Britain's high score on this component for the 1870s and 1880s points to the unfavorable effects of emigration and capital outflows[7] on domestic investment and economic growth rates.[8]

Component 3 suggests another complex of influences slowing economic growth among successful industrializers. Slower increases in per capita income were associated with small populations and, consequently, with limited domestic markets, relatively scanty agricultural resources, and more persistent transportation barriers. Switzerland's high scores derive from its special

---

[6]The phrase "high development levels" summarizes the first four variables listed in component 2, class 1, in table 4-2. Associated together are low percentages of the labor force in agriculture, high levels of development of techniques in industry, high levels of development of inland transportation, and high degrees of urbanization. We infer the retardation in industrial growth from the absence of systematic connections in this component between high development levels and industrial and agricultural improvements. Britain scores high on this component for the period following 1870.

[7]We do not measure capital outflows directly, but the importance of capital outflows, typical of colonizers and other countries with heavy foreign investment, is inferred from Britain's low score on foreign dependence.

[8]Because of the inclusion of our new indicator of the extent of shift in the composition of exports, we are able to give a more reliable interpretation of this component here than we could give in our earlier study (Adelman and Morris 1980).

Table 4-2
Patterns of Industrialization:
Principal Components Analysis for Class 1
(Substantial Early Industrialization through Autonomous Market System Growth)[a]

Variable	Principal Component		
	1	2	3
Rate of improvement in techniques in industry	.23	.05	.08
Rate of improvement in techniques in industry (lagged)	.22	.13	.04
Rate of growth of exports	.18	−.11	.17
Rate of improvement in techniques in agriculture	.17	−.07	.03
Direction of change in real wages in industry	.22	−.03	−.00
Direction of change in real wages in agriculture	.21	−.18*	−.10
Level of per capita income	.20	.15	.08
Level of development of techniques in agriculture	.22	.11	−.03
Strength of national representative institutions	.21	.01	−.10
Extent of political stability	.18	−.06	−.14
Socioeconomic character of political leadership	.19	.03	.14
Predominant form of land tenure and holding	.22	−.16	.03
Favorableness of land institutions to improvements	.21	−.02	−.07
Percentage of labor force in agriculture	.13	−.37	−.04
Level of development of techniques in industry	.18*	.21	.04
Level of development of inland transportation	.21*	.37	−.17*
Extent of urbanization	.16	.47	−.09
Degree of shift in export structure	.15	−.23	.06
Net immigration	.13	−.33	−.19*
Rate of change in per capita income	.15	−.05	−.21
Total population	.14	.04	−.29
Relative abundance of agricultural resources	.11	−.27*	−.30
Rate of improvement in inland transportation (lagged)	.17*	.10	−.22
Level of development of market system (composite)	.13	.00	.38
Rate of spread of market system (composite)	.15	−.06	.23
Rate of spread of market system, lagged (composite)	.13	−.07	.48
Favorableness of attitudes toward entrepreneurship	.22*	.05	.23
Rate of improvement in techniques in agriculture (lagged)	.14	−.10	.04
Rate of population growth (lagged)	.14	−.08	−.13
Concentration of landholdings	.12	.12	−.11
Extent of illiteracy	.07	.06	−.06
Rate of spread of primary education (lagged)	.15	−.11	−.03
Colonial status	.07	−.13	.14
Degree of foreign economic dependence	.04	−.04	−.04
Extent of domestic economic role of government	.11	.09	.11

[a]See the introductory section to the statistical analysis in chapter three for a discussion of how to read the components results and of the way we interpret them. Variables are listed within components on which they have primary high loadings in the order in which they are discussed in the text. Variables with secondary high loadings (marked with asterisks) also are important to the interpretation.

problems of size, resource scarcities, and terrain. The favorable market institutions and social attitudes apparent in this component did not fully offset these retarding influences.

Taken together, countries that industrialized early shared three important sets of initial institutions favorable to widespread industrialization: legal institutions for a market system, political institutions responsive to changing economic interests, and land institutions where cultivators benefited from improvements. Secondary component scores show two sources of retardation: one relating to foreign trade performance, and the other to domestic resource and size constraints.

Class 2: Later Substantial Industrialization Promoted by National Governments

Class 2 consists of four countries: Russia, Italy, Germany, and Japan. These countries were moderately backward in the early nineteenth century compared with those in class 1. Prodded by direct government measures, they subsequently industrialized quickly yet unevenly. By the end of the century their surges of industrial expansion involved both consumer and complex intermediate goods. All four countries had relatively large populations, but only Germany had become a major industrial power by 1914.[9]

There were serious social and political hindrances to labor and capital flows in class 2 countries during the early nineteenth century. Capitalist agriculture was quite limited, being found in Germany only in East Prussia and parts of the Rhineland, and in Italy only in the Po Valley.[10] German mobility restrictions and remnants of feudal ties persisted until after 1850; significant agricultural improvements came only late in the century. In Russia, it was more than two decades after serfdom was abolished in 1861 that substantial labor migration became possible; agriculture remained backward. In southern Italy, peasant ties to landlords constrained labor mobility and agricultural development was slow. And Japanese institutional restrictions on factor markets were removed only with the Meiji reforms of the 1870s.

Nowhere in class 2 was there effective political integration before the last few decades of the century. Nor were there parliamentary systems responsive to new economic interest groups. Russia and Japan did not adopt parliamentary systems; Italy's constitutional monarchy was marked by regional dis-

---

[9]While somewhat similar to class 4 in chapter three, this class incorporates a wider range of performance, including Russia before 1890 and Germany after 1870.

[10]It should be noted that in Japan, commercialization in agriculture had proceeded slowly but steadily for more than a century before the Meiji reforms of the 1870s. Note that, strictly speaking, capitalist agriculture involves not only production for profit but substantial use of wage labor.

cords and unstable alliances; and Germany's parliamentary system remained firmly under the influence of large landlords.

Governments promoted industrialization, although not always successfully. In Italy, for example, some government subsidies and transportation investments are even thought to have hindered industrial expansion.[11] Typically, government promotion of particular industries and selective importation of advanced technologies contributed to marked contrasts between advanced and backward sectors. Although expatriate influences did not dominate government economic policies in these countries, foreign capital inflows and foreign entrepreneurship were at times very significant.

The timing and pace of industrialization varied considerably. Industrialization in Germany began before political unification in 1871, increasing rapidly until Germany became a world power by 1914. In Japan, the institutional reforms of the 1870s were followed by a major spurt of industrialization in the 1890s which transformed selected sectors before 1914. In Italy and Russia, economic stagnation, erratic growth, and severe setbacks persisted until the 1880s, and were later interspersed with periods of sustained industrial advances.

The components analysis for class 2 countries, presented in table 4-3, indicates the national governments' vital role in accelerating industrialization. In component 1, leading institutional influences were government removal of restrictions on factor markets,[12] land systems favorable to productivity improvements, and active government promotion of industry. Productivity-enhancing land arrangements included capitalist or family holdings of moderate size under independent or at least fairly secure tenure. Associated with these influences were increased industrialization, export expansion, and economic growth rates; larger populations; export diversification,[13] and higher levels of agricultural productivity. But very high proportions of their populations remained in agriculture and were illiterate. Certain of the variables indicate this persistent gap between advancing industry and lagging agriculture—a gap that is much wider in class 2 than in class 1. This interpretation accords with Germany's and Japan's high scores after 1890 and Italy's and Japan's low scores in the 1850s and 1860s.

The contrast between the results for classes 1 and 2 is greater than indicated by the associations among variables in the component alone. The country data (appendix tables A51 through A53) show that class 2 countries rank lower on agricultural productivity and on variables representing land and market institutions. In class 1, the positive association between the two sets of variables reflects mainly an increase in the geographical scope of market in-

[11] See Fenoaltea (Italy) 1969.

[12] Represented by rate of spread of market system, which is measured in part by removal of institutional restrictions on markets.

[13] Represented by the high secondary loading on shifts in export structure.

Table 4-3
Patterns of Industrialization:
Principal Components Analysis for Class 2
(Later Substantial Industrialization Promoted by National Governments)[a]

Variable	Principal Component		
	1	2	3
Extent of domestic economic role of government	.21	.06	−.01
Level of development of market system (composite)	.26	−.03	−.25*
Rate of spread of market system (composite)	.23	−.08	−.17*
Concentration of landholdings	.21	−.18*	.20*
Rate of improvement in techniques in industry	.20	.13	.17*
Rate of growth of exports	.19	.14	.03
Rate of change in per capita income	.17	.15	−.00
Total population	.23	−.15	.02
Percentage of labor force in agriculture	.26	−.23*	−.20*
Rate of improvement in techniques in agriculture	.14	.21	−.02
Level of development of techniques in agriculture	.18*	.23	−.15
Extent of illiteracy	.19*	−.40	−.12
Favorableness of land institutions to improvements	.19*	.24	−.18*
Predominant form of land tenure and holding	.21*	.25	−.19*
Level of development of inland transportation	.14	.25	.24*
Degree of shift in export structure	.19*	.24	−.13
Relative abundance of agricultural resources	.14	−.23	.04
Degree of foreign economic dependence	.15	−.28	−.04
Level of development of techniques in industry	.13	.04	.20
Rate of improvement in techniques in industry (lagged)	.17*	.11	.19
Rate of improvement in inland transportation (lagged)	.16	.10	.28
Rate of spread of market system, lagged (composite)	.14	−.05	−.34
Direction of change in real wages in industry	.17*	−.23*	.33
Direction of change in real wages in agriculture	.12	−.14	.32
Colonial status	.12	−.09	−.19
Level of per capita income	.14	.02	.14
Rate of improvement in techniques in agriculture (lagged)	.10	.15	−.08
Rate of population growth (lagged)	.14	−.08	.05
Net immigration	.12	−.14	−.08
Rate of spread of primary education (lagged)	.13	.14	.14
Extent of urbanization	.11	.07	−.04
Favorableness of attitudes toward entrepreneurship	.11	.04	.14
Socioeconomic character of political leadership	.13	.02	.09
Strength of national representative institutions	.13	−.04	.10
Extent of political stability	.12	−.13	.01

[a]See the introductory section to the statistical analysis in chapter three for a discussion of how to read the components results and of the way we interpret them. Variables are listed within components on which they have primary high loadings in the order in which they are discussed in the text. Variables with secondary high loadings (marked with asterisks) also are important to the interpretation.

stitutions, while in class 2, the same association indicates some success in removing institutional restrictions on marketization and a reduction in the importance of communal or very insecure tenancies.

Another contrast between the two classes is found in the agricultural concomitants of industrial change. In class 1, rising agricultural productivity and agricultural wages accompanied industrialization. In contrast, with industrialization in class 2, the populations failed to shift from agriculture, remained largely illiterate, and did not benefit from a systematic improvement in agricultural wages. Some surplus above subsistence in agriculture was still required in class 2 for substantial industrial change to result, as indicated by the measure of the *level* of agricultural productivity in this component. We will discuss this further in chapter five (agricultural development) and chapter seven (the course of poverty).

A third contrast between classes 1 and 2 is in the political sphere. Class 1 experienced the typical political concomitants of Western European economic success: increasing representation of rising economic interests, stronger national parliamentary systems, and greater political stability. In class 2, the only political variable in the primary pattern was direct government economic activity.

This primary pattern for class 2, together with other class characteristics, strongly suggests that even though national governments were successful in pushing industrialization, economic improvements in agriculture were hindered by unfavorable initial institutions. The most important hindrances appear to have been legal or social barriers to the extension of market transactions and the inhibiting character of the political power structure.

Component 2 summarizes an alternative path of industrialization accompanied by more successful agricultural transformation. Germany's high scores indicate that its experience was not fully captured by the primary class pattern. Here we find rising agricultural productivity associated with greater literacy and with land systems that encouraged improved methods on freehold farms or on moderate-size family farms.[14] Agricultural achievements also were greater, with better transport and faster adaptations to the changing structure of international markets and a more rapid shift of population out of agriculture.[15] Russia's low component scores reinforce an interpreta-

---

[14]We infer this association with land systems from our definition of the indicator of the favorableness of land institutions to improvements. See chapter five for a description of this indicator.

[15]Adaptation to international markets is inferred from our indicator on shifts in export structure. Contrasts between high-scoring Germany and low-scoring Russia account for the high negative loading of resource abundance and the high positive loading of foreign dependence. Russia had more resources and depended more on foreign capital and skills than Germany. In contrast with class 1 achievements, we do not find Germany's agricultural progress translated into industrial wage increases. Indeed, country data show average wage declines in the 1850s and 1860s (Spree [Germany] 1977).

tion that ties agricultural success to human capital and the characteristics of land institutions. We will discuss this further in chapter five.

Component 3, interpreted with signs reversed, underlines characteristics of the Japanese experience with industrialization before 1890. A slow start on industrialization is linked with transportation bottlenecks. Rapid removal of market restrictions and rapid commercialization are associated with quite favorable land institutions, but agricultural improvements did not follow systematically and average real wages were negatively affected. Component scores for Japan before 1890, which are high on the "reverse" pattern, support our interpretation of a rather specific early Japanese pattern of economic change.[16]

Class 3: Late Modest Industrial Growth Following Primary Export Expansion in Countries Where Land Is Fairly Abundant

Class 3 consists of eight agricultural countries, European or European-settled, where primary export expansion in the last quarter of the nineteenth century was eventually followed by the development of small, modestly mechanized manufacturing. The class includes three Scandinavian countries (Denmark, Norway, and Sweden), three colonies settled by the British (Canada, Australia, and New Zealand), as well as Argentina and Brazil. Until 1850, their economies were characterized by considerable local self-sufficiency or, if newly settled, by dependence on imported goods. Lack of transportation was a critical barrier to domestic market expansion. There were few institutional restrictions on commodity markets, but some labor market restrictions remained in 1850: remnants of feudalism in Scandinavia, convict labor in Australia, and slavery in Brazil. After the major transportation breakthrough by railroads in the 1870s and 1880s, domestic farming and export production spread more rapidly, but import substitution proceeded slowly because domestic markets were small, critical inputs were scarce, and there was a strong comparative advantage in primary production. With favorable foreign markets, greatly improved transportation systems, and expanded exports, per capita income grew at a rapid rate in almost all class 3 countries late in the century.

[16]Colonial status is included in this component because two countries, Germany and Japan, that scored low on the reverse pattern (which we interpret to reflect specific Japanese experience) owned colonies after 1890. Japan owned no colonies, thus having a higher score than Germany and Italy on a variable defined so that colonies ranked highest and owners of colonies lowest. Thus, in this component, Japan's particular pattern of market institutional development is positively associated with independence from colonial domination (but no ownership of colonies).

The difference between component 3, class 2, in our present analysis and component 3, class 2, in our earlier analysis of industrialization (Adelman and Morris 1980) is not surprising. With important additions in variables, such as export and wage indicators, as well as score revisions, stability of associations in third components for small samples cannot always be expected.

The pace and structure of industrialization varied in response to natural resource constraints, domestic and ocean transport, income distribution from exports, agricultural progress, and other influences. As exports to Europe expanded, domestic processing increased and formed the nucleus of small manufacturing sectors: iron in Sweden; wool in Australia, Argentina, and New Zealand; wheat in Argentina and, later, Canada; dairy products in Denmark and, later, New Zealand; meat products in Argentina, Australia, and New Zealand; and coffee in Brazil.

The stimulus to domestic markets varied with the character of export proceeds and population size. Except for Brazil, the population of class 3 countries did not exceed 5 million until the last quarter of the century, if then. Although Brazil had more people, poverty there constrained market size. Large-scale immigration accompanied land settlement in Australia, New Zealand, Argentina, and later, Canada. In contrast, Scandinavian emigration increased land availability.

Where export proceeds were widely distributed among the population, as in Denmark, Sweden, Canada, and later, Australia, export expansion induced increased domestic manufacture. But where proceeds were concentrated, as in Brazil and Argentina, it stimulated domestic production to a lesser degree. Wherever domestic farming expanded significantly in response to urban area food needs, agricultural income was widely distributed and contributed to a larger domestic market, as in Scandinavia and, ultimately, in the British colonies.

Industrialization in class 3 countries was quite modest. Only in Sweden was there considerable industry as iron ore resources led to low-cost iron manufacture. Consumer goods—foodstuffs, beverages, clothing, printed matter, and building materials—were produced near where they were consumed. Production of intermediate goods was primarily limited to tools used in producing goods for export, except in Sweden, where the beginnings of textile and agricultural machinery production were evident.

Political characteristics varied among class 3 countries. The Scandinavian countries had limited constitutional monarchies where suffrage expanded gradually. Most British colonies gained decentralized domestic representative governments during the latter half of the century. Brazil and Argentina had monarchies with negligible representation of rising economic groups. In Brazil, Argentina, and New Zealand, major political or military conflicts impeded economic expansion for a time, particularly during the third quarter of the century.

Table 4-4 presents the principal components analysis for class 3. Component 1 delineates the foreign-promoted primary export expansion typical of the land-abundant British colonies, which led, with a considerable lag, to the modest industrial growth characteristic of class 3 countries.[17] Here govern-

---

[17]The subsequent industrial growth is not evident in the component associations. It is inferred

Table 4-4
Patterns of Industrialization:
Principal Components Analysis for Class 3
(Late Modest Industrial Growth Following Primary Expansion;
Countries Where Land Fairly Abundant)[a]

Variable	Principal Component		
	1	2	3
Rate of growth of exports	.21	−.15	−.02
Degree of foreign economic dependence	.21	−.18*	−.14
Rate of spread of market system, lagged (composite)	.26	−.19*	−.04
Level of development of market system (composite)	.20	−.07	.03
Rate of population growth (lagged)	.22	−.16	.18*
Relative abundance of agricultural resources	.27	−.20*	−.03
Favorableness of attitudes toward entrepreneurship	.21	.14	.10
Level of development of techniques in agriculture	.16	.20	−.10
Rate of improvement in techniques in agriculture	.16	.18	.11
Rate of improvement in inland transportation (lagged)	.14	.17	.06
Concentration of landholdings	.21*	−.30	.15
Predominant form of land tenure and holding	.23*	.29	−.03
Favorableness of land institutions to improvements	.18*	.21	.01
Degree of shift in export structure	.11	.22	−.14
Extent of illiteracy	.11	−.38	−.21*
Net immigration	.18*	−.34	.17*
Rate of change in per capita income	.18*	.13	−.36
Direction of change in real wages in industry	.17*	.09	−.22
Direction of change in real wages in agriculture	.10	.11	−.20
Colonial status	.19*	−.11	.21
Level of per capita income	.18*	.08	.29
Extent of urbanization	.12	.03	.27
Percentage of labor force in agriculture	.19*	−.09	−.29
Rate of spread of primary education (lagged)	.17*	.15	.18
Extent of domestic economic role of government	.16	.10	.17
Socioeconomic character of political leadership	.16	.13	.23
Strength of national representative institutions	.18*	−.05	−.37
Level of development of techniques in industry	.10	.11	.01
Level of development of inland transportation	.09	.15	−.01
Total population	.07	−.04	−.09
Rate of improvement in techniques in industry	.16	.05	−.01
Rate of improvement in techniques in industry (lagged)	.13	.10	.02
Rate of improvement in techniques in agriculture (lagged)	.10	.15	−.01
Extent of political stability	.11	.11	−.14
Rate of spread of market system (composite)	.08	−.01	.02

[a]See the introductory section to the statistical analysis in chapter three for a discussion of how to read the components results and of the way we interpret them. Variables are listed within components on which they have primary high loadings in the order in which they are discussed in the text. Variables with secondary high loadings (marked with asterisks) also are important to the interpretation.

ments removed legal restrictions on land and labor markets and expatriate capital, entrepreneurship, and immigration, and thus population increased dramatically. Where market institutions were established, land resources abundant, agricultural enterprises large, and initial per capita income fairly high, these developments led to increasing per capita income growth rates. Our results indicate that this dynamic export expansion pattern was faster and benefited industrial workers more wherever rising indigenous socioeconomic groups had gained some political representation, attitudes had become moderately favorable to entrepreneurship, and governments had invested in primary education and had taken measures to consolidate individual property rights. Australia, Canada, and New Zealand score high for the period of buoyant world markets at the end of the century, while Brazil and Norway score low for the 1850s and 1860s, when restrictions on factor markets were still important.[18]

While the associations in component 1 summarize the average pattern for the class and explain the largest amount of total variance, the residual standard deviations are quite large, reflecting the heterogeneity of the class. Components 2 and 3 describe alternative patterns that differ significantly from the primary pattern.

Component 2 describes a pattern of generalized agricultural improvement and modest industrial growth from primary-export expansion. The three Scandinavian countries in the period after 1890 have the highest scores. Agricultural improvements proceeded more rapidly wherever transportation linked major regions of the country. For countries more poorly endowed in land resources, the broader the base of landholdings (and the more favorable the tenure conditions), the more diversified exports, and the greater public investment in education, the more widespread was agricultural progress. Land scarcity stimulated faster net emigration (indicated by the minus sign of the migration variable). The countries that score low on this component are Brazil in 1850 and 1870 and Argentina in 1850, where large-scale plantation enterprise still predominated, small-scale commercial farming expanded only slowly, and income distribution within agriculture remained concentrated.

Component 3 underlines the direct role of fast population growth and international migration in slowing increases in per capita income and in both industrial and agricultural wages. Australia, which scores high on the primary pattern, with its fast rate of aggregate export expansion, scores high on component 3 too because the rise in its GNP had largely been absorbed by exceptional rates of population growth and immigration. The remaining vari-

---

from the common characteristic of class 3 that modest industrialization took place late in the nineteenth or early in the twentieth century.

[18]In Brazil there was slavery, and in Norway there were remainders of communal production systems.

ables also characterize Australia: colonial dependence, high per capita income, a high urbanization rate, substantial investment in literacy, a large government economic role, the influence of indigenous business on political leadership, but underdeveloped national parliamentary institutions. Sweden's low score represents the contrasting case, where vast rates of emigration from a labor-surplus economy helped raise per capita income.[19]

Class 4: Negligible Industrialization in Export-Oriented, Densely Settled Peasant Economies

Class 4 consists of four agricultural economies: Burma, China, Egypt, and India. In these countries agriculture was relatively backward, expatriates dominated trade, there was very little modern industrial growth in the nineteenth century, and political systems tended to be autocratic and often were unstable.

In 1850, agriculture in these countries was mostly subsistence peasant production. Except in Burma, an unfavorable ratio of population to land was a major cause of poverty; everywhere only primitive tools were used; and in many areas farms had become too small to support a family. During the latter half of the nineteenth century, Western laws arrived, encouraging land sales and mortgaging, which accelerated the commercialization of agriculture and production for export. Foreign capital flowed into specialized agricultural exports: cotton in Egypt; rice in Burma; cotton, rice, and jute in India; silk in China. But the proceeds from peasant production for export provided little if any income above subsistence for the average cultivator.

A small number of factories processed primary products for export, and in India there were some textile factories. But factory production for the domestic market was on a minute scale in all four countries. Except in China, where foreigners dominated only the treaty ports, traditional handicraft industries declined under colonial rule with the impact of free trade and the drop in indigenous demand for luxuries. In all four countries domestic savings went into land and traditional valuables; domestic entrepreneurship went mainly into trading.

Table 4-5 presents the components analysis for class 4. Component 1 summarizes a narrow range of variations in socioeconomic characteristics around a low average level of achievement. The key dynamic force expressed here is a dualistic spread of markets promoted by expatriates. But these processes did

---

[19]Component 3, class 3, is very different from our earlier runs (Adelman and Morris 1980). With the explicit inclusion of an indicator of export expansion, Australia's spectacular export performance could be much better explained by component 1, and thus its score on component 1 became much higher. Component 3 captures that aspect of Australian performance not captured by component 1: immigration and population growth so great that striking export expansion and GNP growth did not succeed in raising per capita income.

Table 4-5
Patterns of Industrialization:
Principal Components Analysis for Class 4
(Negligible Industrialization in Export-Oriented, Densely Settled
Peasant Economies)[a]

Variable	Principal Component		
	1	2	3
Degree of foreign economic dependence	.32	.10	−.25*
Colonial status	.30	−.04	−.16
Net immigration	.20	.06	.19*
Percentage of labor force in agriculture	.33	−.09	.26*
Extent of illiteracy	.34	−.06	−.02
Rate of spread of market system (composite)	.25*	.45	.21*
Direction of change in real wages in agriculture	.10	−.25	−.13
Direction of change in real wages in industry	.08	−.20	−.18*
Predominant form of land tenure and holding	.24*	−.42	.10
Concentration of landholdings	.17*	.31	−.07
Rate of population growth (lagged)	.20*	.22	−.10
Total population	.25*	−.50	.00
Level of development of inland transportation	.08	.10	−.19
Rate of improvement in inland transportation (lagged)	.10	.10	−.20
Extent of domestic economic role of government	.13	.05	−.54
Relative abundance of agricultural resources	.14	.02	.25
Level of development of market system (composite)	.31*	.08	.39
Level of per capita income	.06	.07	.13
Level of development of techniques in industry	.06	−.06	−.06
Level of development of techniques in agriculture	.07	.13	−.02
Rate of change in per capita income	.07	.11	−.15
Rate of improvement in techniques in industry	.14	−.03	−.03
Rate of improvement in techniques in industry (lagged)	.11	−.01	−.10
Rate of improvement in techniques in agriculture	.07	.02	−.08
Rate of improvement in techniques in agriculture (lagged)	.05	−.00	−.06
Favorableness of land institutions to improvements	.13	−.10	−.00
Rate of spread of primary education (lagged)	.04	−.06	−.07
Extent of urbanization	.07	.03	−.03
Favorableness of attitudes toward entrepreneurship	.05	.04	−.03
Rate of growth of exports	.13	.10	−.12
Degree of shift in export structure	.04	−.00	.02
Socioeconomic character of political leadership	.03	−.00	.07
Strength of national representative institutions	.06	−.05	.01
Extent of political stability	.06	.03	−.04
Rate of spread of market system, lagged (composite)	.14	.02	−.07

[a]See the introductory section to the statistical analysis in chapter three for a discussion of how to read the components results and of the way we interpret them. Variables are listed within components on which they have primary high loadings in the order in which they are discussed in the text. Variables with secondary high loadings (marked with asterisks) also are important to the interpretation.

not lead to industrial development, agricultural progress, or increases in average income and wages. In general, greater colonial domination quickly loosened communal restrictions on land use and transfer, accelerated land and labor commercialization,[20] increased the number of very large and very small landholdings, and led to slightly more immigration. Faster population growth followed. Where populations were large, overwhelmingly agricultural, and illiterate these transformations occurred quickly. Egypt after 1890 and India during 1870–1890 have the highest component scores; the lowest scores are those of Burma and China at midcentury, before the entry of colonial powers.

Component 2, on which Egypt scores high and China scores low for all three periods, indicates institutional and social conditions that aggravated the negative effects of rapid marketization on the agricultural and industrial poor. More market-oriented institutions caused wages in agriculture and industry to fall where insecure tenancies with concentrated landownership were prevalent and population grew without increases in productivity. In China, marketization slowed wherever small peasant holdings and severe land scarcity led to negligible agricultural surpluses above subsistence. But since marketization proceeded more slowly in China, its negative consequences were reduced. We find nothing in the secondary pattern of covariations among land structure, population, and marketization that would have favored domestic market growth for industry. China's large population was too poor to be an asset.

Component 3 involves the construction of transportation systems by colonial governments. (We reverse signs for the interpretation.) Transportation improvements were accelerated by direct foreign domination. Egypt in the 1890s, the high-scoring country on the "reverse" pattern, had fairly good foreign-financed transportation for its class and proportionately less population in agriculture than did China, the low-scoring country, but Egypt had fewer agricultural resources. The lagged transportation variable is negatively related to the primary and secondary market institutional variables. The secondary industrial wage variable suggests that transportation improvements contributed to very modest wage increases affecting a minute proportion of factory labor forces. In general, neither significant industrial progress nor agricultural development followed colonial investments in transportation.

In summary, in a class defined by foreign-stimulated export expansion, unfavorable land population ratios, and negligible industrialization, none of the changes summarized by the included variables (expanding market institutions, population growth, government construction of infrastructure) led to economic improvement of any quantitative significance.

[20] This point is inferred from country data on the performance of countries in individual types of markets as well as from our results.

Measures of Statistical Fit

The differentiation of industrial development embodied in our typology led to well-separated samples. Table 4-6 compares the total own-class variance of class observations (the diagonal elements in the table) with their variance when fitted to the other class models (the off-diagonal elements). In all pairwise comparisons, the own-class variance of the country observations is significantly lower than their other-class variances. The least difference obtained is 18 percent (when observations for class 2 are fitted to the model for class 3); all other differences exceed 34 percent.

None of the country observations is misclassified in this set of results. That is, each observation is closer to its own class model than to any other class model. As we explain in chapter two, the statistical method calculates the distance of each country observation from each class model as measured by its standard deviation when the observations are fitted to each class model (table 4-7).

Distance measures for the countries whose industrial patterns were too different to classify show the Netherlands closest to class 1 for the period after 1870 and Spain closest to class 2 in all three periods. The Netherlands was probably close to class 1 because its high level of commercialization facilitated industrial and agricultural change simultaneously, and the government's role was minimal. Except for its industrial pattern, Spain's characteristics were very similar to Italy's.

The Importance of Variables for Between- and Within-Class Variations

Table 4-8 presents statistical measures of the importance of individual variables in discriminating between classes and in explaining variations within classes. Column 1 provides a measure of each indicator's importance in dis-

Table 4-6
Patterns of Industrailization:
Cluster Distance Matrix for Principal Components Analyses

	Class 1	Class 2	Class 3	Class 4
Class 1	14.7	26.9	29.0	51.7
Class 2	19.1	15.0	17.7	21.5
Class 3	40.3	37.5	16.0	49.3
Class 4	635,000	376,000	499,000	10.1

NOTE: See text for explanation.

Table 4-7
Patterns of Industrialization:
Degree of Fit for Principal Components Analyses
(Residual Standard Deviations for Three Classes Closest to Each Country Observation)

Country and Year	Assigned Class	Class to Which Closest	Residual S.D.— Closest Class	Class to Which 2d Closest	Residual S.D.—2d Closest Class	Class to Which 3d Closest	Residual S.D.—3d Closest Class
Belgium 1850	1	1	16	2	19	3	23
France 1850	1	1	16	2	19	3	23
Great Britain 1850	1	1	19	2	19	3	27
Switzerland 1850	1	1	14	3	21	2	25
United States 1850	1	1	12	3	24	2	26
Belgium 1870	1	1	14	2	21	3	27
France 1870	1	1	13	2	22	3	26
Great Britain 1870	1	1	12	2	24	3	29
Switzerland 1870	1	1	13	3	23	2	26
United States 1870	1	1	11	2	26	3	27
Belgium 1890	1	1	17	2	27	3	31
France 1890	1	1	14	2	24	3	27
Great Britain 1890	1	1	15	2	25	3	29
Switzerland 1890	1	1	15	3	24	2	27
United States 1890	1	1	18	2	27	3	27
Germany 1850	2	2	16	3	24	1	25
Italy 1850	2	2	16	4	19	3	22
Japan 1850	2	2	17	4	18	3	27
Russia 1850	2	2	11	3	22	4	24
Germany 1870	2	2	13	1	18	3	22
Italy 1870	2	2	21	4	26	3	27

Japan 1870	2	2	11	4	27	3	27
Russia 1870	2	2	12	3	27	4	27
Germany 1890	2	2	13	1	20	3	27
Italy 1890	2	2	15	1	23	3	25
Japan 1890	2	2	14	3	26	1	27
Russia 1890	2	2	19	4	24	3	24
Argentina 1850	3	3	15	2	27	4	29
Australia 1850	3	3	11	2	33	4	33
Brazil 1850	3	3	10	2	22	4	24
Canada 1850	3	3	18	2	27	1	28
Denmark 1850	3	3	19	2	23	1	25
New Zealand 1850	3	3	21	2	27	4	28
Norway 1850	3	3	20	1	23	2	23
Sweden 1850	3	3	19	2	22	1	24
Argentina 1870	3	3	11	2	26	4	29
Australia 1870	3	3	13	2	32	1	36
Brazil 1870	3	3	13	2	18	4	24
Canada 1870	3	3	15	1	25	2	25
Denmark 1870	3	3	16	2	21	1	23
New Zealand 1870	3	3	15	2	30	1	31
Norway 1870	3	3	17	1	23	2	25
Sweden 1870	3	3	14	1	22	2	22
Argentina 1890	3	3	22	1	33	2	33
Australia 1890	3	3	14	1	34	2	36
Brazil 1890	3	3	13	2	25	4	30
Canada 1890	3	3	17	1	20	2	27
Denmark 1890	3	3	17	1	22	2	25
New Zealand 1890	3	3	13	1	30	2	31
Norway 1890	3	3	13	1	19	2	24

Table 4-7 (continued)

Country and Year	Assigned Class	Class to Which Closest	Residual S.D.— Closest Class	Class to Which 2d Closest	Residual S.D.—2d Closest Class	Class to Which 3d Closest	Residual S.D.—3d Closest Class
Sweden 1890	3	3	19	1	20	2	26
Burma 1850	4	4	8	2	15	3	22
China 1850	4	4	8	2	18	3	26
Egypt 1850	4	4	12	2	20	3	22
India 1850	4	4	14	2	17	3	23
Burma 1870	4	4	10	2	19	3	23
China 1870	4	4	7	2	19	3	27
Egypt 1870	4	4	13	2	20	3	27
India 1870	4	4	9	2	20	3	26
Burma 1890	4	4	9	2	18	3	25
China 1890	4	4	10	2	20	3	27
Egypt 1890	4	4	10	2	21	3	29
India 1890	4	4	8	2	22	3	29
Netherlands 1850	0	2	18	3	20	1	21
Spain 1850	0	2	16	3	21	4	25
Netherlands 1870	0	1	15	2	19	3	20
Spain 1870	0	2	21	3	24	1	26
Netherlands 1890	0	1	15	2	21	3	22
Spain 1890	0	2	15	3	19	4	22

NOTE: The years 1850, 1870, and 1890 following country names in column 1 are shorthand for our three cross sections: 1850–1870, 1870–1890, and 1890–1914. As noted in chapter two and in appendix tables A51 through A53, some variables refer to the initial year of each period, some refer to the entire period, and a few lagged variables refer to the preceding period.

Table 4-8
Patterns of Industrialization:
Importance of Variables to Between-Class and Within-Class Variations,
All Classes Together[a]

Variable	Between-Group Relevance	Within-Group Relevance
Extent of illiteracy	19.3	.79
Degree of foreign economic dependence	15.7	.61
Total population	12.2	.72
Favorableness of attitudes toward entrepreneurship	11.5	.58
Socioeconomic character of political leadership	10.9	.64
Relative abundance of agricultural resources	10.4	.59
Rate of spread of market system (composite)	8.6	.63
Colonial status	8.2	.49
Rate of improvement in techniques in industry	8.0	.71
Level of per capita income	7.9	.61
Level of development of techniques in agriculture	7.4	.73
Rate of improvement in techniques in industry (lagged)	6.0	.63
Strength of national representative institutions	5.1	.35
Level of development of inland transportation	3.2	.70
Predominant form of land tenure and holding	3.2	.71
Level of development of techniques in industry	4.5	.63
Concentration of landholdings	4.1	.59
Rate of improvement in techniques in agriculture	2.4	.58
Rate of improvement in techniques in agriculture (lagged)	3.6	.57
Degree of shift in export structure	3.7	.56
Net immigration	2.3	.55
Favorableness of land institutions to improvements	2.3	.55
Direction of change in real wages in industry	3.7	.55
Extent of urbanization	3.2	.54
Rate of spread of market system, lagged (composite)	4.9	.52
Extent of domestic economic role of government	2.7	.50
Percentage of labor force in agriculture	2.8	.43
Rate of change in per capita income	1.9	.34
Rate of improvement in inland transportation (lagged)	1.0	.26
Rate of population growth (lagged)	2.7	.45
Rate of spread of primary education (lagged)	1.8	.11
Rate of growth of exports	1.2	.13
Extent of political stability	3.7	.34
Direction of change in real wages in agriculture	2.1	.33
Level of development of market system (composite)	2.1	.15

[a]Variables with between-group relevance over 5.0 are listed in descending order by that measure (column 1: 19.3–5.1). The remaining variables that have measures of within-group relevance over .50 are listed in descending order by the within-group measure (column 2: .71–.50).

criminating among the four "types" of industrialization, *taking all classes together.*[21]

The most important variables with ratios of between-group relevance over 5.0 (column 1) have strong political, social, or institutional content. The degree of literacy and foreign domination of national economic policies appear to be the most critical forces explaining differences among country groups in industrialization patterns. The social status of entrepreneurs and the political influence of rising business and commercial classes are next most important in accounting for contrasts between successful Western European industrialization, the more modest industrial growth of backward European countries and some primary exporting countries, and the absence of industrial growth in densely settled foreign-dominated primary exporting countries. Colonial status reinforced economic dependence for the colonies. But it gave access to overseas resources, imports, and export markets to colonizers who had assets and skills, thereby strongly contributing to the shaping of economic opportunities. Of the variables describing domestic institutions, the development of market institutions stands out. How rapidly market institutions expanded helped determine which classes of countries were best able to achieve modest industrial growth by the end of the nineteenth century. Conventional economic influences also are important in explaining contrasts in industrialization patterns among country classes: a large population and a high level of per capita income made it possible for industry to capture economies of scale by relying on domestic markets. Abundance of agricultural resources helped account for differences among classes of countries in the extent of their reliance on comparative advantages in agriculture. The level of agricultural technology, indicative of the agricultural surplus and of the rural market for manufactures, also substantially influenced success in industrialization. Lagged and current improvements in industrial technology are among the significant variables because they are used to define the classes in the industrialization typology.

Column 2 measures each variable's contribution to a statistical explanation of within-class variations, taking all classes together; thus, it does not give weight to variables with high explanatory power within only one class. Some of the same features are as important to within-class variations among countries as to between-class variations. When countries are grouped by structure and speed of industrial expansion, variables determining the potential domestic market size and agricultural resource abundance explain which countries *within* the groups perform best industrially.

---

[21] As explained in chapter three, this measure compares the unexplained variance of all country observations when fitted to their "correct" class models with their unexplained variance when fitted to the "wrong" class models. The higher the ratio of the unexplained variance with "incorrect" assignments to that with "correct" assigments, the greater the contribution of the variable to the correct assignment of country observations.

The important political and social variables are the same, with one exception. The strength of representative political systems was important in grouping countries by industrialization paths, but once grouped, the political influence of rising socioeconomic groups on government policies mattered more than either the number of political parties or electoral participation. The high explanatory power of literacy is as striking in column 2 as in column 1. The result that foreign economic dependence mattered more within groups than between groups is consistent with the wide variations in extent of foreign dependence within classes 3 and 4.

The character of land tenure and holding systems is important in explaining the nature of industrial change within classes. In class 1, it was closely related to the extent of simultaneous advances in industry and agriculture, in classes 2 and 3 to the secondary patterns of agricultural improvements, and in class 4 to the pattern of rapid marketization. The major purpose of chapter five is to explore these findings further.

CONCLUSION

Our study of patterns of industrialization confirms our thesis that the structure and extent of industrial expansion can be explained only with models that incorporate institutional influences. The following propositions are consistent with the results presented in this chapter.

1. Neoclassical models of economic growth are fully appropriate only for the class of early successful industrializers. By 1850, these countries had passed a critical threshold in economic and institutional development: legal institutions had secured property rights; market institutions enabled rapid expansion of exchanges of land, labor, and capital; land tenure arrangements encouraged cultivators to respond to market opportunities; and political institutions allowed rising business and commercial interests to influence government economic policies. Once these institutions supported the effective functioning of markets, capitalist industrialization interacted continuously with social, political, and institutional transformations to raise average living standards.

2. In the backward countries of Western Europe, industrialization was sharply dualistic. The initial conditions of economic backwardness determined the structure of industrial expansion. National governments that were firmly entrenched responded strongly to the economic and political challenges posed by early industrialization outside their borders. They unified their countries politically, removed institutional barriers to the growth of market systems, and substituted government demand and foreign inputs for missing development "prerequisites" such as capital, skills, and a home market for industrial goods. But these substitutions did not compensate for the backwardness of agriculture in these countries. Domestic markets for manufactured goods were severely constrained by the small agricultural surplus

and by the concentrated landholdings narrowing its distribution. Industrialization was substantial only where governments promoted more equity in land distribution and invested significantly in rural education.

3. In countries where comparative advantage favored primary production, industrialization was modest. Patterns of industrial expansion varied with resource abundance, foreign dependence, political power structure, and land institutions. In land-abundant dependent countries where laws secured property rights and enabled the unimpeded functioning of land and labor markets, primary exports expanded rapidly and per capita income rose. But improvements in food agriculture and wages did not follow unless indigenous socioeconomic groups gained sufficient political clout to reorient government economic policies toward domestic market expansion. In small European countries heavily dependent on trade, high levels of agricultural productivity, made possible by favorable land institutions, helped exports expand rapidly. Productive agriculture and substantial investment in education furthered modest industrialization. International migration affected per capita income and the size of the domestic market everywhere. In the small, trade-dependent European countries, emigration raised average rural income by reducing labor surpluses. In land-abundant European-settled countries, massive immigration accelerated export expansion and enlarged the domestic market but slowed the growth of per capita income.

4. In poor, densely populated peasant societies, industrial growth was limited to a few processing factories. Colonial governments promoted exports by eliminating communal restrictions on land transfer and use and by investing in transportation and ports. But given low agricultural productivity and inadequate skills and education, commercialization increased peasant indebtedness and led to loss of land, thus reducing the incomes of the agricultural poor and severely limiting the size of the domestic market. Political dependency forestalled tariff protection of indigenous industry, further limiting its development.

Thus, patterns of industrialization were strongly influenced by institutions—foreign-dependence relations, legal arrangements determining market functioning, land tenure systems, and political power structures. The importance of institutions lay primarily in their shaping of the structure of economic activity and of the diffusion of economic growth. But economic influences also were important, since they largely determined comparative advantage, factor supplies, and market opportunities.

5 Patterns of Agricultural Development

In the early phases of economic development land institutions, agricultural change, and industrial growth interact to varying degrees. While economic historians have always paid attention to agricultural technology, interest in the interdependence between agriculture and industry has grown rapidly since 1945 along with the greater concern about underdeveloped countries. Neoclassical theorists have analyzed the multiple positive roles of agriculture in industrial expansion: its supplying labor, food, raw materials, capital, and entrepreneurship to the nonagricultural sector; its foreign exchange earnings through export expansion; and its provision of markets for industrial goods. There are also gains from economies of scale and from externalities based on the on-the-job learning that comes to workers, technicians, and entrepreneurs with the shift from agriculture to industry.

Our hypothesis is that as countries develop, the role of agriculture changes dynamically, and the institutional influences important to these varied roles are different. Some countries start the process of modern economic growth with primary-export expansion.[1] In these agricultural countries, the existence of an agricultural surplus above subsistence is essential for the simultaneous expansion of primary exports and food for a growing population. During this phase, agriculture must earn foreign exchange to buy improved technology and know-how in marketing. Agriculture may at first be the most significant source of domestic savings and entrepreneurship, but as urban demand grows for both industrial and agricultural products, an increasing marketable agricultural surplus is needed to feed the growing nonagricultural labor force. In densely settled agricultural countries the only way to increase the surplus enough is to raise agricultural productivity.[2] Population growth raises the productivity increase required to produce a surplus.

As countries become more industrialized, the importance of an agricultural surplus declines; the increasing supply of manufactured exports can be exchanged for imported food. The importance of agriculture as a supplier of labor and foreign exchange also declines with the shift toward manufacturing.[3]

At the beginning of industrialization, the agricultural surplus must serve yet another function: It must provide sufficient income for the mostly agricultural population to consume industrial products. Without this important source of demand, industry is unlikely to expand or even get started.[4] Al-

---

[1] Modern economic growth in much of Western Europe began before 1850, but our study focuses on export expansion after 1850. Thus, our analysis of the beginnings of primary-export expansion presumes that in at least one advanced industrialized country consumers and producers provided market demand for primary exports.

[2] Immigration provided an alternative source of labor.

[3] This shift sometimes increased the indirect role of agriculture in providing materials for the domestic processing of primary products for export.

[4] An exception would be small countries that form a larger trading area with each other.

though the other various functions of agriculture decline with industrialization, the role of agriculture in providing a home market for consumer goods remains crucial until high levels of industrialization are achieved. And agriculture's role as a demander of intermediate goods such as fertilizer and tools increases steadily during this phase.

In countries where unsettled land is abundant, labor, capital, and food may be imported during the initial phase of agricultural export expansion. In this case the key roles of agriculture are to earn foreign exchange for financing food imports and to provide land for settlement. However, as urban areas grow and the land becomes increasingly settled, the importance of a domestic agricultural sector capable of feeding the population increases greatly. Otherwise, agricultural export earnings would not be sufficient to pay for the import needs of a rapidly growing immigrant population. Furthermore, if domestic industry did not expand, export earnings would also have to cover imports of nonfood consumer goods. Thus, for countries with a strong comparative advantage in primary production, agriculture continues to be important as a source of foreign exchange earnings, domestic savings, and domestic demand.

We start the analysis with certain expectations based on the existing literature (chapter one). Given the various ways in which land systems affected economic performance, the distribution of income, and the structure of political power, we expect the legal institutional conditions for secure individual titles to land to be fundamental for growth through export expansion. Supplying labor to the nonagricultural sector requires that customary ties of labor to the land be eliminated, as Marxian analyses stress. Given the successful experience of Western Europe, we expect a wide distribution of land to combine with an agricultural surplus in promoting the early development of a domestic market. These institutional conditions for rising agricultural productivity are complex, involving both secure titles to the fruits of investment and holdings large enough to provide a surplus above subsistence. The provision of savings and skilled entrepreneurship also depends on enterprises large enough to warrant the risks of expansion.

Historical case studies provide hypotheses about the institutional consequences of economic change. We expect expanding demand for agricultural products to induce rapid shifts to production for the market. Neoclassical studies lead us to expect expanding opportunities for exports to induce legal changes and institutional rearrangements facilitating their exploitation. Dependency theory leads us to expect institutional changes in dependent countries reinforcing the position of landed elites and limiting the spread of benefits from export expansion.

In this chapter we use our empirical findings in two ways: (1) to delineate precisely how institutions helped or constrained agricultural and thus industrial performance, and (2) to seek to understand how economic changes induced institutional responses in agriculture that differed by type of country and by phase in the evolution of agriculture.

We consider three broad scenarios for successful agricultural performance. The first is typical of large Western European countries where a long history of agricultural improvements provided the base for a growth process directed from the beginning at the domestic market. Because this scenario precedes our study period, only its outcome is evident in our results. The second scenario deals with economies with settled populations, countries where export expansion provided the stimulus for modern economic growth. The third scenario describes countries with rich empty lands, economies where export expansion was made possible only by inflows of immigrants and capital. Actual historical patterns may be understood as variations on these scenarios, the variations being caused by differences in the interactions between institutional influences and economic changes during successive phases of the evolution of agriculture and industry.

Such a study could not be attempted with only conventional quantitative variables. Classification schemes are needed that rank different countries and periods by characteristics of their land systems. We now turn, therefore, to a discussion of the construction of such ranking schemes. The definitions of the categories in each scheme, the assignment of each country and period, and the sources on which each of the 69 assignments (3 for each country) are based are listed in the tables of the data appendix.

The Land Institutional Variables

Our brief review of the literature on land institutional influences suggested two features of importance to economic performance. One is the system of land tenure and holding, which includes the legal and customary system under which land is owned and the terms under which it is cultivated by nonowners—the security of tenancy, the type of rent paid, or the arrangements for cultivation by wage earners, serfs, or slaves. The particular cultivation system greatly affects the incentive to adopt improvements. The second is the size distribution of landholdings. This feature relates closely to how income is distributed within agriculture, and because of its impact on savings, investment, and the domestic market, it determines the rate of adoption of technological improvements in agriculture.

We constructed one variable for each of these two features, plus another composite variable in which conditions of tenure and scale of enterprise were combined and ranked by their joint expected impact on the incentives to adopt improvements, according to a priori judgment. The three variables permitted us to capture the historical complexity of the connections between land institutions and agricultural performance, and helped summarize relationships differing greatly both among and within groups of countries. (Our statistical method fortunately permits the use of such intercorrelated variables.)[5]

Predominant Form of Land Tenure and Holding

This variable groups countries into seven land tenure and holding classes. The scheme involved both grouping countries and ranking the groups. We grouped countries by the "predominance" of a particular land system—that is, by the proportion of land cultivated under that system—with adjustments for "subdominant" characteristics. Countries where private owners with secure land titles used primarily family labor to cultivate were grouped together. Given the paucity of quantitative data, we could not take full account of the variety of tenancy forms in countries where nonowners did most of the cultivating. Instead we distinguished only between reasonably secure fixed cash tenancies and a variety of less secure rental and sharecropping systems. The remaining countries were grouped according to whether large estates controlling both crops and methods were cultivated by tenants, serfs, or slaves. Communal production arrangements were grouped in a separate category.

There is no unique way to rank systems of land tenure and holding, but we selected a principle suggested by Boserup (1963): the degree of control the direct cultivator of the basic operational unit had over methods of production and choice of crops. At the top of the continuum were countries where most of the land was farmed by cultivators with full rights of ownership, the remaining lands being farmed by tenants with considerable de facto security of tenure. In the second category were countries where "independent" peasants cultivated without full ownership rights or where feudal obligations were moderate. Third came countries characterized by a predominance of fixed cash rents and reasonable security of tenure (the nontenant sector being mainly independent cultivators).[6] Also in the third category were countries where capitalist tenants (or tenant-managers) participated directly in cultivation. Fourth came countries characterized either by short-term tenancy with fixed rents or by sharecropping with little security of tenure. The last three categories were: fifth, countries where "independent" peasants had significant communal control over the types and methods of cultivation; sixth, countries where large estates controlled crop production, the cultivation be-

---

[5]The use of overlapping variables is not uncommon in statistical analyses, even where components analysis is not the method applied. For example, it is not uncommon to include an indicator of national income and an indicator of aggregate consumption in the same equation.

[6]In ranking forms of tenancy, we stressed practices regarding security of tenure rather than legal provisions. Unfortunately, only a few countries had reliable information on practices regarding compensation for unexhausted improvements, so we could not include this important feature.

ing done either by laborers who lacked alternatives and mobility or by short-term tenants or sharecroppers; and seventh, countries where cultivation was controlled by large estates, the work being done by serfs or other forms of servile labor. It should be emphasized that categories 5 through 7 ranked low only because the direct cultivators did not control crops and methods, and owners did not usually participate directly in cultivation. That is, we did not prejudge the actual conduciveness of particular types of tenure systems to improvements.[7]

Concentration of Landholdings

The purpose of this variable is to group countries by size distribution of land-holdings, but the most common data are figures on the number of holdings by size classes measured in acreage rather than units of ownership. The data vary among countries with respect to size classes and whether or not they include very small holdings and garden plots; that is, they vary with respect to the definition of the word "farm."[8] We wished to exclude both garden plots and, at the other extreme, large public (and even large private) forest holdings and publicly or communally held tracts of rough grazing and waste land. (See Dovring 1965, p. 117.) Conceptually, we sought the distribution of cultivated and pastoral agricultural land only, but frequently had to compromise and use whatever data were available. Another problem was judging the meaning of the data on farm size at the lower end of the distribution. The size of farm necessary to support a family varies greatly by type of crop, land and technology, as is vividly illustrated in table 5-1.

Because of data problems, we constructed a classification scheme that made only gross distinctions based on both quantitative and qualitative information. But choices had to be made among various characteristics of the distribution. For example, should the focus be on the proportion of acreage held by the top, middle, or low quantiles of landholders?

Our guiding principle was to incorporate characteristics indicative of the distribution of the agricultural surplus above subsistence. The degree of concentration at the top of the distribution was clearly important: Both quantitative and descriptive data were used to judge whether 10 percent of the landholders held as much as 75 percent of the agricultural land. The proportion of the holdings below a size sufficient to support a family also was clearly important (providing we eliminated garden plots and other part-time farming ar-

---

[7]Controversy over our assignment of agricultural sectors with slavery or serf labor to a low category can be met by noting that there is no case in our sample where capitalist slavery (such as existed in the United States before 1860) predominated. Since our classifications are based on the dominant form of tenure, the classification for the United States discounts Southern slavery.

[8]For a discussion of the problems of using data on land distribution, see Dovring 1965, pp. 114ff.

Table 5-1
Patterns of Agricultural Development:
Variations in the Size of Farm Necessary to Support a Family

Country or Region	Definition of Minimum Area for a Family	Minimum Area in Acres	Time Period	Source[a]
Japan	"good average-size farm supporting a family"	1.225	1860s	Allen 1962, p. 63
Belgium (East Flanders)	necessary to support a family	10	19th century	Duchesne 1932, pp. 480–481
Belgium (The Ardenne)	necessary to support a family	50	19th century	Duchesne 1932, pp. 480–481
Spain (The Levante)	average holding—"enough to support a family"	1.5	1940	Brenan 1943, p. 100
France	"necessary to support a family"	10	1860s	The Cobden Club, p. 431
Russia (Black-Soil Region)	"minimum support for a soul"	13.75	1875	Yanson, quoted in Gerschenkron 1965, p. 742
Russia (Non-Black-Soil Region)	"minimum support for a soul"	22	1875	Yanson, quoted in Gerschenkron 1965, p. 742
Sweden	minimum for a "livelihood"	125	18th century	Janson 1931, pp. 400–401
Queensland, Australia	"living area"	100–160	19th century	Coghlan 1918, 4:1991–1992
New South Wales, Australia	"living area"	320	19th century	Coghlan 1918, 2:649

[a]See appropriate country sections of the bibliography for full citations. Only the reference for France is in the general section.

rangements),[9] but only broad distinctions could be made based on both descriptive and numerical estimates. A third important dimension was the number of viable family-size farms as a proportion of all farms; a fourth was the proportion of holdings that could be called middle-size as determined by available information on land area. While the definition of "middle-size" could not be precise, the term was used to describe holdings exceeding what a family could cultivate (excluding extra hired labor at harvest time); that is, a farm where some labor was hired year round. Holdings with more than a few permanent hired laborers were considered large.

The final classification for concentration of landholdings grouped the 69 observations into six categories: (1) countries where concentration of landholdings was extreme—where the top 10 percent of landholders probably held over 75 percent of the cultivated land;[10] (2) countries where concentration of landholdings was extreme, even as extreme as in category 1, but the large number of extremely small holdings was overwhelmingly predominant; (3) countries where most of the land was farmed by cultivators with large holdings using considerable amounts of hired labor but where the concentration was much less than in either category 1 or category 2; (4) countries where middle-size landholdings were farmed by families hiring some year-round labor; (5) countries where small viable family-size holdings predominated without extreme parcelization; and (6) countries where small holdings prevailed with extreme parcelization and fragmentation.

Favorableness of Land System to Adoption of Improvements

Neither of the above two land variables alone is suitable for ranking different land systems with respect to their likely economic performance, so we combined the two, thereby constructing a classification scheme by which to rank the favorableness of various systems to improvements. It should be stressed that these rankings are not based on judgments of actual performance in the individual countries in each category. Rather, we have followed the practice common among numerical indexes, that of weighting the components in an index using theoretical or a priori judgments about their *expected* relationship to performance. The judgments we use here, however, are more weakly linked to theory than those used in indexes based on neoclassical reasoning.

The final classification scheme grouped countries into nine categories ranked by a priori judgments about the conduciveness of farm size and tenure conditions to the adoption of agricultural improvements. Classifications are

[9] These holdings were important in countries like Belgium, where farm families had generous work opportunities off the farm.

[10] Note our assumption here that an extreme concentration of landholdings in the absence of a peasant sector represents a larger degree of "concentration" than the same concentration at the top with a large number of small holdings at the bottom.

based on data and judgments regarding the predominant land system as a proportion of the overall cultivated area.

We founded our composite variable on the following propositions: (1) Given the same form of tenure, middle-size and moderately large farms were more conducive to the adoption of technological improvements than very small farms.[11] (2) Given the same form of tenure and assuming that on large nineteenth-century estates aristocratic values about consumption and land accumulation most likely dominated goals of profit maximization, middle-size and moderately large farms were more conducive to the adoption of improvements than extremely large estates. (3) Given the same scale of enterprise, cultivation by an owner-manager was more conducive to the adoption of improvements than cultivation by tenants paying fixed cash rents, even those with security of tenure. We based this assumption on the fact that nineteenth-century tenants were generally not compensated for unexhausted improvements. (4) Given the same scale of enterprise and assuming that fixed cash rents were more conducive to capitalist profit-maximizing behavior, cultivation by tenants paying fixed cash rents with reasonable de facto security of tenure was more favorable to improvements than cultivation by tenants (including sharecroppers) with short, insecure tenures. (5) Assuming that noneconomic goals were more important than profit maximization with slave or serf agriculture, the least favorable arrangements for the adoption of improvements were such communal arrangements. (This would not hold where the predominant system was capitalist slave agriculture, as in the South of the United States, but in no countries in our sample was this sort of system dominant.)[12]

In the final classification scheme, at the top of the spectrum are countries where independent cultivators with middle-size or large farms predominated without extreme concentration of landholdings. Next come countries with mostly middle-size or large farms paying cash rents with reasonable de facto security of tenure. The next two categories differ from the top two in that farms were small but land was not excessively parcelized. Fifth come countries where cultivation was mainly on large centrally managed estates, including pastoral estates. At the lower end of the spectrum are four categories that were judged not very conducive to improvements: sixth, countries where cultivation was by peasants under extreme land parcelization; seventh, countries where cultivation was by short-term, insecure tenures or sharecropping ten-

---

[11] Note, however, that labor was often more efficient on very small holdings than on larger holdings. In Japan, for example, larger landowners in villages had difficulty competing with small landowners because of the lesser efficiency of wage labor compared with family labor (Smith 1959, p. 105).

[12] As noted above, since capitalist slavery in the United States was not the predominant form of land tenure, it had little effect on the classification of the United States with respect to land tenure and holding.

ures; eighth, countries where cultivation was by peasants under a system of communal control of crops and methods; and ninth, countries where serf or slave agriculture predominated.

THE TYPOLOGY

Here we divide our sample by the nature and extent of interactions between industry and agriculture before and during the period of most rapid industrial growth. Two of the classes in the typology include countries where agriculture played a strong positive role in industrialization, mainly the countries of Western Europe and North America, plus Japan. (Recall from chapters three and four the role of agricultural institutional influences in patterns of success.) The smaller of the two top classes includes certain small open economies where a radical and successful shift from extensive cereal production to intensive specialized agriculture for export took place in the last quarter of the nineteenth century. This sample includes Belgium, Denmark, the Netherlands, and Switzerland. In the third class, slow improvements in agriculture constrained but did not prevent the agricultural sector from eventually supplying labor, savings, and a home market sufficient for modest industrialization to take place. This class includes the backward European countries, plus Norway, Argentina, and New Zealand. In the fourth class, export expansion of staples led to neither agricultural improvements nor much industrial growth; the densely settled British colonies, China, and Brazil are the countries in this class.[13]

THE STATISTICAL ANALYSES

In this section we discuss our statistical results on patterns of agricultural development. Readers who have not read the book continuously are referred to chapter two, pages 58–61, and chapter three, pages 74–78, for guidance in interpreting the tables that follow.

Class 1: Strong Positive Role of Agriculture

Class 1 includes Great Britain, France, Germany, the United States, Canada, Japan, and Sweden (see table 5-2). For these countries, a substantial period of gradually rising labor productivity in agriculture preceded the first sustained surge of modern industrial expansion. Then, as industrialization progressed, the agricultural sector played an important role in providing labor, raw materials, and/or capital to the industrial sector and in providing a market for both industrial and agricultural products.

---

[13]Australia was omitted from the typology because it appeared to be less constrained than the other class 3 countries and it clearly did not belong in classes 1, 2, or 4.

Table 5-2
A Typology of Agricultural Development in the Nineteenth and Early Twentieth Centuries

Class	Description of Class	Country	Principal Sources
1	Countries in which a period of sustained increases in agricultural output per agricultural laborer preceded the earliest major spread of factory industry; then during industrialization the agricultural sector played an important role in providing inputs to industry and a domestic market for industrial goods. Excluded from this class is a subset of small open economies described in class 2.	Canada	Easterbrook and Aitken 1956, pp. 482ff.; Firestone 1958, pp. 194–199; Norrie 1975, pp. 410–427
		France	Boserup 1963, p. 207; Bairoch 1973, pp. 470–471; Marczewski 1963, pp. 134–135
		Germany	Boserup 1963, p. 207; Bairoch 1973, p. 471; Hoffmann 1963, pp. 100–104
		Great Britain	Boserup 1963, p. 207; Bairoch 1973, p. 470; Deane 1965, pp. 47–50
		Japan	Tsuru 1963, pp. 148–149; Smith 1959, pp. 92–105; Rosovsky 1966; Dore 1969
		Sweden	Jörberg 1965; Janson 1931, pp. 277ff.
		United States	Danhof 1969, pp. 11–13; Fishlow 1965, pp. 206–207, 225ff.
2	Small open economies sharing the characteristics of class 1; in addition, underwent a radical transformation of their agricultural sectors during the last quarter of the nineteenth century; these are countries in which governments did not protect cereals when the drastic decline in grain prices hit the world market in the 1870s; their agri-	Belgium	Bairoch 1973, p. 471; Van Houtte 1943, pp. 130–152
		Denmark	Jensen 1937; Skrubbeltrang 1951; Youngson 1959
		Netherlands	Brugmans 1961, pp. 288–311; Slichter van Bath 1966; de Jonge 1968, pp. 20–23

	Switzerland	Bergier 1968, pp. 52–57; Hauser 1961, pp. 245–255; Chuard 1901

cultural sectors shifted successfully from grains to intensive specialized agriculture for export.

3		
	Argentina	Díaz Alejandro 1970, pp. 9–11; Ferrer 1967, p. 100; Scobie 1964b, pp. 35–37, 77, 81
	Italy	Zangheri 1969; Luzzatto 1969, pp. 218–219
	New Zealand	Condliffe 1959, pp. 140–143; Simkin 1951, pp. 156–157, 174–175
	Norway	Johnsen 1939, pp. 498–503; Lieberman 1970
	Russia	Gerschenkron 1965
	Spain	Vicens Vives and Nadal Oller 1969, chap. 43

3 Countries where the slow growth of agriculture serving the domestic market delayed the development of industry for several decades during the latter half of the nineteenth century. A lagging agriculture either limited agricultural demand for industrial goods or restricted the supply of labor to industry or both. In spite of this lag, domestic agriculture eventually expanded enough to make possible some significant industrial growth prior to 1914.

4		
	Brazil	Leff 1973; Burns 1970, pp. 216–217; Stein 1957, chap. 8
	Burma	Boserup 1963, p. 204; Hlaing 1964
	China	Hou 1961; Hou 1963; Perkins et al. 1969
	Egypt	Owen 1969, p. 143 and passim; Issawi 1961
	India	Boserup 1963, p. 203; Bhatia 1965; Gadgil 1942

4 Overwhelmingly agricultural countries where the growth of staple exports under the stimulus of expanding European markets was followed by few, if any, improvements in domestic agriculture and industry; levels of agricultural productivity and average income were extremely low in all these countries.

Unclassified	Australia	Morrissey 1970; McGhee 1970, p. 148; Cotter 1970, pp. 120–121; McCarty 1965; Shaw 1946, pp. 84–87

NOTE: Of the sources in this table, the following are listed in the general section of the bibliography: Bairoch 1973 and Boserup 1963.

While all class 1 countries were characterized by strong positive interactions between agriculture and industry, they varied greatly in other respects. Great Britain and France industrialized considerably before the United States and Germany, while Canada, Japan, and Sweden industrialized toward the end of the century. In the United States and Canada, agriculture progressed onto previously uncultivated lands, while in the other countries it was more land intensive. Types of agricultural improvements also varied greatly, with mechanization very important in the United States, moderately important in Germany and Great Britain, and much less so in the other countries. Essential inputs provided by agriculture to industry also varied depending on the type and level of development of the country.

The results for class 1 are found in table 5-3. The primary pattern is somewhat similar to that for the early industrializers (chapter four). Higher levels and rates of agricultural progress are associated with faster industrialization, higher levels and rates of per capita income, significant export expansion, stronger shifts in export structure, and rising average wages in both industry and agriculture. Favorable social attitudes toward entrepreneurship and stronger parliamentary systems also are associated with agricultural and industrial progress. Adoption of agricultural improvements was faster where market institutions were more developed, slower wherever poor transportation hampered commercial agricultural production. Adoption of improvements was more rapid where more of the labor force was in agriculture. The United States, where exploitation of abundant resources helps account for the continuing importance of agricultural labor, scored high after 1870. Japan's pre-1890 score was the lowest.

All countries in the class score in the top four categories of our indicator of conduciveness of land systems to improvements; sharecropping, parcelized holdings, dependent estate or plantation systems, and communal production are nowhere dominant in class 1. The positive association between land tenure and economic progress suggests the stimulus to agricultural progress from independent cultivators with full ownership rights. From the importance of the composite measure of conducive institutions we also infer that both extremes in the distribution of land were less favorable to technological advances: excessive concentration limited the demand for consumption goods, while excessive parcelization limited the agricultural surplus—and income and savings—per family.

Class 1 provides a variation on the Jones and Woolf scenario for Western European economic success (1969), in which the institutional features of land tenure are stressed. The importance of a widely distributed agricultural surplus above subsistence in accelerating industrialization is shown by higher levels of agricultural productivity and by the variables representing land institutions. We infer the importance of agricultural savings and investment (for which we lack quantitative measures) from the historical connections between these influences and agricultural improvements. The indicator of market sys-

Table 5-3
Patterns of Agricultural Development:
Principal Components Analysis for Class 1
(Strong Positive Role of Agriculture)[a]

Variable	Principal Component 1	2
Level of development of techniques in agriculture	.22	.12
Rate of improvement in techniques in agriculture	.17	.01
Rate of improvement in techniques in industry	.20	.19*
Rate of change in per capita income	.19	−.07
Rate of growth of exports	.19	−.13
Degree of shift in export structure	.17	−.16
Direction of change in real wages in industry	.22	−.05
Direction of change in real wages in agriculture	.18	−.05
Favorableness of attitudes toward entrepreneurship	.18	.11
Strength of national representative institutions	.17	−.08
Predominant form of land tenure and holding	.25	−.13
Favorableness of land institutions to improvements	.23	−.03
Level of development of market system (composite)	.18	−.02
Extent of urbanization	.13	.27
Level of development of techniques in industry	.14	.25
Level of development of inland transportation	.18*	.37
Level of per capita income	.17*	.21
Relative abundance of agricultural resources	.16	−.21
Percentage of labor force in agriculture	.17*	−.34
Rate of improvement in techniques in industry (lagged)	.18*	.24
Rate of improvement in inland transportation (lagged)	.16	.17
Rate of spread of market system, lagged (composite)	.16	−.22
Colonial status	.09	−.26
Degree of foreign economic dependence	.09	−.30
Total population	.15	.12
Rate of improvement in techniques in agriculture (lagged)	.14	.02
Rate of population growth (lagged)	.15	−.08
Net immigration	.12	−.11
Concentration of landholdings	.14	.07
Extent of illiteracy	.08	−.10
Rate of spread of primary education (lagged)	.16	−.03
Extent of domestic economic role of government	.14	−.16
Socioeconomic character of political leadership	.16	.10
Extent of political stability	.15	−.06
Rate of spread of market system (composite)	.16	.09

[a]See the introductory section to the statistical analysis in chapter three for a discussion of how to read the components results and of the way we interpret them. Variables are listed within components on which they have primary high loadings in the order in which they are discussed in the text. Variables with secondary high loadings (marked with asterisks) also are important to the interpretation.

tems points to the importance of institutions permitting farm responsiveness to market signals. Market-oriented family farms producing a surplus played a crucial role in raising agricultural productivity and providing a home market for industry. This scenario differs from the Western European pattern summarized by Jones and Woolf in that land abundance gave a comparative advantage in agricultural products, slowing significantly the labor shift out of agriculture.

The second component for class 1 depicts a highly urban industrial pattern in which the roles of domestic agriculture are greatly reduced. Great Britain after 1870 scores highest, given the importance of its industrial sectors and cities, improved transportation, high per capita income, scarce land resources, and a greatly reduced agricultural labor force.[14] Canada at midcentury scores lowest. A rapid pace of industrialization also is included in this component.[15] Finally, the negative coefficients for colonial status and foreign economic dependence underline the vital role of foreign investment in financing imports of food and raw materials to substitute for domestic agricultural resources. A high level of capital outflow to foreign territories was typical of the most industrially advanced nations of the nineteenth century.

If we interpret this component with the signs reversed so that Canada for the period 1850–1870 scores highest,[16] we find a sharply contrasting scenario in which abundant land resources in overwhelmingly agricultural, colonial territories were exploited by foreign capital. Neither transportation networks nor agricultural incomes, however, were yet sufficient to support a domestic industrial sector of any quantitative significance. Information on high- and low-scoring countries makes it clear that foreign economic dependence slowed a shift of resources from agriculture to industry by encouraging primary-product specialization and free trade.

Class 2: Strong Role of Agriculture in Small Countries Undergoing Radical Transformation

Class 2 consists of four small open economies (Belgium, Denmark, the Netherlands, and Switzerland) whose agricultural sectors were radically transformed during the last quarter of the nineteenth century from extensive cultivation to the production of human-capital-intensive crops for export. Export markets became even more important to agriculture than domestic markets.

---

[14]The use of the term "greatly reduced" is based on actual data for the high- and low-scoring countries.

[15]Past improvements in transportation and a slowing of the past expansion of market institutions also are included in this component. The latter is a characteristic of advanced countries, where market systems were quite well established by the middle of the century.

[16]Recall that the indicators of level of development for our earliest cross-section refer to 1850, while the indicators of the rate or structure of expansion (including foreign economic dependence and the other political variables) refer to the period 1850–1870.

Governments provided little protection from the drastic decline in grain prices in the 1870s, but Switzerland, for example, did partially subsidize the shift away from cereals and toward specialized dairy products. This class is more homogeneous than class 1: All four countries had a history of agricultural improvements, low illiteracy rates, and dispersed landholdings; their land systems were conducive to improvements in technology.

The results for class 2 are given in table 5-4. The main pattern is similar to that for class 1, but includes two additional political variables: the socioeconomic character of political leadership and the extent of political stability. Belgium, Switzerland, and Denmark at the end of the century score the highest, Denmark and the Netherlands at midcentury the lowest. The secondary pattern also is similar to that for class 1: a high degree of urbanization and industrialization, a well-developed transportation system, fewer agricultural resources, a high level of foreign investment, and a marked exit of labor from agriculture.[17] The minus signs of the land variables point to the spread of small-scale intensive agriculture on rented farmland. In Belgium, the country with the highest component score, inheritance systems favoring small holdings led agriculturalists to respond to urbanization by increasing the number of fixed cash tenant farms.[18] This component also shows a negative relationship to real wages in agriculture, reflecting the unfavorable medium-term effects of the agricultural crisis of the 1870s and 1880s on class 2 countries—a class defined by governmental support of the radical transformation of agriculture.

Reversing the signs so that Denmark and Switzerland in the 1850s and 1860s score high, we find another scenario, one in which *domestic* exploitation of land resources retained labor in agriculture,[19] and deficiencies in transportation limited the domestic market. However, land institutions providing a wider distribution of surplus and public investments in education contributed to the rising agricultural wages included in this "reverse" pattern.[20]

---

[17] But Belgium, the country with the highest component score, differed from class 1 countries. Foreign capital outflows and a large industrial sector exporting manufactures financed food imports without directly involving Belgium in the exploitation of land resources abroad. Belgian colonial holdings were not a source of food imports to Belgium.

[18] The high score of Belgium also suggests that the multiplicity of small rented commercial holdings was promoted by widespread opportunities for farm families to hold factory jobs in cities.

[19] Our inferences about domestic exploitation of agricultural resources derive from the difference in the range of variations in foreign dependence between classes 1 and 2. In class 1, there was a full range, from countries with colonial holdings to land-abundant colonies developed by European settlers and capital. In class 2, the range narrowed from countries with colonial holdings to countries having a growth structure heavily dependent on trade and moderate foreign capital inflow. None of these trade-dependent class 2 countries was as trade-dependent as Canada in class 1.

[20] The minus sign accompanying the rate of spread of primary education indicates that the

Table 5-4
Patterns of Agricultural Development:
Principal Components Analysis for Class 2
(Strong Role of Agriculture in Small Countries Undergoing Radical Transformation)[a]

Variable	Principal Component	
	1	2
Level of development of techniques in agriculture	.23	.01
Rate of improvement in techniques in agriculture	.19	.02
Rate of improvement in techniques in industry	.21	.08
Rate of improvement in techniques in industry (lagged)	.19	.10
Level of development of techniques in industry	.17	.17*
Level of per capita income	.21	.10
Rate of growth of exports	.19	−.00
Degree of shift in export structure	.17	−.03
Direction of change in real wages in industry	.23	−.07
Favorableness of attitudes toward entrepreneurship	.24	−.01
Strength of national representative institutions	.22	−.08
Socioeconomic character of political leadership	.21	.08
Extent of political stability	.18	−.07
Extent of urbanization	.16	.37
Level of development of inland transportation	.18*	.44
Relative abundance of agricultural resources	.09	−.22
Degree of foreign economic dependence	.07	−.17
Percentage of labor force in agriculture	.14	−.25
Predominant form of land tenure and holding	.24*	−.25
Favorableness of land institutions to improvements	.22*	−.22
Rate of improvement in inland transportation (lagged)	.17*	.28
Rate of spread of primary education (lagged)	.15	−.25
Direction of change in real wages in agriculture	.18*	−.28
Total population	.08	.01
Rate of change in per capita income	.14	−.02
Rate of improvement in techniques in agriculture (lagged)	.14	−.02
Rate of population growth (lagged)	.14	−.06
Net immigration	.11	.12
Concentration of landholdings	.11	−.14
Extent of illiteracy	.06	.12
Colonial status	.09	−.16
Extent of domestic economic role of government	.16	.09
Level of development of market system (composite)	.16	.10
Rate of spread of market system (composite)	.09	−.01
Rate of spread of market system, lagged (composite)	.11	.15

[a]See the introductory section to the statistical analysis in chapter three for a discussion of how to read the components results and of the way we interpret them. Variables are listed within components on which they have primary high loadings in the order in which they are discussed in the text. Variables with secondary high loadings (marked with asterisks) also are important to the interpretation.

Class 3: Lagging Agricultural Output for the Domestic Market

The countries in class 3—Argentina, Italy, New Zealand, Norway, Spain, and Russia—are quite diverse. They include economically dependent countries with generous land resources where institutions slowed the growth of agriculture for the domestic market. In New Zealand at midcentury, Maori communal agriculture was still overwhelmingly important, but as the Maoris were killed off in battle or by epidemic disease, the pattern changed to very large scale pastoral holdings. Only late in the century did farming on smaller-scale operations for the domestic market become important. In Argentina, landownership was highly concentrated and food was produced mostly by subsistence farmers, so agriculture's contribution to the domestic market was very limited. Development of industry toward the end of the century was stimulated more by demand in large urban centers where many immigrants had settled than by rising agricultural demand. In Italy, Spain, and Russia, agriculture was usually carried out by large landowners using poor dependent peasants or by independent subsistence peasants. But the unfavorableness of these institutions for stimulating demand for factory goods was to some extent offset by extremely large populations. Norway was the only class 3 country with wide land distribution, but agriculture there was retarded by a legacy of communal arrangements for production which at midcentury were slowly weakening.

In all class 3 countries the slow growth of agriculture for the domestic market constrained industrial development for several decades during the last half of the nineteenth century because purchases of industrial goods by the agricultural sector were very limited and the food supply expanded slowly. Comparative advantage called for specialization in the export of primary products. Eventually, in all these countries gradual improvements in domestic agriculture raised incomes and increased food supplies sufficiently for at least modest industrial growth to occur. Steady expansion of primary exports eventually induced the construction of domestic factories for processing agricultural products, contributing thereby to the modest levels of industrialization achieved by all the countries in the class before 1914.

Land institutions ranged from forms of communal agriculture in New Zealand and Norway in the middle of the nineteenth century and in Russia after the reform of 1861 to independent freehold cultivation in New Zealand and Norway late in the century. Except in Norway, landholdings were concen-

---

rate of expansion of primary enrollments in all countries in the sample was highest in the early period (the 1830s and 1840s since the variable is lagged) and lowest in the latest period (the 1870s and 1880s), when *levels* of primary enrollments were comparatively high. The significance of rising agricultural wages in the reverse pattern should not be overemphasized, as wage labor was not quantitatively very important in the agricultural labor force in any of these countries.

trated. In the European countries the numerical predominance of peasant holders with small parcels of land was accompanied by land concentration.

The results for class 3 are presented in table 5-5. A dynamic process of foreign-promoted exploitation of abundant land resources for export, stimulated by inflows of labor[21] and capital, gives the best statistical explanation for the substantial variations in the class. Profitable large-scale staple production broke down institutional restrictions on markets to facilitate export expansion but slowed investment in smaller-scale farming and its associated rural demand for consumer goods. Land concentration narrowed the distribution of the proceeds from export expansion, thereby also narrowing the domestic market for consumer goods.[22] Industrial expansion was therefore quite modest. *Ceteris paribus,* abundant land raised per capita income. Somewhat stronger parliamentary institutions, more favorable attitudes toward entrepreneurship, and more solidly established freehold tenures point to late-century developments that contributed to shifts in political structure and economic policies helpful to industrial growth. The association in this component of a larger percentage of the labor force in agriculture with faster export expansion is consistent with the weakness of improvements in agricultural productivity and the extremely modest expansion of industry in this class.[23]

Component 2 summarizes the substantial variations left unexplained by the primary pattern.[24] It describes a conjunction of influences that helped some countries achieve agricultural progress and expand agricultural demand for consumer goods toward the end of the century. Substantial agricultural progress and faster growth of per capita income were associated with smaller, less rural populations, land tenure systems giving more control to the cultivator, reduced concentration of landholdings, more public investment in education, political leaderships less dominated by large landholders, and more favorable attitudes toward entrepreneurship. The high-scoring observa-

---

[21] The variable for population growth included in this component is lagged and the variable representing net immigration is not. However, the similarity of current and past population growth rates in most countries in this class permits us to interpret the inclusion of both variables to suggest immigration as a cause of population growth.

[22] Data on the high-scoring countries (Argentina and New Zealand at the end of the nineteenth century) suggest that they achieved narrowly based modest industrialization without a wide distribution of the agricultural surplus in part because of (1) construction, services, and industry for large, rapidly increasing urban immigrant populations and (2) the importance of industrial processing of exports.

[23] The inclusion of faster industrialization in this component should be interpreted with caution. The high-scoring countries were in the second-lowest industrialization category (fast growth of consumer goods production from a very narrow base) and low-scoring countries were in the bottom category. Only two countries in the entire class scored as high as category C on rate of industrialization (Russia and Italy after 1890).

[24] Recall that our results provide information on the variance and standard deviation for each country as successive components are added. See chapter two.

Table 5-5
Patterns of Agricultural Development:
Principal Components Analysis for Class 3
(Lagging Agricultural Output for the Domestic Market)[a]

Variable	Principal Component	
	1	2
Degree of foreign economic dependence	.24	−.04
Colonial status	.18	.11
Relative abundance of agricultural resources	.25	.10
Rate of growth of exports	.20	.02
Net immigration	.19	.01
Concentration of landholdings	.25	−.25*
Rate of population growth (lagged)	.20	.11
Level of per capita income	.18	.06
Level of development of market system (composite)	.25	−.00
Rate of spread of market system, lagged (composite)	.24	−.10
Rate of improvement in techniques in industry	.17	−.01
Strength of national representative institutions	.18	−.09
Rate of improvement in techniques in agriculture	.11	.22
Rate of change in per capita income	.15	.19
Total population	.15	−.38
Percentage of labor force in agriculture	.24*	−.31
Predominant form of land tenure and holding	.17*	.35
Rate of spread of primary education (lagged)	.16	.24
Extent of illiteracy	.20*	−.50
Socioeconomic character of political leadership	.14	.17
Favorableness of attitudes toward entrepreneurship	.17*	.25
Level of development of techniques in industry	.11	−.04
Level of development of techniques in agriculture	.12	.09
Level of development of inland transportation	.08	.04
Rate of improvement in techniques in industry (lagged)	.13	−.01
Rate of improvement in techniques in agriculture (lagged)	.06	.07
Rate of improvement in inland transportation (lagged)	.15	.08
Favorableness of land institutions to improvements	.14	−.01
Extent of urbanization	.12	.06
Degree of shift in export structure	.10	−.05
Extent of domestic economic role of government	.15	−.05
Extent of political stability	.11	.03
Direction of change in real wages in industry	.12	.01
Direction of change in real wages in agriculture	.09	.05
Rate of spread of market system (composite)	.16	.12

[a]See the introductory section to the statistical analysis in chapter three for a discussion of how to read the components results and of the way we interpret them. Variables are listed within components on which they have primary high loadings in the order in which they are discussed in the text. Variables with secondary high loadings (marked with asterisks) also are important to the interpretation.

tions are New Zealand after 1890 and Norway after 1870, where severe restrictions on markets had finally been removed. The low-scoring cases, Russia until the 1890s and Spain, were much less successful in removing institutional barriers to agricultural improvements.

On the average, the landed elites of class 3 countries had much more political influence than their counterparts in classes 1 and 2; social attitudes toward entrepreneurship were more negative; the distribution of land was much more concentrated (except in Norway); and the control of direct cultivators over production was typically limited. Consequently, positive covariations with rates of economic growth have a somewhat different meaning than in class 1 or 2. Here they indicate the favorable impact of removing severe institutional or political barriers to agricultural improvements on the growth of domestic markets.

Class 4: Overwhelmingly Agricultural Countries with Little Industrial Development

Class 4 consists of five overwhelmingly agricultural countries—Brazil, China, India, Egypt, and Burma—where very little, if any, industrial development occurred (the exceptions being some textile factories and a few export-processing plants). Standards of living were extremely low and agricultural productivity did not advance sufficiently to raise them. All five countries had low levels of productivity and average income and high percentages of the labor force in agriculture. Stimulated by foreign intermediaries and growing foreign markets, staple exports expanded in all class 4 countries at the end of the nineteenth century.

While indigenous entrepreneurs were important in Brazil and China, foreigners dominated in the other three countries. Land institutions varied greatly, ranging from serf or slave farming in Brazil and communal patterns in Burma in 1850 to the predominance of small-scale peasant agriculture and landownership in China and India. Concentration in landholdings ranged from very dispersed in China and India to extremely concentrated in Brazil and Egypt. No class 4 country ranked even moderately high on the variable representing the conduciveness of land institutions to agricultural improvements.

The results for class 4 are given in table 5-6. Component 1 summarizes a pattern of dependent dualistic market expansion in underdeveloped, overwhelmingly agricultural countries with illiterate populations. Typically, marketization proceeded more rapidly where immigration and population growth were greater, agricultural resources were more abundant, short-term tenancies were more important than communal arrangements, and larger landholdings prevailed over parcelization. Expatriates promoted export expansion by influencing governments to free land from restrictions on sales and mortgages and to substitute cash tenancies and sharecropping for com-

Table 5-6
Patterns of Agricultural Development:
Principal Components Analysis for Class 4
(Overwhelmingly Agricultural Countries with Little Industrial Development)[a]

Variable	Principal Component	
	1	2
Degree of foreign economic dependence	.32	.08
Colonial status	.27	−.16
Rate of spread of market system (composite)	.23	.18*
Rate of spread of market system, lagged (composite)	.18	.02
Level of development of market system (composite)	.31	.05
Percentage of labor force in agriculture	.32	−.09
Extent of illiteracy	.33	−.05
Net immigration	.21	.09
Rate of population growth (lagged)	.21	.19*
Rate of growth of exports	.16	.24
Relative abundance of agricultural resources	.19*	.24
Total population	.23*	−.46
Rate of change in per capita income	.10	.20
Predominant form of land tenure and holding	.21*	−.47
Concentration of landholdings	.21*	.40
Direction of change in real wages in agriculture	.09	−.25
Level of per capita income	.06	.02
Level of development of techniques in industry	.07	−.02
Level of development of techniques in agriculture	.08	.13
Level of development of inland transportation	.08	.03
Rate of improvement in techniques in industry	.14	−.02
Rate of improvement in techniques in industry (lagged)	.11	−.04
Rate of improvement in techniques in agriculture	.07	.01
Rate of improvement in techniques in agriculture (lagged)	.06	−.00
Rate of improvement in inland transportation (lagged)	.09	.04
Favorableness of land institutions to improvements	.12	−.15
Rate of spread of primary education (lagged)	.04	−.04
Extent of urbanization	.07	−.00
Favorableness of attitudes toward entrepreneurship	.06	.07
Degree of shift in export structure	.04	−.00
Extent of domestic economic role of government	.12	−.02
Socioeconomic character of political leadership	.04	.02
Strength of national representative institutions	.06	.03
Extent of political stability	.07	−.02
Direction of change in real wages in industry	.08	−.11

[a]See the introductory section to the statistical analysis in chapter three for a discussion of how to read the components results and of the way we interpret them. Variables are listed within components on which they have primary high loadings in the order in which they are discussed in the text. Variables with secondary high loadings (marked with asterisks) also are important to the interpretation.

munal controls. But on the average, neither agricultural improvements nor much industrial growth followed. Undoubtedly, the class characteristics of low initial incomes in agriculture and trade policies that hurt indigenous industry contributed significantly to the lack of industrial expansion. Brazil and Egypt at the end of the nineteenth century have the highest scores, China and Burma in the 1850s the lowest scores, on this component.

Class 4 extremes in land distribution operated against both agricultural improvements and domestic market formation. Where large-scale estates or plantations and countless low-productivity subsistence holdings persisted side by side, the agricultural surplus was concentrated in the hands of a few. Independent tenures could not promote savings, investment, or market demand where holdings were too small to support a family and alternatives to agricultural employment were absent. If signs are reversed so that China's and Burma's scores before foreign penetration are high, we find dispersed small landholdings and less secure individual property rights associated with slower market penetration of agriculture.

The secondary pattern shows an unsuccessful variation of the land-abundant scenario. The removal of severe restrictions on markets and the geographical spread of cash cropping (indicated by the secondary market variable) accelerated the pace of export expansion and the rate of growth of per capita income. Brazil and Egypt score high on this component for the 1850s and 1860s, when international markets for their exports were booming. But land systems greatly restricting cultivator freedom (and thus the agricultural surplus),[25] a marked concentration of landholdings, and mass rural poverty (a class characteristic) prevented significant development of domestic markets. The forces accelerating exports and average income growth had a negative impact on agricultural wages, and faster population growth (in part the consequence of market growth) reduced the amount of land per person.

With signs reversed, this component underlines a land-scarce scenario that limited the agricultural surplus. Here we find the coincidence of very small holdings usually belonging to independent cultivators where the inadequacy of holdings and land scarcity slowed export expansion and growth rates. When the component is viewed from this perspective, China and India score strongly.

Measures of Statistical Fit

Table 5-7 gives the total own-class variance of class observations (the diagonal elements in the table) and their variance when fitted to the other class models

---

[25]The high negative loading of the land tenure variable reflects the fact that the more land abundant expanding countries with high component scores (Brazil and Egypt in the early phase of primary-export expansion) had land systems with large holdings cultivated by slaves or depen-

Table 5-7
Patterns of Agricultural Development:
Cluster Distance Matrix for Principal Components Analyses

	Class 1	Class 2	Class 3	Class 4
Class 1	17.6	28.6	37.8	54.4
Class 2	15.2	15.2	23.9	34.7
Class 3	27.5	32.3	18.0	28.2
Class 4	623,000	754,000	481,000	13.5

NOTE: See text for explanation.

(the off-diagonal elements). In most pairwise comparisons, the own-class variance of each set of observations is significantly lower than its other-class variances. The differentiation of patterns between classes 1 and 2, taken together, and classes 3 and 4 is particularly good. The distance between classes 3 and 4 also is marked; the differentiation between classes 1 and 2 is less so. The lack of substantial separation between classes 1 and 2 is not surprising since they share important characteristics, including a significant role for agriculture in industrial change.

Table 5-8 provides details on the closeness of the characteristics of each country-period observation to the components model for its own and other classes. Only Italy after 1890 violates the clear separation of classes 1 and 2, on the one hand, from classes 3 and 4, on the other. Italy's lack of fit to class 3 for the period after 1890 is probably due to the features of its industrialization that resemble those of the smaller countries of class 1. Its lack of agricultural progress places it properly in class 3 as we have defined it. Hence, we did not consider reclassification. In spite of the overall closeness of classes 1 and 2, the country distances are reasonably consistent with our differentiation between the two classes. The lack of fit of Japan in 1850 is hardly surprising since its industrial growth came only later. Germany after 1890 and the Netherlands in 1850 fit classes 1 and 2 almost equally well—the former perhaps because its agricultural progress late in the century accompanied quite dualistic industrial expansion. As for the latter, in spite of very favorable initial conditions, its agricultural transformation came late. At the lower end of the spectrum, the principal misfit is Argentina during the third quarter of the nineteenth century, a period in which severe political instability and lack of transportation precluded the modest industrial development that came later.

---

dent tenants. (Egypt at midcentury had moderately abundant land per person; Brazil had very abundant land.) In the low-scoring countries (China and Burma in the 1850s and 1860s), fairly independent peasants were quite important.

Table 5-8
Patterns of Agricultural Development:
Degree of Fit for Principal Components Analyses
(Residual Standard Deviations for Three Classes Closest to Each Country Observation)

Country and Year	Assigned Class	Class to Which Closest	Residual S.D. – Closest Class	Class to Which 2d Closest	Residual S.D. – 2d Closest Class	Class to Which 3d Closest	Residual S.D. – 3d Closest Class
Canada 1850	1	1	17	3	19	2	24
France 1850	1	1	14	2	19	3	24
Germany 1850	1	1	19	2	20	3	31
Great Britain 1850	1	1	18	2	22	3	31
Japan 1850	1	4	21	3	23	1	25
Sweden 1850	1	1	13	2	21	3	22
United States 1850	1	1	21	3	24	2	24
Canada 1870	1	1	18	2	20	3	20
France 1870	1	1	11	2	16	3	29
Germany 1870	1	1	18	2	19	3	35
Great Britain 1870	1	1	17	3	23	3	34
Japan 1870	1	1	20	3	25	4	28
Sweden 1870	1	1	15	2	17	3	23
United States 1870	1	1	17	2	21	3	30
Canada 1890	1	1	17	2	20	3	23
France 1890	1	1	13	2	16	3	32
Germany 1890	1	2	20	1	21	3	41
Great Britain 1890	1	1	16	2	23	3	34
Japan 1890	1	1	17	2	24	3	29
Sweden 1890	1	1	20	2	20	3	29
United States 1890	1	1	18	2	21	3	33

Belgium 1850	2	17	1	18	3	26
Denmark 1850	2	15	1	16	3	20
Netherlands 1850	1	18	2	19	3	22
Switzerland 1850	2	14	1	22	3	30
Belgium 1870	2	12	1	18	3	30
Denmark 1870	2	11	1	14	3	23
Netherlands 1870	2	11	1	15	3	27
Switzerland 1870	2	18	1	23	3	35
Belgium 1890	2	13	1	20	3	37
Denmark 1890	2	18	1	20	3	32
Netherlands 1890	2	14	1	18	3	32
Switzerland 1890	2	17	1	19	3	32
Argentina 1850	4	17	3	20	1	27
Italy 1850	3	14	4	20	1	24
New Zealand 1850	3	25	4	25	1	26
Norway 1850	3	20	1	24	4	24
Russia 1850	3	12	4	15	1	29
Spain 1850	3	11	4	19	1	24
Argentina 1870	4	16	3	17	1	27
Italy 1870	3	21	1	26	2	29
New Zealand 1870	3	18	1	26	4	28
Norway 1870	3	17	1	23	2	26
Russia 1870	3	12	4	17	1	26
Spain 1870	3	16	1	23	4	25
Argentina 1890	3	22	1	29	4	31
Italy 1890	1	21	2	23	3	23
New Zealand 1890	3	19	1	27	2	28
Norway 1890	3	17	1	20	2	24
Russia 1890	3	18	4	23	1	25

Table 5-8 (continued)

Country and Year	Assigned Class	Class to Which Closest	Residual S.D. – Closest Class	Class to Which 2d Closest	Residual S.D. – 2d Closest Class	Class to Which 3d Closest	Residual S.D. – 3d Closest Class
Spain 1890	3	3	14	1	21	4	21
Brazil 1850	4	4	14	3	19	1	29
Burma 1850	4	4	15	3	20	1	25
China 1850	4	4	11	3	22	1	26
Egypt 1850	4	4	11	3	21	1	30
India 1850	4	4	15	3	21	1	29
Brazil 1870	4	4	13	3	15	1	28
Burma 1870	4	4	13	3	22	1	28
China 1870	4	4	10	3	23	1	27
Egypt 1870	4	4	15	3	22	1	31
India 1870	4	4	13	3	24	1	28
Brazil 1890	4	4	17	3	18	1	26
Burma 1890	4	4	12	3	22	1	28
China 1890	4	4	11	3	24	1	27
Egypt 1890	4	4	17	3	24	1	31
India 1890	4	4	13	3	26	1	27
Australia 1850	0	3	24	1	32	4	34
Australia 1870	0	3	23	1	29	2	32
Australia 1890	0	3	24	2	30	1	30

NOTE: The years 1850, 1870, and 1890 following country names in column 1 are shorthand for the three cross sections: 1850–1870, 1870–1890, and 1890–1914. As noted in the text and in appendix tables A51 through A53, some variables refer to the initial year of each period, some refer to the entire period, and a few lagged variables refer to the preceding period.

Importance of Variables to Between- and Within-Class Variations

Table 5-9 presents statistical measures of the importance of individual classification schemes in discriminating between classes and in explaining within-class variations.

Column 1 gives a measure of each classification scheme's contribution in discriminating among the four patterns of agricultural and industrial interaction, taking all classes together. Recall that the measure compares the unexplained variance of all country observations when fitted to their "correct" class models with their unexplained variance when fitted to the "wrong" class models. The higher the ratio of the unexplained variance with "incorrect" assignments to that with "correct" assignments, the greater the contribution of a variable to the correct assignment of the observations.

As in the analysis of industrialization, the two most important variables in discriminating among classes defined by the nature of agriculture-industry interactions and type of agriculture are degree of foreign economic dependence and the extent of literacy. The important economic variables accounting for class differences in agriculture-industry interactions are current levels and past rates of improvement of agricultural productivity, which determined the marketable surplus, the supply of savings, and the amount of labor available from domestic sources for early industrial growth; per capita income and the growth of industrial wages, which determined the extent of domestic demand for food agriculture; and the level of technological development in manufacturing. Important institutional variables are the character of land systems, which determined the extent of institutional barriers to agricultural development; and the influence of rising business and commercial classes on political leaderships, which determined whether national policy promoted food agriculture or staple exports.

Foreign economic dependence stands out as an important political variable differentiating types of economic change. In general, in countries with colonial holdings industrial and agricultural change were closely intertwined. By contrast, countries where specialization in primary-export expansion led to very modest or negligible industrial expansion were usually more dependent. Foreign economic dependence was a crucial determinant of trade, transportation, education, and immigration policies, all of which impinged closely on the way agriculture and industry interacted (see chapter six).

The importance of land institutions underlines the finding that all countries where domestic agriculture played a strong positive role in industrial growth score in the top categories for favorableness of land institutions to improvements. In all other countries, land systems were marked by extreme concentration, excessive parcelization, insecure tenancy, or communal control over production. The complexity of relationships between land tenure and development is discussed further in the concluding section of this chapter.

Table 5-9
Patterns of Agricultural Development:
Importance of Classification Schemes to Between-Class and Within-Class
Variations, All Classes Together[a]

Variable	Between-Group Relevance	Within-Group Relevance
Extent of illiteracy	9.0	.47
Degree of foreign economic dependence	8.1	.43
Level of development of techniques in agriculture	7.2	.36
Level of per capita income	6.6	.56
Direction of change in real wages in industry	6.1	.07
Favorableness of land institutions to improvements	5.7	.15
Predominant form of land tenure and holding	5.6	.78
Rate of improvement in techniques in agriculture (lagged)	5.4	.37
Socioeconomic character of political leadership	5.4	.50
Level of development of techniques in industry	5.3	.68
Level of development of inland transportation	3.9	.70
Total population	4.0	.57
Rate of improvement in techniques in industry (lagged)	3.6	.52
Concentration of landholdings	3.6	.52
Rate of improvement in techniques in industry	3.6	.50
Rate of improvement in inland transportation (lagged)	1.2	.27
Relative abundance of agricultural resources	2.1	.25
Rate of change in per capita income	1.5	.18
Rate of improvement in techniques in agriculture	2.8	.48
Percentage of labor force in agriculture	3.0	.29
Rate of population growth (lagged)	1.4	.27
Net immigration	1.3	.08
Rate of spread of primary education (lagged)	1.9	.02
Extent of urbanization	2.0	.46
Favorableness of attitudes toward entrepreneurship	4.8	.49
Colonial status	4.5	.41
Rate of growth of exports	0.9	.12
Degree of shift in export structure	3.2	.18
Extent of domestic economic role of government	1.1	.11
Strength of national representative institutions	4.7	.28
Extent of political stability	2.4	.17
Direction of change in real wages in agriculture	2.0	.29
Level of development of market system (composite)	1.8	−.46
Rate of spread of market system (composite)	1.7	−.01
Rate of spread of market system, lagged (composite)	1.7	.04

[a]Variables with between-group relevance over 5.0 are listed first, in descending order by that measure (column 1: 9.0–5.3). The remaining variables with measures of within-group relevance over .50 are listed in descending order by the within-group measure (column 2: .70–.50).

The political influence of the emerging middle classes is important in explaining between-class variations because of the indirect effects of their increased political power on the supply of domestic entrepreneurship, the direct effects of their expanded influence on government economic policies, and their role in creating a political environment conducive to commercial and industrial expansion.

Column 2 of table 5-9 gives a measure of how well each variable explains statistically the variance *within* classes *for all classes together.* The most important variables explaining within-class variations are land institutions, the adequacy of transportation networks, industrial development, per capita income, total population, and the socioeconomic character of national political leadership. High values for the land tenure and land concentration variables underline the importance of land institutions in explaining variations within all classes. Good transportation networks facilitated exports, enhanced interregional movements of supplies to industry, and extended the size of the domestic market. The importance of level and rate of industrial expansion to agriculture underscores industry's role in demanding agricultural products and supplying agricultural equipment. Total population and average income indicate the potential size of the domestic market. Finally, the variable for the socioeconomic character of national leadership reminds us how the decline in the political power of landed elites encouraged government trade and transportation policics that stimulated domestic food production and industry.

CONCLUSIONS

Given our statistical results, the leading conclusions about institutional influences on the role of agriculture in industrialization are as follows:

1. In predominantly agricultural economies, the character of land tenure systems and the pattern of land distribution were jointly the leading institutional influences on the development of domestic markets. This was true for most of the more developed countries of classes 1 and 2 near the beginning of the study period, when agriculture was still quantitatively important, and throughout the study period for the less developed countries of classes 3 and 4.

2. By contrast, in the more developed countries of classes 1 and 2, with their much-reduced agricultural sectors, rates of industrialization no longer depended on increased agricultural productivity or labor from the agricultural sector. Given the institutions of capitalism—factory enterprises, geographically large transportation enterprises, the financial and commercial networks and concentrated populations of urban centers, the institutions of capital export and foreign investment—domestic urban resources and foreign trade together could substitute for agriculture in providing capital, labor, and markets for industrialization.

3. In land-abundant countries, establishing secure individual titles to

land and removing restrictions on labor mobility were crucial to expanding primary exports. Also important were landholdings sufficiently large to economize on scarce domestic capital and entrepreneurial resources and to capture economies of scale in the production of staples. But institutions that were good for expanding food production and industry for the domestic market differed from those that were good for expanding primary exports. Land concentration eventually slowed domestic-led growth by producing an unequal distribution of income. Further, the organization of production on very large operations also limited the market because dependent laborers received little, if anything, above subsistence.

4. In land-scarce, low-productivity agricultural economies two kinds of institutions posed barriers to both export expansion and domestic market development. Where very small family-owned holdings insufficient to support the family prevailed (and supplementary employment opportunities were limited), neither income for market consumption nor savings for improvements were widely available. Where holdings were large, but the benefits of improvements did not go to the cultivator, the same deficiencies in savings, income, and markets resulted.

5. Colonial institutions or informal coalitions of indigenous landlords and expatriates established laws and institutions that greatly facilitated the marketing of peasant cash crops and plantation crops abroad while simultaneously reducing the profitability of indigenous handicraft industry. In big land-abundant countries, reducing the political power of large landlords led governments to make land accessible to market farmers (thereby serving the expansion of food supplies to urban sectors) and to invest in education and transportation. In land-abundant countries where coalitions of landed elites and expatriate trading interests remained powerful and in densely settled low-productivity colonies, foreign imports undercut domestic manufacturing, transportation served the export sector, and little was invested in education. Growth was then dualistic and had negative backwash effects on the rural poor.

6 Patterns of Foreign Economic Dependence

Between 1850 and 1914 Western European colonial empires expanded, investment extended worldwide, and trade increased dramatically as shipping costs declined. After 1870, most of the manpower and capital flowed to countries with abundant land settled by Europeans, producing extremely fruitful results. When European capital flowed to densely settled peasant economies, it usually contributed to export expansion but frequently was detrimental to indigenous preindustrial systems.

In most of Western Europe and Scandinavia expatriate contributions helped the early process of industrial expansion through purchases of railway bonds, willingness to give short-term credits for trade, and technical skills. Neoclassical economic historians see benefits derived from supplementing domestic savings and skills, while dependency theorists underline the negative effects of foreign penetration as foreign investment substitutes for domestic capital, drains profits from export expansion abroad, and promotes dualistic economic growth. These adverse effects are found in many, but not all, underdeveloped countries. Recently, Marxists have criticized the dependency theorists' view, arguing that foreign penetration expands productive capacity in ways that ultimately promote capitalism even when increases in living standards are negligible. We argue that the consequences for growth and development from increases in foreign ownership, immigration, economic control, skills, management, or loans varied systematically not only with initial factor-endowments and the character of export markets but also with institutional arrangements for production, marketing, and consumption.[1]

Little has been written on the measurement of economic dependence. Single indicators based on colonial status, foreign capital inflows, foreign direct investment, or the repatriation of profits fail to capture the meaning of "dependence" as it is used in the theoretical literature. Accordingly, in this chapter we discuss our operational definition of "foreign economic dependence" and the typology that stratifies our sample, and then we present the results of the components analyses.

DEGREE OF FOREIGN ECONOMIC DEPENDENCE

There is no agreed upon definition of "foreign economic dependence." Historically, countries became dependent economically in diverse ways, some by direct political subjugation and others by various types of economic penetration. In a crucial preliminary step we first identified dimensions of foreign economic dependence that historians and development economists stress as

---

[1]This thesis is drawn from the work of Robert Brenner (1976, 1977) and from case studies of the impact of foreign investment. See, for example, McCarty (Australia) 1973, p. 161.

important to growth and institutional change. Since qualitative aspects were important and quantitative data fragmentary, we then classified our country observations into only three ranked groups for each dimension. Finally, we formed an aggregate classification scheme.

We selected seven dimensions to group observations by heavy, moderate, or only modest dependence. Statistical methods of aggregation were not used to derive the final composite measure. Rather, we assigned weights according to two criteria: (1) heavy weight was given where theoretical reasoning suggested that a dimension played a crucial role in creating dependency; and (2) consistency of final country rankings was sought with the many comparative judgments in the literature about actual country situations. The result was an aggregate scheme of seven categories. Efforts to increase the number of categories either were stymied by the lack of data or introduced distinctions about which there was relatively little consensus in the literature. The dimensions we selected follow.

1. *How much did the expansion of primary exports dominate the structure of economic growth?* We judged countries to be heavily dependent where the structure of domestic expansion was directly linked with the export sector. For example, in Burma, India, and Egypt export expansion to advanced nations overwhelmingly determined the structure of domestic output expansion. The two lowest categories (i.e., the least dependent) described countries where *domestic* markets played an important role in inducing economic expansion.

2. *How important were foreign ownership and control of factory industry?* We judged countries most dependent where foreigners owned factory industry (or had full management control without ownership, as in India). In moderately dependent countries, foreign and domestic interests shared control and earnings. Countries where domestic interests predominated were ranked lowest.

3. *How important were expatriate entrepreneurial and government economic initiatives?* In heavily dependent countries, expatriates took most economic initiatives and established the "rules of the game." India is an example. In nondependent countries, even where foreign capital inflow was great, economic initiatives were overwhelmingly indigenous (e.g., the United States).

4. *To what extent did foreigners own or control foreign trade, distribution, and related financial services?* Foreigners dominated importing firms, those distributing exports, transportation enterprises, and banks serving the foreign trade sector to a much greater extent in heavily dependent countries than in nondependent countries.

5. *Were expanding sectors dependent on specialized foreign technical and administrative skills?* In heavily dependent countries, expatriates provided the most critical of these skills. In moderately dependent countries the main role of foreigners was to train indigenous manpower.

6. *To what extent were governments dependent on foreign loans?* At one extreme were countries such as Egypt, where foreigners financed even ordinary government expenditures; at the other was modest dependence on loans for railroads.

7. *How important were foreign capital inflows in financing domestic investment?* Countries varied from close to half of domestic investment financed by imported capital to a very modest role for foreign capital. (Account could not be taken of foreign capital reinvestment.)

In combining these dimensions into a single ranking scheme, we weighted most heavily the coincidence of heavily dependent production structures with foreign ownership of industry, dominance of trade and distribution, and control over economic initiatives. Dependence on foreign capital and selected foreign skills were given little weight when found alone, and dependent production structures were given only moderate weight when unaccompanied by foreign dominance of domestic institutions.

While some country assignments on individual dimensions were questionable, the aggregate scheme for measuring foreign economic dependence appears quite reliable and consistent with comparative judgments in the literature about individual countries. Individual country classifications and sources are given in the data appendix. The aggregate classification scheme is as follows:

Category A includes countries that showed heavy dependence in all seven dimensions.

Category B includes countries that had heavily dependent production structures and were at least moderately dependent in all other dimensions.

Category C includes countries that had moderately dependent production structures and were at least moderately dependent on all other counts. (Countries were classified C^- if the volume of their foreign trade was very small, the control of trade and distribution showed little dependence, or their dependence on expatriate skills was very modest.)

Category D includes two sorts of countries, both with moderate overall levels of dependence. The first type was at least moderately dependent on foreign capital and skills but had relatively independent production structures. The second had heavily dependent production structures but was only modestly dependent on foreign capital and skills. No countries in this category depended on foreign economic initiatives or experienced expatriate ownership or control of factory industry.

Category E includes countries exhibiting only a trace of dependence.

Category F includes advanced countries with independent production structures; any involvement with foreign loans, skills, or ownership was with countries at similar levels of development.

Category G includes economically advanced countries with no significant dependency features.

THE TYPOLOGY

The typology in table 6-1 stratifies the sample into four subsamples using the foreign-dependence ranking scheme. Each country is assigned to a subsample on the basis of how dependent it had become by the end of the nineteenth century. Class 1 includes countries that became heavily dependent by the end of the nineteenth century (category A). Class 2 includes the more moderately dependent countries (categories B and C). Class 3 (categories D and E) is distinguished from class 2 primarily by the predominance of indigenous entrepreneurial and administrative economic initiatives and the absence of foreign domination of factory industry. In class 4 are the economically advanced

Table 6-1
A Typology of Foreign Economic Dependence in the Nineteenth and Early
Twentieth Centuries

Class	Description of Class	Country
1	Countries that became heavily dependent during the nineteenth century: the expansion of primary exports dominated their domestic growth; expatriates dominated trade, banking, and technical expertise, and financed a substantial part of domestic investment. The "rules of the game" were largely determined by expatriates.	Argentina Burma Egypt India
2	Countries that became at least moderately dependent: domestic growth was at least moderately dependent on exports; factory industry, entrepreneurship, trade, banking, and technical skills were at least partially controlled by foreigners; and economic expansion was at least moderately dependent on foreign capital. On several dimensions dependence was moderate, not heavy.	Brazil Canada China New Zealand Russia Spain
3	Countries where export expansion dominated the structure of domestic growth but where foreign ownership and control of factory industry were very limited and entrepreneurial initiatives were overwhelmingly indigenous. Excluded are economically advanced nations where trade was with nations at similar levels of development. Other features of dependency varied greatly from country to country.	Australia Denmark Italy Japan Norway Sweden
4	Countries that were not significantly dependent. This class includes major colonial powers, major capital exporters, and nations that became advanced economically even though they may have depended on other advanced nations for capital or skills.	Belgium France Germany Great Britain Switzerland
Unclassified		Netherlands United States

SOURCES: Table A46 in data appendix.

nations (categories F and G). Recall that in category F the exchange of foreign skills or capital was with countries at similar levels of development. Two countries were left unclassified. The United States imported capital and did not have colonies during most of the period, but it is not classified as dependent, because its trading and investment relationships were primarily with countries at similar levels of development. The Netherlands was not a major exporter of manufactured goods nor was it as economically advanced as the other countries in class 4.

Countries are assigned to a class on the basis of their situations at the end of the century, but their earlier situations differed greatly. Within any one class, therefore, there is considerable variation in the degree of foreign economic dependence.

The Statistical Results

In this section we discuss our statistical results on patterns of foreign dependence. Readers who have not read the book continuously are referred to chapter two, pages 58–61, and chapter three, pages 74–78, for guidance in interpreting the tables that follow.

Class 1: Heavily Dependent Countries

Countries in class 1 (Argentina, Burma, Egypt, and India) became heavily dependent during the course of the nineteenth century.[2] Although all were dependent, they varied substantially in other respects. In Argentina land was more abundant, per capita income was higher, and a smaller proportion of the population worked in agriculture. Also, the growth in per capita income

---

[2]The expansion of primary exports dominated domestic growth. Expatriates governed foreign trade, modern banking systems, and technical expertise. (In Burma and Egypt they controlled domestic trade as well.) Governments relied on foreign loans for railway construction and other investments. Expatriates established the "rules of the game" except in Argentina. In Argentina, which was the only politically independent country in this class, alliances of indigenous landlords with expatriate exporting interests dominated the political structure, and the expatriate power in these alliances was sufficient to place Argentina in class 1. McCarty ([Australia] 1973) suggests that the Spanish colonial heritage in Argentina led to a situation in which the absence of effective government institutions prevented the construction and operation of railways as well as control over British companies; in contrast, Australia (placed in class 2), with its established parliamentary institutions and competent bureaucracies, was able to construct and operate railways and make financing decisions.

The definition of "expatriate" is difficult but should include resident foreigners who maintain primary national attachment to another country. Where immigration is permanent but a definite cultural identification with another country remains, the distinction between an immigrant and an expatriate is not clear-cut.

Except where otherwise noted, the sources for the country information in this section are those cited in our classification systems in the data appendix.

in Argentina averaged over 2 percent each decade until the end of the century.[3] The other class 1 countries were colonies of Great Britain; none had national parliamentary systems, and in none did emerging indigenous business and labor groups have significant political influence. Land systems varied greatly: By 1890, short-term tenancy predominated in both Egypt and Burma; peasant ownership with strong communal influences prevailed in India; and the latifundia system dominated in Argentina. Landownership was concentrated in Argentina and Egypt, less so in Burma and India.

The statistical results are presented in table 6-2. Component 1 summarizes a familiar pattern of foreign economic exploitation of land resources. Expatriate influences eliminated many institutional restrictions on markets—especially land markets.[4] Expatriate influences and population growth, including immigration, also contributed to the process of export growth. The higher the *level* of market development and the more concentrated the landownership, the faster the *speed* of marketization and the process of export expansion. But these changes did not usually bring benefits in the form of per capita income or wage increases. Nor was export growth associated with greater literacy or shifts from agriculture. Indeed, the reverse holds true. Argentina and Egypt score at the top of the spectrum toward the end of the century, when the British presence and export expansion were greatest. At the lower end of the spectrum is Burma before export expansion began.

Component 2 brings out conditions influencing the rise in per capita income in these heavily dependent expanding countries. Where land was abundant, growth in per capita income was associated with heavy immigration and export expansion. The more land per inhabitant and the smaller the population, the higher the initial average income. Large landholdings, as opposed to a multiplicity of small peasant farms, were associated with successful export expansion. Higher agricultural wages were not, however, associated with rising per capita national income; on the contrary, where per capita income grew faster, agricultural wages rose more slowly.[5]

Argentina at the end of the century scores high on component 2, being a rapidly growing country but one whose proceeds from export expansion were narrowly distributed.[6] If we reverse the signs on the component loadings,

---

[3]More precisely, Argentina was the only one to achieve an average annual rate of growth of over 2 percent for the periods 1850–1870, 1870–1890, and 1890–1914, with the exception of Egypt during the cotton boom of the 1850s and 1860s.

[4]Foreign promotion of the elimination of restrictions on markets is inferred from the inclusion of all three market variables. The establishment of legal conditions favoring market exchanges is an important component in market institutional growth at the lower end of the spectrum.

[5]It should be noted that the variance in wage movements was small in this class, with no country experiencing strong increases.

[6]The inclusion of reduced colonial presence is accounted for by the fact that Argentina was the only politically independent country in the class.

Table 6-2
Patterns of Foreign Economic Dependence:
Principal Components Analysis for Class 1
(Heavily Dependent Countries)[a]

Variable	Principal Component	
	1	2
Degree of foreign economic dependence	.32	−.14
Colonial status	.28	−.28*
Rate of spread of market system (composite)	.18	.03
Rate of spread of market system, lagged (composite)	.18	−.11
Rate of population growth (lagged)	.26	.15
Net immigration	.23	.22*
Level of development of market system (composite)	.27	.15
Extent of illiteracy	.31	−.16
Percentage of labor force in agriculture	.27	−.20*
Rate of change in per capita income	.11	.21
Relative abundance of agricultural resources	.20*	.27
Rate of growth of exports	.19*	.20
Total population	.18*	−.40
Level of per capita income	.10	.19
Concentration of landholdings	.23*	.33
Direction of change in real wages in agriculture	.10	−.18
Favorableness of attitudes toward entrepreneurship	.08	.17
Predominant form of land tenure and holding	.18*	−.25
Level of development of techniques in industry	.06	−.02
Level of development of techniques in agriculture	.09	.12
Level of development of inland transportation	.08	−.01
Rate of improvement in techniques in industry	.14	.00
Rate of improvement in techniques in industry (lagged)	.11	.00
Rate of improvement in techniques in agriculture	.10	.14
Rate of improvement in techniques in agriculture (lagged)	.06	−.03
Rate of improvement in inland transportation (lagged)	.13	.15
Favorableness of land institutions to improvements	.13	−.02
Rate of spread of primary education (lagged)	.06	.09
Extent of urbanization	.09	.16
Degree of shift in export structure	.04	−.00
Extent of domestic economic role of government	.15	−.16
Socioeconomic character of political leadership	.04	.11
Strength of national representative institutions	.09	−.06
Extent of political stability	.06	−.05
Direction of change in real wages in industry	.10	−.10

[a]See the introductory section to the statistical analysis in chapter three for a discussion of how to read the components results and of the way we interpret them. Variables are listed within components on which they have primary high loadings in the order in which they are discussed in the text. Variables with secondary high loadings (marked with asterisks) also are important to the interpretation.

India, the lowest-scoring country, dominates the pattern. Barriers preventing export expansion from contributing to increased per capita income arose from the conjunction of very low average income, an overwhelmingly agricultural population, dense settlement, social attitudes unfavorable to entrepreneurship,[7] and a strong colonial presence. Land tenure included more freehold in India than in high-scoring countries (hence its minus sign), but parcelization and fragmentation posed severe barriers to agricultural progress.

Class 2: Moderately Dependent Countries

In class 2, foreign influences were somewhat less important. Brazil and New Zealand had heavily dependent production structures but were somewhat less dependent on foreign skills and entrepreneurship and experienced less foreign control of industry. Canada, China, Russia, and Spain all had only moderately dependent production structures, but showed considerable variation in other aspects of dependency. There was less foreign penetration in China, though foreigners dominated economic expansion in port areas. While Canada relied most heavily on foreign capital and most industries were foreign owned, industrial decisions were made largely by Canadians.[8] Although Russia relied heavily on both foreign capital and skills to develop factory industry, the Russian government successfully restricted dependency; Russian capital and initiative were important in both domestic and foreign trade. In Spain, expatriate capital and foreign expertise dominated mining and extraction, railways and banking, in sharp contrast to the indigenous Catalan cotton textile industry.

Class 2 is in some respects more diverse than class 1. Land was abundant in Canada, New Zealand, Brazil, and Russia, but very scarce in China. Per capita income, nowhere as high as in Western Europe, varied from moderately high by 1890 in New Zealand and Canada to extremely low in China. Land tenure and holding systems ranged from independent cultivation in New Zealand (after 1870) and Canada to communal control over peasant lands in Russia to cultivation by slaves in Brazil. Landholdings were concentrated in all class 2 countries except Canada and China. Only Canada scores high on the overall characteristics of land systems. While Canada and New Zealand eventually had less than 50 percent of their labor forces in agriculture, the percentage was much higher in the other countries. In addition, political

---

[7]Since all countries in this class have low scores on social attitudes toward entrepreneurship, the inclusion of this variable suggests only that the absence of extremely unfavorable attitudes favored income growth with export expansion.

[8]McCarty ([Australia] 1973, p. 159), for example, indicates that effective control of the railways remained in Canadian hands even where British ownership was large-scale or predominant. This point is also made by Paterson ([Canada] 1976, pp. 13–14).

characteristics were more varied in class 2 than in class 1. Canada and New Zealand, the only colonies, score high on both national leadership and parliamentary systems.

Component 1 for class 2 (table 6-3) is similar to the first component for class 1: strong foreign dependence interacted with resource abundance, market development, export expansion, and demographic change without generating systematic per capita income or wage benefits. Large holdings predominated. But here successful export performance by countries like Canada and New Zealand, with their freehold tenures, yielded a positive relationship between the tenure variable and export growth.

The secondary pattern differs substantially from that for class 1, however. Agricultural productivity improved systematically wherever barriers to market institutions were rapidly eliminated and social, demographic, and political conditions were favorable—that is, where populations were smaller and had begun shifting away from agriculture; literacy was spreading, even among those remaining in agriculture; the indigenous social elite was accepting entrepreneurship; and emerging indigenous commercial, industrial, and labor groups were gaining political influence.[9] Economic expansion, however, did not bring systematic increases in per capita income or wages. Canada and New Zealand toward the end of the century score high on this component; mixed commercial farming spread and exports became more diversified in a political setting that was favorable to economic expansion. China persistently scores low on this component.

Class 3: Modestly Dependent Countries

The heterogeneous countries of class 3—Australia, Denmark, Italy, Japan, Norway, and Sweden—share one common characteristic: For at least several decades of the nineteenth century, changes in production structure were determined largely by expanding foreign trade with economically advanced nations. In addition, all six countries either borrowed abroad for railway construction or attracted foreign investment in mining and industrial enterprises. In contrast with classes 1 and 2, however, foreign ownership and control of factory industry were limited, and entrepreneurial initiatives were largely indigenous. Australia was the most dependent, borrowing heavily abroad for railways, utilities, and construction, while at the same time developing an important domestic market. At the other end of the spectrum, the Scandinavian countries were much less dependent on foreign capital despite its importance in particular sectors of industry and mining.

Typically, class 3 countries had higher per capita income, more literacy,

---

[9]The reason that less representative institutions are included is that the indicator refers to *national* institutions, which were established late in high-scoring Canada and New Zealand.

Table 6-3
Patterns of Foreign Economic Dependence:
Principal Components Analysis for Class 2
(Moderately Dependent Countries)[a]

Variable	Principal Component	
	1	2
Degree of foreign economic dependence	.25	−.08
Colonial status	.20	.05
Relative abundance of agricultural resources	.27	.06
Level of development of market system (composite)	.27	.05
Rate of growth of exports	.20	.05
Net immigration	.21	−.02
Rate of population growth (lagged)	.19	.10
Concentration of landholdings	.23	−.09
Predominant from of land tenure and holding	.20	.11
Rate of improvement in techniques in agriculture	.12	.19
Rate of spread of market system (composite)	.19*	.25
Rate of spread of market system, lagged (composite)	.24*	−.31
Total population	.17*	−.34
Percentage of labor force in agriculture	.26*	−.31
Extent of illiteracy	.22*	−.40
Rate of spread of primary education (lagged)	.13	.19
Favorableness of attitudes toward entrepreneurship	.15	.22
Socioeconomic character of political leadership	.14	.20
Strength of national representative institutions	.13	−.23
Level of per capita income	.14	.16
Level of development of techniques in industry	.10	−.01
Level of development of techniques in agriculture	.11	.13
Level of development of inland transportation	.08	.11
Rate of change in per capita income	.16	.14
Rate of improvement in techniques in industry	.16	.01
Rate of improvement in techniques in industry (lagged)	.12	.01
Rate of improvement in techniques in agriculture (lagged)	.07	.09
Rate of improvement in inland transportation (lagged)	.11	.12
Favorableness of land institutions to improvements	.16	.16
Extent of urbanization	.09	.04
Degree of shift in export structure	.09	.15
Extent of domestic economic role of government	.13	.15
Extent of political stability	.11	−.06
Direction of change in real wages in industry	.10	−.16
Direction of change in real wages in agriculture	.08	−.09

[a]See the introductory section to the statistical analysis in chapter three for a discussion of how to read the components results and of the way we interpret them. Variables are listed within components on which they have primary high loadings in the order in which they are discussed in the text. Variables with secondary high loadings (marked with asterisks) also are important to the interpretation.

and smaller proportions of their population in agriculture than the countries of classes 1 and 2, although none industrialized before World War I.[10] All but Australia had per capita income growth rates over 2 percent per decade until the end of the century. Class 3 land systems ranged from predominantly family farms in Japan and Scandinavia[11] to the Italian mix of small family farms and large holdings under short-term lease arrangements. Export performance varied greatly between countries and over time. This class was also politically diverse, as shown by the full range of scores on national parliamentary systems and leadership. However, these countries shared an absence of foreign political control over their economic policies.

In the primary statistical pattern (table 6-4), export expansion is positively correlated with greater dependence, the building of market institutions, more abundant land resources, faster population growth, a largely agricultural population, and land systems favoring private cultivators with larger holdings. But here the similarity to classes 1 and 2 stops. Gone is the association with immigration and illiteracy. Instead, we see that export expansion led to faster educational expansion and industrial growth, rising industrial wages, and rising per capita income. Economic performance was better where governments took a more active economic role and representative political systems were better developed. The higher the initial level of per capita income, the faster the process of expanding exports and increasing average income.

According to the secondary statistical pattern, per capita income was higher where land was abundant, urbanization was more advanced, a lower proportion of the labor force was in agriculture, and large landholdings (with often insecure property rights) were predominant. Rapid immigration and population growth accelerated urbanization but slowed the rate of increase in per capita income. Australia, the only colony in the class, is at the top of the spectrum for all three periods, while Sweden before 1890 is found at the lower end. (Hence, the colonial-status variable has a positive sign.) In Sweden, growth in per capita income was promoted by a relatively high level of agricultural productivity, the slowing of population growth, an increase in emigration, and the diversification of exports.[12]

Component 3 of this heterogeneous, modestly dependent class summarizes the favorable conditions under which technological improvements in agriculture led to increased agricultural wages: past investment in transportation, a

[10]The exception to this statement is possibly Sweden, where somewhat greater industrialization took place.

[11]In Japan before the Meiji reforms and in Norway before about 1880, peasant farms were constrained by communal or feudal arrangements.

[12]This perspective is gained by reversing the signs in the component. Judging by the predominance of freehold, land tenure was more favorable in countries with low component scores than in those with high scores, but the small size of holdings and less abundant land resources slowed responses to export opportunities.

Table 6-4
Patterns of Foreign Economic Dependence:
Principal Components Analysis for Class 3
(Modestly Dependent Countries)[a]

Variable	Principal Component		
	1	2	3
Rate of growth of exports	.19	.03	−.04
Degree of foreign economic dependence	.17	.02	−.09
Rate of spread of market system, lagged (composite)	.19	−.08	−.15
Relative abundance of agricultural resources	.20	.19*	.11
Favorableness of land institutions to improvements	.21	−.16	−.05
Rate of spread of primary education (lagged)	.18	.02	.12
Rate of improvement in techniques in industry	.17	−.03	.02
Direction of change in real wages in industry	.21	.11	.04
Extent of domestic economic role of government	.19	.00	−.07
Strength of national representative institutions	.19	−.13	.11
Level of per capita income	.18*	.27	.09
Extent of urbanization	.14	.24	.03
Concentration of landholdings	.18*	.28	−.11
Predominant form of land tenure and holding	.24*	−.26	.08
Net immigration	.12	.32	−.13
Rate of population growth (lagged)	.18*	.23	.02
Rate of change in per capita income	.17*	−.33	.14
Colonial status	.17*	.30	−.07
Level of development of techniques in agriculture	.20*	−.22	.03
Degree of shift in export structure	.16	−.32	−.18*
Rate of improvement in techniques in agriculture	.16	−.06	.18
Direction of change in real wages in agriculture	.11	−.08	.31
Rate of improvement in inland transportation (lagged)	.14	−.00	.21
Total population	.12	−.10	−.30
Extent of illiteracy	.10	.02	−.42
Favorableness of attitudes toward entrepreneurship	.19	.10	.24
Extent of political stability	.13	−.05	.20
Percentage of labor force in agriculture	.22*	−.20*	−.35
Level of development of market system (composite)	.23*	.06	−.28
Level of development of techniques in industry	.11	−.04	.14
Level of development of inland transportation	.09	−.09	.14
Rate of improvement in techniques in industry (lagged)	.14	.00	.03
Rate of improvement in techniques in agriculture (lagged)	.11	−.11	.08
Socioeconomic character of political leadership	.16	.12	.15
Rate of spread of market system (composite)	.13	−.06	−.08

[a]See the introductory section to the statistical analysis in chapter three for a discussion of how to read the components results and of the way we interpret them. Variables are listed within components on which they have primary high loadings in the order in which they are discussed in the text. Variables with secondary high loadings (marked with asterisks) also are important to the interpretation.

smaller, more literate population, more favorable social attitudes toward entrepreneurship, reduced domestic political conflict, and a substantial shift of the population from agriculture made possible by fewer restrictions on factor markets.[13] Australia, Sweden, and Denmark late in the century had the highest scores while Japan and Italy before 1890 had the lowest.

Class 4: Nondependent Countries

The five countries of class 4 were largely nondependent: Great Britain, France, and Germany were both major colonial powers and leading capital exporters before 1914; Belgium also had large colonial holdings, and for its size, exported relatively large amounts of capital; Switzerland was a major capital exporter but did not have colonies.

Portfolio investment in railways and government bonds were the major forms of foreign investment. Foreign trade amounted to 14–15 percent of national incomes. There was much foreign trade among class 4 countries. By the end of the century all had become major exporters of manufactured goods. Indigenous entrepreneurship was overwhelmingly dominant, although in some countries foreigners had owned or dominated some sectors of industry in the earlier part of the century. By the end of the century, the importance of colonies ranged from Great Britain, which reaped major economic benefits from colonies, to Germany, which gained little if anything from either trade with or investment in colonies.

As is evident in the results presented in table 6-5, this group of nondependent nations developed successfully internally; expanded agriculture, industry, and exports; and achieved high levels of per capita income and raised wages within a favorable institutional, social, and political framework without important dependence on foreign capital. Their economic success was undoubtedly helped by colonial holdings and foreign investments—a defining characteristic of the class. (There is so little variation within this class with respect to colonial status that the colonial variable has little explanatory power.) The secondary pattern portrays a deterioration in export performance at higher levels of per capita income, industrialization, urbanization, and domestic market development. The adverse movements of both agricultural wages and investment in education within this pattern suggest negative effects of substantial investment abroad on domestic growth.

Measures of Statistical Fit

The separation between the four components of our model can be read from table 6-6. Table 6-7 presents the distances of each country-period observation

---

[13] The inclusion of a smaller shift in export structure results from the high score of Australia, which was late in diversifying its agriculture compared with the other countries in the class.

Table 6-5
Patterns of Foreign Economic Dependence:
Principal Components Analysis for Class 4
(Nondependent Countries)[a]

Variable	Principal Component 1	Principal Component 2
Rate of improvement in techniques in agriculture	.17	−.05
Level of development of techniques in agriculture	.23	.11
Rate of improvement in techniques in industry	.24	−.01
Rate of improvement in techniques in industry (lagged)	.23	.08
Rate of improvement in inland transportation (lagged)	.18	.13
Level of per capita income	.20	.19*
Direction of change in real wages in industry	.23	−.10
Predominant form of land tenure and holding	.23	−.22*
Favorableness of land institutions to improvements	.21	−.06
Favorableness of attitudes toward entrepreneurship	.21	.10
Socioeconomic character of political leadership	.18	.09
Strength of national representative institutions	.20	−.04
Extent of political stability	.19	−.12
Rate of growth of exports	.18*	−.23
Degree of shift in export structure	.15	−.20
Level of development of techniques in industry	.18*	.20
Extent of urbanization	.16	.46
Percentage of labor force in agriculture	.13	−.36
Level of development of inland transportation	.22*	.34
Level of development of market system (composite)	.13	.19
Direction of change in real wages in agriculture	.22*	−.30
Rate of spread of primary education (lagged)	.15	−.22
Total population	.14	.02
Relative abundance of agricultural resources	.09	−.06
Rate of change in per capita income	.15	.03
Rate of improvement in techniques in agriculture (lagged)	.13	−.03
Rate of population growth (lagged)	.12	.05
Net immigration	.09	−.02
Concentration of landholdings	.13	.03
Extent of illiteracy	.07	.07
Colonial status	.07	−.16
Degree of foreign economic dependence	.03	−.03
Extent of domestic economic role of government	.14	−.05
Rate of spread of market system (composite)	.15	−.07
Rate of spread of market system, lagged (composite)	.10	.12

[a]See the introductory section to the statistical analysis in chapter three for a discussion of how to read the components results and of the way we interpret them. Variables are listed within components on which they have primary high loadings in the order in which they are discussed in the text. Variables with secondary high loadings (marked with asterisks) also are important to the interpretation.

Table 6-6
Patterns of Foreign Economic Dependence:
Cluster Distance Matrix for Principal Components Analyses

	Class 1	Class 2	Class 3	Class 4
Class 1	14.8	15.5	17.4	27.4
Class 2	22.3	16.9	22.0	33.2
Class 3	33.5	26.7	17.1	29.5
Class 4	947,000	779,000	522,000	15.5

NOTE: See text for explanation.

from its own and other classes. Recall that the cluster distance matrix compares total own-class variance (the diagonal elements) with variance when observations are fitted to other class models. Class 4 (nondependent) is well separated from all dependent classes. Class 3 countries (modestly dependent) fit the class 3 model substantially better than other class models. Class 2 countries (moderately dependent) show less separation from the models of adjacent classes. Class 1 countries (heavily dependent) fit their own and the class 2 model quite well probably because the primary component patterns for both classes are very similar. But the countries in class 2, with its secondary pattern of more widely diffused growth, do not fit the consistently narrow growth pattern of class 1.

Given the heterogeneity of the country groups in respects other than dependency, the fit of individual observations to their classes is surprisingly good. Class 2 (moderately dependent) is most diverse, including, for example, Spain, which resembles Italy (class 3) except for its greater dependence, and China, which resembles India and Egypt (class 1) except for its lesser dependence. (The statistical analysis misclassifies China for the earliest period and Spain after 1870.) To illustrate further, Argentina (class 1) and Australia (class 3) had similar primary export expansions but quite different dependency features closely related to their contrasting extents of growth diffusion. Both are correctly classified in table 6-7.

Importance of Variables to Between- and Within-Class Variations

Table 6-8 presents the statistical measures of the importance of individual variables in discriminating variations between and within classes. (See chapter three, the last section before the chapter conclusion, for a description of how these measures are constructed.) Foreign economic dependence is, of course, the most important variable in discriminating between classes since it was used to construct the typology. (Colonial status, a related variable, also is important.) The illiteracy and agricultural level variables underline two further influences on domestic carry-over from foreign-promoted export expansion. Four of the other variables with between-group relevance above 5.0 rep-

Table 6-7
Patterns of Foreign Economic Dependence:
Degree of Fit for Principal Components Analyses
(Residual Standard Deviations for Three Classes Closest to Each Country Observation)

Country and Year	Assigned Class	Class to Which Closest	Residual S.D.—Closest Class	Class to Which 2d Closest	Residual S.D.—2d Closest Class	Class to Which 3d Closest	Residual S.D.—3d Closest Class
Argentina 1850	1	1	17	3	17	2	19
Burma 1850	1	1	13	2	14	3	14
Egypt 1850	1	1	17	2	21	3	23
India 1850	1	1	15	2	16	3	21
Argentina 1870	1	1	10	2	16	3	17
Burma 1870	1	1	13	2	17	3	20
Egypt 1870	1	1	18	2	21	3	23
India 1870	1	1	14	2	19	3	25
Argentina 1890	1	1	19	2	22	3	24
Burma 1890	1	1	13	2	19	3	21
Egypt 1890	1	1	18	2	23	3	25
India 1890	1	1	12	2	23	3	26
Brazil 1850	2	2	18	1	19	3	24
Canada 1850	2	2	16	3	25	1	27
China 1850	2	1	18	2	18	3	20
New Zealand 1850	2	2	24	1	24	3	28
Russia 1850	2	2	14	1	17	3	20
Spain 1850	2	3	15	2	15	1	18
Brazil 1870	2	2	15	1	19	3	23
Canada 1870	2	2	15	3	23	1	30
China 1870	2	2	17	1	18	3	23

New Zealand 1870	2	2	18	1	22	3	22
Russia 1870	2	2	14	1	18	3	19
Spain 1870	2	2	18	3	19	1	22
Brazil 1870	2	2	20	1	23	3	26
Canada 1890	2	2	14	3	26	1	33
China 1890	2	2	17	1	19	3	25
New Zealand 1890	2	2	17	3	20	1	30
Russia 1890	2	2	19	1	22	3	23
Spain 1890	3	3	16	2	17	1	20
Australia 1850	3	3	12	2	25	1	25
Denmark 1850	3	3	19	2	19	4	24
Italy 1850	3	3	12	2	17	1	17
Japan 1850	3	3	20	2	20	1	23
Norway 1850	3	3	20	2	20	1	24
Sweden 1850	3	3	20	2	26	4	27
Australia 1870	3	3	14	2	24	1	27
Denmark 1870	3	3	14	2	19	4	21
Italy 1870	3	3	22	2	24	1	26
Japan 1870	3	3	14	2	24	1	27
Norway 1870	3	3	18	2	22	4	26
Sweden 1870	3	3	16	4	23	2	28
Australia 1890	3	3	14	4	31	2	33
Denmark 1890	3	3	20	4	22	2	26
Italy 1890	3	3	22	4	23	2	25
Japan 1890	3	3	16	4	26	2	28
Norway 1890	3	3	14	4	22	2	24
Sweden 1890	3	3	16	4	21	2	34
Belgium 1850	4	4	16	3	21	2	30
France 1850	4	4	17	3	19	2	25
Germany 1850	4	4	15	3	21	2	33

Table 6-7 (continued)

Country and Year	Assigned Class	Class to Which Closest	Residual S.D.— Closest Class	Class to Which 2d Closest	Residual S.D.—2d Closest Class	Class to Which 3d Closest	Residual S.D.—3d Closest Class
Great Britain 1850	4	4	17	3	26	2	33
Switzerland 1850	4	4	15	3	22	2	34
Belgium 1870	4	4	14	3	25	2	34
France 1870	4	4	13	3	21	2	31
Germany 1870	4	4	15	3	22	2	38
Great Britain 1870	4	4	12	3	27	2	38
Switzerland 1870	4	4	18	3	24	2	39
Belgium 1890	4	4	17	3	29	2	40
France 1890	4	4	12	3	22	2	35
Germany 1890	4	4	16	3	27	2	43
Great Britain 1890	4	4	17	3	26	2	41
Switzerland 1890	4	4	19	3	23	2	35
Netherlands 1850	0	3	18	4	21	2	26
United States 1850	0	3	21	4	21	2	30
Netherlands 1870	0	4	16	3	21	2	32
United States 1870	0	4	20	3	23	2	36
Netherlands 1890	0	4	17	3	25	2	37
United States 1890	0	4	22	3	26	2	36

NOTE: The years 1850, 1870, and 1890 following country names in column 1 are shorthand for the three cross sections: 1850–1870, 1870–1890, and 1890–1914. As noted in chapter two and in appendix tables A51 through A53, some variables refer to the initial year of each period, some refer to the entire period, and a few lagged variables refer to the preceding period.

Table 6-8
Patterns of Foreign Economic Dependence:
Importance of Classification Scheme to Between-Class and Within-Class
Variations, All Classes Together[a]

Variable	Between-Group Relevance	Within-Group Relevance
Degree of foreign economic dependence	17.1	.30
Extent of illiteracy	8.3	.61
Level of development of techniques in agriculture	6.4	.59
Rate of improvement in techniques in industry (lagged)	6.4	.28
Colonial status	6.0	.54
Rate of improvement in techniques in industry	5.9	.33
Direction of change in real wages in industry	5.7	.23
Level of development of techniques in industry	5.0	.50
Level of per capita income	3.0	.63
Socioeconomic character of political leadership	4.4	.63
Extent of urbanization	2.7	.61
Favorableness of attitudes toward entrepreneurship	2.9	.60
Degree of shift in export structure	3.7	.51
Level of development of inland transportation	3.1	.38
Percentage of labor force in agriculture	3.3	.45
Total population	1.8	.48
Relative abundance of agricultural resources	3.7	.34
Rate of change in per capita income	1.3	.36
Rate of improvement in techniques in agriculture	1.3	.47
Rate of improvement in techniques in agriculture (lagged)	3.3	.45
Rate of improvement in inland transportation (lagged)	1.0	.20
Rate of population growth (lagged)	3.1	.48
Net immigration	3.0	.39
Predominant form of land tenure and holding	1.6	.30
Concentration of landholdings	2.0	.40
Favorableness of land institutions to improvements	2.0	.24
Rate of spread of primary education (lagged)	1.4	.13
Rate of growth of exports	0.8	.14
Extent of domestic economic role of government	1.5	.33
Strength of national representative institutions	3.7	.30
Extent of political stability	4.3	.36
Direction of change in real wages in agriculture	4.1	.41
Level of development of market system (composite)	2.5	−.03
Rate of spread of market system (composite)	1.5	.25
Rate of spread of market system, lagged (composite)	2.3	.10

[a]Variables with between-group relevance over 5.0 are listed first, in descending order by that measure (column 1: 17.1–5.0). The remaining variables that have measures of within-group relevance over .50 are listed in descending order by the within-group measure (column 2: .63–.51).

resent industrialization and its benefits. This is consistent with our finding that the less dependent the class of countries, the more foreign-promoted exports diffused growth to the domestic urban-industrial sector.

Variables with within-group relevance measures of over .50 were levels of socioeconomic development (urbanization and literacy, agricultural and industrial achievements, and per capita income); colonial status, the nature of political leadership, and attitudes toward entrepreneurship; and shifts in export structure. These variables reinforce our conclusion in the next section that domestic social and political influences were overwhelmingly important in determining whether export expansion favored indigenous economic initiatives and diffused economic benefits.

Summary and Conclusions

In all three dependent classes of countries, rising foreign investment and increased dependence accelerated *export* expansion and *aggregate* economic growth and also promoted immigration and market institutions. Not surprisingly, where land was abundant and immigration substantial, export-led growth was faster. Foreign-promoted export expansion and more rapid market institutional development went hand in hand, no matter what the degree of dependence. Marketization in turn reduced communal controls over the use of land, weakened social restrictions on population growth, and promoted enlarged landholdings. Our statistical results underline the pervasiveness of these connections.

But the results show striking contrasts among classes in the consequences of export expansion. In the heavily dependent class, primary-export expansion did not, on the average, lead to increased productivity or to increases in average wages in either agriculture or industry. Nor was it usually accompanied by increases in literacy. Only where land resources were exceptionally abundant did per capita income rise as a result of export growth. In general, the faster the average income rose, the *slower* the average wages in agriculture increased. Here, the country data suggest that the great profitability of land-intensive exports may have slowed investment in improved production methods for agricultural wage goods.

In the class of more moderately dependent countries the results show favorable impacts of foreign-promoted export expansion on agricultural productivity and a relative shift of labor out of agriculture where social and political conditions favored indigenous economic initiatives and reductions in illiteracy. On the average, however, neither per capita income nor wages rose.

Only in the third of the dependent classes did increased foreign investment and skills systematically contribute to dispersion of economic benefits through modest industrialization, agricultural improvements, rising per capita income, and higher wages in both agriculture and industry.

The political concomitants of export growth also varied systematically across the three dependent classes. The common feature of the heavily dependent class was the political dominance of the country by expatriates, whether through direct colonial control or through alliances with indigenous landed elites. In the more moderately dependent class, increased political influence for indigenous groups other than large landholders was the crucial systematic requisite for the spread of agricultural improvements. In the least dependent group, national representative institutions, an active economic role on the part of the government, and domestic political stability systematically favored industrialization and a wider spread of income benefits; government investment in education also favored the complementary process of agricultural improvements.

In our results, then, the spread effects of aggregate export expansion were systematically greater where indigenous merchants, entrepreneurs, and small farmers gained more political clout. These results suggest that successful development depends in large part on political influences. The hypothesis suggested by our results is that the distribution of political power was a major determinant of economic policies. The structure of political power affected greatly the pattern of economic expansion and thus the distribution of benefits from growth.

Often, the outcome of earlier political and socioeconomic changes not captured by our data was closely related to the structures of political and socioeconomic power. When trading opportunities expanded dramatically in the last quarter of the nineteenth century, these structures mattered greatly to the subsequent pattern of development. In heavily dependent countries, for example, earlier foreign political aggression, often economically motivated, had destroyed or altered preexisting socioeconomic systems in ways that greatly limited the size of the domestic market and hence domestic benefits from export expansion. In less heavily dependent countries, rising economic groups—manufacturers, farmers, traders, and wage earners—gained influence in the political system as economic changes increased their economic strength. The gain of political power by rising domestic groups led to government policies that were more likely to increase domestic benefits from export growth.

Our results help identify the sorts of policies that we reason varied most with the political influence of expatriates and the indigenous classes with which they were allied; our results point to land policies, immigration policies, and investment in education. In addition, data on high- and low-scoring countries suggest the importance of tariff policies and the structure of transportation investment.

There are two perspectives from which to view these policies. First is their impact on the aggregate rate of export expansion. Second is their impact on the distribution of the proceeds from export expansion. The thesis suggested by our results is that in countries exporting primary products, stronger expatriate political influence led to policies that accelerated export expansion but narrowed the distribution of its proceeds: land policies that more aggressively destroyed communal arrangements for land use and promoted land concentration; trade policies that promoted primary exports but hurt indigenous small-scale manufacturing; immigration policies that kept the price of labor low; financial policies that served exclusively the expansion of exports; and transportation policies that stressed railways from the interior to ports rather than connections furthering internal trade.

In contrast, where indigenous manufacturers, wage earners, or small farmers were politically influential in a setting of export expansion, they supported different land, tariff, immigration, financial, and transportation policies. The destruction of communal land arrangements, land alienation, and land engrossment tended to proceed more slowly. Governments were less likely to subsidize immigration in periods of unemployment and low wages and more likely to support rural banking institutions. Public investment more often included feeder roads for marketing agricultural wage goods, rural public schools, and other types of social investment in rural areas.

Whether expanding exports and increasing foreign economic dependence led to increased political power for expatriates and the classes with which they were allied depended greatly on their preexisting institutional, socioeconomic, and political structures. As the results for class 1 (heavily dependent) show, where small-scale farmers and indigenous manufacturers were poor, uneducated, and without experience in political participation, export expansion was much more likely to lead to powerful political alliances between large primary producers and foreign export interests. The resultant economic policies severely restricted distribution of the benefits from additional exports. Direct colonial power in conditions of poverty and illiteracy proved even less likely to produce economic policies favoring the dispersion of benefits.

In contrast, as the results for class 3 (the least dependent class) show, where initially a class of indigenous farmers producing for the domestic market had a surplus above subsistence and sufficient education to participate in the political process, foreign economic dependence was much less likely to affect their participation in the political process and thus economic policies. Under these circumstances, increases in foreign economic dependence more often took the form of inflows of capital and skills, but foreign control over management decisions seldom followed even where foreigners held considerable equity.

Nor did increased foreign economic dependence in rich lands sparsely settled by relatively educated foreigners with some experience of political participation lead, on the average, to greater political dominance by colonial powers. Rather, the increased political influence of rising, fairly literate groups of domestic small-scale factory owners, farmers, and even workers helped promote public investment in education that in turn favored increased political participation. Both developments contributed to conditions favorable to public provision of knowledge about new agricultural methods.

Our results do not show that technological conditions and crop patterns determined the institutional and distributional consequences of export expansion predicted by staple theories of growth. Dependent countries exporting grain, for example, did not systematically experience wider growth than those exporting cotton or coffee or wool. Two explanations are consistent with the data on countries that score high and low in our results. First, in the nineteenth century, economies of scale in grain and most other crops were not significant, so both independent family holdings and large-scale management of tenant farmers were equally productive. Second, institutional conditions established well before the nineteenth century determined whether economic expansion induced political transformations and government policies conducive to the spread of growth.

In sum, our results support fully neither neoclassical nor dependency approaches to foreign trade and investment. Each theory applies fully only to one extreme of the range of foreign dependence. The neoclassical model of growth, institutional change, and "trickle down" applies fully only to the nondependent countries of class 4. The thesis of dependency theory that foreign-promoted export expansion failed to benefit most of the population is confirmed fully only for the heavily dependent countries of class 1. For countries with intermediate levels of dependence, features of both models are present. While increased foreign dependence led to faster export growth everywhere, the consequences varied according to the level of dependence of the country. In class 2 (moderately dependent countries), the primary pattern resembles the heavily dependent pattern of class 1, but the secondary pattern captures the favorable impacts of foreign capital and skills. In class 3 (modestly dependent countries), both primary and tertiary patterns reflect the neoclassical story of the benefits of foreign trade and investment. The key to these findings, and thus to widespread economic growth, is an indigenous entrepreneurial scope for adapting institutions to changing economic opportunities. Heavy foreign economic dependence precluded government land, tariff, educational, financial, and transportation policies that would have created an effective scope for responsive indigenous institutional change.

7 The Course of Poverty

In this chapter we analyze the impact of institutional change on poverty.[1] We have reviewed a considerable body of theory explaining low levels of economic development and poor dynamic economic performance (chapter one), but we have not yet discussed explicitly the eclectic literature on the causes of poverty in the early phases of nineteenth-century economic growth. With rare exceptions, this literature consists of "partial" hypotheses about the relative importance of various influences on poverty; grand theories are rare.[2] Here we summarize theses on the impacts of marketization, demographic change, industrialization, and colonialism, respectively, on poverty in the nineteenth century.

THESES ON THE CAUSES OF POVERTY

Marketization

One major theme relates to the spread of market institutions. The neoclassical theory of *institutional* change underlines positive long-term aspects of market institutional growth. Private property rights and the commercialization of property were crucial to the success of industrialization and to the eventual reduction of poverty (North and Thomas 1970). In contrast, according to Marxian theory, the "freeing" of labor as the capitalist system penetrated agriculture, increased poverty. In the Marxian model, under preindustrial property relations, commercialization had led to increased extraction of surplus from land-bound laborers and, given static technology, to declining incomes (Brenner 1976).

Marketization caused the terms of trade between agriculture and industry to have increased relevance for poverty. Where agricultural improvements lagged during the first surge of industrialization, as in Belgium for a time (Lis 1982), or remained slight, as in Russia (Portal 1965), rising food prices reduced the real incomes of both urban people and landless agricultural workers. In contrast, where increases in agricultural productivity kept pace with the expanding urban labor force, agricultural and industrial trade contributed to increased urban wages, as in Scandinavia (Söderberg 1982) and probably in Great Britain (Williamson 1982). Markets provided opportunities for those with skills and assets, but where assets were not sufficient to cover periods of unfavorable returns, market expansion added price risk to ordinary production risk. The result was often increased loss of remaining assets, including land (Wright [United States] 1978).

---

[1] The impacts of dynamic economic or geographic change on poverty differ depending on how they affect market institutions, land systems, dependency relationships, and political institutions. They also vary with initial institutional and resource conditions—a thesis developed by Robert Brenner in his studies of the transition from feudalism to capitalism (1976, 1977).

[2] The most well known is that of Karl Marx.

Demographics

Demographics also influenced the course of poverty. From the middle of the eighteenth century in Western Europe, populations surged partly because of improved agricultural productivity and nutrition (McKeown 1978). But where economic opportunities did not expand enough to absorb the additional labor force, as in Scandinavia, poverty increased significantly (Söderberg [Sweden] 1982). In contrast, where the population increase coincided with expanding agriculture and cottage industry markets, as in Belgium, complex interactions occurred among several factors—population change, land systems, regional soil types, and increases in cottage industry. These interactions, explored in the rich literature on "protoindustry" (Fisher 1973), determined regional and national impacts on the poor. Population growth stimulated productivity improvements and attracted cottage industry, thereby raising incomes (Mokyr [Netherlands] 1975). But population growth also produced typical Malthusian outcomes (Malthus 1914).

Fertility had a role in these processes, but its interactions with mortality are not well understood (Grigg 1980). Wherever economic growth persisted over long periods, fertility rates eventually declined. But there were also major preindustrial cases where small peasant holdings predominated and where families were systematically limited; for example, France (Grantham 1975), Japan (Smith 1959), and Bavaria (Lee 1977).

Internal migration had positive and negative effects. It reduced poverty in poor rural areas of emigration but increased it in urban areas of immigration wherever work opportunities did not expand fast enough to absorb the additional workers (Jones [Great Britain] 1964).

International migration interacted with poverty in several ways. First, it directly affected the labor supply. Emigration from labor surplus areas contributed to tighter labor markets and rising wages for those remaining, as in Scandinavia (Semmingsen [Norway] 1940; Janson [Sweden] 1931). In areas of immigration, the additional labor relieved labor shortages and dampened wage increases, as in Burma with Indian immigration (Furnivall 1931) and at times in European overseas settlements (Lebergott [United States] 1964; Coghlan [Australia] 1918). The net impact depended, of course, on both the economic opportunities and the patterns of international capital flows. Where foreign capital moved with migrants, investment stimulated increased employment and wages in immigration areas, but capital outflows from emigration areas tended to slow domestic investment and depress employment and wages (Thomas 1973).

Industrialization

The relationship between poverty and industrialization has been much disputed. There is contrasting evidence on whether poverty increased or decreased and on its intensity during the early decades of industrialization. Even where the evidence clearly points to *lower* incomes with faster industrialization, conflicting interpretations abound. Some authors use cross-sectional comparisons to suggest that lower wages favored faster industrialization (Romano [Italy] 1982; Mokyr [Belgium] 1976), while others give evidence that industrialization lowered incomes and increased the number of poor (Lis and Soly [Belgium] 1977). Some regional cross sections show that faster industrialization induced higher real incomes, as in Scandinavia in the latter part of the century (Söderberg [Sweden] 1982). Despite these differences, economic historians agree that, in the long run, industrialization in Europe brought about a substantial rise in average real income and a reduction in poverty.

The Marxian model gives yet another slant on the relation between industrialization and poverty. The core dynamic—the drive to increase the surplus above laborers' subsistence—leads to more capital-intensive techniques and in combination with population growth and rural-urban migration creates an industrial reserve army (Marx 1930). Marxian theorists predict that real wages will be reduced over the long run unless the predominant means of increasing the surplus is cheapening wage goods through technical innovation.

Colonialism

The literature on foreign dependence documents the pervasive impact of formal and informal colonial institutions on poverty. Legal "reforms" inducing land and labor marketization broke down communal organization and protections against land alienation and landlessness (Furnivall [Burma] 1931; Bhatia [India] 1964). Tariff policies favoring foreign imports destroyed indigenous handicrafts (Hlaing [Burma] 1964; Chaudhuri [India] 1968), while immigration policies favoring the export sector tended to reduce average wages (Hlaing [Burma] 1964). Transportation policies brought poverty above the famine level by greatly reducing interregional transport costs, but promoted marketization leading to crises of "entitlements" during regional harvest failures even where aggregate food supplies were adequate (Sen 1977). As dependency theorists illustrate, colonialism also had negative impacts when political alliances among expatriate exporting interests, domestic landowners, and indigenous merchants promoted staple-export expansion with a dualistic rather than a wider regional distribution of benefits (Baran 1968).

Colonialism had major positive impacts on poverty wherever immigration and capital flowed together into empty lands (Thomas 1973). But even in these land-abundant countries results were varied: In Australia poverty was successfully reduced, but in Argentina it was not. There is a growing literature about the causes of such disparate outcomes in land-abundant European-settled countries. But most comparative studies stress differences in the character of government and political influences. Argentina's failure is usually blamed on political alliances among indigenous landed and commercial elites and expatriate interests which kept wages down and restricted access to land. Australia's success is seen as due to government policies favoring domestic consumption. After heavy gold-rush immigration broke the political domination of large landholders there, labor's political power increased greatly and family farmers gained access to land for food production around the expanding cities (Wheelwright 1974; McCarty 1973; Moran 1970).

We conclude from this brief literature review that influences on poverty must be analyzed within the overall framework of the causes of economic backwardness and dynamic economic performance. The literature suggests strongly that the course of poverty is determined by the economic and institutional processes of change that we analyzed in chapters three through six.

THE TYPOLOGY

We constructed the typology by combining data on twenty-year changes in per capita income and in average wages in agriculture and industry[3] with descriptive information about the proportion of the population affected by these changes.[4] We also observed changes in the proportion of the population in extreme poverty over time, partially ranking countries by these changes over the entire period. The partial rankings for 1850 are based on our earlier work (Adelman and Morris 1978a). Table 7-1 indicates the composition of the four classes and gives the main sources of information upon which the classifications are based. The countries excluded from the typology are listed at the end of the table.[5]

In judging the proportion of populations in poverty between 1850 and 1914, we defined the extremely poor by one or more of the following criteria: (1) those who were starving or destitute; (2) those whose food consumption was marked by a recurrent inadequacy in the supply of their respective staples; and (3) those with poor health conditions as indicated by extreme overcrowding, unusually high mortality rates, and/or disease. Thus, the extremely poor exclude all whose diets may have lacked important nutrients but whose food consumption was marked by an abundance of their particular staple plus some regular consumption of meat, dairy products, fish, or

---

[3]While these proxies for changes in standards of living have well-known deficiencies, our data permit us to interpret them and judge their validity in particular results by their correlations with other variables, such as levels and changes in industrial and agricultural productivity.

[4]The limitations of wage series for evaluating standard-of-living changes are well known. Among other things, wage series fail to take account of unemployment or underemployment; in low-income countries they refer to only a small part of the population, and they fail to capture family incomes that typically depend on multiple sources of income.

[5]An explanation of our omission of six countries from the typology is given later in this chapter.

Table 7-1
A Typology of the Course of Poverty in the Nineteenth and Early Twentieth Centuries

Class	Description of Class	Country	Principal Sources
1	Countries where substantial industrialization began at the latest toward the middle of the nineteenth century and where poverty during the first half of the century was increasingly concentrated among casual or unemployed urban workers, handicraft workers, and the landless or near landless in agricultural areas of labor surplus. In all but Britain, the numbers in extreme poverty increased early in the century. In the latter half of the century, widely based economic growth and industrialization resulted in reductions in poverty, the absorption of labor, and fairly steady rises in average wages.	Belgium	Dechesne 1932, pp. 388, 396, 409-419, 464-487; Chlepner 1956, pp. 49, 110-111; Lis and Soly 1977, pp. 460-486; Ducpétiaux 1850, pp. 65, 78ff.; Avondts et al. 1979, p. viii; Neyrinck 1944, pp. 182-183
		France	Clapham 1936, pp. 18, 160; Levasseur 1969, pp. 260, 704, 714-716, 723; Henderson 1961, pp. 118-126; Grantham 1975, p. 317; Lévy-Leboyer 1968a, pp. 794-795
		Germany	Hamerow 1969, pp. 39-41, 44-50, 69-70; Wunderlich 1961, pp. 8-11; Kuczynski 1945, pp. 23-33, 64-81, 108-142; Desai 1968, p. 125
		Great Britain	Deane 1965, chap. 15; Usher 1920, pp. 364-365; O'Brien and Engerman 1981; Williamson 1982; Jones 1964; Clapham 1930, 1932, 1938
		Switzerland	Wittmann 1963, pp. 595-603; Rappard 1914, chap. 6, pp. 285-287; Kneschaurek 1964, pp. 139-145; Siegenthaler 1964, p. 426
2	Agricultural economies dominated by family farming where increases in extreme poverty among the landless occurred during the first half of the nineteenth century alongside surges in population growth and with negligible industrialization; at the same time, among those *with* land, gradually rising productivity was associated with improved living standards. The latter	Denmark	Hovde 1943, 2:621-622; Nielsen 1933, pp. 503-505, 530-531; Youngson 1959, pp. 217-218, 223, 229-230; Pedersen 1930, p. 313; Hansen 1976, pp. 255-279
		Norway	Drake 1969, pp. 54ff.; Hovde 1943, 2:621-622; Larsen 1948, pp. 462-463; Hodne 1975; Semmingsen 1940, passim; Lieberman 1970, p. 71; Johnsen 1939, p. 521
		Sweden	Montgomery 1939, pp. 60-61; Janson 1931, pp. 82-83, 422ff.; Hovde 1943, 1:287, 2:621-622, 651; Youngson 1959,

half of the nineteenth century was marked by major emigration abroad from areas of surplus agricultural population, and specialized agriculture and small-scale industry expanded greatly.

pp. 166, 176–177; Dahmén 1970, p. 16; Jörberg 1961, p. 11; Jörberg 1972; Söderberg, 1982; Bagge et al. 1935

No.	Description	Country	References
3	Densely populated, low-productivity, predominantly peasant economies where there was no marked long-term trend in the extent of extreme poverty in the early nineteenth century; fluctuations in poverty were associated primarily with variations in harvests. During the latter half of the century, regional increases in extreme poverty were most often associated with increased dependence on the market for subsistence, land parcelization, indebtedness, and loss of land to nonagriculturalists.	Burma	Hlaing 1964, pp. 120–125; Furnivall 1931, pp. 42–43, 75–77, 97–98; Tun Wai 1969, pp. 47–50
		China	Fairbank et al. 1960, pp. 5–6; Perkins et al. 1969, pp. 26ff.; Condliffe 1932, p. 16; Williams and Zimmerman 1935, p. 416
		Egypt	Hershlag 1964, pp. 81, 120–121; Crouchley 1938, p. 362; Owen 1969, pp. 109–110, 238–245; Dicey 1881, pp. 110–111
		India	Gadgil 1942, chaps. 2, 5; Blyn 1966, pp. 142, 154; Bhatia 1965, pp. 136–137; M. Mukerji 1965, pp. 676–682; Kuczynski 1965, pp. 609ff.
		Russia	Lyashchenko 1949, p. 462; Gerschenkron 1965, pp. 776–779; Dobb 1948, pp. 42–45; Crisp 1978, pp. 407–408
4	Sparsely settled land-abundant countries where extreme poverty during the first half of the nineteenth century was largely among urban families of immigrants or in regions of subsistence farming. Fluctuations in extreme poverty during the latter half of the nineteenth century were mainly associated with waves of immigration and cyclical fluctuations in primary-product markets; where domestic markets expanded significantly as independent farms spread and small-scale industry grew, most of the poor	Argentina	Díaz Alejandro 1970, pp. 40–41; Williams and Zimmerman 1935, pp. 217–218; Cortés Conde 1976, pp. 144–147; Randall 1977, 2: 118; Scobie 1964b, pp. 6–8, 14, chap. 3, pp. 67, 122–129; Ferns 1960, pp. 442ff.
		Australia	Coghlan 1918, 1:432–441, 457–458, 2:696–697, 743, 1020–1025, 1044–1049, 3:1266–1267, 1449, 1502–1503; Grundy 1970, passim; Butlin 1962, p. 158
		Canada	Tucker 1936, p. 157; Innis 1935, pp. 195–196; Easterbrook and Aitken 1956, pp. 395, 484–486

Table 7-1 (continued)

Class	Description of Class	Country	Principal Sources
	were eventually absorbed in quite widely based growth.	New Zealand	Sutch 1969, pp. 32–34, 43–45, 65, 82–90, chap. 7, p. 168; Scholefield 1909, pp. 168–169; Simkin 1951, chap. 11
Unclassified		Brazil	Conrad 1972, pp. 24–25; Stein 1957, pp. 46, 62; Jobim 1944, p. 99; Foerster 1919, pp. 283–289
		Italy	Seton-Watson 1967, pp. 22–23; Schmidt 1939, p. 13; Clough 1964, p. 101; Luzzatto 1969, pp. 221–225; Zangheri 1969, pp. 28–29; Romano 1982
		Japan	Crawcour 1965, pp. 25–27; Smith 1959, pp. 110–112, 159–166, chap. 9; Lockwood 1954, pp. 7–8, 138–145; Tussing 1966, passim; Minami and Ono 1979, p. 233
		Netherlands	Brugmans 1961, pp. 188–191, 426–431; de Jonge 1968, pp. 17, 287–291; Mokyr 1975, passim; de Meere 1979, p. 10
		Spain	Carr 1966, pp. 3–22, 32–37; Brenan 1943, pp. 108–109, 118
		United States	Ware 1964, pp. 15, 39–41; Jones 1960, pp. 117–122, 130–132; Kuczynski 1946, passim; Hansen 1925, p. 32; Lebergott 1960, p. 493; Rees and Jacobs 1961, p. 121

NOTES: In Great Britain, the process of reducing extreme poverty and increasing average wages began in the first half of the nineteenth century. There is considerable controversy over the timing and extent of these changes. See Taylor (Great Britain) 1975.

Of the sources in this table, the following are listed in the general section of the bibliography: Foerster 1919, Henderson 1961, and Williams and Zimmerman 1935.

pulses. This poverty line lies above the level of near starvation and destitution and below a rigorously determined level of diet adequacy.

Fragmentary and descriptive data as well as wage series were used to sketch broad outlines of what happens to the poor. The imprecision of the concept "extreme poverty" is a direct reflection of the paucity of data. While a more precise concept could easily have been defined—for example, a poverty line based on minimum nutritional requirements—the conceptual resolution is of little relevance without appropriate data. Using judgments about the course of relative poverty, we grouped countries whose experience with poverty was sufficiently similar to allow variations within a class to represent common processes of change affecting poverty. (See table 7-1.)

Class 1 consists of Western European countries where poverty was substantially reduced through widespread industrialization in the latter half of the nineteenth century. Class 1 countries shared the favorable agricultural transformations and political developments of earlier centuries that added up to the "European Miracle" (Jones 1981). But the timing and pace of their industrialization varied considerably, with Britain being the first to industrialize and Germany the last. Typically, during the early years of the nineteenth century, population growth coincided with some increase in per capita food production, but except for Great Britain, the proportion of the population in extreme poverty also increased and average real wages declined somewhat.[6] At midcentury, class 1 countries sometimes faced considerable regional labor surpluses. Between 1850 and 1914, all of these countries were successful in significantly reducing the proportion of their population in extreme poverty and substantially raising average real wages. Because our data (except for a few lagged variables) do not go back to the first half of the century, when

---

[6]The sources cited in table 7-1 suggest an increase in the extent of extreme poverty over several decades for Germany, Belgium, Switzerland, and possibly France. However, the role of industrialization in that increase is highly controversial. In Germany the surge of poverty *preceded* the surge in industrialization of the 1840s and was concentrated in rural areas (Saalfeld 1984). Average real wages in manufacturing (mainly urban) did not rise significantly until the 1860s (ibid.), but per capita food consumption rose during the 1850s (Teuteberg 1976). In France poverty was concentrated in urban areas, particularly Paris, where per capita food consumption fell during the first half of the century along with average real wages (Philippe 1970; Levasseur 1969; Perroux 1955); meanwhile, nationwide average real wages were rising slightly (Perroux 1955). In Belgium per capita food consumption in Antwerp fell during the first half of the century (Lis and Soly 1977), and agricultural poverty in Flanders increased (Ducpétiaux 1850); nationwide estimates are not available. In Switzerland poverty increased greatly during the early decades of the century when British competition undercut Swiss domestic industries, but as modern industry spread in rural areas where factory workers often had plots of land, the proportion in extreme poverty was not as high as in other countries (Wittmann 1963). Great Britain is an exception in that both per capita food consumption and average real wages for the country as a whole were rising at least slightly in most of the decades studied. The "standard-of-living debate" over the course of average wages has little to say about the proportion of the population in extreme poverty—a question apparently not settled by data available in Williamson (1982).

poverty was increasing, our statistical analysis for this group of industrializers with favorable agricultural conditions relates to the process of poverty reduction.

Class 2 consists of the three Scandinavian countries (Norway, Denmark, and Sweden) where the proportion of the population in extreme poverty increased during the first half of the nineteenth century owing to an increase in population that greatly exceeded the expansion in economic opportunities. Class 2 countries were overwhelmingly agricultural economies with initially small populations where independent peasant holdings with secure titles to land prevailed.[7] Agricultural output per capita rose steadily even throughout the period when the number in poverty increased. While the living standards of those with access to land rose steadily (except during temporary subsistence crises), the number of underemployed landless workers increased dramatically; by midcentury there were substantial labor surpluses.[8] During the second half of the century, expanded domestic employment opportunities and heavy emigration abroad contributed to a striking decline in the proportion of the population in poverty. Once again, our statistical analysis relates only to this process of poverty reduction in the latter half of the century.

Class 3 consists of five densely populated low-productivity economies,[9] overwhelmingly agricultural, with poor transportation systems and with no marked change in the proportion of the population in extreme poverty over the century: India, Burma, and Egypt were colonies, and Russia and China experienced limited foreign dependency. While the class shared the characteristic of having landholding and tenure systems unfavorable to improvements in agricultural productivity, the systems themselves were diverse. Small independent holdings predominated in China and India—too small, on the average, to support a family. Short-term tenancy and small holdings were common in Egypt and Lower Burma, while various communal and landlord

[7]Firm individual titles to land came later in Norway than in Sweden and Denmark.

[8]The increase in poverty in Norway and Denmark before 1850 is inferred from striking data on the rise in the proportion of the landless and near landless together with descriptive data on their living standards (Lieberman [Norway] 1970; Jensen [Denmark] 1937; Hovde [Denmark and Norway] 1943). Data on real day wages in agriculture for Sweden show sharp declines for the latter half of the eighteenth century, rises in the first two decades of the nineteenth, and declines again in the 1820s, 1830s, and 1840s (Jörberg 1972). With respect to the proportion in poverty, Söderberg (1982) points to "ample evidence" of a process of polarization and increasing income inequality around the middle decades of the century that prevented the rising per capita output from trickling down to the poorest strata of the population. He cites the extent of poverty as close to 20 percent of the population for 1826, 1851, and 1871. Only after midcentury did emigration and expansionary forces lead to a striking reduction in the proportion of the population in poverty in Sweden.

[9]Russia was considerably less densely populated than the other countries; Burma was not nearly as densely populated as Egypt, India, and China.

controls over cultivation were prevalent in Russia and Upper Burma.[10] Countries in the class shared significant aggregate export expansion and uneven commercialization, which tended to increase indebtedness and loss of land among small cultivators. Extreme poverty was associated with inadequate land, age-old cultivation methods, and the absence of supplementary employments, among other factors. The character of subsistence crises over the century changed from being a matter of recurrent regional food deficits to one of having inadequate purchasing power when faced with harvest failure as dependence on the market increased. And except for Russia and parts of the Chinese countryside, foreign competition tended to undercut and destroy indigenous handicraft industries.

Class 4 consists of four land-abundant countries settled by Europeans: Canada, Australia, New Zealand, and Argentina. Argentina was dominated by British export interests to an even greater extent than the three colonies. All experienced massive immigration, foreign capital inflows, and export expansion based on the exploitation of agricultural resources (e.g., hides and furs, wool, grain, meat). The extent of poverty in these countries followed long swings in demand for staples, immigration, investment, and the international terms of trade. No significant long-term trend in the extent of poverty was apparent until the end of the nineteenth century. The worst poverty tended to occur in urban areas whenever heavy immigration coincided with a downswing in the demand for staples. Areas cultivated by poor subsistence farmers, usually ethnically distinct groups, also were found. In all class 4 countries except Canada large landholdings were prevalent, with landowners dominating the political process throughout most of the century. Poverty reduction was most successful where independent family farms spread, as in Canada and in late-century Australia, thereby providing a domestic market for the growth of small-scale industry.

Six countries were excluded from the typology. Our experience with the disjoint principal components technique indicates that a minimum of three countries (yielding nine observations) is required in a class to give reliable results of general interest. Among the unclassified countries, poverty patterns were too diverse to either form a group of three countries with reasonably similar courses of poverty or add any of these countries to the other classes. In the United States, land abundance and heavy immigration led to an initial structure of poverty resembling that in class 4, but the labor absorption process associated with rapid industrialization in the later nineteenth century was more like that of Western Europe. In Spain and Italy, poverty was aggravated by labor displacements associated with limited industrialization and foreign imports, as in other European countries; yet the impacts of commer-

---

[10]In our definition of the land tenure variable, insecure short-term tenancies and small holdings are ranked higher than tenancies subject to communal controls over production.

cialization in agriculture were much more like those in the peasant economies of class 3. In the Netherlands, early nineteenth-century labor surpluses in cities were associated with population growth and economic stagnation (the end result of a long decline from the high level of seventeenth-century commercial capitalism), while the eventual absorption of labor through moderate industrial growth and the expansion of specialized agriculture followed the Scandinavian path. In Brazil, poverty was similar in some ways to that of class 4 countries, but it was strongly marked by the special characteristics of Brazilian slavery. Finally, slow commercialization during the Tokugawa period apparently produced much less extreme poverty in Japan than in the class 3 peasant economies, while the course of poverty in the later nineteenth century reflected characteristics unique to Japan: heavy taxation of an increasing agricultural surplus, and the government's policy of locating labor-intensive industry in rural areas to absorb underemployed labor.

THE STATISTICAL RESULTS

The statistical results for the four classes are presented in tables 7-2 through 7-5. For a discussion of how to read the tables and the way we interpret them, see the introductory section to the statistical analysis in chapter three.

Class 1: Western European Industrializers with Favorable Agricultural Conditions

Table 7-2 presents the results for class 1—a class characterized by eventual widespread industrialization and a substantial reduction in poverty. Our results analyze only the reductions in poverty that occurred after midcentury.

Component 1 indicates how the leading features of Western European industrialization discussed in chapter four interacted to reduce poverty. High levels of per capita income, agricultural productivity, and industrial techniques, and substantial rates of industrial and agricultural advance, transportation improvements, and export expansion combined to raise industrial and agricultural wages.[11] Institutional change contributed to Western Europe's relative success in diffusing the benefits of growth to the poor. Agricultural wages rose faster where farms were cultivator owned rather than tenant run and neither very large nor very small, and where levels and rates of agricultural improvements were greater.[12] Agricultural and industrial im-

---

[11]Note that variables with high secondary loadings (marked with asterisks in table 7-2) are particularly important in the interpretation of this component.

[12]The inclusion of the land tenure variable in the primary component expresses the average positive relationship for this class between greater independence of landownership and agricultural improvements. The inclusion of the variable representing favorableness of land institutions

Table 7-2
The Course of Poverty:
Principal Components Analysis for Class 1
(Western European Industrializers with Favorable Agricultural Conditions)[a]

Variable	Principal Component		
	1	2	3
Level of per capita income	.20	.19*	.20*
Level of development of techniques in agriculture	.23	.11	.04
Rate of improvement in techniques in industry	.24	−.01	−.06
Rate of improvement in techniques in industry (lagged)	.23	.08	−.01
Direction of change in real wages in industry	.22	−.10	.05
Predominant form of land tenure and holding	.23	−.22*	−.02
Favorableness of land institutions to improvements	.21	−.06	−.09
Extent of urbanization	.16	.46	−.03
Percentage of labor force in agriculture	.13	−.36	−.16
Level of development of techniques in industry	.18*	.20	.15
Level of development of market system (composite)	.13	.19	−.14
Level of development of inland transportation	.22	.34	−.13
Degree of shift in export structure	.15	−.20	.12
Direction of change in real wages in agriculture	.22*	−.30	.23*
Total population	.14	.02	−.24
Rate of improvement in techniques in agriculture	.17*	−.05	.18
Rate of growth of exports	.18*	−.23*	−.28
Rate of change in per capita income	.15	.03	−.29
Rate of improvement in inland transportation (lagged)	.18*	.13	−.29
Extent of illiteracy	.07	.07	−.24
Rate of spread of primary education (lagged)	.15	−.22*	−.30
Favorableness of attitudes toward entrepreneurship	.21*	.10	.23
Socioeconomic character of political leadership	.18*	.09	.24
Strength of national representative institutions	.20*	−.04	.25
Extent of political stability	.19*	−.12	.29
Relative abundance of agricultural resources	.09	−.06	−.09
Rate of improvement in techniques in agriculture (lagged)	.13	−.03	.04
Rate of population growth (lagged)	.12	.05	−.02
Net immigration	.09	−.02	.00
Concentration of landholdings	.13	.03	−.14
Colonial status	.07	−.16	.05
Degree of foreign economic dependence	.03	−.03	−.05
Extent of domestic economic role of government	.14	−.05	.03
Rate of spread of market system (composite)	.15	−.07	−.06
Rate of spread of market system, lagged (composite)	.10	.12	−.05

[a]See the introductory section to the statistical analysis in chapter three for a discussion of how to read the components results and of the way we interpret them. Variables are listed within components on which they have primary high loadings in the order in which they are discussed in the text. Variables with secondary high loadings (marked with asterisks) also are important to the interpretation.

provements in living standards were greater in nations where representative systems were stronger and more stable and where emerging industrial, commercial, and working classes had greater political influence. As discussed in earlier chapters, political influences were important because their impact on government economic policies helped diffuse economic growth more widely.

Component 2 summarizes a highly urbanized and industrialized pattern of development leading to greater rural poverty—a pattern that characterized Great Britain in the 1870s and 1880s, as noted in chapter four. Here, greater urbanization, a less agricultural labor force, higher per capita income, higher productivity in industry, more developed market institutions, and better transportation systems are associated with a retardation in export expansion due to a failure to adapt export structure to greatly increased international competition. Agricultural wages suffered where overseas grain imports caused European grain prices and profits to fall.[13] The inclusion of land tenure, a secondary variable with a minus sign, indicates a specifically British pattern in which capitalist tenantry rather than cultivator ownership was associated with high levels of urbanization and development. This pattern contrasts with that in Germany and Switzerland, countries scoring low on this component, where cultivator ownership predominated and the export sector changed more radically in response to international competition. The inclusion of the spread of primary education (lagged), another secondary variable with a minus sign, also underlines contrasting British and Continental experiences: In Britain, government did not give extensive support to primary education during the early decades of rapid industrialization; in Germany and Switzerland, governments financed primary education widely and early.

Component 3 describes an ultimately successful pattern of response to severe international competition by a small open economy—a pattern typical of Switzerland during the last decades of the nineteenth century. Here agriculture reacted to the undercutting of domestic grain prices with a widespread shift to intensive dairy farming (a process summarized by the variable for improvement in techniques in agriculture). Incomes of agricultural wage earners and small agriculturalists rose modestly.[14] The component shows a slowing of export expansion, per capita income growth, and transportation improvements. But it also shows social and political conditions that would

---

expresses the average favorable impact of the combination of independent tenure arrangements and land distributions avoiding the extremes of excessively small or large landholdings.

[13] As noted in the introduction to the statistical results in chapter three, we apply descriptive information on countries and periods indicated by low and high component scores in interpreting second and third components that summarize alternative or supplementary patterns heavily influenced by specific country experience. Our discussion here is of that type.

[14] The agricultural wage variable ranks countries by the direction of change in agricultural wages for all countries where the wage labor force is not negligible. For countries with very little agricultural wage labor—for example, Switzerland—judgments about the direction of income change for agriculturalists with small holdings have been included in the ranking of the country.

favor economic progress later: widespread literacy,[15] attitudes favoring entrepreneurship, leaderships and parliamentary institutions responsive to capitalist interests, and political stability. In the short run, however, these conditions could not prevent the slowing of export and per capita income growth caused by severe international competition.

Thus, three quite diverse patterns associated with substantial long-run reductions in poverty appear in this class of countries that shared land systems, market institutions, and political conditions favorable to widespread industrialization. The primary pattern depicts technical progress, industrialization, and rising living standards (including those of the poor). But the two secondary scenarios portray difficulties in adjusting to foreign competition, which constrained significantly the spread of the benefits of growth to the poor.

Class 2: Adjustments to Malthusian Poverty

Table 7-3 presents the results for the less industrialized and more literate class 2 countries. By 1914, this class had made a successful start on industrial growth, moderately aided by foreign capital, but in 1850 these countries were still experiencing quite severe labor surpluses and substantial agricultural poverty caused in part by preindustrial population growth.

In component 1, favorable land systems, political institutions and social attitudes, achievements in agriculture, and fairly adequate land resources are associated with faster export expansion, rising industrial wages, and higher levels and rates of increase of per capita income. This pattern, typical of Denmark and Sweden after 1890,[16] resembles the primary pattern for class 1 except for the significant omission of an increase in agricultural wages. Descriptive evidence shows that rural labor surpluses caused by much earlier population growth (not captured by the two-decade lag of our variable) worked against income increases for the agricultural poor,[17] and this helps account for the absence of the agricultural wage variable from this component.

The institutions favoring growth include viable family cultivation conducive to agricultural improvements (indicated by primary and secondary land variables), more developed marketing arrangements, and strengthened parliamentary systems open to peasant influence. Favorable social attitudes toward capitalist endeavors and increased dependence on foreign capital

---

[15]There is a minus sign on the loading for the spread of primary education because of Switzerland's very early success in achieving widespread literacy. The education variable classifies countries by success in *expanding* primary education.

[16]Norway before 1870 scored lowest on this component.

[17]Note that just over half of the variables referred to in this paragraph are secondary variables marked by asterisks in table 7-3.

Table 7-3
The Course of Poverty:
Principal Components Analysis for Class 2
(Adjustments to Malthusian Poverty)[a]

Variable	Principal Component		
	1	2	3
Predominant form of land tenure and holding	.29	.02	.08
Strength of national representative institutions	.19	−.11	−.08
Favorableness of attitudes toward entrepreneurship	.23	−.05	−.08
Level of development of techniques in agriculture	.22	−.13	.09
Relative abundance of agricultural resources	.21	.16	−.18*
Level of per capita income	.17	.01	.00
Degree of foreign economic dependence	.17	.09	−.02
Level of development of inland transportation	.09	−.27	.04
Rate of improvement in inland transportation (lagged)	.13	−.38	−.04
Percentage of labor force in agriculture	.23*	.27	−.02
Rate of change in per capita income	.21*	−.24	.01
Rate of spread of market system, lagged (composite)	.21*	.20	.12
Level of development of market system (composite)	.23*	.28	−.05
Rate of spread of primary education (lagged)	.20*	.44	−.07
Colonial status	.13	.18	−.02
Net immigration	.07	.09	.18
Direction of change in real wages in agriculture	.12	−.26*	−.43
Direction of change in real wages in industry	.22*	.07	−.40
Concentration of landholdings	.13	−.01	.20
Favorableness of land institutions to improvements	.22*	−.09	.39
Rate of improvement in techniques in agriculture	.16	−.17*	.21
Rate of growth of exports	.17*	−.01	.27
Degree of shift in export structure	.16	−.10	.22
Extent of political stability	.15	−.14	−.34
Level of development of techniques in industry	.12	−.14	.01
Total population	.08	.05	.00
Rate of improvement in techniques in industry	.16	−.03	−.08
Rate of improvement in techniques in industry (lagged)	.14	−.01	−.03
Rate of improvement in techniques in agriculture (lagged)	.12	−.09	.14
Rate of population growth (lagged)	.16	.13	.07
Extent of illiteracy	.04	.05	−.01
Extent of urbanization	.09	−.08	−.06
Extent of domestic economic role of government	.15	−.15	.05
Socioeconomic character of political leadership	.15	−.07	−.03
Rate of spread of market system (composite)	.09	−.04	−.11

[a]See the introductory section to the statistical analysis in chapter three for a discussion of how to read the components results and of the way we interpret them. Variables are listed within components on which they have primary high loadings in the order in which they are discussed in the text. Variables with secondary high loadings (marked with asterisks) also are important to the interpretation.

helped both export expansion and growth. The crucial economic influence favoring growth was fairly high agricultural productivity, which made possible both labor transfers out of agriculture and rapid primary-export expansion. A considerable agricultural surplus was essential for the influences summarized by components 2 and 3 to reduce agricultural poverty by the end of the century.

Component 2 underlines the negative impact of severe transportation bottlenecks in heavily agricultural economies on economic growth, agricultural productivity, agricultural wages, and living standards. This unfavorable pattern, characteristic of Norway before 1890, explains statistical variance *not* accounted for by the first component's complex of favorable institutions, economic growth, and higher industrial wages. Neither success in reducing market institutional restrictions (indicated by positive loadings for the two market variables) nor the spread of primary education into rural areas offset the barriers posed by poor transportation.[18] Transportation breakthroughs in Sweden and Denmark contributed to the greater success of these countries in raising agricultural productivity and wages.

In component 3, emigration from areas of labor surplus and poverty is associated with rising agricultural and industrial wages. This is the familiar Scandinavian path to poverty reduction. Emigration reduced poverty by supplementing the processes described by components 1 and 2. We reverse the signs for our interpretation in order to discuss the correlates of greater net emigration.[19] Associated with increased emigration are the institutional and economic causes of poverty: excessive land parcelization, slower improvements in agriculture, and poorer export performance.[20] Also included are the consequences of emigration: rising agricultural and industrial wages.[21] Emi-

---

[18]The inclusion of colonial status in component 2 is accounted for by Norway's union with Sweden into the twentieth century, which made Norway politically dependent on Sweden.

[19]The continuum for "net immigration" extends from high net immigration at the top of the scale to high net emigration at the bottom of the scale. Since all Scandinavian countries were at the lower end of the scale, a negative association between agricultural wage movements and net immigration means faster wage increases with increased net emigration.

[20]The variable for lagged population growth is not included here since the population growth that caused preindustrial labor surpluses preceded emigration by more than two decades.

[21]The inclusion of *more* abundant agricultural resources (a secondary variable) with more emigration is explained by the nature of the resources variable. It is based on a classification of countries according to Colin Clark's quantification of "standard farmland" per person. (See the introduction to the data appendix.) The accessibility of land by transport is not taken into account. Thus, in terms of "land resources per person," Norway had more cultivable land per person than either Sweden or Denmark.

The inclusion of increased political stability with more emigration is the outcome of small variations within a class of politically quite stable countries. Denmark had the lowest rate of emigration. It also experienced less land parcelization because national legislation prevented the breakup of small holdings; Denmark in the 1880s and 1890s suffered the most severe, although nonviolent, constitutional turmoil. Once again, we note associations in second and third components that reflect fairly specific country characteristics.

gration as a means of poverty reduction was most important in high-scoring Norway, where preindustrial population growth and land parcelization were greatest.[22]

In sum, the results for class 2 show the strong negative impact of earlier population growth on rural living standards in heavily agricultural countries. The primary pattern points to institutions and human resources that favored successful export-led economic growth and benefited small industrial work forces. But these influences were not sufficient to overcome rural poverty in the presence of widespread rural underemployment. Transportation breakthroughs helped reduce rural poverty by enlarging markets and providing incentives for agricultural improvements. Emigration overcame poverty by directly reducing labor surpluses and thereby benefiting both industrial and agricultural workers.

Class 3: High-Poverty, Low-Productivity Agricultural Economies

Table 7-4 gives the results for class 3. None of the dynamic influences in the primary pattern raised per capita income or wages: not foreign economic exploitation of land resources, or the freeing of land from communal restrictions, or the faster marketization promoted by colonial powers, or population growth, or the sharply dualistic export expansion that characterized the class.[23] These processes were associated with greater illiteracy, more labor in agriculture, modest immigration, and a greater concentration of landholdings. On the average, incomes did not rise. Country studies show that colonial enforcement of free trade destroyed handicraft industries, thereby reducing alternatives to agricultural employment. India and Egypt, the most colonially and economically dependent, score highest; Burma and China, in the earlier decades when foreigners were not dominant, score lowest.

In the secondary cluster, the faster per capita income increases accompanying agricultural commercialization led, on the average, to reduced incomes for the agricultural poor.[24] This decline in income was more pronounced where prior population growth had been greater, cultivators lacked indepen-

---

[22]High and low scores here refer to scores on the pattern with signs reversed, where more emigration is associated with more political stability.

[23]Note once again that secondary variables, marked by asterisks in the tables, are important to our interpretation. The freeing of land from communal restrictions is important in differentiating among countries at the lower end of the spectrum for the market development variable. The replacement of communal tenure systems by independent or individual tenant cultivation also leads to a higher score on the land tenure variable, accounting for the positive sign of its secondary loading on this component. Immigration was modest in this class, but tended to occur more where colonial governments promoted it.

[24]Recall again that in classifying countries with respect to the agricultural wage variable, we included judgments about changes in the incomes of small holders in those countries having extremely small agricultural wage labor forces.

Table 7-4
The Course of Poverty:
Principal Components Analysis for Class 3
(High-Poverty and Low-Productivity Agricultural Economies)[a]

Variable	Principal Component		
	1	2	3
Degree of foreign economic dependence	.30	.09	−.19*
Level of development of market system (composite)	.32	−.11	−.18*
Rate of spread of market system, lagged (composite)	.17	.00	.00
Extent of illiteracy	.33	−.03	.07
Percentage of labor force in agriculture	.32	−.09	.13
Net immigration	.20	.02	−.02
Rate of change in per capita income	.09	.26	.23*
Direction of change in real wages in agriculture	.07	−.19	.05
Rate of population growth (lagged)	.20*	.23	−.10
Predominant form of land tenure and holding	.21*	−.51	−.06
Concentration of landholdings	.19*	.40	.18*
Extent of domestic economic role of government	.14	.19	.10
Total population	.26*	−.40	.38*
Level of development of techniques in industry	.08	.03	.22
Direction of change in real wages in industry	.07	−.04	.26
Relative abundance of agricultural resources	.17*	.09	.25
Colonial status	.25*	−.14	−.40
Socioeconomic character of political leadership	.05	.07	.23
Rate of spread of market system (composite)	.27*	.22*	−.43
Level of per capita income	.07	.08	.07
Level of development of techniques in agriculture	.07	.14	−.04
Level of development of inland transportation	.08	.11	−.06
Rate of improvement in techniques in industry	.15	.03	.14
Rate of improvement in techniques in industry (lagged)	.12	.04	.11
Rate of improvement in techniques in agriculture	.07	.04	.01
Rate of improvement in techniques in agriculture (lagged)	.05	.02	.01
Rate of improvement in inland transportation (lagged)	.10	.13	−.00
Favorableness of land institutions to improvements	.12	−.15	.08
Rate of spread of primary education (lagged)	.05	.00	.13
Extent of urbanization	.06	.01	−.02
Favorableness of attitudes toward entrepreneurship	.06	.07	.09
Rate of growth of exports	.14	.15	.02
Degree of shift in export structure	.04	−.01	.00
Strength of national representative institutions	.07	−.06	.06
Extent of political stability	.09	−.01	−.02

[a]See the introductory section to the statistical analysis in chapter three for a discussion of how to read the components results and of the way we interpret them. Variables are listed within components on which they have primary high loadings in the order in which they are discussed in the text. Variables with secondary high loadings (marked with asterisks) also are important to the interpretation.

dence, and large landholdings prevailed. A larger government economic role (nowhere very large) was associated with the removal of institutional barriers to commercialization.[25] Top component scores go to Egypt during the rapid expansion of cotton exports in the 1850s and 1860s and Russia during the strong growth of grain exports toward the end of the century. Descriptive evidence indicates that Russian exports of grain during subsistence crises contributed to increased agricultural poverty. Low component scores go to China before 1890, when the agricultural economy was relatively stagnant and the large population was extremely poor.

Component 2 underlines land arrangements that caused increased agricultural poverty in countries with very low productivity: insecure cultivator titles, parcelization of peasant land plots, and concentration of landownership. Foreign-promoted commercialization often led to the replacement of extended-family or communal land arrangements by individual holdings with poorly defined titles and leases. These land institutions had a negative effect on the poor. Descriptive evidence shows that indebtedness and alienation from the land rose as communal protections declined and the peasants' market dependence increased.

Component 3 portrays an alternative pattern that was typical of high-scoring Russia—the only path to poverty reduction apparent in this class of countries. A small modern industrial sector raised per capita income and industrial wages for a tiny fraction of the population, but brought no systematic increases in agricultural wages. Favorable conditions for this modest industrial success were a large population forming a home market for industry, abundant agricultural resources, land inequality concentrating the limited investable surplus for staple-export expansion, government subsidization of large-scale industry, and constraints on foreign penetration by a powerful national state bureaucracy. The minus signs of the primary variable for colonial status and the secondary variable for foreign dependence, together with the positive loading for reductions in landed-elite political power, suggest that national government and domestic classes dominated the political system.[26] Descriptions of Russia, the only nation in the class where industry grew significantly, show that trade restrictions and government subsidies to industry enhanced industrial growth.

In sum, in low-productivity, overwhelmingly agricultural economies, foreign penetration, export expansion, and marketization failed to benefit the agricultural poor. Rapid marketization where there were small agricultural

---

[25]The inclusion of total population in this component with a high negative loading underlines the weight of China, with its enormous population and comparative economic stagnation, at the bottom of the component spectrum.

[26]The inclusion of the spread of market institutions (a primary variable) and the level of market institutional development (a secondary variable) with minus signs is a peculiarity that cannot be explained by contrasting the characteristics of countries with high and low component scores.

surpluses and land tenures limiting incentives for improvements worsened the position of the agricultural poor, even where average national income was increasing. Where an independent government subsidized industry and a large population provided a home market, workers in a handful of modern factories benefited. But even there, low initial levels of productivity and unfavorable agricultural institutions precluded systematic increases in rural living standards.

Class 4: Cyclical Poverty in Dependent Land-Abundant Countries

Table 7-5 presents the results for class 4—a class characterized by cyclical poverty. In the primary pattern the familiar trio of colonialism, foreign dependence, and abundant land is associated with higher rates of immigration and export expansion. But the component incorporates no consistent upward trend in wages or per capita income. Rather, it summarizes the complex conditions for successful export expansion that characterized the three British colonies late in the nineteenth century.[27] Rapid population growth and the development of market institutions in preceding decades had relieved labor shortages and reduced transaction costs. Higher initial per capita income helped enlarge the investable surplus. Greater dependence on foreign capital, entrepreneurship, marketing, and technical expertise relieved domestic shortages of inputs. Domestic institutional influences created a fairly favorable climate for the concurrent expansion of domestic supplies of entrepreneurship and capital. Land systems provided more secure ownership rights without extreme land inequality.[28] Fairly favorable social attitudes toward indigenous entrepreneurship, moderate reductions in landed-elite political power, and the growth of national parliamentary systems strengthened domestically controlled class alliances and ultimately reduced agricultural poverty by leading to the favorable conjunction of influences depicted in component 2.

The lack of correlation between wage and per capita income increases and export expansion is in part due to the failure of living standards to rise steadily. But it may also be due to the fact that the time periods for our data do not coincide with the cyclical fluctuations in export expansion, terms of trade, employment, and output that plagued countries dependent on primary ex-

---

[27] Scoring lowest on this component was New Zealand in the period before the British established their dominance over the Maori.

[28] All three land variables and the political variables have secondary high loadings. Scoring high on the land tenure variable were countries with secure landownership rights, whether to pastoral estates or family farms. Scoring high on the land concentration variable were countries with systems of large pastoral estates lacking an important peasant sector. Scoring high on the composite land variable were countries where independent landownership was combined with medium-size independent family farms (e.g., Canada). Scoring lower were countries characterized by a predominance of large, leased pastoral estates (e.g., Australia).

Table 7-5
The Course of Poverty:
Principal Components Analysis for Class 4
(Cyclical Poverty in Land-Abundant Dependent Countries)[a]

Variable	Principal Component		
	1	2	3
Colonial status	.23	−.05	−.09
Degree of foreign economic dependence	.21	−.17*	−.12
Relative abundance of agricultural resources	.28	−.19*	−.06
Net immigration	.24	−.21*	.20*
Rate of growth of exports	.22	−.12	.04
Rate of population growth (lagged)	.24	−.07	.17*
Rate of spread of market system, lagged (composite)	.27	−.24*	−.07
Level of per capita income	.19	.09	.14
Favorableness of attitudes toward entrepreneurship	.20	.05	−.09
Rate of improvement in techniques in agriculture	.16	.31	−.01
Direction of change in real wages in agriculture	.10	.21	.14
Rate of improvement in inland transportation (lagged)	.14	.30	.08
Level of development of inland transportation	.08	.23	−.09
Percentage of labor force in agriculture	.14	−.24	−.16
Extent of illiteracy	.11	−.39	.05
Rate of spread of primary education (lagged)	.16	.19	−.06
Socioeconomic character of political leadership	.17*	.20	−.08
Rate of change in per capita income	.15	−.09	−.39
Extent of urbanization	.14	.19*	.29
Predominant form of land tenure and holding	.20*	.14	−.31
Concentration of land holdings	.23*	−.10	.40
Favorableness of land institutions to improvements	.17*	.03	−.29
Degree of shift in export structure	.08	.07	−.35
Strength of national representative institutions	.20*	−.08	.21
Level of development of techniques in industry	.08	.15	.04
Level of development of techniques in agriculture	.12	.12	−.06
Total population	.06	−.03	−.02
Rate of improvement in techniques in industry	.15	.05	−.00
Rate of improvement in techniques in industry (lagged)	.12	.13	−.01
Rate of improvement in techniques in agriculture (lagged)	.08	.14	−.10
Extent of domestic role of government	.16	.16	.03
Extent of political stability	.11	.16	.10
Direction of change in real wages in industry	.13	.07	.12
Level of development of market system (composite)	.15	−.09	−.02
Rate of spread of market system (composite)	.07	.03	.10

[a]See the introductory section to the statistical analysis in chapter three for a discussion of how to read the components results and of the way we interpret them. Variables are listed within components on which they have primary high loadings in the order in which they are discussed in the text. Variables with secondary high loadings (marked with asterisks) also are important to the interpretation.

ports. The literature cites these fluctuations as important determinants of changes in industrial and construction wages in countries characterized by heavy immigration, foreign capital flows, and foreign settlement (Thomas 1973). Our results do not reject the importance of these fluctuations in explaining changes in standards of living.

Components 2 and 3 show two special conjunctions of influences on standards of living, favorable and unfavorable, respectively. Component 2 depicts a favorable conjunction of influences raising agricultural productivity and wages: transportation breakthroughs (as in class 3), urbanization and shifts of labor out of agriculture, the spread of literacy into agriculture, the slowing of immigration (a secondary variable), reduced political power for the landed elite, and an associated lessening of foreign dependence. Dependence was significantly reduced late in the century in the countries that scored high, Australia and New Zealand. (By then, settler populations had become much larger compared with available land resources.) In the conclusion to chapter six we discussed in detail how reduced political power of landed and foreign elites enabled governments to promote tariff, education, transportation, and immigration policies that helped diffuse the benefits of growth more widely.

Component 3 underlines the unfavorable impact of heavy immigration on per capita income growth and poverty. The experience of Australia (the country with the highest component scores) weighs heavily in this component as well as in components 1 and 2. Exceptionally heavy immigration lowered per capita income even where aggregate GNP was rising sharply. Other variables in this component reflect an Australian pattern that contrasts sharply with that of low-scoring Canada. Massive immigration greatly enlarged Australia's cities. Slowness to establish secure property rights in land favored powerful large-scale squatters over small holders. The concentration of landholdings characteristic of pastoral economies narrowed the distribution of export proceeds and slowed export diversification.[29]

In sum, our results for this class of land-abundant dependent countries show no consistent pattern of success in reducing poverty. Fluctuations in living standards related to cyclical variations in rates of primary-export expansion were a class characteristic. Where alliances of domestic landed elites and foreign interests controlled economic policy, export-led growth failed to

---

[29] As noted elsewhere, land concentration had positive and negative consequences. It concentrated the investable surplus but narrowed the distribution of the proceeds of export expansion. In the composite land variable, the British pastoral economies by the end of the nineteenth century ranked above Argentina and Brazil because of their greater success in establishing independent tenures. The inclusion of a positive loading for national representative systems is a peculiarity that cannot be explained by contrasting the countries with the highest and lowest component scores. Neither Australia after 1890 nor Canada before 1870 scored well on this variable because in each case *regional* parliaments dominated the political scene. It may be a weakness of the variable that it does not incorporate judgments about the strength of both national and regional representative institutions.

induce widespread favorable economic changes. Agricultural productivity and wages improved consistently only where the political power of landed elites and dependence on foreigners were reduced significantly. Heavy immigration furthered export expansion but worked against increases in per capita income and wages.

Measures of Statistical Fit

Table 7-6 gives the own-class variance of class observations (the diagonal elements in the table) and their variance when fitted to the other class models (the off-diagonal elements). The own-class variance of each set of country observations is substantially lower than its other-class variances. Class 4 is extremely distant from all the other classes, which is not so surprising, considering the political barriers to poverty reduction in this class. Class 2 is relatively close to class 1, reflecting in part the similarity of the Scandinavian primary pattern of growth-promoting and poverty-reducing forces to that of other Western European countries, and also to class 4, reflecting the closeness of its secondary patterns to those of the land-abundant countries—that is, the crucial role played by transportation breakthroughs and the positive aspects of moderate levels of foreign dependency.

Table 7-7 shows a very good fit of country observations to their assigned components models, with neither misclassifications nor borderline cases among the 17 countries included in the typology. The positions of the unclassified countries are of considerable interest. The United States up to 1890 approached both the Scandinavian and the land-abundant patterns, reflecting the favorable institutions of the former and the land abundance and migration patterns of the latter. By the final decade of the century, the United States approached the Western European pattern of poverty reduction. Italy persisted for several decades close to the low-productivity agricultural pattern, only late in the century coming closer to the more favorable Western European model. Japan did the same, but more rapidly. The Netherlands moved quite soon from the mixed Scandinavian scenario to the Western Eu-

Table 7-6
The Course of Poverty:
Cluster Distance Matrix for Principal Components Analyses

	Class 1	Class 2	Class 3	Class 4
Class 1	14.1	23.4	42.4	28.0
Class 2	20.3	11.9	29.5	17.8
Class 3	40.4	38.7	11.6	35.0
Class 4	662,000	523,000	680,000	15.5

NOTE: See text for explanation.

Table 7-7
The Course of Poverty:
Degree of Fit for Principal Components Analyses
(Residual Standard Deviations for Three Classes Closest to Each Country Observation)

Country and Year	Assigned Class	Class to Which Closest	Residual S.D. – Closest Class	Class to Which 2d Closest	Residual S.D. – 2d Closest Class	Class to Which 3d Closest	Residual S.D. – 3d Closest Class
Belgium 1850	1	1	15	2	21	4	25
France 1850	1	1	13	2	21	4	27
Germany 1850	1	1	9	2	23	4	28
Great Britain 1850	1	1	13	2	25	4	28
Switzerland 1850	1	1	15	2	23	4	28
Belgium 1870	1	1	15	2	25	4	26
France 1870	1	1	12	2	20	4	25
Germany 1870	1	1	15	2	20	4	30
Great Britain 1870	1	1	12	2	26	4	30
Switzerland 1870	1	1	9	2	23	4	28
Belgium 1890	1	1	16	2	26	4	30
France 1890	1	1	13	2	21	4	27
Germany 1890	1	1	17	2	25	4	32
Great Britain 1890	1	1	17	4	27	2	29
Switzerland 1890	1	1	17	2	21	4	26
Denmark 1850	2	2	14	4	20	1	26
Norway 1850	2	2	12	4	21	3	25
Sweden 1850	2	2	15	4	21	1	22
Denmark 1870	2	2	10	4	16	1	23
Norway 1870	2	2	10	4	19	1	25
Sweden 1870	2	2	13	1	19	4	22

Table 7-7 (continued)

Country and Year	Assigned Class	Class to Which Closest	Residual S.D.– Closest Class	Class to Which 2d Closest	Residual S.D.– 2d Closest Class	Class to Which 3d Closest	Residual S.D.– 3d Closest Class
Denmark 1890	2	2	11	4	18	1	24
Norway 1890	2	2	11	4	18	1	22
Sweden 1890	2	2	9	1	21	4	27
Burma 1850	3	3	14	4	23	2	25
China 1850	3	3	9	2	26	4	26
Egypt 1850	3	3	11	4	25	1	32
India 1850	3	3	14	4	27	2	33
Russia 1850	3	3	11	4	21	2	29
Burma 1870	3	3	11	4	25	2	29
China 1870	3	3	9	4	28	2	29
Egypt 1870	3	3	13	4	29	1	32
India 1870	3	3	13	4	30	2	32
Russia 1870	3	3	11	4	23	2	27
Burma 1890	3	3	8	4	26	2	29
China 1890	3	3	11	1	29	2	29
Egypt 1890	3	3	14	4	30	1	32
India 1890	3	3	13	2	32	4	33
Russia 1890	3	3	11	1	27	4	28
Argentina 1850	4	4	14	3	26	2	29
Australia 1850	4	4	18	2	30	3	32
Canada 1850	4	4	14	2	18	3	33
New Zealand 1850	4	4	18	3	27	2	27
Argentina 1870	4	4	11	3	25	2	29
Australia 1870	4	4	14	2	29	1	35

Canada 1870	4	4	15	2	18	1	30
New Zealand 1870	4	4	16	2	25	3	31
Argentina 1890	4	4	21	2	32	1	35
Australia 1890	4	4	13	2	32	1	33
Canada 1890	4	4	15	2	19	1	28
New Zealand 1890	4	4	16	2	27	1	31
Brazil 1850	0	3	17	4	20	2	31
Italy 1850	0	3	17	4	24	2	25
Japan 1850	0	3	19	2	24	1	25
Netherlands 1850	0	2	19	1	20	4	22
Spain 1850	0	3	21	4	23	2	26
United States 1850	0	2	23	4	24	1	28
Brazil 1870	0	3	15	4	20	2	30
Italy 1870	0	3	24	1	26	2	28
Japan 1870	0	1	24	2	26	4	29
Netherlands 1870	0	1	14	2	20	4	22
Spain 1870	0	2	26	4	27	1	27
United States 1870	0	2	22	4	25	1	26
Brazil 1890	0	3	20	4	24	1	29
Italy 1890	0	1	20	2	24	3	27
Japan 1890	0	1	18	2	24	4	30
Netherlands 1890	0	1	14	2	22	4	22
Spain 1890	0	2	23	1	26	4	29
United States 1890	0	1	22	2	26	4	30

NOTE: The years 1850, 1870, and 1890 following country names in column 1 are shorthand for the three cross sections: 1850–1870, 1870–1890, and 1890–1914. As noted in chapter two and in appendix tables A51 through A53, some variables refer to the initial year of each period, some refer to the entire period, and a few lagged variables refer to the preceding period.

ropean pattern. Like Italy, Spain started close to the low-productivity pattern, but ended up closer to the Scandinavian model. Brazil remained near the low-productivity model throughout, in spite of its great land abundance. (We did not assign it to class 3, because its resource abundance made it strikingly different.) Thus, the distance measure usually confirmed our initial judgment about the divergent courses of poverty in the countries we excluded from the typology.

Measures of the Importance of Individual Variables

Table 7-8 presents statistical measures of the importance of individual variables in discriminating between classes and "explaining" within-class variations. Column 1 gives a measure of between-group relevance, *taking all classes together*. By far the most important variable discriminating among classes is literacy. Foreign dependence, a major influence accounting for class differences in the diffusion of growth and thus poverty reduction (chapter six), is second. Next, population size differentiates between the class of late industrializers with large populations and other, mainly smaller, countries with modest industrial growth because population significantly influenced labor supply and the size of the domestic market. Then comes a conjunction of influences that set apart the Western European path of widespread industrialization by raising per capita income and average wages in industry and agriculture: more productive agriculture (including shifts of labor out of agriculture), resource abundance, favorable land institutions, transportation development, technological advance in industry, and favorable attitudes toward capitalist entrepreneurship. Colonial status differentiates classes where poverty was reduced most (classes 1 and 2) from classes with sharply dualistic growth where poverty reduction was less widespread (classes 3 and 4). International migration and resource abundance impinged on poverty in contrasting ways in Scandinavia (class 2), where emigration raised homeland agricultural incomes, and in land-abundant dependent countries (class 4), where immigration slowed income increases. Migration and resource patterns differentiated both classes 3 and 4 from classes 1 and 2.

The exceptionally high relevance of literacy to between-class differences requires further comment. In classes 1 and 2, where poverty was substantially reduced by 1914, literacy rates already exceeded 50 percent in 1850. Here, the technology of mixed animal-crop farming that spread rapidly in the last quarter of the century required "superior" inputs, among which was literacy (Schultz 1964). Thus, literacy discriminates between classes 1 and 2, on the one hand, and class 3 with its high illiteracy and class 4 where literacy rates varied greatly, on the other. Literacy's political impacts also serve to distinguish among classes. Literacy promoted fairly effective representative institutions in classes 1 and 2 and the increased power of nonelite groups in national political leaderships in class 4. In contrast, in high-poverty class 3, low liter-

Table 7-8

The Course of Poverty:

Importance of Classification Schemes to Between-Class and Within-Class Variations, All Classes Together[a]

Variable	Between-Group Relevance	Within-Group Relevance
Extent of illiteracy	26.9	.59
Degree of foreign economic dependence	14.0	.32
Total population	11.8	.61
Percentage of labor force in agriculture	10.7	.43
Rate of improvement in techniques in industry (lagged)	9.0	.58
Level of development of techniques in agriculture	8.7	.51
Rate of improvement in techniques in industry	8.5	.48
Direction of change in real wages in industry	7.6	.62
Colonial status	7.4	.38
Relative abundance of agricultural resources	7.2	.11
Rate of spread of market system (composite)	6.8	.46
Level of development of techniques in industry	6.6	.82
Favorableness of attitudes toward entrepreneurship	6.0	.31
Predominant form of land tenure and holding	5.9	.65
Favorableness of land institutions to improvements	5.8	.51
Level of development of inland transportation	5.6	.62
Direction of change in real wages in agriculture	5.3	.69
Net immigration	5.2	.09
Rate of improvement in techniques in agriculture	4.5	.71
Extent of urbanization	4.0	.63
Concentration of landholdings	4.2	.62
Extent of political stability	3.6	.61
Rate of improvement in techniques in agriculture (lagged)	4.3	.60
Socioeconomic character of political leadership	3.8	.56
Rate of improvement in inland transportation (lagged)	2.4	.54
Level of per capita income	4.4	.37
Rate of change in per capita income	2.1	.42
Rate of population growth (lagged)	3.3	.26
Rate of spread of primary education (lagged)	4.6	.41
Rate of growth of exports	1.3	.08
Degree of shift in export structure	4.9	.49
Extent of domestic economic role of government	1.3	.35
Strength of national representative institutions	5.0	.34
Level of development of market system (composite)	3.5	−.10
Rate of spread of market system, lagged (composite)	4.9	−.08

[a]Variables with between-group relevance over 5.0 are listed in descending order by that measure (column 1: 26.9–5.2). The remaining variables that have within-group relevance over .50 are listed in descending order by the within-group measure (column 2: .71–.54). For an explanation of both measures see the text discussion of table 3-9.

acy aggravated extremely dualistic growth, during which rising foreign dependence increased inequity.

Column 2 gives a measure of how well each variable "explains" within-class variations, taking all classes together. The most important variables are the development of technology in industry, technical improvements in agriculture, rising agricultural wages, land tenure and distribution, rising industrial wages, and population—influences consistently associated with poverty reduction through successful industrialization. Urbanization, also an important variable, was associated with failures to raise living standards in secondary components in the Western European and dependent land-abundant results. In Western Europe, grain agriculture was hard hit by international competition in the most highly industrialized and urbanized countries because of their comparative disadvantage in grain. In some land-abundant countries, high degrees of urbanization for their development levels were caused by heavy immigration, which slowed the growth of per capita income. Transportation improvements, literacy, and the socioeconomic structure of political leadership also were important in accounting for within-class variations. Inland transportation was a key influence raising agricultural productivity and wages (class 2). Wider literacy helped the political power of non-landed groups, especially in land-abundant dependent countries, thereby changing economic policies in ways that reduced poverty in agriculture (class 4), as discussed in chapter six. In poor agricultural economies (class 3), wider literacy had no positive effects. On the contrary, since their labor forces lacked commercial experience and since export expansion failed to induce sufficient expansion of nonagricultural employments to absorb population growth, economic change increased illiteracy by raising the proportion of uneducated agriculturalists in the adult population.

Summary and Conclusions

Several features of the interaction of poverty with the processes of economic and institutional change studied in chapters three through six emerge from the results presented in this chapter.

1. Where substantial industrial and agricultural advances were made concurrently in a favorable institutional setting, industrialization eventually became a strong force for long-term increases in per capita income and industrial and agricultural wages. Transportation networks linking rural and urban areas were crucial to this positive role of industrialization. Institutions essential to broad-based growth in these countries were developed market institutions facilitating factor flows between sectors and regions; agricultural institutions providing incentives for cultivators to adopt improvements and a widely distributed substantial agricultural surplus; and political systems reasonably responsive to the needs of rising indigenous entrepreneurial groups.

2. The influences governing the course of agricultural wages and rural

poverty varied by type of country. In the advanced industrial countries, the secondary force that reinforced the impact of industrialization in ultimately reducing poverty was success in transforming agriculture and in expanding manufacturing in the face of greatly intensified international competition in the last quarter of the nineteenth century. In both Scandinavian labor-surplus countries and dependent land-abundant countries, transportation breakthroughs were crucial in raising agricultural productivity and wages and in reducing poverty in rural areas. Before such breakthroughs, agricultural wages systematically lagged behind the wages of the very small industrial labor force.

3. The internationalization of factor markets had a potent effect on both rural and urban poverty. Emigration from Scandinavia in the last quarter of the nineteenth century quickly led to increased wages by eliminating regional labor surpluses. By contrast, immigration and capital flows into land-abundant countries relieved labor shortages or produced urban labor surpluses that dampened the forces for wage increases created by primary-export expansion.

4. Export expansion affected poverty quite differently in diverse institutional settings. In the labor-surplus countries of Scandinavia, export expansion and emigration combined to reduce poverty because widespread literacy and land systems conducive to a substantial and broadly dispersed agricultural surplus made possible broad-based economic growth. In the advanced industrial countries, substantial expansion of manufactured exports eventually benefited wages because market, land, and political institutions provided incentives and opportunities for economic expansion while spreading the benefits from expansion fairly widely. By contrast, in dependent land-abundant countries, institutions were considerably less favorable. Here, living standards rose only where political changes enabled indigenous governments to overcome transportation barriers to domestic market growth and to make land more accessible to family farmers serving cities. Living standards did not rise where political alliances of expatriate and landed elites limited access to land and built transportation networks that served domestic markets poorly. Finally, in low-productivity, overwhelmingly agricultural countries, export expansion did not benefit the poor. On the contrary, the greater the expansion of exports and spread of agricultural commercialization, the more negative the impact on the real incomes of the rural poor, even when per capita income was increasing.

5. Political influences were critical determinants of the spread effects of economic growth, particularly for the poor. Where private economic initiatives were reasonably free of the exercise of arbitrary state power and where representative institutions permitted the incorporation of new domestic business interests, economic growth eventually trickled down to the poor. The decline in the power of landed elites made more likely the adoption of state land, transport, tariff, and education policies that would help diffuse growth

more widely. By contrast, where large agricultural export and foreign trade interests were strongly allied and dominated the political system, state economic policies had negative impacts on the poor. The destruction of communal protections from land alienation, inadequate feeder roads within agriculture, the destruction of handicrafts by free trade, and illiteracy combined to limit the economic opportunities of the very poor and to increase the economic risks they faced in expanding their participation in the market, whether as wage earners or as producers.

8 Conclusion

The industrialization of Western Europe, especially Great Britain, caused world economic opportunities to expand dramatically and upset severely the balance of political and economic power. The responses were striking, but differed greatly across and within countries. In some large countries, politically strong governments actively promoted industrialization; their success varied greatly. Some small nations expanded enormously their primary exports to the British market; because of their well-developed human resources and favorable land institutions, export expansion led to substantial domestic growth. In European-settled land-abundant countries, migration of capital and people initiated a strong flow of primary products back to Europe. The penetration of markets and the massive inflows of settlers and capital radically altered these societies, with positive and negative consequences. In poor, densely settled countries with valuable raw materials and food crops, European capital and skills caused sharply dualistic economic and social change. The commercialization of these economies undermined traditional institutions and revolutionized lives, expanding opportunities for those with skills and assets and destroying the livelihoods of those without them. Thus, national responses to Western European industrialization varied greatly, as did the success of the strategies that nations adopted.

Whether the force for economic change was an external political challenge, expanding foreign markets, capital accumulation, technological innovation, or population growth, institutions determined both the speed and the pattern of development. The neoclassical theory that resources, technology, and comparative advantage determined development patterns does not adequately explain variations either across or within strategies. On the contrary, institutions determined if and how economic development and its benefits spread across sectors and regions. This is not to say that conventional economic influences were unimportant. Among countries with fairly similar institutions, growth of per capita GNP, rapid export increases, and rates of industrialization were closely associated with expanding economic opportunities and supplies of inputs.

INSTITUTIONS MATTERED MOST

In all our results, institutions mattered most in distinguishing between country groups experiencing more successful and less successful economic development, *as judged by the diffusion of economic growth and its benefits.*

How Economic Institutions Mattered

Widespread industrialization occurred only where market institutions and legal conditions for their effective functioning were present, as seen in chapters three (market expansion) and four (industrialization).[1] The reverse did not hold. That is, the development of market institutions did not by itself assure substantial industrialization.[2] This result is consistent with the theses of Marx, Polanyi, and the neoclassical institutionalists: "freeing" land and labor from feudal and mercantilist restrictions and establishing clear property rights are essential for the development of successful industrial capitalism.

The role of responsive agricultural institutions in providing labor, capital, and markets for industrial expansion is underlined in chapter five.[3] Countries where agriculture's contribution to industrial expansion was significant also scored high on the incentives for cultivator improvements provided by their land institutions. But favorable institutions did not assure successful agricultural industrial interactions.[4]

Foreign dominance of domestic economic institutions (chapter six) hampered significantly the diffusion of economic growth and its benefits. True, increased foreign inputs and influence accelerated aggregate export expansion and sometimes economic growth rates.[5] But in country groups more heavily dependent economically on foreigners, economic growth and its benefits spread less widely outside the export sector, judging by the course of agricultural productivity, per capita income, incomes of the agricultural poor, and industrial wages.[6] Growth diffused successfully to the domestic economy only where domestic interests dominated government tariff, immigration, education, and transportation policies.[7] The reverse proposition did not hold. Domestic dominance of government policy did not assure widely beneficial economic growth.[8]

As seen in chapter seven, an essential condition for substantial poverty reduction was agricultural institutions that both responded to market signals and provided a wide distribution of the agricultural surplus.[9] Extensive industrialization, made possible by well-developed market institutions and reasonable agricultural incentive structures, was a strong impetus for long-term rises in average living standards[10] (however inequitable its initial consequences). But it was not the only route to poverty reduction. Primary-export

[1] Developed market institutions is a characteristic of class 1 countries in chapter four (industrialization).

[2] Class 1, component 1, in chapter two (market expansion).

[3] Class 1, component 1, and class 2, component 1, in chapter five (agricultural development).

[4] Component 2 of classes 1, 2, and 3 in chapter five (agricultural development).

[5] Component 1 of classes 1, 2, and 3 in chapter six (foreign dependence).

[6] Note the lack of wage and productivity improvements in the results for class 1 and the lack of wage improvements in the results for class 2 in chapter six (foreign dependence).

[7] Class 2, component 2, and class 3, component 1, in chapter six (foreign dependence).

[8] Note the low component scores of Japan and Italy before 1890 on component 3 of class 3 in chapter six (foreign dependence).

[9] Component 1 of classes 1 and 2 in chapter seven (poverty).

[10] Class 1, component 1, in chapter seven (poverty).

expansion with modest industrial growth reduced poverty significantly where agricultural institutions and distribution of the agricultural surplus were favorable.[11] Here again, appropriate institutions were necessary but not sufficient.[12]

Thus, in all facets of development, institutions shaped the impact of resource accumulation on the diffusion of growth and its benefits.

How Political Institutions Mattered

At critical junctures in our results, political institutions mattered greatly. With rare exceptions, economic growth and its benefits did not diffuse far where domestic landed elites aligning with foreign export interests dominated the political process. In all countries undergoing substantial industrialization, domestic commercial and industrial classes had or gained significant power in national leaderships.[13] In more politically diverse country groups— for example, land-abundant dependent countries—economic growth spread far only when landed elites no longer dominated domestic economic policies.[14]

Thus, our results indicate that institutions were critical to the diffusion of economic growth—especially institutions determining how market systems functioned, how agriculture responded to expanding opportunities, how the agricultural surplus was distributed, and who controlled national economic policies.

How Other Economic Influences Mattered

We cannot conclude from our results that appropriate institutions alone assured successful dispersed economic development. Other economic influences were crucial as well. Export markets and initial resources counted everywhere.[15] Extensive and rapid industrialization occurred only where ini-

---

[11]Class 2, components 1 and 2, in chapter seven (poverty).

[12]Note the lag of several decades before Canada scored high on components that included rising agricultural wages in class 4, component 2, in chapter seven (poverty).

[13]A characteristic of countries industrializing substantially (class 1) in chapter four (industrialization).

[14]For the spread of agricultural improvements, see class 2, component 2, in chapter three (market expansion); and for the spread of wage benefits, see class 4, component 2, in chapter seven (poverty).

[15]Export growth is included in component 1 seventeen out of twenty times across all classes in all results. It is not included for three classes of very low productivity dependent economies. On nine of the seventeen occasions, greater abundance of land resources was associated with faster export growth. On six occasions, higher agricultural productivity was associated with export growth instead of land abundance. On two occasions, both greater abundance of land resources and higher agricultural productivity were associated with export growth.

tial agricultural development yielded a significant economic surplus above subsistence, export opportunities expanded, and better techniques were adopted in both industry and agriculture.[16] Where rapid primary-export expansion led to domestic growth, crucial causes were growing export markets and abundant land resources.[17] (But technical improvements in agriculture could substitute for abundant land.)[18] Where export expansion led nowhere domestically, low economic productivity, very limited economic surpluses above subsistence, and low levels of human capital contributed to that failure.[19]

THE ADAPTABILITY OF INSTITUTIONS WAS IMPORTANT

Inappropriate institutions impeded economic development. Even institutions that were effective in getting development under way later proved inadequate for continued economic progress. Our results for moderately backward European countries and for dependent land-abundant countries illustrate this point most clearly.

How Institutional Needs in Moderately Backward European Countries Changed

Governments in moderately backward countries devised substitutes for missing development "prerequisites," as underscored by Gerschenkron (1962a and 1970). The economic institutions and policies that substituted for missing capital, skills, and home markets often worked well to initiate industrial growth.[20] But as industrialization proceeded, they proved inadequate to diffuse growth to a broad spectrum of industries and to agriculture. At first, government demand for military supplies and intermediate goods, for example, was substituted for narrow home markets. But governments could not provide the breadth of consumer demand necessary for a transition to broad industrialization. Ultimately, the failure of agricultural institutions to achieve a significant and widespread distribution of the agricultural surplus blocked the rise of a domestic market for industry.[21]

---

[16]Class 1, component 1, in chapter four (industrialization).

[17]Class 1, component 1, in chapter three (market expansion); class 3, components 1 and 2, in chapter four (industrialization); component 1 of classes 1 and 2 in chapter five (agricultural development); and class 3, component 1, in chapter six (foreign dependence).

[18]See note 15.

[19]Class 4 in chapters four and five (industrialization and agricultural development); class 1 in chapter six (foreign dependence); and class 3 in chapter seven (poverty).

[20]Class 4, component 1, in chapter three (market expansion); and class 2, component 1, in chapter four (industrialization).

[21]Class 4, component 2, in chapter three (market expansion); and class 2, component 2, in chapter four (industrialization).

Political actions and laws that provided stability and "freed" internal trade helped industry begin to grow. But once industrialization got started, these were not enough. Additional "prerequisites" became operative. Government institutions administratively capable of financing and promoting industry in the face of weak private institutions were needed;[22] and political responses to the economic interests of new classes became important. Failure to incorporate middle-class interests into the political process limited the spread of modern industry by impeding land, education, and transportation policies responsive to rising indigenous capitalist interests.[23]

Thus, in backward Europe, not only did development "prerequisites" change across different phases of industrial growth, but the effectiveness of institutional substitutions shifted systematically as well.

How Institutional Needs in Dependent Land-Abundant Countries Changed

Foreign-dominated institutions were a powerful force in inducing institutional changes that initiated strong primary-export expansion. In alliance with landed elites, they pushed laws that would create a market system and promoted large holdings that could generate a surplus quickly. Foreign trade, capital, credit, and migration successfully substituted for scarce domestic capital, industry, and skills.[24] Imports provided food that domestic agricultural institutions could not supply.

The returns to rapid marketization with foreign inputs were very high. But institutions that were good for export expansion brought neither systematic agricultural improvements nor consistently rising standards of living.[25] Widely distributed export proceeds were required for the creation of a home market.[26] Massive foreign immigration into urban areas could substitute only temporarily for agricultural institutions that could provide a home market and increasing supplies of food.[27] Imports could no longer supply sufficient food for rapidly growing populations.[28]

---

[22] Note the importance of the government's economic role in the results cited in note 20.

[23] Inferred from components 2 and 3 of class 2 in chapter four (industrialization) and from country data. Note the importance in these components of the spread of literacy and transportation and the reduced foreign dependence in patterns showing agricultural improvements and rising wages.

[24] Class 2, component 1, in chapter three (market expansion).

[25] Note the absence of rising wages and agricultural improvements in class 2, component 1, in chapter three (market expansion), and in class 4, component 1, in chapter seven (poverty).

[26] For this favorable conjunction accompanied by improvements in agricultural productivity and wages, see class 4, component 2, in chapter seven (poverty); for this conjunction accompanied by improvements in agricultural productivity, see class 2, component 2, in chapter three (market expansion).

[27] Illustrated by slow progress in improving agricultural techniques in countries with low component scores (Argentina and Brazil in the results referred to in note 26).

[28] Inferred from country histories.

As in backward Europe, political institutions good for early growth proved inadequate as land-abundant dependent countries grew economically. At first, the establishment of political stability (especially the cessation of wars with indigenous groups) and the support of powerful landed elites for laws creating market systems were crucial political forces for export expansion.[29] But later, as in Europe, failures of political institutions to adapt to the needs of rising domestic industrial and commercial classes blocked the diffusion of economic growth and its benefits.[30]

Substitutes for Missing Prerequisites Worked in Early Phases of Development but Not in Later Ones

As discussed in the previous sections, government actions, foreign trade, and international capital and labor flows launched economic growth in countries lacking the institutions required for long-term development. But our results show that their effectiveness in substituting for missing institutional "prerequisites" declined as growth proceeded, regardless of initial economic conditions and the development strategy chosen. Substitutions for favorable institutional conditions that worked well in the early phases of growth proved inadequate for the transition to later phases. Thus, the concept of a fixed set of initial conditions for which substitutes could be found is deficient. Rather, the institutional conditions for success varied not only across development strategies but also at different phases along a given growth path.

No Unique Paths of Change Were Found

Our findings contradict the proposition that all countries undergo similar progressions of economic and institutional change. Nor are they consistent with the "uniqueness hypothesis," according to which each country's experience is a special case. Rather, they suggest that there are a small number of typical paths of change. Reappearing in our results are five different paths of economic development characterized by contrasting progressions of change as well as marked variations in growth patterns along each path: two industrial paths, two agricultural paths, and one balanced-growth path.[31] The interaction of institutions with economic development differed along each path.

[29]Based on country information on the cessation of wars and inferences from (1) the association of large holdings, the rapid establishment of legal conditions for markets, and more rapid export expansion in class 4, component 1, in chapter three (market expansion), and class 4, component 1, in chapter seven (poverty); and (2) the political concomitants of wider growth in land-abundant countries evident in class 2, component 2, in chapter three (market expansion) and in class 4, component 2, in chapter seven (poverty).

[30]Evident from data on countries with low component scores in the results referred to in note 26.

[31]Footnotes in this section indicate which components for which class and chapter reflect each of the five paths of growth we discuss. In our discussion we focus on the dominant features of

The Industrial Paths of Growth

One path of growth followed by the firstcomers to the industrial revolution (e.g., Great Britain and France), led to widespread industrialization, a substantial quantity of manufactured exports, and generalized improvements in agriculture.[32] Successful industrialization was closely linked with prior agricultural development, the evolution of market systems, and political institutions that limited the political power of landed elites.

A second industrial path of growth was followed by latecomers to the industrial revolution with large populations (e.g., Germany, Italy, Japan, and Russia).[33] Britain's industrialization and military victories over Napoleon and Prussia posed severe economic, political, and military challenges. To catch up with the firstcomers, the latecomers adopted measures for political unification, legal reforms that facilitated factor mobility and market exchanges, and policies for promoting import substitution. Tariffs were a major weapon for initiating industrialization and for protecting grain producers. Their populations were so large that even a small percentage of cultivators with surpluses could produce a total agricultural surplus sufficient to provide a market for a start on manufacturing.

Along this growth path, success with inward-oriented industrialization varied greatly. Growth was everywhere dualistic, most industry was small scale, and agriculture lagged behind industrial expansion. Agricultural improvements diffused significantly only where land institutions provided incentives for increasing the agricultural surplus; a large number of landholdings yielded a surplus; and governments supplied not only transportation linking domestic markets but also agricultural extension programs and substantial public education—as in Germany and Japan. Where, in contrast, governments neglected a backward food agricultural sector and transportation was severely inadequate—as in Russia, Italy, and Spain—industrialization remained limited or erratic.

The Agricultural Paths of Growth

Countries following agricultural paths of growth concentrated on primary-export expansion. These paths resembled inward-oriented industrialization

---

each path. Variations among subsets of nations along each path are fully discussed in the relevant chapters. Points about specific countries are not footnoted. The reader is referred to the country sections of the bibliography for further information on individual countries.

[32] For the results reflecting the industrial path followed by the firstcomers to the industrial revolution, see chapter three (market expansion), class 1, component 1; chapter four (industrialization), class 1, component 1; and chapter seven (poverty), class 1, component 1.

[33] For the results reflecting the industrial path followed by the latecomers to the industrial revolution, see chapter three (market expansion), class 4, component 1; and chapter four (industrialization), class 2, component 1.

in several respects: (1) resources and policy were focused on a limited segment of the economy, and growth was sharply dualistic; (2) weak cultivator incentives in food agriculture kept productivity low so that agricultural improvements usually lagged behind both export expansion and per capita income growth; (3) large landholdings concentrated the limited marketable surplus, investing it in export expansion; and (4) because food production increased slowly and export benefits were concentrated, faster economic growth worsened the distribution of income.

Countries exporting primary products had different types of initial conditions, which resulted in different growth paths. In land-abundant countries (Australia, Argentina, Canada, and New Zealand), rich resources attracted foreign labor, capital, and entrepreneurship.[34] Expatriates provided crucial technical, financial, and marketing skills. On the average, the greater the degree of foreign economic dependence, the faster the rate of economic change. Indigenous large landowners and expatriate trading interests pushed laws that "freed" land transactions, promoted large landholdings, and subsidized immigration. Industrialization came late, was modest, and occurred behind tariff barriers. Its positive impacts on the rest of the economy were greatest where domestic manufacturers, small farmers, and labor gained power at the expense of landed elites, as in Australia and New Zealand. Here, tariffs were levied to protect infant industries, and land policies increasingly favored small and moderate landholdings; small farms provided food to cities, and industry expanded the production of wage goods and agricultural implements. In contrast, where the political power of landed elites continued to be strong, as in Argentina and Brazil, most food was supplied by low-productivity tenant farmers, and luxury goods were important in both imports and production.

In densely populated agricultural countries (Burma, China, Egypt, and India), low levels of productivity sharply constrained the supply of food, raw materials, and incomes with which to purchase manufactured goods.[35] Expatriates dominated trade and there was little modern industrial growth. Commercialization was accelerated by Western laws encouraging land sales and mortgages that were introduced in the latter half of the nineteenth century. Export expansion proceeded rapidly, but agricultural progress was minimal. Nor did average income or wages increase. Thus, primary-export expansion in land-scarce countries resulted in the development of foreign enclaves that had little positive impact on the rest of the economy.

[34] For the results reflecting the agricultural path followed by dependent land-abundant countries, see chapter three (market expansion), class 2, component 1; and chapter seven (poverty), class 4, component 1.

[35] For the results reflecting the agricultural path followed by densely populated, low-productivity agricultural countries, see chapter four (industrialization), class 4, component 1; chapter five (agricultural development), class 4, component 1; chapter six (foreign dependence), class 1, component 1; and chapter seven (poverty), class 3, component 1.

The Balanced-Growth Path

A few small European nations—Belgium, Denmark, the Netherlands, Switzerland, and Sweden—followed paths of export expansion that involved both heavy trade dependence and, by the end of the century, widespread domestic economic growth.[36] Substantial agricultural progress preceded their industrialization. In the last quarter of the century, extensive agriculture was widely replaced by mixed intensive farming. Drastic declines in grain prices accelerated this shift toward livestock, dairy products, or other specialized high-value crops, since governments did not protect grain farmers.

These countries started with favorable institutions and human resources. In some countries, agrarian reforms that preceded industrialization created land institutions that provided most farmers with land and incentives. In all of them, agricultural surpluses were significant and widely distributed, parliamentary institutions usually functioned fairly well, and literacy rates were high. These favorable conditions contributed to the diversification of exports, per capita income growth, and industrialization. Deficiencies in natural resources led these countries to specialize in skill-intensive exports. The smallness of their internal markets put pressure on them to develop production processes that were internationally competitive.

In sum, the interactions between institutions and economic change were strikingly different along the five development paths typical of nineteenth-century experience with economic development. Of the five paths, only two resulted in sustained, widespread domestic growth: the industrialization strategy of the firstcomers to the industrial revolution, and the balanced-growth strategy of the small, open, European economies. The important common features of these two strategies were functioning factor markets; land tenure systems that gave incentives and property rights to small cultivators; effective parliamentary institutions; open trade strategies; and substantial improvements in agricultural productivity preceding industrialization.

NO SINGLE THEORETICAL FRAMEWORK APPLIES UNIVERSALLY

None of the theories reviewed in chapter one applies universally to the nineteenth-century experience of all the countries we have studied. But each of them is valid for a particular range of countries and periods.

---

[36]For the results reflecting the balanced-growth path followed by small, open, European economies, see chapter five (agricultural development), class 2, component 1; and chapter seven (poverty), class 2, component 1. Chapter four (industrialization), class 3, component 2, also reflects some characteristics of the balanced-growth path.

Classical and Neoclassical Theories

Our results strongly support the emphasis of classical writers on expanding exports, but not their predictions about consequent increases in the division of labor, productivity improvements, and rising agricultural output. Nor does our study consistently confirm the classical thesis regarding the benefits of free trade. Score analysis for successful industrializers shows no systematic connection between trade restrictions and economic performance or living standards.[37] In small open economies combining primary exports with small-scale industry, free trade and cheap grain imports caused an ultimately beneficial shift to specialized high-value agriculture.[38] In contrast, in heavily dependent countries, unrestricted imports and rapid primary-export expansion had a negative effect on the agricultural poor.[39]

Neoclassical growth theory applies without major qualification only to economically advanced industrializing countries, a small part of our sample. Where market institutions were well developed by 1850, rapid industrialization went hand in hand with increasing factor supplies and technical change in industry and agriculture. But in our results, these economic changes were closely correlated with political institutional influences that contributed to observed economic transformations.[40]

Neoclassical institutional theories do not successfully explain why export expansion in underdeveloped countries failed in many instances to provide the dynamic benefits of foreign trade expansion stressed by Mill. This failure is a major theme of this book. Our results do not show that the domestic impacts of export expansion were primarily dependent on techniques and resources.[41] Rather, as noted, we found patterns of export expansion and their impacts to be heavily dependent on the characteristics of institutions. In land-abundant countries, political power and the distribution of land strongly conditioned the impact of surging exports.[42] In densely settled, very poor countries, expatriate dominance and unfavorable land tenure systems vitally influenced outcomes, as pointed out by Hirschman (1977). Primary-export expansion produced few benefits in poor countries, where negative final-de-

---

[37] Recall that we do not have a measure of the extent of trade restrictions. We infer the impact of trade barriers in two ways. We analyze data on countries that score high or low on components summarizing economic performance; or we study the common characteristics of a class in conjunction with the class results relating to economic performance.

[38] Class 2, component 1, in chapter five (agricultural development).

[39] Class 1, component 1, in chapter six (foreign dependence), and class 4, component 2, in chapter five (agricultural development).

[40] Class 1, component 1, in chapter three (market expansion); class 1, component 1, in chapter four (industrialization); and class 1, component 1, in chapter seven (poverty).

[41] Nor would they seem primarily dependent on prices. While we do not have measures of prices, there is no reason to expect them to be closely correlated with the statistically important influences in our results.

[42] See notes 25, 26, and 27.

mand linkages (destroying indigenous handicraft industries), "alien" technological linkages, and negative fiscal linkages precluded any beneficial effects
from export expansion.[43] Internal sociostructural and political conditions
that discouraged investment in industry and in domestic transportation limited the spread of economic growth.[44] Narrow land distributions and politically powerful landlords also contributed to the poor performance in diffusing
growth,[45] a finding that confirms the analysis of Senghaas and Menzel (1978).

Thus, neoclassical theories fail to explain the variety of development experience that characterized the latter half of the nineteenth century because
they do not incorporate the diverse institutional requirements and political
conditions that determined the transmission of export-led growth to the domestic sector.

Dependency Theory

Our study does not fully support the dependency school's approaches to foreign trade and investment. Increased foreign dependence led everywhere to
more rapid export increases, but the consequences varied greatly.[46] Only in
very heavily dependent countries was the completely pessimistic dependency
theory confirmed.[47] In moderately dependent countries, the more optimistic,
neoclassical theory about benefits from foreign investment became relevant
as well.[48] Within all strategies, above-average equity in land distributions and
success in wresting political power from landed elites increased domestic car-
ryover from export expansion.[49]

In dependent countries, political conditions established long before the beginning of the nineteenth century had a great deal to do with whether export

[43]Country data and results from class 4, component 1, in chapter four (industrialization);
class 4, component 1, in chapter five (agricultural development); class 1, component 1, in chapter six (foreign dependence); and class 3, component 1, in chapter 7 (poverty).

[44]Country data and results: for land-abundant countries, class 2 in chapter three (market
expansion), and class 4 in chapter seven (poverty); for low-productivity densely settled countries,
class 4 in chapters four and five (industrialization and agricultural development), class 1 in chapter six (foreign dependence), and class 3 in chapter seven (poverty).

[45]Classes 1 and 2 in chapter six (foreign dependence).

[46]Component 1 of classes 1, 2, and 3 in chapter six (foreign dependence).

[47]Inferred from the absence of wage increases or agricultural improvements in class 1 results
in chapter six (foreign dependence).

[48]Inferred from the inclusion of agricultural improvements in class 2, component 2, in chapter six (foreign dependence).

[49]In class 4, component 2, in chapter three (market expansion), and class 2, component 2, in
chapter four (industrialization). Where domestic elites dominated, agricultural improvements
were associated with above-average favorable land institutions for the class. In class 2, component 2, in chapter three (market expansion), and class 4, component 2, in chapter seven (poverty), which were marked by decreased foreign dependence, agricultural improvements were associated with the increased political influence of rising capitalist classes. (In the latter set of
results, rising agricultural wages were included as well.)

expansion induced changes in the structure of political power. Beneficial growth was blocked where European political conquests not only destroyed indigenous societies but also gave inordinate power to descendants of the conquerors. Economic changes that elsewhere might have induced political upheaval had little effect. Tenacious alliances between landed elites, urban merchants, and a few large manufacturers precluded economic policies that would spread the benefits of export expansion.[50]

Marx

Our findings support Marx's thesis that "freeing" labor and land from the "fetters" of feudalism was necessary for industrial capitalism to evolve. But they also support the views of Polanyi and neoclassical historians on the need for market institutions with which to spread industrial capitalism.

Our results contradict Marx's predictions about capitalism in underdeveloped countries. Rather, they support Paul Baran's view (1968) that foreign penetration fostered political alliances of landed elites, wealthy merchants, and industrial monopolists that blocked the transformation of some underdeveloped countries into capitalist systems. What mattered was which class dominated the economic policies of the state—above all, the policies affecting tariffs, transportation, and education.[51]

Our results also refute Marx's prediction that in the long run, industrialization would immiserize the industrial working class. After 1850 in advanced countries, rising industrial real wages and more rapid industrialization (both measured for two-decade periods) went hand in hand.[52] This does not mean that after 1850, industrial working conditions improved, workers became happier, or real wages did not decline in the short run. Nor does it mean that incomes or conditions in family artisan shops improved or that the number or proportion in extreme poverty declined (since the data refer to the average wages of the employed, mainly in the factory sector). Finally, the result does not invalidate the proposition that rapid industrialization reduced wages or increased extreme poverty in its early stage. Our wage and income data refer to the second half of the nineteenth and the early twentieth century.

Only in densely settled underdeveloped countries do our results show systematic negative impacts of economic growth on wages. Here commercializa-

[50]Inferred from histories of Argentina and Brazil and the low scores of both countries on components expressing the wider diffusion of growth in land-abundant countries; see class 2, component 2, in chapter three (market expansion), and class 4, component 2, in chapter seven (poverty).

[51]See the earlier discussion of land-abundant dependent countries and notes 24, 25, and 26.

[52]Class 1, component 1, in chapters three, four, and seven (market expansion, industrialization, and poverty, respectively).

tion, not industrialization, worsened the condition of workers in agriculture in some countries and periods.[53]

In sum, our study delimits the historical validity of leading development theories. Classical and neoclassical growth models apply to a few successful industrializers and institutionally favored small export economies in Western Europe. Marx's analysis of institutional conditions for capitalism, while valid for Europe, is not valid for the historical experience of underdeveloped countries. Staple and neoclassical institutional models pertain only where institutions brought about effective agricultural industrial interactions. Their critics highlight the negative impacts of the absence of such institutions. Dependency theory works for heavily dependent countries, but fails to explain beneficial dependent scenarios. Neomarxist institutional theories account better for dependent-country successes by focusing on the role of ascending national bourgeoisies in obtaining economic policies that favored domestic growth. But they have little to say about nondependent paths of growth. Thus, no model applies without major qualification to more than a subset of countries.

SUMMARY COMMENTS

To summarize, institutions mattered most in determining if and how economic growth was diffused in the nineteenth and early twentieth centuries. Initial institutions determined the strategy and the timing of development. But no set of institutions was uniquely appropriate either across all strategies or for all phases within a given strategy. Institutions good for a start on growth proved inadequate for its diffusion. Governments could and did find institutional substitutes for missing prerequisites: skills, capital, and home markets. But both the prerequisites and the effectiveness of the substitutes varied as development proceeded. Failure to adapt domestic institutions to provide widely dispersed income and political responsiveness to rising capitalist classes precluded the diffusion of growth.

Whether the cause of a start on growth was the expansion of economic opportunities or an outside political challenge, the consequences were determined by institutions. Institutions governed the distribution of export proceeds, the impact on food agriculture, and government policies determining indigenous economic responses in industry. Laws and institutions governing how well markets functioned, land tenure and holding arrangements determining cultivator incentives, and political systems influencing government responsiveness to rising capitalist interests were foremost causes of divergent paths of growth and development. Neoclassical theory to the contrary, comparable resource endowments and export opportunities in no way assured similar patterns and speeds of economic growth.

---

[53]Class 1, component 2, in chapter six (foreign dependence), and class 4, component 2, in chapter five (agricultural development).

Appropriate institutions, while necessary, were not sufficient for economic development. Conventional economic influences mattered—particularly agricultural technology, an abundance of land, human capital, and export markets. Among countries with similar institutions, economic influences were leading determinants of variations in the pattern and speed of growth. But no economic theory—classical, neoclassical, dependency, or staple—statistically accounts for the development patterns of more than a small subset of nineteenth-century societies.

Thus, diversity in growth patterns, diversity in institutions, and diversity in applicable theories were the hallmarks of the process of nineteenth-century development.

Data Appendix

The Demographic Variables

The Human Capital and Socioinstitutional Variables

The Politicoinstitutional Variables

The Market Institutional Variables

Comparative Country Classifications

INTRODUCTORY NOTE

The appendix tables contain the classification systems, country scores, and data sources. The last name of the author and date of publication fully identify most sources. Where an author published more than once in the same year, the letters "a," "b," "c," and so on, are given after the year of publication to distinguish the sources. Where two different authors with the same last name published in the same year, the first initial is used to distinguish them. The full references are listed in the bibliography in a general section and in 23 country sections. Most sources appear in the appropriate country sections, but occasionally the source for one country is a book or an article about another country. In such cases the appropriate country section of the bibliography is given in brackets following the author's name. A note in each table lists the sources that can be found in the general section of the bibliography; the reader will find the remaining sources in the indicated country sections.

The following text discusses the procedures we followed in constructing the variables, the conceptual problems we faced, and the sources important in our decisions about definitions.

THE ECONOMIC VARIABLES (TABLES A1-A23)

The Income Variables (Tables A1–A4)

We include two income variables: per capita income (1850, 1870, 1890), and rate of change in per capita income (1850–1870, 1870–1890, 1890–1914). We categorize country observations into six groups for the first variable and five groups for the second. The income variables are substantially changed from those in our earlier papers because of the large volume of work that has been published since our earlier classifications were prepared.

The conceptual and measurement problems with historical national income data are numerous and well known. For most countries, published income estimates are based in part on fragmentary data and informed guesses. For example, an estimate of the labor force in a given sector is frequently multiplied by a weighted average annual income across broad occupational groups computed from fragmentary data to obtain aggregate sectoral labor income (see Zwingli and Ducret [Switzerland] 1964). Occasionally, national income "data" are obtained by estimating aggregate production functions (Teijl [Netherlands] 1971). Sometimes, estimating procedures and sources are not given (Bairoch, 1976; Gasser [Switzerland] 1962). These and other inadequacies in the comparative data led us to use categories even where point estimates existed. We sought divisions between categories that would be insensitive to variations among available point estimates. Multiple estimates or detailed information on procedures helped give a rough idea of the range of these variations. Where no such indications existed, we sought to group together country observations for which available point estimates lay close together.

Level of Per Capita Income (Tables A1 and A2)

In our classification by level of per capita income, we relied heavily on the published estimates of Bairoch (1976) and Maddison (1979). For countries not covered by these authors, we relied on comparative judgments in country studies. Table A1 gives our classifications and sources. Table A2 gives indexes based on the estimates of Bairoch and Maddison and the classification each estimate would yield in our scheme.

Rate of Change in Per Capita Income (Tables A3 and A4)

Our classification by average annual rate of change in per capita income is presented in table A3. A discussion of the sources for each country is found in table A4. These discussions indicate where the country classfications used in our earlier papers have been substantially changed by revisions in published national income estimates or in our own estimating procedures.

The Industrialization Variables (Tables A5 and A6)

The industrialization variables are discussed in the first part of chapter four. Table A5 presents the classification scheme for level of development of techniques in industry; table A6, the scheme for rate of improvement in techniques in industry.

The Agricultural Variables (Tables A7–A14)

The agricultural variables include classification schemes summarizing the level and rate of improvement in techniques in agriculture (tables A7 and A8), the percentage of the labor force in agriculture (tables A9–A13), and the abundance of agricultural resources relative to population (table A14).

Level of Development of Techniques in Agriculture (Table A7)

This scheme summarizes the spread of four types of improvements, weighting them by their probable importance in increasing output per man: the use of horse-drawn iron or steel machines; the use of improved crop rotations, irrigation systems, and fertilizers; the use in animal farming of enclosures, stock breeding, and supplementary feeding; and the use within farms of diversified crop and animal farming.

Greatest importance was given to the adoption of labor-saving machinery. We concentrated on machinery used in harvesting since harvesting was usually the major production bottleneck. Improved iron and steel plows were weighted next most heavily because information on their use helped rank the less advanced countries. Next in importance were crop rotations, seed selection, irrigation systems, and fertilizers, all of which contributed significantly to raising total factor productivity. Here we checked the likelihood that increased total factor productivity would lead to increased labor productivity; increasing population density sometimes lowered output per man significantly, offsetting potential gains in labor productivity from land-intensive improvements. Weighted third most heavily was the spread of crop diversification and mixed animal-crop farming, which raised substantially the value of output; this aspect was used to help rank more advanced countries having broadly similar structures of preferences. In our study period (1850–1914) diversification in more advanced countries was an important cause of increases in the value of output. The final type of improvement, the use in animal farming of enclosures, stock breeding, and supplementary feeding, was given significant weight in ranking countries where pastoral farming was very important.

Using these components, we classified the 69 country observations into seven ranked categories. The top two categories discriminate among countries in which improved plows and horse-drawn harvesting machinery as well as improved crop rotations, fertilizers, and mixed animal-crop farming were important. In the third category improved crop rotations and natural fertilizers were widespread, but little machinery was in use. The fourth and fifth categories were reserved for improvements restricted to one or two regions of a country or one of two outputs. In the sixth and seventh categories were countries that showed few improvements; those where increasing population density had significantly reduced output per man were ranked lowest.

The major sources of information were country case studies, which provided quite diverse descriptive and quantitative data. The preliminary ranking of countries and periods was cross-checked against comparative statistical information in Mulhall (1899) and Clark (1957).

Rate of Improvement in Techniques in Agriculture (Table A8)

This classification ranks countries by the improvements listed above and weights most heavily labor-saving improvements. The top two categories include the striking spread of agricultural improvements on all large farms and on many small farms. In the top category the adoption of labor-saving machinery contributed significantly to raising output per man. In the second category land-saving biochemical and organizational improvements and/or a major shift from grain to mixed farming were the major sources of productivity improvement. In the third and fourth categories these same improvements spread only to large farms; in the third the adoption of labor-saving machinery was most important, and in the fourth the adoption of improved crop rotations and drainage was most important. The fifth category included varied combinations of lesser improvements; the sixth, very few improvements; and the seventh, negligible improvements.

The greatest challenge lay in defining categories so that the wealth of descriptive information and fragmentary numerical data could be used to group countries. The breakpoints between categories were selected by careful study of countries on both sides of potential divisions; where possible, the breakpoints were placed where there were discontinuities in the continuum of agricultural improvements.

Percentage of the Labor Force in Agriculture (Tables A9–A13)

Tables A10 through A13 give a multiplicity of estimates and guesstimates on the percentage of the labor force or population in agriculture. Table A9 gives the classification scheme. (Data for 1914 are included even though they were not used in the study.) The problems with these data are familiar. Few are based on properly constructed census data. Definitions of "economically active" varied greatly. Sometimes only guesstimates on the percentage of the population in agriculture or in agricultural areas were available. Where data on the agricultural labor force were lacking, we assumed that the ratio of the agricultural labor force to the total labor force had the same relationship to the ratio of the agricultural population to the total population as in similar countries. Another problem with the data, especially for the earlier part of the study period, was the lack of a clear dividing line between the industrial and agricultural labor forces owing to the importance of industrial supplementary employments in agricultural areas. Given these problems, the multiplicity of estimates for some countries is not surprising. In categorizing the data, we attempted to choose breakpoints between categories that were relatively insensitive to choices among alternative estimates.

Relative Abundance of Agricultural Resources (Table A14)

The purpose of this classification is to group countries by the abundance of agricultural resources compared with population size. Data on total land are misleading because of wide variations in the quality of land. Nor are data on cultivated land suitable since land with immediate potential for cultivation was also important to economic development. We therefore used the estimates of Colin Clark (1957) on the quantity of cultivable land, adjusted for different qualities of land. For 22 of our 23 countries, Clark calculated total area "equivalents in standard farm land." Clark defined standard farmland as land with the climate of the principal temperate and subtropical farming regions of the world, weighting other regions according to characteristics of temperature and the quantity and regularity of rainfall. For example, the measure of land in tropical climates where double-cropping is possible is twice that of standard farmland, while the measure of land in arid climates is one-thirtieth that of standard farmland. (For details, see Clark 1957, pp. 305ff.) The climatic classification is based on Thornwaite (1933). For each country, the areas of land in nine climatic zones were calculated, given their appropriate weights, and then summed. Table A14 gives both total land areas and total standard farmland equivalents. The population per square kilometer was then calculated for each country for 1850, 1870, and 1890.

Since this procedure for estimating the relative abundance of cultivable land is very crude, we set up a classification scheme consisting of only five categories. Among the deficiencies of the estimates of cultivable land for our purposes is the fact that they relate to the 1930s, by which time areas of forest and irrigated land had changed, as had techniques of, for example, dry farming. They also take no account of difficulties of access due to topography. Because of these and other deficiencies, we sought to define categories that would give stability-of-country rankings throughout our study period. These rankings changed only where population density changed significantly. Note c in table A14 gives the classification scheme, and columns 6–8 of the table give the individual classifications.

The present classification scheme differs from that used in our first three published papers (Adelman and Morris 1978b, 1979, 1980). In the earlier classification, we incorporated judgments about institutional access to land and did not use the criterion for judging land availability that Clark supplies. The present measure is conceptually more straightforward and suits better a study of the role of land availability in economic development.

The Transportation Variables (Tables A15 and A16)

Tables A15 and A16 present two classification schemes for data on inland transportation. We used statistics to cross-check classifications based on descriptive characteristics of the overall transportation system. We relied heavily on the country studies listed in the bibliography. Substantial additional research was done on almost all countries in order to revise these classifications for the present book.

Level of Development of Inland Transportation (Table A15)

We grouped countries by level of development of inland transportation using three broad criteria: long-distance transportation between large urban centers suitable for mass shipment of goods, transportation among smaller towns and cities forming an interregional network, and all-weather feeder transportation within agricultural regions. The top category scored high on all three. The next-to-the-top category differed in that waterways and roads rather than railways were most important in the interregional network. In countries in the third category some important populated region was poorly served by interregional transportation and lacked all-weather feeder roads in agricultural regions. Countries in the fourth category scored still lower because railways radiated from a single city or port, thus failing to provide a network for interregional trade. In the bottom category were countries with very few railways or all-weather roads.

The resultant classification scheme stresses the extent and type of transportation used for goods shipment. In judging transportation between cities, we ranked railways above good waterways, and both of these above roads, because of their speed and reliability the year round. We ranked lower those systems that radiated from a major city or port, because they failed to serve interregional as well as international trade. We gave considerable weight to the suitability of roads in agricultural regions to the shipment of goods by cart or carriage rather than pack animal.

Rate of Improvement in Inland Transportation, Lagged (Table A16)

This classification ranks "breakthroughs" in transportation above improvements or extensions in established transportation systems. A breakthrough occurred where railways or canals replaced carts or pack animals in interregional or long-distance trade, thereby enormously reducing transportation costs. Thus, the highest-scoring countries were those where transportation improvements permitted for the first time mass shipments of goods between major populated regions. The second-highest score went to countries where extensive cross-connections were built or important extensions into lightly populated regions were made following major breakthroughs in earlier periods. Widespread substitution of improved means of transport in systems already providing good interregional mass shipment of goods came next in the classification scheme. At the bottom were two categories: one for the linking up of two major regions, which still left other important regions unserved; and the other for small beginnings.

This variable is lagged. That is, the scores are based on the two-decade period preceding our measurement period. A lag is needed to capture the impact of transportation investments on the pace and structure of growth.

The Export Variables (Tables A17–A21)

Rate of Growth of Total Real Exports (Tables A17–A20)

Table A17 presents the classification scheme for the rate of growth of total real exports. Indices of the growth of current exports were deflated using the most appropriate price index available. The suitability of these indices varied greatly. Wholesale price indices from Mitchell (1976, p. 735) were used for European countries since, according to the notes in Mitchell, these countries were heavily dependent on price series for traded commodities. For some countries the rate of growth of exports in current values was adjusted using extremely crude information on price changes. Tables A18–A20 give country estimates for exports in current prices and real exports, as well as the years to which they refer and the sources on which they are based.

The data on exports suffer from the usual deficiencies of historical data and have an additional unique source of unreliability. External trade consists of "general trade," which includes commodities in transit, and "special" exports produced to some degree within the country. We wished to exclude "goods in transit," but definitions varied so greatly that this source of inconsistency remains.

Because of the many inconsistencies in the estimates, we divided our 23 countries into only three categories by probable average annual rates of real export growth: over 4 percent, between 2 percent and 4 percent, and less than 2 percent. We created a special category for fast export growth from a very small export base (judging by the probable percentage of exports in national income at the beginning of each study period). We ranked this category below fast growth from a moderate or large export base. Close study of the data and their deficiencies persuaded us that the data would not support any additional distinctions. We preferred fewer, more reliable distinctions to a larger number of less reliable ones.

Shift in Structure of Export Sector (Table A21)

The classification given in table A21 is crude. We started with estimates of the structure of exports for the beginning and end of each period (1850–1870, 1870–1890, and 1890–1914). We then calculated the percentage point change in the share of exports originating in the following sectors: primary products, primary processed products, manufactured consumer goods, and manufactured intermediate goods. Countries were categorized by the largest percentage point change in the share registered for an individual sector. At the top were the small number with over a 10 percentage point change. Next came those with between a 5 and 10 percentage point change. After these were those with between a 2 and 5 percentage point change. In the bottom category, percentage point changes were less than 2. Where data were deficient, descriptive information on changes in export structure was used.

The percentage point "shifts" were of varied sorts: primary to primary processed, primary or primary processed to manufactured consumer goods, or manufactured consumer goods to manufactured intermediate goods, or any of the less likely movements in the opposite direction. Thus, this classification suggests the responsiveness of production-for-export to the changing composition of international demand. The data did not permit a more detailed index.

The Wage Variables (Tables A22 and A23)

Our classification of real wage changes indicates only the probable direction of average change and whether upward changes were strong or moderate. Where the net change in wage levels was small over the period as a whole, we ranked countries lower if average wages fluctuated sharply. At the bottom were countries where wages probably declined throughout the period.

The problems we encountered with the wage data were enormous. Wage indices varied in the weighting of occupations, the basis of wage calculations (weekly, hourly, monthly, annual), and overall coverage. Our conversion of wage rates to a common annual rate ignored varying extents of unemployment across countries. The use of quite varied price indices to construct series for real wages introduced a further major source of incomparability across countries.

Direction of Change in Average Real Wages in Industry (Table A22)

Table A22 presents the classifications and sources for the course of wages in the industrial sector. Wage data were better for industry than for other sectors of the economy. However, they were sometimes seriously incomplete, relating to only one or two categories of worker or referring to overly short periods. The latter cases are explained in the notes to table A22.

Direction of Change in Average Real Wages or Income of Employed Agricultural Poor (Table A23)

Data for the agricultural sector posed additional problems for countries with very small permanent agricultural wage labor forces. For these countries, fragmentary data on wage changes were hardly meaningful. Here we substituted fragmentary numerical data and qualitative statements on the economically active agricultural poor, including small agricultural tenants as well as agricultural laborers. For the rare cases where small tenants and wage laborers experienced changes in real income in different directions, we weighted our estimates according to the composition of the laboring population. All these cases are explained in the notes to table A23.

THE DEMOGRAPHIC VARIABLES (TABLES A24-A34)

Tables A25 through A29 give estimates of total population for each country for 1830, 1850, 1870, 1890, and 1914. Table A24 presents our classification scheme for total population in 1850, 1870, and 1890, and table A30 our scheme for the average annual rate of growth of population during three periods: 1830-1850, 1850-1870, and 1870-1890.

Total Population (Tables A25-A29)

We include total population because it indicates roughly the size of the potential labor force and one important dimension of the size of the internal market. Because of varying age structures, skills, and work opportunities, population is not a sensitive indicator of labor supply. Nor is it a particularly good indicator of the internal market since it ignores age and income. Given these and other deficiencies, we introduce population into our statistical analyses in categorized form.

Rate of Population Growth, Lagged (Table A30)

The rate of growth of population is introduced with a lag. The rationale for introducing a lag is clear when population is viewed as an indicator of labor force, because of the lag between birth and entry into the labor force. The particular lag we chose was determined by the data we had available. When population is viewed as an indicator of internal market size, the argument for a lag is less valid, for here the lag is based on delayed responses of productive and consumptive activities to changing population.

Importance of Net Immigration (Tables A31–A34)

This classification groups countries according to the direction and importance of immigration compared with changes in total population. It is presented in table A31. The data on which it is based are given in tables A32, A33, and A34.

At the top of the spectrum, net immigration accounted for an important part of population change. Net immigration was compared with the increase in population. (Thus, immigration was viewed as accounting for half of population change when it formed 50 percent of the increase in population.) At the bottom of the spectrum, net emigration accounted for an important part of population change. Net emigration was compared with the amount by which population would have increased without emigration (population change plus emigration). This very crude procedure is indicative of only rough orders of magnitude.

Migration can be viewed as the movement of a labor force or the movement of people. Its economic importance lies in its impacts on the labor force and on the internal market. Net migration figures do not show either effect very precisely. First, since a higher proportion of migrants than of population tend to be of working age, the ratios we used understate the change in labor force caused by migration. (This should not bias our grouping of countries very much, however.) Second, migration data ignore variations in the skills of immigrants and in the structure of the jobs they leave and acquire, both of which affect changes in the labor force induced by migration. Third, viewed from the standpoint of the impact of people on the internal demand for consumer goods, migration estimates take no account of variations in income gained or lost through migration. Finally, net decadal migration underestimates the impact of seasonal migration among countries. In some of the countries we studied, these impacts were considerable, as, for example, with Italian migration to Argentina in the late nineteenth century. None of these conceptual deficiencies of migration data are special to our use of them, however. Furthermore, the problems were somewhat reduced because we grouped the data, seeking only a six-way classification.

We depart slightly in this scheme from our usual periodization. Migration data are widely computed by decades that start with, for example, 1851 or 1871. Consequently, the periods for this indicator are 1851–1870, 1871–1890, and 1891–1910 unless otherwise noted. Tables A32–A34 give the data on the basis of which the migration ratios were computed; table A31 gives the classification system. The change in population used to compute the migration ratios was taken from tables A26–A28 except for the third period, where the population for 1910 was used because most estimates referred to that year. The cutoffs between categories were selected to achieve reliability in the groupings. Estimates close to the cut-offs were assigned minuses or pluses as appropriate.

THE HUMAN CAPITAL AND SOCIOINSTITUTIONAL VARIABLES (TABLES A35-A41)

Extent of Adult Illiteracy (Table A35)

The construction of an indicator of literacy or illiteracy posed problems of both definition and data. Definitions of literacy vary among countries: literacy sometimes includes both reading and writing and sometimes not; criteria vary as to what constitutes literate reading. Intercountry comparisons pose problems because literacy rates vary with the age structure of the population; during periods of increasing literacy, younger populations become literate faster.

Historical data generally refer to illiteracy. Common sources of information are studies of illiteracy among military recruits and data on the proportion of brides and bridegrooms unable to sign marriage registers. The consistency of rates of illiteracy among bridegrooms and military recruits suggests that these data can serve with some reliability as indicators of illiteracy (Cipolla 1969, p. 116). However, both are unsatisfactory guides to literacy because of the existence of widespread semiliteracy. Those few studies which distinguish degrees of literacy suggest that semiliteracy was pervasive in Western Europe in the latter half of the nineteenth century. Cipolla (1969) cites the major extent of semiliteracy among military recruits in France during the period 1881–1900: of over six million recruits during the period, 8 percent could not read or write, 3 percent had an elementary school degree (a proxy for ability to read and write), while 89 percent were apparently semiliterates of varying degrees (ibid., pp. 11–12). It is not clear whether the ranking of countries by illiteracy would differ from the ranking by effective literacy. Studies of Switzerland suggest a significantly lesser degree of semiliteracy there than in France, for example (ibid.).

We grouped the data because we felt that point estimates would produce spurious precision. We selected breakpoints between categories where there were marked gaps in the ordering of country estimates. Difficult cases are explained in detail in the notes to table A35.

Rate of Spread of Primary Education, Lagged (Table A36)

As governments, industry, and humanitarians became interested in the spread of education in the latter half of the nineteenth century, studies were made of its international extent (Barnard 1854 and 1872, Levasseur 1897, and U.S. Bureau of Education 1891 and 1893, among others). These studies provided us with generous data on the extent of primary education.

Although data on primary-school enrollments are abundant, they have a number of deficiencies. Some estimates refer to the number inscribed on the rolls, some to enrollments in the month of maximum attendance, some to average attendance. The length of school year, extent of inclusion of private schools, and ages covered by the term "primary school" varied. Furthermore, to calculate the ratio of enrollments to school-age population requires information on children by age group, and such data were often not available. (Most often the age group was 6–14 years, but it varied.) Finally, attendance does not indicate the quality of education received. (Since age distributions varied greatly, enrollments compared with population indicated only gross orders of magnitude.)

Because of these many problems, we grouped observations into only five groups by the change in the percentage of children aged 6–14 years who were in school. We ranked more highly percentage point changes that resulted in a substantial proportion of children enrolled. Where data on age distribution were not available, we assumed that the 6–14 age group formed the same percentage of the total population as in other countries at similar levels of development; we then tested the sensitivity of each country assignment to alternative reasonable assumptions about the 6–14 age group. We concentrated our cross-checks on those cases where the assignment proved sensitive to our assumption about age distribution. Cross-checks were obtained from the past course of population change, estimates of literacy among army conscripts and brides and bridegrooms for particular dates, and fragmentary quantitative information and qualitative statements in histories of education.

The top category and the bottom two categories were not difficult to constitute. The top category included countries with a percentage point increase of at least 15 in primary-school enrollment ratios that achieved at least three-quarters coverage by the end of the study period; data for these countries were relatively good. The lowest category included countries where qualitative statements indicated extremely low levels of literacy. The second-to-bottom category was defined to include countries where increases in enrollment ratios of less than 10 percentage points were accompanied by the passage of new laws, improvements in attendance, a lengthening of the school year, and the opening of schools in areas previously not covered by the school system. Most difficult was the distinction between categories B and C. For all these countries we used every possible cross-check and checked the sensitivity of our assignments to reasonable alternative assumptions.

We have lagged the spread of primary education since both social and private returns to investment in primary education took place with a lag. The indicator is defined with a two-decade lag. Thus, any correlation with average income growth relates to educational advances that took place two decades earlier than the per capita income change.

Predominant Form of Land Tenure and Holding (Table A37)
Concentration of Landholdings (Table A38)
Favorableness of Land System to the Adoption of Improvements (Table A39)

These three land variables are discussed in the first part of chapter five (agricultural development).

Extent of Urbanization (Table A40)

This variable measures the proportion of the population living in towns and cities of over 10,000 people. We chose this size for convenience, because the study by Weber

(1967) provided estimates for the majority of the countries in our sample. One could argue that the full impact of urbanization in promoting economies of scale, market expansion, technological change, labor mobility, pol'tical participation, and changes in attitudes took place only in cities with a population well over 10,000. However, we decided not to undertake the much larger research effort necessary to develop a variable for the proportion of the population living in larger cities. The data were categorized for two reasons. First, small differences in estimates have little meaning, because of data deficiencies (variations in the definition of "towns" and in the coverage and reliability of the data, among others). Second, categorization permits the classification of countries for which only fragmentary numerical and descriptive data on urbanization were available.

Favorableness of Attitudes toward Entrepreneurship (Table A41)

This classification scheme is the only one in our set of variables that is based exclusively on soft data. Its construction was made possible by the literature of the 1950s and 1960s, in which many informed judgements were made comparing attitudes toward entrepreneurship in different countries (e.g., Gerschenkron 1962a, Hirschmeier [Japan] 1964, Landes [France] 1963, Landes 1965a, Owen [Egypt] 1969, and Sawyer [United States] 1954). We group countries by the extent to which the established social elite had favorable attitudes toward entrepreneurial success—particularly entrepreneurial success with factory enterprise. We judge attitudes as of about 1850, 1870, 1890. In classifying country observations, we do not judge whether attitudes toward entrepreneurship helped or hindered economic growth. Thus, Russia was classified in a category defined by unfavorable attitudes in spite of evidence that these attitudes did not much hamper economic growth (Gerschenkron 1962a). India was ranked low in spite of evidence of successful entrepreneurship within groups looked down on by the social elite. Thus, the variable does not measure the extent to which successful capitalists emerged within groups not accepted by the established social elite.

The establishment of a classification scheme posed less difficulty than we expected. The difficulties lay in assigning those countries for which we lacked informed comparative judgments. In the top category we placed countries where nonelite businessmen could achieve social recognition in their lifetimes through mercantile or industrial success. In the third category we placed countries where recognition of entrepreneurial success went for the most part to economically successful members of the social elite, except for the rare outsiders who became extremely wealthy. Between these two categories we placed countries that had two distinct cultures or regions, one resembling countries in the first category, the other resembling countries in the third category. The bottom three categories similarly included two different cases with provision in between for countries with two distinct cultures or regions. In the most highly ranked of the three categories, the social elite approved of successful commercial exploitation of inherited land or mineral holdings but not of independent industrial and trading activities. In the lowest category elite recognition of capitalist entrepreneurship was uncommon. In the intermediate category were countries in which one region or culture resembled the higher category and another resembled the lower category.

THE POLITICOINSTITUTIONAL VARIABLES (TABLES A42-A47)

Extent of Domestic Economic Role of Government (Table A42)

This scheme ranks countries according to the extent of selected types of government economic activity that directly raised domestic investment. These include investment by government enterprises and government measures to subsidize investment in the private sector—for example, tax exemptions, land grants, and subsidized credit. Measures subsidizing transportation, industry, and agriculture were included. We excluded tariffs, most activities of banking institutions, agricultural price or income maintenance programs, and military production. Also excluded were government actions establishing a legal framework for the operation of markets.

Since statistics on government investment were scarce, we established descriptive criteria (specified in table A42) that in combination grouped countries into five categories. We excluded judgments about the effectiveness of government actions promoting investment. For example, we gave weight to the importance of government investment in railways but did not evaluate whether this investment was misdirected.

The scheme is thus a narrow indicator of the economic "role" of the government. Its coverage is also different from that of the complex of government policies referred to by Gerschenkron in his discussion of "forced draft" industrialization versus "autonomous" industrialization (1968). Gerschenkron cites "the complex of policies through which governments became directly concerned with the establishment and conduct of industrial enterprises" (p. 83), including the provision of finance, purchase of industrial products, measures to assure a labor supply, and various forms of subsidy to industry. We included only direct measures that promoted both industrial and nonindustrial investment and direct government provision of transportation.

The top three categories included countries whose governments probably financed the greater part of investment in transportation; they were differentiated by how actively government promoted investment in industry and agriculture. The fourth category included countries in which governments financed a significant, but not predominant, part of transportation investment and provided negligible financing to industry and agriculture. The lowest category included countries where the absolute size of the government was extremely small, although governments usually financed an important part of the small national investment in transportation.

Country studies were used to obtain descriptive and numerical information.

Socioeconomic Character of National Political Leadership (Table A43)

Our purpose in this scheme was to group countries by the division of political power at the national level between large landowners or traditional bureaucratic elites, on the one hand, and rising industrial and commercial interests, on the other. Political influence was classified as direct or indirect. Direct influence was inferred when rising economic groups were represented in a national legislature or had leaders in the upper level of the executive branch actively promoting their interests. Data on the importance of various coalitions in parliaments were used where available. Indirect influence was inferred from the character of the legislation or executive orders put into effect. For example, where social legislation was passed in the absence of direct representation of workers, we inferred that the workers' political influence was indirect.

Since this scheme is based mainly on descriptive information about the general order of magnitude of political influence, no more than four categories could be distinguished. At the top were those few countries where rising business, commercial, and working classes had a direct controlling share of political power at the national level. The second category was defined by the sharing of political power between rising economic groups and traditional landed or bureaucratic elites. In the third category, landed or bureaucratic elites controlled political institutions, but their actions were significantly influenced by the rising economic power of business or working-class groups. The lowest category included countries where indigenous traditional landed elites or colonial powers were in full control, the political influence of other groups being negligible.

Political and economic histories were the main sources of information for this classification scheme.

Strength of National Representative Institutions (Table A44)

We discussed this classification scheme in chapter two to illustrate our procedures for constructing qualitative variables. The descriptive information used in classifying countries came mainly from country political histories.

Extent of Political Stability (Table A45)

This scheme is based on three dimensions of political stability that are indicative of continuity in political institutions and the extent of political conflict. We stress these dimensions because we deem them important to the effective functioning of market systems and because it was relatively easy to obtain descriptive information about them. We eschewed more complex definitions of "political stability" because of conceptual, measurement, and data problems. Specifically, the included dimensions were continuity in national political decision making, frequency of intense nonviolent political strife, and extent of domestic violence.

Four categories were distinguished. In countries at the top there was little strife or violence, and there was continuity of national decision making. Next came countries that experienced frequent government changes (which did not, however, upset the existing institutional framework), much nonviolent political strife, and little violence. The third category was marked by major government reorganizations, frequent nonviolent strife, and some violence in most regions. The lowest category was reserved for disruptions in national decision making by civil war or revolution, intense political strife, and a great deal of domestic violence.

Political histories provided most of the descriptive information used to classify countries.

Degree of Foreign Economic Dependence (Table A46)

This classification scheme is discussed in the first part of chapter six (foreign economic dependence).

Colonial Status (Table A47)

This variable groups countries by their colonial status, with colonies at the upper end of the spectrum. Intermediate along the spectrum are countries that show other forms of economic dependence. In this classification a colony is defined as "any non-self-governing territory under the overwhelming economic and political influence of another country." More strictly, a colony is "any territory where the conditions of life (social, economic, and political) are defined for the whole population in considerable measure by a minority different from the local majority in culture, history, beliefs, and often race" (*Encyclopaedia Britannica* 1969, 6:85).

In our classification scheme we distinguished between colonies that fully met the above definition of a colony and colonies where the majority of the local population were settlers of the same original nationality, culture, and race as the governing colonial power. Where a country such as the United States or Russia had moved population overland into new territories inhabited by populations of another culture and history during the previous two decades, that country was classified as a colonial power for that period but not for later years.

THE MARKET INSTITUTIONAL VARIABLES (TABLES A48–A50)

In chapter three we discussed the classification schemes for the twelve market variables we published in 1978 (Adelman and Morris 1978b). Because of cost and space constraints, these schemes are not reproduced in this book, but each is described briefly below. The classification schemes, country assignments, and sources for the individual variables used to construct each composite index are published in Adelman and Morris 1978b. Our limited resources did not permit us to update the research on which these variables were based.

For the present set of statistical analyses, we formed three composite variables to summarize the level of development of market institutions, the current rate of spread of market institutions, and the past rate of spread of market institutions.

Level of Development of Market Institutions (Composite) (Table A48)

Table A48 gives the component scores for our 69 country observations from a single-component principal components analysis using four variables representing the level of development of land, capital, labor, and commodity markets. The criteria for categorizing countries and periods with respect to the composite variable are given in the note to the table. Brief descriptions of the variables follow.

Level of development of domestic commodity markets. This scheme classifies country observations into nine categories on the basis of qualitative and fragmentary quantitative information on (1) the extent to which production was for the market, (2) the extent to which unrestricted internal trade was legal, (3) the geographical scope of specialized marketing institutions (e.g., staple exchanges or chain stores), and (4) the range of commodities for which regional or national marketing institutions existed.

The spectrum of commodity market development represented by the classification scheme ranges from economies where local self-sufficiency prevailed in 1850 to the advanced industrial economies of the early twentieth century, which had national or multiregional marketing institutions for a wide range of manufactured goods and specialized exchanges for agricultural staples. Intermediate along the scale were two sets of economies: those where commercialization and the geographical expansion of trade proceeded simultaneously in many areas of the country, first within the framework of weakening premodern restrictions and then within a more favorable framework; and those where commodity market expansion was highly dualistic whether dominated by foreign merchants or promoted by national governments.

Level of development of domestic labor markets. This classification scheme stresses (1) the extent of domestic interregional labor flows, (2) the proportion of the labor force dependent exclusively on wages for income, and (3) the strength of legal or customary impediments to labor mobility. With respect to (1), persistent regional labor surpluses and gross differences among regions in laborers' wages were assumed to indicate barriers to mobility. As for (2), fragmentary quantitative data were used together with qualitative information on the importance of subsistence agriculture, the closeness of direct ties between agriculture and cottage industry, and the persistence of nonmonetary payments and obligations. Because the data were poor, only five categories could be distinguished.

The spectrum represented by the scheme ranges from economies where hired labor was quite important to those where nonmarketed or unfree labor prevailed. At the upper end of the spectrum were two categories of countries with quite widespread wage labor and no overwhelming cultural or geographical impediments to mobility. The lower of these two was distinguished by the persistence of labor surpluses or scarcities or of nonmarketed labor in sectors or regions probably involving more than one-quarter of the population. At the lower end of the spectrum were three categories where nonmarketed labor was extremely important and labor mobility limited: those without significant legal or customary impediments to labor mobility; those with moderate legal or customary restraints preventing movements of labor (major settlement laws or poor laws significantly hampering mobility or communal organization of the work force); and, at the bottom, those where de facto slavery or bonded labor was widespread.

Level of development of domestic capital markets. In this classification scheme "domestic capital markets" are defined as domestic banking and nonbanking financial intermediaries that provided finance for investment. These include institutions providing short-term credit that financed investment indirectly. The scheme includes the development of markets for securities, including the use of government securities to provide marketable forms of capital. But it excludes government use of fiscal means to finance investment. Foreign financial intermediaries were given little weight compared with domestic ones.

The classification of countries into six classes is based on historical characteristics of capital market growth: the extent of legal restrictions on interest rates or the issuing of securities; the importance and degree of specialization of credit institutions; and the development of markets for government, transportation, and industrial securities.

At the bottom of the scale were countries with rudimentary capital institutions, the more developed of which had small-scale banks discounting bills of exchange and providing short-term finance for commerce. In the countries intermediate along the scale there were limited domestic markets for government securities and private railway securities and extensive urban markets for short-term loanable funds, but markets for industrial securities were lacking. Countries farther up the scale were characterized by substantial trading of government, railway, and public utility securities on stock exchanges, well-developed urban short-term credit markets, and some significant development of long-term financing of industry through domestic financial intermediaries. At the top, countries with more developed markets were characterized by substantial trading of industrial securities on stock exchanges as well as networks of specialized institutions for marketing securities.

Level of development of domestic land markets.   This variable is described in chapter three (market expansion).

Rate of Spread of Market Institutions, Current (Composite) (Table A49)
Rate of Spread of Market Institutions, Lagged (Composite) (Table A50)

Tables A49 and A50 give the component scores for our 69 country observations from single-component principal components analyses using four variables representing the rate of spread of market systems. The current form of the variable refers to the periods 1850–1869, 1870–1889, and 1890–1914. The lagged form refers to the periods 1830–1849, 1850–1869, and 1870–1889.

Rate of spread of domestic commodity markets.   This classification scheme groups countries into only four broad classes, one of which is a residual category. The top category is reserved for countries where a striking expansion of internal commodity markets took place following widespread commercialization in most regions of the country or a major enlargement of the geographic area of that country's competitive trade. Included in the second category were countries where the spread of commercialization or the enlargement of the area of trade was important but did not affect either a major region or a major segment of the population. The lowest category was reserved for countries and periods where descriptive data suggested a very limited spread of markets; such data included export expansions proceeding from an insignificant base. All countries and periods not clearly assignable to the top two categories or the bottom one were assigned to the residual (third) category.

Rate of spread of domestic labor markets.   This scheme classifies country observations into only four broad groups, one of which is a residual category. The distinctions between categories are necessarily crude as a consequence of poor data. The top category includes cases where there was a rapid expansion of wage labor and a marked *increase* in interregional transfers of labor (including movements into unsettled lands and movements of harvest labor). The second category includes cases where a rapid spread of wage labor and an increase in labor mobility either did not affect important geographical regions or was constrained by the persistence of labor ties with both industry and agriculture. The fourth category consists of cases where very little spread of wage labor took place and where there were no significant increases in interregional transfers of labor. All cases not assigned to the first, second, and fourth categories were assigned to the residual (third) category.

Rate of spread of domestic capital markets. In this scheme, countries and periods are grouped into only four categories, one of which is a residual category. Countries in category A experienced a rapid expansion of banking and nonbanking institutions for financing investment in industry and agriculture. In countries in category B, the expansion of capital markets was limited primarily to a major spread of banking institutions and small extensions in the marketing of securities; the spread of banking facilities usually failed to include a major sector of the economy such as agriculture. In the countries of category D, little spread of capital market institutions occurred. All cases not clearly assignable to categories A, B, or D were assigned to the residual category, C.

Rate of spread of domestic land markets. This classification scheme divides countries and periods into only four categories, one of which is a residual category. The highest category includes cases in which the monetization of land transactions proceeded very rapidly and the volume of land transactions increased greatly; it also includes cases of a rapid spread of specialized institutions for the sale and mortgaging of land. The second highest category shares the characteristics of the highest one except that the spread of land markets did not occur in some important regions of the country. The fourth category includes cases where there was little spread of land markets, while the third category includes all observations not assigned to the other three categories.

As noted above, see Adelman and Morris 1978b for classification schemes, country assignments, and sources.

NOTES ON USAGE

Readers should note the following points in reading the data appendix. There are several kinds of tables. The typical table (e.g., tables A5 through A8) lists the categories and their definitions in the two left-hand columns, gives the countries and periods assigned to each category in the middle column, and in the right-hand column lists the sources used in making each country assignment. The number of categories varies, but is usually five or six. As already noted, sources are identified by author's last name and year of publication; ambiguities in such references are resolved by adding "a," "b," or "c" to the year or by including the author's first initial, as appropriate. The full citations for most references are located in the relevant country section of the bibliography. For those few located in the section for another country, the name of that country is given in brackets after the author's name. Of the sources cited, those in the general section of the bibliography are listed in a note at the end of each table.

Pluses and minuses following country names are assigned in two ways. Sometimes the category's definition specifies country characteristics that require a plus or minus. More often, pluses or minuses indicate cases that are borderline, but for which the weight of the evidence points more strongly to one category than another.

A question mark following a country assignment indicates that the information in the sources cited is insufficient to classify the country with great confidence. These assignments should be treated as "guesstimates." The absence of a question mark means that we are quite confident about *ranking* a country observation below observations having higher letter scores and above those having lower letter scores. Occasionally, no sources are cited for a case flagged with a question mark. In these instances we have used a wide range of uncited information to arrive at a guesstimate.

A second type of table (e.g., tables A10 through A13) presents the basic quantitative data we used to classify countries. Here, a separate table for each time period gives available quantitative estimates with their sources. Multiple estimates for a given year or period are helpful in selecting breakpoints between categories that are relatively insensitive to our choice of a particular estimate. (Two tables, A13 and A29, give data for 1914 that we did not use.)

A third type of table accompanies the quantitative data tables; these tables present classification schemes without listing sources (e.g., tables A24, A30, and A31).

Tables with the single years 1850, 1870, and 1890 in the title refer to level of achievement by these dates. Tables with periods of two or more decades in the title refer to characteristics of the periods listed: 1850-1870, 1870-1890, and 1890-1914 for the unlagged variables; and 1830-1850, 1850-1870, and 1870-1890 for the lagged variables. Two variables are included in both lagged and unlagged form: the rate of improvement in techniques in industry (table A6) and the rate of improvement in techniques in agriculture (table A8). Hence, classifications for four time periods are listed in the tables in which these variables appear.

The time periods given in the titles of tables are approximate. For qualitative variables denoting achievements by a given year or descriptive characteristics of longer periods, this point is obvious. In tables that classify countries by characteristics of periods of two or more decades, the approximate nature of the periods is flagged by the overlap of a year in defining the periods. For quantitative variables for which we give tables of basic data, the precise dates of the data used to classify each country observation are given. (The dating of qualitative achievements is of course approximate.)

One final point: The sources listed in the tables are the ones we consulted. Our limited resources did not permit us to include references to the primary data in the sources we consulted. To have done so would have required that we verify these references—a job well beyond the monetary means at our disposal.

Tables

Table A1

Classification Scheme for Level of Per Capita Income, 1850, 1870, 1890[a]

Description of Category	Country and Year	Sources
Category A Level of per capita income was probably over 80 percent of that of the United Kingdom in 1890.	Australia 1850, 1870, 1890	Maddison 1979, p. 425; Mulhall 1899, p. 320; Cole and Deane 1965, p. 35
	Belgium 1890	Bairoch 1976b, p. 286; Maddison 1979, p. 425; Mulhall 1899, p. 320
	Great Britain 1870, 1890	Bairoch 1976b, p. 286; Maddison 1979, p. 425; Mulhall 1899, p. 320; Paige et al. 1961, pp. 37, 47
	Switzerland 1890	Bairoch 1976b, p. 286; Maddison 1979, p. 425; Mulhall 1899, p. 320
	United States 1890	Bairoch 1976b, p. 286; Maddison 1979, p. 425; Mulhall 1899, p. 320; Paige et al. 1961, pp. 37, 47
Category B Level of per capita income was probably under 80 percent but over 60 percent of that of the United Kingdom in 1890.	Belgium 1870	Bairoch 1976b, p. 286; Maddison 1979, p. 425; Mulhall 1899, p. 320
	Canada 1890	Maddison 1979, p. 425; Mulhall 1899, p. 320; Paige et al. 1961, pp. 37, 47

Table A1 (continued)

Description of Category	Country and Year	Sources
	Denmark 1890	Bairoch 1976b, p. 286; Maddison 1979, p. 425; Mulhall 1899, p. 320; Paige et al. 1961, pp. 37, 42
	France 1890	Bairoch 1976b, p. 286; Maddison 1979, p. 425; Mulhall 1899, p. 320
	Netherlands 1870, 1890	Bairoch 1976b, p. 286; Maddison 1979, p. 425; Mulhall 1899, p. 320; Paige et al. 1961, p. 37
	New Zealand 1890?	Simkin 1951, chap. 10; Sutch 1969, pp. 107–108
	Switzerland 1870	Bairoch 1976b, p. 286; Maddison 1979, p. 425; Mulhall 1899, p. 320
	United States 1870	Maddison 1979, p. 425; Mulhall 1899, p. 320; Paige et al. 1961, pp. 37, 47
Category C Level of per capita income was probably under 60 percent but over 40 percent of that of the United Kingdom in 1890.	Argentina 1890	Mulhall 1899, p. 320
	Belgium 1850	Bairoch 1976b, p. 286; Maddison 1979, p. 425
	Canada 1870	Maddison 1979, p. 425; Paige et al. 1961, pp. 37, 47
	Denmark 1870	Bairoch 1976b, p. 286; Maddison 1979, p. 425; Paige et al. 1961, pp. 37, 47

Table A1 (continued)

Description of Category	Country and Year	Sources
	France 1850, 1870	Bairoch 1976b, p. 286; Maddison 1979, p. 425
	Germany 1870, 1890(+)	Bairoch 1976b, p. 286; Maddison 1979, p. 425; Mulhall 1899, p. 320; Paige et al. 1961, pp. 37, 47
	Great Britain 1850	Bairoch 1976b, p. 286; Maddison 1979, p. 425
	Italy 1870, 1890	Bairoch 1976b, p. 286; Maddison 1979, p. 425; Paige et al. 1961, pp. 37, 47; Mulhall 1899, p. 320
	Netherlands 1850	Bairoch 1976b, p. 286
	New Zealand 1870?	Simkin 1951, chap. 9; Sutch 1969, pp. 84-85
	Norway 1850, 1870, 1890	Bairoch 1976b, p. 286; Maddison 1979, p. 425; Mulhall 1899, p. 320; Paige et al. 1961, pp. 37, 47
	Spain 1850, 1870, 1890	Bairoch 1976b, p. 286; Mulhall 1899, p. 320
	Sweden 1890	Bairoch 1976b, p. 286; Maddison 1979, p. 425; Mulhall 1899, p. 320; Paige et al. 1961, p. 37
	Switzerland 1850	Bairoch 1976b, p. 286
	United States 1850	Maddison 1979, p. 425

Table A1 (continued)

Description of Category	Country and Year	Sources
Category D Level of per capita income was probably under 40 percent but over 30 percent of that of the United Kingdom in 1890.	Argentina 1850?, 1870?	Scobie 1964b, passim
	Canada 1850?	Tucker 1936, passim
	Denmark 1850	Bairoch 1976b, p. 286; Maddison 1979, p. 425
	Germany 1850	Bairoch 1976b, p. 286; Maddison 1979, p. 425
	Italy 1850	Bairoch 1976b, p. 286; Maddison 1979, p. 425
	Russia 1870	Bairoch 1976b, p. 286; Cole and Deane 1965, p. 20
	Sweden 1870	Bairoch 1976b, p. 286; Maddison 1979, p. 425; Paige et al. 1961, pp. 37, 47
Category E Level of per capita income was probably under 30 percent but over 20 percent of that of the United Kingdom in 1890.	Burma 1850?, 1870?, 1890?	Hlaing 1964, pp. 118–119
	Egypt 1870?	Hershlag 1964, passim
	Japan 1850?, 1870, 1890	Maddison 1979, p. 425; Paige et al. 1961, pp. 37, 47
	New Zealand 1850?	Simkin 1951, chap. 8; Sutch 1969, pp. 61–62

Table A1 (continued)

Description of Category	Country and Year	Sources
	Russia 1850, 1890	Balroch 1976b, p. 286; Mulhall 1899, p. 320
	Sweden 1850	Balroch 1976b, p. 286; Maddison 1979, p. 425
Category F Level of per capita income was probably under 20 percent of that of the United Kingdom in 1890.	Brazil 1850?, 1870, 1890?	Furtado 1963, p. 164
	China 1850?, 1870?, 1890?	Perkins et al. 1969, passim
	Egypt 1850?, 1890?	Hershlag 1964, p. 86
	India 1850, 1870, 1890	Sarkar 1917, p. 185; Banerjea 1920, p. 63

Note: Of the sources in this table, the following are listed in the general section of the bibliography: Balroch 1976b, Cole and Deane 1965, Gerschenkron 1961a, Maddison 1979, Mitchell 1976, Mulhall 1899, and Paige et al. 1961.

ᵃ The classifications in this table are based on the Maddison (1979) and Balroch (1976b) data referred to in table A2. Countries that were not included by Maddison or Balroch were classified by comparison with a country that was included, whenever such a comparison was available in an additional source.

Table A2

Indexes of Level of Per Capita Income, Selected Countries,
1850, 1870, 1890[a]

(Per capita income in the United Kingdom in 1890=100)

Country and Year	Index and Classification Based on Bairoch 1976b, p. 286		Index and Classification Based on Maddison 1979, pp. 425–427	
Australia				
1850			101	A
1870			110	A
1890			138	A
Belgium				
1850	52	C	53	C
1870	73	B	77	B
1890	80	A	98	A
Canada				
1870			51	C
1890			73	B
Denmark				
1850	33	D	41	C-
1870	43	C	47	C
1890	64	B	59	C+
France				
1850	42	C	44	C
1870	56	C	52	C
1890	66	B	66	B
Germany				
1850	40	C-	34	D
1870	54	C	44	C
1890	68	B	58	C+
Italy				
1850	35	D	44 (1861)	C
1870	40	D	46	C
1890	40	C	46	C

Table A2 (continued)

Country and Year	Index and Classification Based on Bairoch 1976b, p. 286		Index and Classification Based on Maddison 1979, pp. 425–427	
Japan				
1850				
1870			20	E
1890			28	E
Netherlands				
1850	54	C		
1870	64	B	68	B
1890	75	B	87 (1900)	A
Norway				
1850	45	C	38 (1865)	C
1870	54	C	40	C
1890	67	B	50	C
Russia				
1850	22	E		
1870	32	D		
1890	23	E		
Spain				
1850	40	C		
1870	42	C		
1890	41	C		
Sweden				
1850	27	E	29 (1861)	E
1870	31	D	34	D
1890	45	C	46	C
Switzerland				
1850	50	C		
1870	70	B	65	B
1890	90	A	82	A
United Kingdom				
1850	58	C	57	C
1870	80	A	80	A
1890	100	A	100	A

Table A2 (continued)

Country and Year	Index and Classification Based on Bairoch 1976b, p. 286	Index and Classification Based on Maddison 1979, pp. 425-427	
United States			
1850		48	C
1870		64	B
1890		90	A

a The indexes in this table were derived from the data available in Bairoch 1976b, p. 286, and Maddison 1979, pp. 425-427. The level of per capita income in the United Kingdom in 1890 was set equal to 100 and then comparative values were computed for the different countries and years. Note that these data refer to the United Kingdom, whereas most other data for this study refer to Great Britain only. Since we seek to rank observations only partially, the inconsistency is not important.

Table A3

Classification Scheme for Rate of Change in Per Capita Income,
1850-1870, 1870-1890, 1890-1914[a]

Description of Category	Country and Period
Category A Significant growth of per capita income (probably over 2 percent average annual)	Argentina 1890-1914 Brazil 1890-1914 Canada 1890-1914 Denmark 1890-1914 Japan 1890-1914 New Zealand 1850-1870 Russia 1890-1914 Sweden 1890-1914 United States 1870-1890, 1890-1914

Category B
Moderate growth of per
capita income (probably
between 1 and 1.9
percent average annual)
	Australia 1870-1890
	Belgium 1850-1870?, 1890-1914
	Canada 1850-1870, 1870-1890
	Denmark 1870-1890
	Egypt 1850-1870
	France 1850-1870, 1870-1890(-),
	   1890-1914
	Germany 1850-1870, 1870-1890(+),
	   1890-1914
	Great Britain 1850-1870, 1870-1890
	Italy 1890-1914
	Japan 1870-1890
	Norway 1870-1890, 1890-1914
	Sweden 1850-1870, 1870-1890
	United States 1850-1870(-)

Category C Very modest growth of per capita income (probably between .5 and 1 percent average annual)	Argentina 1870-1890 Belgium 1870-1890 Brazil 1850-1870 Denmark 1850-1870 Egypt 1890-1914 Great Britain 1890-1914 India 1870-1890 Netherlands 1850-1870, 1870-1890, 1890-1914

Table A3 (continued)

Description of Category	Country and Period
	New Zealand 1870-1890, 1890-1914(+) Russia 1850-1870 Spain 1890-1914 Switzerland 1850-1870(+), 1890-1914
Category D Negligible growth of per capita income	Argentina 1850-1870 Brazil 1870-1890 Burma 1850-1870, 1870-1890, 1890-1914 China 1870-1890, 1890-1914 India 1850-1870, 1890-1914 Italy 1850-1870, 1870-1890 Japan 1850-1870 Norway 1850-1870 Spain 1850-1870
Category D- Decline in per capita income (not necessarily a marked decline)	Australia 1850-1870, 1890-1914 China 1850-1870 Egypt 1870-1890 Russia 1870-1890 Spain 1870-1890 Switzerland 1870-1890

a See table A4 for sources and exact time periods of estimates.

Table A4

Sources for Classification of Countries with Respect to Rate of
Change in Per Capita Income

The following paragraphs give the sources on which the
classifications are based and brief notes on the type of data used and
the rationale for the classification. The following sources cited
below will be found in the general section of the bibliography:
Bairoch 1976b, Cole and Deane 1965, Gerschenkron 1962a, Maddison 1979,
Mitchell 1976, Mulhall 1899, and Paige et al. 1961.

Argentina

   The sources consulted are Cole and Deane 1965, Díaz Alejandro 1970,
Peterson 1964, and Randall 1977a.

   Estimates of GDP (in 1950 prices) are available for 1900-1914.
Estimates of growth prior to 1900 have to be based on data concerning
the growth of exports and qualitative information. There is no
evidence to suggest that GNP per capita was growing during the 1850-
1870 period. Cole and Deane (1965, p. 39) postulate that aggregate
national income expanded at about the same rate as population. Data
on quantities of exports suggest that export growth may have provided
modest per capita GNP growth in the 1870-1890 period and rapid growth
in the 1890-1914 period.

Australia

   The sources consulted are Butlin 1962 and 1964, and Cole and Deane
1965.

   Estimates of GPD at factor cost in constant prices are available for
1861-1914. Butlin's estimates are based on the value added by
productive enterprises (1962, p. 6).

Belgium

   The sources consulted are Bairoch 1976b and Maddison 1979.
Estimates of GNP, in 1960 U.S. prices, for the 1850-1913 period are
available in Bairoch 1976b. Estimates of GDP, in 1970 U.S. prices for
that period are available in Maddison 1979. Both Bairoch and Maddison
indicate that they used gross output estimates derived from movements
in agricultural and industrial output available in J. Gadisseur,
"Contribution à l'Etude de la Production Agricole en Belgique de 1846
à 1913," *Revue Belge d'Histoire Contemporaine*, 4 (1973). Maddison
(1977) indicates that service output was assumed to move with
employment in services, and these figures were obtained from Bairoch
1968.

Table A4 (continued)

Different growth rates are indicated by Bairoch and Maddison for the 1870-1890 period, and, having no further information on the methods of calculation utilized in these sources, we used an average of the two growth rates for classificatory purposes.

Brazil

The sources consulted are Graham 1968, Leff 1972c, and Randall 1977b, vol. 3.

GNP data are not available for the years 1850-1914; thus our estimates of GNP growth are based on export growth, qualitative information, and Leff's estimates of GNP growth, which are dependent on growth of the deflated currency supply.

Burma

The sources consulted are Hlaing 1964 and Tun Wai 1961.

Data on NDP are available only for the years 1900-1914. Estimates of growth before this time are based on export, wage, and price information in conjunction with qualitative information.

Canada

The sources consulted are Firestone 1958 and 1960.

Estimates of GNP in constant market prices are available for 1850-1914. Firestone's estimates are based on value added by the economic sector (1960, pp. 241-245).

China

The sources consulted are Hou 1965 and Perkins et al. 1969.

Estimates of GNP growth are based on estimates of agricultural yields, growth of exports, and qualitative information.

Denmark

The sources consulted are Bjerke and Ussing 1958, Hansen 1970, and Youngson 1959.

Estimates of annual rates of growth of national income are available for 1855-1913 in Hansen. Estimates of NDP, using a flow-of-incomes approach, are available for 1870-1914 in Bjerke and Ussing. These sources suggest the same classification scheme, which is confirmed by

Table A4 (continued)

---

qualitative information.

Egypt

The sources consulted are Owen 1969, Issawi 1966, and Hansen 1979.

Estimates of national income or product are not available for the period 1850-1887. Our classification is based on an index of the buying power of exports in Issawi, information on agricultural output and exports in Owen, and other qualitative information in these sources.

The classification for 1850-1870 and 1870-1890 is based on the index of buying power of exports with the assumption that the nonexport sector experienced negligible growth per capita (as judged by qualitative information) and that exports constituted 30-40 percent of GNP (based on cotton as a percentage of total agricultural output; cotton as a percentage of production of wheat, beans, barley, and cotton; and cotton exports as a percentage of total exports).

Hansen provides per capita income estimates for 1887-1912. His estimates were based on his indexes of rural and urban real value added per capita. These indexes were based on series of agricultural output, output of the railway system, and the volume of foreign trade. Hansen's estimates, combined with the procedure described above, form the basis of our classification for 1890-1914.

France

The sources consulted are Bairoch 1976b, Kindleberger 1964, Mitchell 1976, and Perroux 1955.

Estimates of various measures of national income are available for the entire period covered by our study. The average annual growth rates that result are remarkably close to one another, with the slight differences appearing to be attributable to different averaging periods.

Germany

The sources consulted are Hoffmann et al. 1965 and Mitchell 1976. Our classification is based on Hoffmann's estimates of net national product in market prices for 1913.

Table A4 (continued)

___

Great Britain

The sources consulted are Deane 1968, Feinstein 1972, and Mitchell 1976.

Estimates of GNP at factor cost in constant prices are available in Deane and Feinstein. Estimates of annual rates of growth of GNP from these sources result in the same classification.

Our present classifications for 1850-1870 and 1870-1890 differ from our earlier classifications, which were based on earlier estimates by Deane. Deane's new estimates of growth rates are lower than her older estimates primarily due to a difference in her deflation procedure (Deane 1968, p. 97).

India

The sources consulted are Mukerjee 1969 and Saini 1969.

Estimates of per capita national income are available in Mukerjee. Saini notes that these estimates are based on statistical evidence that is of doubtful validity, but his conclusions, based on manufacturing output, employment, agricultural production, and wheat and rice exports, support the same classifications.

Italy

The sources consulted are Gerschenkron 1962a, Maddison 1970, Mitchell 1976, and Seton-Watson 1967.

Estimates of GNP in constant market prices are available in Maddison and Mitchell. The data from these sources lead to the same classifications.

Japan

The sources consulted are Hanley and Yamamura 1977, Ohkawa et al. 1957, Ohkawa and Rosovsky 1973, and Bank of Japan, Statistics Dept. 1966.

Estimates of NDP in constant market prices are available for 1880-1914 in Ohkawa et al. 1957. Their method of estimation was primarily value added by sector, with the data on the various sectors taken primarily from official statistics. Qualitative information indicates that per capita growth was negligible in the pre-1868 period and minimal in the 1870s. We assumed a per capita growth rate of .6 percent or below for the 1870s in our classification. The present

Table A4 (continued)

---

classification for the 1870-1890 period is lower than our previous
classification due to this qualitative information.

Netherlands

The sources consulted are de Jonge 1968, Mitchell 1976, Teijl 1971,
and van Stuivenberg 1967.

Teijl provides two alternative sets of estimates of national income
for 1850-1910. One method of estimation is based on assumptions
regarding the relationship between national income and tax yields.
The second method utilizes a Cobb-Douglas production function (with
labor and energy inputs) estimated for the period 1900-1940. GDP
estimates for 1850-1900 are then determined from labor and energy
inputs for these years. Mitchell provides the official estimates of
NNP in constant market prices for 1900-1914. The classifications
indicated by these three sets of data coincided, with the exception of
the first period. The production function method indicates a
classification of C, as opposed to a D+ classification indicated by
the tax yield method. We chose the higher classification based on
qualitative information primarily in de Jonge.

New Zealand

The sources consulted are Condliffe 1959 and Simkin 1951.

Estimates of national income or product are not available for the
1850-1914 period. Our classifications are based on agricultural
output, the growth of population involved in manufacturing, the growth
of exports, and other qualitative information from the above sources.

Norway

The major sources consulted are Aukrust and Bjerke 1959, Lieberman
1970, and Mitchell 1976.

Estimates of GDP in constant market prices are available for 1865-
1914 in Mitchell. Aukrust and Bjerke and Lieberman provide data for
1900-1914 which lead to the same classification for the 1890-1914
period as the Mitchell data. On the basis of qualitative information
and agricultural production data available in the above sources, we
assumed a negligible per capita GDP growth rate for the period prior
to 1865.

Table A4 (continued)

Russia

The sources consulted are Crisp 1976 and Goldsmith 1961.

Goldsmith provides data on agricultural output and the rate of growth of industrial output for 1860-1914. Assuming that agricultural output accounted for the major portion of national income prior to 1890, and that per capita GDP growth for 1850-1860 was below .6 percent, our classifications are C and D- for 1860-1870 and 1870-1890 respectively. National income in the final period was assumed to be somewhat more influenced by the growth of industrial output than in the earlier periods. Crisp provides estimates of per capita GNP for 1897 and 1913 which confirm our classification based on Goldsmith's data.

Spain

The sources are Bairoch 1976b and Vicens Vives and Nadal Oller 1969.

Estimates of GNP growth per capita are available in Bairoch for 1850-1913. These estimates are based primarily on the volume of agriculture and industrial production and secondarily on the volume of exports and labor force statistics. The data on agriculture and livestock production for the 1860-1900 period in Vicens Vives and Nadal Oller are consistent with the classification based on Bairoch's estimates.

Sweden

The sources consulted are Fridlizius 1963, Mitchell 1976, and Youngson 1959.

Estimates of GDP in constant market prices are available in Mitchell for 1861-1914. We adopted the classification for 1861-1870 for the entire first period based on per capita export growth for the 1850-1870 period and on qualitative information in Youngson.

Switzerland

The source consulted is Gasser 1962.

Gasser gives a chart of real net national product in constant prices. We based our classification on his indicated trend growth.

Table A4 (continued)

United States

The sources consulted are Gallman 1960 and 1966 and U.S. Dept.
of Commerce, Bureau of the Census 1966.

Gallman provides estimates of value added by agriculture, mining,
manufacturing, and construction for 1850-1870. These estimates are
the basis of our classification for the first period. Kendrick's and
Kuznet's estimates of GNP in the 1966 Department of Commerce study are
the basis for our classifications of the 1870-1890 and the 1890-1914
periods. These estimates of GNP are based on the market value of
final goods and services.

Table A5

Classification Scheme for Level of Development of Techniques in Industry, 1850, 1870, 1890

Description of Category	Country and Year	Sources
Category A Countries where both the spinning and weaving of cotton and woolen textiles were predominantly mechanized, as judged by the probable proportion of the work force in factories using inanimate power. In addition, in a considerable range of consumer goods industries, most employees were in factories. Finally, there was a well-developed machinery industry where the fabrication or use of interchangeable parts was quite common.	Belgium 1890 Great Britain 1890	Lincke 1911, p. 172 Clapham 1938, pp. 81–82, 174–195; Wilson 1965, pp. 191–192
Category B Countries where, as in category A, both spinning and weaving of cotton and woolen textiles were predominantly mechanized. Countries in this category differed from those in A in that, outside of	Belgium 1870 France 1890(–)	Dechesne 1932, pp. 435, 439, 441; Linden 1920, p. 299 Clapham 1936, pp. 247, 259; Lincke 1911, p. 197

Table A5 (continued)

Description of Category	Country and Year	Sources
textiles, while there were some factories in many consumers goods industries, they did not usually predominate. These countries also had well-developed machinery industries where the fabrication or use of interchangeable parts was quite common.	Germany 1890	Clapham 1936, pp. 284–285; Lincke 1911, p. 167
	Great Britain 1870	Clapham 1932, pp. 77, 82–97; Clough and Cole 1946, p. 557; Richardson 1965, p. 129
	Switzerland 1890	Hauser 1961, pp. 212–237; Kneschaurek 1964, pp. 146–148; Lincke 1911, pp. 55, 111; Wartmann 1901, pp. 175–176
	United States 1870(–), 1890	Hughes 1970, p. 132; Lincke 1911, pp. 178–179; North 1965, pp. 682–696; Strassmann 1959, pp. 130–157; U.S. Dept. of Commerce, Bureau of the Census, 1960, p. 409
Category C Countries where both cotton spinning and cotton weaving were predominantly mechanized, but other textile industries were not. Outside of textiles, factories existed in a considerable number of consumer goods industries, especially food processing, but they did not usually predominate.[a] The	Australia 1890(–)	Butlin 1962, pp. 60–63, 164, 166; Butlin 1964, p. 207; Fitzpatrick 1969, pp. 182–183, 252–263
	Belgium 1850	Chlepner 1956, p. 47; Clapham [France] 1936, pp. 58–59; Dechesne 1932, pp. 395–396, 431, 439–440; Landes 1965a, p. 393
	Denmark 1890(–)	Drachmann 1915, pp. 24–26; Galenson 1952, p. 9; Jensen 1937, p. 156; Jürberg 1973, pp. 408–412

Table A5 (continued)

Description of Category	Country and Year	Sources
overwhelming majority of factories were small horsepower. These countries produced a few lines of specialized machinery such as farm, agricultural processing, or textile machinery, but did not have a well-developed machinery industry fabricating or using interchangeable parts. Excluded from this category are countries where the work force in factories using inanimate power was probably less than 1 percent of the labor force (calculated using three-fifths of the population as a proxy for the labor force where data were lacking).	France 1870(-)?	Bogart 1942, pp. 338-343; Clapham 1936, pp. 241-242, 246, 249-251; Landes 1965a, p. 449
	Germany 1870(-)?	Bogart 1942, p. 43; Clapham 1936, pp. 199, 297; Landes 1965a, p. 449
	Great Britain 1850	Clapham 1932, pp. 23, 25, 28, 32-34, 82, 97; Lipson 1969, pp. 20-21
	Netherlands 1870(-), 1890	Brugmans 1961, pp. 201-213, 324-332; de Jonge 1968, pp. 90, 106, 167-168
	Sweden 1890	Dahmén 1970, pp. 16-20; Jürberg 1958, p. 129
	Switzerland 1870	Hunold 1954, p. 9; Kneschaurek 1964, pp. 146-147; Rappard 1914, pp. 194-195
Category D Countries where cotton spinning was predominantly mechanized but cotton weaving was not. In a number of consumer goods industries	Australia 1870	Butlin 1962, pp. 60-63, 164, 166; Fitzpatrick 1969, pp. 182-183, 262-263; Sinclair 1975, p. 94
	Canada 1890	Firestone 1960, pp. 230, 239

Table A5 (continued)

Description of Category	Country and Year	Sources
there were some factories using inanimate power but they did not usually predominate.a In most cases there were a small number of machinery factories in a few specialized lines. Where there was no machinery production at all, the country is classified D-. Included in this category are late industrializers where textiles were largely imported but factories of small horsepower existed in a considerable number of other consumer goods industries. Also included in this category are countries meeting the criteria of category C except that factory workers were probably less than one percent of their labor force.	Denmark 1870(+)	Glamann 1960, p. 117; Jörberg 1973, pp. 408–412; Youngson 1959, pp. 199, 100, 215, 217
	France 1850(–)	Clapham 1936, pp. 63–70, 259; Henderson 1961, pp. 118, 158; Landes 1965a, p. 449; Neufeld [Italy] 1961, p. 142
	Germany 1850	Clapham 1936, p. 297; Henderson 1961, p. 21; Landes 1965a, p. 443; Minchinton 1973, p. 103; Neufeld [Italy] 1961, p. 142
	Japan 1890	Hirschmeier 1964, p. 93; Miyamoto et al., 1965, p. 558
	New Zealand 1890(+)	Condliffe 1959, p. 164; Simkin 1951, pp. 63, 155
	Norway 1890(–)	Hodne 1975, pp. 260–261; Johnsen 1939, p. 515; Lieberman 1970, pp. 118, 128–130, 155
	Russia 1850(–), 1870, 1890(+)	Blackwell 1968, pp. 42–45; Dobb 1948, p. 36; Portal 1965, pp. 808–810, 815–817, 820–823

Table A5 (continued)

Description of Category	Country and Year	Sources
	Spain 1870(-), 1890(+)	Lincke 1911, pp. 172-173; Nadal 1973, pp. 615, 618; Nadal 1975, pp. 196, 207; Vicens Vives and Nadal Oller 1969, pp. 672-674
	Sweden 1870	Dahmén 1970, pp. 16-20
	Switzerland 1850	Kneschaurek 1964, p. 139; Landes 1965a, p. 397; Rappard 1914, pp. 199-203
	United States 1850(+)	Hughes 1970, p. 132; North 1965, p. 683
Category E Countries where power spinning of cotton was established but did not predominate over hand-spinning, and cotton weaving was generally by hand. Other textile industries were not mechanized. There were a few factories of small horsepower in other consumer goods industries (for example, water-driven flour mills) but no factories making machinery.	Argentina 1890(+)	Cole and Deane 1965, p. 39; Filiol 1961, p. 43; Wythe 1945, pp. 80-83
	Brazil 1870, 1890	Burns 1970, p. 146; Graham 1968, p. 14; Normano 1968, p. 100; Wythe et al. 1949, p. 160
	Canada 1870	Firestone 1960, pp. 225-230; Jones 1946, p. 308
	China 1890	Allen 1965, p. 901; Hou 1965, p. 278; King 1965, pp. 14-17; Tawney 1932, p. 111

Table A5 (continued)

Description of Category	Country and Year	Sources
	Denmark 1850	Jörberg 1973, pp. 408-412; Youngson 1959, pp. 199-200
	India 1870, 1890	Allen 1965, pp. 910-912; Buchanan 1934, p. 139; Chandra 1966, pp. 71-72; Sen 1966, pp. 30-31, 34-35, 44-45, 50-51; Sundara Rajan 1955, p. 121; Thorner 1960, p. 219
	Italy 1850, 1870, 1890(+)	Albrecht-Carrié 1950, p. 51; Clough 1964, pp. 20, 64, 82, 89-90; Gerschenkron 1962a, pp. 392-398; Gille 1973, pp. 292-293; Lincke 1911, pp. 170-171; Luzzato 1969, p. 221; Neufeld 1961, p. 142; Salvadori 1965, p. 112; Schmidt 1939, p. 12; Seton-Watson 1967, pp. 18, 81; Mack Smith 1959, p. 153
	Netherlands 1850	de Jonge 1968, pp. 90, 97, 106, 167
	New Zealand 1870	Simkin 1951, pp. 63, 137; Sutch 1969, p. 99
	Norway 1870	Johnsen 1939, p. 520; Jörberg 1973, pp. 429-431; Lieberman 1970, p. 122; Soltow 1965, p. 6
	Spain 1850(+)	Nadal 1975, pp. 196, 614, 671-678; Vicens Vives and Nadal Oller 1969, p. 670

Table A5 (continued)

Description of Category	Country and Year	Sources
	Sweden 1850	Hovde 1943, 1: 241, 252, 258-259; Janson 1931, p. 80; Youngson 1959, p. 157
Category F Countries where there were either no factories using inanimate power or a very few low-horsepower ones, in one or two sectors. In the latter case, the country is classified F+.	Argentina 1850, 1870	Ferns 1960, p. 363
	Australia 1850	Butlin 1962, pp. 60-63, 164; Cotter 1970, p. 248; Fitzpatrick 1969, pp. 182-183, 262-263; Shaw 1955, pp. 268-269; Sinclair 1975, p. 83
	Brazil 1850(+)	Burns 1970, p. 146; Graham 1968, p. 14
	Burma 1850, 1870, 1890(+)	Hlaing 1964, p. 137; Resnick 1970, p. 57; Tun Wai 1961, p. 38
	Canada 1850	Firestone 1960, pp. 226, 228-230; Jones 1946, p. 308; Tucker 1936, pp. 8, 21, 23
	China 1850, 1870	Allen 1965, p. 901; Fairbank et al., 1960, p. 19; Hou 1963, pp. 279, 286; King 1965, pp. 14-17; Tawney 1932, p. 111
	Egypt 1850, 1870, 1890(+)	Commission du Commerce et de l'Industrie 1966, pp. 452-453; Crouchley 1938, p.

Table A5 (continued)

Description of Category	Country and Year	Sources
	India 1850	135; Grunwald and Ronall 1960, p. 183; Issawi 1966, pp. 365, 372.
	Japan 1850, 1870	Chandra 1966, pp. 71-72; Gadgil 1942, p. 197; Sen 1966, pp. 30-31, 34-35, 44-45, 50-51
		Allen 1965, p. 876; Lockwood 1954, p. 17; Miyamoto et al., 1965, p. 558; Rosovsky 1966, pp. 99-100
	New Zealand 1850	Sutch 1969, p. 99
	Norway 1850(+)	Drake 1969, pp. 79-81; Hodne 1975, p. 256; Jørberg 1973, p. 427; Lieberman 1970, pp. 118, 122

Note: Of the sources in this table, the following are listed in the general section of the bibliography: Bogart 1942, Clough and Cole 1946, Cole and Deane 1965, Gerschenkron 1962a, Gille 1973, Henderson 1961, Hughes 1970, Landes 1965a, Lipson 1969, and Minchinton 1973. Lincke [Switzerland] 1911 is cited for many countries other than Switzerland; by exception, its location in the Switzerland section of the bibliography is not noted each time it appears as a source for another country.

a The few instances in which they predominated occurred when a new product not previously produced for the market was introduced with factory production.

Table A6

Classification Scheme for Rate of Improvement in Techniques in Industry,
1830–1850, 1850–1870, 1870–1890, 1890–1914

Description of Category	Country and Period	Sources
Category A Countries where significant across-the-board industrialization from a substantial base took place. Specifically (1) at the beginning of the period at least 25 percent of GDP probably originated in industry, and factory production was already important--it predominated in cotton textiles; (2) the average annual rate of growth of industrial output during the period was probably over 3 percent; and (3) qualitative information indicates that additions to industrial capacity involving, for the most part, factory production were significant in both consumer goods and machinery industries.	Belgium 1850–1870, 1890–1914(−) Germany 1870–1890, 1890–1914(+) Great Britain 1850–1870	Cammaerts 1921, p. 324; Chlepner 1956, pp. 47, 179; Dechesne 1932, pp. 435, 439–441; Landes 1965a, pp. 423, 449; League of Nations 1945, p. 130; Lewinski 1911, p. 162; Linden 1920, pp. 299–300; Mitchell 1976, pp. 489, 737; van Houtte 1943, pp. 179–180 Bogart 1942, pp. 320–331; Fisher 1976, pp. 536–542; Hoffmann 1963, pp. 104–115; Jostock 1955, p. 103; Landes 1965a, pp. 423, 446, 449; League of Nations 1945, p. 130; Lincke 1911, p. 166; Mitchell 1976, pp. 355, 799, 801; Patel 1963, p. 70 Aldcroft 1968, p. 13; Clapham 1932, pp. 28–33, 77, 80, 82–97, 114–119; Clough and Cole 1946, p. 557; Landes 1965a, pp. 423, 449; Marczewski [France] 1965, p. cxxxvi; Mitchell 1976, pp. 355, 800, 804; Patel 1963, p. 70

Table A6 (continued)

Description of Category	Country and Period	Sources
	United States 1890–1914(+)	Davis et al., 1965, p. 267; Hughes 1970, pp. 132, 133; League of Nations 1945, p. 130; Lincke 1911, pp. 178–179; North 1965, pp. 696–703; Patel 1963, p. 70; U.S. Dept. of Commerce, Bureau of the Census 1960, pp. 139–140, 409
Category B Countries where moderate across-the-board industrialization from a substantial base took place. Specifically, countries are included in this category if they meet either all the criteria for Category A except that the average annual rate of growth of output in industry during the period was probably between 1.5 percent and 3 percent; or, alternatively, all the criteria for Category A except that at the beginning of the period only between 20 and 25 percent of GDP probably originated in industry.	Belgium 1830–1850(-), 1870–1890	Baudhuin 1928, pp. 246–247; Cammaerts 1921, p. 324; Chlepner 1956, p. 47; Clapham [France] 1936, pp. 57, 281, 285; Craeybeckx 1970, p. 188; Dechesne 1932, pp. 395, 431–440; Hague 1963, p. 376; Landes 1965a, pp. 394–395, 405, 449; Landes 1969, pp. 187, 221; League of Nations 1945, p. 130; Lewinski 1911, pp. 162, 320; Linden 1920, pp. 299–300; Mitchell 1976, pp. 489, 737; van Houtte 1943, pp. 179–180
	France 1830–1850, 1850–1870, 1870–1890(-), 1890–1914	Bogart 1942, pp. 336–343; Clapham 1936, pp. 70, 259; Crouzet 1970, pp. 62–89; Fohlen 1970, pp. 203, 207, 213, 214; Henderson 1961, pp. 118, 158; Landes 1965a, pp. 423, 449; League of Nations 1945, p. 130; Lévy Leboyer 1968a, p. 790; Lincke 1911, p. 170;

Table A6 (continued)

Description of Category	Country and Period	Sources
Countries are classified B-If, although at least 20 percent of GDP probably originated in Industry, the factory sector was nevertheless small compared with the nonfactory sector.		Markovitch 1966c, pp. 120–123; Mitchell 1976, pp. 355, 359, 799, 801; Patel 1963, p. 70
	Germany 1850–1870(–)	Fisher 1976, pp. 536–542; Hamerow 1969, pp. 16–21, 33, 78; Henderson 1961, pp. 31–36; Hoffmann 1963, pp. 104–115; Jostock 1955, p. 103; Landes 1965a, pp. 423, 446, 449; Mitchell 1976, pp. 355, 799, 801
	Great Britain 1830–1850, 1870–1890, 1890–1914	Aldcroft 1968, p. 13; Clapham 1932, pp. 175–195; Clough and Cole 1946, p. 557; Habakkuk 1967, p. 189; Habakkuk and Deane 1963, pp. 80, 82; Landes 1965a, pp. 423, 449; League of Nations 1945, p. 130; Lincke 1911, pp. 174–176; Marczewski [France] 1965, p. cxxxvi; Mitchell 1976, pp. 355, 800, 804; Patel 1963, p. 70; Richardson 1965, p. 129; Wilson 1965, pp. 191–193
	Switzerland 1850–1870(+)?, 1870–1890?, 1890–1914?	Hauser 1961, pp. 212–237; Hunold 1954, p. 9; Kneschaurek 1964, pp. 139, 141, 146–148, 155; Landes 1965a, p. 396; Landes 1969, pp. 189, 242, 243, 275, 276; Lincke 1911, pp. 55, 111; Rappard 1914, pp. 194–195; Swiss Office for the

Table A6 (continued)

Description of Category	Country and Period	Sources
	United States 1850–1870(–), 1870–1890(+)	Development of Trade 1931, p. 34; Wartmann 1901, pp. 175–180
		Davis et al. 1965, p. 477; Gallman 1966, pp. 26, 43; Hughes 1970, p. 132; Hunter 1951, pp. 470–472, 477, 498, 500; Landes 1965a, p. 449; Landes 1969, p. 221; League of Nations 1945, p. 130; North 1965, pp. 682–703; Patel 1963, p. 70; Strassmann 1959, pp. 130–157; U.S. Dept. of Commerce, Bureau of the Census 1960, pp. 139–140
Category C Countries where rapid industrialization from a narrow base involving factory production of both consumer goods and machinery took place. (1) In these countries growth started from a very narrow base. (Industry was probably less than 20 percent of GDP and mechanization had barely started.) (2) Average annual rates of industrial growth during the period were very high, usually over 5 percent. Finally, (3)	Australia 1890–1914(–)	Butlin 1962, pp. 460–461; Butlin 1964, p. 22; Cotter 1970, p. 248; Fitzpatrick 1949, pp. 262–263; Sinclair 1976, p. 168; Thompson 1970, pp. 83, 87
	Canada 1890–1914(–)	Bertram 1963, pp. 170–183; Firestone 1958, pp. 186–189, 206–209, 221; Firestone 1960, pp. 224–239; League of Nations 1945, p. 130; Marr and Paterson 1980, p. 22; Wittke 1941, p. 284
	Germany 1830–1850(–)	Bogart 1942, p. 93; Henderson 1961, p. 21; Hoffmann 1968, pp. 104–115;

Table A6 (continued)

Description of Category	Country and Period	Sources
additions to industrial capacity involved the spread of factory production of both consumer goods and machinery. Countries where only a single kind of machinery (such as agricultural or dairy) was produced are classified C-.	Italy 1890-1914	Kaufhold 1976, pp. 334, 336-338; Landes 1965a, p. 449
		Clough 1964, pp. 64, 95-97; Fenoaltea 1968, p. 146; Gerschenkron 1962a, pp. 392-398, 401; Landes 1965a, p. 449; League of Nations 1945, p. 130; Lincke 1911, pp. 170, 171; Mitchell 1976, pp. 355, 799, 802; Neufeld 1961, pp. 536, 539; Patel 1963, p. 70; Seton-Watson 1967, pp. 285-287; Schmidt 1939, p. 12
	Japan 1890-1914	Allen 1965, p. 876; Hirschmeier 1964, p. 93; League of Nations 1945, p. 130; Miyamoto et al. 1965, p. 558; Ohkawa et al. 1957, pp. 81-82; Ohkawa 1979, p. 35; Patel 1963, p. 70
	Netherlands 1890-1914	Brugmans 1961, pp. 324-332; de Jonge 1968, pp. 495, 496; Landes 1965a, p. 449
	Russia 1890-1914	Cole and Deane 1965, pp. 21, 22; Crisp 1976, p. 111; Dobb 1948, p. 36; Goldsmith 1961, pp. 462, 463; League of Nations 1945, p. 130; Lincke 1911, p. 173; Mitchell 1976, p. 355; Portal 1965, pp. 823, 834, 837, 843, 844, 852; Rimlinger 1961, pp. 209-211

Table A6 (continued)

Description of Category	Country and Period	Sources
	Sweden 1890–1914?	Dahmén 1970, pp. 16–22; Hildebrand 1960, p. 281; Jörberg 1969, p. 277; League of Nations 1945, p. 130; Lincke 1911, p. 172; Mitchell 1976, pp. 355, 800, 803; Patel 1963, p. 70; Thomas 1941, pp. 112, 113, 116–123, 128
	Switzerland 1830–1850(–)	Biucchi 1973, pp. 631–634; Kneschaurek 1964, pp. 139, 141, 155; Landes 1965a, p. 397
	United States 1830–1850	Davis et al. 1965, pp. 80–82; Gallman 1966, p. 26; Landes 1965a, p. 449; North 1963, pp. 45–46, 49–52; North 1965, p. 683
Category D Countries where rapid industrialization from a narrow base took place involving mainly additions to factory consumer goods production.	Argentina 1870–1890, 1890–1914	Cole and Deane 1965, p. 39; Díaz Alejandro 1970, pp. 418, 419, 428, 449; Pendle 1955, p. 62; Scobie 1964a, pp. 177–179; Wythe 1949, pp. 82, 83
	Australia 1870–1890	Butlin 1962, pp. 165, 166, 460, 461; Cotter 1970, p. 248; Fitzpatrick 1969, pp. 182, 183; McGhee 1970, p. 165; Sinclair 1976, p. 94; Thompson 1970, pp. 83, 87–88

Table A6 (continued)

Description of Category	Country and Period	Sources
	Brazil 1890-1914	Burns 1970, pp. 146, 258-260; Joblm 1944, pp. 98, 198, 199; Normano 1968, pp. 99, 100, 108; Tyler 1976, p. 13; Wythe 1955, pp. 70, 160
	Canada 1870-1890(+)	Bertram 1963, pp. 170-183; Firestone 1958, pp. 186-189, 206-209, 221; Firestone 1960, pp. 224-239; Marr and Paterson 1980, p. 22
	Denmark 1870-1890, 1890-1914	Drachmann 1915, pp. 21, 24-26; Galenson 1952, p. 9; Glamann 1960, p. 124; Hansen 1970, pp. 8, 11, 14, 64, 65; Jørberg 1973, pp. 410-412; Youngson 1959, pp. 199, 200, 215, 217
	Japan 1870-1890(-)	Allen 1965, pp. 876-877; Lockwood 1954, p. 17; Ohkawa et al. 1957, p. 81; Rosovsky 1966, pp. 99, 100
	Italy 1870-1890(-)	Albrecht-Carrié 1950, p. 12; Clough 1964, pp. 82, 95-97; Fenoaltea 1968, p. 146; Gerschenkron 1962a, p. 402; Landes 1965a, p. 449; League of Nations 1945, p. 130; Mitchell 1976, pp. 355, 799, 802; Neufeld 1961, pp. 140-142; Patel 1963, p. 70; Salvadori 1965, p. 112; Seton-Watson 1967, pp. 80, 81; Mack Smith 1959, p. 153

Table A6 (continued)

Description of Category	Country and Period	Sources
	Netherlands 1870–1890	Brugmans 1961, pp. 201–213; de Jonge 1968, pp. 167–168, 495–496; Landes 1965a, p. 449
	New Zealand 1870–1890, 1890–1914	Condliffe 1959, pp. 143, 164–166, 247–252; League of Nations 1945, p. 130; Lloyd Prichard 1970, pp. 147–149, 189–193, 200, 406, 413; Scholefield 1909, p. 295; Simkin 1951, pp. 63, 137, 155; Sutch 1969, p. 99
	Norway 1870–1890(–), 1890–1914	Blegen 1931, pp. 4–5; Bull 1960, pp. 267, 268; Drachmann 1915, p. 95; Glass and Grebenick 1965, p. 61; Hodne 1975, pp. 260–261; Johnsen 1939, pp. 515, 520; Larsen 1948, p. 500; Lieberman 1970, pp. 118, 128–130, 155; Mitchell 1976, pp. 357, 800; Nielsen [Denmark] 1933, pp. 542, 544
	Russia 1870–1890(–)	Cole and Deane 1965, pp. 21–22; Crisp 1976, p. 111; Gerschenkron 1968, pp. 434–435; Goldsmith 1961, pp. 462–463, 468, 472; Henderson 1961, pp. 215–217; Landes 1965a, p. 449; Landes 1969, p. 236; League of Nations 1945, p. 130; Lyashchenko 1949, pp. 487, 493–494; Mitchell 1976, p. 355; Portal 1965, pp. 810, 815–817, 820–823

Table A6 (continued)

Description of Category	Country and Period	Sources
	Spain 1890-1914(-)	Lincke 1911, pp. 172-173; Mitchell 1976, p. 357; Nadal 1973, p. 618
	Sweden 1870-1890(+)	Dahmén 1970, pp. 16-22; Heckscher 1954, pp. 219, 226; Hildebrand 1960, pp. 279, 280; Jörberg 1965, pp. 24-26, 33; Jörberg 1969, p. 277; Landes 1965a, p. 449; League of Nations 1945, p. 130; Mitchell 1976, pp. 355, 800, 803; Paige et al. 1961, appendix p. 8; Patel 1963, p. 70; Thomas 1941, pp. 112, 113, 116-123, 128
Category E Countries where small beginnings of industrial expansion involved primarily factory processing of natural products with sometimes also very small beginnings of factory consumer goods production.	Australia 1830-1850, 1850-1870(+)	Cotter 1970, p. 248; Shaw 1946, pp. 77-78, 268, 269; Sinclair 1976, pp. 44-45, 54-55, 79, 83; Thompson 1970, p. 87
	Brazil 1870-1890	Burns 1970, pp. 146, 258-260; Jobim 1944, pp. 198, 199; Wythe 1955, pp. 70, 160
	Burma 1870-1890(-)?, 1890-1914	Gadgil [India] 1942, pp. 151, 154; Hlaing 1964, pp. 101-107, 137; Levin 1960, p. 212; Resnick 1970, pp. 57, 58

Table A6 (continued)

Description of Category	Country and Period	Sources
	Canada 1830–1850, 1850–1870	Firestone 1958, p. 221; Firestone 1960, pp. 224–230, 235; Jones 1946, p. 308; Marr and Paterson 1980, p. 22; Tucker 1936, pp. 8, 21, 23
	China 1870–1890(–), 1890–1914	Allen 1965, pp. 874, 901; Clark 1932, pp. 78–79; Cowan 1964, p. 84; Eckstein et al. 1968, pp. 3–4; Fairbank et al. 1960, p. 19; Hou 1965, pp. 278, 286; King 1965, pp. 14–19; Tawney 1932, pp. 111, 196
	Denmark 1830–1850, 1850–1870	Glamann 1960, p. 22; Hansen 1970, pp. 8, 11, 14; Hornby 1969, p. 26; Jörberg 1973, pp. 408–411; Youngson 1959, pp. 199, 200, 217
	Egypt 1830–1850, 1870–1890, 1890–1914	Commission du Commerce et de l'Industrie 1966, pp. 452–453; Crouchley 1938, p. 135; Grunwald and Ronall 1960, p. 183; Hershlag 1964, pp. 122–123; Issawi 1966a, pp. 365, 372; McCoan 1877, pp. 287–289; Owen 1969, p. 295
	India 1850–1870, 1870–1890, 1890–1914(+)	Allen 1965, pp. 910–913; Bisht and Namboodripad 1965, p. 201; Buchanan 1934, pp. 136–139, 297; Chandra 1966, pp. 61, 71–72; Fukazawa 1965, pp. 227, 228; Gadgil 1942, pp. 71, 74–75, 114–116,

Table A6 (continued)

Description of Category	Country and Period	Sources
		184, 197; Maddison 1970, pp. 65-66; Sarkar 1917, pp. 40, 193; Sen 1966, pp. 31, 34, 44, 51; Sundara Rajan 1955, p. 121
	Italy 1830-1850, 1850-1870	Clough 1964, pp. 89, 90; Fenoaltea 1968, p. 146; Landes 1965a, p. 449; Luzzatto 1969, pp. 221, 222; Mitchell 1976, pp. 355, 799, 802; Neufeld 1961, pp. 536, 539; Seton-Watson 1967, p. 18; Mack Smith 1959, p. 153
	Netherlands 1830-1850, 1850-1870	Brugmans 1969, pp. 68-70; Dhondt and Brunier 1973, pp. 35-36; Eyck [Germany] 1950, p. 63; de Jonge 1968, pp. 90, 106, 167, 493, 495-496; Landes 1965a, p. 449
	Norway 1830-1850, 1850-1870	Drachmann 1915, pp. 95-96; Drake 1969, pp. 79-81; Hodne 1975, p. 256; Johnsen 1939, pp. 516-518, 520; Lieberman 1970, pp. 118, 122, 128-129; Mitchell 1976, p. 800; Nielsen [Denmark] 1933, pp. 469, 542; Soltow 1965, p. 6
	Russia 1830-1850, 1850-1870	Blackwell 1968, pp. 42-45; Cole and Deane 1965, pp. 21-22; Goldsmith 1961, pp. 462-463; Henderson 1961, p.

Table A6 (continued)

Description of Category	Country and Period	Sources
		215; Landes 1965a, p. 449; Lyashchenko 1949, p. 486; Mitchell 1976, p. 355; Portal 1965, pp. 808–810
	Spain 1830–1850, 1850–1870, 1870–1890?	Carr 1966, pp. 390–392; Higgin 1886, pp. 66, 70; Landes 1965a, p. 449; Nadal 1973, pp. 614, 615, 618; Nadal 1975, pp. 196, 207; Vicens Vives and Nadal Oller 1969, pp. 666, 670–678, 688–689
	Sweden 1830–1850, 1850–1870	Dahmén 1970, p. 20,; Hildebrand 1960, pp. 279–280; Hovde 1943, 1:241, 252, 258–259; Janson 1931, pp. 80, 355; Landes 1965a, p. 449; Mitchell 1976, pp. 355, 800, 803; Söderlund 1952, p. 108; Youngson 1959, p. 157
Category F Countries where industrial expansion involved primarily the growth of hand-manufactures or artisan industry. Included in this category are countries where, in addition, a very few factories were built for the export sector.	Argentina 1850–1870	Cole and Deane 1965, p. 39; Ferns 1960, p. 363; Pendle 1955, p. 62; Scobie 1964a, pp. 177–179; Wythe 1949, pp. 82, 83
	Brazil 1850–1870	Burns 1970, p. 146; Graham 1968, p. 14; Joblim 1944, pp. 198, 199; Wythe 1955, p. 70

Table A6 (continued)

Description of Category	Country and Period	Sources
	Burma 1850–1870	Gadgil [India] 1942, p. 107; Hlaing 1964, pp. 101–107, 137; Tun Wai 1961, pp. 38–39
	China 1830–1850, 1850–1870	Allen 1965, pp. 874, 901; Eckstein et al. 1968, pp. 3–4; Hou 1965, pp. 278, 286; Tawney 1932, pp. 111, 196
	Egypt 1850–1870	Crouchley 1938, p. 135; Issawi 1966a, pp. 365, 372; McCoan 1877, pp. 287–289
	Japan 1830–1850?, 1850–1870	Lockwood 1954, p. 17; Rosovsky 1966, p. 99; Smith 1959, pp. 78–80
	New Zealand 1850–1870	Condliffe 1959, p. 39; Lloyd Prichard 1970, pp. 76, 100–102, 148, 402; Simkin 1951, pp. 124, 137; Sutch 1969, p. 99
Category G Countries where the growth of industry was insignificant.	Argentina 1830–1850	Cole and Deane 1965, p. 39; Ferns 1960, p. 363; Pendle 1955, p. 62; Scobie 1964a, pp. 177–179; Wythe 1949, pp. 82–83
	Brazil 1830–1850	Jobim 1944, pp. 198–199; Wythe 1955, p. 70

Table A6 (continued)

Description of Category	Country and Period	Sources
	Burma 1830-1850?	Gadgil [India] 1942, p. 107; Hlaing 1964, pp. 101-107, 137; Tun Wai 1961, pp. 38-39
	India 1830-1850	Gadgil 1942, p. 184; Maddison 1970, pp. 64-65; Sen 1966, p. 31
	New Zealand 1830-1850	Lloyd Prichard 1970, pp. 43, 60; Sutch 1969, p. 99

Notes: This table provides classifications of countries and periods for both the unlagged and lagged indicators of the rate of improvement in techniques in industry. The classifications for the unlagged variable refer to the periods 1850-1870, 1870-1890, and 1890-1914. Those for the lagged variable refer to the periods 1830-1850, 1850-1870, and 1870-1890.

Of the sources in this table, the following are listed in the general section of the bibliography: Bogart 1942, Cole and Deane 1965, Clough and Cole 1946, Gerschenkron 1962a and 1968, Glass and Grebenick 1965, Hague 1963, Henderson 1961, Hughes 1970, Landes 1965a and 1969, League of Nations 1945, Maddison 1970, Minchinton 1973, Mitchell 1976, and Patel 1963. Lincke [Switzerland] 1911 is listed for several countries other than Switzerland; by exception, its location in the Switzerland section of the bibliography is not noted each time it appears as a source for another country.

Table A7

Classification Scheme for Level of Development of Techniques in Agriculture, 1850, 1870, 1890

Description of Category	Country and Year	Sources
Category A Countries in which farms probably producing the greater part of the value of national output of cereals, rice, and livestock products used (1) animal-drawn cast-iron or steel plows and animal-drawn harvesting machinery; (2) enclosures and some systematic stock-breeding in the production of animals; (3) improved crop rotations as indicated by the production of clover and/or beet crops and the absence of fallow, and a significant amount of natural fertilizer, but very little chemical fertilizer. In addition, in these countries, the individual farms using improvements typically practiced some degree of mixed crop and animal farming. Countries are classified A+ if the level of mechanization is unusually	Belgium 1890 (-)	Bublot 1957, pp. 221-224, 235; Dechesne 1932, pp. 469-471; Rowntree 1910, pp. 178-182; van Houtte 1943, pp. 143-144
	Germany 1890	Bogart 1942, pp. 278, 280-283; Clapham 1936, pp. 215-220; Cole and Deane 1965, p. 16; Hoffmann 1963, pp. 101-103
	Great Britain 1870, 1890(+)	Chambers and Mingay 1966, pp. 189-190; Clapham 1932, pp. 268-276; Clapham 1938, pp. 89-90; Collins 1969, pp. 74, 75; Ernle 1936, pp. 387-392
	Netherlands 1890 (-)	Brugmans 1961, pp. 288, 289
	Sweden 1890	Andersson 1956, pp. 12-13; Jörberg 1969, p. 265; Montgomery 1939, pp. 154-155
	United States 1870(-), 1890	Danhof 1951, pp. 140-143; Rogin 1931, pp. 91-95, 118-125, 175-176, 198-199

Table A7 (continued)

Description of Category	Country and Year	Sources
high. They are classified A— if high-yield intensive agriculture predominates and there are harvesting machines only on large farms.		
Category B Countries in which farms producing a significant portion of, but probably not the greater part of, the value of national output of cereals, rice, and livestock products used the types of improvements listed in Category A. Excluded from this category, however, are countries meeting these criteria in which improvements are limited to a geographically extremely restricted part of the agricultural sector or to the production of only one or two types of output.	Belgium 1870	Bublot 1957, pp. 213, 219–221, 235; Dechesne 1932, pp. 454–455; de Lavaleye 1870, pp. 249–251; van Houtte 1943, pp. 143–144
	Canada 1890(−)	Easterbrook and Aitken 1956, pp. 402–405, 482–486; Jones 1946, pp. 309–317; Youngson 1965, pp. 185, 196–197
	Denmark 1870(−), 1890	Jensen 1937, pp. 168–171, 261–262, 264–265; Tracy 1964, pp. 108–112; Youngson 1959, pp. 202–213
	France 1870(−), 1890	Barral 1979, pp. 360–361; Clapham 1936, p. 170; Laurent 1976b, pp. 672–674, 678–684; Marczewski 1965, pp. liv–lv
	Germany 1870	Clapham 1936, p. 215; Hoffmann 1963, pp. 101–103

Table A7 (continued)

Description of Category	Country and Year	Sources
	Great Britain 1850(+)	Clough and Cole 1946, pp. 425–427; Ernle 1936, chap. 17; Orwin and Whetham 1964, pp. 3–11
	Japan 1890	Nakamura 1966, pp. 251–269, 291–295; Sawada 1965, pp. 339–340
	Netherlands 1870(−)	Brugmans 1961, p. 254
	Sweden 1870	Østerud 1978, pp. 162–163
	Switzerland 1870(−), 1890	Chuard 1901, pp. 28–45; Hauser 1974, pp. 603–606
	United States 1850	Danhof 1951, pp. 139–140; Rogin 1931, pp. 24–26, 34, 75–79, 83
Category C Countries in which improved crop rotation schemes and/or irrigation schemes (as appropriate) and some use of natural fertilizers were widespread in the agricultural sector but in which the other classes of improvements listed in Category A were negligible. Excluded from this category	Belgium 1850	Bublot 1957, pp. 219–221
	Denmark 1850	Hansen 1976, pp. 142–144; Jensen 1937, pp. 168–169; Youngson 1959, pp. 194–195
	France 1850	Laurent 1976b, pp. 672–674, 678–682
	Germany 1850(−)	Clapham 1936, pp. 214–217; Hoffmann 1963, pp. 101–103

Table A7 (continued)

Description of Category	Country and Year	Sources
are countries meeting these criteria which had extremely high ratios of population to cultivated land in the agricultural sector as indicated by descriptive statements giving evidence of negligible returns to labor at the intensive margin, extremely high population density, and/or pervasive underemployment in the agricultural sector.	Japan 1850(-), 1870(-)	Hayami et al. 1975, p. 70; Smith 1959, pp. 92-97, 211
	Netherlands 1850	de Jonge 1968, pp. 20-23
	Sweden 1850	Janson 1931, p. 76; Montgomery 1939, pp. 58-59; Østerud 1978, p. 162
	Switzerland 1850	Bergier 1968, pp. 54-55; Chuard 1901, pp. 26-27, 51-52; Hauser 1974, pp. 599-602
Category D Countries in which the production of only one or two types of output, and/or production in one or two very restricted regions, was characterized by the use of the first three types of improvements listed in Category A (as appropriate to their products), while the predominant part of the agricultural sector (as judged by both area of cultivated	Argentina 1890(-)	Díaz Alejandro 1970, pp. 143-145; Ferrer 1967, p. 100; Wythe et al. 1949, pp. 80-81
	Australia 1870(-), 1890	Cotter 1970, pp. 120-121; Fitzpatrick 1969, pp. 66-67; Shaw 1946, pp. 84-86
	Canada 1870	Hamelin and Roby 1971, pp. 193-195; Jones 1946, pp. 309-317; Morton 1949, p. 320
	Egypt 1890(-)	Issawi 1966a, p. 364; O'Brien 1966, p. 4

Table A7 (continued)

Description of Category	Country and Year	Sources
land and population) was characterized by the absence of these improvements. Countries meeting these criteria in which the ratio of cultivated land to the agricultural labor force was extremely high are classified D+; those in which it was extremely low are classified D-.	Italy 1890(-)	Cohen 1972, p. 88; Foerster 1919, pp. 82, 115-119
	New Zealand 1890	Gould [Australia] 1976, p. 19; Scholefield 1909, p. 180
	Norway 1890	Hodne 1975, pp. 150, 156-158; Johnsen 1939, pp. 498-502
Category E Countries in which the use of the first three types of improvements listed in Category A was not significant, but in which either (1) one or two crops or a very restricted geographical area were characterized by large-scale production using improvements based upon a substantial division of labor (without machinery); or (2) improved rotations and diversification of commercial crops by individual farmers	Brazil 1890	Clark 1957, fn. p. 302; Graham 1968, pp. 29-31
	Burma 1890	Furnivall 1931, pp. 74ff., 98-99; Wickizer and Bennett 1941, p. 256
	Italy 1850, 1870	Luzzatto 1969, pp. 218-219; Neufeld 1961, p. 20; Zangheri 1969, pp. 36-37
	Norway 1850(-), 1870	Johnsen 1939, p. 501; Lieberman 1970, pp. 58-59, 74-75
	Russia 1890	Dobb 1948, pp. 40-43; Gerschenkron 1965, pp. 777-778; Lyashchenko 1949, p. 465

Table A7 (continued)

Description of Category	Country and Year	Sources
characterized some significant regions of the country; and (3) the ratio of cultivated land to the agricultural labor force was not extremely unfavorable as shown by the absence, in at least some major regions, of widespread indications of negligible returns to labor at the intensive margin of cultivation and the absence of indications that cultivable land was unavailable.	Spain 1870, 1890	Higgin 1886, pp. 86-87, 94, 99
Category F Countries in which there was not significant use of the four classes of improvements listed in Category A, but in which the ratio of cultivated land to the agricultural force was very favorable as indicated by evidence on the widespread existence of a surplus above subsistence, lack of famine, and possibilities for relatively easy acquisition of land.	Argentina 1850, 1870(+)	Brown 1979, pp. 140-143; Rennie 1945, p. 76; Scoble 1964a, pp. 85-86; Scoble 1964b, p. 35
	Australia 1850	Cotter 1970, p. 120; McGhee 1970, p. 148; Morrissey 1970, p. 105
	Brazil 1850, 1870	Graham 1968, pp. 10-13
	Burma 1850, 1870	Furnivall 1931, p. 43
	Canada 1850	Burt 1944, pp. 136-137; Jones 1946, pp. 61, 196; Jones 1967, passim; Létourneau 1950, pp. 113-114

Table A7 (continued)

Description of Category	Country and Year	Sources
	New Zealand 1850, 1870	Condliffe 1959, pp. 140-143; Simkin 1951, p. 156
Category G Countries resembling those in Category F in that there was not significant use of the four classes of improvements listed in Category A, but the ratio of cultivated land to the agricultural labor force was either only moderately favorable or extremely unfavorable. Countries of the latter type are classified G-. Extremely unfavorable ratios of cultivated land in the agricultural labor force are judged to prevail where descriptive evidence indicates serious overpopulation, negligible returns to labor at the intensive margin of cultivation, and periodic famine.	China 1850(-), 1870(-), 1890(-)	Perkins et al. 1969, p. 70; Tawney 1932, pp. 27, 46-50
	Egypt 1850, 1870	McCoan 1877, chap. 12
	India 1850(-), 1870, 1890	Davis 1951, p. 209
	Russia 1850, 1870	von Haxthausen 1847, 1:127, 129, 235
	Spain 1850	Vicens Vives and Nadal Oller 1969, pp. 645-646

Note: Of the sources in this table, the following are listed in the general section of the bibliography: Bogart 1942, Clough and Cole 1946, Clark 1957, Cole and Deane 1965, Østerud 1978, and Tracy 1964.

Table A8

Classification Scheme for Rate of Improvement In Techniques In Agriculture, 1830–1850, 1850–1870, 1870–1890, 1890–1914

Description of Category	Country and Period	Sources
Category A Countries where agricultural productivity Improved significantly during the period primarily, but not exclusively, through a striking spread of varied types of labor-saving machinery such as harvesting machinery and threshers which were Introduced on most larger holdings and also on many (but not necessarily a majority of) small holdings. In most cases, there was also a major Increase In the use of fertilizer. The stock-raising countries in this category were characterized by major Improvements In fencing and a wider spread of stock-breeding.	Argentina 1890–1914	Ferber 1967, pp. 100–101
	Australla 1890–1914	McLean 1973, pp. 569–571
	Belglum 1890–1914	Bublot 1957, pp. 222–224; Chlepner 1945, p. 178
	Canada 1890–1914	Buckley 1955, pp. 22, 24; Hartland 1955, p. 19; Norrie 1975, p. 417
	Denmark 1890–1914	Jensen 1937, pp. 168–171
	Germany 1890–1914	Bogart 1942, pp. 278–283; Clapham 1936, pp. 216–218; Rolfes 1976, pp. 518–520
	United States 1870–1890?, 1890–1914	Rogin 1931, pp. 91–95, 118–125, 175–176
Category B Countries where agricultural productivity Improved significantly during the	Great Britain 1890–1914	Clapham 1938, pp. 89–90; Ernle 1936, pp. 386–391

Table A8 (continued)

Description of Category	Country and Period	Sources
period primarily, but not exclusively, through a striking spread of land-saving biochemical and organizational improvements or a major shift from cereals to mixed farming significantly raising the value of output per acre. As in Category A, these improvements spread to most larger holdings and also to many (but not necessarily a majority of) small holdings.	Japan 1890-1914	Landes 1965b, p. 163
	Netherlands 1890-1914	Brugmans 1961, pp. 308-309
	New Zealand 1890-1914(+)	Scholefield 1909, pp. 76-79, 152-153; Simkin 1951, pp. 174-175
	Switzerland 1870-1890(-), 1890-1914	Chuard 1901, pp. 28-41, 51; Hauser 1974, pp. 603-605
Category C Countries where agricultural productivity improved significantly during the period through the adoption of varied kinds of labor-saving machinery, but where, in contrast with Category A, the spread was almost exclusively to larger holdings. Also included in this category are countries where the spread of machinery to large farms was somewhat less complete, but	Belgium 1870-1890(-)	Bublot 1957, pp. 221-222; Dechesne 1932, pp. 467-469
	Canada 1870-1890	Hamelin and Roby 1971, pp. 193-197, 202; Jones 1946, p. 310; Norrie 1975, p. 417
	Denmark 1870-1890	Jensen 1937, pp. 264-265; Youngson 1959, pp. 203-208
	France 1870-1890(-), 1890-1914	Barral 1979, pp. 360-361; Bogart 1942, pp. 299-301; Laurent 1976b, pp. 681-682

Table A8 (continued)

Description of Category	Country and Period	Sources
where there was a wide spread of improved rotations.	Germany 1850–1870, 1870–1890	Cole and Deane 1965, p. 16; Haushofer 1963, chaps. 2–3
	Sweden 1890–1914	Menzel 1980c
	United States 1830–1850, 1850–1870	Danhof 1951, pp. 139–140; Rogin 1931, pp. 24–26, 34, 75–76, 79
Category D		
Category D includes several kinds and mixes of moderate improvements in agricultural productivity during the period but not in all major regions. Three groups of countries are included: (1) countries (classified D+) where a mixture of labor-saving and land-saving improvements spread to most, but by no means all, larger holdings. These countries differ from those in Category C in that only one or two types of machinery—usually improved plows—were involved and a	Australia 1870–1890(+)	McLean 1973, pp. 569–570
	Belgium 1830–1850?, 1850–1870(+)	Bublot 1957, pp. 220–221
	Canada 1850–1870(–)	Hamelin and Roby 1971, pp. 197, 201
	Denmark 1830–1850, 1850–1870	Hansen 1976, pp. 142–144; Youngson 1959, pp. 194–195
	France 1830–1850, 1850–1870(–)	Clapham 1936, p. 170; Kindleberger 1964, pp. 211–213; Knowles 1932, p. 57; Laurent 1976b, pp. 672–674, 681
	Germany 1830–1850	Clapham 1936, pp. 214–217; Franz 1976, pp. 307–314

Table A8 (continued)

Description of Category	Country and Period	Sources
significant minority of larger holdings were not affected; (2) countries (classified D) where improvements in productivity were mainly, though not exclusively, land-saving—for example, improved drainage and rotations. These countries differ from those in Category B either in that the improvements affected almost exclusively larger holdings or in the slow pace of improvements. (Also, not all major regions saw improvements.) Machinery improvements, where they occurred, mainly involved better plows; (3) countries (classified D-) where the use of machinery spread to a small proportion of larger holdings and where, unlike the case of D+ countries, land-saving improvements were quite limited.	Great Britain 1830-1850(+), 1850-1870(+)	Chambers and Mingay 1966, p. 189; Clapham 1932, pp. 268-275; Ernle 1936, pp. 364-376
	Japan 1830-1850(-), 1850-1870(-), 1870-1890	Ohkawa and Rosovsky 1965, p. 67; Sawada 1965, pp. 340-343; Smith 1959, pp. 92-105
	Netherlands 1830-1850, 1850-1870(-), 1870-1890(-)	Brugmans 1961, pp. 254, 292-295; de Jonge 1968, pp. 20-23
	New Zealand 1870-1890(-)	Condliffe 1959, p. 143; Gould [Australia] 1976, p. 19; Scholefield 1909, p. 180; Simkin 1951, pp. 174-175
	Norway 1890-1914	Johnsen 1939, pp. 498-503
	Sweden 1830-1850, 1850-1870(-), 1870-1890(+)	Janson 1931, p. 76; Jörberg 1961, p. 10; Jörberg 1969, pp. 263-265; Youngson 1959, p. 173
	Switzerland 1830-1850, 1850-1870(+)	Chuard 1901, pp. 26-45, 51-52; Hauser 1974, pp. 599-606

Table A8 (continued)

Description of Category	Country and Period	Sources
Category E Countries where the improvements described in Category D occurred in one major region; or improvements were limited to the production of only a single crop; or very small improvements took place over a fairly large geographic area.	Australia 1850–1870(+)	Barnard 1958, pp. 14–17
	Brazil 1870–1890, 1890–1914	Clark 1957, p. 302; Graham 1968, pp. 29–31
	Burma 1870–1890(–), 1890–1914	Andrus 1947, pp. 17–18; Furnivall 1931, pp. 74ff., 93, 99
	Canada 1830–1850	Easterbrook and Aiken 1956, p. 279
	Egypt 1870–1890(–), 1890–1914	Issawi 1966a, p. 364; O'Brien 1966, pp. 4–7; Owen 1969, pp. 143, 253–254
	Great Britain 1870–1890	Clapham 1970, pp. 83–84, 88–90; Ernle 1936, pp. 382–383
	India 1870–1890, 1890–1914	Bhatia 1965; Blynn 1966
	Italy 1890–1914(+)	Cohen 1972, p. 88; Foerster 1919, pp. 82, 115–116; Seton-Watson 1967, pp. 288–289
	Norway 1850–1870, 1870–1890(+)	Hodne 1975, pp. 150, 155–158; Johnsen 1939, pp. 498–502
	Russia 1870–1890, 1890–1914(+)	Dobb 1948, pp. 40–43; Gerschenkron 1965, p. 777; Lyashchenko 1949, p. 465

Table A8 (continued)

Description of Category	Country and Period	Sources
	Spain 1870–1890(–), 1890–1914	Madariaga 1930, pp. 157–158; Vicens Vives and Nadal Oller 1969, pp. 646–653
Category F Countries where improvements in agricultural productivity were negligible.	Argentina 1830–1850, 1850–1870(+), 1870–1890(+)	Díaz Alejandro 1970, p. 149; Ferrer 1967, p. 100; Scobie 1964b, pp. 35, 77, 85–86; Williams 1920, p. 27; Wythe 1949, pp. 80–81
	Australia 1830–1850	Cotter 1970, p. 120; McGhee 1970, p. 148
	Brazil 1830–1850, 1850–1870	Graham 1968, pp. 10–13
	Burma 1830–1850, 1850–1870	Furnivall 1931, p. 43
	China 1830–1850, 1850–1870, 1870–1890, 1890–1914	Hou 1963, p. 298; Perkins et al. 1969, p. 70
	Egypt 1830–1850, 1850–1870	McCoan 1877, chap. 12
	India 1830–1850, 1850–1870	Bhatia 1965, pp. 119–185 passim

Table A8 (continued)

Description of Category	Country and Period	Sources
	Italy 1830–1850, 1850–1870, 1870–1890	Eckaus 1961, p. 303; Luzzatto 1969, p. 219; Neufeld 1961, p. 20
	New Zealand 1830–1850, 1850–1870	Condliffe 1959, pp. 140–143; Simkin 1951, p. 156
	Norway 1830–1850	Lieberman 1970, pp. 58–59, 64–65, 74–75
	Russia 1830–1850, 1850–1870	von Haxthausen 1847, 1:127, 129, 235
	Spain 1830–1850, 1850–1870	Vicens Vives and Nadal Oller 1969, pp. 645–648

Notes: This table provides classifications of countries and periods for both the unlagged and lagged indicators of improvements in agricultural productivity. The classifications for the unlagged variable refer to the periods 1850–1870, 1870–1890, and 1890–1914. Those for the lagged variable refer to the periods 1830–1850, 1850–1870, and 1870–1890.

Of the sources in this table, the following are listed in the general section of the bibliography: Bogart 1942 and Cole and Deane 1965.

Table A9

Classification Scheme for Percentage of Labor Force in Agriculture, 1850, 1870, 1890

Description of Category	Country and Year
Category A Over 70 percent of labor force engaged in agriculture	China 1850, 1870, 1890 Japan 1850, 1870, 1890 Norway 1850 Russia 1850, 1870, 1890 Sweden 1850
Category B 61-70 percent of labor force engaged in agriculture	Brazil 1850, 1870, 1890 Burma 1850, 1870, 1890 Egypt 1850, 1870, 1890 Germany 1850 India 1850, 1870, 1890 Italy 1850 Spain 1850, 1870, 1890 Sweden 1870 United States 1850
Category C 51-60 percent of labor force engaged in agriculture	Canada 1850 Denmark 1850, 1870 France 1850 Italy 1870, 1890 New Zealand (including Maoris) 1850(-) Norway 1870 Sweden 1890 Switzerland 1850 United States 1870 Argentina 1850?
Category D 41-50 percent of labor force engaged in agriculture	Argentina 1870 Australia 1850? Belgium 1850 Canada 1870, 1890 Denmark 1890 France 1870, 1890 Germany 1870, 1890 Netherlands 1850 Norway 1890

Table A9 (continued)

Description of Category	Country and Year

	Switzerland 1870
	United States 1890
Category E 31–40 percent of labor force engaged in agriculture	Argentina 1890 Australia 1870 Belgium 1870 Netherlands 1870? New Zealand 1870, 1890 Switzerland 1890
Category F 21–30 percent of labor force engaged in agriculture	Australia 1890 Belgium 1890 Great Britain 1850 Netherlands 1890
Category G 20 percent or less of labor force engaged in agriculture	Great Britain 1870, 1890

Table A10

Percentage of Labor Force in Agriculture, 1850

Country	Estimate	Total or Active Population	Year of Estimate	Source
Argentina	Not available			
Australia	Not available			
Belgium	50.9	Active	1846	Bairoch 1968, p. 88
	51	Active	1846	Bairoch 1973, p. 468
	51	Total	1846	Chlepner 1956, p. 13
	45.6	Active	1856	Mulhall 1899, p. 431
Brazil	Not available			
Burma	Not available			
Canada	54	Active	1851	Firestone 1960, p. 229
China	Not available			
Denmark	58.3	Active	1834	Skrubbeltrang 1951, p. 91
	57.5	Total	1834	Bjerke 1955, p. 129
	55.2	Active	1845	Nielsen 1933, p. 542
	60	Active	1850	Bairoch 1973, p. 468
	49.4	Total	1850	Bairoch 1968, p. 91
	50	Active	1850	Cipolla 1974, p. 30
	54.4	Total	1855	Bjerke 1955, p. 129
	53.3	Active	1860	Nielsen 1933, p. 542

Table A10 (continued)

Country	Estimate	Total or Active Population	Year of Estimate	Source
Egypt	Not available			
France	50	Total	1850	Dovring 1965, p. 604
	52	Active	1850	Cipolla 1974, p. 30
	61.3	Total	1851	Mulhall 1899, p. 428
	51.7	Active	1856	Bairoch 1968, p. 97
	54	Active	1856	Bairoch 1973, p. 468
	51.4	Active	1856	Kindleberger 1964, p. 215
Germany	60	Total	1860	Hamerow 1969, p. 57
	52	Active	1861	Hoffmann 1963, p. 103
Great Britain	26	Active	1841	Bairoch 1973, p. 468
	15.5	Total	1850	Rowntree [Belgium] 1910, p. 214
	16	Active	1850	Checkland 1964, p. 215
	22.2	Active	1850	Clark 1957, p. 514
	27.6	Active (U.K.)	1850	Mulhall 1899, p. 420
	22	Active	1850	Cipolla 1974, p. 30
	21.9	Active	1850	Bairoch 1968, p. 99
	26.5	Active (U.K.)	1861	Feinstein 1972, table 131
India	Not available			
Italy	70	Active	1850	Dovring 1965, p. 609
	59.2	Active	1861	Neufeld 1961, p. 528
	62	Active	1860	U.S. Dept. of Commerce, Bureau of the Census [United States] 1966, p. 103
	75	Total	1862	Seton-Watson 1967, p. 284

Table A10 (continued)

Country	Estimate	Total or Active Population	Year of Estimate	Source
Japan	80	Active	1853	Miyamoto et al. 1965, p. 54
	80	Total	1860	Crawcour 1965, p. 25
Netherlands	53	Active	1849	Balroch 1973, p. 468
	40	Active	1849	Cole and Deane 1965, p. 13
	44	Active	1849	de Jonge 1968, p. 19
	44.2	Active	1849	Balroch 1968, p. 110
	37.4	Active	1859	Balroch 1968, p. 110
New Zealand	41.6[a]	Active (% of laborers)	1858	Simkin 1951, p. 122
	23.5[a]	Active	1861	Clark 1957, p. 517
	60[b]	Active	1850	Pool 1977; Simkin 1951
Norway	90	Total	1845	Semmingsen 1954, p. 179
	65	Active	1850	Cipolla 1974, p. 30
	66.6	Total	1865	Blegan 1931, p. 2
	60.8	Total	1865	Mulhall 1899, p. 431
	64.1	Total	1865	Lieberman 1970, p. 13
Russia	90	Active	1850	Cipolla 1974, p. 31
	90	Rural population	1850	Crisp 1976, p. 73
	82.4	Active	1867	Mulhall 1899, p. 429
Spain	70	Active	1850	Cipolla 1974, p. 30
	66.3	Active	1860	Balroch 1968, p. 93

Table A10 (continued)

Country	Estimate	Total or Active Population	Year of Estimate	Source
Sweden	80.9	Total	1840	Montgomery 1939, p. 61
	80	Total	1850	Dahmén 1970, p. 13
	65	Active	1850	Cipolla 1974, p. 30
	75	Active	1850	Youngson 1959, p. 175
	75	Active	1861	Cole and Deane 1965, p. 46
	64	Active	1860	Bairoch 1968, p. 115
	67	Active	1860	Bairoch 1973, p. 468
Switzerland	57.4	Active	1850	S.G.S.V. 1964, p. 139
	57.4	Active	1850	Bergier 1968, p. 58
United States	64	Active	1850	Bairoch 1968, p. 54
	65	Active	1850	Cipolla 1974, p. 30
	64.5	Active	1850	Clark 1957, p. 520
	65	Active	1850	Bairoch 1973, p. 468
	63	Active	1850	U.S. Dept. of Commerce, Bureau of the Census 1960, p. 74

Notes: Those countries for which quantitative estimates are not available are classified on the basis of estimates for later years together with qualitative information from a wide range of sources on changes in the importance of the agricultural labor force between 1850 and the earliest years for which estimates are available.

Of the sources in this table, the following are listed in the general section of the bibliography: Bairoch 1968 and 1973, Cipolla 1974, Clark 1957, Dovring 1965, Encyclopaedia Britannica 1910-1911, and Mulhall 1899.

Table A10 (continued)

a Does not include the Maoris.

b These percentages include the Maoris. On the basis of information in Pool 1977 and Simkin 1951, we assumed that approximately 40-45 percent of the Maoris were in the labor force and 70-80 percent of the Maori labor force was engaged in agriculture. These assumptions give the following range of estimates for the percentage of the total labor force in agriculture: 1850, 51-60 percent; 1870, 31-40 percent; 1890, 31-40 percent. Note that this affects our classification only in the earliest period, when the Maoris constituted the majority of the population.

Table A11

Percentage of Labor Force in Agriculture, 1870

Country	Estimate	Total or Active Population	Year of Estimate	Source
Argentina	41	Active	1869	Randall 1977a, p. 247
Australia	43.9	Active (plus mining)	1870	Clark 1957, p. 510
	38	Active	1870	Kuznets 1958, p. 143
Belgium	44.4	Active	1866	Bairoch 1968, p. 88
	35.6	Active	1880	Mulhall 1899, p. 431
Brazil	61.3	Active	1872	Bairoch 1968, p. 47
Burma	61	Active	1881	Hlaing 1964, p. 119
Canada	50	Active	1870	Firestone 1960, p. 229
	50	Active	1870	Kuznets 1958, p. 142
China	Not available			
Denmark	47.8	Active	1870	Bairoch 1968, p. 91
	52.3	Total	1870	Bjerke 1955, p. 129
	51.1	Active	1880	Nielsen 1933, p. 542
	46.9	Active	1880	Mulhall 1899, p. 431
Egypt	61.7	Total	1882	Nahas 1901, p. 130

Table A11 (continued)

Country	Estimate	Total or Active Population	Year of Estimate	Source
France	43	Active	1866	Clark 1957, p. 513
	49.8	Active	1866	Bairoch 1968, p. 97
	50	Total	1872	Mulhall 1899, p. 428
	49.3	Active	1876	Kindleberger 1964, p. 215
	48.8	Total	1881	Mulhall 1899, p. 428
	48	Active	1881	Tracy 1964, p. 38
Germany	50	Total	1850	Hamerow 1969, p. 57
	45	Total	1850	Dovring 1965, p. 605
	41.8	Active	1882	Mulhall 1899, p. 428
	43	Total	1882	Bogart 1942, p. 319
	46.7	Active	1882	Bairoch 1968, p. 84
	43	Active	1882	Tracy 1964, p. 38
	49	Active	1871	Hoffmann et al. 1965, p. 205
	47	Active	1882	Bairoch 1973, p. 468
Great Britain	15	Active	1870	Clark 1957, p. 514
	19.1	Active (U.K.)	1870	Mulhall 1899, p. 420
	15.3	Active	1870	Bairoch 1968, p. 99
	21.7	Active (U.K.)	1870	Feinstein 1972, table 131
	12	Active	1881	Tracy 1964, p. 38
India	50.7	Active	1881	Clark 1957, p. 515
	74	Active	1881	Thorner 1960, p. 224
	74	Active	1901	Thorner 1960, p. 224

Table A11 (continued)

Country	Estimate	Total or Active Population	Year of Estimate	Source
Italy	51	Active	1871	Clark 1957, p. 516
	64	Active	1871	Bairoch 1973, p. 468
	61	Active	1871	Bairoch 1968, p. 107
	54	Active	1870	Cole and Deane 1965, p. 26
	61.4	Active	1871	Neufeld 1961, p. 528
	56.8	Active	1881	Neufeld 1961, p. 528
	51.4	Active	1881	Bairoch 1968, p. 106
	45.8	Active	1881	Clark 1957, p. 516
Japan	76.4	Active	1870	Clark 1957, p. 516
	75-80	Active	1870	Ohkawa and Rosovsky 1965, p. 54
	84.9	Active	1872	Bairoch 1968, p. 74
	85	Active	1875	Nakamura 1966, p. 144
	82.3	Active	1880	Ohkawa 1957, p. 28
	82	Active	1880	Nakamura 1966, p. 144
Netherlands	Not available			
New Zealand	32.4[a]	Active (% of laborers)	1871	Simkin 1951, p. 135
	27.5[a]	Active	1874	Simkin 1951, p. 155
	30.5[a]	Active	1874	Clark 1957, p. 517
	31[a]	Active	1874	Kuznets 1958, p. 143
	37[b]	Active	1870	Pool 1977; Simkin 1951
Norway	26.8[c]	Active	1875	Bairoch 1968, p. 109
	58.7	Total	1875	Blegen 1931, p. 2
	48.8	Active	1875	Clark 1957, p. 517

Table A11 (continued)

Country	Estimate	Total or Active Population	Year of Estimate	Source
	50	Total	1875	Mulhall 1899, p. 431
	49	Active	1875	Kuznets 1958, p. 143
Russia	89	Total (% of peasants)	1872	Mulhall 1899, p. 429
Spain	70.3	Active	1877	Bairoch 1968, p. 92
Sweden	61	Active	1870	Bairoch 1968, p. 115
	55.5	Active	1870	Clark 1957, p. 518
	64	Active	1870	Kuznets 1958, p. 143
	72	Total	1870	Montgomery 1939, p. 61
	72	Total	1870	Drachmann 1915, p. 63
	61	Total	1880	Drachmann 1915, p. 63
Switzerland	41.4	Active	1870	Mulhall 1899, p. 431
	42.4	Active	1880	S.G.S.V. 1964, p. 139
	42.4	Active	1880	Bairoch 1968, p. 116
	32.7	Active	1880	Clark 1957, p. 519
	42	Active	1880	Bairoch 1973, p. 468
	40.1	Total	1880	Mulhall 1899, p. 431
United States	50.2	Active	1870	Bairoch 1968, p. 53
	50.8	Active	1870	Clark 1957, p. 520
	53	Active	1870	U.S. Dept. of Commerce, Bureau of the Census 1960, p. 74

Table A11 (continued)

Notes: Those countries for which quantitative estimates are not available are classified on the basis of estimates for later years together with qualitative information from a wide range of sources on changes in the importance of the agricultural labor force between 1870 and the earliest years for which estimates are available.

Of the sources in this table, the following are listed in the general section of the bibliography: Bairoch 1968 and 1973, Bogart 1942, Clark 1957, Cole and Deane 1965, Kuznets 1958, Mulhall 1899, and Tracy 1964.

a Does not include the Maoris.

b These percentages include the Maoris. On the basis of information in Pool 1977 and Simkin 1951, we assumed that approximately 40–45 percent of the Maoris were in the labor force and 70–80 percent of the Maori labor force was engaged in agriculture. These assumptions give the following range of estimates for the percentage of the total labor force in agriculture: 1850, 51–60 percent; 1870, 31–40 percent; 1890, 31–40 percent. Note that this affects our classification only in the earliest period, when the Maoris constituted the majority of the population.

c This estimate does not include servants working in agriculture (see Bairoch 1968).

Table A12

Percentage of Labor Force in Agriculture, 1890

Country	Estimate	Total or Active Population	Year of Estimate	Source
Argentina	39.2	Active	1900	Díaz Alejandro 1970, p. 8
Australia	26.5	Active	1890	Clark 1957, p. 510
	23.3	Active	1890	Butlin 1964, p. 196
	30.7	Active	1890	Fitzpatrick 1949, p. 197
	25	Active	1900	Cipolla 1974, p. 31
	32	Active	1901	Bairoch 1968, p. 121
Belgium	32	Active	1890	Bairoch 1968, p. 87
	18.2	Active	1890	Clark 1957, p. 511
	26	Active	1895	Rowntree 1910, p. 214
	27	Active	1900	Cipolla 1974, p. 30
Brazil	64.6	Active	1900	Bairoch 1968, p. 47
Burma	Not available			
Canada	43.5	Active	1890	Firestone 1960, p. 229
	45.7	Active	1891	Urquhart and Buckley 1965, p. 59
	42	Active	1900	Cipolla 1974, p. 30
	42	Active	1900	Firestone 1960, p. 229
	43.6	Active	1901	Clark 1957, p. 511
China	Not available			

Table A12 (continued)

Country	Estimate	Total or Active Population	Year of Estimate	Source
Denmark	44.8	Active	1890	Bairoch 1968, p. 87
	45.9	Total	1890	Bjerke 1955, p. 129
	45.9	Active	1890	Nielsen 1933, p. 542
	42.4	Active	1900	Clark 1957, p. 512
	46.6	Active	1901	Bairoch 1968, p. 87
	41.1	Active	1901	Nielsen 1933, p. 542
Egypt	63.8	Total	1897	Nahas 1901, p. 130
	70.3	Active	1907	Clark 1957, p. 512
France	47	Active	1886	Bairoch 1968, p. 97
	45	Total	1891	Tracy 1964, p. 38
	45.3	Active	1896	Kindleberger 1964, p. 215
	42	Active	1900	Cipolla 1974, p. 30
	33	Active	1901	Clark 1957, p. 513
Germany	43	Active	1890	Hoffmann et al. 1965, p. 205
	41	Active	1895	Tracy 1964, p. 38
	35.5	Total	1895	Dovring 1965, p. 605
	39.9	Active	1895	Bairoch 1968, p. 83
	36	Total	1895	Bogart 1942, p. 319
	35	Active	1895	Cipolla 1974, p. 30
Great Britain	10.4	Active	1890	Clark 1957, p. 514
	10.7	Active	1890	Bairoch 1968, p. 99
	15.3	Active (U.K.)	1890	Feinstein 1972, table 131
	5.1	Total	1901	Rowntree [Belgium] 1910, p. 214
	8	Total	1901	Tracy 1964, p. 38

Table A12 (continued)

Country	Estimate	Total or Active Population	Year of Estimate	Source
India	61	Total	1890	Pillai 1925, p. 59
	61.7	Total	1891	Chakrabarti et al. 1965, p. 45
	66.5	Total	1901	Chakrabarti et al. 1965, p. 45
	62.4	Active	1901	Sinha 1965, p. 113
	73	Total	1901	Sarkar 1917, p. 59
	67.1	Active	1901	Bairoch 1968, p. 70
Italy	58.8	Active	1901	Bairoch 1968, p. 106
	48.9	Active	1901	Clark 1957, p. 516
	59.8	Active	1901	Neufeld 1961, p. 527
Japan	67	Active	1887	Clark 1957, p. 516
	76.1	Active	1890	Ohkawa 1957, p. 28
	76.1	Active	1890	Bairoch 1968, p. 74
	76	Active	1890	Nakamura 1966, p. 144
	71	Active	1900	Cipolla 1974, p. 30
Netherlands	32.9	Active	1889	Bairoch 1968, p. 110
	28.5	Active	1899	Clark 1957, p. 517
New Zealand	27.2[a]	Active	1891	Simkin 1951, p. 155
	30.1[a]	Active	1891	Clark 1957, p. 517
	36.2[a]	Active	1896	Bairoch 1968, p. 123
	28.3[a]	Active	1896	Simkin 1951, p. 155
	38.5	Active	1896	Condliffe 1930, p. 226
	35[b]	Active	1890	Pool 1977; Simkin 1951
	30	Active	1900	Cipolla 1974, p. 30

Table A12 (continued)

Country	Estimate	Total or Active Population	Year of Estimate	Source
Norway	49.6	Active	1890	Balroch 1968, p. 109
	48.7	Total	1890	Blegen 1931, p. 2
	30	Active	1890	Clark 1957, p. 517
	41	Active	1900	Cipolla 1974, p. 30
Russia	75	Total	1897	Cole and Deane 1965, p. 20
	58.6c	Active	1897	Balroch 1968, p. 119
	85	Active	1900	Cipolla 1974, p. 31
Spain	69.4	Active	1887	Balroch 1968, p. 92
	69	Active	1887	Clark 1957, p. 518
	68	Active	1900	Cipolla 1974, p. 30
Sweden	59.2	Active	1890	Balroch 1968, p. 114
	49.2	Active	1890	Clark 1957, p. 518
	61	Active	1890	Cole and Deane 1965, p. 46
	62.1	Total	1890	Montgomery 1939, p. 141
	56	Total	1899	Drachmann 1915, p. 63
	54	Active	1900	Cipolla 1974, p. 36
Switzerland	36.4	Active	1888	Hunold 1954, p. 9
	37.4	Active	1888	S.G.S.V. 1964, p. 139
	37.4	Active	1888	Bergier 1968, p. 58
	27.1	Active	1900	Clark 1957, p. 519
	34.6	Active	1900	Balroch 1968, p. 116
	35	Active	1900	Cipolla 1974, p. 30

Table A12 (continued)

Country	Estimate	Total or Active Population	Year of Estimate	Source
United States	42.8	Active	1890	Bairoch 1968, p. 53
	43.1	Active	1890	Clark 1957, p. 520
	42	Active	1890	U.S. Dept. of Commerce, Bureau of the Census 1960, p. 74
	38	Active	1900	Cipolla 1974, p. 30

Notes: Those countries for which quantitative estimates are not available are classified on the basis of estimates for later years together with qualitative information from a wide range of sources on changes in the importance of the agricultural labor force between 1890 and the earliest years for which estimates are available.

Of the sources in this table, the following are listed in the general section of the bibliography: Bairoch 1968, Bogart 1942, Cipolla 1974, Clark 1957, Cole and Deane 1965, Dovring 1965, and Tracy 1964.

[a] Does not include the Maoris.

[b] These percentages include the Maoris. On the basis of information in Pool 1977 and Simkin 1951, we assumed that approximately 40-45 percent of the Maoris were in the labor force and 70-80 percent of the Maori labor force was engaged in agriculture. These assumptions give the following range of estimates for the percentage of the total labor force in agriculture: 1850, 51-60 percent; 1870, 31-40 percent; 1890, 31-40 percent. Note that this affects our classification only in the earliest period, when the Maoris constituted the majority of the population.

[c] Excludes family workers in agriculture (see Bairoch 1968, p. 119).

Table A13

Percentage of Labor Force in Agriculture, 1914

Country	Estimate	Total or Active Population	Year of Estimate	Source
Argentina	23.6	Active	1914	Clark 1957, p. 510
	26	Active	1914	Randall 1977a, p. 247
	16.8	Active	1919	Bairoch 1968, p. 37
Australia	24.8	Active	1911	Clark 1957, p. 510
	30.4	Active	1911	Fitzpatrick 1969, p. 197
	24.2	Active	1911	Bairoch 1968, p. 121
Belgium	23.2	Active	1910	Bairoch 1968, p. 88
	17.6	Active	1910	Clark 1957, p. 511
	16	Active	1910	Chlepner 1956, p. 109
Brazil	70.5	Active	1920	Bairoch 1968, p. 47
	67.9	Active	1940	Clark 1957, p. 511
	61	Active	1950	Cipolla 1974, p. 30
Burma	73	Active	1931	Hlaing 1964, p. 119
Canada	34.2	Active	1911	Urquhart and Buckley 1965, p. 59
	40	Active	1911	Clark 1957, p. 511
	37.1	Active	1914	Bairoch 1968, p. 48
China	75	Rural as % of total	1930	Remer 1968, p. 24
	75	Rural as % of total	1930	Condliffe 1932, p. 19

Table A13 (continued)

Country	Estimate	Total or Active Population	Year of Estimate	Source
Denmark	37.3	Active	1911	Clark 1957, p. 512
	41.7	Active	1911	Balroch 1968, p. 87
	36.1	Total	1911	Bjerke 1955, p. 129
Egypt	64.1	Active	1917	Clark 1957, p. 512
France	43	Active	1906	Tracy 1964, p. 38
	30.1	Active	1911	Clark 1957, p. 513
	41.7	Active	1911	Kindleberger 1964, p. 215
	41	Active	1911	Balroch 1968, p. 96
	43	Active	1913	Friedlaender and Oser 1953, p. 210
Germany	29	Total	1907	Bogart 1942, p. 319
	36.8	Active	1907	Balroch 1968, p. 83
	34.5	Active	1913	Hoffmann et al. 1965, p. 205
Great Britain	7.8	Active	1911	Clark 1957, p. 514
	8.8	Active	1911	Balroch 1968, p. 98
	11.5	Active (U.K.)	1911	Feinstein 1972, T131
India	71.9	Active	1911	Balroch 1968, p. 70
	75	Active (males)	1911	Thorner 1960, p. 224
	68.2	Active	1911	Clark 1957, p. 515
	71	Total	1911	Pillai 1925, p. 59
	72.2	Total	1911	Chakrabarti et al. 1965, p. 45
	76	Active (males)	1921	Thorner 1960, p. 224

Table A13 (continued)

Country	Estimate	Total or Active Population	Year of Estimate	Source
Italy	45.4	Active	1911	Clark 1957, p. 516
	57	Total	1911	Seton-Watson 1967, p. 284
	55.4	Active	1911	Bairoch 1968, p. 106
	56.1	Active	1911	Neufeld 1961, p. 527
Japan	63	Active	1910	Bairoch 1968, p. 73
	48	Active	1912	Clark 1957, p. 516
	59.2	Active	1914	Ohkawa et al. 1957, p. 28
	59	Active	1915	Nakamura 1966, p. 144
Netherlands	24.7	Active	1909	Clark 1957, p. 517
	29.4	Active	1909	Bairoch 1968, p. 110
	21.1	Active	1920	Clark 1957, p. 517
New Zealand	26.1	Active	1911	Bairoch 1968, p. 123
	27.9	Active	1916	Clark 1957, p. 517
	31	Active	1916	Condliffe 1930, p. 226
Norway	39.5	Active	1910	Bairoch 1968, p. 109
	27.9	Active	1916	Clark 1957, p. 517
	35.6	Total	1920	Lieberman 1970, p. 13
Russia	66.6	Total	1913	Crisp 1976, p. 5
	82	Active	1926	Bairoch 1973, p. 468
	86.1	Active	1926	Bairoch 1968, p. 119

Table A13 (continued)

Country	Estimate	Total or Active Population	Year of Estimate	Source
Spain	56.3	Active	1910	Bairoch 1968, p. 92
	71.1	Active	1910	Nadal 1973, p. 616
	67	Active	1910	Clark 1957, p. 518
Sweden	46.2	Active	1910	Bairoch 1968, p. 114
	40.8	Active	1910	Clark 1957, p. 518
	48.8	Active	1910	Montgomery 1939, p. 141
	48	Active	1911	Cole and Deane 1965, p. 46
Switzerland	25.6	Active	1910	Bairoch 1968, p. 116
	25.7	Active	1910	Hunold 1954, p. 9
	26.8	Active	1910	S.G.S.V. 1964, p. 139
	22.4	Active	1910	Clark 1957, p. 519
	26.8	Active	1910	Bergier 1968, p. 59
United States	31.6	Active	1910	Bairoch 1968, p. 53
	32	Active	1910	Clark 1957, p. 520
	31	Active	1910	U.S. Dept. of Commerce, Bureau of the Census 1960, p. 74

Notes: The data in this table are not utilized in our study. They are provided for the interest of the reader.

Of the sources in this table, the following are listed in the general section of the bibliography: Bairoch 1968 and 1973, Bogart 1942, Cipolla 1974, Clark 1957, Cole and Deane 1965, Friedlaender and Oser 1953, and Tracy 1964.

Table A14

Relative Abundance of Agricultural Resources, 1850, 1870, 1890

Country	Total Land Area In Thousands of sq. kms.[a]	Standard Farmland In Thousands of sq. kms.[a]	Population per sq. km. of Standard Farmland[b] 1850	1870	1890	Classification in Ranking Scheme of Five Categories[c] 1850	1870	1890
Argentina	2,793	812	1.5	2.1	4.9	A	A	A
Australia	7,704	1,532	.3	1.1	2.0	A	A	A
Belgium	30	28	155.9	172.4	216.8	E	E	E
Brazil	8,511	8,867	.8	1.1	1.6	A	A	A
Burma[d]	384	384	20.8	20.9	25.5	A	C	C
Canada	9,350	4,752	.5	.8	1.0	A	A	A[e]
China	9,736	4,086	100.3	85.7	94.2	D	D	D
Denmark	43	39	36.3	45.8	55.7	C	C	C
Egypt	1,000	50	89.6	105	194.3	D	D	E
France	551	525	68.2	68.6	72.6	C	C	C
Germany	353	338	98.9	121.5	146.2	D	D	D
Great Britain	244	229	90.9	113.9	144.2	D	D	D
India[f]	4,288	3,052	57.3	83.6	92.4	C	D	D
Italy	301	249	97.8	107.6	122.7	D	D	D
Japan	369	369	72.9	94.7	108.8	C	D	D
Netherlands	33	32	95.5	111.9	141.0	D	D	D
New Zealand	268	268	.3	1.1	2.5	A	A	A
Norway	309	270	5.2	6.4	7.4	B	B	B
Russia[h]	22,273	11,089	5.9	7.6	10.6	B	B	B
Spain	503	268	57.6	60.2	65.5	C	C	C
Sweden	410	376	9.2	11.1	12.7	B	B	B

Table A14 (continued)

Country	Total Land Area in Thousands of sq. kms.[a]	Standard Farmland in Thousands of sq. kms.[a]	Population per sq. km. of Standard Farmland[b]			Classification in Ranking Scheme of Five Categories[c]		
			1850	1870	1890	1850	1870	1890
Switzerland	41	22	108.8	121.3	132.6	D	D	D
United States	7,702	4,772	4.9	8.4	13.2	A-	B	B

[a] Clark 1957, table 33, facing p. 309. For an explanation of standard farmland, see our discussion of the agricultural variables in the introduction to the data appendix.

[b] Population estimates are from tables A26-A28 below.

[c] The ranking scheme is as follows:

Class	Population per sq. km. of Standard Farmland
A	<5
B	>5 <15
C	>15 <80
D	>80 <150
E	>150

[d] The estimate used is that of total land area cited in Encyclopaedia Britannica 1910, 4:838. In his discussion of table 33, Clark (1957) indicates that land in Burma is almost all potential farmland.

[e] In our statistical analyses, this score is incorrectly entered as A+.

Table A14 (continued)

f The estimate used addresses India and Pakistan, as do the population estimates.

g An average of 1845 and 1855 population figures was used in this calculation.

h This estimate applies to the U.S.S.R. It was assumed that this estimate would indicate the same classification as an estimate for pre-Soviet Russia.

Table A15

Classification Scheme for Level of Development of Inland Transportation, 1850, 1870, 1890

Description of Category	Country and Year	Sources
Category A Countries where (1) the major urban centers and ports were linked by railways; (2) towns and cities throughout the Important populated sections of the country were served by a transportation system consisting mainly of railways, supplemented by all-weather roads and improved waterways suitable for mass shipment of goods; and (3) the agricultural sector was served by a reasonably good network of short-haul railways, waterways, and roads for which local public or semipublic institutions provided maintenance. Countries meeting these criteria where all railway linkages were with one central city—that is, where the railway system did not provide cross-linkages—are classified A-.	Belgium 1870, 1890(+)	Clapham [France] 1936, pp. 339-340; Dechesne 1932, p. 422; Linden 1920, pp. 298-299; Rowntree 1910, p. 283
	France 1870(-), 1890?	Clapham 1936, pp. 339-340; Girard 1965, pp. 239-240; Léon 1976b, pp. 248, 250, 293-297; Moulton and Lewis 1925, p. 48
	Germany 1890	Clapham 1936, p. 350; Clough and Cole 1946, pp. 589-590; Knight et al. 1928, p. 554
	Great Britain 1850, 1870, 1890	Clapham 1932, chap. 5, pp. 205-207; Clapham 1939, p. 94; Clough and Cole 1946, p. 587; Girard 1965, pp. 229-231
	Netherlands 1890	Brugmans 1961, pp. 366, 369; Clapham 1936, pp. 339-340
	United States 1890	Danhof 1969, pp. 4-7; Girard 1965, pp. 250-251, 253; Healy 1951, pp. 370-375

Table A15 (continued)

Description of Category	Country and Year	Sources
Category B Countries in the B category differ from those in Category A primarily because railways formed a less important part of the transportation system. Specifically, (1) as in A, the major urban centers and ports were linked by railways; (2) the transportation system served towns and cities in all populated sections of the country, mainly through roads and improved waterways, but also to an important extent through railways; and (3) the agricultural sector was served by a system of waterways and roads maintained by local public or semipublic institutions; there were relatively few short-haul feeder railways. Countries meeting criteria (1) and (2) where, however, local institutions for maintaining feeder roads in agriculture were frequently nonexistent or	Belgium 1850	Clapham [France] 1936, pp. 339–340; Dechesne 1932, pp. 377, 379; Mitchell 1973, p. 789
	Canada 1890?	Easterbrook and Aiken 1956, pp. 409–411, 417–418, 424, 431–432; Firestone 1960, pp. 219–221; Girard 1965, p. 254; Guillet 1966, chap. 10; Hamelin and Roby 1971, p. 156; Innis 1957, pp. 74–76
	Denmark 1890?	Encyclopaedia Britannica 1910, 8:25; Olsen 1962, pp. 224–225
	France 1850(−)	Clapham 1936, pp. 105, 339–340; Léon 1976b, pp. 247–248, 262
	Germany 1870(+)	Clapham 1936, pp. 155, 339–340, 345–346
	Italy 1890(−)	Clapham 1936, pp. 339–340; Clough 1964, pp. 66–67; Fenoaltea 1968, map on p. 229; Mulhall 1899, p. 517
	Netherlands 1870	Brugmans 1961, pp. 227–228; Edmundson 1922, p. 415

Table A15 (continued)

Description of Category	Country and Year	Sources
Inadequate are classified B-.	Switzerland 1890(-)?	Clough and Cole 1946, p. 591; Georg 1901, pp. 245, 275-278; Hauser 1961, pp. 291-292
	United States 1870?	Davis et al. 1972, pp. 493-495; Girard 1965, pp. 245, 250-251; Healy 1951, pp. 366-368
Category C The countries of Category C met the first two criteria for Category B over the greater part of the populated area of the country but differed from B countries in that some important populated region was not served by the transportation network and in most parts of the country the feeder roads system in agriculture was less well maintained. Specifically, (1) over the greater part of the populated area of the country, the major urban centers and ports were linked by railways and the transportation system	Australia 1890	Barnard 1958, p. 184; Butlin 1965, p. 152; Fitzpatrick 1949, pp. 157-159; McGhee 1970, pp. 175-176
	Egypt 1870, 1890(+)	Crouchley 1938, pp. 112-115, 116-117; Hershlag 1964, pp. 104-107, 123-124; McCoan 1877, pp. 228, 390; Owen 1969, pp. 77, 213
	Germany 1850(+)	Clapham 1936, pp. 150-157, 215, 345-350, 352-355; Clough and Cole 1946, pp. 444, 454
	Japan 1890?	Encyclopaedia Britannica 1911, 15:191-192
	Netherlands 1850(-)	Brugmans 1961, pp. 227-228; Clough and Cole 1946, p. 444; Girard 1965, p. 236

Table A15 (continued)

Description of Category	Country and Year	Sources
served towns and cities mainly through locally maintained roads and improved waterways; (2) some major populated region was not served by an all-weather transportation system (road, rail, waterway), and this unserved populated area was either an important subsistence sector from which marketed crops went out on dirt tracks by cart, mule, or barrel or it was an area where commercial pastoral or agricultural occupation had preceded the establishment of a transportation system; (3) C countries also differed from B countries in that in all parts of the country local institutions for maintaining roads and waterways in the agricultural sector were often nonexistent or inadequate. Excluded from Category C are countries where the mainline transportation network linked commercial centers or areas to	New Zealand 1890	Butlin 1961, p. 230; Condliffe 1959, p. 38; Scholefield 1909, pp. 262–263, 270, 275; Simkin 1951, pp. 151, 154–155; Sutch 1969, pp. 98–99
	Spain 1890(–)?	Cameron 1961, p. 259; Ramos Oliveira 1946, pp. 250–251; Vicens Vives and Nadal Oller 1969, p. 691
	Sweden 1890?	Encyclopaedia Britannica 1911, 26: map facing 190, 193; Jörberg 1973, p. 443
	Switzerland 1870?	Bonjour et al. 1952, p. 294; Clough and Cole 1946, p. 591; Georg 1901, pp. 268–271, 273; Martin 1926, pp. 272–273
	United States 1850?	Danhof 1969, pp. 4–5; Girard 1965, pp. 231–232; Healy 1951, pp. 126–127

Table A15 (continued)

Description of Category	Country and Year	Sources
ports only, while cross-links suitable for internal trade between towns (road, rail, waterway) were nonexistent over the major part of the country.	Argentina 1890	McGann 1966, pp. 16-19; Scobie 1964a, p. 86; Scobie 1964b, pp. 89-91
Category D The countries in Category D resemble those in Category C in that the important urban centers and ports were linked by railways, some important populated region was not served by the all-weather transportation system, and local institutions for maintaining roads and waterways were frequently nonexistent or inadequate. The major difference from C countries is that the railway system, while linking the main commercial centers with the major ports, failed to provide cross-links suitable for internal trade among towns.	Brazil 1890	Burns 1970, pp. 144-145; Graham 1968, pp. 30, 53-54, 58-60, 64-67, 126-127
	Burma 1890(-)	Encyclopaedia Britannica 1910, 4:843; Hlaing 1964, p. 109; Tun Wai 1961, pp. 45, 59-60, 86-89
	Canada 1870?	Firestone 1960, pp. 218-219; Guillet 1966, chaps. 7-8; Hamelin and Roby 1971, pp. 149, 197; Innis 1935, p. 169; Jones 1946, pp. 233-234
	India 1890(-)	Buchanan 1934, pp. 180, 184; Maddison 1970, p. 71
	Italy 1870	Clapham 1936, p. 350; Eckaus 1961, pp. 288-289; Fenoaltea 1968, map on p. 228

Table A15 (continued)

Description of Category	Country and Year	Sources
	Norway 1890	Hodne 1975, pp. 202-205; Lieberman 1970, pp. 123, 131
	Russia 1890	Girard 1965, pp. 254-255; Henderson 1961, pp. 223-225
	Spain 1870(-)?	Cameron 1961, pp. 263-264; Nadal 1973, p. 551; Vicens Vives and Nadal Oller 1969, pp. 680-681
Category E Countries where the overwhelming part of the populated country was not served by long-distance transportation other than natural waterways and where short-distance transport was mainly via dirt tracks suited to pack animals. In most of these countries there were a few railway lines or a few all-weather roads between urban centers (or from urban centers to ports) or some good long-distance waterways.	Argentina 1850(-), 1870	McGann 1966, pp. 1-2, 18-19; Scoble 1964b, p. 11, map 4
	Australia 1850(-), 1870	Barnard 1958, pp. 11, 82, 182-183; Shaw 1946, pp. 90-91
	Brazil 1850(-), 1870	Burns 1970, pp. 137, 144-145; Graham 1968, p. 14
	Burma 1850(-), 1870	Encyclopaedia Britannica 1910, 4:843; Hiaing 1964, p. 109; Tun Wai 1961, pp. 45-46
	Canada 1850(+)	Guillet 1966, chaps. 2-4; Hamelin and Roby 1971, pp. 143-144; Innis 1957, pp. 69-70; Tucker 1936, pp. 26-27

Table A15 (continued)

Description of Category	Country and Year	Sources
	China 1850, 1870, 1890	Hou 1965, pp. 59, 62; Perkins et al. 1969, pp. 119–120, 146–151; Tawney 1932, p. 87; Vinacke 1926, pp. 126–127, 130
	Denmark 1850, 1870(+)	Hansen 1976, pp. 138–139; Olsen 1962, pp. 223, 237
	Egypt 1850?	al-Hitta 1966, pp. 407–409; Owen 1969, pp. 75–77
	India 1850, 1870	Bhatia 1965, p. 123; Buchanan 1934, pp. 182–183; Dubey 1965, pp. 327–331; Gadgil 1942, pp. 18–19, 131–134; Shrimali 1965, pp. 760–761; Sundara Rajan 1955, pp. 220–221
	Italy 1850	Clough 1964, pp. 27, 66–69, 71; Clough and Cole 1946, p. 451; Eckaus 1961, pp. 288–289; Mitchell 1973, pp. 789–793; Neufeld 1961, pp. 149–153; Seton-Watson 1967, p. 18
	Japan 1850, 1870	Allen 1962, pp. 90, 212; Allen 1965, pp. 880–881
	New Zealand 1850(–), 1870(–)	Condliffe 1959, p. 30; Encyclopaedia Britannica 1911, 19:454; Fitzpatrick 1949, pp. 161–162; Simkin 1951, pp. 144–145

Table A15 (continued)

Description of Category	Country and Year	Sources
	Norway 1850(-), 1870	Blegen 1931, pp. 9-10; Hodne 1975, pp. 202-204
	Russia 1850, 1870	Blackwell 1968, pp. 262, 269; Henderson 1961, p. 222; Mavor 1925, p. 371; Portal 1965, p. 813
	Spain 1850(-)	Clough and Cole 1946, p. 450; Higgin 1886, pp. 64-65; Vicens Vives and Nadal Oller 1969, pp. 680-681
	Sweden 1850, 1870(+)	Heckscher 1954, p. 213; Hovde 1943, p. 262; Jörberg 1973, pp. 439-440; Montgomery 1939, p. 104; Youngson 1959, p. 157
	Switzerland 1850(-)	Clough and Cole 1946, p. 451; Georg 1901, pp. 238-240, 242; Hauser 1961, p. 285

Note: Of the sources in this table, the following are listed in the general section of the bibliography: Cameron 1961, Clough and Cole 1946, *Encyclopaedia Britannica* 1910-1911, Girard 1965, Henderson 1961, Jörberg 1973, Knight et al. 1928, Mitchell 1973, and Mulhall 1899.

Table A16

Classification Scheme for Rate of Improvement of Inland Transportation (Lagged), 1830-1850, 1850-1870, 1870-1890

Description of Category	Country and Period	Sources
Category A Countries where a major breakthrough in the development of a transportation network occurred during the period. These are countries where (1) at the beginning of the period, the transportation network failed to link together the major populated regions of the country (with transport suitable for mass shipment of goods), and (2) during the period the expansion of the transportation network was sufficient to link together the major urban centers and also to link together the major populated regions of the country. This category excludes countries where the establishment of a railway system substituted for a good network of canals and roads	Argentina 1870-1890	Ferrer 1967, p. 228; Girard 1965, pp. 256-257; McGann 1966, pp. 10-11, 16-18; Scobie 1964a, pp. 86, 137; Scobie 1964b, pp. 38-39, 42, 61
	Australia 1870-1890	Fitzpatrick 1949, pp. 144, 157-159
	Belgium 1830-1850	Clough and Cole 1946, pp. 453-454; Mitchell 1973, p. 789
	Denmark 1870-1890	Hansen 1970, pp. 64, 73; Mitchell 1973, p. 789; Youngson 1959, pp. 201, 214-215
	France 1850-1870	Girard 1965, pp. 239-240; Mitchell 1973, pp. 789-793
	Germany 1830-1850	Clough and Cole 1946, pp. 453-454; Henderson 1961, pp. 20-21; Mitchell 1973, pp. 789-792
	Great Britain 1830-1850(-)	Clough and Cole 1946, pp. 450-451; Girard 1965, pp. 225-231, 243; Mitchell 1973, pp. 789-794

Table A16 (continued)

Description of Category	Country and Period	Sources
linking major populated regions.	Italy 1850–1870	Clough 1964, pp. 27, 66–69, 71; Eckaus 1961, pp. 288–289; Mitchell 1973, pp. 789–793; Neufeld 1961, pp. 149–153; Seton-Watson 1967, p. 21
	New Zealand 1870–1890	Butlin 1961, p. 230; Condliffe 1959, p. 38; Scholefield 1909, pp. 262–263, 270, 275; Simkin 1951, pp. 154–155
	Sweden 1870–1890	Hecksher 1954, p. 241–244; Jörberg 1965, pp. 134–135; Mitchell 1973, pp. 789–794; Montgomery 1939, pp. 104–105, 123–124
	Switzerland 1870–1890	Clough and Cole 1946, p. 591; Georg 1901, pp. 275–278; Mitchell 1973, p. 789
	United States 1830–1850	Danhof 1969, pp. 4–5; Davis et al. 1972, pp. 482–484, 492–493; Girard 1965, pp. 231–232; Healy 1951, pp. 120–127
Category B Countries where the first major breakthrough in the transportation system had occurred in an earlier period, but, during this period, major work completing the main lines of the transportation system	Belgium 1850–1870	Chlepner 1956, pp. 82–83; Dechesne 1932, pp. 421–422; Girard 1965, pp. 234–235; Linden 1920, pp. 298–299
	Germany 1850–1870	Knight et al. 1928, pp. 554–555; Mitchell 1973, pp. 789–793

Table A16 (continued)

Description of Category	Country and Period	Sources
was done. Examples would be the completion of important cross-links in the system, major extensions into regions previously unsettled or into lightly populated subsistence areas, or the construction of branch lines.	Italy 1870–1890	Clough 1964, pp. 66, 69, 71; Mitchell 1973, pp. 789–794; Neufeld 1961, pp. 149–153
	Netherlands 1850–1870?	Brugmans 1961, pp. 227–228, 230; Edmundson 1922, p. 415; Mitchell 1973, p. 789
	United States 1850–1870	Fishlow 1972, pp. 493–495, 500–501; Girard 1965, pp. 245–251; Healy 1951, pp. 366–368

Category C1
Countries in which widespread improvements in the transportation system consisted for the most part of the substitution of improved means of transportation rather than the laying down of the initial means of mass-goods transport. For example, railways may have substituted for canal transport, or macadam roads for dirt roads, or branch railways for good roads or for coastal waterways. Thus, at the

	Belgium 1870–1890	Chlepner 1956, pp. 86–87; Clapham [France] 1936, pp. 339–340; Girard 1965, p. 235
	Canada 1850–1870	Easterbrook and Aiken 1956, pp. 298–300, 305–308, 311–312, 370–377; Firestone 1960, pp. 218–219; Parker 1966, pp. 207, 219–225
	Egypt 1850–1870	al-Hitta 1966, pp. 408–411; Crouchley 1938, pp. 112–117; McCoan 1877, pp. 228, 390; Owen 1969, pp. 77, 213
	France 1870–1890	Clapham 1936, pp. 339–340, 350–357; Knight et al. 1928, pp. 598–599; Mitchell 1973, pp. 789–794

Table A16 (continued)

Description of Category	Country and Period	Sources
beginning of the period, the main lines of the transportation system were pretty fully laid out.	Germany 1870–1890	Clough and Cole 1946, pp. 589–590; Knight et al. 1928, p. 554; Mitchell 1973, pp. 789–794
	Great Britain 1850–1870, 1870–1890	Clough and Cole 1946, p. 587; Girard 1965, pp. 229, 231, 249–250; Mitchell 1973, pp. 789–794
	Netherlands 1830–1850?, 1870–1890?	Edmundson 1922, p. 415; Girard 1965, p. 236
Category C2 Countries in which improvements in the transportation system consisted of linking up frontier areas to the rest of the country by the most advanced form of transport (i.e., railway). In these countries at the beginning of this period the areas that were densely settled were connected by a system for the mass transportation of goods (either canals or railways).	Canada 1870–1890	Easterbrook and Aiken 1956, pp. 409–411, 417–418, 424, 431–432; Firestone 1960, pp. 219–221; Innis 1935, p. 190; Innis 1957, pp. 74–76
	Egypt 1870–1890	al-Hitta 1966, pp. 406, 409; Hershlag 1964, pp. 105–107, 123–124; McCoan 1877, pp. 229, 231, 246–247; Owen 1969, pp. 213, 319
	United States 1870–1890	Danhof 1969, pp. 4–7; Davis et al. 1972, pp. 500–503; Girard 1965, pp. 250–253; Healy 1951, pp. 370–375; Knowles 1936, pp. 93–94

Table A16 (continued)

Description of Category	Country and Period	Sources
Category D Countries where a breakthrough linked two major regions of a country but left large areas of the rest of the country without a transportation system for the mass shipment of goods; for example, the construction of a major interregional canal or the first surge of railway building when major long-distance lines were put in, which nevertheless left large gaps in the rest of the system. In both cases, two or more regions were linked up between which there had not previously been much trade in bulky agricultural products. The classification is based on the first period of utilization of the new transportation rather than on the dates of construction. A score of D- signifies a breakthrough involving regions of lesser importance as judged	Argentina 1850–1870(–)	Ferrer 1967, p. 228; Girard 1965, pp. 256–257; McGann 1966, pp. 10–11; Scoble 1964a, p. 86
	Australia 1850–1870	Fitzpatrick 1949, pp. 121–122, 144, 157–159
	Brazil 1850–1870(–), 1870–1890	Burns 1970, pp. 144–145; Graham 1968, pp. 26–30, 51–67, 126–127
	Burma 1870–1890(–)	Tun Wai 1961, pp. 45, 59–60, 86–89; Hlaing 1964, p. 109
	Canada 1830–1850	Easterbrook and Aiken 1956, pp. 260–261, 268–270; Parker 1966, pp. 204–212
	Denmark 1850–1870(–)	Hovde 1943, 1:226–269; Mitchell 1973, p. 789; Youngson 1959, pp. 200–201, 214–215
	Egypt 1830–1850(–)	al-Hitta 1966, pp. 407–409; Owen 1969, p. 77
	France 1830–1850	Buchanan 1955, p. 165; Léon 1976c

Table A16 (continued)

Description of Category	Country and Period	Sources
by population or involving a lesser geographical span.	India 1850–1870(–), 1870–1890	Bhatia 1965, p. 123; Buchanan 1934, pp. 182–183; Dubey 1965, pp. 327–333; Gadgil 1942, pp. 18–19, 131–134; Shrimali 1965, pp. 760–761; Sundara Rajan 1955, pp. 220–221
	Italy 1830–1850(–)	Clough 1964, p. 26; Mitchell 1973, pp. 789–791
	Japan 1870–1890?	Allen 1962, pp. 90, 212; Allen 1965, pp. 880–881; Hirschmeier 1964, pp. 140–141; Hirschmeier 1965, pp. 226–230; Lockwood 1954, p. 14
	New Zealand 1850–1870(–)	Condliffe 1959, p. 30; Simkin 1951, pp. 144–145
	Norway 1850–1870(–), 1870–1890	Derry 1957, p. 159; Hodne 1975, pp. 202–217; Hovde 1943, p. 266; Johnsen 1939, p. 495; Lieberman 1970, p. 123; Mitchell 1973, p. 789; Soltow 1965, p. 29
	Russia 1830–1850(–), 1850–1870, 1870–1890	Cameron 1961, pp. 275–283; Crisp 1976, pp. 17, 24, 160; Girard 1965, pp. 241, 254–255; Karpovich 1960, p. 2; Mavor 1925, pp. 381, 363–364, 371–373; Mitchell 1973, pp. 789–793

Table A16 (continued)

Description of Category	Country and Period	Sources
	Spain 1830–1850(–), 1850–1870(–), 1870–1890	Cameron 1961, pp. 248, 259, 263–264, 274–275; Carr 1966, p. 409; Girard 1965, pp. 240–241; Higgin 1886, pp. 64–65, 80–81; Mitchell 1973, p. 789; Nadal 1973, pp. 549–553
	Sweden 1850–1870	Girard 1965, p. 236; Heckscher 1954, pp. 240–241; Mitchell 1973, pp. 789–794; Montgomery 1939, p. 104
	Switzerland 1850–1870	Bonjour 1952, p. 294; Clough and Cole 1946, p. 591; Georg 1901, pp. 268–271; Martin 1926, pp. 272–273; Mitchell 1973, p. 789
Category E Countries in this category did not improve their inland transportation systems significantly during the period. If one or two small railway lines were built or a few canals were opened or improved for short hauls, the country is classified with a (+).	Argentina 1830–1850	Ferrer 1967, p. 228; Girard 1965, pp. 256–257; McGann 1966, pp. 17–18
	Australia 1830–1850	Fitzpatrick 1949, p. 121; Shaw 1946, pp. 89–90
	Brazil 1830–1850	Graham 1968, pp. 14, 25–26, 30
	Burma 1830–1850, 1850–1870	Hlaing 1964, p. 109

Table A16 (continued)

Description of Category	Country and Period	Sources
	China 1830–1850(+), 1850–1870, 1870–1890	Allen 1965, pp. 905–906; Hou 1965, pp. 59–60, 62
	Denmark 1830–1850(+)	Nielsen 1933, p. 482; Youngson 1959, pp. 200–201, 214–215
	India 1830–1850	Dubey 1965, pp. 327–328; Gadgil 1942, pp. 18–19
	Japan 1830–1850, 1850–1870?	Allen 1962, pp. 90, 212; Allen 1965, pp. 880–881
	New Zealand 1830–1850	Condliffe 1953, p. 30; Encyclopaedia Britannica 1911, 19:454.
	Norway 1830–1850	Derry 1957, p. 159; Hodne 1975, pp. 208–215, 226; Lieberman 1970, pp. 122–123
	Sweden 1830–1850(+)	Girard 1965, p. 236; Hovde 1943, p. 262; Mitchell 1973, pp. 789–794
	Switzerland 1830–1850	Henderson 1961, p. 147; Mitchell 1973, p. 789

Note: Of the sources in this table, the following are listed in the general section of the bibliography: Buchanan 1955, Cameron 1961, Clough and Cole 1946, Encyclopaedia Britannica 1910–1911, Girard 1965, Henderson 1961, Mitchell 1973, Knight et al. 1928, and Knowles 1932.

Table A17

Classification Scheme for Rate of Growth of Total Real Exports,
1850-1870, 1870-1890, 1890-1914

Description of Category	Country and Period
Category A Rapid rate of growth of real exports (probably over 4 percent average annual rate of growth) from a moderate or large base	Argentina 1890-1914(+) Australia 1850-1870, 1870-1890(+) Belgium 1870-1890, 1890-1914 Brazil 1850-1870(-), 1890-1914 Canada 1850-1870(-)?, 1890-1914(+) Denmark 1890-1914 France 1850-1870 Germany 1850-1870(+), 1890-1914(+) Great Britain 1850-1870 Japan 1890-1914(+) Netherlands 1850-1870(+) New Zealand 1890-1914? Spain 1870-1890(+) Sweden 1850-1870(+) Switzerland 1850-1870 United States 1870-1890, 1890-1914
Category B Rapid rate of growth of real exports (probably over 4 percent average annual rate of growth) from a very small base	Argentina 1850-1870, 1870-1890 Burma 1870-1890 Egypt 1850-1870 India 1850-1870(-) Italy 1850-1870(-) Japan 1870-1890 New Zealand 1850-1870 Russia 1850-1870 Spain 1850-1870(-)
Category C Moderate growth of real exports (probably less than 4 percent but greater than 2 percent average annual growth rate)	Australia 1890-1914(+) Belgium 1850-1870(+) Brazil 1870-1890 Burma 1890-1914(+)? China 1890-1914 Denmark 1850-1870, 1870-1890 Egypt 1890-1914 France 1870-1890, 1890-1914 Germany 1870-1890

Table A17 (continued)

Description of Category	Country and Period
	Great Britain 1870-1890, 1890-1914
	India 1870-1890, 1890-1914(-)
	Italy 1890-1914(+)
	Netherlands 1870-1890, 1890-1914
	New Zealand 1870-1890
	Norway 1850-1870, 1870-1890, 1890-1914(+)
	Russia 1870-1890, 1890-1914
	Sweden 1870-1890(+), 1890-1914
	Switzerland 1870-1890(+), 1890-1914
	United States 1850-1870
Category D Slow or negligible growth of real exports (probably less than 2 percent average annual growth rate)	Burma 1850-1870(-) Canada 1870-1890 China 1850-1870, 1870-1890 Egypt 1870-1890? Italy 1870-1890 Japan 1850-1870(-) Spain 1890-1914

Table A18

Average Annual Rate of Growth of Exports, 1850–1870

Country	Real Exports (%)	Sources	Exports In Current Prices (%)	Sources
Argentina	8 (1864–1870)	Randall 1977a, p. 224	7.3 (1864–1870)	Randall 1977a, p. 218
Australia	4.3 (1861–1870)	Butlin 1962, pp. 396, 410	2.8 (1861–1870)	Butlin 1962, p. 410
Belgium	6.4 (1861–1873)	Bairoch 1973, p. 25		
Brazil	3.7	Mitchell 1976, pp. 489, 737	4.9	Mitchell 1976, p. 489
	4.5	Randall [Argentina] 1977a, p. 216		
Burma	Negligible	Hlaing 1964, pp. 91–94		
Canada			8	Marr and Paterson 1980, p. 142
China	1.5 (1867–1870)	Hou 1965, p. 231	4.6 (1864–1871)	Hou 1965, p. 231
Denmark	3.3	Olsen 1962, p. 229		
Egypt	7.7	McCoan 1877, p. 392	7.5	McCoan 1877, p. 391

Table A18 (continued)

Country	Real Exports (%)	Sources	Exports In Current Prices (%)	Sources
France	5.7 (1860–1870) 4 5.6	Bairoch 1973, p. 25 Mitchell 1976, pp. 490, 737 Lévy-Leboyer 1968, Inserts	4.9	Mitchell 1976, p. 490
Germany	6.7 (1860–1870) 5.7	Bairoch 1973, p. 25 Hoffmann et al. 1965, p. 530		
Great Britain	3.8 (1860–1870) 4.4 4.2	Bairoch 1973, p. 25 Imlah 1958, pp. 96–98 Mitchell 1976, pp. 490, 737	5.3	Mitchell 1976, p. 492
India			5.4	Chandra 1966, p. 143
Italy	5.5 (1862–1870) 6.3 (1861–1870)	Bairoch 1973, p. 25 Mitchell 1976, pp. 490, 737	5.2	Mitchell 1976, p. 490
Japan	Not available			
Netherlands	>5.2	Bairoch 1973, p. 26	5.5	Mitchell 1976, p. 490
New Zealand	>13.3 rapid	Lloyd Prichard 1970, pp. 78, 109, 112, 182 Simkin 1951, pp. 92–93	13.3	Lloyd Prichard 1970, pp. 78, 109

Table A18 (continued)

Country	Real Exports (%)	Sources	Exports In Current Prices (%)	Sources
Norway	3.4 (1865–1870)	Central Bureau of Statistics of Norway 1966, p. 130	3.4	Mitchell 1976, p. 490
Russia	7 (1860–1870) >5.2	Barkai 1973, p. 340 Bairoch 1973, p. 26	6.7	Mitchell 1976, p. 490
Spain	4.3 ≈5.2	Mitchell 1976, pp. 490, 737 Bairoch 1973, p. 26	6.1	Mitchell 1976, p. 490
Sweden	6.7 6.6 (1860–1870) 7.3	Fridlizius 1963, p. 89 Mitchell 1976, pp. 490, 737 Bairoch 1973, p. 25	7.5	Mitchell 1976, p. 490
Switzerland	<5.2	Bairoch 1973, p. 26	3.9 (1840–1879)	Bosshardt and Nydeggar 1964, p. 324
United States	3.4	U.S. Dept. of Commerce, Bureau of the Census 1960, p. 544; Kravis 1972, p. 389	5	U.S. Dept. of Commerce, Bureau of the Census 1960, p. 544

Note: Of the sources in this table, the following are listed in the general section of the bibliography: Bairoch 1973 and Mitchell 1976.

Table A19

Average Annual Rate of Growth of Exports, 1870–1890

Country	Real Exports (%)	Sources	Exports In Current Prices (%)	Sources
Argentina	13.7 7.8	Díaz Alejandro 1970, p. 474 Randall 1977a, p. 224	2.1	Randall 1977a, p. 218
Australia	5.9	Butlin 1962, pp. 396, 410	2.7	Butlin 1962, p. 410
Belgium	2.8 4.1	Bairoch 1973, p. 25 Mitchell 1976, pp. 489, 737	3.7	Mitchell 1976, p. 489
Brazil	2.5	Randall [Argentina] 1977a, p. 224		
Burma			6.2 4.6 (1875–1890)	Encyclopaedia Britannica 1910, 4:843 Hlaing 1964, p. 110
Canada	1.1 1	Firestone 1958, p. 142 Urquhart and Buckley 1965, p. 175	1	Hamelin and Roby 1971, appendix
China	1.2	Hou 1965, p. 231	1.4	Hou 1965, p. 231
Denmark	2.2 (1880–1890) 3.5 2.9	Bairoch 1973, p. 25 Olsen 1962, p. 229 Bjerke 1955, p. 149	1.4	Mitchell 1976, p. 489

Table A19 (continued)

Country	Real Exports (%)	Sources	Exports In Current Prices (%)	Sources
Egypt			1.2	Issawi 1966a, p. 373
France	2.35 2.9 2.5	Balroch 1973, p. 25 Mitchell 1976, pp. 490, 737 Lévy-Leboyer 1968, inserts	1.4	Mitchell 1976, p. 490
Germany	2.25 2.6 3	Balroch 1973, p. 25 Hoffmann et al. 1965, p. 530 Mitchell 1976, p. 737 and Friedlaender and Oser 1953, p. 277	1.7 2.7	Stolper et al. 1967, p. 30 Borchardt 1967, p. 30 Friedlaender and Oser 1953, p. 277
Great Britain	2.65 2.9 2.7	Balroch 1973, p. 25 Imlah 1958, pp. 96-98 Mitchell 1976, pp. 492, 737	1.4	Mitchell 1976, p. 492
India			3.2	Chandra 1966, p. 143
Italy	.65 .8	Balroch 1973, p. 25 Mitchell 1976, pp. 490, 737	.8	Mitchell 1976, p. 490
Japan	7	Taniguchi 1937, p. 240		
Netherlands	>2.9	Balroch 1973, p. 26	5.1	Mitchell 1976, p. 490
New Zealand	3.5 or ≈3.5 slow	Lloyd Prichard 1970, pp. 109, 160-161 Simkin 1951, pp. 92-93	3.5	Lloyd Prichard 1970, pp.

Table A19 (continued)

Country	Real Exports (%)	Sources	Exports in Current Prices (%)	Sources
Norway	2.9 2.95	Central Bureau of Statistics of Norway 1966, p. 130 Bairoch 1973, p. 25	2.4	Mitchell 1976, p. 490
Russia	3.4 >2.9	Barkal 1973, p. 340 Bairoch 1973, p. 26	3.3	Mitchell 1976, p. 490
Spain	5.3 ≈2.9	Mitchell 1976, pp. 490, 737 Bairoch 1973, p. 26	4	Mitchell 1976, p. 490
Sweden	3.2 4.2 3.5	Fridlizius 1963, p. 89 Mitchell 1976, pp. 490, 737 Bairoch 1973, p. 25	3.6	Mitchell 1976, p. 490
Switzerland	<2.9 6	Bairoch 1973, p. 26 Brugmans [Netherlands] 1961, p. 382	.8 (1879–1887)	Bosshardt and Nydeggar 1964, p. 324
United States	1.9 (1879–1890) 4.6	U.S. Dept. of Commerce, Bureau of the Census 1960, p. 540 U.S. Dept. of Commerce, Bureau of the Census 1960, p. 540; Kravis 1972, p. 389	4.1	U.S. Dept. of Commerce, Bureau of the Census 1960, p. 540

Note: Of the sources in this table, the following are listed in the general section of the bibliography: Bairoch 1973, Encyclopaedia Britannica 1910–1911, and Mitchell 1976.

Table A20

Average Annual Rate of Growth of Exports, 1890–1914

Country	Real Exports (%)	Sources	Exports in Current Prices (%)	Sources
Argentina	8.8 5.4	Díaz Alejandro 1970, p. 474 Randall 1977a, p. 224	8.7	Randall 1977a, p. 218
Australia	3.3	Butlin 1962, pp. 396, 410	3.3	Butlin 1962, p. 410
Belgium	3.9 (1890–1910) 4.3	Balroch 1973, p. 25	4.9	Mitchell 1976, p. 489
Brazil	4.8	Mitchell 1976, pp. 489, 737 Randall [Argentina] 1977a, p. 216		
Burma			5 5.7	Encyclopaedia Britannica 1910, 4:843 Hlaing 1964, p. 110
Canada	5.1 6.2	Firestone 1958, p. 142 Urquhart and Buckley 1965, p. 175	6.9	Hou 1965, p. 231
China	3.8	Hou 1965, p. 231	6	Mitchell 1976, p. 489
Denmark	3.75 (1890–1910) 4 5.6	Balroch 1973, p. 25 Olsen 1962, p. 229 Bjerke 1955, p. 149		

Table A20 (continued)

Country	Real Exports (%)	Sources	Exports In Current Prices (%)	Sources
Egypt	2.9	Birnberg and Resnick 1975, p. 278	3.8	Birnberg and Resnick 1975, p. 278
France	2.15 (1890–1910) 2.3 2.9	Balroch 1973, p. 25 Lévy-Leboyer 1968, Inserts Mitchell 1976, pp. 490, 737	3.6	Mitchell 1976, p. 490
Germany	4.95 (1890–1910) 5.4 4.4	Balroch 1973, p. 25 Hoffmann et al. 1965, p. 530 Mitchell 1976, pp. 490, 737	4.7 4.9 5 4.9	Friedlaender and Oser 1953, p. 277 Stolper et al. 1967, p. 30 Mitchell 1976, p. 490 Stolper et al. 1967, p. 30
Great Britain	2.6 2.4 2.7	Imlah 1958, pp. 96–98 Balroch 1973, p. 25 Mitchell 1976, pp. 492, 737	3.2	Mitchell 1976, p. 492
India	2	Birnberg and Resnick 1975, p. 284	4.1 3.5	Birnberg and Resnick 1975, p. 284 Chandra 1966, p. 143
Italy	3.55 (1890–1910) 4	Balroch 1973, p. 25 Mitchell 1976, pp. 490, 737	4.6	Mitchell 1976, p. 490
Japan	8.1 8.1	Lockwood 1954, p. 13 Taniguchi 1937, p. 240		

Table A20 (continued)

Country	Real Exports (%)	Sources	Exports In Current Prices (%)	Sources
Netherlands	>3.15	Bairoch 1973, p. 26	4.6	Mitchell 1976, p. 490
New Zealand	≤4 to >4 rapid	Lloyd Prichard 1970, pp. 160, 202, 182 Simkin 1951, pp. 92-93	4.0	Lloyd Prichard 1970, pp. 160, 202
Norway	2.7 (1890-1910) 2.85 (1890-1910) 3.7	Central Bureau of Statistics of Norway 1966, p. 130 Bairoch 1973, p. 25	4.9	Mitchell 1976, pp. 490, 737
Russia	3.5 >3.15	Barkai 1973, p. 340 Bairoch 1973, p. 26	3.5	Mitchell 1976, p. 490
Spain	-.3 3.15	Mitchell 1976, pp. 490, 737 Bairoch 1973, p. 26	1	Mitchell 1976, p. 490
Sweden	3.3 3.5 2.4 (1890-1910)	Fridlizius 1963, p. 89 Mitchell 1976, pp. 490, 737 Bairoch 1973, p. 25	4.4	Mitchell 1976, p. 490
Switzerland	<3.15 8	Bairoch 1973, p. 26 Brugmans [Netherlands] 1961, p. 382	2.8 (1887-1913) 3	Bosshardt and Nydeggar 1964, p. 324 Mitchell 1976, p. 492

Table A20 (continued)

Country	Real Exports (%)	Sources	Exports In Current Prices (%)	Sources
United States	4	U.S. Dept. of Commerce, Bureau of the Census 1960, p. 544	4.4	U.S. Dept. of Commerce, Bureau of the Census 1960, p. 544
	4.1	Kravis 1972, p. 389		

Note: Of the sources in this table, the following are listed in the general section of the bibliography: Bairoch 1973, Encyclopaedia Britannica 1910-1911, and Mitchell 1976.

Table A21

Classification Scheme for Degree of Shift in Structure of Export Sector, 1850-1870, 1870-1890, 1890-1914

Description of Category	Country and Period	Sources
Category A Very strong shift in structure of exports between primary, primary processed, manufactured consumer, and manufactured intermediate goods	Denmark 1890-1914?	Youngson 1959, pp. 210-212
	Germany 1890-1914	Hoffmann et al. 1965, p. 154; Olsen [Denmark] 1962, p. 232
	Japan 1870-1890 1890-1914	Yamazawa and Yamamoto 1979, p. 134; Taniguchi 1937, p. 241 Lockwood 1954, p. 354
	United States 1870-1890, 1890-1914	U.S. Dept. of Commerce, Bureau of the Census 1960, pp. 544-545
Category B Moderate shift in structure of exports between primary, primary processed, manufactured consumer, and manufactured intermediate goods	Belgium 1890-1914?	
	Canada 1850-1870?, 1870-1890, 1890-1914	Firestone 1958, p. 156; Marr and Paterson 1980, p. 16; Menzel 1981, pp. 98-99
	Denmark 1870-1890	Youngson 1959, pp. 210, 212
	Germany 1850-1870, 1870-1890	Hoffmann et al. 1965, p. 153
	Italy 1850-1870, 1870-1890, 1890-1914	Instituto Centrale di Statistica 1968, p. 102

Table A21 (continued)

Description of Category	Country and Period	Sources
	Netherlands 1870–1890?, 1890–1914	de Jonge 1968, pp. 353–354
	Sweden 1850–1870, 1870–1890	Fridlizius 1963, pp. 8–31
	Switzerland 1850–1870, 1870–1890, 1890–1914	Bosshardt and Nydeggar 1964, p. 324
	United States 1850–1870	U.S. Dept. of Commerce, Bureau of the Census 1960, pp. 544–545
Category C Slight shift in structure of exports between primary, primary processed, manufactured consumer, and manufactured intermediate goods	Belgium 1850–1870?, 1870–1890?	
	France 1850–1870 1870–1890 1890–1914	Weiller 1971, p. 811 Friedlaender and Oser 1953, p. 269 Broder 1976, p. 344
	Great Britain 1850–1870 1870–1890, 1890–1914	Mitchell and Deane 1971, p. 303 Deane and Cole 1967, p. 31
	Netherlands 1850–1870	de Jonge 1968, pp. 353–354
	New Zealand 1890–1914	Simkin 1951, pp. 176–177
	Norway 1850–1870 1870–1890, 1890–1914	Hodne 1973, p. 110 Lieberman 1970, p. 128
	Spain 1850–1870, 1870–1890, 1890–1914	Nadal 1973, p. 618

Table A21 (continued)

Description of Category	Country and Period	Sources
	Sweden 1890–1914	Fridlizius 1963, pp. 8–31
Category D Negligible or no shift in structure of exports	Argentina 1850–1870 1870–1890 1890–1914	Youngson 1965, p. 192 Díaz Alejandro 1970, p. 474 Randall 1977a, p. 218
	Australia 1850–1870, 1870–1890, 1890–1914	Butlin 1953, p. 30
	Brazil 1850–1870 1870–1890, 1890–1914	Silva 1953, p. 8 Leff 1973, p. 684
	Burma 1850–1870, 1870–1890, 1890– 1914	Hlaing 1964, p. 110
	China 1850–1870 1870–1890, 1890–1914	Hyde [Japan] 1973, p. 216 Allen and Donnithorne 1954, pp. 22–23
	Denmark 1850–1870?	Youngson 1959, pp. 210–212
	Egypt 1850–1870, 1870–1890, 1890– 1914	Owen 1969, pp. 126, 307
	India 1850–1870, 1870–1890, 1890– 1914	Chakrabarti et al. 1965, p. 302

Table A21 (continued)

Description of Category	Country and Period	Sources
	Japan 1850–1870?	Lockwood 1954, p. 315
	New Zealand 1850–1870, 1870–1890	Condliffe 1959, p. 149
	Russia 1850–1870, 1870–1890, 1890–1914	Carson 1959, p. 121

Note: Of the sources in this table, the following are listed in the general section of the bibliography: Friedlaender and Oser 1953 and Youngson 1965.

Table A22

Classification Scheme for Direction of Change in Average Real Wages in Industry, 1850–1870, 1870–1890, 1890–1914

Description of Category	Country and Period	Sources
Category A Average real wages in industry showed a strong upward movement.	Australia 1850–1870	Butlin 1962, p. 158; Kuczynski [Great Britain] 1972a, p. 105
	Denmark 1870–1890, 1890–1914	Hansen 1976, pp. 255–279; Olsen 1962, p. 211; Pedersen 1930, p. 313
	Great Britain 1870–1890	Bogart 1942, p. 237; Bowley 1895, p. 381; Clapham 1938, p. 465; Kuczynski 1972b, p. 90; Phelps Brown 1973, p. 66
	Japan 1890–1914	Lockwood 1954, p. 144; Minami and Ono 1979, p. 233; Ohkawa et al. 1957, p. 243
	Norway 1870–1890	Central Bureau of Statistics of Norway 1966, p. 142; Dahmén [Sweden] 1970, p. 16; Hodne 1975, p. 143; Larsen 1948, p. 462
	Sweden 1870–1890, 1890–1914	Bagge et al. 1935, p. 305; Dahmén 1970, p. 16; Phelps Brown 1973, pp. 66–67
	Switzerland 1850–1870	Siegenthaler 1964, p. 426

Table A22 (continued)

Description of Category	Country and Period	Sources
	United States 1870–1890	Hansen 1925, p. 33; Kuczynski 1946a, pp. 81, 153; Lebergott 1964, pp. 524, 528; Rees 1961, p. 121
Category B Average real wages in industry showed an upward movement, but not a strong one.	Argentina 1850–1870,[a] 1890–1914	Cortés Conde 1976, pp. 144–147; Randall 1977a, pp. 64–89, 234
	Australia 1870–1890	Butlin 1962, p. 158; Coghlan 1918, 3:1239; Kuczynski [Germany] 1945, p. 105
	Belgium 1850–1870, 1870–1890, 1890–1914	Chlepner 1945, p. 181; Mitchell 1976, pp. 184, 742; Neyrinck 1944, pp. 182–183
	Brazil 1890–1914	Stein[b] 1957, pp. 62–65
	Burma 1850–1870	Tun Wai 1961, pp. 47–50
	Canada 1850–1870, 1870–1890, 1890–1914	Bertram and Percy 1979, pp. 307–309; Cairncross 1953, p. 59; Firestone 1958, pp. 77c, 207; Parker[a] 1966, abstract p. 2 and pp. 2–3, 6, 58–86; Urquhart and Buckley 1965, pp. 93–96, 291
	Denmark 1850–1870	Hansen 1976, p. 255; Pedersen 1930, p. 313

Table A22 (continued)

Description of Category	Country and Period	Sources
	France 1850–1870, 1870–1890, 1890–1914	Kuczynski 1946b, pp. 97, 128, 162; Levasseur 1969, p. 715; Lévy-Leboyer 1968, p. 795; Phelps Brown 1973, pp. 66–67
	Germany 1870–1890, 1890–1914	Desai 1968, p. 125; Kuczynski 1945, p. 128; Phelps Brown 1973, p. 66
	Great Britain 1850–1870, 1890–1914	Bogart 1942, pp. 236, 465; Bowley 1895, p. 381; Clapham 1938, p. 466; Kuczynski 1972b, pp. 89, 130; Phelps Brown 1973, p. 66
	Italy 1870–1890, 1890–1914	Clough 1964, p. 382; Mitchell 1976, pp. 185, 744; Neufeld 1961, p. 540; Seton-Watson 1967, p. 296
	Netherlands 1870–1890, 1890–1914	de Jonge 1968, pp. 287–503; de Meere 1979, p. 10
	Norway 1850–1870, 1890–1914	Central Bureau of Statistics of Norway 1966, p. 142; Dahmén [Sweden] 1970, p. 16; Hodne 1975, p. 143; Johnsen 1939, p. 521
	Russia 1870–1890	Crisp[d] 1978, pp. 407–408
	Sweden 1850–1870	Bagge et al. 1935, p. 305; Phelps Brown 1973, p. 66; Youngson 1959, p. 182

Table A22 (continued)

Description of Category	Country and Period	Sources
	Switzerland 1890–1914	Siegenthaler 1964, p. 426
	United States 1890–1914	Hansen 1925, p. 33; Kuczynski 1946a, pp. 81, 153; Lebergott 1964, p. 524; Rees 1961, p. 121
Category C Average real wages in industry were reasonably stable with no clear trend.	Australia 1890–1914	Kuczynski [Great Britain] 1972a, pp. 105, 107
	Brazil 1850–1870, 1870–1890	Leff 1972a, p. 248; Stein[e] 1957, pp. 62–63
	Burma 1890–1914	Tun Wai 1961, pp. 90–93
	China 1870–1890?	
	India 1870–1890, 1890–1914	Bhatia 1967, p. 231; Buchanan 1934, p. 350; Kuczynski [Great Britain] 1972a, p. 51; K. Mukerji 1965, p. 657; M. Mukerji 1965, p. 678
	Japan 1850–1870?	Hanley and Yamamura[f] 1977, pp. 69–91; Sumiya and Taira 1979, pp. 126, 137, 183
	Netherlands 1850–1870	de Jonge 1968, pp. 287–288

Table A22 (continued)

Description of Category	Country and Period	Sources
	New Zealand 1890–1914	Kuczynski [Great Britain] 1972a, p. 129; Scholefield 1909, p. 232
	Russia 1890–1914	Crisp 1978, pp. 407–408
	Spain 1870–1890?	Témine et al.[g] 1979, pp. 102–107
	Switzerland 1870–1890	Siegenthaler 1964, p. 426
Category D		
Average real wages in Industry fluctuated with no clear trend.	China 1850–1870?	Perkins et al.[h] 1969, chap. 7
	Egypt 1870–1890, 1890–1914	Issawi[i] 1966a, pp. 426–427, 433
	New Zealand 1850–1870	Sutch[j] 1969, pp. 84–85
	Spain 1850–1870	Témine et al.[h] 1979, pp. 102–103, 114
	United States 1850–1870	Hansen 1925, p. 32; Kuczynski 1946a, pp. 49, 81; Lebergott 1960, p. 493
Category E		
Average real wages in Industry showed a downward movement.	Argentina 1870–1890	Cortés Conde 1976, pp. 144–147; Randall 1977a, p. 118
	Burma 1870–1890	Tun Wai 1961, pp. 47–50

Table A22 (continued)

Description of Category	Country and Period	Sources
	China 1890–1914	Williams and Zimmerman 1935, p. 416
	Egypt 1850–1870	Issawi 1966a, pp. 368–369, 451
	Germany 1850–1870	Kuczynski 1945, p. 78
	India 1850–1870	K. Mukerji 1965, p. 657
	Italy 1850–1870	Neufeld 1961, pp. 40–44, 158–174
	Japan 1870–1890	Minami and Ono 1979, p. 233; Ohkawa 1967, p. 243
	New Zealand 1870–1890	Campbell 1976, p. 75; Kuczynski [Great Britain] 1972a, pp. 114, 129–130; Sutch 1969, p. 89
	Russia 1850–1870	Crisp[m] 1978, p. 408
	Spain 1890–1914	Carr 1966, p. 438; Témine et al. 1979, p. 104

Note: Of the sources in this table, the following are listed in the general section of the bibliography: Bogart 1942, Phelps Brown 1973, Mitchell 1976, and Williams and Zimmerman 1935.

[a] Qualitative statements about the beginning of industry.

[b] Cotton industry workers.

Table A22 (continued)

c Real consumer expenditure per capita.

d St. Petersburg workers.

e Cotton mill workers.

f Qualitative statements about longer periods.

g Guestimate based on general qualitative statements.

h Inferred from statements about subsistence crises and labor force in industry. In China, the amount of wage labor in industry was close to negligible.

i Statements about urban poor and trends in industry.

j Qualitative statements.

k 1900-1924.

l Statements about urban poor, trends in industry, and available labor force.

m St. Petersburg workers.

Table A23

Classification Scheme for Direction of Change in Average Real Wages or Income of the Employed Agricultural Poor, 1850–1870, 1870–1890, 1890–1914[a]

Description of Category	Country and Period	Sources
Category A Average real wages in agriculture showed strong upward movement.	Denmark 1870–1890	Pedersen 1930, pp. 313–314
	Norway 1870–1890, 1890–1914	Central Bureau of Statistics of Norway 1966, p. 142; Hodne 1975, p. 143; Larsen 1948, p. 462; Mitchell 1976, p. 192
	Sweden 1870–1890, 1890–1914	Bagge et al. 1935, p. 305; Dahmén 1970, p. 16; Jörberg 1972, pp. 42, 49
Category B Average real wages in agriculture showed an upward movement, but not a strong one.	Argentina 1850–1870, 1890–1914	Brown 1979, p. 164 Cortés Conde 1976, p. 146; Williams 1920, p. 197
	Australia 1890–1914	Kuczynski [Great Britain] 1972a, p. 104
	Belgium 1890–1914	Mahaim 1904, p. 436; Mitchell 1976, p. 743; Rowntree 1910, pp. 204–205, 231–247
	Burma 1850–1870	Tun Wai 1961, pp. 48–50

Table A23 (continued)

Description of Category	Country and Period	Sources
	Canada 1850–1870?, 1870–1890, 1890–1914	Buckley and Urquhart 1965, pp. 93–96, 291; Firestone[b] 1958, p. 77; Jones[c] 1946, p. 306; Parker[c] 1966, abstract p. 2 and pp. 2–3, 6, 20, 58–91, 98–120
	Denmark 1850–1870, 1890–1914	Pedersen 1930, pp. 313–314
	Egypt 1850–1870	Issawi 1961, p. 373; Owen[d] 1969, pp. 110, 127, 148
	France 1850–1870, 1890–1914	Grantham 1975, p. 347; Kindleberger 1964, pp. 232–235; Kuczynski 1946b, p. 130; Mitchell 1976, p. 742; Sée 1951, pp. 332–333
	Germany 1870–1890, 1890–1914	Ashley 1904, pp. 75, 77, 83; Kuczynski 1945, pp. 129–132; Mitchell 1976, pp. 191, 742
	Great Britain 1850–1870, 1870–1890, 1890–1914	Clapham 1938, p. 100; Hartwell 1972, p. 43; Jones 1964, pp. 328, 338; Kikuchi [Japan] 1979, p. 66; Kuczynski 1972b, pp. 89, 130; Usher 1920, p. 504
	India 1890–1914	Bhatia 1967, p. 231; Buchanan 1934, p. 351; M. Mukerji 1965, p. 678

Table A23 (continued)

Description of Category	Country and Period	Sources
	Italy 1890-1914	Mack Smith 1959, pp. 245-246; Seton-Watson[d] 1967, pp. 290, 296, 316
	Japan 1870-1890, 1890-1914	Ishii[b] 1937, p. 165; Lippit 1978, p. 66; Minami and Ono 1979, p. 233; Ohkawa and Shinohara[b] 1979, p. 342
	Netherlands 1870-1890, 1890-1914	de Jonge 1968, pp. 287-289, 503; de Meere 1979, p. 10
	Norway 1850-1870	Central Bureau of Statistics of Norway 1966, p. 142; Hodne 1975, p. 143; Mitchell 1976, p. 192
	Switzerland 1850-1870(-)?, 1890-1914	Gruner[e] 1968, pp. 88-89, 139; Hauser[f] 1974, p. 607
	United States 1850-1870, 1890-1914	Lebergott 1960, pp. 493, 524-540
Category C Average real wages in agriculture were reasonably stable with no clear trend.	Australia 1870-1890	Kuczynski [Great Britain] 1972a, p. 104
	Brazil 1850-1870, 1890-1914	Eisenberg 1977, p. 358; Furtado 1963, p. 168; Reis 1977, p. 383
	France 1870-1890	Kindleberger 1964, pp. 232-235; Kuczynski 1946b, p. 130

Table A23 (continued)

Description of Category	Country and Period	Sources
	India 1850–1870, 1870–1890	Gadgil 1942, p. 92; M. Mukerji, 1965, pp. 678–685
	Japan 1850–1870?	Hanley and Yamamura[g] 1977, pp. 69–91; Sumiya and Taira 1979, pp. iii, 95, 158–161
	Netherlands 1850–1870	de Jonge 1968, pp. 287–288
	New Zealand 1890–1914	Kuczynski [Great Britain] 1972a, pp. 128–131
	Sweden 1850–1870	Bagge et al. 1935, p. 305; Janson 1931, p. 83; Mitchell 1976, pp. 191, 742
	Switzerland 1870–1890?	Hauser[h] 1961, p. 246
Category D Average real wages in agriculture fluctuated; no clear trend.	Australia 1850–1870	Kuczynski [Great Britain] 1972a, p. 104
	Burma 1870–1890	Hlaing 1964, p. 121
	China 1870–1890, 1890–1914	Condliffe[d] 1932, p. 16; Feuerwerker[d] 1969, pp. 3–15; Mallory[d] 1926, pp. 5–36

Table A23 (continued)

Description of Category	Country and Period	Sources
	Egypt 1870–1890, 1890–1914	Owen[d] 1969, pp. 126, 148, 232–235, 264–267
	New Zealand 1850–1870	Sutch[d] 1969, pp. 84–85
Category E Average real wages in agriculture showed downward movements.	Argentina 1870–1890	Cortés Conde 1976, p. 146; Randall 1977, 2:119; Williams 1920, p. 197
	Belgium[f] 1850–1870, 1870–1890	Dechesne 1932, p. 483; de Laveleye 1870, p. 269; Mahaim 1904, p. 436; Mitchell 1976, p. 743; Rowntree 1910, p. 113
	Brazil 1870–1890	Eisenberg 1977, p. 358; Reis 1977, p. 383
	Burma 1890–1914	Hlaing 1964, p. 121; Tun Wai 1961, pp. 90–92
	China 1850–1870	Feuerwerker[d] 1969, p. 5
	Germany 1850–1870	Hamerow 1969, p. 40; Kuczynski 1945, pp. 28, 74, 77; Mitchell 1976, pp. 191, 742
	Italy 1850–1870, 1870–1890	Neufeld 1961, pp. 40–44, 158–174; Seton-Watson 1967, p. 85

Table A23 (continued)

Description of Category	Country and Period	Sources
	New Zealand 1870–1890	Sutch[d] 1969, pp. 84, 89
	Russia 1850–1870, 1870–1890, 1890–1914	Carson 1959, pp. 121–125; Gerschenkron 1965, pp. 778–779; Lyashchenko[d] 1949, p. 382
	Spain 1850–1870, 1870–1890, 1890–1914	Malefakis[d] 1970, pp. 5–6; Vicens Vives and Nadal Oller[b] 1969, pp. 645–649
	United States 1870–1890	Lebergott 1964, pp. 524–540

Note: Of the sources in this table, the following is listed in the general section of the bibliography: Mitchell 1976.

[a] Where the agricultural poor consisted overwhelmingly of small peasants, including tenants, rather than wage earners, their position rather than just the position of wage earners has been taken into account. Where different groups—for example, wage earners and small peasants—experienced differing trends, these have been weighted according to their rough relative importance in the population; this procedure is always indicated in table notes. Unless so noted, the classifications are based on directions of change in average real wages.

[b] Per capita real consumption.

[c] Qualitative statements about farmers or timber workers.

[d] Qualitative statements.

Table A23 (continued)

e Inferred from qualitative statements about poor peasants, considerable immigration, and employment in countryside of German paupers between 1850 and 1870, and slight net upward trend in real wages of contruction workers that followed downward trend in the 1850s.

f Based on qualitative statements about rising welfare of small peasants and data on rising agricultural wages for 1901-1913.

g Qualitative statements about longer periods.

h Inferred from qualitative statements about widespread crisis among agricultural peasants and their greatly increased indebtedness and bankruptcy, together with statements about the scarcity and increased costliness of agricultural laborers, who were, however, a very small proportion of the agricultural poor.

i Categorized on the basis of tenants' real income since they made up the majority of the agricultural poor.

Table A24

Classification Scheme for Total Population, 1850, 1870, 1890

Description of Category	Country and Year
Category A Population probably over 100,000,000	China 1850, 1870, 1890 India 1850, 1870, 1890 Russia 1890
Category B Population probably over 50,000,000 and less than 100,000,000	Russia 1850, 1870 United States 1890
Category C Population probably over 25,000,000 and less than 50,000,000	France 1850, 1870, 1890 Germany 1850, 1870, 1890 Great Britain 1870, 1890 Italy 1870, 1890 Japan 1850, 1870, 1890 United States 1870
Category D Population probably over 15,000,000 and less than 25,000,000	Great Britain 1850 Italy 1850 Spain 1850, 1870, 1890 United States 1850
Category E Population probably over 5,000,000 and less than 15,000,000	Belgium 1890 Brazil 1850, 1870, 1890 Burma 1870, 1890 Egypt 1870, 1890
Category F Population probably over 1,000,000 and less than 5,000,000	Argentina 1850, 1870, 1890 Australia 1870, 1890 Belgium 1850, 1870 Burma 1850 Canada 1850, 1870, 1890 Denmark 1850, 1870, 1890 Egypt 1850 Netherlands 1850, 1870, 1890 Norway 1850, 1870, 1890 Sweden 1850, 1870, 1890 Switzerland 1850, 1870, 1890
Category G Population probably less than 1,000,000	Australia 1850 New Zealand 1850, 1870, 1890

Table A25

Total Population, 1830 (in thousands)

Country	Population	Census or Official/ Unofficial Estimate	Year	Sources
Argentina	675	Unofficial	1837	Ferrer 1967, p. 227
Australia	200	Unofficial	1840	Condliffe 1965, p. 171
Belgium	4,090	Census	1831	Mitchell 1976, p. 19
Brazil	3,800	Unofficial	1834	Normano 1968, p. 81
	5,340	Unofficial	1830	Normano 1968, p. 81
Burma	4,000	Unofficial	1830	Cowan 1964, p. 51
Canada	910	Unofficial	1830	Mulhall 1899, p. 455
China	374,600	Unofficial	1819	Perkins 1969, p. 213
Denmark	1,231	Census	1834	Mitchell 1976, p. 19
Egypt	2,540	Unofficial	1821	Hershlag 1964, p. 110
	3,500	Unofficial	1836	Issawi 1966a, p. 373
France	32,569	Census	1831	Mitchell 1976, p. 20
Germany	28,237	Census	1834	Mitchell 1976, p. 20
Great Britain	16,261	Census	1831	Mitchell 1976, p. 24

Table A25 (continued)

Country	Population	Census or Official/ Unofficial Estimate	Year	Sources
India	130,000	Unofficial	1834	Davis 1951, p. 25
Italy	21,212	Official	1833	Mitchell 1976, p. 21
Japan	29,680	Unofficial	1834	Honjo 1965, p. 155
Netherlands	2,613	Census	1829	Mitchell 1976, p. 22
New Zealand	2 (whites) 120 (Maoris)	Official Unofficial	1840 1840	Simkin 1951, p. 117 Pool 1977, p. 235
Norway	1,195	Census	1835	Mitchell 1976, p. 22
Russia	56,100	Unofficial	1830	Mitchell 1976, p. 26
Spain	14,660	Unofficial	1834	Mitchell 1976, p. 27
Sweden	2,888	Census	1830	Mitchell 1976, p. 23
Switzerland	2,190	Census	1837	Mitchell 1976, p. 24
United States	12,901	Official	1830	U.S. Dept. of Commerce, Bureau of the Census 1960, p. 7

Note: Of the sources in this table, the following are listed in the general section of the bibliography. Mitchell 1976 and Mulhall 1899.

Table A26

Total Population, 1850 (In thousands)

Country	Population	Census or Official/ Unofficial Estimate	Year	Sources
Argentina	1,200	Unofficial	1852	Pendle 1963, p. 60
Australia	440	Unofficial	1850	Mulhall 1899, p. 454
	400	Unofficial	1850	Condliffe 1965, p. 171
Belgium	4,337	Census	1846	Mitchell 1976, p. 19
Brazil	7,000	Unofficial	1850	Graham 1968, p. 10
	7,678	Unofficial	1856	Normano 1968, p. 81
Burma	<8,000			Table A27 of this appendix
Canada	2,483	Census	1851	Firestone 1960, p. 229
China	410,000 (±25)	Unofficial	1850	Perkins et al. 1969, p. 216
Denmark	1,415	Census	1850	Mitchell 1976, p. 19
Egypt	4,480	Unofficial	1846	Hershlag 1964, p. 110
France	35,783	Census	1851	Bogart 1942, p. 240
Germany	33,413	Census	1852	Mitchell 1976, p. 20
Great Britain	20,817	Census	1851	Mitchell 1976, p. 24

Table A26 (continued)

Country	Population	Census or Official/ Unofficial Estimate	Year	Sources
India	175,000	Unofficial	1855	Davis 1951, p. 25
Italy	24,351	Census	1852	Mitchell 1976, p. 19
Japan	26,908	Kuni census data	1850	Hanley and Yamamura 1977, p. 52
	30,000	Unofficial	1850	Miyamoto et al. 1965, p. 541
Netherlands	3,057	Census	1849	Mitchell 1976, p. 22
New Zealand	22 (whites)	Unofficial	1850	Simkin 1951, p. 117
	56 (Maoris)	Unofficial	1852	Thomson 1859, p. 325
Norway	1,328	Census	1845	Blegen 1931, p. 5
	1,490	Census	1855	Mitchell 1976, p. 22
Russia	65,077	Official	1851	Mitchell 1976, p. 26
Spain	15,445	Census	1857	Mitchell 1976, p. 23
Sweden	3,471	Census	1850	Mitchell 1976, p. 23
Switzerland	2,393	Census	1850	Mitchell 1976, p. 24
United States	23,192	Census	1850	U.S. Dept. of Commerce, Bureau of the Census 1960, p. 7

Note: Of the sources in this table, the following are listed in the general section of the bibliography: Bogart 1942, Mitchell 1976, and Mulhall 1899.

Table A27

Total Population, 1870 (in thousands)

Country	Population	Census or Official/ Unofficial Estimate	Year	Sources
Argentina	1,737	Census	1869	Ferrer 1967, p. 227
Australia	1,652	Census	1870	Mulhall 1899, p. 454
Belgium	4,828	Census	1866	Mitchell 1976, p. 19
Brazil	10,112	Census	1872	Normano 1968, p. 81
Burma	8,007	Adjusted census data	1871	Davis [India] 1951, p. 236
Canada	3,673	Census	1870	Firestone 1960, p. 229
China	350,000 (±25)	Unofficial	1873	Perkins et al. 1969, p. 216
Denmark	1,785	Census	1870	Mitchell 1976, p. 19
Egypt	5,250	Census	1871	Issawi 1966a, p. 373
France	36,103	Census	1872	Mitchell 1976, p. 20
Germany	41,059	Census	1871	Mitchell 1976, p. 20
Great Britain	26,072	Census	1871	Mitchell 1976, p. 24
India	255,166	Adjusted census data	1871	Davis 1951, p. 27

Table A27 (continued)

Country	Population	Census or Official/ Unofficial Estimate	Year	Sources
Italy	26,801	Census	1871	Mitchell 1976, p. 21
Japan	34,940	Official	1872	Ohkawa 1957, p. 140
Netherlands	3,580	Census	1869	Mitchell 1976, p. 22
New Zealand	256 (whites) 47 (Maoris)	Census Census	1871 1874	Hamilton 1947, p. 138 Pool 1977, p. 58
Norway	1,735	Official	1870	Central Bureau of Statistics of Norway 1966, p. 24
Russia	84,500	Unofficial	1870	Mitchell 1976, p. 26
Spain	15,645 16,622	Census Census	1860 1877	Mitchell 1976, p. 23 Mitchell 1976, p. 23
Sweden	4,165	Census	1870	Mitchell 1976, p. 23
Switzerland	2,669	Census	1870	Mitchell 1976, p. 24
United States	39,905	Census	1870	U.S. Dept. of Commerce, Bureau of the Census 1960, p. 7

Note: Of the sources in this table, the following are listed in the general section of the bibliography: Mitchell 1976 and Mulhall 1899.

Table A28

Total Population, 1890 (In thousands)

Country	Population	Census or Official/ Unofficial Estimate	Year	Sources
Argentina	3,955	Census	1895	Ferrer 1967, p. 227
Australia	3,022	Census	1891	Butlin 1964, p. 12
Belgium	6,069	Census	1890	Mitchell 1976, p. 19
Brazil	14,334	Census	1890	Normano 1968, p. 81
Burma	9,778	Adjusted census data	1891	Davis [India] 1951, p. 236
Canada	4,820	Census	1890	Firestone 1960, p. 229
China	385,000 (±25)	Unofficial	1893	Perkins et al. 1969, p. 216
Denmark	2,172	Census	1890	Mitchell 1976, p. 19
Egypt	9,715	Census	1897	Issawi 1966, p. 373
France	38,133	Census	1891	Mitchell 1976, p. 19
Germany	49,428	Census	1890	Mitchell 1976, p. 20
Great Britain	33,029	Census	1891	Mitchell 1976, p. 24
India	282,134	Census	1891	Davis 1951, p. 27

Table A28 (continued)

Country	Population	Census or Official/ Unofficial Estimate	Year	Sources
Italy	30,300	Official	1890/91	Mitchell 1973, p. 747
Japan	40,164	Official	1890	Ohkawa 1957, p. 140
Netherlands	4,511	Census	1889	Mitchell 1976, p. 22
New Zealand	634 (whites) 42 (Maoris)	Census Census	1891 1892	Scholefield 1909, p. 180 Levasseur 1897, p. 315
Norway	2,001	Census	1890	Mitchell 1976, p. 21
Russia	117,800	Unofficial	1890	Mitchell 1976, p. 26
Spain	17,550	Census	1887	Mitchell 1976, p. 23
Sweden	4,785	Census	1890	Mitchell 1976, p. 23
Switzerland	2,918	Census	1888	Mitchell 1976, p. 24
United States	63,056	Census	1890	U.S. Dept. of Commerce, Bureau of the Census 1960, p. 7

Note: Of the sources in this table, the following are listed in the general section of the bibliography: Mitchell 1976 and Levasseur 1897.

Table A29

Total Population, 1914 (In thousands)

Country	Population	Census or Official/ Unofficial Estimate	Year	Sources
Argentina	7,885	Census	1914	Ferrer 1967, p. 227
Australia	4,455	Census	1911	Gregory 1916, p. 12
Belgium	7,424	Census	1910	Mitchell 1976, p. 19
Brazil	30,636	Census	1920	Normano 1968, p. 81
Burma	12,288	Adjusted census data	1911	Davis [India] 1951, p. 236
Canada	7,116	Census	1910	Firestone 1958, p. 46
China	430,000 (±25)	Unofficial	1913	Perkins et al. 1969, p. 216
Denmark	2,921	Census	1916	Mitchell 1976, p. 19
Egypt	12,751	Census	1917	Issawi 1966a, p. 373
France	39,192	Census	1911	Mitchell 1976, p. 19
Germany	64,926	Census	1910	Mitchell 1976, p. 20
Great Britain	40,831	Census	1911	Mitchell 1976, p. 24
India	302,985	Adjusted census data	1911	Davis 1951, p. 27

Table A29 (continued)

Country	Population	Census or Official/ Unofficial Estimate	Year	Sources
Italy	34,671	Census	1911	Mitchell 1976, p. 21
Japan	51,856	Official	1913	Ohkawa et al. 1957, p. 141
Netherlands	5,858	Census	1909	Mitchell 1976, p. 22
New Zealand	1,150	Census	1915	Condliffe 1959, p. 252
Norway	2,498	Official	1915	Central Bureau of Statistics of Norway 1966, p. 24
Russia	160,700	Unofficial	1910	Mitchell 1976, p. 24
Spain	19,927	Census	1910	Mitchell 1976, p. 23
Sweden	5,713	Census	1915	Mitchell 1976, p. 23
Switzerland	3,753	Census	1910	Mitchell 1976, p. 24
United States	99,118	Census	1914	U.S. Dept. of Commerce, Bureau of the Census 1960, p. 7

Notes: The data in this table are not utilized in this study. They are provided for the interest of the reader.

Of the sources in this table, the following is listed in the general section of the bibliography: Mitchell 1976.

Table A30

Classification Scheme for Rate of Population Growth (Lagged),
1830-1850, 1850-1870, 1870-1890[a]

Description of Category	Country and Period
Category A Population growth probably over 3 percent	Argentina 1830-1850, 1870-1890 Australia 1830-1850, 1850-1870, 1870-1890(-) Canada 1830-1850 New Zealand 1850-1870, 1870-1890 United States 1830-1850
Category B Population growth probably 2 percent or over, but less than 3 percent	Argentina 1850-1870 Brazil 1830-1850(-)[b] Canada 1850-1870 Egypt 1830-1850, 1870-1890 India 1850-1870 United States 1850-1870, 1870-1890

Category C
Population growth
probably 1 percent or
over but less than 2
percent
	Belgium 1870-1890(-)
	Brazil 1850-1870, 1870-1890(+)
	Burma[c] 1830-1850, 1850-1870,
	   1870-1890(-)
	Canada 1870-1890
	Denmark 1850-1870, 1870-1890(-)
	Egypt 1850-1870
	Great Britain 1830-1850,
	   1850-1870, 1870-1890
	India 1830-1850
	Netherlands 1870-1890
	Norway 1830-1850, 1850-1870(-)
	Russia 1850-1870, 1870-1890
	Sweden 1830-1850(-), 1850-1870(-)

Category D Population growth probably over .5 percent, but less than 1 percent	Belgium 1850-1870 China 1870-1890(-) Denmark 1830-1850(+) France 1830-1850 Germany 1830-1850(+), 1850-1870, 1870-1890 India 1870-1890(-)

Table A30 (continued)

Description of Category	Country and Period
	Italy 1830-1850, 1850-1870, 1870-1890 Japan 1850-1870, 1870-1890 Netherlands 1830-1850, 1850-1870 Norway 1870-1890 Russia 1830-1850 Sweden 1870-1890 Switzerland 1830-1850, 1850-1870, 1870-1890(-)
Category E Population growth probably between 0 and .5 percent	Belgium 1830-1850 China 1830-1850 France 1850-1870, 1870-1890 Japan 1830-1850 Spain 1830-1850, 1850-1870, 1870-1890
Category F Population growth probably negative	China 1850-1870 New Zealand 1830-1850[d]

[a] The average annual growth rates in this table are based on the data in tables A25-A29.

[b] We used an average of the two population estimates available for the 1830s.

[c] Two sets of estimates are available for Burma in 1891 (Hlaing 1964, p. 96; and Davis 1951, p. 236) and both are based on the Census of India. We chose the Davis estimate because he attempted corrections for boundary changes taking the definition of Burma as it existed in the 1920s.

[d] Including the Maoris, the classification is F; excluding the Maoris, the classification would be A+.

Table A31

Classification Scheme for Net Immigration,
1850-1870, 1870-1890, 1890-1914

Description of Category	Country and Period
Category A Net immigration was probably more than one-third of the increase in population.	Argentina 1870-1890, 1890-1914 Australia 1850-1870, 1870-1890 Canada 1890-1914 New Zealand 1850-1870, 1870-1890, 1890-1914 United States 1850-1870, 1870-1890, 1890-1914
Category B Net immigration was probably less than one-third, but more than one-tenth, of the increase in population.	Argentina 1850-1870 Australia 1890-1914 Brazil 1870-1890, 1890-1914
Category C Net immigration was clearly positive, but was probably less than one-tenth of the increase in population.	Belgium 1870-1890, 1890-1914 Brazil 1850-1870 Burma 1850-1870, 1870-1890, 1890-1914? China 1870-1890, 1890-1914 Egypt 1850-1870?, 1870-1890, 1890-1914 Italy 1850-1870? Russia 1850-1870, 1870-1890
Category D Net emigration was positive, but was probably less than one-tenth of the sum of population change plus net emigration.	Belgium 1850-1870 Canada 1850-1870 China 1850-1870 Denmark 1850-1870? France 1870-1890, 1890-1914 Germany 1890-1914 India 1850-1870, 1870-1890, 1890-1914 Japan 1850-1870, 1870-1890, 1890-1914 Netherlands 1870-1890, 1890-1914 Russia 1890-1914 Spain 1850-1870? Switzerland 1890-1914

Table A31 (continued)

Description of Category	Country and Period
Category E Net emigration was probably less than one-third, but more than one-tenth, of the sum of the population change plus net emigration.	Canada 1870-1890 Denmark 1870-1890, 1890-1914 France 1850-1870 Germany 1850-1870, 1870-1890 Netherlands 1850-1870 Norway 1850-1870 Spain 1870-1890, 1890-1914 Sweden 1850-1870 Switzerland 1850-1870
Category F Net emigration was probably more than one-third of the sum of population change plus net emigration.	Great Britain 1850-1870, 1870-1890, 1890-1914 Italy 1870-1890, 1890-1914 Norway 1870-1890, 1890-1914 Sweden 1870-1890, 1890-1914 Switzerland 1870-1890

Table A32

Net Immigration, 1850-1870

Country and Period	Estimated Net Immigration, Emigration (-)	Sources
Argentina		
1850s	30,000 (gross?)	Ferns 1960, p. 340
1857-1860	11,100	Díaz Alejandro 1970, p. 23
1861-1870	76,600	Díaz Alejandro 1970, p. 23
1857-1870	88,000	Davie 1949, p. 449
1857-1870	87,694	Ferenczi 1929, p. 543
Australia		
1861-1870	166,600	Butlin 1964, p. 28
1851-1860	740,000	Davie 1949, p. 426
1860-1870	190,514	Ferenczi 1929, p. 543
Belgium		
1851-1870	-26,158	Ferenczi 1929, p. 603
Brazil		
1861-1870	98,000 (gross)	Ashworth 1962, p. 188
1851-1870	212,162 (gross)	Burns 1970, p. 187
1851-1870	219,318 (gross)	Davie 1949, p. 456
1851-1870	214,893 (gross)	Ferenczi 1929, p. 549
Burma		
1862-1872	64,000[a]	Hlaing 1964, p. 96
Canada		
1861-1870	283,000 (gross)	Ashworth 1962, p. 188
1851-1870	560,993 (gross)	Ferenczi 1929, p. 360
1851-1871	-16,000	McDougall 1961, p. 172
1851-1871	-68,000	Marr and Paterson 1980, p. 173
China		
1851-1870	-269,292 (gross)	Ferenczi 1929, p. 929
Denmark	Not available[b]	Lassen 1966, p. 157
Egypt		
1836-1878	65,000 (gross)	Issawi 1966a, p. 365

Table A32 (continued)

Country and Period	Estimated Net Immigration, Emigration (-)	Sources
France		
1857-1870	-61,498 (gross)	Ferenczi 1929, p. 677
Germany		
1851-1870	-1,256,012 (gross)	Ferenczi 1929, p. 692
Great Britain		
1851-1870	-3,910,000	Mitchell 1976, p. 140
India		
1851-1870	-420,315 (gross)	Ferenczi 1929, p. 904
Italy	Not available[b]	Foerster 1919, pp. 4-6
Japan	Not available[b]	Davie 1949, p. 318
Netherlands		
1865-1870	-20,200	Mitchell 1976, p. 139
1851-1870	-83,400 (gross)	Ferenczi 1929, p. 139
New Zealand		
1840-1853	2-3 thousand	Davie 1949, p. 432
1860-1864	132,000 (gross)	Davie 1949, p. 432
1861-1870	195,000 (gross)	Ashworth 1962, p. 188
1853-1870	147,574	Ferenczi 1929, pp. 1000, 1005
Norway		
1851-1870	-133,968 (gross)	Ferenczi 1929, p. 748
Russia		
1850-1869	232,300	Mitchell 1976, pp. 140, 143
1851-1870	312,201	Ferenczi 1929, p. 796
Spain	Not available[b]	Vicens Vives and Nadal Oller 1969, p. 622; Nadal 1975, p. 23
Sweden		
1851-1870	-139,347	Ferenczi 1929, p. 757

Table A32 (continued)

Country and Period	Estimated Net Immigration, Emigration (−)	Sources
Switzerland		
1850–1870	−67,000	Menzel 1979, p. 135
United States		
1860	2,598,214 (gross)	<u>Encyclopaedia Britannica</u> 1911, 18:429
1870	2,314,824 (gross)	<u>Encyclopaedia Britannica</u> 1911, 18:429
1861–1870	3,051,000 (gross)	Ashworth 1962, p. 188
1851–1860	2,598,000 (gross)	U. S. Dept. of Commerce, Bureau of the Census 1960, p. 57
1861–1870	2,314,000 (gross)	U. S. Dept. of Commerce, Bureau of the Census 1960, p. 57

Note: Of the sources in this table, the following are listed in the general section of the bibliography: Ashworth 1962, Davie 1949, Ferenczi 1929, Mitchell 1976, and <u>Encyclopaedia Britannica</u> 1910–1911.

[a] Calculated on the assumption that the net increase in the number of Indians in Burma is a reasonable proxy for net immigration during this period.

[b] Countries for which quantitative data are not available are classified using qualitative information from the sources cited.

Table A33

Net Immigration, 1870-1890

Country and Period	Estimated Net Immigration, Emigration (-)	Sources
Argentina		
1871-1880	85,100	Díaz Alejandro 1970, p. 23
1881-1890	637,700	Díaz Alejandro 1970, p. 23
1871-1890	723,000	Davie 1949, p. 449
1871-1890	722,989	Ferenczi 1929, p. 543
Australia		
1870-1889	565,900	McGhee 1970, p. 182
1870-1890	574,600	Butlin 1964, p. 28
1871-1890	574,545	Ferenczi 1929, p. 947
Belgium		
1870-1889	65,100	Mitchell 1976, pp. 137, 138, 141
1871-1890	55,367	Ferenczi 1929, p. 603
Brazil		
1871-1880	219,000 (gross)	Ashworth 1962, p. 188
1881-1890	531,000 (gross)	Ashworth 1962, p. 188
1870-1888	582,472 (gross)	Burns 1970, p. 187
1871-1890	750,034 (gross)	Davie 1949, p. 456
1871-1890	750,034 (gross)	Ferenczi 1929, p. 549
Burma		
1872-1881	383,000 (gross)	Hlaing 1964, p. 96
Canada		
1871-1880	220,000 (gross)	Ashworth 1962, p. 188
1881-1890	886,000 (gross)	Ashworth 1962, p. 188
1881-1890	886,177 (gross)	Davie 1949, p. 417
1871-1890	1,105,960 (gross)	Ferenczi 1929, p. 360
1871-1891	-194,000	McDougall 1961, p. 172
1871-1891	-290,000	Marr and Paterson 1980, p. 173
China		
1876-1890	354,199	Ferenczi 1929, pp. 927-931
Denmark		
1871-1890	-120,215 (gross)	Ferenczi 1929, p. 667

Table A33 (continued)

Country and Period	Estimated Net Immigration, Emigration (−)	Sources
Egypt		
1873–1877	64,561	Ferenczi 1929, p. 1033
France		
1871–1890	−175,720 (gross)	Ferenczi 1929, p. 677
Germany		
1871–1890	−1,968,391 (gross)	Ferenczi 1929, pp. 692, 697
Great Britain		
1871–1890	−3,061,800	Mitchell 1976, p. 140
India		
1871–1890	−323,994 (gross)	Ferenczi 1929, p. 904
1878–1890	−105,311	Ferenczi 1929, pp. 904–906
Italy		
1871–1890	−3,056,510 (gross)	Mitchell 1976, p. 139
	−1,458,000	Clough 1964, p. 381
Japan		
prior to 1876	Not available[a]	Davie 1949, p. 318
1876–1890	−44,472 (gross)	Ferenczi 1929, p. 934
Netherlands		
1871–1890	−42,900	Mitchell 1976, p. 139
New Zealand		
1871–1880	197,000 (gross)	Ashworth 1962, p. 188
1881–1890	150,000 (gross)	Ashworth 1962, p. 188
1871–1890	125,833	Ferenczi 1929, pp. 1000, 1005
Norway		
1871–1890	−269,922 (gross)	Ferenczi 1929, p. 748
Russia		
1870–1889	471,100	Mitchell 1976, pp. 140, 143
1871–1890	485,637	Ferenczi 1929, p. 796
Spain		
1882–1890	−148,385	Ferenczi 1929, p. 849

Table A33 (continued)

Country and Period	Estimated Net Immigration, Emigration (-)	Sources
Sweden		
1875-1890	-406,586	Ferenczi 1929, p. 757
Switzerland		
1871-1890	-121,891 (gross)	Ferenczi 1929, p. 764
1870-1888	-110,000	Menzel 1979, p. 135
United States		
1871-1880	3,709,000 (gross)	Ashworth 1962, p. 188
1881-1890	7,655,000 (gross)	Ashworth 1962, p. 188
1871-1890	8,138,847 (gross)	Ferenczi 1929, p. 394
1871-1890	8,058,804 (gross)	U.S. Dept. of Commerce, Bureau of the Census 1960, p. 57

Note: Of the sources in this table, the following are listed in the general section of the bibliography: Ashworth 1962, Davie 1949, Ferenczi 1929, and Mitchell 1976.

[a] Classified with help of qualitative information from the source cited.

Table A34

Net Immigration, 1890-1914

Country and Period	Estimated Net Immigration, Emigration (-)		Sources
Argentina			
1891-1900	319,900		Díaz Alejandro 1970, p. 23
1901-1910	1,120,200		Díaz Alejandro 1970, p. 23
1891-1910	1,440,000		Davie 1949, p. 449
1891-1914	1,830,165		Ferenczi 1929, p. 543
Australia			
1901-1910	652,000	(gross)	Ashworth 1962, p. 188
1890	24,600		McGhee 1970, p. 182
1901-1905	-16,793		Davie 1949, p. 427
Belgium			
1906-1910	57,278		Davie 1949, p. 427
1891-1914	286,636		Ferenczi 1929, p. 947
1890-1914	125,700		Mitchell 1976, pp. 137-138, 141
1891-1914	125,900		Ferenczi 1929, p. 603
Brazil			
1891-1900	1,144,000	(gross)	Ashworth 1962, p. 188
1901-1910	691,000	(gross)	Ashworth 1962, p. 188
1891-1910	1,834,769	(gross)	Davie 1949, p. 456
1891-1914	2,415,796	(gross)	Ferenczi 1929, p. 550
1899-1907	101,184		Ferenczi 1929, pp. 550, 555
Burma			
1891-1901	1,039,000	(gross?)	Hlaing 1964, p. 96
Canada			
1891-1900	321,000	(gross)	Ashworth 1962, p. 188
1901-1910	1,453,000	(gross)	Ashworth 1962, p. 188
1891-1900	321,302	(gross)	Davie 1949, p. 417
1901-1910	1,453,391	(gross)	Davie 1949, p. 417
1891-1914	3,348,218	(gross)	Ferenczi 1929, p. 361
1891-1911	679,000		McDougall 1961, p. 172
1891-1911	534,000		Urquhart and Buckley 1965, p. 22

Table A34 (continued)

Country and Period	Estimated Net Immigration, Emigration (-)	Sources
China		
1900-1914	823,507	Ferenczi 1929, pp. 928
Denmark		
1891-1914	-156,914 (gross)	Ferenczi 1929, p. 667
Egypt		
France		
1892-1914	-118,872 (gross)	Ferenczi 1929, p. 680
Germany		
1891-1914	-888,401 (gross)	Ferenczi 1929, p. 697
Great Britain		
1891-1914	-3,043,000	Mitchell 1976, p. 140
India		
1891-1914	-203,343	Ferenczi 1929, p. 904
Italy		
1891-1914	-11,458,500 (gross)	Mitchell 1976, p. 139
1890-1910	-2,391,000	Clough 1964, p. 381
Japan		
1890-1914	-692,428 (gross)	Ferenczi 1929, p. 934
Netherlands		
1890-1914	-61,000	Mitchell 1976, pp. 139, 143
New Zealand		
1891-1900	197,000 (gross)	Ashworth 1962, p. 188
1901-1910	347,000 (gross)	Ashworth 1962, p. 188
1891-1914	144,856	Ferenczi 1929, pp. 1000, 1005
Norway		
1891-1914	-379,534 (gross)	Ferenczi 1929, p. 751
Russia		
1890-1914	1,027,200	Mitchell 1976, pp. 140, 143
1891-1914	-1,045,594	Ferenczi 1929, p. 796

Table A34 (continued)

Country and Period	Estimated Net Immigration, Emigration (-)	Sources
Spain		
1891-1914	-694,110	Ferenczi 1929, p. 849
Sweden		
1891-1914	-379,534	Ferenczi 1929, p. 751
Switzerland		
1891-1914	-116,044 (gross)	Ferenczi 1929, p. 764
United States		
1891-1900	5,998,000 (gross)	Ashworth 1962, p. 188
1901-1910	13,702,000 (gross)	Ashworth 1962, p. 188
1911-1920	11,410,000 (gross)	Ashworth 1962, p. 188
1891-1914	11,891,065 (gross)	Ferenczi 1929, pp. 394, 471
1891-1914	16,616,081 (gross)	U.S. Dept. of Commerce, Bureau of the Census 1960, p. 56

Note: Of the sources in this table, the following are listed in the general section of the bibliography: Ashworth 1962, Davie 1949, Ferenczi 1929, and Mitchell 1976.

Table A35

Classification Scheme for Extent of Adult Illiteracy, 1850, 1870, 1890

Description of Category	Country and Year	Sources
Category A Countries in which the adult illiteracy rate was higher than 90 percent	Brazil 1850[a]	Graham 1968, p. 17
	Egypt 1850, 1870, 1890	Hershlag 1964, p. 114; Lloyd 1933, p. 109; Tignor 1966, p. 324
	India 1850, 1870, 1890	Sidhanta 1965, p. 45
	Russia 1850, 1870	Cipolla 1969, pp. 114, 118; Levasseur 1897, p. 221; Roach 1964, p. 111
Category B Countries in which the adult illiteracy rate was higher than 80 percent but lower than 90 percent	Argentina 1850[b]	Díaz Alejandro 1970, p. 425
	Brazil 1870[c]	Graham 1968, p. 17
	China 1850, 1870, 1890[d]	Banks 1971, p. 213; Levasseur 1897, p. 292
	Russia 1890	Cipolla 1969, pp. 118, 120, 128
	Spain 1850	Gannes and Repard 1936, p. 185

Table A35 (continued)

Description of Category	Country and Year	Sources
Category C Countries in which the adult illiteracy rate was higher than 70 percent but lower than 80 percent	Argentina 1870	Díaz Alejandro 1970, p. 425
	Brazil 1890(+)[e]	Levasseur 1897, p. 488; Spiegel 1949, p. 90
	Burma 1890	Encyclopaedia Britannica 1910, 4:841
	Italy 1850	Cipolla 1969, p. 115; Neufeld 1961, p. 126
	Japan 1850	Crawcour 1965, p. 34; Levasseur 1897, p. 277
	Spain 1870	Cipolla 1969, p. 115; Levasseur 1897, pp. 177, 571
Category D Countries in which the adult illiteracy rate was higher than 60 percent but lower than 70 percent	Burma 1850, 1870[f]	Cipolla 1969, table 6 and pp. 113–114; Hagen 1956, pp. 10, 22
	Italy 1870(+)	Levasseur 1897, p. 192; Neufeld 1961, p. 126
	Japan 1870	Crawcour 1965, p. 34
	New Zealand 1850?9	Lynd 1945, p. 355

Table A35 (continued)

Description of Category	Country and Year	Sources
Category E Countries in which the adult illiteracy rate was higher than 50 percent but lower than 60 percent	Argentina 1890	Cochran and Reina 1962, p. 34; Díaz Alejandro 1970, p. 425
	Italy 1890	Cipolla 1969, pp. 118, 124; Levasseur 1897, p. 571
	Spain 1890	Cipolla 1969, p. 128; Vilar 1967, p. 82
Category F Countries in which the adult illiteracy rate was higher than 40 percent but lower than 50 percent	Belgium 1850[h]	Barnard 1872, p. 456; Cipolla 1969, p. 115
	France 1850	Cipolla 1969, p. 115
	Japan 1890[i]	Crawcour 1965, p. 34; Levasseur 1897, p. 287
Category G Countries in which the adult illiteracy rate was higher than 30 percent but lower than 40 percent	Australia 1850?[j]	Cipolla 1969, p. 115
	Belgium 1870	Cipolla 1969, p. 127
	Canada 1850[k]	Greer 1978, p. 327
	France 1870(-)	Cipolla 1969, p. 127
	Great Britain 1850	Cipolla 1969, p. 115; Lynd 1945, p. 355

Table A35 (continued)

Description of Category	Country and Year	Sources
Category H Countries in which the adult illiteracy rate was higher than 20 percent but lower than 30 percent	Australia 1870	Mulhall 1899, p. 242
	Belgium 1890	Cipolla 1969, p. 127
	Canada 1870(-)[l]	Greer 1978, p. 327
	Germany 1850	Cipolla 1969, pp. 113, 115
	Great Britain 1870	Lynd 1945, p. 367
	Netherlands 1850	Barnard 1854, pp. 595-597; Cipolla 1969, p. 113; Levasseur 1897, p. 29
	New Zealand 1870	Mulhall 1899, p. 242
	United States 1850[m]	Barnard 1872, p. 875; Fishlow 1966, p. 46
Category I Countries in which the adult illiteracy rate was higher than 10 percent but lower than 20 percent	Canada 1890[n]	Greer 1978, p. 327; Mulhall 1899, p. 455
	France 1890	Cipolla 1969, pp. 123-124
	Germany 1870[o]	Cipolla 1969, p. 118; Levasseur 1897, p. 571
	Netherlands 1870, 1890(-)[p]	Barnard 1872, p. 456; Levasseur 1897, pp. 29, 571

Table A35 (continued)

Description of Category	Country and Year	Sources
	New Zealand 1890(-)	Mulhall 1899, p. 242
	Norway 1850?9	Barnard 1854, p. 623; Barnard 1872, pp. 484-485; Cipolla 1969, p. 113
	United States 1870(+), 1890	U.S. Dept. of Commerce, Bureau of the Census 1960, p. 214
Category J Countries in which the adult illiteracy rate was lower than 10 percent	Australia 1890	Levasseur 1897, p. 571
	Denmark 1850?r, 1870, 1890	Cipolla 1969, p. 115; Danstrup 1948, p. 91; Hovde 1943, 2:603; Levasseur 1897, pp. 240-246, 502
	Germany 1890	Cipolla 1969, p. 118; Levasseur 1897, p. 571
	Great Britain 1890	Cipolla 1969, pp. 123-125
	Norway 1870, 1890	Barnard 1854, p. 623; Cipolla 1969, p. 113
	Sweden 1850(+), 1870, 1890	Cipolla 1969, p. 115; Levasseur 1897, pp. 227, 571
	Switzerland 1850, 1870, 1890	Cipolla 1969, pp. 113, 118; Levasseur 1897, pp. 146, 348, 571

Table A35 (continued)

Note: Of the sources in this table, the following are listed in the general section of the bibliography: Banks 1971, Barnard 1854, Barnard 1872, Cipolla 1969, Encyclopaedia Britannica 1910–1911, Levasseur 1897, Mulhall 1899, and Roach 1964.

a Brazil 1850: Inferred from assumption that (1) illiteracy among free persons was over 80 percent (in 1877, it was 78 percent according to Graham 1968, p. 17) and (2) the 2 million slaves in 1850 were illiterate. (The estimate of the number of slaves is from Graham 1968, p. 161.)

b Argentina 1850: Inferred to be over 80 percent in 1850, given that it was 77 percent in 1869 (Díaz Alejandro 1970, p. 425).

c Brazil 1870: Inferred from (1) report that illiteracy among free persons in 1877 was 78 percent (Graham 1968, p. 17) and (2) assumption that the more than one million slaves were illiterate.

d China 1850–1890: guesstimate based on the fact that in 1919 only 1 percent of the population was enrolled in primary schools (Banks 1971, p. 213), and that, nevertheless, during the latter half of the nineteenth century a majority of boys went to temple schools for several years (Levasseur 1897, p. 292).

e Brazil 1890: Inferred from an illiteracy rate of 84 percent in 1881 and 74 percent in 1900.

f Burma 1850, 1870: based on Hagen's statement that there was less illiteracy in Burma in the early nineteenth century than in Western Europe (males only). Assuming that the rate among Burmese males was the same as that of Western Europe about 1850, about 30 percent (Cipolla 1969, table 6 and pp. 113–114), and assuming a female rate of 100 percent gives an overall illiteracy rate of 65 percent. Illiteracy then increased under colonial rule (Hagen 1956, p. 22).

g New Zealand 1850: based on the assumption that illiteracy among the European population was the same as in England, about 38 percent (Lynd 1945, p. 355), and that illiteracy among the Maoris was at least 80 percent. The Maoris constituted about 72 percent of the population (see tables A25–A28).

h Belgium 1850: based on the assumption that Cipolla's estimate of illiteracy of 45–50 percent refers to the census year of 1846.

Table A35 (continued)

i Japan 1890: In 1868, 40–50 percent of boys and only 15 percent of girls were getting any kind of formal schooling (Crawcour 1965, p. 34); thus, literacy among older adult women cannot have been much over half that of men in 1890. Averaging (1) the illiteracy rate among military recruits in 1891, 27 percent (Levasseur 1897, p. 287), and (2) a 50 percent higher assumed illiteracy rate for women in that age group, and making a small upward adjustment for greater illiteracy among older members of the population, we get a very probable adult illiteracy rate of over 40 percent.

j Australia 1850: based on the assumption that the rate of illiteracy in Australia was 25 percent higher than that given for England and Wales by Cipolla (1969, p. 115).

k Canada 1850: The rate of adult literacy (ability to read and write) in Quebec was 43 percent in 1839 (for those over the age of 15) and 64.6 percent in 1861 (for those over the age of 20) (Greer 1978, p. 327). We assume, therefore, that adult literacy in Quebec was in the neighborhood of 54 percent in 1850. According to the census of 1891, the literacy of the Ontario educational cohort educated between 1842 and 1861 was 88.6 percent and that of the cohort educated before 1841 was 79.3 percent. (Ibid.; rates for males and females have been averaged.) Assuming that cohorts educated earlier had lower literacy rates, it seems plausible to suppose that the adult literacy rate in Ontario in 1850 was not much above 70 percent. Weighting Ontario twice as heavily as Quebec (see note n below) gives a guesstimate for the nation of over 60 percent and under 70 percent literacy. We thus assign Canada in 1850 to the category of illiteracy over 30 percent and under 40 percent.

l Canada 1870: If we interpolate between the 64.6 percent adult literacy rate for Quebec in 1861 and the 70.4 percent rate in 1891 (Greer 1978, p. 327), we get between 66 and 67 percent for 1870. According to the 1891 census, the literacy rate for the educational cohort of 1862–1871 was 63.9 percent for men and 72.5 percent for women, with the literacy of cohorts educated earlier much lower (ibid.). Hence, 65 or 66 percent would appear to be a plausible estimate for Quebec in 1870. For Ontario, the estimate for the pre–1841 educational cohort, 79.3 percent (the 1891 census, ibid.), gives a reasonable lower bound to our estimate for 1870, while the estimate of 88.6 percent for the 1842–1861 educational cohort gives a reasonable upper bound. If we weight Ontario twice as heavily as Quebec (see note n below), we obtain a range guesstimate for Canada as a whole of 75 to 80 or 81 percent. This suggests a categorization of between 20 and 30 percent illiteracy, but closer to 20 percent.

Table A35 (continued)

m United States 1850: According to Barnard (1872, p. 875), there were 2,872,111 whites and blacks over the age of 21 who could neither read nor write. If we assume between 2/5 and 3/5 of the population over 21, that gives an illiteracy rate of between 21 and 31 percent. Illiteracy was undoubtedly less among those between the ages of 10 and 21 than among those over 21, given primary-school enrollments of 38 percent in 1840 and over 50 percent in 1850 (Fishlow 1966, p. 46). A classification at the lower end of the range for this category appears reasonable.

n Canada 1890: According to the 1891 census, all educational cohorts in Ontario who were less than 40 years old had, on the average, literacy rates of over 90 percent and those between 40 and 60 had average literacy rates of over 80 percent. Quebec's literacy rate was 70 percent (Greer 1978, p. 327). Weighting Ontario twice as heavily as Quebec gives an overall national literacy rate of between 80 and 90 percent. The weights are crude. French Canadians constituted 30 percent of the population in 1881 (Mulhall 1899, p. 455). We have assumed that literacy in Quebec represents that of French Canadians and that literacy in Ontario represents that for the rest of Canadians. It is likely that we have somewhat overestimated the literacy of both.

o Germany 1870: based on the assumption that the 12.2 percent illiteracy rate in Prussia in 1871 (Levasseur 1897, p. 571) was not substantially less than that for Germany as a whole.

p Netherlands 1870: It is assumed that the rate of female illiteracy was not much higher than that of male conscripts in 1870, 16.3 percent (Levasseur 1897, p. 29), so that adult illiteracy is likely to have been over 10 percent. Illiteracy was reported in 1857 to have been below 20 percent (Barnard 1872, p. 456).

Netherlands 1890: Since the rate of illiteracy among male conscripts was not brought below 11 percent until 1885 (Levasseur 1897, p. 571), it seems likely that adult illiteracy in 1890 was still above 10 percent.

q Norway 1850: a guesstimate based on (1) Barnard's statement (1854, p. 623) that primary education was generally diffused in 1850, with 14 percent of the population receiving instruction in public schools by 1837, and (2) offsetting reports that attendance was poor and the school "year" lasted only a few weeks in many rural areas in the 1860s (Barnard 1872, pp. 484–485).

Table A35 (continued)

r Denmark 1850: a guesstimate based on the estimate for Sweden, 10 percent (Cipolla 1969, p. 115), together with clear indications that primary education spread earlier and farther in Denmark than in Sweden. See Levasseur 1897, pp. 245–246, and Hovde 1943, p. 603, on Denmark; Levasseur 1897, p. 502, and Barnard 1854, p. 622, on Sweden.

Table A36

Classification Scheme for Rate of Spread of Primary Education (Lagged), 1830–1850, 1850–1870, 1870–1890

Description of Category	Country and Period	Sources
Category A Countries where the percentage of children 6–14 in school probably increased by at least 15 percentage points during the period and by the end of the period over three-quarters of this age group were probably in school	Australia 1870–1890	Fitzpatrick 1946, pp. 205, 207; Levasseur 1897, pp. 294, 307, 310, 312, 565; Mulhall 1899, p. 454; Partridge 1968, pp. 31–32, 33–35
	Denmark 1830–1850	Barnard 1854, p. 619; Barnard 1872, p. 472; Hovde 1943, 2:603; Tracy 1964, p. 108
	Germany 1830–1850	Barnard 1854, pp. 89, 139; Hamerow 1969, p. 279; Levasseur 1897, pp. 112, 120, 125, 131–132, 595; Roach 1964, p. 109
	Great Britain 1870–1890	Banks 1971, p. 233; Levasseur 1897, p. 12; Lynd 1945, p. 367; Trevelyan 1937, pp. 354–355
	Netherlands 1830–1850	Barnard 1854, pp. 596–597; Barnard 1872, p. 412; Levasseur 1897, p. 565
	New Zealand 1870–1890(–)	Condliffe and Airey 1954, p. 141; Levasseur 1897, pp. 313–319; Sinclair 1961, p. 139; Sutch 1941, pp. 75–76
	Norway 1850–1870	Barnard 1872, pp. 481–484, 495; Derry 1957, p. 163; Levasseur 1897, pp. 238, 565

Table A36 (continued)

Description of Category	Country and Period	Sources
	Sweden 1850-1870?	Barnard 1854, p. 622; Levasseur 1897, pp. 234, 502
	Switzerland 1830-1850	Barnard 1854, pp. 341-342, 348; Levasseur 1897, pp. 140, 348
Category B Countries where the percentage of children 6-14 in school probably increased by at least 15 percentage points during the period but by the end of the period less than three-quarters, yet more than one-half, of this age group was probably in school	Belgium 1830-1850	Barnard 1854, pp. 583-587; Ducpétiaux 1850, pp. 99-100; Mitchell 1976, pp. 19, 750
	Canada 1830-1850?	Greer 1978, p. 327
	France 1830-1850	Barnard 1854, pp. 391-397; Barnard 1872, pp. 227, 292-293; Hazen 1968, p. 199; Mitchell 1976, pp. 20, 750
	Japan 1870-1890	Banks 1971, p. 221; Hirschmeier 1964, p. 124; Levasseur 1897, pp. 277, 279-280
	Norway 1830-1850	Barnard 1854, p. 623; Barnard 1872, pp. 481-484, 495; Levasseur 1897, p. 235
	Sweden 1830-1850	Barnard 1854, p. 622; Levasseur 1897, pp. 502, 508
	United States 1830-1850	Fishlow 1966, pp. 41-43, 46, 49; Morison 1965, p. 530; North 1966, p. 85; Roach 1964, p. 116

Table A36 (continued)

Description of Category	Country and Period	Sources
Category C Countries where the percentage of children 6-14 in school probably increased by at least 10 percentage points during the period but by the end of the period less than a majority, yet more than one-third of this age group was probably in school. Also included in this category are countries meeting the end-of-period criteria for Category A or B where the probable increase in the percentage of children 6-14 in school was between 10 and 15 percentage points.	Argentina 1870–1890	Banks 1971, pp. 207–208; Díaz Alejandro 1970, pp. 27–28; Klemm 1968, p. 412; Levasseur 1897, p. 565
	Australia 1850–1870	Fitzpatrick 1946, p. 206; Partridge 1968, pp. 8, 17
	Belgium 1850–1870	Banks 1971, p. 209; Barnard 1854, pp. 397–398; Levasseur 1897, pp. 36–39; Mitchell 1976, pp. 19, 750
	Canada 1850–1870?, 1870–1890	Greer 1978, p. 327
	France 1850–1870, 1870–1890	Banks 1971, p. 217; Barnard 1872, pp. 292, 337; Hazen 1968, p. 199; Levasseur 1897, pp. 82, 89, 91, 565; Mitchell 1976, table J1 and pp. 20, 750, 754; Thomson 1968, p. 27
	Germany 1870–1890	Banks 1971, pp. 217–218; Laishley 1968, pp. 387, 393; Lynd [Great Britain] 1945, p. 358; Mitchell 1976, p. 755
	Great Britain 1830–1850	Levasseur 1897, p. 1; Lynd 1945, pp. 355–356; Mitchell 1976, p. 752; Trevelyan 1937, pp. 27–28

Table A36 (continued)

Description of Category	Country and Period	Sources
	Italy 1850–1870, 1870–1890	Banks 1971, p. 221; Barnard 1872, pp. 49, 609–610; Levasseur 1897, pp. 180–181, 191; Mitchell 1976, pp. 751–752; Neufeld 1961, p. 127; Roach 1964, p. 111; Mack Smith 1959, p. 260
	New Zealand 1850–1870	Sutch 1941, pp. 73–75
	Norway 1870–1890	Banks 1971, p. 230; Levasseur 1897, pp. 238, 565; Mitchell 1976, pp. 752, 757
	Spain 1850–1870, 1870–1890	Banks 1971, pp. 229–230; Barnard 1872, pp. 643–645, 656; Gannes and Repard 1936, p. 185; Levasseur 1897, pp. 176, 565
	United States 1850–1870?, 1870–1889?	Morison 1965, p. 530; North 1966, p. 85; Roach 1964, p. 116
Category D Countries where some significant spread of primary education took place during the period, with new laws passed, improvements in attendance, modest increases in enrollment, and	Argentina 1850–1870	Pendle 1963, pp. 50–51
	Australia 1830–1850	Fitzpatrick 1946, pp. 205–206; Partridge 1968, p. 8
	Denmark 1850–1870, 1870–1890	Barnard 1854, p. 619; Lassen 1966, p. 143; Levasseur 1897, pp. 240–246, 565; Mitchell 1976, p. 754

Table A36 (continued)

Description of Category	Country and Period	Sources
lengthening of the school year among possible developments, but quantitative progress was not sufficient to meet the criteria for Categories A through C	Germany 1850-1870	Banks 1971, pp. 217-218; Hamerow 1969, pp. 277-279; Levasseur 1897, pp. 99-139, 595-601
	Great Britain 1850-1870	Banks 1971, p. 233; Lowndes 1937, p. 355; Mitchell 1976, p. 752; Trevelyan 1937, pp. 354-355
	India 1870-1890	Dasgupta 1969, pp. 368-371; Sidhanta 1965, pp. 734, 738
	Netherlands 1850-1870, 1870-1890?	Banks 1971, p. 225; Barnard 1872, pp. 415, 454-455; Levasseur 1897, pp. 24-25, 28, 565; Mitchell 1976, pp. 751-752
	New Zealand 1830-1850	Condliffe and Airey 1954, p. 141; Levasseur 1897, p. 313; Sutch 1941, pp. 520-558
	Russia 1850-1870, 1870-1890	Banks 1971, p. 233; Barnard 1872, pp. 528-529, 548-549; Levasseur 1897, pp. 221, 565; Murray 1962, p. 188
	Spain 1830-1850	Barnard 1872, p. 643; Gannes and Repard 1936, p. 185; Levasseur 1897, p. 175
	Sweden 1870-1890	Banks 1971, p. 231; Levasseur 1897, pp. 230, 234; Mitchell 1976, p. 758

Table A36 (continued)

Description of Category	Country and Period	Sources
	Switzerland 1850–1870, 1870–1890	Banks 1971, p. 231; Barnard 1854, pp. 341–342; Levasseur 1897, pp. 140, 146; Mitchell 1976, pp. 758–759
Category E Countries where the spread of primary education during the period was quantitatively small and the qualitative improvements mentioned under Category D were not significant	Argentina 1830–1850	Scobie 1964b, p. 63
	Belgium 1870–1890	Levasseur 1897, pp. 33, 34, 36–39, 565; Mitchell 1976, pp. 752–753; Rowntree 1910, pp. 257–263
	Brazil 1830–1850, 1850–1870, 1870–1890	Banks 1971, p. 210; de Azevedo 1971, pp. 383, 392–393, 406; Klemm 1968, p. 412; Graham 1968, p. 17; Levasseur 1897, pp. 488–489; Wythe et al. 1949, p. 256
	Burma 1830–1850, 1850–1870(–), 1870–1890(–)	Cady 1958, pp. 59, 96–97; Encyclopaedia Britannica 1910, 4:841; Hagen 1956, pp. 10, 22
	China 1830–1850, 1850–1870, 1870–1890	Levasseur 1897, p. 292
	Egypt 1830–1850, 1850–1870(–), 1870–1890	Hershlag 1964, pp. 90, 114; Heyworth-Dunne 1968, pp. 360–361, 389, 390; Levasseur 1897, pp. 578–579; McCoan 1877, pp. 215–225; Tignor 1966, pp. 39, 321, 323

Table A36 (continued)

Description of Category	Country and Period	Sources
	India 1830-1850, 1850-1870	Dasgupta 1969, pp. 368-371; Roach 1964, p. 118; Sharma 1948, p. 47; Sidhanta 1965, p. 738
	Italy 1830-1850	Levasseur 1897, p. 180; Mitchell 1976, p. 751
	Japan 1830-1850, 1850-1870?	Crawcour 1965, pp. 34-35; Lippit 1978, p. 59; Owen [Egypt] 1969, p. 363; Rosovsky 1966, pp. 106-107
	Russia 1830-1850	Blackwell 1968, pp. 341-342; Levasseur 1897, p. 207

Note: Of the sources in this table, the following are listed in the general section of the bibliography: Banks 1971, Barnard 1854, Barnard 1872, Hazen 1968, Klemm 1968, Laishley 1968, Levasseur 1897, Mitchell 1976, Mulhall 1899, Murray 1962, Roach 1964, Thomson 1968, and Tracy 1964.

Table A37

Classification Scheme for Predominant Form of Land Tenure and Holding, 1850, 1870, 1890

Description of Category	Country and Year	Sources
Category A Countries where the greater part of the cultivated land was farmed by independent cultivators who owned most of the land they farmed and had full rights of ownership. The remaining land was generally cultivated by tenants paying fixed cash rents who had either reasonable de facto security of tenure or some recompense for unexhausted improvements. Included in this category with a minus sign are countries where independent cultivators and tenants of the type just described were about equally important, judging by the amount of cultivated land they farmed. Also included in this category with a minus sign are cases where at least two-thirds of the land was farmed by independent peasants, but the remainder was farmed by tenants with little or no security of tenure. Included with "independent" peasants are those	Canada 1850, 1870, 1890	Menzel 1981, p. 89; Parker 1966, pp. 88–128, 133–135, 143–153
	China 1850(−), 1870(−), 1890(−)	Perkins et al. 1969, pp. 87, 100–104; Tawney 1932, p. 34
	Denmark 1850, 1870, 1890	Rowntree [Belgium] 1910, pp. 113–114; Hertel 1937, p. 22; Skrubbeltrang 1951, pp. 93, 119
	France 1850(−), 1870(−), 1890(−)	Friedlaender and Oser 1953, pp. 212–213; Leslie 1870, pp. 336, 355; Rowntree [Belgium] 1910, pp. 113–114
	Germany 1850, 1870, 1890	Clapham 1936, pp. 198–199; Rowntree [Belgium] 1910, pp. 113–114
	India 1870(−), 1890(−)	Gadgil 1942, pp. 63–64, 166; Khusro 1965, pp. 181–184
	Japan 1890	Allen 1962, p. 64; Smith 1959, p. 163
	New Zealand 1870(−), 1890	Condliffe 1959, pp. 199, 206

Table A37 (continued)

Description of Category	Country and Year	Sources
who held lifetime or heritable tenancies that gave de facto rights of ownership.	Norway 1870, 1890	Hodne 1975, pp. 136–137; Larsen 1948, p. 462
	Sweden 1850, 1870, 1890	Janson 1931, pp. 50–52, 402
	Switzerland 1850, 1870, 1890	Swiss Office for the Development of Trade 1931, p. 29
	United States 1850(–), 1870(–), 1890(–)	Danhof 1951, p. 134; Danhof 1969, pp. 87–94; Gray 1973, II, chap. 27; U.S. Dept. of Commerce, Bureau of the Census 1960, pp. 278–279
Category B Countries where the greater part of the cultivated land was farmed by peasant cultivators whose ownership rights were constrained by various types of feudal obligations in taxes, kind, and services. "Ownership" rights included rights against eviction.	Japan 1850, 1870	Miyamoto et al. 1965, p. 544
Category C Countries where the greater part of the cultivated land was farmed by	Australia 1890(–)	Gregory 1916, pp. 111–115

Table A37 (continued)

Description of Category	Country and Year	Sources
cultivators paying fixed cash rents who had either reasonable de facto security of tenure or some form of recompense for unexhausted improvements. The remaining land was cultivated by independent operators who had full rights of ownership. Included in this category are countries where short leases prevailed but long de facto tenures were quite widespread (and where compensation for unexhausted improvements was important in practice although not assured legally). A plus rating is assigned where compensation for unexhausted improvements was provided for legally. Also included in this category with a minus sign are cases where the greater part of the cultivated land was held in pastoral leases that in practice were fairly secure with low payments but provided little legal security of tenure.	Belgium 1850, 1870, 1890	de Laveleye 1870, pp. 258-259; Rowntree 1910, pp. 113-114; van Houtte 1943, p. 132
	Great Britain 1850, 1870, 1890(+)	Clapham 1932, pp. 252-257, 260-261; Clapham 1938, pp. 116-117
	Netherlands 1850, 1870, 1890	Baasch 1927, p. 486; Brugmans 1961, pp. 305-306

Table A37 (continued)

Description of Category	Country and Year	Sources
Category D Countries where the greater part of the cultivated land was farmed by short-term tenants paying fixed rents in cash or kind with, in practice, little security of tenure or recompense for unexhausted improvements.	Australia 1850(−), 1870(+)	Coghlan 1918, vol. 1, pt. 3, chaps. 4–5; vol. 2, pt. 5, chap. 4
	Argentina 1890	Díaz Alejandro 1970, pp. 155–156; Scoble 1964b, pp. 48–49, 52
	Brazil 1890	Burns 1970, pp. 199–200; Foerster 1919, pp. 291–293
Included with a minus rating are cases where short-term sharecropping tenantry predominated, with little security of tenure or recompense for unexhausted improvements.	Burma 1890	Furnivall 1931, pp. 93–95
Also included with a minus rating are cases where the greater part of	Egypt 1870(−)?, 1890(−)	Baer 1966, p. 85; Owen 1969, pp. 243–244
the cultivated land was used by squatters for large sheep runs without any legal rights to occupancy; most of the remaining land was held by cultivators who either were independent or held leases from the government.	Italy 1890	Foerster 1919, pp. 71, 74–80, 113–116
Category E Countries where the greater part of the cultivated land was farmed by peasants with title to their land;	Burma 1850, 1870	Furnivall 1931, pp. 50–57, 84–87, 93–95; Tun Wai 1961, p. 60

Table A37 (continued)

Description of Category	Country and Year	Sources
however, many of them were subject to communal controls over type and method of cultivation which originated in the prevalence of open field methods of cultivation or in widespread fragmentation of landholdings.	India 1850	Bhatia 1964, passim
	New Zealand 1850(-)	Sutch 1969, pp. 21-22
	Norway 1850	Blegen 1931, p. 5; Lieberman 1970, pp. 65-69, 73
Included with a minus sign are cases where fully communal agriculture predominated.	Russia 1870, 1890?	Mavor 1925, p. 341; Tuma 1965, pp. 76-78
Category F Countries where the predominant form of land tenure and holding was a system of large estates or latifundia, centrally managed, usually not by the owner, with cultivation by hired laborers or tenants on short-term leases, usually sharecroppers. The remaining land not under this form of tenure and holding was usually cultivated by independent peasants holding full title to their land.	Argentina 1850?, 1870?	Burgin 1946, pp. 254-255; Díaz Alejandro, 1970, p. 38; Ferrer 1967, p. 97; Hanson 1938, p. 10
	Italy 1850, 1870	Clough 1964, p. 101
	Spain 1850, 1870, 1890	Brenan 1943, chap. 6

Table A37 (continued)

Description of Category	Country and Year	Sources
Category G		
Countries where the predominant form of land tenure and holding was a system of large estates, centrally managed, usually not by the owner, with cultivation by serfs or other forms of servile labor. The remaining land not under this system of tenure and holding was usually cultivated by independent peasants holding full title to their land.	Brazil 1850, 1870 Egypt 1850(+) Russia 1850	Burns 1970, p. 57 McCoan 1877, p. 374 Lyashchenko 1949, chap. 17

Note: Of the sources in this table, the following are listed in the general section of the bibliography: Friedlaender and Oser 1953 and Foerster 1919.

Table A38

Classification Scheme for Concentration of Landholdings, 1850, 1870, 1890

Description of Category	Country and Year	Sources
Category A Countries with an extreme concentration of landholdings with the top 10 percent of landholders holding at least 75 percent of the cultivated land. Excluded are countries where the overwhelming proportion of landholders were peasants with very small holdings using no year-round hired labor. Included with a minus sign are countries where there were quite a few small agricultural holdings but not enough to constitute the overwhelming proportion of landholders.	Argentina 1850?, 1870, 1890(-)	Díaz Alejandro 1970, pp. 151-154; Ferrer 1967, p. 97; McGann 1966, pp. 21, 31-32
	Australia 1850?, 1870?, 1890?	Coghlan 1918, 2:648, 655, 1007; 3:1374, 1393; 4:1970, 1986; Fitzpatrick 1969, pp. 142-143, 396
	Brazil 1850?, 1870? 1890?	Reis 1977, pp. 372-373
	New Zealand 1870, 1890(-)	Condliffe 1930, pp. 142-143; Scholefield 1909, pp. 168, 181; Simkin 1951, p. 173
Category B Countries with an extreme concentration of landholdings, but not necessarily meeting the criterion that the top 10 percent hold at least 75 percent of the cultivated land, where, judging by available numbers, peasants	Egypt 1850, 1870, 1890	Baer 1962, chap. 2; Dicey 1881, pp. 110-111; Hershlag 1964, p. 120; Owen 1969, pp. 61, 238-239
	Italy 1850(-), 1870(-), 1890(-)	Clough 1964, p. 100; Foerster 1919, p. 69; Schmidt 1939, pp. 5-6

Table A38 (continued)

Description of Category	Country and Year	Sources
having very small holdings and using no year-round hired labor were overwhelmingly predominant	Russia 1850, 1870, 1890	Dobb 1948, p. 43; Lyashchenko 1949, p. 462; Tuma 1965, pp. 77-79
	Spain 1850(-), 1870(-), 1890(-)	Merin 1938, pp. 142-143; Ramos Oliveira 1946, pp. 234-235
Category C Countries where the predominant scale of holdings was large, but where the concentration of land-holdings was considerably less than in the countries of Categories A and B. "Large" means that hired labor undertook the greater part of cultivation. Countries where a significant part of the cultivated land was characterized by small holdings using little or no permanent hired labor are classified C-.	Germany 1850(-), 1870(-), 1890(-)	Clapham 1936, pp. 199-200; Great Britain Board of Agriculture and Fisheries 1916, p. 12
	Great Britain 1850, 1870, 1890	Chambers and Mingay 1966, p. 132; Ernle 1936, p. 429; Great Britain Board of Agriculture and Fisheries [Germany] 1916, p. 12
Category D Countries where the greater part of the cultivated land was exploited on middle-size holdings using permanent hired labor.	Canada 1850(-)?, 1870(-)?, 1890(-)?	Menzel 1981, p. 92; Parker 1966, pp. 88-128, 133-135, 143-153; Urquhart and Buckley 1965, pp. 351-352

Table A38 (continued)

Description of Category	Country and Year	Sources
Where there were also important geographical regions dominated by small holdings using little or no permanent hired labor, the country is classified D-.	Denmark 1850, 1870, 1890	Nielsen 1933, pp. 528-529
	United States 1850(-), 1870(-), 1890(-)	Danhof 1951, p. 134; U.S. Dept. of Commerce, Bureau of the Census, pp. 279-280
Category E Countries where the greater part of the cultivated land was exploited on small holdings using little permanent hired labor. Excluded are countries meeting this criterion where extreme parcelization and fragmentation of holdings were widespread.	Burma 1850, 1870, 1890(+)	Christian 1942, p. 112; Furnivall 1931, pp. 59-61, 99
	France 1850, 1870, 1890	Clapham 1936, pp. 160-165
	India 1850?	Bhatia 1965, pp. 136-137
	Japan 1850, 1870, 1890	Allen 1962, pp. 63-64; Hirschmeier 1964, pp. 107-108; Smith 1959, pp. 106-107, 162-163
	Netherlands 1850(-), 1870(-), 1890(-)	Baasch 1927, p. 486; Brugmans 1961, p. 305
	Sweden 1850, 1870, 1890	Heckscher 1954, pp. 168-169; Janson 1931, pp. 82, 400-403
	Switzerland 1850(-), 1870(-), 1890(-)	Landmann 1928, p. 70; Soloveytchik 1954, p. 104

Table A38 (continued)

Description of Category	Country and Year	Sources
Category F Countries where the greater part of the cultivated land was exploited on very small holdings, with parcelization of holdings and fragmentation of holdings widespread	Belgium 1850(+), 1870(+), 1890(+)	de Laveleye 1870, p. 244; Linden 1920, pp. 301, 323; Rowntree 1910, p. 567
	China 1850, 1870, 1890	Condliffe 1932, p. 36; Tawney 1932, p. 40
	India 1870, 1890	Bhatia 1965, pp. 136–137; Gadgil 1942, pp. 166–167
	Norway 1850, 1870, 1890	Hodne 1975, pp. 135–136; Semmingsen 1954, p. 182
Category G Countries where identifiable individual holdings were uncommon because of the prevalence of communal agriculture.	New Zealand 1850	Sutch 1969, chap. 1

Table A39

Classification Scheme for Favorableness of Land System to Adoption of Improvements, 1850, 1870, 1890[a]

Description of Category	Country and Year
Category A Countries where ownership by independent cultivators farming large or middle-size holdings predominated but without an extreme concentration of land-holdings. Countries where there was also an important sector of small farms without permanent hired labor are classified A-.	Canada 1850(-), 1870(-), 1890(-) Denmark 1850, 1870, 1890 Germany 1850(-), 1870(-), 1890(-) United States 1850(-), 1870(-), 1890(-)
Category B Countries where the predominant form of cultivation was by tenants paying fixed cash rents and having reasonable de facto security of tenure, and where middle-size or large farms predominated, but without an extreme concentration of landholdings.	Great Britain 1850, 1870, 1890
Category C Countries where ownership by independent cultivators farming small but viable family-size holdings predominated. Included with a minus rating are countries where peasant independence was constrained by feudal obligations for taxes in kind, cash, or services. Also classified C- are countries countries cultivation by tenants on family-size holdings (with reasonable security of tenure) was as important as that by independent cultivators.	France 1850(-), 1870(-), 1890(-) Japan 1850(-), 1870(-), 1890 Sweden 1850, 1870, 1890 Switzerland 1850, 1870, 1890

Table A39 (continued)

Description of Category	Country and Year

Category D
Countries where cultivation by
tenants paying fixed cash rents
with reasonable de facto
security of tenure on viable
family-size holdings
predominated. Also included are
countries with an important
sector of holdings too small to
support a family but where
alternative employment in
industry was widespread.

Belgium 1850, 1870, 1890
Netherlands 1850, 1870, 1890

Category E
Countries where large, centrally
managed agricultural or pastoral
estates cultivated by hired
laborers predominated

Argentina 1850
Australia 1850, 1870, 1890(+)
Italy 1850, 1870
New Zealand 1870, 1890(+)
Spain 1850, 1870, 1890

Category F
Countries where cultivation by
peasants with extremely small
holdings, often insufficient to
support a family, predominated,
and where opportunities for
supplementary employment in
industry were not widespread

China 1850, 1870, 1890
Egypt 1870, 1890
India 1870, 1890
Norway 1870, 1890

Category G
Countries where cultivation by
tenants with short-term insecure
tenures, including sharecropping
arrangements, predominated.
Countries where sharecropping
arrangements predominated are
classified G+.

Argentina 1870?, 1890
Brazil 1890
Burma 1890
Italy 1890(+)

Table A39 (continued)

Description of Category	Country and Year
Category H Countries where the predominant land system was cultivation by peasants with title to their land but with some form of communal control over type of crop and method of production.	Burma 1850, 1870 Egypt 1850 India 1850 New Zealand 1850 Norway 1850 Russia 1870, 1890
Category I Countries where the predominant land system was large estates cultivated by serfs, slaves, or other forms of servile labor	Brazil 1850, 1870 Russia 1850

[a] For sources, see the country references in tables A37 and A38.

Table A40

Classification Scheme for Extent of Urbanization, 1850, 1870, 1890

Description of Category	Country and Year	Sources
Category A Countries in which 30 percent or more of the population lived in towns of 10,000 or more inhabitants	Australia 1870, 1890	Butlin 1965, pp. 156–157; Weber 1967, pp. 140–141
	Belgium 1890	Weber 1967, p. 116
	Great Britain 1850(–), 1870, 1890	Weber 1967, pp. 144, 151
	Netherlands 1870, 1890	Brugmans 1961, pp. 188–189; Weber 1967, p. 115
Category B Countries in which 20 percent or more (but less than 30 percent) of the population lived in towns of 10,000 or more inhabitants	Argentina 1890	Díaz Alejandro 1970, p. 424; Scobie 1964a, pp. 131–132; Weber 1967, p. 135
	Australia 1850	Weber 1967, pp. 140–141
	Belgium 1850, 1870	Weber 1967, p. 116
	France 1870, 1890	Weber 1967, p. 71
	Germany 1890(–)	Weber 1967, p. 90; Jostock 1955, p. 97
	Italy 1890	Clough 1964, p. 136

Table A40 (continued)

Description of Category	Country and Year	Sources
	Netherlands 1850	Brugmans 1961, pp. 188-189
	New Zealand 1890	Scholefield 1909, p. 194
	United States 1890	U.S. Dept. of Commerce, Bureau of the Census 1960, p. 14; Weber 1967, p. 39
Category C Countries in which 10 percent or more (but less than 20 percent) of the population lived in towns of 10,000 or more inhabitants	Argentina 1870	Díaz Alejandro 1970, p. 424
	Brazil 1890(-)	Weber 1967, p. 134
	Canada 1870?, 1890	Higgins and Lerner 1950, pp. 235-236; Weber 1967, p. 132
	China 1890?	Not available[a]
	Denmark 1870, 1890	Weber 1967, pp. 112-113
	Egypt 1870?, 1890	Weber 1967, p. 137
	France 1850	Weber 1967, p. 71
	Germany 1870?	Jostock 1955, p. 97; Weber 1967, p. 90
	Italy 1850?, 1870?	Clough 1964, p. 136

Table A40 (continued)

Description of Category	Country and Year	Sources
	Japan 1850, 1870, 1890	Hanley and Yamamura 1977, pp. 65, 66, 97, 152, 304, 351; Sumiya and Taira 1979, pp. 117, 119, 121; Weber 1967, p. 129
	Norway 1870?, 1890	Derry 1957, pp. 181–182; Weber 1967, p. 113
	Spain 1850, 1870?, 1890(+)	Higgin 1886, p. 24; Weber 1967, pp. 118–119
	Sweden 1870?, 1890	Weber 1967, pp. 109–110
	Switzerland 1870, 1890	Soloveytchik 1954, p. 290; Weber 1967, p. 117
	United States 1850, 1870	U.S. Dept. of Commerce, Bureau of the Census 1960, p. 14; Weber 1967, p. 39
Category D Countries in which less than 10 percent of the population lived in towns of 10,000 or more inhabitants	Argentina 1850	Díaz Alejandro 1970, p. 424; McGann 1966, p. 31; Pendle 1955, p. 60
	Brazil 1850, 1870	Weber 1967, p. 134
	Burma 1850?, 1870?, 1890?	Not available[a]
	Canada 1850	Higgins and Lermer 1950, pp. 235–236; Weber 1967, p. 132
	China 1850?, 1870?	Not available[a]

Table A40 (continued)

Description of Category	Country and Year	Sources
	Denmark 1850	Weber 1967, pp. 112–113
	Egypt 1850?	Not available[a]
	Germany 1850(+)?	Köllmann 1976, p. 22
	India 1850, 1870, 1890	Davis 1951, p. 127; Gadgil 1942, p. 158; Weber 1967, p. 125; Woytinski and Woytinski 1953, p. 116
	New Zealand 1850, 1870	Weber 1967, p. 140
	Norway 1850	Weber 1967, p. 113
	Russia 1850, 1870, 1890(+)	Blackwell 1968, pp. 97, 427; Weber 1967, pp. 107–109
	Sweden 1850	Weber 1967, pp. 109–110
	Switzerland 1850	Soloveytchik 1954, p. 290; Weber 1967, p. 117

Note: Of the sources in this table, the following are listed in the general section of the bibliography: Weber 1967 and Woytinski and Woytinski 1953.

[a] Those countries and years for which quantitative estimates are not available are classified on the basis of estimates for later years together with qualitative information on urbanization from a wide range of sources on the growth in the importance of cities.

Table A41

Classification Scheme for Favorableness of Attitudes toward Entrepreneurship, 1850, 1870, 1890

Description of Category	Country and Year	Sources
Category A Countries where social recognition of capitalist entrepreneurial success by the established social elite was indicated by a combination of the following: official recognition of capitalist achievements by the crown; intermarriage between the elite and the children of industrial entrepreneurs of nonelite background; and the retention of industrial entrepreneurs in industry rather than their early retirement to landownership. Two groups of countries are classified A–: (1) countries meeting the criteria of A for the most part, but with less strong recognition of the three kinds mentioned than in countries classified A; and (2) countries with little industry and thus few of the overt signs of social	Australia 1890(–)	Mayer 1966, passim; Rosecrance 1964, pp. 282–291, 306
	Belgium 1850(–), 1870(–), 1890	Chlepner 1956, p. 192; Linden 1920, pp. 301–302; Van Houtte 1943, pp. 176–177
	Denmark 1890(–)	Danstrup 1948, pp. 104, 111; Jensen 1937, p. 106; Youngson 1959, p. 204
	Great Britain 1870(–), 1890(–)	Crouzet 1981, p. 20; Thane 1981, pp. 219–221; Trevelyan 1937, pp. 274–275
	New Zealand 1890(–)	Brady 1958, pp. 262, 282
	Norway 1890	Semmingsen 1954, pp. 8, 185, 195
	Sweden 1890(–)	Jörberg 1965, p. 21; Semmingsen [Norway] 1954, p. 168
	Switzerland 1850(–), 1870, 1890	Braun 1967, pp. 555–557, 563; Landes 1965a, p. 397
	United States 1890	Sawyer 1952, p. 22

Table A41 (continued)

Description of Category	Country and Year	Sources
recognition mentioned, but with a social elite that included some large bankers and merchants and that had quite open attitudes toward capitalist entrepreneurship and innovation compared with countries in lower categories.	Australia 1850(+), 1870(+)	Brady 1958, pp. 133-137
Category B Countries where there were two different cultures, one of which met the criteria for Category A and the other of which met the criteria of Category C. Also included and classified B+ are countries where a recently created, exclusively landed elite that was very commercially oriented opposed industrial interests on	Canada 1850, 1870, 1890	Brady 1958, pp. 3-4, 9, 26-27, 92, 97, 114; Easterbrook and Aiken 1956, p. 257; Jones 1967, p. 125; McRae 1964, pp. 245-246; Tucker 1936, pp. 11, 24-25
	New Zealand 1870(-)	Brady 1958, pp. 262, 285; Merrill 1954, passim
economic grounds, but gave less attention to social distinctions per se than countries in lower categories.	United States 1850, 1870	Gray 1973, 1:495-500; Sawyer 1954, pp. 376-379

Table A41 (continued)

Description of Category	Country and Year	Sources
Category C Countries where social recognition of capitalist entrepreneurs, by those with inherited social position and wealth, went largely to the sons of those with inherited position and wealth and to a small number of nonelite capitalist entrepreneurs who became <u>extremely</u> wealthy compared with those who were already part of the elite. Also included in this category are countries where the social elite recognized socially those with wealth accumulated in mercantile activities but had much less respect for those who accumulated wealth in industrial activities.	Denmark 1850, 1870(+)	Danstrup 1948, pp. 104, 111; Jensen 1937, pp. 105–106; Youngson 1959, p. 204
	France 1850?, 1870(+), 1890(+)	Landes 1963, pp. 348–349; Palmade 1972, pp. 153, 212–214, 218, 225; Sawyer 1952, pp. 15–19
	Germany 1870(−), 1890(−)	Gerschenkron 1962a, p. 64; Kocka 1981, p. 463; Landes 1965a, p. 281; Parker 1954, p. 32
	Great Britain 1850?	Crouzet 1981, p. 20; Rose 1981, pp. 256, 261–262
	Netherlands 1850, 1870, 1890(+)?	Brugmans 1961, pp. 89, 195–198; Griffiths 1979, pp. 40–43; Landheer 1943a, pp. 182–183
	New Zealand 1850	Brady 1958, pp. 262, 285
	Norway 1850, 1870(+)?	Semmingsen 1954, pp. 168, 185, 191, 195–199
	Sweden 1850?, 1870?	Janson 1931, pp. 45, 60; Söderland 1952, p. 71

Table A41 (continued)

Description of Category	Country and Year	Sources
Category D Countries where elitist attitudes toward capitalist entrepreneurship in one major region met the criteria for Category C, while elitist attitudes in another major region met the criteria for Category E. Countries are classified D+ if in one of the regions there was considerable social respect for large accumulations of mercantile wealth.	Argentina 1850, 1870, 1890(+)	Fillol 1961, pp. 28–29; Goodrich 1964, pp. 79–80; Scoble 1964a, pp. 130, 150–152, 171–173, Scoble 1964b, p. 13
	Germany 1850	Hamerow 1969, pp. 66–67; Hamerow 1972, pp. 49–50
	Italy 1850, 1870, 1890	Clough and Livi 1963, pp. 361–362; Foerster 1919, pp. 77, 117; Neufeld 1961, p. 147
	Spain 1870(–), 1890	Carr 1966, pp. 431–433; Vilar 1967, p. 75
Category E Countries where social recognition of newly successful entrepreneurs was granted to only a small number who were <u>extremely</u> successful in primary-export production and in the process became very large landowners. Even here recognition was more often given by the government than by the established landed elite. In these countries large	Brazil 1850, 1870, 1890	Burns 1970, p. 138; Graham 1968, pp. 16–17, 31, 204–205, 212
	Egypt 1870(–), 1890?	Commission du Commerce et de l'Industrie 1966, pp. 452–453; Issawi 1961, p. 12; Owen 1969, pp. 363–366
	Japan 1890	Hirschmeier 1964, p. 172; Landes 1965b, p. 170; Marshall 1967, pp. 49–50; Moore 1966, pp. 286–288
	Russia 1850, 1870, 1890	Gerschenkron 1962a, p. 60

Table A41 (continued)

Description of Category	Country and Year	Sources
accumulations of mercantile wealth were not regarded by the established social elite as a basis for social acceptance.		
Category F Countries where social recognition of capitalist entrepreneurship by the established social elite was not common	Burma 1850?, 1870?, 1890?	Furnivall 1931, pp. 31–41, 91, 159–163, 168; Hagen 1956, p. 23
	China 1850, 1870, 1890	Allen 1965, pp. 901–902; Beckman 1962, p. 153; Cowan 1964, p. 96; Moore 1966, pp. 178–179
	Egypt 1850	Fahmy 1954, pp. 96–97, 126–127; Hershlag 1964, p. 23
	India 1850, 1870?, 1890	Allen 1965, pp. 909, 916; Bhatia 1964, pp. 100–101; Maddison 1970, p. 65
	Japan 1850(+), 1870(+)	Landes 1965b, p. 170; Moore 1966, pp. 235, 237; Smith 1959, pp. 176–177
	Spain 1850	Tortella 1972, pp. 94–95

Note: Of the sources in this table, the following are listed in the general section of the bibliography: Brady 1958, Gerschenkron 1962a, Landes 1965a, and Moore 1966.

Table A42

Classification Scheme for Extent of Domestic Economic Role of Government, 1850–1870, 1870–1890, 1890–1914

Description of Category	Country and Period	Sources
Category A Countries where national or regional governments financed the greater part of investment in inter-regional transportation, owned and managed the greater part of inter-regional transportation networks (as judged by the proportion of mileage owned), directly owned or subsidized a considerable number and variety of industrial enterprises, and provided some subsidization of inputs to agriculture	Germany 1890–1914?	Clough and Cole 1946, p. 590; Kirkaldy and Evans 1924, p. 75; McPherson 1910, pp. 57–58; Stolper et al. 1967, p. 41
	Japan 1870–1890, 1890–1914	Allen 1965, pp. 876, 890; Hayami et al. 1975, pp. 176–177, 207; Hirschmeier 1964, pp. 140–141; Horie 1965, pp. 183–208; Landes 1965b, pp. 94, 102–103; Lockwood 1954, pp. 14–15; Sawada 1965, pp. 331–334
	New Zealand 1890–1914(–)?	Airey 1947b, p. 93; Condliffe 1959, p. 221; Hamilton 1947, p. 154; Rowe and Rowe 1968, p. 60
Category B Countries where (as in Category A) national or regional governments financed the greater part of investment in	Australia 1850–1870, 1870–1890, 1890–1914	Fitzpatrick 1969, pp. 264–265, 294, 310–311; 54–55; McGee 1970, pp. 136–137, 145; Shann 1948, pp. 436, 441–442; Shaw 1946, pp. 78, 90; Sinclair 1976, p. 93

Table A42 (continued)

Description of Category	Country and Period	Sources
Interregional transportation and owned and managed the greater part of interregional networks.	Belgium 1870–1890, 1890–1914	Chlepner 1956, pp. 83–88; Girard 1965, p. 235; Kirkaldy and Evans 1924, pp. 76–77; Linden 1920, p. 298; McPherson 1910, p. 31
National or regional governments provided some financing of investment in industry (but rarely through ownership), or governments supported such investments in agriculture as irrigation projects or extensive improvements in agricultural knowledge.	Canada 1890–1914	Caves and Holton 1961, pp. 234–238; Easterbrook and Aitken 1956, pp. 390–391; Innis 1935, pp. 76–81; Wittke 1941, pp. 252–253
	Egypt 1890–1914?	Hershlag 1964, p. 122; Owen 1969, pp. 316–320
	India 1890–1914(–)	Chandra 1966 p. 68; Gadgil 1942, pp. 123–131, 214, 219–220; Sen 1966, pp. 4, 12, 32–39, 63–65, 75–79
	Italy 1870–1890, 1890–1914	Clough 1964, pp. 67–70; Cohen 1972, pp. 70–71; Gershenkron 1962a, pp. 79–84; McPherson 1910, pp. 77–85
	Russia 1890–1914?	Carson 1959, pp. 116–117, 122–137; Gershenkron 1962a, p. 48; Henderson 1961, pp. 224–225; Kahan 1967, pp. 467, 476–477; McPherson 1910, pp. 34–35, 73; Portal 1965, pp. 824–825, 870–871
	Sweden 1890–1914(?)	Heckscher 1954, pp. 254, 259; Hedin 1967, p. 5; Jörberg 1965, p. 20; Menzel 1980c, p. 116; Montgomery 1939, pp. 123–124; Sandberg 1978, p. 655

Table A42 (continued)

Description of Category	Country and Period	Sources
Category C Countries where (as in Categories A and B) national or regional governments financed the greater part of investment in interregional transportation. However, national or regional governments owned and managed only a few main lines of transportation networks (if any) and provided very little financing of investment in industry or agriculture.	Belgium 1850–1870	Chlepner 1956, pp. 30–31, 83–87, 199; Kirkaldy and Evans 1924, p. 76; Linden 1920, pp. 277–279, 298
	Canada 1850–1870, 1870–1890	Caves and Holton 1961, pp. 233–237; Easterbrook and Aiken 1956, p. 317; McInnis 1959, pp. 258–261; Wittke 1941, p. 142
	Denmark 1850–1870?, 1870–1890?, 1890–1914?	Jensen 1937, pp. 146–149, 178–179; Olsen 1962, pp. 224–225
	France 1890–1914?	Clough 1939, pp. 237–238; Kindleberger 1964, p. 188
	Germany 1850–1870, 1870–1890	Clough and Cole 1946, p. 454; Henderson 1961, pp. 46–47; Kirkaldy and Evans 1924, pp. 74–75; Stolper et al. 1967, pp. 39–41
	India 1850–1870, 1870–1890	Allen 1965, pp. 908–912; Chandra 1966, pp. 68, 176; Sundara Rajan 1955, pp. 27–28
	Italy 1850–1870	Clough 1964, pp. 67–69, 96–97; Luzzato 1969, p. 205; McPherson 1910, pp. 77–81; Neufeld 1961, p. 130
	Netherlands 1850–1870, 1870–1890, 1890–1914	Brugmans 1961, pp. 226–229, 250–252, 286, 291, 302, 311–312, 370; McPherson 1910, pp. 28, 60–61

Table A42 (continued)

Description of Category	Country and Period	Sources
	Norway 1890-1914	Kellhau 1944, p. 161
	Russia 1870-1890	Ellison 1965, p. 535; Gershenkron 1962a, p. 48; Henderson 1961, pp. 202, 224
	Sweden 1850-1870, 1870-1890	Heckscher 1954, pp. 223, 232; Hildebrand 1960, pp. 276-277, 284-285; Hovde 1943, 1:269; Jörberg 1965, p. 20; Montgomery 1939, pp. 104-105, 123; Thomas 1941, p. 126
	Switzerland 1890-1914?	Landmann 1928, pp. 24-27
Category D Countries where national or regional governments financed a significant part of investment in inter-regional transportation but (in contrast with higher categories) not a predominant part. As in Category C, they owned and managed only a few main lines (if any) of inter-regional transportation networks and provided very little financing of	Argentina 1850-1870, 1870-1890, 1890-1914	Ferns 1960, p. 418; Ferrer 1967, p. 93; McGann 1966, pp. 65-66; Pendle 1955, p. 49; Scoble 1964a, pp. 138-139; Scoble 1964b, pp. 61, 90-91, 133, 138-139; Wythe 1949, p. 95
	Brazil 1870-1890, 1890-1914	Graham 1968, pp. 218-219, 230; Stein 1957, pp. 81, 86-87, 94-97
	Burma 1890-1914	Cady 1958, pp. 94-95, 102-103; Furnivall 1931, pp. 71-72; Hagen 1956, pp. 13-14
	Egypt 1850-1870, 1870-1890?	Crouchley 1938, pp. 132, 135; Hershlag 1964, pp. 95, 106-109; Landes 1958, p. 31; Owen 1969, pp. 212, 214-215

Table A42 (continued)

Description of Category	Country and Period	Sources
Investment in Industry or agriculture.	France 1850-1870?, 1870-1890?	Clough 1939, pp. 235-239; Clough and Cole 1946, pp. 588-589; Girard 1965, p. 244; Henderson 1961, p. 112; Kindleberger 1964, pp. 185-186; Kirkaldy and Evans 1924, pp. 71-73; McPherson 1910, pp. 48, 52
	Great Britain 1850-1870, 1870-1890, 1890-1914	Edelstein 1981, pp. 70-80; Floud 1981, pp. 13-16
	New Zealand 1870-1890?	Condliffe 1959, pp. 31-34
	Russia 1850-1870	Blackwell 1968, p. 263; Clough and Cole 1946, p. 590; Ellison 1965, p. 535; Henderson 1961, pp. 202, 222-223; McPherson 1910, pp. 72-73
	Spain 1850-1870(-)? 1890-1914(-)?	Higgin 1886, p. 40; Tortella 1972, pp. 94-95; Vicens Vives and Nadal Oller 1969, pp. 646-647
	Switzerland 1850-1870, 1870-1890	Baumgartner 1964, pp. 220-221, 226-227; Bonjour et al. 1952, pp. 294, 296, 323; Georg 1901, pp. 268-278; McPherson 1910, pp. 67, 70; Oechsli 1922, pp. 401-402
	United States 1850-1870 1870-1890, 1890-1914	Chandler 1978, p. 41; Davis et al. 1972, pp. 649-545; Hughes 1977, pp. 70-77

Table A42 (continued)

Description of Category	Country and Period	Sources
Category E Countries where the direct role of the government was extremely small but where governments were the major providers of finance for the little physical overhead capital and the few factories that existed.	Brazil 1850–1870?	Burns 1970, pp. 148–149; Graham 1968, pp. 216–221; Stein 1957, p. 81
	Burma 1850–1870, 1870–1890	Cady 1958, pp. 94–95; Furnivall 1931, pp. 71–72
	China 1850–1870(–), 1870–1890(–), 1890–1914(–)	Allen 1965, pp. 901–905; Beckman 1962, p. 153; Cowan 1964, pp. 100–102
	Japan 1850–1870?	Allen 1965, pp. 875–876; Crawcour 1965, pp. 43–44; Horie 1965, p. 202; Lockwood 1954, p. 14
	New Zeal and 1850–1870?	Lloyd Pritchard 1970, pp. 118–127
	Norway 1850–1870, 1870–1890	Hovde 1943, 1:266–269; Kellhau 1944, pp. 160–161; Østensjø 1963, pp. 148–149
	Spain 1870–1890	Higgin 1886, p. 40; Tortella 1972, pp. 94–95; Vicens Vives and Nadal Oller 1969, pp. 646–647

Note: Of the sources in this table, the following are listed in the general section of the bibliography: Clough and Cole 1946, Gerschenkron 1962b, Girard 1965, Henderson 1961, Kirkaldy and Evans 1924, and McPherson 1910.

Table A43

Classification Scheme for Socioeconomic Character of National Political Leadership, 1850–1870, 1870–1890, 1890–1914

Description of Category	Country and Period	Sources
Category A Countries in which rising classes of indigenous entrepreneurs, businessmen, and wage earners had a predominant direct share of power in national governmental institutions, including direct representation in national parliaments during the period. Countries are classified A– if power was concentrated in the hands of a wealthy bourgeoisie with important parliamentary representation for labor but very little direct labor influence on government decisions.	Australia 1890–1914	Brady 1958, pp. 138–139, 163, 181–211, 247–253; Grundy 1970, pp. 224, 227, 236
	Belgium 1890–1914(–)	Crouzet 1968, p. 513; Encyclopaedia Britannica 1910, 3:679
	France 1890–1914(–)	Crouzet 1968, pp. 514–518; Néré 1962, pp. 313–319
	Netherlands 1890–1914(–)	Albarda 1943, p. 98; Encyclopaedia Britannica 1910, 13:605; Lourens 1943, p. 109
	New Zealand 1890–1914(–)	Airey 1947b, pp. 100–101; Brady 1958, pp. 263–272, 285, 292–300, 324; Senghaas 1982, p. 179
	Switzerland 1870–1890(–), 1890–1914(–)	Buell 1935, pp. 572, 580–581; Encyclopaedia Britannica 1911, 26:260–262 Rappard 1914, pp. 309–312
	United States 1890–1914(–)	Hession and Sardy 1969, pp. 394, 471–499, 576–594

Table A43 (continued)

Description of Category	Country and Period	Sources
Category B Countries in which rising classes of indigenous entrepreneurs, businessmen, and wage earners shared direct power in national governmental institutions with a propertied traditional elite over the greater part of the period, including through direct parliamentary representation. Countries are classified B+ if, in addition, labor had direct parliamentary influence; or if landed elites had no political power and power was in the hands of a wealthy commercial and industrial elite but wage earners had little even indirect political power. Countries are classified B- if rising classes of entrepreneurs and businessmen shared direct power in national governmental institutions with a propertied traditional elite but wage earners had no influence on	Australia 1850–1870, 1870–1890	Brady 1958, pp. 140, 181; Cotter 1970, pp. 127, 129; Grundy 1970, pp. 209–216; McGhee 1970, pp. 151–157; Morrissey 1970, p. 100
	Belgium 1850–1870, 1870–1890	Chlepner 1956, p. 192; Encyclopaedia Britannica 1910, 3:678–679; Eyck 1959, pp. 70–71
	Canada 1850–1870(−)?, 1870–1890(+), 1890–1914(+)	Brady 1958, pp. 3–4, 68, 71–73, 89, 97–99; McCarty [Australia] 1973, p. 159; McInnis 1959, pp. 345ff.
	Denmark 1890–1914(+)	Galenson 1952, pp. 41, 43, 210; Jensen 1937, p. 105; Østerud 1978, p. 200
	France 1870–1890	Néré 1962, pp. 302–307, 310, 312–313
	Germany 1890–1914	Anderson and Anderson 1967, pp. 338, 391; Conze 1962, pp. 280–281, 294–295; Schieder 1962, p. 271
	Great Britain 1850–1870, 1870–1890?, 1890–1914(+)	Moore 1966, pp. 32–33, 37–39; Schieder 1962, pp. 271–272; Thane 1981, pp. 213–214, 219–220; Thomson 1964, pp. 334–336, 341–348
	Italy 1890–1914	Mack Smith 1959, p. 259; Schmidt 1939, pp. 16–17

Table A43 (continued)

Description of Category	Country and Period	Sources
national governmental decisions, not even an indirect effect.	Netherlands 1850–1870(–), 1870–1890	Albarda 1943, p. 99; Encyclopaedia Britannica, 1910, 13:604–605; Lourens 1943, p. 190
	New Zealand 1870–1890	Airey 1947b, pp. 90–91; Sinclair 1961, pp. 147–148
	Norway 1890–1914	Galenson 1949, p. 59; Larsen 1948, p. 465; Lindgren 1959, pp. 31–33
	Sweden 1890–1914(–)	Crouzet 1968, p. 518; Menzel 1980c, pp. 148–149
	Switzerland 1850–1870(+)	Encyclopaedia Britannica 1911, 26:260–261; Rappard 1914, pp. 304–312
	United States 1850–1870(–), 1870–1890(+)	Brock 1962, p. 489; Hession and Sardy 1969, pp. 283–294, 475–476; Potter 1964, pp. 614–615
Category C Countries in which direct political power over national governmental decisions remained in the hands of a national traditional elite, usually propertied, during the period, but the indirect influence of	Argentina 1890–1914	Cochran and Reina 1962, p. 258; Pendle 1963, p. 65; Scoble 1964a, p. 189
	Denmark 1850–1870, 1870–1890	Encyclopaedia Britannica 1910, 8:38; Jensen 1937, pp. 104–105; Østerud 1978, pp. 199–226

Table A43 (continued)

Description of Category	Country and Period	Sources
rising entrepreneurs, businessmen, and wage earners was evident in government actions to promote industry or to take account of the interests of wage earners. Countries are classified C+ where the traditional elite was not landed but nevertheless was very conservative; or where neither the traditional elite nor the rising new groups were in control; or where the propertied elite, while in control, was being transformed by its acquisition of new commercial or industrial interests. Countries are classified C– where only the wealthy commercial and industrial groups had even indirect political influence and wage earners had none.	France 1850–1870(+)	Farmer 1964, pp. 442, 448–449, 451–452
	Germany 1850–1870(–), 1870–1890	Conze 1962, pp. 289–291; Joll 1964, pp. 494–498, 505, 510, 517–521; Schieder 1962, pp. 257–258
	Italy 1870–1890 (–)	Mack Smith 1959, pp. 206–207; Schmidt 1939, pp. 4–7, 9
	Japan 1870–1890(+), 1890–1914(+)	Halliday 1975, pp. 40, 46, 57–60, 62, 64; Lippit 1978, pp. 63–64; Marshall 1967, pp. 44, 46, 118; Moore 1966, pp. 237–241, 276–279, 287; Scalapino 1953, p. 156
	New Zealand 1850–1870	Brady 1958, pp. 267, 285–286, 309
	Norway 1850–1870, 1870–1890(+)	Derry 1957, pp. 190–191; Lindgren 1959, pp. 31–33, 52–55; Østerud 1978, pp. 198–223; Semmingsen 1954, pp. 188–189
	Russia 1850–1870(–), 1870–1890, 1890–1914(+)	Blackwell 1968, p. 192; Lyashchenko 1949, pp. 415–417
	Spain 1870–1890(–)?, 1890–1914(–)	Boyd 1979, pp. 8, 10; Carr 1966, pp. 439, 449–450
	Sweden 1850–1870(–), 1870–1890	Herlitz 1939, pp. 37, 73; Østerud 1978, pp. 201–226

Table A43 (continued)

Description of Category	Country and Period	Sources
Category D Countries in which propertied traditional national or colonial elites were in full control of the national government during the greater part of the period and were not significantly influenced by rising indigenous commercial, industrial, or wage-earning groups. Countries are classified D+ if, instead of being in the control of landed or colonial elites, political life was dominated by the joint power of a monarch and opportunistic nationalist ministers who controlled or circumvented national parliaments.	Argentina 1850–1870(+), 1870–1890(+)	Cardoso and Faletto 1979, pp. 83–85
	Brazil 1850–1870(+), 1870–1890(+), 1890–1914	Cardoso and Faletto 1979, pp. 89–91; Hambloch 1936, pp. 43–45, 58–59, 105–109, 119–121, 154–161, 176; Haring 1958, pp. 56–62
	Burma 1850–1870, 1870–1890, 1890–1914	Furnivall 1931, chaps. 6 and 7
	China 1850–1870, 1870–1890, 1890–1914	Beckman 1962, pp. 147–150
	Egypt 1850–1870(−), 1870–1890(−), 1890–1914	Tignor 1966, pp. 18, 28, 43, 48, 50, 53–55, 103, 123–138; Vatikiotis 1980, pp. 86, 88
	India 1850–1870(−), 1870–1890(−), 1890–1914(−)	Andrews and Mookerjee 1967, pp. 62–63, 67, 87; Misra 1977, pp. 65, 92; Moore 1966, pp. 344–345, 352–355
	Italy 1850–1870(+)	Fenoaltea 1968, p. 419; Mack Smith 1964, pp. 566–576; Schmidt 1939, pp. 4–6; Seton-Watson 1967, p. 24
	Japan 1850–1870(+)	Halliday 1975, pp. 4–12, 14, 19, 23–26, 34–35, 40–46; Harootunian 1970, pp. 401–402

Table A43 (continued)

Description of Category	Country and Period	Sources
	Spain 1850-1870(+)	Boyd 1979, pp. 8, 11, 16, 19, 20-22; Manuel 1938, pp. 6-7; Payne 1973, pp. 455, 459-460, 464

Note: Of the sources in this table, the following are listed in the general section of the bibliography: Anderson and Anderson 1967, Brady 1958, Buell 1935, Cardozo and Faletto 1979, Crouzet 1968, Encyclopaedia Britannica 1910-1911, Moore 1966, Østerud 1978, Schieder 1962, and Senghaas 1982.

Table A44

Classification Scheme for Strength of National Representative Institutions, 1850–1870, 1870–1890, 1890–1914

Description of Category	Country and Period	Sources
Category A Countries in which national representative institutions were well established, as indicated by the regular functioning of cabinet responsibility to the legislature and the regular exercise of legislative lawmaking powers; opposition parties were permitted to operate within the legislature; and there was at least limited male suffrage. Countries meeting these criteria with universal male suffrage are classified A+; those with suffrage extended to the majority of adult males are classified A; and those with suffrage restricted by property requirements to a minority of adult males are classified A-.	Canada 1890–1914	Brady 1958, pp. 67–73; Wittke 1941, p. 316
	France 1890–1914	Anderson and Anderson 1967, pp. 40, 302, 304; Lowell 1914, pp. 34–35
	Great Britain 1850–1870(-), 1870–1890(-), 1890–1914	Kitson Clark 1962, pp. 222, 230–231; Moore 1961, pp. 7–34; Schieder 1962, pp. 255–256; Trevelyan 1937, p. 246
	New Zealand 1890–1914(+)	Brady 1958, p. 266
	Sweden 1870–1890(-), 1890–1914	Arneson 1939, pp. 36–38; Herlitz 1939, pp. 38–39; Rustow 1955, p. 72
	Switzerland 1870–1890, 1890–1914	Encyclopaedia Britannica 1911, 26:260; Oechsli 1922, pp. 407–408; Schieder 1962, pp. 258–260
	United States 1870–1890, 1890–1914	Morison 1965, pp. 792, 983

Table A44 (continued)

Description of Category	Country and Period	Sources
Category B Countries in which national representative institutions were quite well established as indicated by regular sharing of power between a monarch and the legislature in the form of a division in both executive authority and cabinet responsibility; limitations operated upon freedom of political opposition; and the franchise was restricted by property qualifications to a minority of adult males. Countries meeting these criteria in which cabinet responsibility to the legislature had been established are classified B+; those in which cabinet responsibility had not been established are classified B; and those without established cabinet responsibility and with suffrage extremely limited (to only a few percent of adult males) are classified B-.	Argentina 1870–1890(–), 1890–1914(–)	Barager 1968, pp. 8–13, 15–16; Fillol 1961, pp. 47–48; Kirkpatrick 1931, p. 143; McGann 1966, pp. 23–25, 44
	Belgium 1850–1870(–), 1870–1890(–), 1890–1914	Hawgood 1964, pp. 191–192; Huggett 1969, pp. 34–35; Lyon 1969, pp. 45–46, 54
	Canada 1870–1890(+)	Brady 1958, pp. 69–70, 72–73; Wittke 1941, p. 316
	France 1850–1870, 1870–1890(+)	Anderson and Anderson 1967, pp. 38–40, 305; Brogan 1957, pp. 105–106; Lowell 1914, pp. 15, 34–35; Wolf 1963, pp. 242–249, 265
	Germany 1870–1890, 1890–1914	Anderson and Anderson 1967, pp. 294–299; Lowell 1914, pp. 168–169, 184–185; Ullman and King-Hall 1954, pp. 59–60, 75–77
	Italy 1870–1890(–), 1890–1914	Lowell 1914, pp. 130–131, 138; Mack Smith 1959, pp. 138–139, 196–199, 259; Salvadori 1965, pp. 107–108, 110–111; Seton-Watson 1967, pp. 12, 24
	Netherlands 1850–1870(+), 1870–1890(+), 1890–1914(+)	Albarda 1943, pp. 96–99; Barnouw 1944, pp. 188–189; Eyck 1959, pp. 64–65; Landheer 1943a, pp. 181–183

Table A44 (continued)

Description of Category	Country and Period	Sources
	New Zealand 1870–1890(+)	Brady 1958, pp. 265–266; Encyclopaedia Britannica 1911, 19:628; Milne 1966, p. 13
	Norway 1850–1870, 1870–1890, 1890–1914(+)	Arneson 1939, pp. 28–30, 157–159; Larsen 1948, pp. 431–433; Semmingsen 1954, pp. 176–177
	Sweden 1850–1870(+)	Arneson 1939, pp. 36–38; Herlitz 1939, pp. 38–39; Janson 1931, pp. 71–73; Rustow 1955, pp. 18–19
	United States 1850–1870	Hession and Sardy 1969, pp. 302–303, 390–391
Category C Countries in which national representative institutions were established during the twenty-year period prior to the period for which the country is classified; and these institutions were rudimentary as indicated by the brevity of the period since their establishment and/or discontinuities in their functioning and/or very limited	Argentina 1850–1870	Barager 1968, pp. 70–73; Levene 1963, pp. 443, 447, 453; McGann 1966, p. 28
	Australia 1850–1870(−), 1870–1890(−), 1890–1914(+)	Fitzpatrick 1946, pp. 38–39; Gollan 1960, pp. 1–3, 30–31, 50–51, 66–67; McGhee 1970, pp. 150–151; Rosecrance 1964, pp. 290, 303
	Canada 1850–1870(+)	Brady 1958, pp. 41, 67–70; Wittke 1941, pp. 131, 167, 189–190

Table A44 (continued)

Description of Category	Country and Period	Sources
lawmaking powers. Countries meeting these criteria in which there were, in addition, reasonably well-established regional representative institutions and cabinet responsibility to the legislature are classified C+. Also included in this category and classified C- are countries that lacked national representative institutions but in which there were well-established regional representative institutions.	Denmark 1850-1870(+), 1870-1890, 1890-1914	Arneson 1939, pp. 24-25, 147; Danstrup 1948, pp. 102-106; Encyclopaedia Britannica 1910, 8:26; Jensen 1937, pp. 49, 104-105
	Germany 1850-1870	Lowell 1914, pp. 168-169, 184-185; Pollock 1938, pp. 12-13; Ullman and King-Hall 1954, pp. 59-60, 69, 77
	Italy 1850-1870	Lowell 1914, pp. 130-131, 138; Mack Smith 1959, pp. 198-199; Salvadori 1965, pp. 107-108; Seton-Watson 1967, pp. 12, 24
	Japan 1870-1890(-), 1890-1914(-)	Ike 1950, pp. 39-40; Kawabe 1921, pp. 2-5, 47-48, 123-124; Norman 1940, p. 189; Yanaga 1949, pp. 215, 265, 405-406
	New Zealand 1850-1870(+)	Brady 1958, pp. 265-266, 285-286; Condliffe 1959, pp. 83-85; Encyclopaedia Britannica 1911, 19:628; Fitzpatrick 1949, p. 96
	Spain 1870-1890, 1890-1914	Boyd 1979, pp. 8, 10-11, 16, 19-22; Ramos Oliveira 1946, pp. 47, 50-53, 78-93, 105-107

Table A44 (continued)

Description of Category	Country and Period	Sources
	Switzerland 1850-1870(+)	Bonjour et al. 1952, pp. 268-269, 301; *Encyclopaedia Britannica* 1911, 26:259-261; Oechsli 1922, pp. 405-408; Rappard 1936, pp. 21, 24
Category D Countries where national representative institutions were nonexistent or were established late in the period for the first time or were frequently suppressed. Countries in this category with national representative institutions placing constitutional limitations on the monarchy which were frequently suppressed are classified D+; countries in which national representative institutions were established late in the period for the first time also are classified D+. Countries without national representative institutions but with limited local representative institutions are classified D.	Brazil 1850-1870(+), 1870-1890(+), 1890-1914(-)	Freyre 1970, pp. 90, 100; Hambloch 1936, pp. 43-45, 58-59, 105-121, 158, 176; Haring 1958, pp. 56-62
	Burma 1850-1870(-), 1870-1890(-), 1890-1914(+)	Cady 1958, pp. 93-94; Furnivall 1960, pp. 5, 9; Hagen 1956, pp. 12-13
	China 1850-1870(-), 1870-1890(-), 1890-1914(+)	Beckmann 1962, pp. 200-202; Cameron et al. 1960, pp. 34-37; Ch'en 1969, pp. 15, 17
	Egypt 1850-1870(-), 1870-1890(-), 1890-1914(-)	Tignor 1966, pp. 14-55, 103, 123-138, 180-181; Vatikiotis 1980, pp. 49-50, 62, 81-88
	India 1850-1870(-), 1870-1890(-), 1890-1914	Andrews and Mookerjee 1967, pp. 38, 62-67, 79, 87, 96-97; Misra 1977, pp. 65, 74-75, 92

Table A44 (continued)

Description of Category	Country and Period	Sources
Countries without any form of representative institutions are classified D-.	Japan 1850-1870(-)	Buchanan 1951, pp. 360-361; Ike 1950, pp. 39-40; Kawabe 1921, pp. 2-5
	Russia 1850-1870(-), 1870-1890, 1890-1914(+)	Anderson and Anderson 1967, pp. 303-305; Karpovich 1960, pp. 38-49, 111-115; Vernadsky 1961 pp. 247-250, 267-268
	Spain 1850-1870(-)	Ramos Oliveira 1946, pp. 47, 50-53

Note: Of the sources in this table, the following are listed in the general section of the bibliography: Anderson and Anderson 1967, Arneson 1939, Brady 1958, Encyclopaedia Britannica 1910-1911, Hawgood 1960, Lowell 1914, and Schieder 1962.

Table A45

Classification Scheme for Extent of Political Stability, 1850-1870, 1870-1890, 1890-1914

Description of Category	Country and Period	Sources
Category A Countries where during the period there was (1) continuity in national political decision making as indicated by few unauthorized cabinet changes, (2) no marked signs of intense nonviolent political strife in any region, and (3) little or no domestic violence in any region. Included in this category and classified A- are countries meeting these criteria except that (1) a national government was substituted for a system of regional government, or (2) there was some intermittent intense nonviolent political strife in some but not most regions, or (3) the legislative process was paralyzed for a short period by severe conflict between the upper and lower houses of parliament.	Canada 1890-1914	Brady 1958, pp. 18, 41, 67-68, 72, 91, 93, 98, 109, 113, 129-130
	Denmark 1850-1870, 1870-1890(-), 1890-1914	Arneson 1939, pp. 23-24; Danstrup 1948, p. 121; Encyclopaedia Britannica 1910, 8:38-39; 1922, 30:831
	Great Britain 1850-1870, 1870-1890, 1890-1914	Encyclopaedia Britannica 1910, 9:564-582
	Netherlands 1850-1870, 1870-1890, 1890-1914	Encyclopaedia Britannica 1910, 13:604-605; 1922, 31:379
	New Zealand 1890-1914	Brady 1958, pp. 268-269, 286, 288
	Norway 1850-1870, 1890-1914(-)	Encyclopaedia Britannica 1911, 19:812-815
	Sweden 1850-1870, 1870-1890, 1890-1914	Encyclopaedia Britannica 1911, 26:210-214; 1922, 32:631-632
	Switzerland 1850-1870, 1870-1890, 1890-1914	Buell 1935, pp. 562-571; Encyclopaedia Britannica 1911, 26:259-262

Table A45 (continued)

Description of Category	Country and Period	Sources
Category B Countries where during the period (1) there was significant discontinuity in national decision making as indicated by frequent government turnovers, but without upsetting the institutional framework; (2) nonviolent political strife occurred in several regions; but (3) In most regions there was no significant domestic violence. Included in this category and classified B+ are countries meeting the criteria for category A except that either (1) there was some significant domestic violence in one region or (2) there was intermittent intense nonviolent political strife in most regions. Included and classified B- are countries that experienced frequent intense nonviolent political strife and frequent cabinet changes.	Argentina 1890–1914(+)	Barager 1968, p. 10; McGann 1966, p. 30
	Australia 1890–1914	Brady 1958, pp. 134, 183, 204, 225
	Belgium 1850–1870(+), 1870–1890(+), 1890–1914(+)	Encyclopaedia Britannica 1910, 3:678–679
	Brazil 1850–1870(+), 1870–1890(–)	Hambloch 1936, pp. 43–45, 154–161; Haring 1958, pp. 56–62
	Burma 1890–1914(+)?	Encyclopaedia Britannica 1910, 4:845–846
	Canada 1850–1870, 1870–1890(+)	Brady 1958, pp. 24–30, 41, 77; Encyclopaedia Britannica 1910, 5:159–163; Wittke 1941, p. 179
	France 1850–1870(–), 1870–1890(–), 1890–1914(–)	Brogan 1957, pp. 163–164, 179; Lowell 1914, pp. 74–82, 84–85, 104; Soltau 1965, pp. 13–14
	Germany 1850–1870(+), 1870–1890(+), 1890–1914(+)	Dawson 1919, 1:480–482, 487
	New Zealand 1850–1870, 1870–1890	Brady 1958, pp. 267–268, 309

Table A45 (continued)

Description of Category	Country and Period	Sources
	Norway 1870–1890(+)	*Encyclopaedia Britannica* 1911, 19:812–814
	United States 1870–1890, 1890–1914(+)	Hession and Sardy 1969, pp. 474–475, 483–484, 486–488, 590
Category C Countries where during the period (1) significant discontinuity existed in national decision making due to a reorganization in government or change in location of a national government, (2) there was frequent nonviolent political strife in some regions, and (3) there was frequent domestic violence in most regions. Included and classified C+ are countries meeting the first criterion, but where there was frequent nonviolent political strife in most regions and frequent domestic violence in some regions. Also included and regions.	Argentina 1850–1870, 1870–1890	Barager 1968, pp. 10, 72–73; Levene 1963, pp. 462, 478; McGann 1966, p. 30; Williams 1920, pp. 30–31
	Australia 1850–1870(+), 1870–1890(+)	Brady 1958, pp. 183, 204; Cotter 1970, pp. 122–129; Grundy 1970, pp. 217–219; McGhee 1970, p. 173
	Brazil 1890–1914	Hambloch 1936, pp. 43–45, 58–59, 105–109, 119–121, 158, 176; Haring 1958, pp. 56–62
	China 1850–1870, 1870–1890, 1890–1914	Beckman 1962, pp. 146, 150, 156; Li 1956, pp. 47, 95
	Italy 1850–1870, 1870–1890, 1890–1914	Lowell 1914, pp. 137–138; Mack Smith 1959, pp. 30–32, 41; Seton-Watson 1967, pp. 13–14, 25

Table A45 (continued)

Description of Category	Country and Period	Sources
classified C+ are countries that lacked national governments but experienced frequent changes in regional government cabinets not associated with severe domestic violence.	Japan 1870–1890, 1890–1914(+)	Beckman 1962, p. 302; Halliday 1975, pp. 3, 22–30, 68–70; Kawabe 1921, pp. 51, 53–54, 87–88; McLaren 1916, pp. 105, 112, 121, 161–162, 285, 288
	Russia 1850–1870, 1870–1890, 1890–1914	Encyclopaedia Britannica 1911, 23:904–907; Karpovich 1960, pp. 18–19, 38; Vernadsky 1954, p. 231; Vernadsky 1961, pp. 227–230, 261–272
	Spain 1870–1890, 1890–1914	Boyd 1979, pp. 8, 10, 16, 19, 20–22; Manuel 1938, pp. 10–11; Payne 1973, pp. 467–471, 488, 492–500, 585–591, 627; Ramos Oliveira 1946, pp. 50–53, 78–88
Category D Countries that during the period experienced (1) continuous disruption of national decision-making functions through civil war or revolution over most of the period, (2) continuous and intense nonviolent political strife in most regions, and (3) continuous domestic violence in most regions. Included and	Burma 1850–1870(+), 1870–1890(+)	Walinsky 1962, p. 21
	Egypt 1850–1870(+), 1870–1890(+), 1890–1914(+)	Tignor 1966, pp. 18, 28, 43–55, 123–138, 180–181; Vatikiotis 1969, pp. 62, 81, 86, 88
	India 1850–1870, 1870–1890, 1890–1914(+)	Allan et al. 1964, pp. 145, 670; Andrews and Mookerjee 1967, pp. 38, 62–63, 67, 87, 96–97; Misra 1977, pp. 65, 74–75, 92

Table A45 (continued)

Description of Category	Country and Period	Sources
classified D- are countries under foreign rule that experienced fairly continuous violence in most regions, continuous nonviolent political dissent, and sporadic political uprisings. Also classified D+ are countries meeting the main criteria for the category for one decade of the period but not for the other.	Japan 1850-1870	Halliday 1975, pp. 3, 13, 17, 19-21, 23; Harootunian 1970, pp. 32-33, 38, 42; Norman 1940, pp. 41-44, 46-47
	Spain 1850-1870	Payne 1973, pp. 458-464; Ramos Oliveira 1946, pp. 51-53, 78-88
	United States 1850-1870(+)	Hession and Sardy 1969, pp. 298-306, 374, 383-391, 472

Note: Of the sources in this table, the following are listed in the general section of the bibliography: Arneson 1939, Brady 1958, Buell 1935, Encyclopaedia Britannica 1910-1911, Encyclopaedia Britannica 1922, and Lowell 1914.

Table A46

Classification Scheme for Degree of Foreign Economic Dependence, 1850–1870, 1870–1890, 1890–1914

Description of Category	Country and Period	Sources
Category A Countries that were rated as heavily dependent on all seven dimensions of foreign economic dependence[a]	Argentina 1870–1890, 1890–1914	Díaz Alejandro 1970, p. 215; Ferns 1950, pp. 206–207; Ferns 1960, pp. 357, 372, 397, 409, 420, 428–429; Fillol 1961, p. 43; McCarty [Australia] 1973, pp. 160–162; Randall 1977, 2:29–30, 215, 244; Scoble 1964a, pp. 92–93
	Brazil 1850–1870	Burns 1970, p. 141; Graham 1968, pp. 5, 26, 60–61, 73–76, 130, 159; Wythe et al. 1949, pp. 158–159
	Burma 1870–1890, 1890–1914	Andrus 1947, p. 19; Hlaing 1964, pp. 130–131; Tun Wai 1961, pp. 44, 58–59
	Egypt 1850–1870, 1870–1890, 1890–1914	Hershlag 1964, pp. 95–99, 101, 103, 112–116; Issawi 1966, pp. 365–366; Owen 1969, pp. 81–83, 87, 128–129, 174–176, 221, 280–281
	India 1850–1870, 1870–1890, 1890–1914	Bose 1965, pp. 487–495; Islam 1960, pp. 54–55, 59; Lamb 1955, pp. 464, 467–468, 471–472, 474–475, 477–481; Mukerjee 1972, pp. 196–198, 206–210; Sarkar 1917, p. 89; Sen 1966, pp. 32–33, 36–39, 62–65

Table A46 (continued)

Description of Category	Country and Period	Sources
Category B Countries that had heavily dependent production structures and were rated as moderately dependent on all other dimensions	Brazil 1870–1890, 1890–1914	Graham 1968, pp. 5, 54–57, 60–61, 71, 78–79, 137–140, 142, 159; Randall 1977b, p. 232; Wythe et al. 1949, pp. 158–159
	Canada 1850–1870, 1870–1890	Jones 1946, pp. 238, 308–309; Marr and Paterson 1980, pp. 293–294; Paterson 1976, pp. 3, 45; Woodruff 1966, p. 120
	New Zealand 1850–1870, 1870–1890, 1890–1914	Berrill 1963, pp. 294–295; Bloomfield 1968, p. 47; Condliffe 1930, pp. 169, 223; Lloyd Prichard 1970, pp. 172, 209; Simkin 1951, p. 153; Woodruff 1967, p. 138
Category C Countries that had moderately dependent production structures and were rated as moderately dependent on all other counts. Countries were classified C— if the volume of their foreign trade was very small, the control of trade and distribution showed little dependence or their dependence on expatriate	Canada 1890–1914	Berrill 1963, pp. 291–293; Bloomfield 1968, p. 47; Marr and Paterson 1980, pp. 291–295; Paterson 1976, pp. 3, 6–8, 12–14, 43–45, 48–51, 53, 76
	China 1870–1890, 1890–1914	Allen and Donnithorne 1954, pp. 166–167; Hou 1961, p. 40; Hou 1965, pp. 7–8, 52–53, 59–63, 66, 206–207, 214–217; King 1965, p. 93; Remer 1968, pp. 66–69, 79, 115–116; Yang 1952, p. 88
	Italy 1850–1870	Bloomfield 1968, p. 47; Luzzatto 1969, pp. 209–211; Neufeld 1961, pp. 30–32

Table A46 (continued)

Description of Category	Country and Period	Sources
skills was modest.	Norway 1890–1914	Berrill 1963, pp. 296–297; Bloomfield 1968, p. 47; Bull 1960, pp. 266–269; Jörberg 1973, pp. 433–435
	Russia 1850–1870, 1870–1890, 1890–1914	Ashworth 1952, p. 173; Crisp 1976, pp. 159–196; McKay 1970, pp. 24–26, 28–29, 31, 37, 379–381, 383–388
	Spain 1850–1870, 1870–1890, 1890–1914	Nadal 1973, pp. 543, 548–551, 569–570, 583–584, 619–620; Vicens Vives and Nadal Oller 1969, pp. 683–687, 722–725; Vilar 1967, p. 71
Category D Includes two types of countries with moderate overall levels of dependence. Some countries were at least moderately dependent on foreign capital and skills and had no more than modestly dependent production structures. Other countries had heavily dependent production structures and were only modestly dependent on foreign	Australia 1850–1870, 1870–1890, 1890–1914	Barnard 1958, pt. 2; Bloomfield 1968, p. 47; Butlin 1964, pp. 5–6, 29, 31; Butlin 1965, pp. 148–149; Sinclair 1976, pp. 97–98; Woodruff 1966, pp. 139–140
	Denmark 1850–1870, 1870–1890, 1890–1914	Hansen 1970, pp. 3, 7, 16, 28, 33, 63; Jörberg 1973, p. 407; Skrubbeltrang 1951, pp. 118–119; Youngson 1959, pp. 223–225
	Italy 1870–1890, 1890–1914	Bloomfield 1968, p. 47; Cafagna 1973, pp. 287–296, 300–321; Cohen 1972, p. 73
	Japan 1870–1890, 1890–1914	Berrill 1963, pp. 290–291; Landes 1965b, p. 94; Reubens 1955, pp. 179–195, 200, 203, 205, 210, 213, 214–217, 219–222, 228

Table A46 (continued)

Description of Category	Country and Period	Sources
capital and skills. None of the countries in this category depended on foreign economic initiatives or experienced expatriate ownership or control of factory industry.	Norway 1850-1870, 1870-1890	Berrill 1963, pp. 296-297; Bloomfield 1968, p. 47; Bull 1960, pp. 266-269; Hodne 1975, p. 123; Lieberman 1970, p. 117
	Sweden 1850-1870, 1870-1890, 1890-1914	Berrill 1963, p. 296; Bloomfield 1968, p. 47; Heckscher 1954, pp. 246-250; Jörberg 1961, p. 13; Jörberg 1969, p. 267; Youngson 1959, pp. 153, 167-170, 178, 180
Category E Countries that exhibited very small beginnings of the dependent characteristics summarized in Categories A through C	Argentina 1850-1870	Ferns 1950, pp. 206-207; Ferns 1960, pp. 334, 338, 357, 363; Randall 1977, 2:29-30 Scobie 1964b, pp. 26-27, 32-35
	Burma 1850-1870	Andrus 1947, p. 19; Hlaing 1964, pp. 98, 130-131
	China 1850-1870	Allen and Donnithorne 1954, pp. 166-167; Hou 1965, pp. 7-8, 52-53, 59-63, 66; King 1965, p. 93; Remer 1968, pp. 66-68; Yang 1952, p. 88
Category F Advanced countries with nondependent production structures where foreign loans, skills, and owner-	Belgium 1850-1870	Cameron 1961, pp. 348-349, 364, 366; Clapham [France] 1936, pp. 58-59; Dhondt and Bruwier 1973, pp. 30-31; Hague 1968, pp. 376-377; Baudhuin 1928, pp. 328-334

Table A46 (continued)

Description of Category	Country and Period	Sources
ship, if any, involved countries at similar levels of development	Germany 1850–1870	Henderson 1961, p. 73; Kindleberger 1976, pp. 277–279; Woodruff 1973, p. 674, 709
	Japan 1850–1870	Allen 1965, p. 875; Berrill 1963, pp. 290–291; Reubens 1955, p. 180
	Netherlands 1850–1870	Brugmans 1961, pp. 268–270; Brugmans 1969, p. 76
	United States 1850–1870, 1870–1890	Berrill 1963, p. 293–294; Bloomfield 1968, p. 47; McKay [Russia] 1970, p. 16; North 1961, pp. 196–197, 199
Category G Countries that were advanced economically and had no significant dependent features	Belgium 1870–1890, 1890–1914	Cameron 1961, pp. 367–368; Baudhuin 1928, pp. 328–334; Lincke 1911, p. 172
	France 1850–1870, 1870–1890, 1890–1914	Ashworth 1952, p. 173; Berrill 1963, p. 290; Bloomfield 1968, p. 47; Clough 1939, p. 251; Henderson 1961, pp. 189–190; Holmes 1961, p. 175; Lévy-Leboyer 1978, p. 232; Palmade 1972, pp. 195–196; Royal Institute of International Affairs 1937, pp. 123–124; White 1933, pp. 122–123

Table A46 (continued)

Description of Category	Country and Period	Sources
	Germany 1870–1890, 1870–1914	Ashworth 1952, p. 173; Berrill 1963, p. 290; Bloomfield 1968, p. 47; Henderson 1961, p. 73; Royal Institute of International Affairs 1937, pp. 126–128; Woodruff 1973, pp. 674, 709
	Great Britain 1850–1870, 1870–1890, 1890–1914	Ashworth 1952, pp. 170–172; Berrill 1963, pp. 289–290; Bloomfield 1968, p. 74; Woodruff 1966, p. 117; Woodruff 1973, pp. 708–709
	Netherlands 1870–1890, 1890–1914	Brugmans 1961, pp. 382–385; Brugmans 1969, p. 76; de Jonge 1968, pp. 355–356
	Switzerland 1850–1870, 1870–1890, 1890–1914	Bosshardt and Nydegger 1964, pp. 311–313
	United States 1890–1914	Berrill 1963, pp. 293–294; Bloomfield 1968, p. 47; McKay [Russia] 1970, p. 16; North 1961, p. 199

Note: Of the sources in this table, the following are listed in the general section of the bibliography: Ashworth 1952, Berrill 1963, Bloomfield 1968, Cameron 1961, Hague 1963, Henderson 1961, Islam 1960, Royal Institute of International Affairs 1937, Woodruff 1966, and Woodruff 1973.

a See chapter six for a description of the seven dimensions in terms of which this variable is defined.

Table A47

Classification Scheme for Colonial Status, 1850, 1870, 1890

Description of Category	Country and Year	Sources
Category A Countries or territories strictly defined as "colonies" where the national or regional government (whichever was predominant) was run by expatriates. "Expatriates" in the colonies in our sample were British colonial career officers.	Australia 1850, 1870, 1890	Encyclopaedia Britannica 1910, 2:953–954, 964, 966–967, 969; Griffin 1970, p. 105
	Burma 1870(-), 1890	Encyclopaedia Britannica 1910, 4:845
	Canada 1850	Encyclopaedia Britannica 1910, 5:159
	Egypt 1890(-)	Encyclopaedia Britannica 1910, 9:28, 115
	India 1850, 1870, 1890	Encyclopaedia Britannica 1911, 14:389–390, 392–393, 413–417; Maddison 1970, p. 51
Category B Countries that were defined as "colonies" in that they were under the overwhelming economic and political influence of another country but whose national or regional government (whichever was predominant) was run by settlers. In the countries in our sample, "settlers" were British-born immigrants or colonial-born persons of British descent.	Canada 1870, 1890	Encyclopaedia Britannica 1910, 5:161–162, 164
	New Zealand 1850, 1870, 1890	Encyclopaedia Britannica 1911, 19:629–631

Table A47 (continued)

Description of Category	Country and Year	Sources
Category C Countries that were not defined as "colonies," maintaining political independence, but that exhibited a strong, dependent economic relationship with a colonial power or powers.	Argentina 1870, 1890	Encyclopaedia Britannica 1910, 2:471–472; Ferns 1960, pp. 327, 489
	Brazil 1890	Encyclopaedia Britannica 1910, 4:460; Graham 1968, p. 125
	China 1850, 1870(+), 1890(+)	Cowan 1964, p. 80; Encyclopaedia Britannica 1910, 6:177–179, 199–207, 209–212
	Egypt 1850, 1870	Encyclopaedia Britannica 1910, 9:110–114
	Italy 1850(−)	Encyclopaedia Britannica 1911, 15:50–58
	Japan 1870(−)	Encyclopaedia Britannica 1911, 15:194, 202, 211–212, 237–240
	Norway 1850, 1870, 1890	Encyclopaedia Britannica 1911, 19:804, 812–814
Category D Countries that were not defined as "colonies," did not exhibit relationships of strong economic dependence with a colonial power, and did not own colonies.	Argentina 1850	Encyclopaedia Britannica 1910, 2:470–471
	Brazil 1850, 1870	Encyclopaedia Britannica 1910, 4:458, 460

Table A47 (continued)

Description of Category	Country and Year	Sources
	Burma 1850(+)	Encyclopaedia Britannica 1910, 4:844-845
	Denmark 1850, 1870, 1890	Encyclopaedia Britannica 1910, 8:26, 37-39
	Germany 1850	Encyclopaedia Britannica 1911, 11:865, 871, 873
	Italy 1870	Encyclopaedia Britannica 1911, 15:60, 65-68, 72
	Japan 1850(+), 1890	Encyclopaedia Britannica 1911, 15:192, 202, 211-212, 237-241
	Russia 1850	Encyclopaedia Britannica 1911, 23:902-904
	Spain 1850, 1870, 1890	Encyclopaedia Britannica 1911, 25:526, 556, 558-559, 563-564
	Switzerland 1850, 1870, 1890	Encyclopaedia Britannica 1911, 26:259-263
Category E Countries with modest colonial holdings. Included are countries that held colonial territories not larger than the mother country.	Belgium 1850, 1870, 1890	Encyclopaedia Britannica 1910, 3:677, 680
	France 1850, 1870	Encyclopaedia Britannica 1911, 10:799

Table A47 (continued)

Description of Category	Country and Year	Sources
Also included are countries that had, during the two previous decades, acquired contiguous land inhabited by indigenous peoples of a dissimilar culture and language.	Germany 1870	Encyclopaedia Britannica 1911, 11:876–877
	Italy 1890	Encyclopaedia Britannica 1911, 15:72–73, 77–78
	Russia 1870, 1890	Encyclopaedia Britannica 1911, 23:905–907
	Sweden 1850, 1870, 1890	Encyclopaedia Britannica 1911, 26:210–214
	United States 1850, 1870, 1890	Encyclopaedia Britannica 1911, 27:700–701, 703–704, 718, 730–732
Category F Countries with major colonial holdings	France 1890	Encyclopaedia Britannica 1911, 10:799
	Germany 1890	Encyclopaedia Britannica 1911, 11:818
	Great Britain 1850, 1870, 1890	Encyclopaedia Britannica 1911, 4:608–609
	Netherlands 1850, 1870, 1890	Encyclopaedia Britannica 1911, 13:603, 605

Note: Of the sources in this table, the following is listed in the general section of the bibliography: Encyclopaedia Britannica 1910–1911.

Table A48

Component Scores for Composite Indicator of Level of
Development of Market Institutions, 1850, 1870, 1890[a]

	1850		1870		1890	
Country	Score	Classifi-cation	Score	Classifi-cation	Score	Classifi-cation
Argentina	-1.0	D	-.7	D	.2	B-
Australia	-1.0	D	.0	C+	.5	B-
Belgium	.8	B	1.6	A	1.9	A+
Brazil	-1.2	E	-1.2	E	-.6	D
Burma	-1.2	E	-1.1	D	-.5	C-
Canada	-.5	C-	-.1	C	.4	B-
China	-1.2	E	-1.2	E	-1.2	E
Denmark	-.8	D	.2	B-	.7	B
Egypt	-1.7	E-	-1.4	E	-.7	D
France	.5	B-	1.3	A-	1.7	A
Germany	-.1	C	.7	B	1.9	A+
Great Britain	.8	B	1.4	A-	1.7	A
India	-.9	D	-.7	D	-.3	C-
Italy	-.3	C-	-.1	C	.4	B-
Japan	-1.0	D	-1.0	D	-.0	C
Netherlands	.2	B-	.5	B-	.8	B
New Zealand	1.4	E	-.8	D	.8	B
Norway	-1.1	D-	-.8	D	.5	B-
Russia	-1.5	E	-1.0	D	-.3	C-

Table A48 (continued)

Country	1850 Score	1850 Classifi-cation	1870 Score	1870 Classifi-cation	1890 Score	1890 Classifi-cation
Spain	-.5	C-	-.2	C	.4	B-
Sweden	-.4	C	.4	B-	1.1	B+
Switzerland	.2	B-	1.7	A	1.8	A
United States	.7	B	1.6	A	1.8	A

Note: See the introduction to the data appendix for an explanation of this table.

a Each country in each time period was classified using its component score and the following classification scheme:

1.8 < A+		.0 < C+ <	.2
1.4 < A < 1.8		-.2 < C <	.0
1.2 < A- < 1.4		-.5 < C- <	-.2
1.0 < B+ < 1.2		-1.1 < D <	-.5
.6 < B < 1.0		-1.6 < E <	-1.1
.2 < B- < .6		E- <	-1.6

Table A49

Component Scores for Composite Indicator of Rate of Spread
of Market Institutions, 1850-1870, 1870-1890, 1890-1914[a]

Country	1850-1870		1870-1890		1890-1914	
	Score	Classifi-cation	Score	Classifi-cation	Score	Classifi-cation
Argentina	-2.1	D	-.4	C	.5	B
Australia	-.4	C	.8	B	.3	B-
Belgium	1.4	A-	.4	B-	.8	B
Brazil	-1.5	D+	-.6	C	.1	B-
Burma	-1.9	D	-.3	C	-.0	B-
Canada	-.5	D	.1	B-	1.2	B+
China	-2.3	D	-2.1	D	-1.7	D
Denmark	-.3	C	.6	B	1.8	A-
Egypt	-.8	C	-.6	C	-.0	B-
France	1.4	A-	.6	B	.3	B-
Germany	.9	B+	1.9	A-	1.7	A-
Great Britain	1.5	A-	.3	B-	-.5	C
India	-1.1	C-	-.4	C	-.4	C
Italy	-.8	C	.2	B-	.3	B-
Japan	-1.7	D	-.1	C+	1.1	B+
Netherlands	-.8	C	-.1	C+	1.1	B+
New Zealand	-.6	C	.1	B-	.8	B+
Norway	-.7	C	-.3	C	.1	B-
Russia	-.5	C	-.4	C	.4	B-

Table A49 (continued)

Country	1850–1870		1870–1890		1890–1914	
	Score	Classifi-cation	Score	Classifi-cation	Score	Classifi-cation
Spain	−1.1	C−	−.8	C	−.5	C
Sweden	−.3	C	−.2	C+	.3	B−
Switzerland	.8	B	.2	B−	1.2	B+
United States	.7	B	2.2	A+	1.0	B+

Note: See the introduction to the data appendix for an explanation of this table.

a Each country in each time period was classified using its component score and the following classification scheme:

2.2 < A+	−.2 < C+ < −.1
2.0 < A < 2.2	−1.0 < C < −.2
1.4 < A− < 2.0	−1.2 < C− < −1.0
.8 < B+ < 1.4	−1.6 < D+ < −1.2
.4 < B < .8	D < −1.6
−.1 < B− < .4	

Table A50

Component Scores for Composite Indicator of Rate of Spread
of Market Institutions (Lagged), 1830-1850, 1850-1870, 1870-1890[a]

Country	1830-1850		1850-1870		1870-1890	
	Score	Classifi-cation	Score	Classifi-cation	Score	Classifi-cation
Argentina	-.9	D+	-1.4	D	.3	C+
Australia	-.5	C-	.2	C+	1.2	B
Belgium	-.2	C	1.8	A-	.8	B-
Brazil	-1.4	D	-.8	C-	-.1	C
Burma	-1.4	D	-1.1	D+	.3	C+
Canada	-1.1	D+	.0	C	.6	B-
China	-1.4	D	-1.5	D	-1.4	D
Denmark	-.8	C-	.2	C+	1.1	B
Egypt	-1.4	D	-.1	C	.0	C
France	.1	C	1.8	A-	.9	B-
Germany	1.3	B+	1.3	B+	2.1	A
Great Britain	1.2	B	1.8	A-	.7	B-
India	-1.2	D+	-.5	C	.2	C+
Italy	-.8	D+	-.2	C	.7	B-
Japan	-.9	D+	-.9	D+	.5	C+
Netherlands	-1.4	D	-.2	C	.3	C+
New Zealand	-1.4	D	.0	C	.6	B-
Norway	-1.4	D	-.1	C	.3	C+
Russia	-1.4	D	.1	C	.1	C

Table A50 (continued)

Country	1830–1850		1850–1870		1870–1890	
	Score	Classifi-cation	Score	Classifi-cation	Score	Classifi-cation
Spain	-.5	C-	-.5	C-	-.2	C
Sweden	-.5	C-	.3	C+	.2	C+
Switzerland	.4	C+	1.2	B	.6	B-
United States	1.2	B	1.1	B	2.5	A

Note: See the introduction to the data appendix for an explanation of this table.

a Each country in each time period was classified using its component score and the following classification scheme:

2.0	< A		.15 < C+ <	.5
1.6	< A- <	2.0	-.5 < C <	.15
1.3	< B+ <	1.6	-.8 < C- <	-.5
1.0	< B <	1.3	-1.2 < D+ <	-.8
.5	< B- <	1.0	D <	-1.2

Table A51

The Data: 1850-1870 Cross Section

Variable		ARG	AUS	BEL	BRA	BUR	CAN	CHI	DEN	EGY	FRA	GER	GB	IND	ITA	JAP	NTH	NZ	NOR	RUS	SPA	SWE	SWZ	USA
																	Country							
Level of per capita income* (A to F), table Af		D	A	C	F	E	D	F	D	F	C	D	C	F	D	E	C	C	E	E	C	E	C	C
Change In per capita income (A to D), table A3		D	D-	B	C	D	B	D-	C	B	B	B	B	D	D	C	A	D	C	C	D	B	C+	B-
Development of techniques In Industry* (A to F), table A5		F	F	C	D	F	F	F	E	B	B	C	A	D	D	D	D	A	D	D	D	B	C+	B+
Improvement In Industrial techniques (A to F), table A6		F	E+	A	F	F	E	F	F	B-	B	A	C	E	F	F	F	G	F	F	E	B+	B-	D+
Improvement In Industrial techniques, lagged (A to F), table A6		F	E+	A	F	F	E	F	F	B-	B	A	C	E	F	F	F	G	F	F	E	B+	B-	B-
Development of techniques In agriculture* (A to G), table A7		G	E	B-	G	G	F	G	C-	B	C-	B	B+	G	F	C-	F	E-	G	G	G	C	C-	C
Improvement In agricultural techniques (A to F), table A7		F	F	C	F	G-	C	G	C	C	D-	B+	B+	F	C-	D-	F	F	E-	F	F	D-	D+	C
Improvement In agricultural techniques, lagged (A to F), table A8		F+	E+	D+	F	F	D-	F	D	C	C	D+	D+	F	D-	D-	D	F	F	F	E-	D-	D+	C
Percentage of labor In agriculture* (A to G), table A9		F	F	D	F	F	F	F	D	F	D	D+	D	F	F	D	D	F	F	F	F	D	D	C
Abundance of agricultural resources* (A to E) table A14		C	D	D	B	B	C	A	C	B	C	F	B	B	A	D	C-	A	A	B	B	C	B	A-
Development of Inland transportation* (A to E), table A15		E-	E-	B	E-	E+	B-	C+	E-	E	E-	E-	C-	E-	E-	E	E	C-	E-	E	E-	E	E-	C

Table A51 (continued)

Variable	ARG	AUS	BEL	BRA	BUR	CAN	CHI	DEN	EGY	FRA	GER	GB	IND	ITA	JAP	NTH	NZ	NOR	RUS	SPA	SWE	SWZ	USA
															Country								
Improvement in transportation, lagged (A to F), table A16	E	E	A	E	E	D	E+	E+	D-	D	A	A-	E	D-	E	C	E	E	D-	D-	E+	E	A
Growth of exports (A to D), table A17	A	A	C+	A-	D-	C	B	A+	A	A+	C	A	B-	B-	D-	A+	B	C	B	B+	A+	A	C
Shift in structure of export sector (A to D), table A21	D	D	C	D	D	B	D	C	B	C	B	C	D	B	D	C	D	C	C	C	B	B	B
Change in average real wages in industry (A to E), table A22	B	A	B	B	B	B	B	B	E	B	E	B	E	E	C	C	D	B	D	E	B	A	B
Change in average real wages in agriculture (A to E), table A23	B	D	C	C	D	B	B	B	B	B	E	B	E	E	C	C	D	B	D	E	A	B	A
Total population* (A to G), table A24	B	D	E	B	B	F	F	F	F	C	C	D	C	D	C	F	G	F	B	D	C	F	D
Population growth, lagged (A to F), table A30	F	G	F	F	F	A	E	D+	D	D+	E	C	C	C	E	D	F	C	C	E	C-	D	A
Net immigration (A to E), table A31	A	A	E	A	C	A	E	B	C	D	E	F	D	C	D	E	A	E	C	C	E	E	A
Illiteracy* (A to J) table A35	B	A	E	C	C	A	E	B	A	E	F	G	A	C	C	H	D	I	A	B	J+	E	A
Spread of primary education, lagged (A to E), table A36	B	G	F	A	F	G	E	A	E	E	A	C	E	F	E	A	A	B	B	D	B	A	B
Predominant form of land tenure* (A to G), table A37	F	D-	C	G	E	A-	A-	G+	A-	A-	A	C	C	F	B	C	E-	E-	G	F	A	E-	A-
Concentration of land holdings* (A to G), table A38	A	A	F+	A	E	D-	F	B	B	C-	A-	C	E	F	E	L-	G	F	B	B+	A	E-	A-
Favorableness of land institutions* (A to I), table A39	E	D	I	D	H	A-	H	A-	H	C-	A-	B	H	E	C-	D	H	H	I	E	C	C	A-

Table A51 (continued)

Variable	ARG	AUS	BEL	BRA	BUR	CAN	CHI	DEN	EGY	FRA	GER	GB	IND	ITA	JAP	NTH	NZ	NOR	RUS	SPA	SWE	SWZ	USA
Urbanization* (A to D), table A40	D	B	B	D	D	D	D	D	C	D+	A-	D	C	C	B	D	D	D	D	C	D	D	C
Attitudes toward entrepreneurship* (A to F), table A41	B+	A-	E	F	C	F	C	D	C	F	D	F+	D	F	C	C	E	F	C	A-	C	A-	B
Economic role of government (A to E), table A42	D	B	C	E	E	C	E-	C	D	C	D	C	C	E	C	C	E	D	D-	C	D	D	D
Character of political leadership (A to D), table A43	D+	B	B	D+	D	B-	D	C	D-	C+	C-	B	D-	D+	D+	C	C	C	C-	D+	C-	B+	B-
National representative institutions (A to D), table A44	C	C-	B-	D+	D-	C+	D-	D-	D-	C	A-	D-	C	D-	B+	B	D-	D-	C-	D+	B+	C+	B
Political stability (A to D), table A45	C	C+	B+	B+	C	A	D+	D+	B+	B+	A	B-	C	D-	B+	B	A	A	C	C+	A	A	D+
Foreign economic dependence (A to G), table A46	E	D+	F	A	E-	B-	A-	G	G	F	G	A	C	F	F	D-	B	D-	C	C-	D	A	D+
Colonial status* (A to F), table A47	D	A	E	D+	B	A	C	C	E	D	F	A	C-	D+	F	B	F	C	D	D	E	D	D
Development of market institutions* (A to E), table A 48	D	D	B	E+	E	C-	E	E-	B-	C	B	B	C	D	D	B-	B	C	D	D	D	D	E
Spread of market institutions (A to E), table A49	D	C	A-	D+	D	C	C	C	A-	A-	A-	C-	C	C-	C	C	C	C	C-	C-	B	B	B
Spread of market institutions, lagged (A to E), table A50	D+	C-	C	D	D	D	C-	D	C	B	B	D+	D+	D+	D	D	D	D	C-	C+	C-	C+	B

Notes   An asterisk indicates that the classification for a variable refers to the year 1850.   The lagged variables refer to the period 1830–1850.

Table A52

The Data: 1870–1890 Cross Section

Variable	ARG	AUS	BEL	BRA	BUR	CAN	CHI	DEN	EGY	FRA	GER	GB	IND	ITA	JAP	NTH	NZ	NOR	RUS	SPA	SWE	SWZ	USA
Level of per capita income* (A to F), table A1	D	A	B	F	E	C	F	C	E	C	C	A	F	C	E	B	C	C	D	D	D	B	B
Change in per capita income (A to D), table A3	C	B	C	D	D	B	D	B	D-	B-	B+	B	C	B	C	C	C	B	D-	D-	D-	D-	A
Development of techniques in industry* (A to F), table A5	F	D	E	F	F	D+	D+	F	F	C-	C-	B	E	E	F	C-	E	E	D	E	C	C	B-
Improvement in industrial techniques (A to F), table A6	D	D	E	E-	E-	D+	E-	D	E	B-	A	B	E	D-	D	D	D	D-	D	D-	D+	C	B+
Improvement in industrial techniques, lagged (A to F), table A6	F	E-	F	F	F	F	F	E	E	B	A	B	E	E	E	F	E	E	E	E	E	B+	B+
Development of techniques in agriculture* (A to G), table A7	F+	B	F	D	G-	B+	G-	G	B-	A	A	E	G	C-	D	E-	E+	E	G	F	F+	B-	A-
Improvement in agricultural techniques (A to F), table A8	F+	D-	C-	E+	C	C	F	C-	E-	C-	C	E	E	C-	D	D-	D-	E	E-	D+	F	D-	A
Improvement in agricultural techniques, lagged (A to F), table A8	F+	E+	E+	D-	D-	C	F	D-	E-	A-	C	E	F	D	D-	D-	D-	E-	F	D+	E+	B-	A
Percentage of labor in agriculture* (A to G), table A9	D	E	B	D	A	C	B	C	B	D	D	G	B	C	A	C	A	B	A	B	B	D	C
Abundance of agricultural resources* (A to E), table A14	A	A	C	A	D	A	D	C	D	A-	B+	A	D	E	B	E-	E-	C	A	D-	E+	C	B
Development of inland transportation* (A to E), table A15	E	E	E	A	E	E	E	E	E	D+	A	B	E	E	E	E	E	E	E	D-	E+	E	B

Country

Table A52 (continued)

Variable	ARG	AUS	BEL	BRA	BUR	CAN	CHI	DEN	EGY	FRA	GER	GB	IND	ITA	JAP	NTH	NZ	NOR	RUS	SPA	SWE	SWZ	USA
Improvement in transportation, lagged (A to F), table A16	D-	D	B	D-	E	C	E	D-	C	A	B	C	D-	A	E	B	D-	D-	D	D-	C-	D	B
Growth of exports (A to D), table A17	B	A+	A	C	B	D	D	C	C	C	C	C	C	B	B	C	C	C	C	A+	C+	D	A
Shift in structure of export sector (A to D), table A21	D	D	C	D	D	D	D	B	D	C	C	C	C	A	B	B	C	C	D	D	B	B	A
Change in average real wages in industry (A to E), table A22	E	B	B	E	E	B	C	A	D	B	B	A	C	E	E	B	A	A	B	C	A	B	A
Change in average real wages in agriculture (A to E), table A23	E	C	E	E	E	C	A	D	D	B	B	B	A	C	B	B	E	B	E	E	A	C	E
Total population* (A to G), table A24	F	F	F	E	E	F	B	A	F	C	C	C	A	E	E	F	G	F	B	D	C	F	C
Population growth, lagged (A to F), table A30	B	A	D	E	F	A	D	C	E	E	D	C	B	C	A	A	G	C-	C	E	C-	D	B
Net immigration (A to E), table A31	A	A	C	E	C	F	C	E	C	D	F	B	B	D	D	B	E	F	A	E	F	F	A
Illiteracy* (A to J), table A35	C	C	B	E	D	C	C	C	A	C	E	F	C	D	D	I	F	A	C	E	J	J	I+
Spread of primary education, lagged (A to E), table A36	D	C	C	E	C	E	E	D	E-	C	D	D	E	C	D	D	A	A	D	C	A	D	C
Predominant form of land tenure* (A to G), table A37	F	D+	C	A	A-	A	D	E-	A-	A-	D	D	A-	F	C	C	A-	A	E	A	A	E	A-
Concentration of land holdings* (A to G), table A38	A	A	F+	A	E	D-	F	A	B	E	C-	C	F	E	A	E-	A-	F	B-	B-	E	E-	D-
Favorableness of land institutions* (A to I), table A39	G	E	D	H	A-	F	F	A	F	C-	B	C-	F	E	E	D	F	H	E	C	C	D	A-

Table A52 (continued)

Variable	ARG	AUS	BEL	BRA	BUR	CAN	CHI	DEN	EGY	FRA	GER	GB	IND	ITA	JAP	NTH	NZ	NOR	RUS	SPA	SWE	SWZ	USA
Urbanization* (A to D), table A40	C	A	B	D	D	C	D	C	C	B	C	A	C	C	A	A	D	C	D	C	C	C	C
Attitudes toward entrepreneurship* (A to F), table A41	D	B+	A-	E	E	F	C+	E-	C-	C+	B	A-	F	D	F+	C	B-	C+	E	E	D-	C	A
Economic role of government (A to E), table A42	D	B	D	E	C	E-	C	D	D	C	D	D	B	A	C	D	D	E	C	E	C	D	D
Character of political leadership (A to D), table A43	D+	B	B	D+	D	E-	C	D-	C	C	B	B	D-	B-	C-	B	B	C+	C	C-	C	A-	B+
National representative institutions (A to D), table A44	E-	C-	E-	D+	D	C	C	D-		B	A+	B	D-	C-	B+	B+	B+	B	D	C	A-	A	A
Political stability (A to D), table A45	C	C+	B+	D-	B-	C	A-	D+	D-	B+	A+	A	D	B-	C-	A	B+	B+	C	C	A-	A	A
Foreign economic dependence (A to G), table A46	A-	D+	B	A	B-	D-	A	G	G	G	G	A	D+	D	G	B	D	D	D	C	D	A	B
Colonial status* (A to F), table A47	C	A	E	D	A-	B	C-	D	C	E	E	F	A	C-	C-	F	B	C	E	D	E	E	F
Development of market institutions* (A to E), table A 48	D	C+	A	E+	D-	C	E	B-	E	A-	B	A-	D	D-	D+	B-	D	D	D	C	B-	A	E
Spread of market institutions (A to E), table A49	C	B	B-	C	B-	D	B	C	B	A-	B-	B	B-	C+	C+	C	C	C	C	C	C+	B-	A+
Spread of market institutions, lagged (A to E), table A50	D	C+	A-	C-	D+	C	C	C+	A-	B+	A-	C	C	D+	D+	C	C	C	C	C-	C+	B	B

Notes. An asterisk indicates that the classification for a variable refers to the year 1870. The lagged variables refer to the period 1850–1870.

Table A53

The Data: 1890–1914 Cross Section

Variable	Country																						
	ARG	AUS	BEL	BRA	BUR	CAN	CHI	DEN	EGY	FRA	GER	GB	IND	ITA	JAP	NTH	NZ	NOR	RUS	SPA	SWE	SWZ	USA
Level of per capita income* (A to F), table A1	C	A	A	F	E	B	F	B	F	B	C+	A	F	C	E	B	B	C	C	C	C	A	A
Change in per capita income (A to D), table A3	A	D-	B	A	D	A	D	A	C	B	B	C	C	D	B	A	C+	B	A	A	A	A	A
Development of techniques in industry* (A to F), table A5	E+	C-	A	E	F+	E	C-	C-	F+	B-	A+	A	E+	E+	D	D+	D+	D+	D+	D-	D+	B	A+
Improvement in industrial techniques (A to F), table A6	D	C-	A-	D	E	C-	E	D	E	B	A+	B	C	C	C	D	D	C	C-	C	B	B	A+
Improvement in industrial techniques, lagged (A to F), table A6	D	D	B	E	E-	D+	E-	E-	D-	B-	A	B	D-	D-	D-	D-	D-	D-	D-	E	D+	B	B+
Development of techniques in agriculture* (A to G), table A7	D-	D	A-	E	B-	G	B	D-	B	B	A+	A+	D-	D-	B	D	D	D-	E+	E	A	B	A
Improvement in agricultural techniques (A to F), table A8	A	A	A	E	A	F	A	A	C	C	B	B	E	E+	B	B+	B+	E+	E+	E	C	B	A
Improvement in agricultural techniques, lagged (A to F), table A8	F+	D+	C-	D	E-	C	D	C	E-	C-	C	C	D	F	D	D-	D-	D-	E-	E-	C	B-	A
Percentage of labor in agriculture* (A to G), table A9	E	F	F	E	C	D	A	C	B	C	D	G	A	C	A	E	E	D	A	B	C	D	D
Abundance of agricultural resources* (A to E), table A14	A	A	E	A	A+	D	A	B	B	C	D	D	A	D	D	A	A	D	A	B	B	D	A
Development of inland transportation* (A to E), table A15	D	C	A+	D	D-	B	B	C+	A	A	D-	A	D	C	C	A	C	D	D	C-	B	B-	A

Table A53 (continued)

Variable	ARG	AUS	BEL	BRA	BUR	CAN	CHI	DEN	EGY	FRA	GER	GB	IND	ITA	JAP	NTH	NZ	NOR	RUS	SPA	SWE	SWZ	USA
Improvement in transportation, lagged (A to F), table A16	A	A	C	D-	C	E	A	A	C	C	C	C	D	B	D	C	A	D	D	D	A	A	C
Growth of exports (A to D), table A17	A+	C+	A	C+	A+	C	A	C	C	C	A+	C	C-	C+	A+	C	A	C+	C	D	C	C	A
Shift in structure of export sector (A to D), table A21	D	D	B	B	D	D	A	D	A	C	A	A	D	B	A	B	C	C	D	C	C	B	A
Change in average real wages in Industry (A to E), table A22	B	C	B	C	B	E	A	D	B	B	B	B	C	A	B	C	B	B	C	C	A	B	B
Change in average real wages in agriculture (A to E), table A23	B	B	B	C	E	D	A	D	D	B	B	B	B	B	A	B	C	A	E	E	A	B	B
Total population* (A to G), table A24	F	F	E	E	E	F	A	F	E	C	C	C	A	C	C	F	G	F	A	E	F	F	B
Population growth, lagged (A to F), table A30	A	A-	C-	C-	C-	D-	C-	B	B	E	D	F	D-	D	D	A	A	D	D	E	D	D-	B
Net immigration (A to E), table A31	A	B	C	C	A	A	C	C	D	C	C	A	D	C	B	D	A	C	D	C	D	A	A
Illiteracy* (A to J) table A35	E	J	H	G	J	I	A	B	A	I	J	J	A	E	F	J	A-	F	D	I	J	J	C
Spread of primary education, lagged (A to E), table A36	C	A	C	C	B	C	D	E	D	C	C	A	D	F	D	D	F	C	A	D	C	D	C
Predominant form of land tenure* (A to G), table A37	D	C-	B	D	A-	B	A-	D	E	C	C	C+	F	D	B	D	A	D	F	D-	D	C-	A-
Concentration of land holdings* (A to G), table A38	A-	A	F+	D	D	A	D-	A-	C-	A-	A	C	F	G+	C	E+	A-	B-	B+	F	A	E-	A-
Favorableness of land institutions* (A to I), table A39	G	E+	D	A-	G	A+	F	A-	C-	C+	A-	A-	F	C	C	D	E+	D-	H	E	C	C	A-

Table A53 (continued)

Variable	ARG	AUS	BEL	BRA	BUR	CAN	CHI	DEN	EGY	FRA	GER	GB	IND	ITA	JAP	NTH	NZ	NOR	RUS	SPA	SWE	SWZ	USA
Urbanization* (A to D), table A40	B	A	A	C-	D	C	C	C	B	B	B-	A	D	B	C	A	B	C	D+	C+	C	C	B
Attitudes toward entrepreneurship* (A to F), table A41	D+	A-	A	E	F	B	F	A-	E	C+	C-	A-	F	D	E	C+	A-	A	E	D	A-	A	A
Economic role of government (A to E), table A42	D	B	B	D	D	B	E-	C	B	C	A	D	B-	B	A	C	A-	C	B	D-	B	C	D
Character of political leadership (A to D), table A43	C	A	A-	D	D	B+	D	B+	D	A-	B	B+	D-	B	C+	A-	A-	B	C+	C-	B-	A-	A-
National representative institutions (A to D), table A44	B-	C+	B	D-	D+	A	D+	C	D-	A	B	A	D	B	C-	B+	A+	B+	D+	C	A	A	A-
Political stability (A to D), table A45	B+	B	B+	D+	B+	A	C	A	D+	B-	B+	A	D+	C	C+	A	A-	A	C	C	A	A	B+
Foreign economic dependence (A to G), table A46	A-	D-	G	A	A	C-	C	D	A-	F	F	G	A	G	D	B-	B-	C-	C+	C+	D-	G	G
Colonial status* (A to F), table A47	C	A	C	A	B	B	D	A-	F	F	A	F	F	E	D	F	B	C	E	D	E	D	A
Development of market institutions* (A to E), table A48	B-	B-	A+	B-	C-	B-	E	B	D	A	A+	A	C-	B-	C	B	B-	C-	E	B-	B+	A	A
Spread of market institutions (A to E), table A49	B	B	B-	B-	B-	B+	D	A-	B-	B-	A-	C	C	B-	B-	B+	B-	B-	B-	B-	B-	B+	A
Spread of market institutions, lagged (A to E), table A50	C+	B	B-	C+	C+	B-	D	C	C	B	B+	C+	C+	C+	C+	B-	B-	C+	C	C	B+	B+	A

Notes: An asterisk indicates that the classification for a variable refers to the year 1850. The lagged variables refer to the period 1830–1850.

Table A54

The Scoring Scheme

A to I	A to H	A to G	A to F	A to E	A to D	A to C
A^+ 93	A^+ 93	A^+ 93	A^+ 95	A^+ 95	A^+ 97	A^+ 100
A 90	A 90	A 90	A 90	A 90	A 90	A 90
A^- 87	A^- 87	A^- 86	A^- 85	A^- 85	A^- 83	A^- 80
B^+ 83	B^+ 81	B^+ 80	B^+ 75	B^+ 75	B^+ 67	B^+ 60
B 80	B 78	B 77	B 70	B 70	B 60	B 50
B^- 77	B^- 75	B^- 73	B^- 66	B^- 65	B^- 54	B^- 40
C^+ 73	C^+ 70	C^+ 67	C^+ 59	C^+ 55	C^+ 41	C^+ 20
C 70	C 67	C 64	C 55	C 50	C 35	C 10
C^- 67	C^- 64	C^- 60	C^- 51	C^- 45	C^- 29	C^- 01
D^+ 63	D^+ 58	D^+ 53	D^+ 44	D^+ 35	D^+ 16	
D 60	D 55	D 50	D 40	D 30	D 10	
D^- 57	D^- 52	D^- 46	D^- 36	D^- 25	D^- 04	
E^+ 53	E^+ 47	E^+ 40	E^+ 29	E^+ 15		
E 50	E 44	E 37	E 25	E 10		
E^- 47	E^- 41	E^- 33	E^- 21	E^- 05		
F^+ 43	F^+ 35	F^+ 27	F^+ 14			
F 40	F 32	F 23	F 10			
F^- 37	F^- 29	F^- 20	F^- 06			
G^+ 33	G^+ 24	G^+ 13				
G 30	G 21	G 10				
G^- 27	G^- 18	G^- 06				
H^+ 23	H^+ 13					

Table A54 (continued)

A to I	A to H	A to G	A to F	A to E	A to D	A to C
H 20	H 10					
H⁻ 17	H⁻ 07					
I⁺ 13						
I 10						
I⁻ 07						

Bibliography

The bibliography has been organized to serve two purposes: first, it lists the general sources that educated us and influenced our thinking; second, it lists the sources used to rank each of the 23 countries studied with respect to the 35 classification schemes described in the data appendix. It does not include sources listed in the footnotes of the works we cite in the appendix unless we consulted them.

We used mainly secondary sources, national collections of statistical data, and comparative quantitative studies. Secondary books and articles describing institutions and their changes were the most appropriate sources for many of our variables. Primary statistical sources for the individual countries would have been the most appropriate for our quantitative variables. However, limited resources precluded our consulting them systematically in view of the number of countries involved and the length of the period studied.

The comprehensiveness of our search for secondary sources was determined uniquely by the needs of our data preparation. The proportion of appropriate sources consulted varied from country to country according to our prior familiarity with the country and the difficulty of classifying it. The United States and Great Britain were usually relatively easy for us to classify, so the bibliography includes a modest number of sources on them. In the case of most other countries, we required a larger amount of information. In our research on some countries, we were constrained by language, though we were able to cope with French, German, and Dutch, and, painstakingly, with Italian and Spanish.

The cutoff date for the bibliography, with a few exceptions, is the end of 1982, the same as for our statistical analyses. The de facto cutoff for important institutional variables was earlier. Most of the work on the social and political variables was done in the late 1960s; that on the market and land variables, in the early 1970s. Occasionally, later publications were consulted when we were unable to review sources used early in the project. Fortunately, our classifications for these variables are based on descriptions of institutions, which change less frequently than do quantitative estimates. During 1981 and 1982 we revised all the economic and demographic variables, using the resources provided by our 1979 National Science Foundation grant.

Within each section of the bibliography, entries are listed alphabetically by author or editor. Multiple references by a single author or set of authors are ordered by date. Publications in the same year by a single author or set of authors are distinguished by letters following the year of publication, even if they fall in different sections of the bibliography. This arrangement was necessary to permit unambiguous identification of citations in the data appendix. Books about two countries are listed in the sections for both countries; those about more than two countries are listed in the general section. For economy of space, the full information for edited volumes is cited only once within a section; individual entries for articles in these volumes refer the reader to the main entry for further details. Complete publication information is included when only one article from an edited volume, or one volume from a multivolume work, is cited.

In order to facilitate the location of references in libraries, we have often included more information than is usual in bibliographies. Many entries were checked against Library of Congress listings. We regret the errors that undoubtedly remain. We distinguish the particular edition used and sometimes cite two or three editions of the same work because each was used at some time during the project.

I. GENERAL

Adams, John, ed. (1980). Institutional Economics: Contributions to the Development of Holistic Economics: Essays in Honor of Allan G. Gruchy. Boston: Martinus Nijhoff.

Adelman, Irma, and Morris, Cynthia Taft (1968). "Performance Criteria for Evaluating Economic Development Potential." Quarterly Journal of Economics 82 (May): 260-280.

_____ (1971a). "Analysis-of-Variance Techniques for the Study of Economic Development." Journal of Development Studies 7 (October): 93-105.

_____ (1971b). Society, Politics, and Economic Development: A Quantitative Approach. 2d ed. Baltimore: Johns Hopkins Press. Originally published in 1967.

_____ (1972). "The Measurement of Institutional Characteristics of Nations: Methodological Considerations." Journal of Development Studies 9 (April): 111-135.

_____ (1973). Economic Growth and Social Equity in Developing Countries. Stanford: Stanford University Press.

_____ (1978a). "Growth and Impoverishment in the Middle of the Nineteenth Century." World Development 6 (March): 245-273.

_____ (1978b). "Patterns of Market Expansion in the Nineteenth Century: A Quantitative Study." In Research in Economic Anthropology, edited by George Dalton, pp. 231-324. Greenwich, Conn.: JAI Press.

_____ (1979). "The Role of Institutional Influences in Patterns of Agricultural Development in the Nineteenth and Early Twentieth Centuries: A Cross-Section Quantitative Study." Journal of Economic History 39 (March): 159-176.

_____ (1980). "Patterns of Industrialization in the Latter Nineteenth and Early Twentieth Centuries: A Cross-Section Quantitative Study." In Research in Economic History: An Annual Compilation of Research, edited by Paul Uselding, 5:1-83. Greenwich, Conn.: JAI Press.

_____ (1983). "Institutional Influences on Poverty in the Nineteenth Century: A Quantitative Comparative Study." Journal of Economic History 43 (March): 43-55.

Adelman, Irma; Geier, Marsha; and Morris, Cynthia Taft (1969). "Instruments and Goals in Economic Development." American Economic Review, Papers and Proceedings 59 (May): 409-426.

Adelman, Irma; Morris, Cynthia Taft; and Robinson, Sherman (1976). "Policies for Equitable Growth." World Development 4 (July): 561-582.

Adelman, Irma; Morris, Cynthia Taft; and Wold, Svante (1980). "Society, Politics, and Economic Development Revisited." In Quantitative Economics and Development: Essays in Honor of Ta-chung Liu, edited by L. R. Klein, M. Nerlove, and S. C. Tsiang, pp. 2-18. New York: Academic Press.

Adelman, Irma, and Robinson, Sherman (1978). Income Distribution Policy in Developing Countries: A Case Study of Korea. New York: Oxford University Press.

Agarwala, Amar Narrin [Agarwal; and/or Agrawal, Amar Nath], and Singh, S. P., eds. (1958). The Economics of Underdevelopment. New York: Oxford University Press.

Ahluwalia, Montek (1976). "Inequality, Poverty, and Development." Journal of Development Economics 3: 307-342.

Aitken, Hugh G. H., ed. (1959). The State and Economic Growth. Papers of a conference held on October 11-13, 1956, under the auspices of the Committee on Economic Growth. New York: Social Science Research Council.

Anderson, C. Arnold (1965). "Literacy and Schooling on the Development Threshold: Some Historical Cases." Pp. 347-362. (See Anderson and Bowman 1965 below.)

Anderson, C. Arnold, and Bowman, Mary Jean, eds. (1965). Education and Economic Development. Papers of a conference on "The Role of Education in the Early Stages of Development," Chicago, April 4-6, 1963, sponsored by the Committee on Economic Growth, Social Science Research Council. Chicago: Aldine.

Anderson, Eugene Newton, and Anderson, Pauline Safford R. (1967). Political Institutions and Social Change in Continental Europe in the Nineteenth Century. Berkeley and Los Angeles: University of California Press.

Anderson, Perry (1974). Lineages of the Absolutist State. London: New Left Books.

Andrén, Nils Bertel Einar (1964). Government and Politics in the Nordic Countries: Denmark, Finland, Iceland, Norway, Sweden. Stockholm: Almqvist & Wiksell.

Arneson, Ben Albert (1939). The Democratic Monarchies of Scandinavia. New York: D. Van Nostrand.

Ashworth, William (1952). A Short History of the International Economy, 1850-1950. London: Longmans, Green.

_____ (1962). A Short History of the International Economy since 1850. 2d ed. London: Longmans, Green.

_____ (1977). "Typologies and Evidence: Is Nineteenth-Century Europe a Guide to Economic Growth?" Economic History Review, 2d ser. 30 (February): 140-158.

Aydelotte, William Osgood (1971). Quantification in History. Addison-Wesley Series in History. Reading, Mass.: Addison-Wesley.

Bagchi, Amiya Kumar (1972). "Some International Foundations of Capitalist Growth and Underdevelopment." Economic and Political Weekly 7 (August): 1559-1570.

Bairoch, Paul (1965). "Niveaux de développement économique de 1810 à 1910. Annales 20 (November-December): 1091-1117.

_____ (1968). La Population active et sa structure. (See Deldycke et al. 1968 below.)

_____ (1973). "Agriculture and the Industrial Revolution, 1700-1914." Pp. 452-506. (See Cipolla 1973a below.)

_____ (1974). Révolution industrielle de sous-développement. 4th ed. Paris: Mouton.

_____ (1976a). Commerce extérieur et développement économique de l'Europe au XIXᵉ siècle. Civilisations et sociétés 53, École des hautes études en sciences sociales, Centre de recherches historiques. Paris: Mouton.

_____ (1976b). "Europe's Gross National Product: 1800-1975." Journal of European Economic History 5 (Fall): 273-340.

Baldwin, Robert (1971). "Patterns of Development in Newly Settled Regions." In The Economics of Technological Change: Selected Readings, edited by Nathan Rosenberg, pp. 461-479. Baltimore: Penguin Books. Reprinted from Manchester School of Economics and Social Studies 24 (May 1956): 161-179.

Banks, Arthur S. (1971). Cross-Polity Time-Series Data. Assembled by Arthur S. Banks and the staff of the Center for Comparative Political Research, State University of New York at Binghamton. Cambridge: Massachusetts Institute of Technology Press.

Baran, Paul Alexander (1968). The Political Economy of Growth. New York: Modern Reader Paperbacks. Originally published in 1957.

Baran, Paul Alexander, and Hobsbawm, Ernest (1961). "The Stages of Economic Growth: A Review." Kyklos 14: 234-242.

Barber, Bernard (1957). Social Stratification: A Comparative Analysis of Structure and Process. Edited by Robert K. Merton. New York: Harcourt, Brace & World.

Barber, Bernard, and Barber, Elinor G. (1965). European Social Class: Stability and Change. New York: Macmillan.

Barnard, Henry (1854). National Education in Europe: Being an Account of the Organization, Administration, Instruction, and Statistics of Public Schools of Different Grades in the Principal States. 2d ed. New York: Charles B. Norton.

_____ (1872). <u>National Education: Systems, Institutions, and Statistics of Public Instruction in Different Countries</u>. Part II, <u>Europe: Switzerland, France, Belgium, Holland, Denmark, Norway, Sweden, Russia, Turkey, Greece, Italy, Spain</u>. New York: Steiger.

Barrat Brown, Michael [Brown, Michael Barrat] (1971). "A Critique of Imperialism." Pp. 35-69. (See Owen and Sutcliffe 1971 below.)

Barsby, Steven L. (1969). "Economic Backwardness and the Characteristics of Development." <u>Journal of Economic History</u> 29 (September): 449-472.

Bendix, Reinhard, and Lipset, Seymour Martin, eds. (1966). <u>Class, Status, and Power: Social Stratification in Comparative Perspective</u>. 2d ed. New York: Free Press.

Berrill, Kenneth E. (1963). "Foreign Capital and Take-off." Pp. 285-300. (See Rostow 1963 below.)

Binswanger, Hans P. (1978). "Issues in Modeling Induced Technical Change." Pp. 128-163. (See Binswanger and Ruttan 1978b below.)

Binswanger, Hans P. and Ruttan, Vernon W., eds. (1978). <u>Induced Innovation</u>. Baltimore: Johns Hopkins University Press.

Birnberg, Thomas B., and Resnick, Stephen A. (1975). <u>Colonial Development: An Econometric Study</u>. New Haven: Yale University Press.

Black, Cyril Edwin (1966). <u>The Dynamics of Modernization: A Study in Comparative History</u>. New York: Harper & Row.

Black, Eugene Charlton, ed. (1967). <u>European Political History, 1815-1870: Aspects of Liberalism</u>. New York: Harper & Row.

Blalock, Hubert N., Jr. (1961). <u>Causal Inferences in Nonexperimental Research</u>. Chapel Hill: University of North Carolina Press.

Blaug, Mark (1966). "Literacy and Economic Development." <u>School Review</u>, Winter, pp. 303-418.

Bloch, Marc Leopold B. (1953). "Toward a Comparative History of European Societies." Pp. 494-521. (See Lane and Riemersma 1953 below.)

_____ (1966). <u>French Rural History: An Essay on Its Basic Characteristics</u>. Translated by Janet Sondheimer. Berkeley and Los Angeles: University of California Press.

Bloomfield, Arthur Irving (1968). <u>Patterns of Fluctuation in International Investment before 1914</u>. Princeton Studies in International Finance, no. 21. Princeton: International Finance Section, Department of Economics, Princeton University.

Bodenheimer, Susanne (1971). "Dependency and Imperialism: The Roots of Latin American Underdevelopment." <u>Politics and Society</u> 1 (May): 327-357.

Bogart, Ernest Ludlow (1942). <u>Economic History of Europe, 1760-1939</u>. London: Longmans, Green.

Boserup, Ester (1965). The Condition of Agricultural Growth: The Economics of Agrarian Change under Population Pressure. Chicago: Aldine.

Boserup, Mogens (1963). "Agrarian Structure and Take-off." Pp. 201-224. (See Rostow 1963 below.)

Brady, Alexander (1958). Democracy in the Dominions: A Comparative Study in Institutions. 3d ed. Toronto: University of Toronto Press.

Braun, Rudolf; Fischer, Wolfram; Grosskreutz, Helmut; and Volkmann, Heinrich, eds. (1972). Industrielle Revolution: Wirtschaftliche Aspekte. Neue wissenschaftliche Bibliothek no. 50, Geschichte. Cologne: Kiepenheuer & Witsch.

Brenner, Robert (1976). "Agrarian Class Structure and Economic Development in Pre-industrial Europe." Past and Present, no. 70 (February): 30-75.

_____ (1977). "The Origins of Capitalist Development: A Critique of Neo-Smithian Marxism." New Left Review, no. 104 (July-August): 15-91.

Brewer, Anthony (1980). Marxist Theories of Imperialism: A Critical Survey. London: Routledge & Kegan Paul.

Buchanan, Norman Sharpe, and Ellis, Howard Sylvester (1955). Approaches to Economic Development. New York: Twentieth Century Fund.

Buell, Raymond Leslie, ed. (1935). Democratic Governments in Europe. New York: T. Nelson.

Bury, John Patrick Tuer, ed. (1964). The New Cambridge Modern History. Vol. 10, The Zenith of European Power, 1830-1870. Cambridge: Cambridge University Press.

Cairncross, Alexander Kirkland (1962). Factors in Economic Development. London: Allen & Unwin.

Cameron, Meribeth Elliott; Mahoney, Thomas H. D.; and McReynolds, George E. (1960). China, Japan, and the Powers: A History of the Modern Far East. 2d ed. New York: Ronald Press.

Cameron, Rondo E. (1961). France and the Economic Development of Europe, 1800-1914. Princeton: Princeton University Press.

_____, ed. (1972). Banking and Economic Development: Some Lessons of History. New York: Oxford University Press.

Cameron, Rondo E.; Crisp, Olga; Patrick, Hugh T.; and Tilly, Richard H. (1967). Banking in the Early Stages of Industrialization: A Study in Comparative Economic History. New York: Oxford University Press.

Cardoso, Fernando Henrique, and Faletto, Enzo (1979). Dependency and Development in Latin America. Translated by Marjory Mattingly Urquidi. Berkeley and Los Angeles: University of California Press.

Caves, Richard E. (1965). "'Vent for Surplus' Models of Trade and Growth." In Trade, Growth, and the Balance of Payments: Essays in Honor of Gottfried Haberler, edited by Robert E. Baldwin and others, pp. 95-115. Chicago: Rand McNally.

Chenery, Hollis Burnley (1960). "Patterns of Industrial Growth." American Economic Review 50 (September): 624-654.

_____ (1979). Structural Change and Development Policy. New York: Oxford University Press for the World Bank.

Chenery, Hollis Burnley; Shishido, Shuntaro; and Watanabe, Tsungkiko (1962). "The Pattern of Japanese Growth, 1914-1954." Econometrica 30 (January): 98-139.

Cipolla, Carlo M. (1969). Literacy and Development in the West. Baltimore: Penguin Books.

_____ (1974). The Economic History of World Population. 6th ed. Baltimore: Penguin Books.

_____, ed. (1973a). The Fontana Economic History of Europe. Vol. 3, The Industrial Revolution. London: Collins/Fontana Books.

_____, ed. (1973b). The Fontana Economic History of Europe. Vol. 4, pts. 1 and 2, The Emergence of Industrial Societies. London: Collins/Fontana Books.

Clark, Colin (1957). The Conditions of Economic Progress. 3d ed. London: Macmillan.

Clough, Shepard Bancroft, and Cole, Charles Woolsey (1946). Economic History of Europe. Rev. ed. Boston: D. C. Heath.

_____ (1952). Economic History of Europe. 3d ed. Boston: D. C. Heath.

Coatsworth, John H. (1979). "Indispensable Railroads in a Backward Economy: The Case of Mexico." Journal of Economic History 39 (December): 939-960.

Cobden Club (1870). Systems of Land Tenure in Various Countries. A series of essays published under the sanction of the Cobden Club. 2d ed. London: Macmillan.

Cole, W. A., and Deane, Phyllis (1965). "The Growth of National Income." Pp. 1-59. (See Habakkuk and Postan 1965 below.)

Commons, John R. (1959). Institutional Economics: Its Place in Political Economy. 2 vols. Madison: University of Wisconsin Press.

Crafts, N. F. R. (1977). "Industrial Revolution in England and France: Some Thoughts on the Question, 'Why was England first?'" Economic History Review, 2d ser. 30 (August): 429-441.

Crouzet, François (1972a). "Editor's Introduction." Pp. 1-69. (See Crouzet 1972c below.)

_____ (1972b). "Western Europe and Great Britain: 'Catching Up' in the First Half of the Nineteenth Century." Pp. 98-125. (See Youngson 1972 below.)

_____, ed. (1972c). Capital Formation in the Industrial Revolution. London: Methuen.

Crouzet, François M.; Chaloner, William Henry; and Stern, Walter M., eds. (1969). Essays in European Economic History, 1789-1914. New York: St. Martin's Press.

Crouzet, Maurice (1968). "Great Britain, France, the Low Countries, and Scandinavia." Pp. 512-555. (See Mowat 1968 below.)

Davie, Maurice Rea (1949). World Immigration, with Special Reference to the United States. New York: Macmillan.

Davis, Lance E., and North, Douglass C. (1971). Institutional Change and American Economic Growth. Cambridge: Cambridge University Press.

Davis, William Stearns (1922). A Short History of the Near East from the Founding of Constantinople (330 A.D. to 1922). New York: Macmillan.

De Castro, Bruce (1980). "Multinationals and Manufactured Exports from Less Developed Countries." Ph.D. dissertation, The American University.

De Janvry, Alain (1981). The Agrarian Question and Reformism in Latin America. Baltimore: Johns Hopkins University Press.

Deldycke, Tilo; Gelders, H.; and Limbor, Jean Marie (1968). La Population active et sa structure. International Historical Statistics, vol. 1. Brussels: Centre d'économique politique de l'Université libre de Bruxelles.

Deutsch, Karl W. (1953). Nationalism and Social Communication: An Inquiry into the Foundations of Nationality. Cambridge: Published jointly by the Technology Press of the Massachusetts Institute of Technology and John Wiley & Sons.

Dobb, Maurice (1947). Studies in the Development of Capitalism. Rev. ed. New York: International Publishers.

Dovring, Folke (1965). Land and Labor in Europe in the Twentieth Century: A Comparative Survey of Recent Agrarian History. 3d rev. ed. of Land and Labor in Europe, 1900-1950. Edited by Gunther Beyer. Studies in a Social Life, no. 4. The Hague: Martinus Nijhoff.

Drake, Michael, ed. (1969). Population in Industrialization. London: Methuen.

Easterlin, Richard A. (1967). "Effects of Population Growth on the Economic Development of Developing Countries." Annals of the American Academy of Political and Social Science 369 (January): 98-120.

_____ (1981). "Why Isn't the Whole World Developed?" Journal of Economic History 41 (March): 1-19.

Encyclopaedia Britannica (1910), 11th ed., vols. 1-15; (1911), 11th ed., vols. 16 to the end; (1922), 12th ed., vol. 30; (1969), 14th ed., vol. 6.

Feis, Herbert (1930). Europe, the World's Banker, 1870-1914. New Haven: Yale University Press.

Ferenczi, Imre (1929). International Migrations. Vol. 1, Statistics. Edited by Walter F. Willcox. Publications of the National Bureau of Economic Research, nos. 14, 18. New York: Gordon & Breach. Reprinted in 1969.

Fischer, Wolfram (1973). "Rural Industrialization and Population Change." Cambridge Studies in Social History 15 (March): 158-170.

Fishlow, Albert (1965b). "Empty Economic Stages?" Economic Journal 75 (March): 112-125.

_____ (1974). "The New Economic History Revisited." Journal of European Economic History 3 (Fall): 453-467.

Foerster, Robert Franz (1919). The Italian Emigration of Our Times. Cambridge: Harvard University Press.

Fogel, Robert William, and Engerman, Stanley L. (1971). "A Model for the Explanation of Industrial Expansion during the Nineteenth Century: With an Application to the American Iron Industry." In The Reinterpretation of American Economic History, edited by Fogel and Engerman, pp. 148-162. New York: Harper and Row.

Frank, André Gunder (1969). Capitalism and Underdevelopment in Latin America: Historical Studies of Chile and Brazil. Rev. and enl. New York: Monthly Review Press.

_____ (1973). "The Development of Underdevelopment." Pp. 94-104. (See Wilber 1973 below.)

_____ (1979). Dependent Accumulation and Underdevelopment. New York: Monthly Review Press.

Fraser, Stewart E., and Brickman, William W., eds. (1968). A History of International and Comparative Education: Nineteenth-Century Documents. Glenview, Ill.: Scott, Foresman.

Friedlaender, Heinrich E., and Oser, Jacob (1953). Economic History of Modern Europe. Englewood Cliffs, N.J.: Prentice-Hall.

Furtado, Celso (1964). Development and Underdevelopment. Berkeley and Los Angeles: University of California Press.

_____ (1970). Obstacles to Development in Latin America. New York: Doubleday.

_____ (1973). "The Concept of External Dependence in the Study of Underdevelopment." Pp. 118-123. (See Wilber 1973 below.)

Geertz, Clifford (1963). Agricultural Involution: The Process of Ecological Change in Indonesia. Association of Asian Studies, Monographs and Papers, no. 11. Berkeley and Los Angeles: University of California Press.

Gerschenkron, Alexander (1962a). Economic Backwardness in Historical Perspective: A Book of Essays. Cambridge: Harvard University Press.

_____ (1962b). "The Typology of Industrial Development as a Tool of Analysis." Paper presented at the Convention of the International Economic History Association, 1962. In Continuity in History and Other Essays, edited by Gerschenkron, pp. 77-97. Cambridge: Harvard University Press, 1968.

_____ (1970). Europe in the Russian Mirror: Four Lectures in Economic History. Cambridge: Cambridge University Press.

_____, ed. (1968). Continuity in History and Other Essays. Cambridge: Harvard University Press.

Gille, Bertrand (1973). "Banking and Industrialisation in Europe, 1730-1914." Translated by Roger Greaves. Pp. 1-49. (See Cipolla 1973b above.)

Girard, L. (1965). "Transport." Pp. 212-273. (See Habakkuk and Postan 1965 below.)

Glass, David V., and Grebenik, E. (1965). "World Population, 1800-1950." Pp. 60-138. (See Habakkuk and Postan 1965 below.)

Gottheil, Fred M. (1977). "On an Economic Theory of Colonialism." Journal of Economic Issues 11 (March): 83-102.

Grigg, David (1980). Population Growth and Agrarian Change: An Historical Perspective. Cambridge: Cambridge University Press.

Gruchy, Allan G. (1972). Contemporary Economic Thought: The Contribution of Neo-institutional Economics. Clifton, N.J.: Augustus M. Kelley, Publishers.

Habakkuk, H. J. (1955). "Family Structure and Economic Change in Nineteenth-Century Europe." Journal of Economic History 15 (March): 1-12.

Habakkuk, H. J., and Postan, M. M., eds. (1965). The Cambridge Economic History of Europe. Vol. 6, pts. 1 and 2, The Industrial Revolution and After: Incomes, Population, and Technological Change. Cambridge: Cambridge University Press.

Hagen, Everett E. (1962). On the Theory of Social Change: How Economic Growth Begins. A study from the Center for International Studies, Massachusetts Institute of Technology. Homewood, Ill.: Dorsey Press.

Hägerstrand, Porsten (1967). Innovation: Diffusion as a Spatial Process. Translated by Allan Pred. Chicago: University of Chicago Press.

Hague, D. C. (1963). "Summary Record of the Debate." Pp. 301-476. (See Rostow 1963 below.)

Hahn, Frank H., and Matthews, Robert Charles O. (1965). "The Theory of Economic Growth: A Survey." In <u>Surveys of Economic Theory: Growth and Development</u>, 2:1-124. Prepared for the American Economic Association and the Royal Economic Society. London: Macmillan.

Haines, Michael (1979). <u>Fertility and Occupation: Population Patterns in Industrialization</u>. New York: Harcourt Brace Jovanovich.

Hansen, Alvin H. (1925). "Factors Affecting the Trend of Real Wages." <u>American Economic Review</u> 15 (March): 27-42.

Hanson, J. R., II (1980). <u>Trade in Transition: Exports from the Third World, 1840-1900</u>. New York: Academic Press.

Hartwell, R. Maxwell (1965). "The Causes of the Industrial Revolution: An Essay in Methodology." <u>Economic History Review</u>, 2d ser. 18 (April): 164-182.

Hartz, Louis (1964). <u>The Founding of New Societies: Studies in the History of the United States, Latin America, South Africa, Canada, and Australia</u>. New York: Harcourt, Brace & World.

Hawgood, J. A. (1964). "Liberalism and Constitutional Development." Pp. 185-212. (See Bury 1964 above.)

Hayami, Yujiro, and Ruttan, Vernon W. (1971). <u>Agricultural Development: An International Perspective</u>. Baltimore: Johns Hopkins Press.

Hayes, Carlton Joseph (1941). <u>The Rise of Modern Europe</u>. Vol. 16, <u>A Generation of Materialism, 1871-1900</u>. Edited by William L. Langer. New York: Harper & Bros.

Hazen, William B. (1968). "Comparative Education: A Military Viewpoint." Pp. 198-200. (See Fraser and Brickman 1968 above.)

Hempel, Carl G. (1952). "Typological Methods in the Social Sciences." In <u>Science, Language, and Human Thought</u>, 1:65-86. Philadelphia: University of Pennsylvania Press. Reprinted in <u>The Nature and Scope of Social Science: A Critical Anthology</u>, edited by Leonard I. Krimerman, pp. 445-456. New York: Appleton-Century-Crofts, 1969.

Henderson, William O. (1961). <u>The Industrial Revolution on the Continent: Germany, France, Russia, 1800-1914</u>. London: Frank Cass.

_____ (1969). <u>The Industrialization of Europe, 1780-1914</u>. New York: Harcourt, Brace & World.

Hershlag, Zvi Y. (1964). <u>Introduction to the Modern Economic History of the Middle East</u>. Leiden: E. J. Brill.

Hicks, John Richard (1969). <u>A Theory of Economic History</u>. Oxford: Clarendon Press.

_____ (1979). Causality in Economics. New York: Basic Books.

Higgins, Benjamin Howard (1968). Economic Development: Problems, Principles, and Policies. Rev. ed. New York: W. W. Norton. Originally published in 1959.

Hinsley, Francis H., ed. (1962). The New Cambridge Modern History. Vol. 11, Material Progress and World-wide Problems, 1870-1898. Cambridge: Cambridge University Press.

Hirschman, Albert O. (1958). The Strategy of Economic Development. New Haven: Yale University Press.

_____ (1977). "A Generalized Linkage Approach to Development, with Special Reference to Staples." In Essays on Economic Development and Cultural Change in Honor of Bert F. Hoselitz, edited by Manning Nash, pp. 67-98. Economic Development and Cultural Change, vol. 25, supplement. Chicago: University of Chicago Press.

Hoffmann, Walther G. (1958). The Growth of Industrial Economies. Translated by William O. Henderson and William Henry Chaloner. New York: Oceana Publications.

Hovde, Brynjolf J. (1943). The Scandinavian Countries, 1720-1865: The Rise of the Middle Classes. 2 vols. Boston: Chapman & Grimes.

Hughes, Jonathan R. T. (1970). Industrialization and Economic History: Theses and Conjectures. New York: McGraw-Hill.

_____ (1976). "Transference and Development of Institutional Constraints upon Economic Activity." In Research in Economic History: An Annual Compilation of Research, edited by Paul Uselding, 1:45-68. Greenwich, Conn.: JAI Press.

_____ (1977). The Governmental Habit: Economic Controls from Colonial Times to the Present. New York: Basic Books.

Huntington, Samuel P. (1968). Political Order in Changing Societies. New Haven: Yale University Press.

Islam, Nurul (1960). Foreign Capital and Economic Development: Japan, India, and Canada. Studies in Some Aspects of Absorption of Foreign Capital. Rutland, Vt.: C. E. Tuttle.

Jones, Eric Lionel (1968). "Agricultural Origins of Industry." Past and Present, no. 40 (July): 58-71.

_____ (1981). The European Miracle: Environments, Economies, and Geopolitics in the History of Europe and Asia. Cambridge: Cambridge University Press.

Jones, Eric Lionel, and Woolf, Stuart Joseph, eds. (1969). Agrarian Change and Economic Development: The Historical Problems. London: Methuen.

Kan, Aleksandr Sergeevich (1978). Geschichte der Skandinavischen Länder: (Dänemark, Norwegen, Schweden). Berlin: VEB.

Kaplan, Abraham (1964). <u>The Conduct of Inquiry: Methodology for Behavioral</u>
<u>Science</u>. San Francisco: Chandler.

Keirstead, B. S. (1948). <u>The Theory of Economic Change</u>. Toronto:
Macmillan.

Kelley, Allen C., and Williamson, Jeffrey G. (1974). <u>Lessons from Japanese</u>
<u>Development: An Analytical Economic History</u>. Chicago: University of Chicago
Press.

Kemp, Tom (1972). "The Marxist Theory of Imperialism." Pp. 15–33. (See
Owen and Sutcliffe 1972 below.)

Kindleberger, Charles Poor (1951). "Group Behavior and International
Trade." <u>Journal of Political Economy</u> 59 (February): 30–46.

Kirkaldy, Adam Willis, and Evans, Alfred Dudley (1924). <u>The History and</u>
<u>Economics of Transport</u>. 3d ed. London: Isaac Pitman & Sons. Originally
published in 1915.

Klemm, Louis R. (1968). "Systematic Comparisons of American and European
Education." Pp. 409–412. (See Fraser and Brickman 1968 above.)

Knight, Melvin M.; Barnes, Harry Elmer; and Flügel, Felix (1928). <u>Economic</u>
<u>History of Europe in Modern Times</u>. Boston: Houghton Mifflin.

Knowles, Lillian Charlotte A. (1932). <u>Economic Development in the</u>
<u>Nineteenth Century: France, Germany, Russia, and the United States</u>.
London: George Routledge & Sons.

Kuznets, Simon S. (1955). "Economic Growth and Income Inequality."
<u>American Economic Review</u> 45 (March): 1–28.

———— (1958). "Underdeveloped Countries and the Pre-industrial Phase in
the Advanced Countries." Pp. 135–153. (See Agarwala and Singh 1958 above.)

———— (1968). <u>Toward a Theory of Economic Growth, with "Reflections on the</u>
<u>Economic Growth of Modern Nations</u>." New York: W. W. Norton.

———— (1971). <u>Economic Growth of Nations: Total Output and Production</u>
<u>Structure</u>. Cambridge: Harvard University Press.

———— (1979). <u>Growth, Population, and Income Distribution: Selected</u>
<u>Essays</u>. New York: W. W. Norton.

Laishley, R. (1968). "Comparative Educational Charts and Notes on Education
in the United States." Pp. 381–396. (See Fraser and Brickman 1968 above.)

Landes, David S. (1954). "Social Attitudes, Entrepreneurship, and Economic
Development: A Comment." <u>Explorations in Entrepreneurial History</u> 6
(May): 245–272.

———— (1965a). "Technological Change and Development in Western Europe,
1750–1914." Pp. 274–601. (See Habakkuk and Postan 1965 above.)

_____ (1969). <u>The Unbound Prometheus: Technological Change and Industrial Development in Western Europe from 1750 to the Present</u>. Cambridge: Cambridge University Press.

_____, ed. (1966). <u>The Rise of Capitalism</u>. Main Themes in European History. New York: Macmillan.

Landes, David S., and Tilly, Charles, eds. (1971). <u>History as Social Science</u>. Englewood Cliffs, N.J.: Prentice-Hall.

Lane, Frederic Chapin, and Riemersma, Jelle C., eds. (1953). <u>Enterprise and Secular Change: Readings in Economic History</u>. Homewood, Ill.: Richard D. Irwin.

Lazarsfeld, Paul F., and Barton, Allen H. (1951). "Qualitative Measurement in the Social Sciences: Classification, Typologies, and Indices." In <u>The Policy Sciences</u>, edited by Daniel Lerner and Harold D. Lasswell, pp. 155-192. Stanford: Stanford University Press.

League of Nations. Secretariat. Economic, Financial, and Transit Department (1945). <u>Industrialization and Foreign Trade</u>. Mainly the work of Folke Hilgerdt. Geneva: League of Nations.

Lerner, Daniel, and Pevsner, Lucille W. (1958). <u>The Passing of Traditional Society: Modernizing the Middle East</u>. Glencoe, Ill.: Free Press.

Levasseur, Émile (1897). <u>L'Enseignement primaire dans les pays civilisés</u>. Paris: Berger-Levrault.

Lévy-Leboyer, Maurice (1964). <u>Les Banques européenes et l'industrialisation internationale dans la première moitié du XIX siècle</u>. Paris: Presses universitaires de France.

_____ (1968). "Les Processus d'industrialisation: Le Cas de l'Angleterre et de la France." <u>Revue historique</u> 239 (April-June): 281-298.

Lewis, William Arthur (1954). "Economic Development with Unlimited Supplies of Labour." <u>Manchester School of Economics and Social Studies</u> 22 (May): 139-191

_____ (1955). <u>The Theory of Economic Growth</u>. Homewood, Ill.: Richard D. Irwin.

_____ (1958). "Economic Development with Unlimited Supplies of Labour." Pp. 400-449. (See Agarwala and Singh 1958 above.)

_____ (1977). <u>The Evolution of the International Economic Order</u>. Princeton: Princeton University Press.

_____ (1978). <u>Growth and Fluctuation, 1870-1913</u>. London: George Allen & Unwin.

Lipson, E. (1969). "The National Economy (1815-1914)." Pp. 16-42. (See Scoville and La Force 1969 below.)

Liversage, Vincent (1945). Land Tenure in the Colonies. Cambridge: Cambridge University Press.

Lowell, Abbott Lawrence (1914). The Governments of France, Italy, and Germany. Cambridge: Harvard University Press.

Lowndes, George Alfred Norman (1937). The Silent Social Revolution: An Account of the Expansion of Public Education in England and Wales, 1895-1935. London: Oxford University Press.

McClelland, David Clarence (1961). The Achieving Society. New York: Free Press.

McKeown, Thomas (1978). "Fertility, Mortality, and Causes of Death: An Examination of Issues Related to the Modern Rise of Population." Population Studies 32 (November): 535-542.

McKeown, Thomas; Brown, R. G.; and Record, R. G. (1922). "An Interpretation of the Modern Rise of Population in Europe." Population Studies 26 (November): 345-382.

McKinney, John C. (1966). Constructive Typology and Social Theory. New York: Appleton-Century-Crofts.

McPherson, Logan Grant (1910). Transportation in Europe. New York: H. Holt.

Maddison, Angus (1970). "Economic Growth in Western Europe, 1870-1957." Pp. 28-70. (See Scoville and La Force 1970 below.) Reprinted from Banca Nazionale del Lavoro Quarterly Review 12 (March 1959): 58-102.

_____ (1977). "Phases of Capitalist Development." Banca Nazionale del Lavoro Quarterly Review [30] (June): 103-137.

_____ (1979). "Per Capita Output in the Long Run." Kyklos 32, nos. 1-2: 412-429.

_____ (1982). Phases of Capitalist Development. New York: Oxford University Press, 1982.

Malthus, Thomas Robert (1914). An Essay on the Principle of Population. 7th ed. 2 vols. Everyman's Library, nos. 692 and 693. London: J. M. Dent & Sons. Originally published in 1872.

Marczewski, Jean (1965). Introduction à l'histoire quantitative. Geneva: Librarie Droz.

Marx, Karl (1930). Capital. Translated from the 4th German ed. by Eden and Cedar Paul. 2 vols. Everyman's Library, no. 849. London: J.M. Dent & Sons.

Mathias, Peter, and Postan, M. M., eds. (1978). The Cambridge Economic History of Europe. Vol. 7, The Industrial Economies: Capital, Labour, and Enterprise. Pt. 1, "Britain, France, Germany, and Scandinavia." Pt. 2, "The United States, Japan, and Russia." Cambridge: Cambridge University Press.

Mendels, Franklin F. (1972). "Proto-industrialization: The First Phase of the Industrialization Process." Journal of Economic History 32 (March): 241-261.

Menzel, Ulrich (1980a). "Autozentrierte Entwicklung in historischer Perspektive. Dogmengeschichtliche und typologische Aspekte eines aktuellen Konzeptes." Project: Untersuchung zur Grundlegung einer Praxisorientierten Theorie autozentrierter Entwicklung. Forschungsbericht, no. 10. University of Bremen. Mimeographed.

Mill, John Stuart (1961). Principles of Political Economy with Some of Their Applications to Social Philosophy. Edited by W. J. Ashley. New York: Augustus M. Kelley. Originally published in 1909 by Longmans, Green.

Miller, William, ed. (1952). Men in Business: Essays in the History of Entrepreneurship. Cambridge: Harvard University Press.

Milward, Alan S. (1979). "Strategies for Development in Agriculture: The Nineteenth-Century European Experience." Pp. 21-42. (See Smout 1979 below.)

Milward, Alan S., and Saul, S. B. (1979). The Economic Development of Continental Europe, 1780-1870. 2d ed. London: George Allen & Unwin. Originally published in the United States in 1973 by Rowman & Littlefield.

Minchinton, Walter (1973). "Patterns of Demand, 1750-1914." Pp. 77-186. (See Cipolla 1973a above.)

Mitchell, Brian R. (1973). "Statistical Appendix." Pp. 738-820. (See Cipolla 1973b above.)

———— (1976). European Historical Statistics, 1750-1970. New York: Columbia University Press.

Mokyr, Joel (1976a). "Growing-up and the Industrial Revolution in Europe." Explorations in Economic History 13 (October): 371-396.

Moller, Herbert, ed. (1964). Population Movements in Modern European History. New York: Macmillan.

Moore, Barrington, Jr. (1966). Social Origins of Dictatorship and Democracy: Lord and Peasant in the Making of the Modern World. Boston: Beacon Press.

Moore, D. C. (1961). "The Other Face of Reform." Victorian Studies 5 (September): 7-34.

Mowat, Charles L., ed. (1968). The New Cambridge Modern History. Vol. 12, The Shifting Balance of World Forces, 1898-1945. Cambridge: Cambridge University Press. 2d ed. of vol. 12, The Era of Violence, published in 1960 and edited by David Thomson.

Mulhall, Michael G. (1899). The Dictionary of Statistics. 4th ed. London: G. Routledge & Sons.

Munholland, J. Kim (1970). <u>Origins of Contemporary Europe, 1890-1914</u>. New York: Harcourt, Brace & World.

Murray, A. Victor (1962). "Education." Pp. 177-203. (See Hinsley 1962 above.)

Myint, Hla [usually cataloged under Hla Myint, U.] (1968). "Classical Theory of International Trade and the Underdeveloped Countries." In <u>Economics of Trade and Development</u>, edited by James D. Theberge, pp. 188-210. New York: John Wiley & Sons. Originally published in <u>Economic Journal</u> 68 (June 1958): 317-337.

Myrdal, Gunnar (1957). <u>Economic Theory and Under-Developed Regions</u>. London: Gerald Duckworth. A revision of the author's <u>Development and Underdevelopment</u>, published in 1956. The American edition (New York: Harper & Bros.) has the title <u>Rich Lands and Poor</u>.

Nagel, Ernest (1961). <u>The Structure of Science: Problems in the Logic of Scientific Explanation</u>. New York: Harcourt, Brace & World.

Newbery, David M. G. (1975). "The Choice of Rental Contract in Peasant Agriculture." Pp. 109-137. (See Reynolds 1975 below.)

Nicholls, William H. (1963). "An 'Agricultural Surplus' as a Factor in Economic Development." <u>Journal of Political Economy</u> 71 (February): 1-29.

North, Douglass C. (1955). "Location Theory and Regional Economic Growth." <u>Journal of Political Economy</u> 63 (June): 243-258.

_____ (1981). <u>Structure and Change in Economic History</u>. New York: W. W. Norton.

North, Douglass C., and Thomas, Robert Paul (1970). "An Economic Theory of the Growth of the Western World." <u>Economic History Review</u>, 2d ser. 23 (April): 1-17.

_____ (1973). <u>The Rise of the Western World: A New Economic History</u>. Cambridge: Cambridge University Press.

Nurkse, Ragnar (1967). <u>Problems of Capital Formation in Underdeveloped Countries and Patterns of Trade and Development</u>. New York: Oxford University Press. <u>Problems . . .</u> originally published in 1953. <u>Patterns . . .</u> originally published in 1959.

Nussbaum, Frederick L. (1933). <u>A History of the Economic Institutions of Modern Europe: An Introduction to "Der moderne Kapitalismus" of Werner Sombart</u>. New York: F. S. Crofts.

O'Brien, Patrick Karl (1979). "Agriculture and the Industrial Revolution." <u>Economic History Review</u>, 2d ser. 30 (February): 166-181.

Ohlin, Goran (1959). "Balanced Economic Growth in History." <u>American Economic Review, Papers and Proceedings</u> 49 (May): 338-353.

Olson, Mancur, Jr. (1963). "Rapid Economic Growth as a Destabilizing Force." <u>Journal of Economic History</u> 23 (December): 529-552.

_____ (1982). The Rise and Decline of Nations: Economic Growth, Stagflation, and Social Rigidities. New Haven: Yale University Press.

Østerud, Øyvind (1978). Agrarian Structure and Peasant Politics in Scandinavia: A Comparative Study of Rural Response to Economic Change. Oslo: Universitetsforlaget.

Owen, Edward Roger, and Sutcliffe, Robert B., eds. (1971). Studies in the Theory of Imperialism. London: Longmans, Green.

Paige, D. C.; Blackaby, F. T.; and Freund, S. (1961). "Economic Growth: The Last Hundred Years." National Institute Economic Review 16 (July): 24-49.

Palmer, Robin, and Parsons, Neil (1977). The Roots of Rural Poverty in Central and Southern Africa. Berkeley and Los Angeles: University of California Press.

Parker, William N. (1972). Technology, Resources, and Economic Change in the West." Pp. 62-78. (See Youngson 1972 below.)

Parker, William N., and Jones, Eric Lionel, eds. (1975). European Peasants and Their Markets: Essays in Agrarian Economic History. Princeton: Princeton University Press.

Patel, Surendra J. (1963). "Rates of Industrial Growth in the Last Century, 1860-1958." Pp. 68-80. (See Supple 1963 below.)

_____ (1964). "Main Features of Economic Growth over the Century." Indian Economic Journal 11 (January-March): 287-303.

Paukert, F. (1973). "Income Distribution at Different Levels of Development: A Survey of Evidence." International Labour Review, August-September, pp. 97-125.

Phelps Brown, Ernest Henry (1953). Economic Growth and Human Welfare: Three Lectures. Delhi School of Economics, Occasional Papers, no. 7. Delhi: Ranjit.

_____ (1973). "Levels and Movements of Industrial Productivity and Real Wages Internationally Compared, 1860-1970." Economic Journal 83 (March): 58-71.

Phelps Brown, Ernest Henry, and Browne, Margaret H. (1968). A Century of Pay: The Course of Pay and Production in France, Germany, Sweden, the United Kingdom, and the United States of America, 1860-1960. London: Macmillan.

Pirenne, Henri (1914). "The Stages in the Social History of Capitalism." American Historical Review 19 (April): 494-515.

Platt, Desmond Cristopher St. Martin (1980). "British Portfolio Investment Overseas before 1870: Some Doubts." Economic History Review, 2d ser. 33 (February): 1-16.

Polanyi, Karl (1957). The Great Transformation: The Political and Economic Origins of Our Time. Beacon Paperback no. 45. Boston: Beacon Press. Originally published in 1944.

Pollard, Sidney (1973). "Industrialization and the European Economy." Economic History Review, 2d ser. 26 (November): 636-648.

Pressnell, Lewis Seddon, ed. (1960). Studies in the Industrial Revolution. Presented to T. S. Ashton. London: Athlone Press.

Pyatt, F. Graham, and Roe, Alan (1977). Social Accounting for Development Planning with Special Reference to Sri Lanka. Cambridge: Cambridge University Press.

Ranis, Gustav, and Fei, Ching-han (1961). "A Theory of Economic Development." American Economic Review 51 (September): 533-565.

Redlich, Fritz (1970). "Potentialities and Pitfalls in Economic History." In The New Economic History: Recent Papers on Methodology, edited by Ralph L. Andreano, pp. 85-99. New York: John Wiley & Sons.

Reynolds, Lloyd G., ed. (1975). Agriculture in Development Theory. New Haven: Yale University Press.

Ricardo, David (1911). The Principles of Political Economy and Taxation. London: J. M. Dent & Sons; New York: E. P. Dutton.

Ripert, Georges (1951). Aspects juridiques du capitalisme moderne. 2d ed. Paris: R. Pichon & R. Durand-Auzias.

Roach, John (1964). "Education and the Press." Pp. 104-123. (See Bury 1964 above.)

Robinson, Sherman, and Dervis, Kemal (1977). "Income Distribution and Socio-economic Mobility: A Framework for Analysis and Planning." Journal of Development Studies 13 (July): 347-366.

Rosenberg, Nathan (1969). "The Direction of Technological Change: Inducement Mechanisms and Focusing Devices." Economic Development and Cultural Change 18 (October): 1-24.

Rosenberg, Nathan (1971). "Review of The Unbound Prometheus, by David S. Landes." Journal of Economic History 31 (June): 497-500.

Rosenstein-Rodan, P. N. (1958). "Problems of Industrialization of Eastern and Southeastern Europe." Pp. 245-255. (See Agarwala and Singh 1958 above.)

Rosovsky, Henry (1965). "The Take-off into Sustained Controversy." Journal of Economic History 25 (June): 271-275.

_____, ed. (1966). Industrialization in Two Systems: Essays in Honor of Alexander Gerschenkron by a Group of His Students. New York: John Wiley & Sons.

Rostow, Walt Whitman (1956). "The Take-off into Self-Sustained Growth." Economic Journal 66 (March): 25-48.

_____ (1960). The Stages of Economic Growth: A Non-Communist Manifesto. Cambridge: Cambridge University Press.

_____ (1978). The World Economy: History and Prospect. Austin: University of Texas Press.

_____, ed. (1963). The Economics of Take-off into Sustained Growth. Proceedings of a conference held by the International Economic Association. London: Macmillan.

Royal Institute of International Affairs [Great Britain] (1937). The Problem of International Investment. London: Oxford University Press.

Ruttan, Vernon W. (1978a). "Induced Institutional Change." Pp. 327-357. (See Binswanger and Ruttan 1978b above.)

_____ (1978b). "A Postscript on Alternative Paths of Induced Institutional Change." Pp. 409-413. (See Binswanger and Ruttan 1978 above.)

Ruttan, Vernon W., and Binswanger, Hans P. (1978). "Induced Innovation and the Green Revolution." Pp. 358-408. (See Binswanger and Ruttan 1978 above.)

Saul, S. B. (1960). Studies in British Overseas Trade, 1870-1914. Liverpool: Liverpool University Press.

_____ (1972). "The Nature and Diffusion of Technology." Pp. 36-61. (See Youngson 1972 below.)

Sawyer, John Edward (1952). "The Entrepreneur and the Social Order: France and the United States." Pp. 7-22. (See Miller 1952 above.)

Schickele, Rainer (1941). "Effect of Tenure Systems on Agricultural Efficiency." Journal of Farm Economics 23 (February): 185-207.

Schieder, Theodore (1962). "Political and Social Development in Europe." Pp. 243-273. (See Hinsley 1962 above.)

Schultz, Theodore W. (1964). Transforming Traditional Agriculture. Studies in Comparative Economics, no. 3. New Haven: Yale University Press.

_____ (1968). "Institutions and the Rising Economic Value of Man." American Journal of Agricultural Economics 50 (December): 1113-1122.

_____ (1980). "Investment in Entrepreneurial Ability." Scandinavian Journal of Economics 82, no. 4: 437-448.

Schumpeter, Joseph A. (1939). Business Cycles: A Theoretical, Historical, and Statistical Analysis of the Capitalist Process. 2 vols. New York: McGraw-Hill.

_____ (1950). Capitalism, Socialism, and Democracy. 3d ed. New York: Harper & Bros. Originally published in 1942.

Scott, James C. (1972). "The Erosion of Patron-Client Bonds and Social Change in Rural Southeast Asia." Journal of Asian Studies 32 (November): 5-37.

Scoville, Warren C., and La Force, J. Clayburn, eds. (1969a). The Economic Development of Western Europe. Vol. 3, The Eighteenth and Early Nineteenth Centuries. Lexington, Mass.: D. C. Heath.

_____, eds. (1969b). The Economic Development of Western Europe. Vol. 4, The Late Nineteenth and Early Twentieth Centuries. Lexington, Mass.: D. C. Heath.

_____, eds. (1970). The Economic Development of Western Europe. Vol. 5, From 1914 to the Present. Lexington, Mass.: D. C. Heath.

Semmingsen, Ingrid Gaustad (1972). "Emigration from Scandinavia." Scandinavian Economic History Review 20, no. 1: 45-60.

Sen, Amartya K. (1976). "Poverty: An Ordinal Approach to Measurement." Econometrics 44 (March): 219-231.

_____ (1977). "Starvation and Exchange Entitlements: A General Approach and Its Application to the Great Bengal Famine." Cambridge Journal of Economics 1 (March): 33-59.

Senghaas, Dieter (1981). "Self-reliance and Autocentric Development: Historical Experiences and Contemporary Challenges." Bulletin of Peace Proposals 1: 44-51.

_____ (1982). Von Europa lernen: Entwicklungsgeschichtliche Betrachtungen. Frankfurt am Main: Suhrkamp Verlag. Translated by K. H. Kimmig, under the title The European Experience: A Historical Critique of Development Theory. Dover, N.H.: Berg Publishers, 1985.

_____, ed. (1980). Kapitalistische Weltökonomie: Kontroversen über ihren Ursprung und ihre Entwicklungsdynamik. Frankfurt am Main: Suhrkamp Verlag.

Senghaas, Dieter, and Menzel, Ulrich (1978). "Autozentrierte Entwicklung trotz internationalem Kompetenzgefälle: Warum wurden die heutigen Metropolen Metropolen und nicht Peripherien?" Project: Untersuchung zur Grundlegung einer praxisorientierten Theorie autozentrierter Entwicklung. Forschungsbericht, no. 1. University of Bremen. Mimeographed.

_____ (1979). "Länderkurzberichte, Typologie und Auswahl der Fallstudien." Project: Untersuchung zur Grundlegung einer praxisorientierten Theorie autozentrierter Entwicklung. Forschungsbericht, no. 2. University of Bremen. Mimeographed.

Siegenthaler, Jürg K. (1972). "A Scale Analysis of Nineteenth-Century Industrialization." Explorations in Economic History 10 (Fall): 75-107.

Singer, Hans (1950). "The Distribution of Gains between Investing and Borrowing Countries." American Economic Review, Papers and Proceedings 40 (May): 473-485.

Slicher van Bath, B. H. (1963). The Agrarian History of Western Europe, A.D. 500-1850. Translated by Olive Ordish. New York: St. Martin's Press.

Smith, Adam (1910). An Inquiry into the Nature and Causes of the Wealth of Nations. 2 vols. Everyman's Library, nos. 412-413. London: J. M. Dent. Originally published in 1776.

Smout, Thomas Christopher, ed. (1979). The Search for Wealth and Stability: Essays in Economic and Social History Presented to Michael Walter Flinn. London: Macmillan.

Social Science Research Council. Committee on Historical Analysis (1963). Generalization in the Writing of History. Edited by Louis Reichenthal Gottschalk. Chicago: University of Chicago Press.

_____. Committee on Historiography (1954). The Social Sciences in Historical Study. A Report of the Committee on Historiography, Bulletin 64. New York: Social Science Research Council.

Solow, Robert M., and Temin, Peter (1978). "Introduction: The Inputs for Growth." Pp. 1-27. (See Mathias and Postan 1978 above.)

Stabler, J. C. (1968). "Exports and Evolution: The Process of Regional Change." Land Economics 44 (February): 11-23.

Stiglitz, Joseph E., and Uzawa, Hirofumi, eds. (1969). Readings in the Modern Theory of Economic Growth. Cambridge: Massachusetts Institute of Technology Press.

Streeten, Paul (1979). "Development Ideas in Historical Perspective." In Toward a New Strategy for Development, edited by Kim Q. Hill, pp. 21-52. A set of papers commissioned by the Rothko Chapel and presented at a colloquium held in Houston, Texas, on February 3-5, 1977. New York: Pergamon Press.

Supple, Barry E. (1973). "The State and the Industrial Revolution, 1700-1914." Pp. 301-357. (See Cipolla 1973a above.)

_____, ed. (1963). The Experience of Economic Growth: Case Studies in Economic History. New York: Random House.

Svennilson, Ingvar (1954). Growth and Stagnation in the European Economy. Geneva: United Nations, Economic Commission for Europe.

Sylla, Richard Eugene (1977). "Financial Intermediaries in Economic History: Quantitative Research on the Seminal Hypotheses of Lance Davis and Alexander Gerschenkron." In Research in Economic History, suppl. 1, Recent Developments in the Study of Business and Economic History: Essays in Memory of Herman E. Kroos, edited by Robert E. Gallman, pp. 55-80. Greenwich, Conn.: JAI Press.

Thomas, Brinley (1973). Migration and Economic Growth: A Study of Great Britain and the Atlantic Economy. 2d ed. Cambridge: Cambridge University Press. Originally published in 1946.

_____ (1975). "A Plea for an Ecological Approach to Economic Growth." In
Contemporary Issues in Economics, edited by Michael Parkin and A. R. Nobay,
pp. 292-304. Manchester: Manchester University Press.

Thomson, David (1968). "The Transformation of Social Life." Pp. 10-36.
(See Mowat 1968 above.)

Thornthwaite, C. Warren (1933). "The Climates of the Earth." Geographical
Review 23 (July): 433-440.

Tilly, Charles (1975). "Reflections on the History of European
State-Making." In The Formation of National States in Western Europe,
edited by Tilly, pp. 3-83. Studies in Political Development, no. 8.
Princeton: Princeton University Press.

Timmons, John F. (1968). "Agricultural Tenancy." Sec. II of "Land
Tenancy." In International Encyclopedia of the Social Sciences, edited by
David L. Sills, pp. 567-570. New York: Macmillan and Free Press.

Tolstoy, Leo (1942). War and Peace. Translated by Louise and Aylmer
Maude. New York: Simon & Schuster. Originally published in Russian, in 2
parts, 1865 and 1869.

Tracy, Michael (1964). Agriculture in Western Europe. New York: Frederick
A. Praeger.

Tuma, Elias H. (1971). Economic History and the Social Sciences: Problems
of Methodology. Berkeley and Los Angeles: University of California Press.

Tun Wai, U. (1957). "Interest Rates Outside the Organized Money Markets of
Underdeveloped Countries." International Monetary Fund Papers 6
(November): 80-142.

U.S. Bureau of Education (1891). Report of the Commissioner of Education,
1888-1889. Washington, D.C.: Government Printing Office.

_____ (1893). Report of the Commissioner of Education, 1889-1890.
Washington, D.C.: Government Printing Office.

U.S. Department of Commerce. Bureau of Economic Analysis (1972). "The
Measurement of Productivity." Survey of Current Business 52, no. 5, pt. 2
(May): 1-111.

Uno, Kozo (1980). Principles of Political Economy: Theory of a Purely
Capitalist Society. Translated by Thomas T. Sekine. Highlands, N.J.:
Humanities Press.

Veblen, Thorstein (1904). The Theory of Business Enterprise. New York:
Charles Scribner's Sons.

Wallerstein, Immanuel (1974). "The Rise and Future Demise of the World
Capitalist System: Concepts for Comparative Analysis." Comparative Studies
in Society and History 16 (September): 387-415.

Warren, Bill (1980). Imperialism: Pioneer of Capitalism. London: New Left
Books.

Weaver, James, and Berger, Marguerite (1984). "The Marxist Critique of
Dependency Theory: An Introduction." In The Political Economy of
Development and Underdevelopment, 3d ed., edited by Charles K. Wilber, pp.
45-64. New York: Random House.

Weber, Adna Ferrin (1967). The Growth of Cities in the Nineteenth
Century: A Study in Statistics. Ithaca, N.Y.: Cornell University Press,
Cornell Paperbacks. Originally published as Ph.D. dissertation in 1899 for
Columbia University by the Macmillan Co. as vol. 11 of Studies in History,
Economics, and Public Law.

Weeks, John, and Dore, Elizabeth (1979). "International Exchange and the
Causes of Backwardness." Latin American Perspectives 6 (Spring): 62-87.

Wehler, Hans-Ulrich (1975). Modernisierungstheorie und Geschichte.
Göttingen: Vandenhoeck & Ruprecht.

Weisskoff, Richard, and Wolff, Edward (1977). "Linkages and Leakages:
Industrial Tracking in an Enclave Economy." Economic Development and
Cultural Change 25 (July): 607-628.

Wickizer, Vernon D., and Bennett, M. K. (1941). The Rice Economy of Monsoon
Asia. Stanford, Calif.: Food Research Institute.

Wilber, Charles K., ed. (1973). The Political Economy of Development and
Underdevelopment. New York: Random House.

Wilkie, James W., and Reich, Peter, eds. (1980). Statistical Abstract of
Latin America. UCLA Latin American Center Publications, vol. 20. Berkeley
and Los Angeles: University of California Press.

Williams, Faith M., and Zimmerman, Carle C. (1935). Studies of Family
Living in the United States and Other Countries: An Analysis of Material and
Method. U.S. Department of Agriculture Miscellaneous Publications,
no. 223. Washington, D.C.: Government Printing Office.

Wiskemann, Elizabeth (1968). "Germany, Italy, and Eastern Europe."
Pp. 473-511. (See Mowat 1968 above.)

Wold, Herman (1975). "Modelling in Complex Situations with Soft
Information." Paper presented at the Third World Congress of the
Econometrics Society, Toronto, August 21-26, 1975. Group Report no. 5.
University of Göteberg, Department of Statistics. Mimeographed.

_____ (1976a). "On the Transition from Pattern Cognition to Model
Building: The NIPALS (Nonlinear Iterative Least Squares) Approach." Paper
presented at the European Meeting of the Econometric Society, Helsinki,
Finland, August 23-27, 1976. Research Report no. 3, University of
Göteberg, Department of Statistics. Mimeographed.

_____ (1976b). "On the Transition from Pattern Cognition to Model
Building: The NIPALS (Nonlinear Iterative Least Squares) Approach, Part I."
Republication Paper, Uppsala University, Department of Statistics.
Mimeographed.

Wold, Svante (1976). "Pattern Recognition by Means by Disjoint Principal Components Models." Pattern Recognition 8: 127-137.

Woodruff, William (1966). Impact of Western Man: A Study of Europe's Role in the World Economy, 1750-1960. New York: St. Martin's Press.

_____ (1973). "The Emergence of an International Economy, 1700-1914." Pp. 656-737. (See Cipolla 1973a above.)

Woytinsky, Wladimir S., and Woytinsky, Emma S. (1953). World Population and Production: Trends and Outlook. New York: Twentieth Century Fund.

Wrigley, Edward Anthony (1969). Population and History. New York: McGraw-Hill.

Young, Edward (1875). Labor in Europe and America: A Special Report on the Rates of Wages, the Cost of Subsistence, and the Condition of the Working Classes in Great Britain, Germany, France, Belgium, and Other Countries of Europe, Also in the United States and British America. Washington, D.C.: Government Printing Office.

Youngson, A. J. (1959). Possibilities of Economic Progress. Cambridge: Cambridge University Press.

_____ (1965). "The Opening Up of New Territories." Pp. 139-211. (See Habakkuk and Postan 1965 above.)

_____, ed. (1972). Economic Development in the Long Run. New York: St. Martin's Press.

II.   COUNTRY STUDIES

ARGENTINA

Alexander, Robert J. (1969). An Introduction to Argentina. New York: Frederick A. Praeger.

Barager, Joseph R., ed. (1968). Why Perón Came to Power: The Background to Peronism in Argentina. New York: Alfred A. Knopf.

Brown, Jonathan C. (1979). A Socioeconomic History of Argentina, 1776-1860. Cambridge: Cambridge University Press.

Burgin, Miron (1946). The Economic Aspects of Argentine Federalism, 1820-1852. Cambridge: Harvard University Press.

Cochran, Thomas Childs, and Reina, Ruben E. (1962). Entrepreneurship in Argentine Culture: A Study of Torcuato Di Tella and S.I.A.M. Philadelphia: University of Pennsylvania Press. Published in 1971 under the title Capitalism in Argentine Culture.

Cortés Conde, Roberto (1976). "Tendencias en la Evolución de los Salarios Real en Argentina, 1880-1910: Resultados Preliminares." Económica 22 (May): 131-159.

De Janvry, Alain (1978). "Social Structure and Biased Technical Change in Argentine Agriculture." In Induced Innovation, edited by Hans P. Binswanger and Vernon W. Ruttan, pp. 297-323. Baltimore: Johns Hopkins University Press.

Díaz Alejandro, Carlos F. (1970). Essays on the Economic History of the Argentine Republic. New Haven: Yale University Press.

Dyster, Barrie (1979). "Argentine and Australian Development Compared." Past and Present, no. 84 (August): 91-110.

Ferns, H. S. (1950). "Investment and Trade between Britain and Argentina in the Nineteenth Century." Economic History Review, 2d ser. 3: 203-218.

_____ (1960). Britain and Argentina in the Nineteenth Century. Oxford: Clarendon Press.

Ferrer, Aldo (1967). The Argentine Economy. Translated by Marjory J. Urquidi. Berkeley and Los Angeles: University of California Press.

Ferrer, Aldo, and Wheelwright, Edward Lawrence (1974). "Australia and Argentina: A Comparative Study." In Radical Political Economy: Collected Essays, edited by Edward Lawrence Wheelwright, pp. 270-296. Sydney: Australia & New Zealand Book Co.

Fillol, Tomás Roberto (1961). Social Factors in Economic Development. The Argentine Case. Cambridge: Massachusetts Institute of Technology Press.

Goodrich, Carter (1964). "Argentina as a New Country." Comparative Studies in Society and History 7 (October): 70-88.

Hanson, Simon G. (1938). Argentine Meat and the British Market. Stanford: Stanford University Press.

Kirkpatrick, Frederick A. (1931). A History of the Argentine Republic. Cambridge: Cambridge University Press.

Levene, Ricardo (1963). A History of Argentina. Translated and edited by William Spence Robertson. New York: Russell & Russell.

McCarty, J. W. (1973). "Australia as a Region of Recent Settlement in the Nineteenth Century." Australian Economic History Review 13 (September): 148-167.

McGann, Thomas F. (1937). Argentina, the Divided Land. Princeton: D. Van Nostrand.

_____ (1966). Argentina, the Divided Land. Princeton: D. van Nostrand.

Moran, Theodore H. (1970). "The 'Development' of Argentina and Australia." Comparative Politics 3 (October): 71-92.

Pendle, George (1955). <u>Argentina</u>. London: Royal Institute of International Affairs.

_____ (1963). <u>Argentina</u>. 3d ed. London: Oxford University Press.

Peterson, Harold F. (1964). <u>Argentina and the United States, 1810-1960</u>. Albany: State University of New York.

Randall, Laura Regina (1977a). "A Comparative Economic History of Latin America, 1500-1914." Vol. 2, "Argentina." Ann Arbor, Mich.: University Microfilms International.

Rennie, Ysabel F. (1945). <u>The Argentine Republic</u>. New York: Macmillan.

Scobie, James R. (1964a). <u>Argentina: A City and a Nation</u>. New York: Oxford University Press.

_____ (1964b). <u>Revolution on the Pampas: A Social History of Argentine Wheat, 1860-1910</u>. Austin: University of Texas Press.

Whitaker, Arthur P. (1964). <u>Argentina</u>. Englewood Cliffs, N.J.: Prentice-Hall.

Wilkie, James W., and Reich, Peter, eds. (1980). <u>Statistical Abstract of Latin America</u>. UCLA Latin American Center Publications, vol. 20. Berkeley and Los Angeles: University of California Press.

Williams, John Henry (1920). <u>Argentine International Trade under Inconvertible Paper Money, 1800-1900</u>. Harvard Economic Studies, vol. 22. Cambridge: Harvard University Press.

Wythe, George (1945). <u>Industry in Latin America</u>. New York: Columbia University Press.

_____ (1949). <u>Industry in Latin America</u>. 2d ed. New York: Columbia University Press.

AUSTRALIA

Barnard, Alan (1958). <u>The Australian Wool Market, 1840-1900</u>. Carlton, Australia: Melbourne University Press.

Boehm, Ernest Arthur (1965). "Measuring Australian Economic Growth, 1861 to 1938-39." A review of <u>Australian Domestic Product Investment and Foreign Borrowing, 1861-1938/39</u>, by Noel G. Butlin. <u>Economic Record</u> 41 (June): 207-239.

Butlin, Noel G. (1962). <u>Australian Domestic Product, Investment and Foreign Borrowing, 1861-1938/39</u>. Cambridge: Cambridge University Press.

_____ (1964). <u>Investment in Australian Economic Development, 1861-1900</u>. Cambridge: Cambridge University Press.

_____ (1965). "The Shape of the Australian Economy, 1861-1900." Pp. 143-166. (See Drohan and Day 1965 below.) Reprinted from Economic Record 34 (April 1958): 10-29.

Butlin, Sydney James (1961). Australia and New Zealand Bank: The Bank of Australasia and the Union Bank of Australia Limited, 1828-1951. London: Longmans, Green.

Coghlan, Timothy A. (1918). Labour and Industry in Australia. 4 vols. London: Oxford University Press.

Condliffe, John Bell (1965). "The Peopling of Australia." Pp. 169-187. (See Drohan and Day 1965 below.)

_____ (1970). The Development of Australia. New York: Free Press. Originally published in 1964.

Cotter, Richard (1970). "War, Boom, and Depression." Pp. 244-282. (See Griffin 1970 below.)

Davis, Solomon R., ed. (1960). The Government of the Australian States. London: Longmans, Green.

Drohan, Neville T., and Day, John H., eds. (1965). Readings in Australian Economics: Studies in Economic Growth. Melbourne: Cassell of Australia.

Dunsdorfs, Edgars (1956). The Australian Wheat-Growing Industry, 1788-1948. Carlton, Australia: Melbourne University Press.

Dyster, Barrie (1979). "Argentine and Australian Development Compared." Past and Present, no. 84 (August): 91-110.

Ferrer, Aldo, and Wheelwright, Edward Lawrence (1974). "Australia and Argentina: A Comparative Study." In Radical Political Economy: Collected Essays, edited by Edward Lawrence Wheelwright, pp. 270-296. Sydney: Australia & New Zealand Book Co.

Fitzpatrick, Brian (1946). The Australian People, 1788-1845. Carlton, Australia: Melbourne University Press.

_____ (1949). The British Empire in Australia: An Economic History, 1834-1939. 2d ed., rev. and abridged. Carlton, Australia: Melbourne University Press.

_____ (1969). The British Empire in Australia: An Economic History, 1834-1939. Reissue of 2d ed. Melbourne: Macmillan.

Gollan, Robin (1960). Radical and Working Class Politics: A Study of Eastern Australia, 1850-1910. Carlton, Australia: Melbourne University Press in association with the Australian National University.

Gregory, John Walter (1916). Australia. Cambridge: Cambridge University Press.

Griffin, James, ed. (1970). Essays in Economic History of Australia. 2d ed. Milton, Australia: Jacaranda Press. Originally published in 1967.

Grundy, Denis (1970). "Labour." Pp. 207-243. (See Griffin 1970 above.)

Jackson, Robert Vincent (1977). Australian Economic Development in the Nineteenth Century. Canberra: Australian National University Press.

McCarty, John William (1965). "The Staple Approach in Australian Economic History." Pp. 123-142. (See Drohan and Day 1965 above.)

_____ (1973). "Australia as a Region of Recent Settlement in the Nineteenth Century." Australian Economic History Review 13 (September): 148-167.

McGhee, Roger (1970). "The Long Boom, 1860-1890." Pp. 135-185. (See Griffin 1970 above.)

McLean, J. W. (1973). "Growth and Technological Change in Agriculture: Victoria, 1870-1910." Economic Record 49 (December): 560-574.

Mayer, Kurt B. (1966). "Social Stratification in Two Egalitarian Societies: Australia and the United States." In Australian Politics: A Reader, edited by Henry Mayer, pp. 30-56. Melbourne: F. W. Cheshire.

Moran, Theodore H. (1970). "The 'Development' of Argentina and Australia." Comparative Politics 3 (October): 71-92.

Morrissey, Sylvia (1970). "The Pastoral Economy, 1821-1850." Pp. 51-112. (See Griffin 1970 above.)

Partridge, Percy Herbert (1968). Society, Schools, and Progress in Australia. Oxford: Pergamon Press.

Roberts, Stephan Henry (1968). History of Australian Land Settlement 1788-1920. New York: Johnson Reprints. Originally published in 1924.

Rosecrance, Richard N. (1964). "The Radical Culture of Australia." In The Founding of New Societies: Studies in the History of the United States, Latin America, South Africa, Canada, and Australia, edited by Louis Hartz, pp. 275-318. New York: Harcourt, Brace & World.

Shann, Edward Owen G. (1930). An Economic History of Australia. Cambridge: Cambridge University Press.

_____ (1948). An Economic History of Australia. Australian ed. Cambridge: Cambridge University Press.

Shaw, Alan George Lewes (1946). The Economic Development of Australia. Rev. ed. London: Longmans, Green.

_____ (1955). 3d ed. The Economic Development of Australia. London: Longmans, Green.

Sinclair, William Angus (1975). "Economic Growth and Well-being: Melbourne, 1870-1914." Economic Record 51 (June): 153-173.

_____ (1976). The Process of Economic Development in Australia. Cheshire Economic Series. Melbourne: F. W. Cheshire.

Thompson, Allan (1970). "The Enigma of Australian Manufacturing, 1851-1901." Australian Economic Papers 9 (June): 76-92.

BELGIUM

L'Agriculture belge, rapport présenté au nom des sociétés agricoles de Belgique et sous les auspices du gouvernement (1878). Paris: Au siège de la Société des agriculteurs de France.

Annuaire statistique de la Belgique et du Congo belge. Published annually. Brussels: Suprêmesic Lesigne.

Avondts, Gerda; Hannes, J.; Scholliers, E.; Scholliers, Peter; and Vande, Perre P., eds. (1979). Vol. 4, Lonen in de Weverij van het Bedrijf A. Voortman-N.V. Texas, 1835-1925. Brussels: Centrum voor Hedendaagse Sociale Geschiedenis.

Avondts, Gerda, and Scholliers, Peter (1977). De Gentse Textil arbeiders in de 19e en 20e Eeuw. Vol. 5, Gentse Prijzen, Huishuren, en Budgetonderzoeken in de 19e en 20e Eeuw. Brussels: Centrum voor Hedendaagse Sociale Geschiedenis.

Baudhuin, Fern (1928). "Histoire économique de la Belgique." In Histoire de la Belgique contemporaine, 1830-1914, 1:237-348. Brussels: Librairie Albert Dewit.

Bertrand, Louis Philippe (1924). L'Ouvrier belge depuis un siècle. Brussels: L'Églantine.

Bublot, Georges (1957). La Production agricole belge: Étude économique séculaire, 1846-1955. Louvain: Editions E. Mauwelaerts.

Cammaerts, Émile (1921). Belgium from the Roman Invasion to the Present Day. London: T. Fisher Unwin.

Chlepner, Ben Serge (1930). Le Marché financier belge depuis cent ans. Brussels: Librairie Falk fils.

_____ (1945). "Economic Development of Belgium." Pp. 167-186. (See Goris 1945 below.)

_____ (1956). Cent ans d'histoire sociale en Belgique. Brussels: Institut de Sociologie Solvay.

Clough, Shepard Bancroft (1968). A History of the Flemish Movement in Belgium: A Study in Nationalism. New York: Octagon Books. Originally published in 1930.

Craeybeckx, Jan (1970). "The Beginnings of the Industrial Revolution in Belgium." In Essays in French Economic History, edited by Rondo E. Cameron, pp. 187-200. Homewood, Ill.: Richard D. Irwin.

Dechesne, Laurent (1932). <u>Histoire économique et social de la Belgique depuis les origines jusqu'en 1914</u>. Paris: Librairie du Recueil Sirey.

De Laveleye, Émile Louis (1870). "The Land System of Belgium and Holland." In <u>Systems of Land Tenure in Various Countries</u>, edited by the Cobden Club, pp. 233-282. 2d ed. London: Macmillan.

Dhondt, Jan (1969). "The Cotton Industry of Ghent during the French Régime." Translated by Michael B. Palmer. In <u>Essays in European History, 1789-1914</u>, edited by François Crouzet, William Henry Chaloner, and Walter M. Stern, pp. 15-52. London: Edward Arnold.

Dhondt, Jan, and Bruwier, Marinette (1973). "The Low Countries, 1700-1914." In <u>The Fontana Economic History of Europe</u>, vol. 3, pt. 1, <u>The Emergence of Industrial Societies</u>, edited by Carlo M. Cipolla, pp. 329-366. London: Collins/Fontana Books.

Ducpétiaux, Édouard (1850). <u>Mémoire sur le paupérisme dans les Flandres</u>. Brussels: M. Hayez.

Eyck, F. Gunther (1959). <u>The Benelux Countries: An Historical Survey</u>. Princeton: D. Van Nostrand.

Goris, Jan-Albert, ed. (1945). <u>Belgium</u>. United Nations Series, edited by Robert J. Kerner. Berkeley and Los Angeles: University of California Press.

Hollants, Betsie (1950). <u>Social Action and Welfare in Belgium</u>. Art, Life, and Science in Belgium, no. 17. New York: Belgium Government Information Center.

Huggett, Frank Edward (1969). <u>Modern Belgium</u>. New York: Frederick A. Praeger.

Lebrun, Pierre; Bruwier, Marinette; Dhondt, Jan; and Hansotte, Georges (1979). <u>Essai sur la révolution industrielle en Belgique, 1770-1847</u>. Vol. 2, pt. 1, of <u>Histoire quantitative et développement de la Belgique</u>, edited by Pierre Lebrun. Brussels: Palais des Academies.

Lewinski, Jan Stanislaw (1911). <u>L'Évolution industrielle de la Belgique</u>. Brussels: Misch & Thron.

Linden, Herman Vander (1920). <u>Belgium: The Making of a Nation</u>. Translated by Sybil Jane. Oxford: Clarendon Press.

Lis, Catharina (1982). "The Labouring Poor in an Age of Transition, Antwerp, 1770-1860." Synopsis presented to "C" Session ("Causes of Poverty in the Nineteenth Century") at the Eighth International Economic History Congress, Budapest, August 16-20. Mimeographed.

Lis, Catherina, and Soly, H. (1977). "Food Consumption in Antwerp between 1807 and 1859: A Contribution in the Standard of Living Debate." Translated from the Dutch by R. B. Powell. <u>Economic History Review</u>, 2d ser. 30 (August): 460-486.

Lyon, Margot (1971). <u>Belgium</u>. New York: Walker.

Mahaim, E. (1904). "Changes in Wages and Real Wages in Belgium." Journal of the Royal Statistical Society 67, pt. 3 (September): 430-438.

Mokyr, Joel (1974). "The Industrial Revolution in the Low Countries in the First Half of the Nineteenth Century: A Comparative Case Study." Journal of Economic History 34 (June): 365-391.

_____ (1976). Industrialization in the Low Countries, 1795-1850. New Haven: Yale University Press.

Neyrinck, Michel (1944). De lonen in Belgie sedert 1846. Louvain: Em. Warny.

Pirenne, Henri (1932). Histoire de Belgique. Vol. 7, De la révolution de 1830 à la guerre de 1914. 7 vols. Brussels: Maurice Lamertin.

Rowntree, Benjamin Seebohm (1910). Land and Labour: Lessons from Belgium. London: Macmillan.

Scholliers, Peter (1981). "Arbeiders consumptie in transitie, 1890-1930." In Consumptiepatronen en prijsindices, edited by J. Hannes, pp. 30-39. Brussels: V.U.B.

Slicher van Bath, B. H. (1966). "The Rise of Intensive Husbandry in the Low Countries." In Agrarian Conditions in Modern European History, edited by Charles K. Warner, pp. 24-42. New York: Macmillan. Reprinted from John Selwyn Bromley and Ernst Heinrich Kossman, eds., Agrarian Britain and the Netherlands, pp. 130-153. London: Chatto & Windus, 1960.

Van den Eeckhout, Patricia (1980). "Determinaten van het 19e Eeuws Sociaal-Economisch Leven te Brussel. Hun Betekenis voor de Laagste Bevolkingsklassen." Ph.D. dissertation. Vrije Universiteit Brussel, Faculteit der Letteren en Wijsbegeerte, Brussels. Mimeographed.

Van Houtte, J. A. (1943). Esquisse d'une histoire économique de la Belgique. Louvain: Editions Universitas.

BRAZIL

Aguiar, Neuma, ed. (1979). The Structure of Brazilian Development. New Brunswick, N.J.: Transaction Books.

Baklanoff, Eric N., ed. (1969). The Shaping of Modern Brazil. Colloquium on the Modernization of Brazil, Louisiana State University, 1967. Baton Rouge: Published for the Latin American Studies Institute by Louisiana State University Press.

Burns, E. Bradford (1970). A History of Brazil. New York: Columbia University Press.

Conrad, Robert (1972). The Destruction of Brazilian Slavery, 1850-1888. Berkeley and Los Angeles: University of California Press.

de Azevedo, Fernando (1971). <u>Brazilian Culture: An Introduction to the</u> <u>Study of Culture in Brazil</u>. Translated by William Rex Crawford. New York: Hafner Publishing. Originally published in 1950.

Duncan, Kenneth, and Rutledge, Ian, eds. (1977). <u>Land and Labour in Latin</u> <u>America: Essays on the Development of Agrarian Capitalism in the Nineteenth</u> <u>and Twentieth Centuries</u>. Cambridge: Cambridge University Press.

Eisenberg, Peter L. (1977). "The Consequences of Modernization for Brazil's Sugar Plantations in the Nineteenth Century." Pp. 345-368. (See Duncan and Rutledge 1977 above.)

Flory, Thomas (1981). <u>Judge and Jury in Imperial Brazil, 1808-1871: Social</u> <u>Control and Political Stability in the New State</u>. Austin: University of Texas Press.

Frank, André Gunder (1969). <u>Capitalism and Underdevelopment in Latin</u> <u>America: Historical Studies of Chile and Brazil</u>. New York: Monthly Review Press. Originally published in 1967.

Freyre, Gilbert (1970). <u>Order and Progress: Brazil from Monarchy to</u> <u>Republic</u>. Edited by Rod W. Horton. New York: Alfred A. Knopf.

Furtado, Celso (1963). <u>The Economic Growth of Brazil: A Survey from</u> <u>Colonial to Modern Times</u>. Translated by Ricardo W. de Aguiar and Eric Charles Drysdale. Berkeley and Los Angeles: University of California Press.

_____ (1970). <u>Economic Development of Latin America: A Survey from</u> <u>Colonial Times to the Cuban Revolution</u>. Translated by Suzette Macedo. Cambridge: Cambridge University Press.

Graham, Richard (1968). <u>Britain and the Onset of Modernization in Brazil,</u> <u>1850-1914</u>. Cambridge: Cambridge University Press.

Hambloch, Ernest (1936). <u>His Majesty the President of Brazil: A Study of</u> <u>Constitutional Brazil</u>. New York: E. P. Dutton.

Haring, Clarence Henry (1958). <u>Empire in Brazil: A New World Experiment</u> <u>with Monarchy</u>. Cambridge: Harvard University Press.

Jobim, José (1944). <u>Brazil in the Making</u>. New York: Macmillan.

Kuznets, Simon S.; Moore, Wilbert E.; and Spengler, Joseph J., eds. (1955). <u>Economic Growth: Brazil, India, Japan</u>. Durham, N.C.: Duke University Press.

Leff, Nathaniel H. (1972a). "Development and Regional Inequality in Brazil." <u>Quarterly Journal of Economics</u> 86 (May): 243-262.

_____ (1972b). "Economic Retardation in Nineteenth-Century Brazil." <u>Economic History Review</u> 25 (August): 489-507.

_____ (1972c). "A Technique for Estimating Income Trends from Currency Data and an Application to Nineteenth-Century Brazil." <u>Review of Income and</u> <u>Wealth</u> 18 (December): 355-368.

_____ (1973). "Tropical Trade and Development in the Nineteenth Century: The Brazilian Experience." Journal of Political Economy 81 (May-June): 678-696.

Merrick, Thomas W., and Graham, Douglas H. (1979). Population and Economic Development in Brazil, 1800 to the Present. Baltimore: Johns Hopkins University Press.

Mowat, Charles L., ed. (1968). The New Cambridge Modern History. Vol. 12, The Shifting Balance of World Forces, 1898-1945. 2d ed. of vol. 12, The Era of Violence. Cambridge: Cambridge University Press.

Normano, J. F. (1968). Brazil: A Study of Economic Types. New York: Bible & Tannen. Originally published in 1935 by the University of North Carolina Press, Chapel Hill.

Poppino, Rollie E. (1968). Brazil: The Land and People. New York: Oxford University Press.

Prado, Caio, Jr. (1967). The Colonial Background of Modern Brazil. Translated by Suzette Macedo. Berkeley and Los Angeles: University of California Press.

Randall, Laura Regina (1977b). A Comparative Economic History of Latin America, 1500-1914. Vol. 3, Brazil. New York: Columbia University, The Institute of Latin American Studies.

Reis, Jaime (1977). "From Banque to Usina: Social Aspects of Growth and Modernization in the Sugar Industry of Pennambuco, Brazil, 1850-1920." Pp. 369-396. (See Duncan and Rutledge 1977 above.)

Schmitter, Philippe C. (1971). Interest Conflict and Political Change in Brazil. Stanford: Stanford University Press.

Silva, Helio Schlittler (1953). "Tendencias e Carateristicas do Commercio Exterior do Brasil no Seculo XIX." Revista de Historia de Economia Brasileira 1 (June): 5-21.

Spiegel, Henry William (1949). The Brazilian Economy: Chronic Inflation and Sporadic Industrialization. Philadelphia: Blakiston.

Stein, Stanley J. (1957). The Brazilian Cotton Manufacture: Textile Enterprise in an Underdeveloped Area, 1850-1950. Cambridge: Harvard University Press.

Tyler, William G. (1976). Manufactured Export Expansion and Industrialization in Brazil. Tübingen: J. C. B. Mohr.

Wilkie, James W., and Riech, Peter, eds. (1980). Statistical Abstract of Latin America. UCLA Latin American Center Publications, vol. 20. Berkeley and Los Angeles: University of California Press.

Wythe, George (1955). "Brazil: Trends in Industrial Development." Pp. 29-77. (See Kuznets et al. 1955 above.)

Wythe, George; Wight, Royce A.; and Midkiff, Harold M. (1949). Brazil: An
Expanding Economy. New York: Twentieth Century Fund.

BURMA

Adas, Michael (1974). The Burma Delta: Economic Development and Social
Change on an Asian Rice Frontier, 1852-1941. Madison: University of
Wisconsin Press.

Andrus, James Russell (1947). Burmese Economic Life. Stanford: Stanford
University Press.

Cady, John Frank (1958). A History of Modern Burma. Ithaca, N.Y.: Cornell
University Press.

Christian, John LeRoy (1942). Modern Burma: A Survey of Political and
Economic Development. Berkeley and Los Angeles: University of California
Press.

Cook, Bernard Christopher Allen (1957). Burma: Economic and Commercial
Conditions in Burma. London: Her Majesty's Stationery Office.

Cowan, C. D., ed. (1964). The Economic Development of South-East Asia:
Studies in Economic History and Political Economy. London: George Allen &
Unwin.

Furnivall, John S. (1931). An Introduction to the Political Economy of
Burma. Rangoon: Burma Book Club.

_____ (1956). Colonial Policy and Practice: A Comparative Study of Burma
and Netherlands India. New York: New York University Press. Originally
published in 1948.

_____ (1960). The Governance of Modern Burma. 2d ed. enl. New York:
International Secretariat, Institute of Pacific Relations.

Hagen, Everett Einar (1956). The Economic Development of Burma.
International Committee Report, Planning Pamphlet, no. 96. Washington,
D.C.: National Planning Association.

Harvey, Godfrey Eric (1946). British Rule in Burma, 1824-1942. London:
Faber & Faber.

Hlaing, Aye (1964). "Trends of Economic Growth and Income Distribution in
Burma, 1870-1940." Journal of the Burma Research Society 47 (June): 89-148.

Levin, Jonathan V. (1960). The Export Economies: Their Pattern of
Development in Historical Perspective. Cambridge: Harvard University Press.

Resnick, Stephen A. (1970). "The Decline of Rural Industry under Export
Expansion: A Comparison among Burma, Philippines, and Thailand, 1870-1938."
Journal of Economic History 30 (March): 51-73.

Singhal, Damodor P. (1960). The Annexation of Upper Burma. Singapore:
Donald Moore for Eastern Universities Press.

Tun Wai, U. (1961). Economic Development of Burma from 1800 till 1940. Rangoon: Department of Economics, University of Rangoon.

Walinsky, Louis Joseph (1962). Economic Development in Burma, 1951-1960. New York: Twentieth Century Fund.

Wickizer, V. D. and Bennett, M. K. (1941). The Rice Economy of Monsoon Asia. Published in cooperation with the International Secretariat, Institute of Pacific Relations. Stanford: Stanford University Food Research Institute.

CANADA

Aitken, Hugh G. J. (1959). "Defensive Expansionism: The State and Economic Growth in Canada." In The State and Economic Growth, edited by Aitken, pp. 79-114. Papers of a conference held on October 11-13, 1956, under the auspices of the Committee on Economic Growth. New York: Social Science Research Council.

Bertram, Gordon W. (1963). "Economic Growth in Canadian Industry, 1870-1915: The Staple Model and the Take-off Hypothesis." Canadian Journal of Economics and Political Science 29 (May): 159-184.

Bertram, Gordon W., and Percy, Michael B. (1979). "Real Wage Trends in Canada, 1900-1926: Some Provisional Estimates." Canadian Journal of Economics 12 (May): 299-312.

Buckley, Kenneth A. H. (1955). Capital Formation in Canada, 1896-1930. Toronto: University of Toronto Press.

Cairncross, Alexander Kirkland (1953). "Investment in Canada, 1900-13." Home and Foreign Investment, 1870-1913: Studies in Capital Accumulation, pp. 37-64. Cambridge: Cambridge University Press.

Caves, Richard E., and Holton, Richard H. (1961). The Canadian Economy: Prospect and Retrospect. Cambridge: Harvard University Press.

Clark, Samuel Delbert (1942). The Social Development of Canada: An Introductory Study with Select Documents. Toronto: University of Toronto Press.

Easterbrook, William Thomas (1967). "Recent Contributions to Economic History: Canada." Pp. 259-292. (See Easterbrook and Watkins 1967 below.) Reprinted from Journal of Economic History 19 (March 1959): 76-102.

Easterbrook, William Thomas, and Aitken, Hugh G. J. (1956). Canadian Economic History. Toronto: Macmillan of Canada.

Easterbrook, William Thomas, and Watkins, Melville H., eds. (1967). Approaches to Canadian Economic History. Toronto: McClelland & Stewart.

Firestone, O. J. (1958). <u>Canada's Economic Development, 1867-1953. With Special Reference to Changes in the Country's National Product and National Wealth</u>. International Association of Income and Wealth, Income and Wealth Series, no. 7. London: Bowes & Bowes.

_____ (1960). "Development of Canada's Economy, 1850-1900." In <u>Trends in the American Economy in the Nineteenth Century</u>, pp. 217-252. A Report of the National Bureau of Economic Research. Studies in Income and Wealth, vol. 24. Princeton: Princeton University Press.

Fowke, Vernon Clifford (1967). "The National Policy--Old and New." Pp. 237-258. (See Easterbrook and Watkins 1967 above.) Reprinted from <u>Canadian Journal of Economics and Political Science</u> 18 (August 1952): 271-286.

Greer, Allan (1978). "The Pattern of Literacy in Quebec, 1745-1899." <u>Social History/Histoire sociale</u> 11, no. 2: 293-335.

Guillet, Edwin Clarence (1966). <u>The Story of Canadian Roads</u>. Toronto: University of Toronto Press.

Hamelin, Jean, and Roby, Yves (1971). <u>Histoire économique du Quebec, 1851-1896</u>. Montreal: Fides.

Hammond, Bray (1967). "Banking in Canada before Confederation, 1792-1867." Pp. 127-168. (See Easterbrook and Watkins 1967 above.) Reprinted from <u>Banks and Politics in America from the Revolution to the Civil War</u>. Princeton: Princeton University Press, 1957.

Hansen, Marcus Lee (1940). <u>The Mingling of the Canadian and American Peoples</u>. Vol. 1, <u>Historical</u>, completed and prepared for publication by John Bartlet Brebner. New Haven: Yale University Press.

Hartland, Penelope (1955). "Factors in Economic Growth in Canada." <u>Journal of Economic History</u> 15, no. 1: 13-22.

Higgins, Benjamin Howard, and Lermer, Arthur (1950). "Trends and Structure of the Economy." In <u>Canada</u>, edited by George Williams Brown, pp. 222-277. United Nations Series. Berkeley and Los Angeles: University of California Press.

Innis, Harold A. (1933). <u>Problems of Staple Production in Canada</u>. Toronto: Ryerson Press.

_____ (1956). <u>Essays in Canadian Economic History</u>. Edited by Mary Quayle Innis. Toronto: University of Toronto Press.

_____ (1967). "The Fur Trade." Pp. 20-27. (See Easterbrook and Watkins 1967 above.) Reprinted from <u>The Fur Trade in Canada: An Introduction to Canadian Economic History</u>. Rev. ed. Toronto: University of Toronto Press, 1956. Originally published in 1930.

Innis, Mary Quayle (1935). <u>An Economic History of Canada</u>. Toronto: Ryerson Press.

Jones, Robert Leslie (1946). History of Agriculture in Ontario, 1613-1880. University of Toronto Studies, History and Economics Series, vol. 11. Toronto: University of Toronto Press.

_____ (1967). "French-Canadian Agriculture in the St. Lawrence Valley, 1815-1850." Pp. 110-125. (See Easterbrook and Watkins 1967 above.) Reprinted from Agricultural History 16 (July 1942): 137-148.

Létourneau, Firmin (1950). Histoire de l'agriculture (Canada français). Montreal: L'Imprimerie populaire.

Lithwick, Norman Harvey (1967). Economic Growth in Canada: A Quantitative Analysis. Toronto: University of Toronto Press.

Lower, A. R. M. (1967). "The Trade in Square Timber." Pp. 28-48. (See Easterbrook and Watkins 1967 above.) Reprinted from University of Toronto Studies, History and Economics Series, vol. 6, Contributions to Canadian Economics. Toronto: University of Toronto Press, 1933.

McDougall, Duncan M. (1961). "Immigration into Canada, 1851-1920." Canadian Journal of Economics and Political Science 27 (May): 162-175.

_____ (1971). "Canadian Manufactured Commodity Output, 1870-1915." Canadian Journal of Economics 4 (February): 21-36.

McInnis, Edgar (1959). Canada: A Political and Social History. Rev. and enl. New York: Holt, Rinehart & Winston.

McRae, Kenneth D. (1964). "The Structure of Canadian History." In The Founding of New Societies: Studies in the History of the United States, Latin America, South Africa, Canada, and Australia, edited by Louis Hartz, pp. 219-274. New York: Harcourt, Brace & World.

Mackintosh, William Alexander (1967). "Economic Factors in Canadian History." Pp. 1-15. (See Easterbrook and Watkins 1967 above.) Reprinted from Canadian Historical Review 4 (March 1923): 12-25.

Marr, William L., and Paterson, Donald G. (1980). Canada: An Economic History. Toronto: Macmillan of Canada.

Menzel, Ulrich (1981). "Der Entwicklungsweg Kanadas (1846-1930). Ein Beitrag zum Konzept autozentrierter Entwicklung." Project: Untersuchung Grundlegung einer Praxisorientierten Theorie Autozentrierter Entwicklung. Forschungsbericht no. 12. University of Bremen. Mimeographed.

Morton, William Lewis (1949). "Agriculture in the Red River Colony." Canadian Historical Review 30 (December): 305-321.

Neufeld, Edward Peter (1972). The Financial System of Canada: Its Growth and Development. New York: St. Martin's Press.

Norrie, K. H. (1975). "The Rate of Settlement of the Canadian Prairies, 1870-1911." Journal of Economic History 35 (June): 410-427.

Parker, Keith Alfred (1966). "The Staple Industries and Economic
Development, Canada, 1851-1967." Ph.D. dissertation, University of
Maryland.

Paterson, Donald G. (1976). <u>British Direct Investment in Canada,
1890-1914</u>. Toronto: University of Toronto Press.

Pentland, H. Clare (1959). "The Development of a Capitalistic Labour Market
in Canada." <u>Canadian Journal of Economics and Political Scien</u>ce 25
(November): 450-461.

Rose, John Holland; Newton, Arthur Percival; and Benians, Edward A., eds.
(1930). <u>The Cambridge History of the British Empire</u>. Vol. 6, <u>Canada and
Newfoundland</u>. Cambridge: Cambridge University Press.

Tucker, William Norman (1936). <u>The Canadian Commercial Revolution,
1845-1851</u>. New Haven: Yale University Press.

Urquhart, Malcolm C., and Buckley, Kenneth A. H., eds. (1965). <u>Historical
Statistics of Canada</u>. Cambridge: Cambridge University Press.

Watkins, Melville H. (1963). "A Staple Theory of Economic Growth."
<u>Canadian Journal of Economics and Political Science</u> 29 (May): 141-158.

Wilson, J. Donald; Stamp, Robert M.; and Audet, Louis-Philippe, eds.
(1970). <u>Canadian Education: A History</u>. Ontario: Prentice-Hall of Canada.

Wittke, Carl Frederick (1941). <u>A History of Canada</u>. 3d ed. New York:
F. S. Crofts.

Young, John Humphrey (1955). "Comparative Economic Development: Canada and
the United States." <u>American Economic Review, Papers and Proceedings</u> 45
(May): 80-93.

CHINA

Allen, George Cyril (1965). "The Industrialization of the Far East." In
<u>The Cambridge Economic History of Europe</u>, vol. 6, pt. 2, <u>The Industrial
Revolution and After: Income, Population and Technological Change</u>, edited by
H. J. Habakkuk and M. M. Postan, pp. 873-923. Cambridge: Cambridge
University Press.

Allen, George Cyril, and Donnithorne, Audrey Gladys (1954). <u>Western
Enterprise in Far Eastern Economic Development: China and Japan</u>. London:
George Allen & Unwin.

Beckmann, George M. (1962). <u>The Modernization of China and Japan</u>. New
York: Harper & Row.

Bland, John Otway P. (1912). <u>Recent Events and Present Policies in China</u>.
Philadelphia: J. B. Lippincott.

Cameron, Meribeth Elliott; Mahoney, Thomas H. D.; and McReynolds, George E. (1960). *China, Japan, and the Powers: A History of the Modern Far East*. 2d ed. New York: Ronald Press.

Ch'en, Jerome (1969). "Historical Background." Pp. 1-40. (See Gray 1969 below.)

Clark, Grover (1932). *Economic Rivalries in China*. New Haven: Published for the Carnegie Endowment for International Peace by Yale University Press.

Condliffe, John Bell (1932). *China To-Day: Economic*. Boston: World Peace Foundation.

Cowan, Charles Donald, ed. (1964). *The Economic Development of China and Japan: Studies in Economic History and Political Economy*. London: George Allen & Unwin.

Eckstein, Alexander; Galenson, Walter; and Liu, Ta-chung, eds. (1968). *Economic Trends in Communist China*. Chicago: Aldine.

Fairbank, John King; Eckstein, Alexander; and Yang, Lien-sheng (1960). "Economic Change in Early Modern China: An Analytic Framework." *Economic Development and Cultural Change* 9 (October): 1-26.

Feuerwerker, Albert (1958). *China's Early Industrialization: Sheng Hsuan-huai (1844-1916) and Mandarin Enterprise*. Cambridge: Harvard University Press.

———— (1969). *The Chinese Economy, ca. 1870-1911*. Michigan Papers in Chinese Studies, no. 5. Ann Arbor: Center for Chinese, University of Michigan.

Gray, Jack, ed. (1969). *Modern China's Search for a Political Form*. London: Oxford University Press.

Hou, Chi-ming (1961). "External Trade, Foreign Investment, and Domestic Development: The Chinese Experience, 1850-1937." *Economic Development and Cultural Change* 10 (October): 21-41.

———— (1963). "Economic Dualism: The Case of China, 1840-1937." *Journal of Economic History* 23 (September): 277-297.

———— (1965). *Foreign Investment and Economic Development in China, 1840-1937*. Cambridge: Harvard University Press.

King, Frank H. H. (1965). *Money and Monetary Policy in China, 1845-1895*. Harvard East Asian Studies, no. 19. Cambridge: Harvard University Press.

Lee, Mabel Ping-hua (1921). *The Economic History of China, with Special Reference to Agriculture*. Studies in History, Economics, and Public Law, vol. 99, no. 1 (Columbia University Studies in the Social Sciences, no. 225). New York: Columbia University Press.

Li, Chien-Nung (1956). *The Political History of China, 1840-1928*. New York: D. Van Nostrand.

Lippit, Victor D. (1978). "Economic Development in Meiji Japan and Contemporary China: A Comparative Study." <u>Cambridge Journal of Economics</u> 2 (March): 55-81.

Mallory, Walter Hampton (1926). <u>China: Land of Famine</u>, edited by G. M. Wrigley. American Geographical Society Special Publication no. 6. New York: American Geographical Society.

Morse, Hosea Ballou (1921). <u>The Trade and Administration of China</u>. 3d rev. ed. London: Longmans, Green.

Perkins, Dwight Heald; Wang, Yeh-chien; Hsiao, Kuo-ying Wang; and Su, Yung-ming (1969). <u>Agricultural Development in China, 1368-1968</u>. Chicago: Aldine.

Remer, Charles Frederick (1968). <u>Foreign Investments in China</u>. New York: Howard Fertig. Originally published in 1933 by Macmillan, New York.

Rozman, Gilbert (1973). <u>Urban Networks in Ch'ing China and Tokugawa Japan.</u> Princeton: Princeton University Press.

Tawney, Richard Henry (1932). <u>Land and Labour in China</u>. London: George Allen & Unwin.

Vinacke, Harold Monk (1926). <u>Problems of Industrial Development in China: A Preliminary Study</u>. Princeton: Princeton University Press.

Yang, Lien-sheng (1952). <u>Money and Credit in China: A Short History</u>. Harvard-Yenching Institute Monograph Series, vol. 12. Cambridge: Harvard University Press.

DENMARK

Birch, John Henry S. (1938). <u>Denmark in History</u>. London: John Murray.

Bjerke, Kjeld Haakon (1955). "The National Product of Denmark, 1870-1952." In <u>Income and Wealth</u>, ser. 5, edited by Simon S. Kuznets, pp. 123-151. [Usually catalogued under International Association for Research in Income and Wealth, Income and Wealth.]   London: Bowes & Bowes.

Bjerke, Kjeld Haakon, and Ussing, Niels (1958). <u>Studies Over Danmarke Nationalproduct, 1870-1950</u>. Københavens Universitets Økonomiske Institute. Copenhagen: G. E. C. Gad.

Danstrup, John (1948). <u>A History of Denmark</u>. Translated by Verner Lindberg. Copenhagen: Wivel.

_____ (1949). 2d ed. (See Danstrup 1948 above.)

Drachmann, Povl (1915). <u>The Industrial Development and Commercial Policies of the Three Scandinavian Countries</u>. Edited by Harald Westergaard. Oxford: Clarendon Press.

Galenson, Walter (1952). <u>The Danish System of Labor Relations: A Study in Industrial Peace</u>. Cambridge: Harvard University Press.

Glamann, Kristoff (1960). "Industrialization as a Factor in Economic Growth in Denmark since 1700." In Contributions [and] Communications, pp. 115-128. Proceedings of the First International Conference of Economic History, Stockholm, 1960. Paris: Mouton.

Goldmark, Josephine Clara (1936). Democracy in Denmark. Pt. 1, Democracy in Action. Washington, D.C.: National Home Library Foundation.

Hansen, Svend Aage (1970). Early Industrialisation in Denmark. Københavens Universitet, Institut for Økonomisk Historie, publication no. 1. Copenhagen: G.E.C. Gads.

_____ (1976). Økonomisk Vaekst i Danmark. Vol. 1, 1720-1914. Københavens Universitet, Institut for Økonomisk Historie, publication no. 6. Copenhagen: G.E.C. Gads.

Hertel, Hans Axel Valdemar (1937). A Short Survey of Agriculture in Denmark. 3d ed. Royal Agricultural Society of Denmark. Copenhagen: Frederiksberg Bogtrykkeri.

Hollman, Anton H. (1936). Democracy in Denmark. Pt. 2, The Folk High School. Translated by Alice G. Brandeis. Washington, D.C.: National Home Library Foundation.

Hornby, Ove (1969). "Industrialization in Denmark and the Loss of the Duchies." Scandinavian Economic History Review 17, no. 1: 23-57.

Hornby, Ove, and Mogensen, Gunnar Viby (1974). "The Study of Economic History in Denmark: Recent Trends and Problems." Scandinavian Economic History Review 22, no. 1: 61-87.

Hovde, Brynjolf J. (1943). The Scandinavian Countries, 1720-1865: The Rise of the Middle Classes. 2 vols. Boston: Chapman & Grimes.

Jensen, Einar (1937). Danish Agriculture, Its Economic Development: A Description and Economic Analysis Centering on the Free Trade Epoch, 1870-1930. Copenhagen: J. H. Schultz.

Jörberg, Lennart (1973). "The Nordic Countries, 1850-1914." Translated by Paul Britten Austin. In The Fontana Economic History of Europe, vol. 4, pt. 2, The Emergence of Industrial Societies, edited by Carlo M. Cipolla, pp. 375-487. London: Collins/Fontana.

Lassen, Aksel (1966). "The Population of Denmark, 1660-1960." Scandinavian Economic History Review 14, no. 2: 134-157.

Menzel, Ulrich (1980b). "Der Entwicklungsweg Dänemarks (1880-1940)." Project: Untersuchung zur Grundlegung einer praxisorientierten Theorie autozentrierter Entwicklung. Forschungsbericht, no. 8. University of Bremen. Mimeographed.

Nielsen, Axel Edward H. (1933). Dänische Wirtschaftsgeschichte. Jena: Gustav Fischer.

Olsen, Erling Heymann (1962). <u>Danmarks Økonomiske Historie siden 1750</u>. Copenhagen: G. E. C. Gads.

Pedersen, Jørgen (1930). <u>Arbejdslønnen i Danmark: Under Skiftende Konjunkturer i Perioden ca. 1850-1913</u>. Copenhagen: I Konjunkturer Nos Gyldendal.

Samsöe, Jens (1928). <u>Die Industrialisierung Dänemarks</u>. Edited by Bernhard Harms. Probleme der Weltwirtschaft Schriften des Institute für Weltwirtschaft und Seeverkehren und der Universität Kiel, no. 44. Jena: Gustav Fischer.

Skrubbeltrang, Fridley Sørensen (1951). <u>Agricultural Development and Rural Reform in Denmark</u>. Agricultural Studies, no. 22. Rome: Food and Agriculture Organization of the United Nations, Agricultural Division, April.

Youngson, A. J. (1959). <u>Possibilities of Economic Progress</u>. Cambridge: Cambridge University Press.

EGYPT

Baer, Gabriel (1959). "The Dissolution of the Egyptian Village Community." <u>Die Welt des Islams</u>, n. s. 6, nos. 1-2: 56-70.

_____ (1962). <u>A History of Landownership in Modern Egypt, 1800-1950</u>. London: Oxford University Press.

_____ (1966). "Land Tenure in Egypt and the Fertile Crescent, 1800-1950." Pp. 79-90. (See Issawi 1966b below.)

La Commission du Commerce et de l'Industrie (1966). "Beginnings of Industrialisation, 1916." Pp. 452-460. (See Issawi 1966b below.)

Crouchley, Arthur Edwin (1938). <u>The Economic Development of Modern Egypt</u>. London: Longmans, Green.

Dicey, Edward (1881). <u>England and Egypt</u>. London: Chapman & Hall.

Fahmy, Moustafa (1954). <u>La Révolution de l'industrie en Égypte et ses conséquences sociales au 19e siècle (1880-1850)</u>. Leiden: E. J. Brill.

Grunwald, Kurt, and Ronall, Joachim O. (1960). <u>Industrialization in the Middle East</u>. New York: Council for Middle Eastern Affairs Press.

Hansen, Bent (1979). "Income and Consumption in Egypt, 1886/1887 to 1937." <u>International Journal of Middle East Studies</u> 10 (February): 27-47.

Hershlag, Zvi Y. (1964). <u>Introduction to the Modern Economic History of the Middle East</u>. Leiden: E. J. Brill.

Heyworth-Dunne, James (1968). <u>An Introduction to the History of Education in Modern Egypt</u>. London: Frank Cass. Originally published in 1939 by Luzac, London.

al-Hitta, Ahmad Ahmad (1966). "The Development of Transport, 1800-1870." Pp. 406-415. (See Issawi 1966b below.)

Issawi, Charles Philip (1954). *Egypt at Mid-Century: An Economic Survey*. Rev. ed. Published under the auspices of the Royal Institute of International Affairs. London: Oxford University Press. Originally published in 1947 under the title, *Egypt, an Economic and Social Analysis*.

_____ (1961). "Egypt since 1800: A Study in Lopsided Development." *Journal of Economic History* 21 (March): 1-25.

_____ (1966a). "The Economic Development of Egypt, 1800-1960." Pp. 406-415. (See Issawi 1966b below.) Reprint of Issawi, "Egypt since 1800: A Study in Lopsided Development," *Journal of Economic History* 21 (March 1961): 1-25.

_____, ed. (1966b). *The Economic History of the Middle East, 1800-1914: A Book of Readings*. Chicago: University of Chicago Press.

Landes, David S. (1958). *Bankers and Pashas: International Finance and Economic Imperialism in Egypt*. London: Heinemann.

Lévi, I. G. (1918). "La Distribution du crédit en Égypte et la menace d'une crise de spéculation." *L'Égypte contemporaine*, no. 37 (February): 113-132.

Lloyd, George Ambrose Lloyd (1933). *Egypt since Cromer*. Vol. 1. London: Macmillan.

McCoan, James C. (1877). *Egypt as It Is*. New York: Henry Holt.

Mansfield, Peter (1971). *The British in Egypt*. New York: Holt, Rinehart & Winston.

Marlowe, John (1965). *A History of Modern Egypt and Anglo-Egyptian Relations, 1800-1956*. 2d ed. Hamden, Conn.: Archon.

Nahas, Joseph F. [Nahhas, Yusuf] (1901). *Situation économique et sociale du fellah égyptien*. Edited by Arthur Rousseau. Thèse pour le doctorat. Paris: Librairie nouvelle de droit & de jurisprudence.

O'Brien, Patrick Karl (1966). *The Revolution in Egypt's Economic System: From Private Enterprise to Socialism, 1952-1965*. London: Oxford University Press.

Owen, Edward Roger J. (1969). *Cotton and the Egyptian Economy, 1820-1914: A Study in Trade and Development*. Oxford: Clarendon Press.

Safran, Nadav (1961). *Egypt in Search of Political Community: An Analysis of the Intellectual and Political Evolution of Egypt, 1804-1952*. Cambridge: Harvard University Press.

al-Sayyid, Afaf Lutfi (1968). *Egypt and Cromer: A Study in Anglo-Egyptian Relations*. New York: Frederick A. Praeger.

Steward, Desmond (1958). *Young Egypt*. London: Allan Wingate.

Tignor, Robert L. (1966). <u>Modernization and British Colonial Rule in Egypt,</u> <u>1882-1914</u>. Princeton: Princeton University Press.

Vatikiotis, Panayiotis J. (1969). <u>The Modern History of Egypt</u>. New York: Frederick A. Praeger.

_____ (1980). <u>The History of Egypt</u>. 2d ed. of <u>The Modern History of</u> <u>Egypt</u>. Baltimore: Johns Hopkins University Press.

FRANCE

Augé-Laribé, Michel (1912).   <u>Évolution de la France agricole</u>. Paris: Librairie Armand Colin.

Barral, Pierre (1979). "Un Secteur dominé: La Terre." Pp. 351-397. (See Braudel and Labrouse 1979 below.)

Bastid, Marianne (1978). "Les Mondes asiatiques." Pp. 529-558. (See Léon 1978b below.)

Baudrillart, Henri Joseph Léon (1885). <u>Les Populations agricoles de la</u> <u>France</u>. 3 vols. Paris: Librairie Hachette.

Bloch, Marc Leopold B. (1966). <u>French Rural History: An Essay on Its Basic</u> <u>Characteristics</u>. Translated by Janet Sondheimer. Berkeley and Los Angeles: University of California Press. Originally published in French in 1931.

Bogart, Ernest Ludlow (1942). <u>Economic History of Europe, 1760-1939</u>. London: Longmans, Green.

Bouvier, Jean (1978). "Les Mécanismes de domination." Pp. 455-472. (See Léon 1978b below.)

Braudel, Fernand, and Labrousse, Ernest, gen. eds. (1976). <u>Histoire</u> <u>économique et sociale de la France</u>. Vol. 3, <u>L'Avènement de l'ère</u> <u>industrielle (1789-années 1880)</u>. Paris: Presses Universitaires de France.

Braudel, Fernand, and Labrousse, Ernest (1979). <u>Histoire économique et</u> <u>sociale de la France</u>. Vol. 4, <u>L'Ère industrielle et la société</u> <u>d'aujourd'hui (siècle 1880-1980)</u>. Paris: Presses Universitaires de France.

Broder, André (1976). "Le Commerce extérieur: L'Échec de la conquête d'une position internationale." Pp. 305-346. (See Braudel and Labrousse 1976 above.)

Brogan, Denis William (1957). <u>The French Nation from Napoleon to Pétain,</u> <u>1814-1940</u>. London: Hamish Hamilton.

Cameron, Rondo E. (1961). <u>France and the Economic Development of Europe,</u> <u>1800-1914: Conquests of Peace and Seeds of War</u>. Princeton: Princeton University Press.

_____ (1963). "Economic Growth and Stagnation in France, 1815-1914." Pp. 328-339. (See Supple 1963 below.) Reprinted with omissions from <u>Journal of Modern History</u> 30 (March 1958): 1-13.

_____ (1967). "France, 1800-1870." In Banking in the Early Stages of Industrialization: A Study in Comparative Economic History, edited by Rondo E. Cameron, Olga Crisp, Hugh T. Patrick, and Richard H. Tilly, pp. 100-128. New York: Oxford University Press.

Cameron, Rondo E.; Mendels, Franklin F.; and Ward, Judith P., eds. (1970). Essays in French Economic History. Homewood, Ill. Richard D. Irwin.

Campbell, Peter (1965). French Electoral Systems and Elections since 1789. 2d ed. Hamden, Conn.: Archon Books.

Caron, François (1978a). "La Croissance économique." Pp. 69-134. (See Léon 1978b below.)

_____ (1978b). "Facteurs et mécanismes de l'industrialisation." Pp. 135-206. (See Léon 1978b below.)

Clapham, John Harold (1936). The Economic Development of France and Germany, 1815-1914. 4th ed. Cambridge: Cambridge University Press.

Clough, Shepard Bancroft (1939). France: A History of National Economics, 1789-1939. New York: Charles Scribner's Sons.

_____ (1946). "Retardative Factors in French Economic Development in the Nineteenth and Twentieth Centuries." Journal of Economic History, suppl. 6 (December): 91-102.

Crafts, N. F. R. (1977). "Industrial Revolution in England and France: Some Thoughts on the Question, 'Why Was England First?'" Economic History Review, 2d ser. 30 (August): 429-441.

Crouzet, François (1970). "Essai de construction d'un indice annuel de la production industrielle française au XIX siècle. Annales E.S.C. 25 (January-February): 56-99.

Daumard, Adeline (1976a). "Caractères de la société bourgeoise." Pp. 829-844. (See Braudel and Labrousse 1976 above.)

_____ (1976b). "Diversité des milieux supérieurs et dirigeants." Pp. 931-960. (See Braudel and Labrousse 1976 above.)

_____ (1976c). "La Hiérarchie des biens et des positions." Pp. 845-896. (See Braudel and Labrousse 1976 above.)

_____ (1976d). "Progrès et prise de conscience des classes moyennes." Pp. 897-930. (See Braudel and Labrousse 1976 above.)

Farmer, Paul (1964). "The Second Empire in France." In The New Cambridge Modern History, vol. 10, The Zenith of European Power, 1830-70, edited by John Patrick Tuer Bury, pp. 185-212. Cambridge: Cambridge University Press.

Fohlen, Claude (1970). "The Industrial Revolution in France." Pp. 201-225. (See Cameron 1970 above.)

_____ (1978). "Entrepreneurship and Management in France in the Nineteenth Century." In The Cambridge Economic History of Europe, vol. 7, pt. 1, The Industrial Economies: Capital, Labour, and Enterprise, edited by Peter Mathias and M. M. Postan, pp. 347-381. Cambridge: Cambridge University Press.

Garrier, Gilbert, ed. (1978). La Domination du capitalisme, 1840-1914. Vol. 4 of Histoire économique et sociale du monde, edited by Pierre Léon. Paris: Librairie Armand Colin.

Golob, Eugene Owen (1944). The Méline Tariff: French Agriculture and Nationalist Economic Policy. Studies in History, Economics, and Public Law, no. 506. New York: Columbia University Press.

Grantham, George William (1975). "Scale and Organization in French Farming, 1840-1880." In European Peasants and Their Markets: Essays in Agrarian Economic History, edited by William N. Parker and Eric L. Jones, pp. 293-326. Princeton: Princeton University Press.

Heywood, Colin (1981). "The Role of the Peasantry in French Industrialization, 1815-80." Economic History Review, 2d ser. 34: 359-376.

Hoselitz, Bert [Berthold] Frank (1956). (May be cataloged under Universities--National Bureau Committee for Economic Research.) "Entrepreneurship and Capital Formation in France and Britain since 1700." In Capital Formation and Economic Growth, pp. 291-337. A conference of the Universities-National Bureau Committee for Economic Research. Special Conference Series, no. 16. Princeton: Princeton University Press.

Kemp, Tom (1962). "Structural Factors in the Retardation of French Economic Growth." Kyklos 15, no. 2: 325-352.

Kindleberger, Charles Poor (1961). "Foreign Trade and Economic Growth: Lessons from Britain and France, 1850-1913." Economic History Review, 2d ser. 14 (December): 289-305.

_____ (1964). Economic Growth in France and Britain, 1851-1950. Cambridge: Harvard University Press.

Kuczynski, Jürgen (1936). Labour Conditions in Western Europe, 1820 to 1935. New York: International Publishers.

_____ (1946). A Short History of Labour Conditions under Industrial Capitalism. Vol. 4, France: 1700 to the Present Day. London: Frederick Muller.

Labrousse, Ernest (1976a). "À livre ouvert sur les élans et les vicissitudes des croissances." Pp. 961-1024. (See Braudel and Labrousse 1976 above.)

Landes, David S. (1963). "French Entrepreneurship and Industrial Growth in the Nineteenth Century." Pp. 340-353. (See Supple 1963 below.) Reprinted with omissions from Journal of Economic History 9 (May 1949): 45-61.

Laurent, Robert (1976a). "Les Mutations de la société rurale." Pp. 739-769. (See Braudel and Labrousse 1976 above.)

_____ (1976b). "Tradition et progrès: Le Secteur agricole." Pp. 619-735. (See Braudel and Labrousse 1976 above.)

Léon, Pierre (1976a). "L'Affermissement du phénomène d'industrialisation." Pp. 475-618. (See Braudel and Labrousse 1976 above.)

_____ (1976b). "La Conquête de l'espace national." Pp. 241-273. (See Braudel and Labrousse 1976 above.)

_____ (1976c). "L'Épanouissement d'un marché national." Pp. 275-304. (See Braudel and Labrousse 1976 above.)

_____ (1978). "L'Amérique latine." Pp. 573-590. (See Garrier 1978 above.)

Lequin, Yves (1978). "Les Hiérarchies de la richesse et du pol voir." Pp. 299-354. (See Léon 1978b above.)

Leslie, Thomas Edward Cliffe (1870). "The Land System of France." In Systems of Land Tenure in Various Countries, edited by the Cobden Club, pp. 335-359. 2d ed. London: Macmillan.

Leuilliot, Paul (1957). "The Industrial Revolution in France: Some Reflections Inspired by a Recent Study by Arthur Louis Dunham." Journal of Economic History 17 (June): 245-254.

Levasseur, Émile (1969). Histoire des classes ouvrières et de l'industrie en France de 1789 à 1870. New York: AMS Press. Reprint of 2d ed. Paris A. R. Rousseau, 1903-1904.

Lévy-Leboyer, Maurice (1968a). "La Croissance économique en France au XIXe siècle: Résultats préliminaires." Annales E.S.C. 23 (July-August): 788-807.

_____ (1968b). "Les Processus d'industrialisation: Le Cas de l'Angleterre et de la France." Revue historique 239 (April-June): 281-298.

_____ (1976). "La Spécialisation des établissements bancaires." Pp. 431-471. (See Braudel and Labrousse 1976 above.)

Marczewski, Jan [Jean] (1961). "Some Aspects of the Economic Growth of France, 1660-1958." Economic Development and Cultural Change 9 (April): 369-386.

_____ (1965). "Le Produit physique de l'économie française de 1789 à 1913 (comparaison avec la Grande-Bretagne)." Cahiers de L'I.S.E.A. 4 (July): vii-cliv.

Markovitch, T. J. (1965). "L'Industrie française de 1789 à 1964: Sources et méthodes." Cahiers de L'I.S.E.A. 4 (July): 1-234.

_____ (1966a). "L'Industrie française de 1789 à 1964: Analyse des faits." Cahiers de L'I.S.E.A. 5 (May): 1-264.

_____ (1966b). "L'Industrie française de 1964: Analyse des faits (suite)." Cahiers de L'I.S.E.A. 6 (June): 1-285.

_____ (1966c). "L'Industrie française de 1789 à 1964: Conclusions générales." Cahiers de L'I.S.E.A. 7 (November): 1-324.

Moulton, Harold Glenn, and Lewis, Cleona (1925). The French Debt Problem. New York: Macmillan.

Néré, J. (1962). "The French Republic." In The New Cambridge Modern History, vol. 11, Material Progress and World-wide Problems, 1870-1898, edited by Francis H. Hinsley, pp. 300-322. Cambridge: Cambridge University Press.

Newell, William H. (1973). "The Agricultural Revolution in Nineteenth-Century France." Journal of Economic History 33 (December): 697-731.

Palmade, Guy P. (1972). French Capitalism in the Nineteenth Century. Translated by Graema M. Holmes. New York: Barnes & Noble. Originally published in 1961.

Pautard, Jean (1965). Les Disparités régionales dans la croissance de l'agriculture française. Paris: Gauthier-Villars.

Perroux, François (1955). "Prise de vue sur la croissance de l'économie française, 1780-1950." In Income and Wealth, ser. 5, edited by Simon S. Kuznets, pp. 41-78. [Usually cataloged under International Association for Income and Wealth, Income and Wealth.] London: Bowes & Bowes.

Philippe, Robert (1970). "Une Opération pilote: L'Étude du ravitaillement de Paris au temps de Lavoisier." In Pour une histoire de l'alimentation, edited by J. J. Hémardinquer. Cahiers des annales, no. 28. Paris: Librairie Armand Colin.

Ripert, Georges (1951). Aspects juridiques du capitalisme moderne. 2d ed. Paris: Librairie générale de droit et de jurisprudence.

Roehl, Richard (1976). "French Industrialization: A Reconsideration." Explorations in Economic History 13 (July): 233-281.

Sawyer, John Edward (1951). "Social Structure and Economic Progress: General Propositions and Some French Examples." American Economic Review 41 (May): 321-329.

_____ (1952). "The Entrepreneur and the Social Order: France and the United States." In Men in Business: Essays in the History of Entrepreneurship, edited by William Miller, pp. 7-22. Cambridge: Harvard University Press.

Sée, Henri (1951). Histoire économique de la France: Les Temps modernes (1789-1914), vol. 2, Paris: Librairie Armand Colin. Originally published in 1942.

Soltau, Roger Henry (1965). French Parties and Politics, 1871-1921: With a New Supplementary Chapter Dealing with 1922-1930. New York: Russell & Russell. Originally published in 1930.

Supple, Barry E., ed. (1963). <u>The Experience of Economic Growth: Case Studies in Economic History</u>. New York: Random House.

Valensi, Lucette (1978). "Le Monde musulman." Pp. 501-528. (See Léon 1978b above.)

Weiller, Jean Sylvain (1971). "Long-run Tendencies in Foreign Trade: With a Statistical Study of French Foreign Trade Structure, 1871-1939." <u>Journal of Economic History</u> 31 (December): 804-821.

White, Harry Dexter (1933). <u>The French International Accounts, 1880-1913</u>. Harvard Economic Studies, vol. 40. Cambridge: Harvard University Press.

Wolf, John Baptist (1963). <u>France, 1814-1919: The Rise of a Liberal-Democratic Society</u>. New York: Harper & Row, Harper Torchbooks. Originally published in 1940 by Prentice-Hall, under the title <u>France: 1815 to the Present</u>.

GERMANY

Abel, Wilhelm (1966). "Der Pauperismus in Deutschland: Eine Nachlese zu Literaturberichten." In <u>Wirtschaft, Geschichte und Wirtschaftgeschichte</u>, edited by Wilhelm Abel, Knut Borchardt, Hermann Kellenbenz, and Wolfgang Zorn, pp. 284-298. Stuttgart: Gustav Fischer.

Ashley, William James (1904). <u>The Progress of the German Working Classes in the Last Quarter of a Century</u>. London: Longmans, Green.

Berthold, Rudolf (1979). "Die Entstehung der deutschen Landmaschinen- und Düngemittelindustrie zwischen 1850 und 1870." Pp. 245-266. (See Lärmer 1979b below.)

Bog, Ingomar; Franz, Günther; Kaufhold, Karl Heinrich; Kellenbenz, Hermann; and Zorn, Wolfgang, eds. (1974). <u>Wirtschaft und Gesellschaft in der Zeit der Industrialisierung</u>. Vol. 3 of <u>Wirtschaftliche und soziale Strukturen im säkularen Wandel: Festschrift für Wilhelm Abel zum 70. Geburtstag</u>. Shriftenreihe für Ländliche Soziale Fragen no. 70. Hannover: M. & H. Schaper.

Borchardt, Knut (1976a). "Wirtschaftliches Wachstum und Wechsellagen 1800-1914." Pp. 198-275. (See Zorn 1976 below.)

_____ (1976b). "Zur Frage des Kapitalmangels in der ersten Hälfte des 19. Jahrhunderts in Deutschland." Pp. 216-236. (See Braun et al. 1976b below.)

Borscheid, Peter (1979). "Arbeitskräftepotential, Wanderung und Wohlstandsgefälle." Pp. 230-247. (See Fremdling and Tilly 1979 below.)

Braun, Rudolf (1976a). "Zur Entstehung eines ländlichen 'Fabrikherren'-Standes." Pp. 94-107. (See Braun et al. 1976b below.)

Braun, Rudolf; Fischer, Wolfram; Grosskreutz, Helmut; and Volkmann, Heinrich, eds. (1976b). <u>Industrielle Revolution: Wirtschaftliche Aspekte</u>. Cologne: Kiepenheuer & Witsch.

Bruck, Werner Friedrich [Brook, Warner Frederick] (1938). <u>Social and Economic History of Germany from William II to Hitler, 1888-1938: A Comparative Study</u>. Cardiff: Oxford University Press.

Clapham, John Harold (1936). <u>Economic Development of France and Germany, 1815-1914</u>. 4th ed. Cambridge: Cambridge University Press.

Conze, Werner (1962). "The German Empire." In <u>The New Cambridge Modern History</u>, vol. 11, <u>Material Progress and World-wide Problems, 1870-1898</u>, edited by Francis H. Hinsley, pp. 274-295. Cambridge: Cambridge University Press.

_____ (1976). "Sozialgeschichte, 1850-1918." Pp. 602-684. (See Zorn 1976 below.)

Dawson, William H. (1919). <u>The German Empire, 1867-1914, and the Unity Movement</u>. 2 vols. London: George Allen & Unwin.

Desai, Ashok V. (1968). <u>Real Wages in Germany, 1871-1913</u>. Oxford: Clarendon Press.

Dickler, Robert A. (1975). "Organization and Change in Productivity in Eastern Prussia." In <u>European Peasants and Their Markets: Essays in Agrarian Economic History</u>, edited by William N. Parker and Eric L. Jones, pp. 269-292. Princeton: Princeton University Press.

Eyck, Erich (1950). <u>Bismarck and the German Empire</u>. London: George Allen & Unwin.

Fischer, Wolfram (1963). "Government Activity and Industrialization in Germany (1815-1870)." Pp. 83-94. (See Rostow 1963 below.)

_____ (1976). "Bergbau, Industrie und Handwerk, 1850-1914." Pp. 527-562. (See Zorn 1976 below.)

Forbes, Ian L. D. (1978). "German Informal Imperialism in South America before 1914." <u>Economic History Review</u>, 2d ser. 31 (August): 384-398.

Franz, Günther (1976). "Landwirtschaft, 1800-1850." Pp. 276-320. (See Zorn 1976 below.)

Fremdling, Rainer, and Tilly, Richard H. (1976). "German Banks, German Growth, and Econometric History." <u>Journal of Economic History</u> 36 (June): 416-424.

_____, eds. (1979). <u>Industrialisierung und Raum: Studien regionalen Differenzierung in Deutschland des 19. Jahrhunderts</u>. Historisch-Sozialwissenschaftliche Forschungen, vol. 7. Stuttgart: Klett-Cotta.

Great Britain. Board of Agriculture and Fisheries (1916). <u>The Recent Development of German Agriculture</u>. Prepared by Thomas H. Middleton. London: His Majesty's Stationery Office.

Hamerow, Theodore S. (1969). The Social Foundations of German Unification, 1858-1871. Vol. 1, Ideas and Institutions. Princeton: Princeton University Press.

_____ (1972). The Social Foundations of German Unification, 1858-1871. Vol. 2, Struggles and Accomplishments. Princeton: Princeton University Press.

Harnisch, Hartmut (1979). "Bevölkerungsgeschichtliche Probleme der industriellen Revolution in Deutschland." Pp. 267-340. (See Lärmer 1979b below.)

Haushofer, Heinz (1963). Die deutsche Landwirtschaft im technischen Zeitalter. Stuttgart: Eugen Ulmer.

Hoffmann, Walther G. (1963). "The Take-off in Germany." Pp. 95-118. (See Rostow 1963 below.)

Hoffmann, Walther G., and Müller, Josep Heinz (1959). Das deutsche Volkseinkommen, 1851-1957. Tübingen: Mohr.

Hoffmann, Walther G.; Grumbach, Franz; and Hesse, Helmut (1965). Das Wachstum der deutschen Wirtschaft seit der Mitte des 19. Jahrhunderts. Berlin: Springer.

Joll, James (1964). "Prussia and the German Problem, 1830-66." In The New Cambridge Modern History, vol. 10, The Zenith of European Power, 1830-1870, edited by John Patrick Tuer Bury, pp. 493-521. Cambridge: Cambridge University Press.

Jostock, Paul (1955). "The Long-term Growth of National Income in Germany." In Income and Wealth, ser. 5, edited by Simon S. Kuznets, pp. 41-78. [Usually cataloged under International Association of Income and Wealth, Income and Wealth]. London: Bowes & Bowes.

Kaufhold, Karl Heinrich (1976). "Handwerk und Industrie, 1800-1850." Pp. 321-368. (See Zorn 1976 below.)

Kindleberger, Charles Poor (1975). "Germany's Overtaking of England, 1806-1914, Part I." Weltwirtschaftliches Archiv 111, no. 2:253-281; ". . . Part II," 111, no. 3:477-504.

Kocka, Jürgen (1978). "Entrepreneurs and Managers in German Industrialization." Pp. 442-587. (See Mathias and Postan 1978 below.)

_____ (1981). "Capitalism and Bureaucracy in German Industrialization before 1914." Economic History Review 34 (August): 453-468.

Köllmann, Wolfgang (1976). "Bevölkerungsgeschichte, 1800-1970." Pp. 9-50. (See Zorn 1976 below.)

Kuczynski, Jürgen (1945). Germany, 1800 to the Present Day. Vol. 3, pt. 1, of A Short History of Labour Conditions under Industrial Capitalism. London: Frederick Muller.

Lärmer, Karl (1979a). "Zur Problematik der Periodisierung der Geschichte
der Produktivkräfte im 19. Jahrhundert--Ein Diskussionsbeitrag."
Pp. 13-42. (See Lärmer 1979b below.)

_____, ed. (1979b). <u>Studien zur Geschichte der Produktivkräfte</u>.
Berlin: Akademie-Verlag.

Lee, J. J. (1978). "Labour in German Industrialization." Pp. 442-491.
(See Mathias and Postan 1978 below.)

Lee, William Robert (1977). <u>Population Growth, Economic Development, and
Social Change in Bavaria, 1750-1859</u>. New York: Arno Press.

_____ (1979). "Regionale Differenzierung im Bevölkerungswachstum
Deutschlands im frühen neunzehnten Jahrhundert." Pp. 192-224. (See
Fremdling and Tilly 1979 above.)

Mathias, Peter, and Postan, M. M., eds. (1978). <u>The Cambridge Economic
History of Europe</u>. Vol. 7, <u>The Industrial Economies: Capital, Labour, and
Enterprise</u>. Pt. 1, "Britain, France, Germany, and Scandinavia." Cambridge:
Cambridge University Press.

Matz, Klaus-Jürgen (1980). <u>Pauperismus und Bevölkerung: Die gesetzlichen
Ehebeschränkungen in den süddeutschen Staaten während des 19. Jahrhundert</u>.
Stuttgart: Klett-Cotta.

Morier, Robert Burnett David (1870). "Agrarian Legislation of Prussia
during the Present Century." In <u>Systems of Land Tenure in Various
Countries</u>, edited by the Cobden Club, pp. 285-334. London: Macmillan.

Müller, Hans-Heinrich (1979). "Die Entwicklung des Ackerbaus und der
Aufschwung der landwirtschaftlichen Nebenindustrie von 1800 bis 1870 (Die
Bedeutung des Kartoffel- und Zuckerübenanbaus)." Pp. 215-243. (See Lärmer
1979b above.)

Neuberger, Hugh, and Stokes, Houston H. (1974). "German Banks and German
Growth, 1882-1913: An Empirical View." <u>Journal of Economic History</u> 23
(September): 710-731.

Parker, William N. (1954). "Entrepreneurial Opportunities and Response in
the German Economy." <u>Explorations in Entrepreneurial History</u> 7
(October): 26-36.

Pollock, James Kerr (1938). <u>The Government of Greater Germany</u>. Princeton:
D. Van Nostrand.

Rassow, Peter, ed. (1953). <u>Deutsche Geschichte im Überblick: Ein Handbuch</u>.
Stuttgart: J. B. Metzlersche Verlagsbuchhandlung.

Rolfes, Max (1976). "Landwirtschaft, 1850-1914." Pp. 495-526. (See Zorn
1976 below.)

Rostow, Walt Whitman, ed. (1963). <u>The Economics of Take-off into Sustained
Growth</u>. London: Macmillan.

Saalfeld, Diedrich (1974). "Lebensstandard in Deutschland, 1750-1860, Einkommensverhältnisse und Lebenshaltungs-kosten städtischer Populationen in der Übergangsperiode zum Industriezeitalter." Pp. 417-443. (See Bog et al. 1974 above.)

_____ (1984). "Lebensverhältnisse der Unterschichten Deutschlands im neunzehnten Jahrhundert." International Review of Social History 29, 2:215-253.

Spree, Reinhard (1977). Die Wachstumszyklen der deutschen Wirtschaft von 1840 bis 1880. Berlin: Duncker & Humblot.

Stolper, Gustav; Hauser, Karl; and Borchardt, Knut (1967). The German Economy, 1870 to the Present. Translated by Toni Stolper. New York: Harcourt, Brace and World. Originally published in 1940 under the title German Economy, 1870-1940: Issues and Trends.

Teuteberg, Hans J. (1976). "Die Nahrung der sozialen Unterschichten im spät 19. Jahrhundert." In Studien zur Medizingeschichte im neunzehnten Jahrhundert, vol. 6, Ernährung und Ernährungslehre im 19. Jahrhundert, pp. 288-302. Göttingen: Vandenhoeck & Ruprecht.

Tilly, Richard H. (1966). "The Political Economy of Public Finance and the Industrialization of Prussia, 1815-1866." Journal of Economic History 26 (December): 484-497.

_____ (1967). "Germany, 1815-1870." In Banking in the Early Stages of Industrialization: A Study in Comparative Economic History, edited by Rondo E. Cameron et al., pp. 151-182. New York: Oxford University Press.

_____ (1969). "Soll und Haben: Recent German Economic History and the Problem of Economic Development." Journal of Economic History 29 (June): 298-319.

_____ (1976). "Verkehrs- und Nachrichtenwesen, Handel, Geld-, Kredit- und Versicherungswesen, 1850-1914." Pp. 563-596. (See Zorn 1976 below.)

_____ (1978). "Capital Formation in Germany in the Nineteenth Century." Pp. 382-491. (See Mathias and Postan 1978 above.)

_____ (1980). Kapital, Staat und sozialer Protest in der deutschen Industrialisierung: Gesammelte Aufsätze, vol. 41. Göttingen: Vandenhoeck & Ruprecht.

Tipton, Frank B., Jr. (1974). "Farm Labor and Power Politics: Germany, 1850-1914." Journal of Economic History 34 (December): 951-979.

Ullman, Richard K., and King-Hall, Stephen (1954). German Parliaments: A Study of the Development of Representative Institutions in Germany. London: Hansard Society.

Wehler, Hans-Ulrich (1975). Modernisierungstheorie und Geschichte. Göttingen: Vandenhoeck & Ruprecht.

Winkel, Harald (1974). "Zur Preisentwicklung landwirtschaftlicher Grundstücke in Niederbayern, 1830-1870." Pp. 565-577. (See Bog et al. 1974 above.)

Wiskemann, Elizabeth (1968). "Germany, Italy, and Eastern Europe." In The New Cambridge Modern History, vol. 12, The Shifting Balance of World Forces, 1898-1945, edited by Charles L. Mowat, pp. 473-511. Cambridge: Cambridge University Press.

Wünderlich, Frieda (1961). Farm Labor in Germany, 1810-1945: Its Historical Development within the Framework of Agricultural and Social Policy. Princeton: Princeton University Press.

Zorn, Wolfgang, ed. (1976). Handbuch der Deutschen Wirtschafts- und Sozialgeschichte. Vol. 2, Das 19. und 20. Jahrhundert. Stuttgart: Ernst Klett.

GREAT BRITAIN

Aldcroft, Derek Howard, ed. (1968). The Development of British Industry and Foreign Competition, 1875-1914: Studies in Industrial Enterprise. London: George Allen & Unwin.

Ashton, Thomas S. (1969). The Industrial Revolution, 1760-1830. Reprinted with revisions. London: Oxford University Press. Originally published in 1948.

Ashworth, William (1965). "Changes in the Industrial Structure, 1914." Yorkshire Bulletin of Economic and Social Research 17 (May): 61-74.

Baines, Dudley E. (1981). "The Labour Supply and the Labour Market, 1860-1914." Pp. 144-174. (See Floud and McCloskey 1981b below.)

Bowley, Arthur Lyon (1895). "Comparison of the Rates of Increase of Wages in the United States and Great Britain, 1860-1891." Economic Journal 5 (September): 369-383.

Caird, James (1967a). English Agriculture in 1850-51. 2d ed. New York: Augustus M. Kelley. Originally published in 1852.

_____ (1967b). The Landed Interest and the Supply of Food. 5th ed. New York: Augustus M. Kelley. Originally published in 1878.

Cairncross, Alexander Kirkland (1953). Home and Foreign Investment, 1870-1913: Studies in Capital Accumulation. Cambridge: Cambridge University Press.

_____ (1958). "The English Capital Market before 1914." Economica, n.s. 25 (May): 142-146.

Chambers, Jonathan David, and Mingay, G. E. (1966). The Agricultural Revolution, 1750-1880. London: B. T. Batsford.

Checkland, Sydney George (1959). "Growth and Progress.: The Nineteenth-Century View in Britain." Economic History Review, 2d ser. 12 (August): 49-62.

_____ (1964). The Rise of Industrial Society in England, 1815-1885. London: Longmans, Green.

Clapham, John Harold (1930). An Economic History of Modern Britain. Vol. 1, The Early Railway Age, 1820-1850. 2d ed. Reprinted with corrections. Cambridge: Cambridge University Press. First edition published in 1926.

_____ (1932). An Economic History of Modern Britain. Vol. 2, Free Trade and Steel, 1850-1886. Cambridge: Cambridge University Press.

_____ (1938). An Economic History of Modern Britain. Vol. 3, Machines and National Rivalries (1887-1914) with an Epilogue (1914-1929). Cambridge: Cambridge University Press.

Collins, Edward John Thomas (1969). "Harvest Technology and Labour Supply in Britain, 1790-1870." Economic History Review, 2d ser. 22 (December): 453-473.

Crafts, N. F. R. (1977). "Industrial Revolution in England and France: Some Thoughts on the Question, 'Why Was England First?'" Economic History Review, 2d ser. 30 (August): 429-441.

Crouzet, François (1981). "The Social Background of Industrialists during the Industrial Revolution in Britain." Paper presented at a Columbia University economic history seminar, Fall 1981. Mimeographed.

_____, ed. (1972). Capital Formation in the Industrial Revolution. London: Methuen.

David, Paul A. (1970). "Labour Productivity in English Agriculture, 1850-1914: Some Quantitative Evidence on Regional Differences." Economic History Review, 2d ser. 23, no. 3: 504-514.

Deane, Phyllis (1965). The First Industrial Revolution. Cambridge: Cambridge University Press.

_____ (1968). "New Estimates of Gross National Product for the United Kingdom, 1830-1914." Review of Income and Wealth 14 (June): 95-112.

Deane, Phyllis, and Cole, W. A. (1967). British Economic Growth, 1688-1959: Trends and Structure. 2d ed. Cambridge: Cambridge University Press. Originally published in 1962.

Edelstein, Michael (1981). "Foreign Investment and Empire, 1860-1914." Pp. 70-98. (See Floud and McCloskey 1981b below.)

Ernle, Rowland Edmund Prothero (1936). English Farming, Past and Present. Edited by A. D. Hall. 5th ed. London: Longmans, Green.

Feinstein, Charles Hilliard (1972). <u>National Income, Expenditure, and Output of the United Kingdom, 1855-1965</u>. Studies in the National Income and Expenditure of the United Kingdom, no. 6. Cambridge: Cambridge University Press.

_____ (1981). "Capital Accumulation and the Industrial Revolution." Pp. 128-142. (See Floud and McCloskey 1981a below.)

Floud, Roderick (1981). "Britain, 1860-1914: A Survey." Pp. 1-26. (See Floud and McCloskey 1981b below.)

Floud, Roderick, and McCloskey, Donald N., eds. (1981a). <u>The Economic History of Britain since 1700</u>. Vol. 1, <u>1700-1860</u>. Cambridge: Cambridge University Press.

_____, eds. (1981b). <u>The Economic History of Britain since 1700</u>. Vol. 2, <u>1860 to the 1970s</u>. Cambridge: Cambridge University Press.

Ford, Alec George (1981). "The Trade Cycle in Britain, 1850-1914." Pp. 27-49. (See Floud and McCloskey 1981b above.)

Habakkuk, H. J. (1967). <u>American and British Technology in the Nineteenth Century: The Search for Labour-saving Inventions</u>. Cambridge: Cambridge University Press.

Habakkuk, H. J., and Deane, Phillis (1963). "The Take-off in Britain." In <u>The Economics of Take-off into Sustained Growth</u>, edited by Walt Whitman Rostow, pp. 63-82. Proceedings of a conference held by the International Economic Association. London: Macmillan.

Hall, A. Ross (1957). "A Note on the English Capital Market as a Source of Funds for Home Investment before 1914." <u>Economica</u>, n.s. 24 (February): 59-66.

Hartwell, R. Maxwell (1972). "The Consequences of the Industrial Revolution in England for the Poor." In Hartwell et al., <u>The Long Debate on Poverty: Eight Essays on Industrialization and "The Condition of England."</u> IEA Readings, no. 9. London: Institute of Economic Affairs.

_____, ed. (1967). <u>The Causes of the Industrial Revolution in England</u>. London: Methuen.

Hawke, G. R., and Higgins, J. P. P. (1981). "Transport and Social Overhead Capital." Pp. 227-252. (See Floud and McCloskey 1981a above.)

Hoffmann, Walther G. (1955). <u>British Industry, 1700-1950</u>. Translated by William O. Henderson and William Henry Chaloner. Oxford: Basil Blackwell.

Hueckel, Glenn R. (1981). "Agriculture during Industrialisation." Pp. 182-203. (See Floud and McCloskey 1981a above.)

Imlah, Albert Henry (1958). <u>Economic Elements in the Pax Britannica: Studies in British Foreign Trade in the Nineteenth Century</u>. Cambridge: Harvard University Press.

Jefferys, James B., and Walters, Dorothy (1955). "National Income and Expenditure of the United Kingdom, 1870-1952." In <u>Income and Wealth</u>, ser. 5, edited by Simon S. Kuznets, pp. 1-40. [Usually cataloged under International Association of Income and Wealth, Income and Wealth.] London: Bowes & Bowes.

Jones, Eric Lionel (1964). "The Agricultural Labour Market in England, 1793-1872." <u>Economic History Review</u>, 2d ser. 17 (December): 322-338.

Kindleberger, Charles Poor (1961). "Foreign Trade and Economic Growth: Lessons from Britain and France, 1850 to 1913." <u>Economic History Review</u>, 2d ser. 14 (December): 289-305.

_____ (1964). <u>Economic Growth in France and Britain, 1851-1950</u>. Cambridge: Harvard University Press.

Kitson Clark, G. (1962). <u>The Making of Victorian England</u>. London: Methuen.

Knaplund, Paul (1962). "Great Britain and the British Empire." In <u>The New Cambridge Modern History</u>, vol. 11, <u>Material Progress and World-wide Problems, 1870-1898</u>, edited by Francis H. Hinsley, pp. 383-410. Cambridge: Cambridge University Press.

Kuczynski, Jürgen (1936). <u>Labour Conditions in Western Europe, 1820 to 1935</u>. New York: International Publishers.

Kuczynski, Jürgen (1972a). <u>The British Empire, 1800-1944</u>. Vol. 1, pt. 2, of <u>A Short History of Labour Conditions under Industrial Capitalism in Great Britain and the Empire</u>. Reissue of 2d ed. New York: Barnes & Noble. Originally published in 1945.

_____ (1972b). <u>Great Britain, 1750-1944</u>. Vol. 1, pt. 1, of <u>A Short History of Labour Conditions under Industrial Capitalism in Great Britain and the Empire</u>. Reissue of 2d ed. New York: Barnes & Noble. Originally published in 1944.

Landes, David S. (1960). "The Structure of Enterprise in the Nineteenth Century." In <u>Histoire Contemporaine</u>, vol. 5 of International Committee of Historical Sciences [sometimes cataloged under International Congress of Social Sciences], <u>Rapports</u> (Proceedings of the Ninth International Congress of the Historical Sciences, Stockholm, August 21-28, 1960). Göteborg: Almqvist & Wiksell.

Lynd, Helen Merrell (1945). <u>England in the Eighteen-Eighties: Toward a Social Basis for Freedom</u>. London: Oxford University Press.

McCloskey, Donald N. (1981). "The Industrial Revolution, 1780-1860: A Survey." Pp. 103-127. (See Floud and McCloskey 1981a above.)

Mathias, Peter, and Postan, M. M., eds. (1978). <u>The Cambridge Economic History of Europe</u>. Vol. 7, <u>The Industrial Economies: Capital, Labour, and Enterprise</u>. Pt. 1, "Britain, France, Germany, and Scandinavia." Cambridge: Cambridge University Press.

Mitchell, Brian R., and Deane, Phyllis (1971). <u>Abstract of British Historical Statistics</u>. Cambridge: Cambridge University Press.

O'Brien, Patrick Karl, and Engerman, Stanley Lewis (1981). "Changes in Income and Its Distribution during the Industrial Revolution." pp. 164-181. (See Floud and McCloskey 1981a above.)

O'Grada, Carmal (1981). "Agricultural Decline, 1850-1914." Pp. 175-198. (See Floud and McCloskey 1981b above.)

Orwin, Christabel Susan, and Whetham, Edith Hall (1964). History of British Agriculture, 1846-1914. Hamden, Conn.: Archon Books.

Paish, George (1911). "Great Britain's Capital Investments in Individual Colonial and Foreign Countries." Journal of the Royal Statistical Society 74, pt. 2 (January): 167-187.

Payne, Peter L. (1978). "Industrial Entrepreneurship and Management in Great Britain." Pp. 180-230. (See Mathias and Postan 1978 above.)

Platt, Desmond Christopher St. Martin (1980). "British Portfolio Investment Overseas before 1870: Some Doubts." Economic History Review, 2d ser. 33 (February): 1-16.

Pollard, Sidney (1978). "Labour in Great Britain." Pp. 97-179. (See Mathias and Postan 1978 above.)

Redford, Arthur (1964). Labour Migration in England, 1800-1850. Edited and revised by William Henry Chaloner. 2nd ed. Manchester: Manchester University Press.

Richardson, H. W. (1965). "Retardation in Britain's Industrial Growth, 1870-1913." Scottish Journal of Political Economy 12 (June): 125-149.

Rose, Michael Edward (1981). "Social Change and the Industrial Revolution." Pp. 253-275. (See Floud and McCloskey 1981a above.)

Saul, S. B. (1960). Studies in British Overseas Trade, 1870-1914. Liverpool: Liverpool University Press.

Sheppard, David K. (1971). The Growth and Role of U.K. Financial Institutions, 1880-1967. London: Methuen.

Taylor, Arthur John, ed. (1975). The Standard of Living in Britain in the Industrial Revolution. London: Methuen.

Thane, Pat (1981). "Social History, 1860-1914." Pp. 198-238. (See Floud and McCloskey 1981b above.)

Thompson, Francis Michael L. (1957). "The Land Market in the Nineteenth Century." Oxford Economic Papers, n. s. 9 (October): 285-308.

Thomson, David (1964). "The United Kingdom and Its World-wide Interests." In The New Cambridge Modern History, vol. 10, The Zenith of European Power, 1830-1870, pp. 331-356, edited by John Patrick Tuer Bury. Cambridge: Cambridge University Press.

Tranter, N. L. (1981). "The Labour Supply, 1780-1860. Pp. 204-226. (See Floud and McCloskey 1981a above.)

Trevelyan, George Macaulay (1937). British History in the Nineteenth Century and After (1782-1919). 2d ed. London: Longmans, Green. Originally published in 1922 under the title British History in the Nineteenth Century (1782-1901).

Usher, Abbott Payson (1920). An Introduction to the Industrial History of England. Boston: Houghton Mifflin.

Von Tunzelmann, George Nicholas (1981). "Technical Progress during the Industrial Revolution." Pp. 143-163. (See Floud and McCloskey 1981a above.)

Williamson, Jeffrey G. (1982). " 'Trickle-Down' during the First Industrial Revolution." Paper presented to "C" Session ("Causes of Poverty in the Nineteenth Century") at the Eighth International Economic History Congress. Budapest, August 16-20. Mimeographed.

Wilson, Charles (1965). "Economy and Society in Late Victorian Britain." Economic History Review, 2d ser. 18 (August): 225-474.

INDIA

Agarwal, Amar Nath [Agrawal, and/or Agarwala, Amar Narain] (1975). Indian Economy: Nature, Problems, and Progress. Delhi: Vikas.

Allan, John; Haig, T. Wolseley; and Dodwell, Henry Herbert (1964). The Cambridge Shorter History of India. Edited by Henry Herbert Dodwell. New Delhi: S. Chand.

Allen, George Cyril (1965). "The Industrialization of the Far East." In The Cambridge Economic History of Europe, vol. 6, pt. 2, The Industrial Revolution and After: Income, Population, and Technological Change, edited by H. J. Habakkuk and M. M. Postan, pp. 875-923. Cambridge: Cambridge University Press.

Andrews, Charles Freer, and Mookerjee, Girija K. (1967). The Rise and Growth of Congress in India, 1832-1920. 2d ed. Meerut, India: Meenekshi Prakashan.

Bagchi, Amiya Kumar (1976). "De-Industrialization in India in the Nineteenth Century: Some Theoretical Implications." Journal of Development Studies 12 (January): 135-164.

Bhatia, B. M. (1964). "Disintegration of Village Communities in India." Pp. 88-101. (See Ganguli 1964 below.)

_____ (1965). "Agriculture and Co-operation." Pp. 119-161. (See Singh 1965 below.)

_____ (1967). Famines in India: A Study in Some Aspects of the Economic History of India (1860-1965). 2d ed. Bombay: Asia Publishing House.

Bhatt, V. V. (1963a). <u>Aspects of Economic Change and Policy in India,</u>
<u>1800-1960</u>. Bombay: Allied Publishers.

_____ (1963b). "A Century and a Half of Economic Stagnation in India."
<u>Economic Weekly</u> 15, nos. 28-30 (July): 229-236.

Bisht, R. S., and Namboodripad, M. P. N. (1965). "Iron and Steel
Industry." Pp. 201-222. (See Singh 1965 below.)

Blyn, George (1966). <u>Agricultural Trends in India, 1891-1947: Output,</u>
<u>Availability, and Productivity</u>. Philadelphia: University of Pennsylvania
Press.

Bose, Arun (1965). "Foreign Capital." Pp. 485-527. (See Singh 1965
below.)

Buchanan, Daniel Houston (1934). <u>The Development of Capitalistic Enterprise</u>
<u>in India</u>. New York: Macmillan.

Chakrabarti, Sudhindra Chandra; Kundu, Junja Bihari; and Patra, Madan Mohan
(1965). <u>Economic Development of India</u>. Calcutta: Nababharat.

Chandra, Bipan (1966). <u>The Rise and Growth of Economic Nationalism in</u>
<u>India: Economic Policies of Indian National Leadership, 1880-1905</u>. New
Delhi: People's Publishing House.

Chaudhuri, K. N. (1968). "India's International Economy in the Nineteenth
Century: An Historical Survey." <u>Modern Asian Studies</u> 2 (January): 31-50.

Chaudhuri, M. K., ed. (1969). <u>Trends of Socio-economic Change in India,</u>
<u>1871-1961: Proceedings of a Seminar</u>. Translated by the Indian Institute of
Advanced Study. Simla, India: Indian Institute of Advanced Study.

Das Gupta, Ajit (1972). "Study of the Historical Demography of India." In
<u>Population and Social Change</u>, edited by David V. Glass and Roger Revelle,
pp. 419-435. London: Edward Arnold.

Dasgupta, B. N. (1969). "Trends of Change in the Educational Structure and
Pattern." Pp. 368-386. (See Chaudhuri 1969 above.)

Davis, Kingsley (1951). <u>The Population of India and Pakistan</u>. Princeton:
Princeton University Press.

Dubey, Vinod (1965). "Railways." Pp. 327-347. (See Singh 1965 below.)

Dutt, R. C. (1950). <u>The Economic History of India</u>. 7th ed. London:
Routledge & Kegan Paul.

Fukazawa, Hachiro (1965). "Cotton Mill Industry." Pp. 223-259. (See Singh
1965 below.)

Gadgil, D. R. (1942). <u>The Industrial Evolution of India in Recent Times</u>.
4th ed. Calcutta: Geoffrey Cumberlege and Oxford University Press.

Ganguli, Birendranath N. (1946). <u>Reconstruction of India's Foreign Trade</u>.
London: Oxford University Press.

_____, ed. (1964). Readings in Indian Economic History: Proceedings of the First All-India Seminar on Indian Economic History, 1961. New York: Asia Publishing House.

Harnetty, Peter H. (1971). "Cotton Exports and Indian Agriculture, 1861-1870." Economic History Review, 2d ser. 24 (August): 414-429.

Khusro, A. M. (1965). "Land Reforms since Independence." Pp. 181-200. (See Singh 1965 below.)

Kuczynski, Jürgen (1965). "Condition of Workers (1880-1950)." Pp. 609-637. (See Singh 1965 below.)

Kumar, Dharma, and Desai, Meghnad, eds. (1982). The Cambridge Economic History of India. Vol. 2, c.1751-c.1970. Cambridge: Cambridge University Press.

Kuznets, Simon S.; Moore, Wilbert E.; and Spengler, Joseph J., eds. (1955). Economic Growth: Brazil, India, Japan. Durham, N.C.: Duke University Press.

Lamb, Helen B. (1955). "The 'State' and Economic Development in India. Pp. 464-495. (See Kuznets et al. 1955 above.)

Loveday, Alexander (1914). The History and Economics of Indian Famines. London: G. Bell & Sons.

Maddison, Angus (1970). "The Historical Origins of Indian Poverty." Banca Nazionale del Lavóro Quarterly Review 92 (March): 31-81.

Misra, Banket Bihari (1977). The Bureaucracy in India: An Historical Analysis of Development up to 1947. New York: Oxford University Press.

Morison, Theodore (1916). The Economic Transition in India. London: John Murray. Originally published in 1911.

Morris, Morris David (1963). "Towards a Reinterpretation of Nineteenth-Century Indian Economic History." Journal of Economic History 23 (December): 606-618.

_____ (1967). "Values as an Obstacle to Economic Growth in South Asia: An Historical Survey." Journal of Economic History 27 (December): 588-607.

Morris, Morris David, and Stein, Burton (1961). "The Economic History of India: A Bibliographic Essay." Journal of Economic History 21 (June): 179-207.

Mukerjee, M. (1969). "Long-term Changes in the National Income of India Since 1971." Pp. 742-752. (See Chaudhuri 1969 above.)

Mukerjee, Tapan (1972). "Theory of Economic Drain: Impact of British Rule on the Indian Economy, 1840-1900." In Economic Imperialism: A Book of Readings, edited by Kenneth E. Boulding and Tapan Mukerjee, pp. 195-213. Ann Arbor: University of Michigan Press.

Mukerji, K. (1965). "Levels of Living of Industrial Workers."
Pp. 638-660. (See Singh 1965 below.)

Mukerji, Karuna May (1972). "The Growth of the Land Market in India: A Long
Period Analysis." Arthaniti 15 (January and July): 1-16.

Mukerji, M. (1965). "National Income." Pp. 661-703. (See Singh 1965
below.)

Panandikar, S. G. (1965). "Banking." Pp. 414-443. (See Singh 1965 below.)

Pillai, Purushottoma Padmanabha (1925). Economic Conditions in India.
London: George Routledge & Sons.

Saini, Krishan G. (1969). "The Growth of the Indian Economy, 1860-1960."
Review of Income and Wealth 15 (September): 247-263.

Sanderson, Gorham D. (1951). India and British Imperialism. New York:
Bookman Associates.

Sarkar, Jadunath (1917). Economics of British India. 4th ed. Calcutta:
M. C. Sarkar & Sons. Originally published in 1909.

Sen, Sunil Kumar (1966). Studies in Economic Policy and Development of
India (1848-1926). Calcutta: Progressive Publishers.

Shrimali, P. D. (1965). "The Public Sector." Pp. 756-770. (See Singh 1965
below.)

Sidhanta, Ranjana (1965). "Education." Pp. 725-755. (See Singh 1965
below.)

Singh, V. B., ed. (1965). Economic History of India, 1857-1956. Bombay:
Allied Publishers.

Sinha, J. N. (1965). "Demographic Trends." Pp. 104-118. (See Singh 1965
above.)

Sovani, N. V. (1954). "British Impact on India before 1850-57." Cahiers
d'histoire mondiale 1 (April): 857-882.

Sundara Rajan, V. (1955). An Economic History of India, 1757-1947. Baroda,
India: East and West Book House.

Thorner, Daniel (1960). "'De-Industrialisation' in India, 1881-1931." In
Contributions [and] Communications, pp. 217-226. Proceedings of the First
International Conference of Economic History, Stockholm, 1960. Paris:
Mouton.

Thorner, Daniel, and Thorner, Alice (1961). Land and Labour in India.
Bombay: Asia Publishing House.

Varshney, Roshan Lal (1954). India's Foreign Trade during and after the
Second World War. Banaras, India: Kitab Mahal Allahabad.

_____ (1965). "Foreign Trade." Pp. 444-484. (See Singh 1965 above.)

ITALY

Acerbo, Giacomo (1961). "L'agricultura italiana dal 1861 ad oggi."
Pp. 108-169. (See L'economia italiana dal 1861 al 1961 below.)

Albrecht-Carrié, René (1950). Italy from Napoleon to Mussolini. New
York: Columbia University Press.

Cafagna, Luciano (1973). "Italy 1830-1914." In The Fontana Economic
History of Europe, vol. 4, pt. 1, The Emergence of Industrial Societies,
edited by Carlo M. Cipolla, pp. 279-328. London: Collins/Fontana Press.

Castronova, Valerio (1975). "La storia economica." In Storia d'Italia,
vol. 4, pt. 1, Dall'unità a oggi, pp. 5-506. Turin: Giulio Einaudi.

Clough, Shepard Bancroft (1964). The Economic History of Modern Italy. New
York: Columbia University Press.

Clough, Shepard Bancroft, and Livi, Carlo (1956). "Economic Growth in
Italy: An Analysis of the Uneven Development of North and South." Journal
of Economic History 16 (September): 334-349.

_____ (1963). "Economic Growth in Italy: An Analysis of the Uneven
Development of North and South." In The Experience of Economic Growth:
Case Studies in Economic History, edited by Barry E. Supple, pp. 354-366.
New York: Random House. Reprinted, with omissions, from Journal of
Economic History 16 (September 1956): 334-339.

Cohen, Jon S. (1972). "Italy, 1861-1914." In Banking and Economic
Development: Some Lessons of History, edited by Rondo E. Cameron, pp. 58-
90. New York: Oxford University Press.

Dore, R. P. (1969). "Agricultural Improvements in Japan, 1870-1900." In
Agrarian Change and Economic Development: The Historical Problems, edited by
Eric Lionel Jones and Stuart Joseph Woolf, pp. 95-122. London: Methuen.

Eckaus, Richard S. (1961). "The North-South Differential in Italian
Economic Development." Journal of Economic History 21 (September): 285-317.

L'economia italiana dal 1861 al 1961: Studi nel 1º centenario dell'unità
d'Italia (1961). Biblioteca della rivista "economia e storia," no. 6.
Milan: Dott. A. Giuffre.

Fenoaltea, Stefano (1968). "Public Policy and Italian Industrial Policy,
1861-1913." Ph.D. dissertation, Harvard University. Mimeographed.

_____ (1969). "Public Policy and Italian Industrial Development,
1861-1913." Journal of Economic History 29 (March): 176-179.

_____ (1981). "Railways and the Development of the Italian Economy to
1914." Paper presented at Duke University, Durham, N.C., in January.
Mimeographed.

Foerster, Robert Franz (1919). The Italian Emigration of Our Times. Cambridge: Harvard University Press.

_____ (1969). The Italian Emigration of Our Times. Reprint of 1919 and 1929 editions. New York: Arno Press and New York Times.

Fuà, Giorgio (1965). Notes on Italian Economic Growth, 1861-1964. Milan: Dott. A. Giuffre.

Gerschenkron, Alexander (1955). "Notes on the Rate of Industrial Growth in Italy, 1881-1913." Journal of Economic History 15 (December): 360-375. Reprinted in Economic Backwardness in Historical Perspective, by Alexander Gerschenkron (Cambridge: Harvard University Press, 1962).

Hearder, Harry, and Waley, Daniel Philip, eds. (1963). A Short History of Italy: From Classical Times to the Present Day. Cambridge: Cambridge University Press.

Istituto centrale di statistica [usually cataloged under Italy, Istituto . . . statistica] (1968). Sommario di statistiche storiche dell'Italia, 1861-1965. Rome.

Izzo, Luigi (1965). Storia delle relazioni commerciali tra l'Italia e la Francia dal 1860 al 1875. Naples: Edizioni Scientifiche Italiane.

King, Bolton, and Okey, Thomas (1909). Italy To-Day. New and enl. ed. London: J. Nisbet.

Luzzatto, G. (1969). "The Italian Economy in the First Decade after Unification." In Essays in European Ecoomic History, 1789-1914, edited by François Crouzet, William Henry Chaloner, and Walter M. Stern, pp. 203-225. New York: St. Martin's Press.

Mack Smith, Denis (1959). Italy: A Modern History. Ann Arbor: University of Michigan Press.

_____ (1964). "Italy." In The New Cambridge Modern History, vol. 10, The Zenith of European Power, 1830-1870, edited by John Patrick Tuer Bury, pp. 552-576. Cambridge: Cambridge University Press.

Mori, Giorgio (1975). "The Genesis of Italian Industrialization." Journal of European Economic History 4 (Spring): 79-94.

Neufeld, Maurice F. (1961). Italy: School for Awakening Countries. The Italian Labor Movement in Its Political, Social, and Economic Setting from 1800 to 1960. Ithaca: New York State School of Industrial and Labor Relations, Cornell Unversity.

Romano, Roberto (1982). "Some Thoughts on the Relationship between Rural Poverty, Worker's Poverty, and Industrialization: The Case of Lombardy in the Nineteenth Century." Paper presented to "C" Session ("Causes of Poverty in the Nineteenth Century") at the Eighth International Economic History Congress, Budapest, August 16-20. Mimeographed.

Salvadori, Massimo (1965). Italy. Englewood Cliffs, N.J.: Prentice-Hall.

Schmidt, Carl Theodore (1939). *The Corporate State in Action: Italy under Fascism*. New York: Oxford University Press.

Seton-Watson, Christopher (1967). *Italy from Liberalism to Fascism, 1870-1925*. London: Methuen.

Tagliacarne, Guglielmo (1961). "La bilancia internazionale dei pagamenti dell'Italia nel primo centenario dell'unità." Pp. 313-359. (See *L'economia Italiana dal 1861 al 1961* above.)

Tremelloni, Roberto (1961). "Gli ultimi cent'anni dell'industria italiana, 1861-1961." Pp. 187-230. (See *L'economia Italiana dal 1861 al 1961* above.)

Trevelyan, Janet Penrose W. (1956). *A Short History of the Italian People from the Barbarian Invasion to the Present Day*. 4th ed. rev. London: George Allen & Unwin.

Vannutelli, Cesare (1961). "Occupazione e salari dal 1861 al 1961." Pp. 560-596. (See *L'economia Italiana dal 1861 al 1961* above.)

Vaussard, Maurice (1950). *Histoire de l'Italie contemporaine, 1870-1946*. Paris: Hachette.

Wiskemann, Elizabeth (1968). "Germany, Italy, and Eastern Europe." In *The New Cambridge Modern History*, vol. 12, *The Shifting Balance of World Forces, 1898-1945*, edited by Charles L. Mowat, pp. 473-511. Cambridge: Cambridge University Press. 2d ed. of vol. 12, *The Era of Violence*, published in 1960 and edited by David Thomson.

Zangheri, R. (1969). "The Historical Relationship between Agricultural and Economic Development in Italy." In *Agrarian Change and Economic Development: The Historical Problems*, edited by Eric L. Jones and Stuart Joseph Woolf, pp. 23-39. London: Methuen.

JAPAN

Allen, George Cyril (1962). *A Short Economic History of Modern Japan, 1867-1937, with a Supplementary Chapter on Economic Recovery and Expansion, 1945-1960*. 2d ed. New York: Frederick A. Praeger.

_____ (1965). "The Industrialization of the Far East." In *The Cambridge Economic History of Europe*, vol. 6, pt. 2, *The Industrial Revolution and After: Income, Population, and Technological Change*, edited by H. J. Habakkuk and M. M. Postan, pp. 873-923. Cambridge: Cambridge University Press.

Allen, George Cyril, and Donnithorne, Audrey Gladys (1954). *Western Enterprise in Far Eastern Economic Development: China and Japan*. New York: Macmillan.

Bank of Japan. Statistics Department [Nihon Ginko. Tokeikyoku] (1966). *Hundred-Year Statistics of the Japanese Economy*. Tokyo: Statistics Department, Bank of Japan.

Beckmann, George M. (1962). The Modernization of China and Japan. New York: Harper & Row.

Black, Cyril Edwin; Jansen, Marius E.; Levine, Herbert S.; Levy, Marion J., Jr.; Rosovsky, Henry; Rozman, Gilbert; Smith, Henry D., II; and Starr, S. Frederick (1975). The Modernization of Japan and Russia: A Comparative Study. New York: Free Press.

Buchanan, Daniel Houston (1951). "Differential Economic Progress: Some Cases, Comparisons, and Contrasts: Japan versus 'Asia.'" American Economic Review 41 (May): 359-366.

Cameron, Meribeth Elliott; Mahoney, Thomas H. D.; and McReynolds, George E., eds. (1960). China, Japan, and the Powers: A History of the Modern Far East. New York: Ronald Press.

Crawcour, E. Sydney (1963). "The Japanese Economy on the Eve of Modernization." Journal of the Oriental Society of Australia 2 (June): 34-41.

_____ (1965). "The Tokugawa Heritage." Pp. 17-44. (See Lockwood 1965 below.)

Halliday, Jon (1975). A Political History of Japanese Capitalism. New York: Pantheon Books.

Hanley, Susan Bell, and Yamamura, Kozo (1971). "A Quiet Transformation in Tokugawa Economic History." Journal of Asian Studies 30 (February): 373-384.

_____ (1977). Economic and Demographic Change in Preindustrial Japan, 1600-1868. Princeton: Princeton University Press.

Harootunian, Harry D. (1970). Toward Restoration: The Growth of Political Consciousness in Tokugawa Japan. Publications of the Center for Japanese and Korean Studies. Berkeley and Los Angeles: University of California Press.

Hattori, Yukimasa (1904). The Foreign Commerce of Japan since the Restoration, 1869-1900. Johns Hopkins University Studies in Historical and Political Science, ser. 22, nos. 9-10. Baltimore: Johns Hopkins Press.

Hayami, Yujiro; Akino, Masakatsu; Shintani, Masahiko; and Yamada, Saburo (1975). A Century of Agricultural Growth in Japan: Its Relevance to Asian Development. Minneapolis: University of Minnesota Press.

Hirschmeier, Johannes (1964). The Origins of Entrepreneurship in Meiji Japan. Harvard East Asian Series, no. 17. Cambridge: Harvard University Press.

_____ (1965). "Shibusawa Eiichi: Industrial Pioneer." Pp. 209-247. (See Lockwood 1965 below.)

Honjo, Eijiro (1965). The Social and Economic History of Japan. New York: Russell & Russell. Originally published in 1935.

Tsuchiya, Takao (1977). _An Economic History of Japan_. Translated by Michitaro Shidehara. Philadelphia: Porcupine Press. Translated from the Japanese in _The Transactions of the Asiatic Society of Japan_, 2d ser. 15 (December 1937).

Tsuru, Shigeto (1963). "The Take-off in Japan, 1868-1900." In _The Economics of Take-off into Sustained Growth_, edited by Walt Whitman Rostow, pp. 139-150. London: Macmillan.

Tussing, Arlon (1966). "The Labor Force in Meiji Economic Growth: A Quantitative Study of the Yamanashi Prefecture." _Journal of Economic History_ 26 (March): 59-92.

Yamamura, Kozo (1973). "Toward a Reexamination of the Economic History of Tokugawa Japan, 1600-1867." _Journal of Economic History_ 33 (September): 509-546.

_____ (1978). "Entrepreneurship, Ownership, and Management in Japan." Pp. 215-264. (See Mathias and Postan 1978 above.)

Yamazawa, Ippei, and Yamamoto, Yuzo (1979). "Trade and Balance of Payments." Pp. 134-158. (See Ohkawa and Shinohara 1979 above.)

Yanaga, Chitoshi (1949). _Japan since Perry_. New York: McGraw-Hill.

NETHERLANDS

Albarda, Johan Willem (1943). "Constitutional and Political Aspects." Pp. 91-106. (See Landheer 1943b below.)

Baasch, Ernst (1927). _Holländische Wirtschaftsgeschichte_. Jena: Gustav Fischer.

Barnouw, Adriaan Jacob (1944). _The Making of Modern Holland: A Short History_. New York: W. W. Norton.

Blok, Petrus Johannes (1912). _History of the People of the Netherlands_. Pt. 5, _Eighteenth and Nineteenth Centuries_. Translated by Oscar A. Bierstadt. New York: G. P. Putnam's Sons.

Brugmans, Izaak J. (1961). _Paardenkracht en Mensenmacht: Sociaal-Economische Geschiedenis van Nederland, 1795-1940_. The Hague: Martinus Nijhoff.

_____ (1969). "Nederlands Overgang van onderontwikkeld Gebied tot Industrieland." _De Economist_ 117 (January-February): 73-85.

De Blocq van Kuffeler, Victor J. R. (1915). [Usually cataloged under Netherlands (Kingdom 1815-), Department van Landbouw, Nijverheid en Handel.] _Ports and Waterways_, vol. 12 of _A General View of the Netherlands_. 25 vols. (pamphlets). Leiden: E. Ydo.

De Jonge, Jan A. (1968). _De Industrialisatie in Nederland tussen 1850 en 1914_. Amsterdam: Scheltema & Holkema.

Horie, Yasuzō (1965). "Modern Entrepreneurship in Meiji Japan." Pp. 183-208. (See Lockwood 1965 below.)

Hyde, Francis Edwin (1973). _Far Eastern Trade, 1850-1914_. New York: Harper & Row, Barnes & Noble Import Division.

Ike, Nobutaka (1950). _The Beginnings of Political Democracy in Japan_. Baltimore: Johns Hopkins Press.

Ishii, Ryoichi (1937). _Population Pressure and Economic Life in Japan_. London: P. S. King & Son.

Kawaba, Kisaburo (1921). _The Press and Politics in Japan: A Study of the Relation between the Newspaper and the Political Development of Modern Japan_. Chicago: University of Chicago Press.

Kelley, Allen C., and Williamson, Jeffrey G. (1971). "Writing History Backwards: Meiji Japan Revisited." _Journal of Economic History_ 31 (December): 729-776.

_____ (1974). _Lessons from Japanese Development: An Analytical Economic History_. Chicago: University of Chicago Press.

Kikuchi, Masao, and Hayami, Yujiro (1978). "Agricultural Growth against a Land Resource Constraint: A Comparative History of Japan, Taiwan, Korea, and the Philippines." _Journal of Economic History_ 38 (December): 839-864.

Kuznets, Simon S.; Moore, Wilbert, E.; and Spengler, Joseph J., eds. (1955). _Economic Growth: Brazil, India, Japan_. Durham, N.C.: Duke University Press.

Landes, David S. (1965b). "Japan and Europe: Contrasts in Industrialization." Pp. 93-182. (See Lockwood 1965 below.)

Levine, Solomon B. (1965). "Labor Markets and Collective Bargaining in Japan." Pp. 633-667. (See Lockwood 1965 below.)

Lippit, Victor O. (1978). "Economic Development in Meiji Japan and Contemporary China: A Comparative Study." _Cambridge Journal of Economics_ 2 (March): 55-81.

Lockwood, William Wirt (1954). _The Economic Development of Japan: Growth and Structural Change, 1868-1938_. Princeton: Princeton University Press.

_____ (1968). _The Economic Development of Japan: Growth and Structural Change, 1868-1938_. Expanded ed. Princeton: Princeton University Press.

_____, ed. (1965). _The State and Economic Enterprise in Japan: Essays in the Political Economy of Growth_. Princeton: Princeton University Press.

McLaren, Walter Wallace (1916). _A Political History of Japan during the Meiji Era, 1867-1912_. London: George Allen & Unwin.

Marshall, Byron K. (1967). _Capitalism and Nationalism in Prewar Japan: The Ideology of the Business Elite, 1868-1941_. Stanford: Stanford University Press.

Mathias, Peter, and Postan, M. M., eds. (1978). The Cambridge Economic History of Europe. Vol. 7, The Industrial Economies: Capital, Labour, and Enterprise. Pt. 2, "The United States, Japan, and Russia." Cambridge: Cambridge University Press.

Minami, Ryoshin, and Ono, Akira (1979). "Wages." Pp. 229–340. (See Ohkawa and Shinohara 1979 below.)

Miyamoto, Mataji; Sakudo, Yotaro; and Yasuba, Yasukichi (1965). "Economic Development in Preindustrial Japan, 1859–1894." Journal of Economic History 25 (December): 541–565.

Nakamura, James I. (1965). "Growth of Japanese Agriculture, 1875–1920." Pp. 249–324. (See Lockwood 1965 above.)

——— (1966). Agricultural Production and the Economic Development of Japan, 1873–1922. Princeton: Princeton University Press.

——— (1981). "Human Capital Accumulation in Premodern Rural Japan." Journal of Economic History 41 (June): 263–281.

Norman, E. Herbert (1940). Japan's Emergence as a Modern State: Political and Economic Problems of the Meiji Period. New York: International Secretariat, Institute of Pacific Relations.

Ogura, Takekazu, ed. (1967). Agricultural Development in Modern Japan. Translated by the Japanese FAO Association. Rev. ed. Tokyo: Fuji. Originally published in 1963.

Ohkawa, Kazushi [Okawa, Kazushi] (1979). "Aggregate Growth and Product Allocation." Pp. 3–33. (See Ohkawa and Shinohara 1979 below.)

Ohkawa, Kazushi [Okawa, Kazushi], and Rosovsky, Henry (1960). "The Role of Agriculture in Modern Japanese Economic Development." Economic Development and Cultural Change 9, pt. 2 (October): 43–67.

——— (1965). "A Century of Japanese Economic Growth." Pp. 47–82. (See Lockwood 1965 above.)

——— (1973). Japanese Economic Growth: Trend Acceleration in the Twentieth Century. Stanford: Stanford University Press.

——— (1978). "Capital Formation in Japan." Pp. 134–165. (See Mathias and Postan 1978 above.)

Ohkawa, Kazushi [Okawa, Kazushi]; Shinohara, Miyohei; Umemura, Mataji; Ito, M.; and Noda, T. (1957). The Growth Rate of the Japanese Economy since 1878. Tokyo: Kinokuniya Bookstore.

Ohkawa, Kazushi [Okawa, Kazushi], and Shinohara, Miyohei, eds. (1979). Patterns of Japanese Economic Development: A Quantitative Appraisal. New Haven: Yale University Press.

Ohkawa, Kazushi [Okawa, Kazushi]; Shinohara, Mihohei; and Unemura, Mataji, eds. (1967). Estimates of Long-term Economic Statistics of Japan since 1868. Vol. 8, Prices. Tokyo: Toyo Keizai Shinposha.

Patrick, Hugh T. (1967). "Japan, 1868–1914." In Banking in the Early Stages of Industrialization: A Study in Comparative Economic History, edited by Rondo E. Cameron, Olga Crisp, Hugh T. Patrick, and Richard H. Tilly, pp. 239–289. New York: Oxford University Press.

Ranis, Gustav (1959). "The Financing of Japanese Economic Development." Economic History Review, 2d ser. 11 (April): 440–454.

Reubens, Edwin P. (1955). "Foreign Capital and Domestic Development in Japan." Pp. 179–228. (See Kuznets et al. 1955 above.)

Rosovsky, Henry (1961). Capital Formation in Japan, 1868–1940. New York: Free Press.

——— (1966). "Japan's Transition to Modern Economic Growth, 1868–1885." In Industrialization in Two Systems: Essays in Honor of Alexander Gerschenkron, edited by Henry Rosovsky, pp. 91–139. New York: John Wiley & Sons.

Rozman, Gilbert (1973). Urban Networks in Ch'ing China and Tokugawa Japan. Princeton: Princeton University Press.

Sawada, Shujiro (1965). "Innovation in Japanese Agriculture, 1880–1935." Pp. 325–351. (See Lockwood 1965 above.)

Scalapino, Robert A. (1953). Democracy and the Party Movement in Prewar Japan: The Failure of the First Attempt. Berkeley and Los Angeles: University of California Press.

Smith, Thomas C. (1959). The Agrarian Origins of Modern Japan. Stanford: Stanford University Press.

——— (1973). "Pre-Modern Economic Growth: Japan and the West." Past and Present, no. 60 (August): 127–160.

Sumiya, Mikio, and Taira, Koji, eds. (1979). An Outline of Japanese Economic History, 1603–1940: Major Works and Research Findings. Tokyo: University of Tokyo Press.

Taira, Koji (1978). "Factory Labour and the Industrial Revolution in Japan." Pp. 308–415. (See Mathias and Postan 1978 above.)

Takenaka, Yasukazu (1969). "Endogenous Formation and Development of Capitalism in Japan." Journal of Economic History 29 (March): 141–162.

Taniguchi, Kichihiko (1973). "Strukturwandlungen des Japanischen Aussenhandels im Laufe des Industrialisierungsprozesses." Weltwirtschaftliches Archiv 46 (July): 237–256.

De Meere, J. M. M. (1979). "Inkomensgroei en ongelijkheid te Amsterdam, 1870-1970." Tijdschrift voor sociale Geschiedenis 13 (March): 3-46.

De Vries, Jan (1978). "Barges and Capitalism: Passenger Transportation in the Dutch Economy, 1632-1839." A.A.G. Bijdragen 21: 33-398.

De Vries, Joh. (1977). "De Twintigste Eeuw." Pp. 261-308. (See Van Stuijvenberg 1977 below.)

Dhondt, Jan, and Bruwier, Marinette (1973). "The Low Countries, 1700-1914." In The Fontana Economic History of Europe, vol. 3, pt. 1, The Emergence of Industrial Societies, edited by Carlo M. Cipolla, pp. 329-366. London: Collins/Fontana Books.

Edmundson, George (1922). History of Holland. Cambridge: Cambridge University Press.

Griffiths, Richard T. (1979). Industrial Retardation in the Netherlands, 1830-1850. The Hague: Martinus Nijhoff.

Landheer, Bartholomew (1943a). "The Social Structure of the Netherlands." Pp. 176-188. (See Landheer 1943b below.)

_____ [Bartholomus], ed. (1943b). The Netherlands. Berkeley and Los Angeles: University of California Press.

Lourens, Marinus Michiel (1943). "Labor." Pp. 189-203. (See Landheer 1943b above.)

Lucas, Henry Stephen (1955). Netherlanders in America: Dutch Immigration to the United States and Canada, 1789-1950. Ann Arbor: University of Michigan Press.

Mokyr, Joel (1974). "The Industrial Revolution in the Low Countries in the First Half of the Nineteenth Century: A Comparative Case Study." Journal of Economic History 34 (June): 365-391.

_____ (1975). "Capital, Labor, and the Delay of the Industrial Revolution in the Netherlands." In Economisch- en sociaal-historisch Jaarboek, 38:280-299. The Hague: Martinus Nijhoff.

_____ (1976b). Industrialization in the Low Countries, 1795-1850. New Haven: Yale University Press.

Raalte, Ernst van (1959). The Parliament of the Kingdom of the Netherlands. London: Hansard Society for Parliamentary Government.

Swierenga, Robert Peter, and Stout, Harry S. (1976). "Socio-economic Patterns of Migration from the Netherlands in the Nineteenth Century." In Research in Economic History, edited by Paul Uselding, 1:298-333. Greenwich, Conn.: JAI Press.

Teijl, J. (1971). "Nationaal Inkomen van Nederland in de Periode 1850-1900." Economisch- en sociaal-historisch Jaarboek 34: 232-262. The Hague: Martinus Nijhoff.

Van Stuijvenberg, J. H., ed. (1977). De Economische Geschiedenis van Nederland. Groningen, Netherlands: Wolters-Noordhoff.

Van Tijn, Th. (1977). "De Periode 1814-1914." Pp. 218-260. (See Van Stuijvenberg 1977 above.)

Vlekke, Bernard H. M. (1945). Evolution of the Dutch Nation. New York: Roy.

NEW ZEALAND

Airey, W. T. G. (1947a). "New Zealand in Evolution, 1840-1880." Pp. 73-88. (See Belshaw 1947 below.)

_____ (1947b). "New Zealand in Evolution, 1880 to the Present." Pp. 89-105. (See Belshaw 1947 below.)

Belshaw, Horace, ed. (1947). New Zealand. Berkeley and Los Angeles: University of California Press.

Butlin, Sydney James (1961). Australia and New Zealand Bank: The Bank of Australasia and the Union Bank of Australia Limited, 1828-1951. London: Longmans, Green.

Campbell, R. J. (1976). "'The Black Eighties'--Unemployment in New Zealand in the 1880s." Australian Economic History Review 16 (March): 67-82.

Condliffe, John Bell (1930). New Zealand in the Making: A Survey of Economic and Social Development. Chicago: University of Chicago Press.

_____ (1959). New Zealand in the Making: A Survey of Economic and Social Development. 2d ed. rev. London: George Allen & Unwin. Originally published in 1936.

Condliffe, John Bell, and Airey, William Thomas G. (1953). A Short History of New Zealand. New rev. 7th ed. Christchurch: Whitcombe & Tombs.

Fitzpatrick, Brian (1949). The British Empire in Australia: An Economic History, 1834-1939. Rev. 2d ed. Carlton, Australia: Melbourne University Press.

Gould, J. D. (1976). "Pasture Formation and Improvement in New Zealand, 1871-1911. Australian Economic History Review 16 (March): 1-22.

Hamilton, W. M. (1947). "The Farming Industries." Pp. 137-163. (See Belshaw 1947 above.)

Hawke, G. R. (1978). "Long-term Trends in New Zealand Imports." Australian Economic History Review 18 (March): 1-28.

Lloyd Prichard, Muriel F. (1970). An Economic History of New Zealand to 1939. Auckland: Collins.

Merrill, Robert S. (1954). "Some Social and Cultural Influences on Economic Growth: The Case of the Maori." Journal of Economic History 14 (December): 401–408.

Miller, Harold Gladstone (1957). New Zealand. London: Hutchinson's University Library. Originally published in 1950.

Milne, Robert Stephen (1966). Political Parties in New Zealand. Oxford: Clarendon Press.

Pool, David Ian (1977). The Maori Population of New Zealand, 1769–1971. Auckland: Auckland University Press.

Rowe, James W., and Rowe, Margaret A. (1968). New Zealand. New York: Frederick A. Praeger.

Scholefield, Guy Hardy (1909). New Zealand in Evolution: Industrial, Economic, and Political. London: T. Fisher Unwin.

Simkin, Colin George F. (1951). The Instability of a Dependent Economy: Economic Fluctuations in New Zealand, 1840–1914. London: Oxford University Press.

Sinclair, Keith (1961). A History of New Zealand. London: Oxford University Press.

Sutch, William Ball (1969). Poverty and Progress in New Zealand: A Reassessment. Rev. ed. Wellington, New Zealand: A. H. & A. W. Reed.

Thomson, Arthur Saunders (1970). The Story of New Zealand: Past and Present--Savage and Civilized. New York: Frederick A. Praeger. Originally published in 1859.

NORWAY

Aukrust, Odd, and Bjerke, Juul (1959). "Real Capital and Economic Growth in Norway, 1900–56." In The Measurement of National Wealth, edited by Raymond W. Goldsmith and Christopher T. Saunders, pp. 80–118. Income and Wealth, ser. 8. [Sometimes cataloged under International Association for Research in Income and Wealth, Income and Wealth.] Chicago: Quadrangle Books.

Blegen, Theodore Christian (1931). Norwegian Migration to America, 1825–1860. 2 vols. Northfield, Minn.: Norwegian-American Historical Association.

Bull, Edvard (1960). "Industrialisation as a Factor in Economic Growth." In Contributions [and] Communications, pp. 261–271. Proceedings of the First International Conference of Economic History, Stockholm, 1960. Paris: Mouton.

Central Bureau of Statistics of Norway (1966). Trends in Norwegian Economy, 1865–1960. Oslo: Central Bureau of Statistics.

Derry, Thomas Kingston (1957). A Short History of Norway. London: George Allen & Unwin.

Drachmann, Povl (1915). <u>The Industrial Development and Commercial Policies of the Three Scandinavian Countries</u>. Edited by Harald Westergaard. Oxford: Clarendon Press.

Drake, Michael (1969). <u>Population and Society in Norway, 1735-1865</u>. Cambridge: Cambridge University Press.

Galenson, Walter (1949). <u>Labor in Norway</u>. Cambridge: Harvard University Press.

Gjerset, Knut (1915). <u>History of the Norwegian People</u>, vol. 2. New York: Macmillan.

Hildebrand, Karl-Gustav (1978). "Labour and Capital in the Scandinavian Countries in the Nineteenth and Twentieth Centuries." In <u>The Cambridge Economic History of Europe</u>, vol. 7, <u>The Industrial Economies: Capital, Labour, and Enterprise</u>, pt. 1, "Britain, France, Germany, and Scandinavia," edited by Peter Mathias and M. M. Postan, pp. 590-628. Cambridge: Cambridge University Press.

Hodne, Fritz (1973). "Growth in a Dual Economy: The Norwegian Experience, 1814-1914." <u>Economy and History</u> 16: 81-110.

_____ (1975). <u>An Economic History of Norway, 1815-1970</u>. Preliminary ed. Trondheim, Norway: Tapir.

Hovde, Brynjolf J. (1943). <u>The Scandinavian Countries, 1720-1865: The Rise of the Middle Classes</u>. 2 vols. Boston: Chapman & Grimes.

Johnsen, Oscar Albert (1939). <u>Norwegische Wirtschaftsgeschichte</u>. Jena: Gustav Fischer.

Jörberg, Lennart (1973). "The Nordic Countries, 1850-1914." In <u>The Fontana Economic History of Europe</u>, vol. 4, pt. 2, <u>The Emergence of Industrial Societies</u>, edited by Carlo M. Cipolla, pp. 375-481. London: Collins/Fontana Books.

Keilhau, Wilhelm C. (1944). <u>Norway in World History</u>. London: Macdonald.

Larsen, Karen (1948). <u>A History of Norway</u>. Princeton: Princeton University Press.

Lieberman, Sima (1970). <u>The Industrialization of Norway, 1800-1920</u>. Oslo: Universitetsforlaget.

Lindgren, Raymond E. (1959). <u>Norway-Sweden Union, Disunion, and Scandinavian Integration</u>. Princeton: Princeton University Press.

Østensjø, Reidar (1963). "The Spring Herring Fishing and the Industral Revolution in Western Norway in the Nineteenth Century." <u>Scandinavian Economic History Review</u> 11, no. 2: 135-155.

Semmingsen, Ingrid Gaustad (1940). "Norwegian Emigration to America during the Nineteenth Century." Translated by Einar Haugen. In Norwegian-American Studies and Records, vol. 11. Northfield, Minn.: Norwegian-American Historical Association.

_____ (1954). "The Dissolution of Estate Society in Norway." Scandinavian Economic History Review 2, no. 2: 166-203.

Soltow, Lee (1965). Toward Income Equality in Norway. Madison: University of Wisconsin Press.

Sörensen, Sigvart (1899). Norway. New York: Peter Fenelon Collier.

RUSSIA

Arnold, Arthur Z. (1937). Banks, Credit, and Money in Soviet Russia. New York: Columbia University Press.

Barkai, Haim (1973). "The Macro-economics of Tsarist Russia in the Industrialization Era: Monetary Developments, the Balance of Payments, and the Gold Standard." Journal of Economic History 33 (June): 339-371.

Black, Cyril Edwin; Jansen, Marius E.; Levine, Herbert S.; Levy, Marion J., Jr.; Rosovsky, Henry; Rozman, Gilbert; Smith, Henry D., II; and Starr, S. Frederick (1975). The Modernization of Japan and Russia: A Comparative Study. New York: Free Press.

Blackwell, William L. (1968). The Beginnings of Russian Industrialization, 1800-1860. Princeton: Princeton University Press.

Carson, George Barr, Jr. (1959). "The State and Economic Development: Russia, 1890-1939." In The State and Economic Growth: Papers, edited by Hugh G. J. Aitken, pp. 115-147. New York: Social Science Research Council.

Crisp, Olga (1967). "Russia, 1860-1914." In Banking in the Early Stages of Industrialization: A Study in Comparative History, edited by Rondo E. Cameron, Olga Crisp, Hugh T. Patrick, and Richard H. Tilly, pp. 183-238. New York: Oxford University Press.

_____ (1976). Studies in the Russian Economy before 1914. London: Macmillan.

_____ (1978). "Labour and Industrialization in Russia." Pp. 308-415. (See Mathias and Postan 1978 below.)

Dobb, Maurice (1948). Soviet Economic Development since 1917. New York: International Publishers.

Ellison, Herbert J. (1965). "Economic Modernization in Imperial Russia: Purposes and Achievements." Journal of Economic History 25 (December): 523-540.

Gerschenkron, Alexander (1963). "The Early Phases of Industrialization in Russia: Afterthoughts and Counterthoughts." In The Economics of Take-off Into Sustained Growth, edited by Walt Whitman Rostow, pp. 151-169. London: Macmillan.

_____ (1965). "Agrarian Policies and Industrialization: Russia, 1861-1917." (See Habakkuk and Postan 1965 below.)

_____ (1970). Europe in the Russian Mirror: Four Lectures in Economic History. Cambridge: Cambridge University Press.

Goldsmith, Raymond W. (1961). "The Economic Growth of Tsarist Russia, 1860-1913." Economic Development and Cultural Change 9 (April): 441-475.

Habakkuk, H. J., and Postan, M. M., eds. (1965). The Cambridge Economic History of Europe. Vol. 6, pt. 2, The Industrial Revolution and After: Incomes, Population, and Technological Change. Cambridge: Cambridge University Press.

Kahan, Arcadius (1967). "Government Policies and the Industrialization of Russia." Journal of Economic History 27 (December): 460-477.

_____ (1978). "Capital Formation during the Period of Early Industrialization in Russia, 1890-1913." Pp. 265-307. (See Mathias and Postan 1978 below.)

Karpovich, Michael (1960). Imperial Russia, 1801-1917. New York: Holt, Rinehart & Winston.

Kaser, M. C. (1978). "Russian Entrepreneurship." Pp. 416-493. (See Mathias and Postan 1978 below.)

Lyashchenko [Liashchenko], Peter I. (1949). History of the National Economy of Russia to the 1917 Revolution. Translated by L. M. Herman. New York: Macmillan.

McKay, John P. (1970). Pioneers for Profit: Foreign Entrepreneurship and Russian Industrialization, 1885-1913. Chicago: University of Chicago Press.

Mathias, Peter, and Postan, M. M., eds. (1978). The Cambridge Economic History of Europe. Vol. 7, The Industrial Economies: Capital, Labour, and Enterprise. Pt. 2, "The United States, Japan, and Russia." Cambridge: Cambridge University Press.

Mavor, James (1925). An Economic History of Russia. Vol. 2, Industry and Revolution. 2d ed. rev. and enl. London: J. M. Dent & Sons.

Owen, Thomas C. (1981). Capitalism and Politics in Russia: A Social History of the Moscow Merchants, 1885-1905. New York: Cambridge University Press.

Portal, Roger (1965). "The Industrialization of Russia." Pp. 801-872. (See Habakkuk and Postan 1965 above.)

Rimlinger, Gaston V. (1961). "The Expansion of the Labor Market in Capitalist Russia, 1861-1917." Journal of Economic History 21 (June): 208-15.

Rosovsky, Henry (1954). "The Serf Entrepreneur in Russia." Explorations in Entrepreneurial History 6 (May): 207-233.

Seton-Watson, Hugh (1952). The Decline of Imperial Russia, 1855-1914. New York: Frederick A. Praeger.

Stephenson, Graham (1969). Russia from 1812 to 1945: A History. New York: Frederick A. Praeger.

Tourguéneff, Nikolai I. [Turgenev, Nikolai Ivanovich] (1847). La Russie et les russes. Vol. 2, Tableau politique et social de la Russie. Paris: Imprimeurs-unis.

Tugan-Baranovsky, Mikhail I. (1970). The Russian Factory in the Nineteenth Century. Translated from the 3d Russian ed. by Arthur Levin and Clara S. Levin. Homewood, Ill.: Richard D. Irwin. Originally published in 1907.

Tuma, Elias H. (1965). Twenty-six Centuries of Agrarian Reform: A Comparative Analysis. Berkeley and Los Angeles: University of California Press.

Vernadsky, George (1954). A History of Russia. 4th ed. rev. New Haven: Yale University Press.

_____ (1961). A History of Russia. 5th ed., rev. New Haven: Yale University Press.

Volin, Lazar (1970). A Century of Russian Agriculture: From Alexander II to Krushchev. Russian Research Center Studies, no. 13. Cambridge: Harvard University Press.

Von Haxthausen, August (1847). Études de la situation intérieure, la Via Nationale et les institutions rurales de la Russie. Vol. 1. Hannover: Hahn. French ed. of Studien über die innern Zustände, das Volksleben und inbesondere die ländlichen Einrichtungen Russlands.

Walkin, Jacob (1962). The Rise of Democracy in Pre-Revolutionary Russia: Political and Social Institutions under the Last Three Czars. New York: Frederick A. Praeger.

SPAIN

Aracil, Rafael, and Bonafé, Marius Garcia, eds. (1976). Lecturas de historia económica de España. Vol. 1, Siglos XVIII y XIX. Barcelona: Oikos-tau.

Barceló y de la Mora, José Luis (1952). Historia económica de España. Madrid: Afrodisio Aguado.

Beck, Earl Ray (1979). A Time of Triumph and of Sorrow: Spanish Politics during the Reign of Alphonso XII, 1874-1885. Carbondale: Southern Illinois University Press.

Boyd, Carolyn P. (1979). <u>Praetorian Politics in Liberal Spain</u>. Chapel
Hill, N.C.: University of North Carolina Press.

Brenan, Gerald (1943). <u>The Spanish Labyrinth: An Account of the Social and
Political Background of the Civil War</u>. Cambridge: Cambridge University
Press.

Carr, Raymond (1966). <u>Spain, 1808-1939</u>. Oxford: Clarendon Press.

De Madariaga, Salvador (1930). <u>Spain</u>. London: Ernest Penn.

Gannes, Harry, and Repard, Theodore (1936). <u>Spain in Revolt</u>. New York:
Alfred A. Knopf.

Harrison, Joseph (1980). "Spanish Economic History: From the Restoration to
the Franco Regime." Essays in Bibliography and Criticism, no. 82. <u>Economic
History Review</u> 33 (May): 259-275.

Hennessy, Charles Alistair M. 91965). <u>Modern Spain</u>. Historical
Association, General Series, no. 59. London: Historical Association.

Higgin, George (1886). <u>Commercial and Industrial Spain</u>. London: Effingham
Wilson. Reprinted, with considerable additions, from <u>Fortnightly Review</u> 44,
n.s. 38 (September 1885): 356-369.

Livi-Bacci [Bacci], Massimo (1968). "Fertility and Population Growth in
Spain in the Eighteenth and Nineteenth Centuries." <u>Daedalus</u> 97 (Spring):
523-535.

Malefakis, Edward E. (1970). <u>Agrarian Reform and Peasant Revolution in
Spain: Origins of the Civil War</u>. New Haven: Yale University Press.

Manuel, Frank Edward (1938). <u>The Politics of Modern Spain</u>. New York:
McGraw-Hill.

Merin, Peter [Bihalji-Merin, Oto] (1938). <u>Spain between Death and Birth</u>.
Translated by Charles Fullman. New York: Dodge.

Nadal, Jordi (1973). "Spain, 1830-1914." In <u>The Fontana Economic History
of Europe</u>, vol. 4, pt. 2, <u>The Emergence of Industrial Societies</u>, edited by
Carlo M. Cipolla, pp. 532-627. London: Collins/Fontana Books.

_____ (1975). <u>El fracaso de la revolución industrial en España,
1814-1913</u>. Barcelona: Ariel.

Payne, Stanley G. (1973). <u>A History of Spain and Portugal</u>. 2 vols.
Madison: University of Wisconsin Press.

Ramos Oliveira, Antonio (1946). <u>Politics, Economics, and Men of Modern
Spain, 1808-1946</u>. Translated by Teener Hall. London: Colloncz.

Ringrose, David R. (1970). <u>Transportation and Economic Stagnation in Spain,
1750-1850</u>. Durham, N.C.: Duke University Press.

Smith, Rhea Marsh (1965). <u>Spain: A Modern History</u>. Ann Arbor: University of Michigan Press.

Témime, Émile; Broder, Albert; and Chastagnaret, Gérard (1979). <u>Histoire de l'Espagne contemporaine, de 1801 à nos jours</u>. Paris: Aubier Montaigne.

Tortella, Gabriel (1972). "Spain, 1829-1874." In <u>Banking and Economic Development: Some Lessons of History</u>, edited by Rondo E. Cameron, pp. 91-121. New York: Oxford University Press.

Trend, John Brande (1965). <u>The Origins of Modern Spain</u>. New York: Russell & Russell. Originally published in 1934.

Vicens Vives, Jaime, and Oller, Jorge Nadal (1969). <u>An Economic History of Spain</u>. Translated by Frances M. López-Morillas. 3d ed. Princeton: Princeton University Press.

Vilar, Pierre (1967). <u>Spain: A Brief History</u>. Translated by Brian Tate. Oxford: Pergamon Press.

SWEDEN

Andersson, Ingvar (1956). <u>A History of Sweden</u>. Translated by Carolyn Hannay. New York: Frederick A. Praeger.

Bagge, Gösta; Lundberg, Erik; and Svennilson, Ingvar (1933). <u>Wages in Sweden, 1860-1930</u>, vol 1. London: P. S. King & Son.

_____ (1935). <u>Wages in Sweden, 1860-1930</u>, vol. 2. London: P. S. King & Son.

Castles, Francis G. (1973). "Barrington Moore's Thesis and Swedish Political Development." <u>Government and Opposition</u> 8 (Summer): 313-331.

Dahmén, Erik (1970). <u>Entrepreneurial Activity and the Development of Swedish Industry, 1919-1939</u>. Translated by Axel Leijonhufvud. Homewood, Ill.: Richard D. Irwin.

Drachmann, Povl (1915). <u>The Industrial Development and Commercial Policies of the Three Scandinavian Countries</u>. Edited by Harald Westergaard. Oxford: Clarendon Press.

Fridlizius, Gunnar (1957). <u>Swedish Corn Export in the Free Trade Era: Patterns in the Oats Trade, 1850-1880</u>. Samhällsverenskap1ige Studier, no. 14, Institute of Economic History, Lund University. Lund: C. W. K. Gleerup.

_____ (1963). "Sweden's Exports, 1850-1960: A Study in Perspective." Translated by W. F. Salisbury. <u>Economy and History</u> 6: 3-100.

Gaunitz, Sven (1979). "Local History as a Means of Understanding Economic Development: A Study of the Timber Frontier in Northern Sweden during the Industrialization Period." <u>Economy and History</u> 22: 38-62.

Heckscher, Eli Filip (1932). "The Place of Sweden in Modern Economic History." Economic History Review 4 (October): 1-22.

_____ (1954). An Economic History of Sweden. Translated by Göran Ohlin. Harvard Economic Studies, vol. 95. Cambridge: Harvard University Press.

Hedin, Lars-Erik (1967). "Some Notes on the Financing of the Swedish Railroads, 1860-1914." Translated by W. F. Salisbury. Economy and History 10: 3-37.

Herlitz, Nils (1939). Sweden: A Modern Democracy on Ancient Foundations. Minneapolis: University of Minnesota Press.

Hildebrand, Karl-Gustaf (1960). "Sweden." In Contributions [and] Communications, pp. 273-285. Proceedings of the First International Conference of Economic History, Stockholm, 1960. Paris: Mouton.

Hinshaw, David (1949). Sweden: Champion of Peace. G. P. Putnam's Sons.

Holgersson, Bengt, and Nicander, Eric (1968). "The Railroads and the Economic Development in Sweden during the 1870s." Translated by W. F. Salisbury. Economy and History 11: 3-51.

Hovde, Brynjolf J. (1943). The Scandinavian Countries, 1720-1865: The Rise of the Middle Classes. 2 vols. Boston: Chapman & Grimes.

Janson, Florence Edith (1931). The Background of Swedish Immigration, 1840-1930. Social Service Monographs, no. 15. Chicago: University of Chicago Press.

Johansson, Østen (1967). The Gross Domestic Product of Sweden and Its Composition, 1861-1955. Stockholm: Almquist & Wiksell.

Jörberg, Lennart (1958). "Some Notes on Swedish Entrepreneurs in the 1870's." Explorations in Entrepreneurial History 10 (April): 128-133.

_____ (1961). Growth and Fluctuations of Swedish Industry, 1869-1912: Studies in the Process of Industrialisation. Stockholm: Almquist & Wiksell.

_____ (1965). "Structural Change and Economic Growth: Sweden in the Nineteenth Century." Economy and History 8: 3-46.

_____ (1969). "Structural Change and Economic Growth: Sweden in the Nineteenth Century." In Essays in European Economic History, 1789-1914, edited by François Crouzet, William Henry Chaloner, and Walter M. Stern, pp. 259-280. New York: St. Martin's Press. Reprinted from Economy and History 8 (1965): 3-46.

_____ (1972). "The Development of Real Wages for Agricultural Workers in Sweden during the Eighteenth and Nineteenth Centuries." Economy and History 15: 41-57.

_____ (1973). "The Nordic Countries, 1850–1914." Translated by Paul Britten Austin. In The Fontana Economic History of Europe, vol. 4, pt. 2, The Emergence of Industrial Societies, edited by Carlo M. Cipolla, pp. 375–487. London: Collins/Fontana Books.

Kuuse, Jan (1971). "Mechanisation, Commercialisation, and the Protectionist Movement in Swedish Agriculture, 1860–1910." Scandinavian Economic Review 19, no. 1: 23–44.

_____ (1977). "Foreign Trade and the Breakthrough of the Engineering Industry in Sweden, 1890–1920." Scandinavian Economic Review 25, no. 1: 1–36.

Lindahl, Olof [Olaf] (1956). Sveriges National Product, 1861–1951. Stockholm: Konjunkturinstitutit. [Also cataloged under Sweden, Konjunkturinstitutet, Meddalandem, ser. B, vol. 20.]

Lindgren, Raymond E. (1959). Norway–Sweden Union, Disunion, and Scandinavian Integration. Princeton: Princeton University Press.

Menzel, Ulrich (1980c). "Der Entwicklungsweg Schwedens (1800–1913). Ein Beitrag zum Konzept autozentrierter Entwicklung." Project: Untersuchung zur Grundlegung einer praxisorientierten Theorie autozentrierter Entwicklung. Forschungsbericht, no. 11. University of Bremen. Mimeographed.

Modig, Hans (1972). "The Backward Linkage Effect of Railroads on Swedish Industry, 1860–1914." Swedish Journal of Economics 74 (September): 356–369.

Montgomery, Gustaf Arthur (1939). The Rise of Modern Industry in Sweden. London: P. S. King & Sons.

Nilsson, Carl-Axel (1978). "'Foreign Trade and the Breakthrough of the Engineering Industry in Sweden': A Comment." Scandinavian Economic Review 26, no. 2: 156–163.

Oakley, Stewart (1966). The Story of Sweden. London: Faber & Faber.

Rustow, Dankwart A. (1955). The Politics of Compromise: A Study of Parties and Cabinet Government in Sweden. Princeton: Princeton University Press.

_____ (1971). "Sweden's Transition to Democracy: Some Notes toward a Genetic Theory." Scandinavian Political Studies 6: 9–26.

Sandberg, Lars (1978). "Banking and Economic Growth in Sweden before World War I." Journal of Economic History 38 (September): 650–680.

Schön, Lennart (1972). "Västernorrland in the Middle of the Nineteenth Century: A Study in the Transition from Small-scale to Capitalistic Production." Economy and History 15: 83–111.

Söderberg, Johan (1982). "Causes of Poverty in Sweden in the Nineteenth Century." Journal of European Economic History 11 (Spring): 369–402.

Söderland, Ernst F. (1960). "The Impact of the British Industrial
Revolution on the Swedish Iron Industry." In <u>Studies in the Industrial
Revolution</u>, edited by Leslie Sedden Pressnell, pp. 52-65. London: Athlone
Press.

_____ (1952). "Swedish Timber Exports, 1850-1900." In <u>Swedish Timber
Exports, 1850-1950: A History of the Swedish Timber Trade</u>, edited by
Söderland, pp. 3-190. Stockholm: Almqvist & Wiksell.

Svanstrom, Ragnar, and Palmstierna, Carl Fredrik (1934). <u>A Short History of
Sweden</u>. Translated by Joan Bulman. Oxford: Clarendon Press.

Thomas, Dorothy Swaine (1941). <u>Social and Economic Aspects of Swedish
Population Movements, 1750-1933</u>. New York: Macmillan.

Tilton, Timothy A. (1974). "The Social Origins of Liberal Democracy: The
Swedish Case." <u>American Political Science Review</u> 68, no. 2: 561-571.

Youngson, A. J. (1959). <u>Possibilities of Economic Progress</u>. Cambridge:
Cambridge University Press.

SWITZERLAND

Baumgartner, Jean-Pierre (1964). "Les transports." Pp. 195-234. (See
S.G.S.V. 1964 below.)

Bergier, Jean François (1968). <u>Problèmes de l'histoire économique de la
Suisse: Population, vie rurale, echanges et trafics</u>. Monographies
d'histoire suisse, vol. 2. Bern: Francke.

Biucchi, Basilio Mario (1973). "Switzerland, 1700-1914." In <u>The Fontana
Economic History of Europe</u>, vol. 4, pt. 2, <u>The Emergence of Industrial
Societies</u>, edited by Carlo M. Cipolla, pp. 628-655. London: Collins/Fontana
Books.

Böhi, Hans (1964). "Hauptzüge einer schweizerischen Konjunkturgeschichte."
Pp. 71-105. (See S.G.S.V. 1964 below.)

Bonjour, Edgar; Offler, Hilary S.; and Potter, G. R. (1952). <u>A Short
History of Switzerland</u>. Oxford: Clarendon Press.

Bosshardt, Alfred, and Nydegger, Alfred (1964). "Die schweizerische
Aussenwirtschaft im Wandel der Zeiten." Pp. 302-327. (See S.G.S.V. 1964
below.)

Braun, Rudolf (1967). "The Rise of a Rural Class of Industrial
Entrepreneurs." Translated by Ann Keep. <u>Cahiers d'histoire mondiale</u> 10,
no. 3: 551-566.

Brooks, Robert Clarkson (1918). <u>Government and Politics of Switzerland</u>.
Edited by David P. Barrows and Thomas H. Reed. Government Handbooks.
Yonkers-on-Hudson, N.Y.: World Book.

Bürgin, Alfred (1959). "The Growth of the Swiss National Economy." In The State and Economic Growth, edited by Hugh G. J. Aitken, pp. 213-236. Papers of a conference held on October 11-13, 1956, under the auspices of the Committee on Economic Growth. New York: Social Science Research Council.

Chuard, Ernest (1901). "L'Agriculture." Pp. 7-75. (See Seippel 1901 below.)

Crawford, Virginia Mary S. (1911). Switzerland To-Day: A Study in Social Progress. London: Sands.

Gasser, Christian (1962). "Die Bodenteuerung vom Standpunkt der Industrie." Schweizerische Zeitschrift für Volkswirtschaft und Statistik 98 (June): 121-143.

Gasser-Stäger, Wilhelm (1964). "Strukturwandlungen in der schweizerischen Landwirtschaft seit dem 19. Jahrhundert." Pp. 106-132. (See S.G.S.V. 1964 below.)

Georg, Alfred Paul Wilhelm (1901). "Voies de communications." Pp. 229-289. (See Seippel 1901 below.)

Gruner, Erich (1968). Die Arbeiter in der Schweiz in 19. Jahrhundert: Soziale Organisation Verhältnis zu Arbeitgeber und Staat. Bern: Francke.

Günther, Reinhold (1901). "La Vie et les moeurs dans la Suisse allemande." Pp. 459-484. (See Seippel 1901 below.)

Hauser, Albert (1961). Schweizerische Wirtschafts- und Sozialgeschichte: Von den Anfangen bis zur Gegenwart. Zurich: Eugen Rentsch.

Hauser, Albert (1974). "Zur Produktivität der schweizerischen Landwirtschaft im 19. Jahrhundert." In Wirtschaftliche und soziale Strukturen im saekularen Wandel. Festschrift für Wilhelm Abel zum 70. Geburtstag (1974), vol. 3, Wirtschaft und Gesellschaft in der Zeit der Industrialiserlung, edited by Ingomar Bog et al., pp. 508-616. Schriftenreihe für Ländliche Sozialfragen, no. 70. Hannover: M. & H. Schaper.

Hünold, Albert C. (1954). The Industrial Development of Switzerland. National Bank of Egypt Fiftieth Anniversary Commemoration Lectures. Cairo: National Bank of Egypt.

Kneschaurek, Francesco (1964). "Wandlungen der schweizerischen Industriestruktur seit 1800." Pp. 133-155. (See S.G.S.V. 1964 below.)

Landmann, Julius (1928). Die Agrarpolitik des schweizerischen Industriestaates. Jena: Gustav Fischer.

Lincke, Bruno (1911). Die schweizerische Maschinenindustrie und ihre Entwicklung in wirtschaftlicher Beziehung. Frauenfeld, Switzerland: Hube.

Martin, William (1926). Histoire de la Suisse: Essai sur la formation d'une confédération d'états. Paris: F. Payot.

Menzel, Ulrich (1979). "Der Entwicklungsweg der Schweiz (1780-1850). Ein Beitrag zum Konzept autozentrierter Entwicklung." Projekt: Untersuchung zur Grundlegung einer praxisorientierten Theorie autozentrierter Entwicklung. Forschungsbericht, no. 5. University of Bremen, October. Mimeographed.

Oechsli, Wilhelm (1922). History of Switzerland, 1499-1914. Translated by Eden and Cedar Paul. Cambridge Historical Series. Cambridge: Cambridge University Press.

Rappard, William E. (1914). La Révolution industrielle et les origines de la protection légale du travail en Suisse. Collection d'études économiques suisses. Bern: Staempfl.

_____ (1936). The Government of Switzerland. Government of Modern Europe Series. New York: D. Van Nostrand.

Ritzmann, Franz (1964). "Die Entwicklung des schweizerischen Geld- und Kreditsystems." Pp. 235-272. (See S.G.S.V. 1964 below.)

Schweizerische Gesellschaft für Statistik und Volkswirtschaft [S.G.S.V.] (1964). Ein Jahrhundert schweizerischer Wirtschaftsentwicklung, Festschrift zum hundertjährigen Bestehen der schweizerischen Gesellschaft für Statistik und Volkswirtschaft, 1864-1964. Reprinted, with the addition of a "Foreword" by Wilhelm Bickel, from the "100. Jahrgang" edition: "Ein Jahrhundert schweizerischer Wirtschaftsentwicklung." Schweizerische Zeitschrift für Volkswirtschaft und Statistik, nos. 1-2 (March-June). Pagination identical in both book and periodical.

Seippel, Paul, ed. (1901). La Suisse au dix-neuvième siècle, vol. 3. Lausanne: F. Payot.

Siegenthaler, Jürg (1964). "Am Lebensstandard schweizerischer Arbeiter im 19. Jahrhundert." Zeitschrift für schweizerische und Statistik Volkswirtschaft 101: 423-444.

Soloveytchik, George (1954). Switzerland in Perspective. London: Geoffrey Cumberlege and Oxford University Press.

Swiss Office for the Development of Trade [Schweizerische Zentrale für Handelsordnung] (1931). Economic and Industrial Switzerland. 2d ed. Lausanne: Swiss Office for the Development of Trade.

Von Greyerz, Hans (1977). "Der Bundesstaat seit 1848." In Handbuch der Schweizer Geschichte, 2:1019-1246. Zürich: Verlag Berichthaus.

Wartmann, H. (1901). "Industrie et Commerce." (See Seippel 1901 above.)

Wittmann, Walter (1963). Die Take-off Periode der schweizerischen Volkswirtschaft." Zeitschrift für die Gesamte Staatswissenschaft 119 (October): 592-615.

Zwingli, Ulrich, and Ducret, Edgar (1964). "Das Sozialprodukt als Wertmesser des langfristigen Wirtschaftswachstums: Das schweizerische Sozialprodukt 1910 und in früheren Jahren." Pp. 328-368. (See S.G.S.V. 1964 above.)

UNITED STATES

Andreano, Ralph Louis, ed. (1965). New Views on American Economic Development: A Selected Anthology of Recent Work. Cambridge: Schenkman Publishing Co.

Bidwell, Percy Wells, and Falconer, John Ironside (1925). History of Agriculture in the Northern United States, 1620-1860. Washington, D.C.: The Carnegie Institution of Washington.

Bowley, Arthur Lyon (1895). "Comparison of the Ratio of Increase of Wages in the United States and in Great Britain, 1860-1891." Economic Journal 5 (September): 369-383.

Brock, W. R. (1962). "The United States." In The New Cambridge Modern History, vol. 11, Material Progress and World-wide Problems, 1870-1898, edited by Francis H. Hinsley, pp. 487-515. Cambridge: Cambridge University Press.

Broude, Henry Walter (1959). "The Role of the State in American Economic Development, 1820-1890." In The State and Economic Growth, edited by Hugh G. J. Aitken, pp. 4-25. New York: Social Science Research Council.

Bruchey, Stuart Weems (1965). The Roots of American Economic Growth, 1607-1861: An Essay in Social Causation. New York: Harper & Row.

Carstensen, Vernon Rosco, ed. (1962). The Public Lands: Studies in the History of the Public Domain. Madison: University of Wisconsin Press.

Chandler, Alfred D. (1978). "The United States: Evolution of Enterprise." In The Cambridge Economic History of Europe, vol. 7, The Industrial Economies: Capital, Labour, and Enterprise, edited by Peter Mathias and M. M. Postan, pp. 70-133. Cambridge: Cambridge University Press.

Cochran, Thomas Childs, and Miller, William (1942). The Age of Enterprise: A Social History of Industrial America. New York: Macmillan.

Conference on Research in Income and Wealth (1960). Trends in the American Economy in the Nineteenth Century. Edited by William N. Parker. A report of the National Bureau of Economic Research, New York. Studies in Income and Wealth, vol. 24. Princeton: Princeton University Press.

_____ (1966). Output, Employment, and Productivity in the United States after 1800. Edited by Dorothy S. Brady. A report of the National Bureau of Economic Research, New York. Studies in Income and Wealth, vol. 30. New York: National Bureau of Economic Research.

Cox, LaWanda Fenleson (1948). "The American Agricultural Wage Earner, 1865-1900." Agricultural History 22 (April): 94-114.

Danhof, Clarence H. (1951). "Agriculture." Pp. 133-153. (See Williamson 1951 below.)

_____ (1969). <u>Change in Agriculture: The Northern United States,</u>
<u>1820-1870</u>. Cambridge: Harvard University Press.

David, Paul A. (1966). "The Mechanization of Reaping in the Antebellum
Midwest." In <u>Industrialization in Two Systems: Essays in Honor of Alexander</u>
<u>Gerschenkron by a Group of His Students</u>, edited by Henry Rosovsky, pp. 3-
39. New York: John Wiley & Sons.

Davis, Lance Edwin (1965). "The Investment Market, 1870-1914: The Evolution
of a National Market." <u>Journal of Economic History</u> 25 (September): 355-399
(including tables).

Davis, Lance Edwin; Hughes, Jonathan R. T.; and McDougall, Duncan
M. (1965). <u>American Economic History: The Development of a National</u>
<u>Economy</u>. Rev. ed. Homewood, Ill.: Richard D. Irwin.

Davis, Lance E.; Easterlin, Richard A.; Parker, William N.; Brady, Dorothy
S.; Fishlow, Albert; Gallman, Robert E.; Lebergott, Stanley; Lipsey, Robert
E.; North, Douglass C.; Rosenberg, Nathan; Smolensky, Eugene; and Temin,
Peter (1972). <u>American Economic Growth: An Economist's History of the</u>
<u>United States</u>. New York: Harper & Row.

Fisher, C. M. (1870). "Farm Land and Land-Laws of the United States." In
<u>Systems of Land Tenure in Various Countries</u>, edited by the Cobden Club, pp.
398-420. 2d ed. London: Macmillan.

Fishlow, Albert (1965a). <u>American Railroads and the Transformation of the</u>
<u>Ante-Bellum Economy</u>. Cambridge: Harvard University Press.

_____ (1966). "The American Common School Revival: Fact or Fancy?" In
<u>Industrialization in Two Systems: Essays in Honor of Alexander Gerschenkron</u>
<u>by a Group of His Students</u>, edited by Henry Rosovsky, pp. 40-67. New
York: John Wiley & Sons.

Fogel, Robert William, and Engerman, Stanley Lewis, eds. (1917). <u>The</u>
<u>Reinterpretation of American Economic History</u>. New York: Harper & Row.

Gallman, Robert E. (1960). "Commodity Output." Pp. 13-71. (See Conference
on Research in Income and Wealth 1960 above.)

_____ (1966). "Gross National Product in the United States, 1834-1909."
Pp. 3-76. (See Conference on Research in Income and Wealth 1966 above.)

Gray, Lewis Cecil (1973). <u>History of Agriculture in the Southern United</u>
<u>States to 1860</u>. 2 vols. Clifton, N.J.: Augustus M. Kelley. Originally
published in 1933.

Habakkuk, H. J. (1967). <u>American and British Technology in the Nineteenth</u>
<u>Century: The Search for Labour-saving Inventions</u>. Cambridge: Cambridge
University Press.

Hansen, Alvin H. (1925). "Factors Affecting the Trend of Real Wages."
<u>American Economic Review</u> 15 (March): 27-42.

Harris, Seymour Edwin, ed. (1961). American Economic History. New York: McGraw-Hill.

Healy, Kent T. (1951a). "American Transportation before the Civil War." Pp. 116-132. (See Williamson 1951 below.)

_____ (1951b). "Transportation." Pp. 366-387. (See Williamson 1951 below.)

Hession, Charles Henry, and Sardy, Hyman (1969). Ascent to Affluence: A History of American Economic Development. Boston: Allyn & Bacon.

Hughes, Jonathan R. T. (1977). The Governmental Habit: Economic Controls from Colonial Times to the Present. New York: Basic Books.

Hunter, Louis C. (1951). "The Heavy Industries." Pp. 474-494. (See Williamson 1951 below.)

Huthmacher, J. Joseph (1962). "Urban Liberalism and the Age of Reform." Mississippi Valley Historical Review 49 (September): 231-241.

Jones, Maldwyn Allen (1960). American Immigration. Chicago: University of Chicago Press.

Kolko, Gabriel (1963). The Triumph of Conservatism: A Reinterpretation of American History. New York: Free Press.

Kravis, Irving B. (1972). "The Role of Exports in Nineteenth Century United States Growth." Economic Development and Cultural Change 20 (April): 387-405.

Kuczynski, Jürgen (1946). The United States of America, 1789 to the Present Day. Vol. 2 of A Short History of Labour Conditions under Industrial Capitalism. 2d ed. London: Frederick Muller. Originally published in 1943.

Landes, William M., and Solmon, Lewis C. (1972). "Compusory Schooling Legislation: An Economic Analysis of Law and Social Change in the Nineteenth Century." Journal of Economic History 32 (March): 54-91.

Lebergott, Stanley (1960). "Wage Trends, 1800-1900." Pp. 449-498. (See Conference on Research in Income and Wealth 1960 above.)

_____ (1964). Manpower in Economic Growth: The American Record since 1800. New York: McGraw-Hill.

Lipsey, Robert E. (1972). "Foreign Trade." Pp. 548-581. (See Davis et al. 1972 above.)

Morison, Samuel Eliot (1965). The Oxford History of the American People. New York: Oxford University Press.

Myers, Margaret G. (1970). A Financial History of the United States. New York: Columbia University Press.

North, Douglass C. (1961). <u>The Economic Growth of the United States,</u> <u>1790-1860</u>. Englewood Cliffs, N.J.: Prentice-Hall.

_____ (1963). "Industrialization in the United States (1815-1860)." In <u>The Economics of Take-off into Sustained Growth</u>, edited by Walt Whitman Rostow, pp. 44-62. London: Macmillan.

_____ (1965). "Industrialization in the United States." In <u>The Cambridge</u> <u>Economic History of Europe</u>, vol. 6, pt. 2, <u>The Industrial Revolution and</u> <u>After: Incomes, Population, and Technological Change</u>, edited by H. J. Habakkuk and M. M. Postan, pp. 693-705. Cambridge: Cambridge University Press.

_____ (1966). <u>Growth and Welfare in the American Past</u>. Englewood Cliffs, N.J.: Prentice-Hall.

Perloff, Harvey S.; Dunn, Edgar S., Jr.; Lampard, Eric E.; and Muth, Richard F. (1960). <u>Regions, Resources, and Economic Growth</u>. Lincoln: University of Nebraska Press.

Peterson, Harold F. (1964). <u>Argentina and the United States, 1810-1960</u>. Albany: State University of New York.

Potter, D. M. (1964). "National and Sectional Forces in the United States." In <u>New Cambridge Modern History</u>, vol. 10, <u>The Zenith of European Power,</u> <u>1830-1870</u>, edited by John Patrick Tuer Bury, pp. 603-630. Cambridge: Cambridge University Press.

Potter, Jim (1960). "Atlantic Economy, 1815-1860: The U.S.A. and the Industrial Revolution in Britain." In <u>Studies in the Industrial Revolution</u>, edited by Leslie Sedden Pressnell, pp. 236-280. London: Athlone Press.

Rees, Albert, and Jacobs, Donald P. (1961). <u>Real Wages in Manufacturing,</u> <u>1890-1914</u>. National Bureau of Economic Research, General ser., no. 70. Princeton: Princeton University Press.

Rogin, Leo (1931). <u>The Introduction of Farm Machinery in Its Relation to</u> <u>the Productivity of Labor in the Agriculture of the United States during the</u> <u>Nineteenth Century</u>. University of California Publications in Economics, vol. 9. Berkeley and Los Angeles: University of California Press.

Rosenberg, Nathan (1971). <u>The Economics of Technological Change: Selected</u> <u>Readings</u>. Baltimore: Penguin Books.

Sawyer, John Edward (1952). "The Entrepreneur and the Social Order: France and the United States." In <u>Men in Business: Essays in the History of</u> <u>Entrepreneurship</u>, edited by William Miller, pp. 7-22. Cambridge: Harvard University Press.

_____ (1954). "The Social Basis of the American System of Manufacturing." <u>Journal of Economic History</u> 14 (December): 361-379.

Schmidt, Louis Bernard (1939). "Internal Commerce and the Development of National Economy before 1860." <u>Journal of Political Economy</u> 47 (December): 798–822.

Strassmann, Wolfgang Paul (1959). <u>Risk and Technological Innovation: American Manufacturing Methods during the Nineteenth Century</u>. Ithaca, N. Y.: Cornell University Press.

Sylla, Richard (1972). "The United States, 1863–1913." In <u>Banking and Economic Development: Some Lessons of History</u>, edited by Rondo E. Cameron, pp. 232–262. New York: Oxford University Press.

_____ (1974). <u>The American Capital Market, 1846–1914</u>. New York: Arno Press.

Taylor, George Rogers (1951). <u>The Transportation Revolution, 1815–1860</u>. Vol. 4 of <u>The Economic History of the United States</u>. New York: Rinehart.

Temin, Peter, ed. (1973). <u>New Economic History: Selected Readings</u>. Baltimore: Penguin Books.

Tryon, Rolla Milton (1966). <u>Household Manufactures in the United States, 1640–1860</u>. New York: Augustus M. Kelley. Originally published in 1917.

U. S. Department of Commerce. Bureau of the Census (1960). <u>Historical Statistics of the United States, Colonial Times to 1957: A Statistical Abstract Supplement</u>. Washington, D.C.: Government Printing Office.

_____ (1966). <u>Long-term Economic Growth, 1860–1965</u>. Washington, D.C.: Government Printing Office.

Ware, Norman (1964). <u>The Industrial Worker, 1840–1850</u>. Chicago: Quadrangle Paperbacks. Originally published in 1924.

Williamson, Harold Francis, ed. (1951). <u>The Growth of the American Economy</u>. 2d ed. Englewood Cliffs, N.J.: Prentice-Hall.

Williamson, Jeffrey G. (1964). <u>American Growth and the Balance of Payments, 1820–1913: A Study of the Long Swing</u>. Chapel Hill: University of North Carolina Press.

_____ (1974). <u>Late Nineteenth-Century American Development: A General Equilibrium History</u>. London: Cambridge University Press.

Williamson, Jeffrey G., and Lindert, Peter H. (1980). <u>American Inequality: A Macroeconomic History</u>. New York: Academic Press.

Wright, Gavin (1978). <u>The Political Economy of the Cotton South: Households, Markets, and Wealth in the Nineteenth Century</u>. New York: W. W. Norton.

Index

Adelman, Irma, 16, 35, 36, 49, 50n, 51, 57, 64, 66n, 67n, 74n, 79n, 104n, 110n, 114n, 181; on poverty and income distribution, 19, 21-22

Agricultural development: patterns of, 125-154; typology of, 133, 134-135

—statistical analyses of, 133-153; lagging agricultural output for domestic market, 141-144; measures of statistical fit, 146-150; overwhelmingly agricultural countries with little industrial development, 144-146; strong positive role of agriculture, 133, 136-138; strong role of agriculture in small countries undergoing radical transformation, 138-140

Agricultural variables, 45-46; level of development of techniques in agriculture, 226-227, 283-289; percentage of labor force in agriculture, 227-228, 297-317; rate of improvement in techniques in agriculture, 227, 290-296; relative abundance of agricultural resources, 228, 318-320

Ahluwalia, Montek, 22

Anderson, Eugene Newton, 46, 55, 56

Anderson, Pauline Safford R., 46, 55, 56

Anderson, Perry, 47, 49

Bagchi, Amiya Kumar, 20

Baldwin, Robert, 22, 23, 31

Baran, Paul Alexander, 17, 19, 31, 96n, 180

Barton, Allen H., 50n, 53

Bhatia, B. M., 180

Black, Cyril Edwin, 18, 46, 47; modernization model, 15, 16

Boserup, Ester, 44

Boserup, Mogens, 128

Brenner, Robert, 10, 11, 155n, 178

Brugmans, Izaak J., 48

Cairncross, Alexander Kirkland, 44, 45

Cameron, Rondo E., 47

Capitalism, 3, 63; classical theories of, 5-8; Gerschenkron on, 12-13; Marx on, 10-11; neoclassical theories of, 8-10; Polanyi

and Hughes on, 13-15; Schumpeter on, 12

Cardoso, Fernando Henrique, 19-20, 31

Chandler, Alfred D., 12

Change, paths of, 214-217; agricultural, 215-216; balanced-growth, 217; industrial, 215. *See also* Institutional change

Chaudhuri, K. N., 48, 180

Chenery, Hollis Burnley, 33, 96n

Cipolla, Carlo M., 47

Clapham, John Harold, 45

Clark, Colin, 193n

Classical development theory, 5-8; 218-219; Jones and Woolf's trade models, 7-8; Lewis's model of dualistic growth, 7

Clough, Shepard Bancroft, 47

Coatsworth, John H., 12

Coghlan, Timothy A., 46, 179

Cole, Charles Woolsey, 47

Colonialism, and poverty, 180-181

Country classifications: for agricultural development, 133-146; for course of poverty, 188-200; for foreign economic dependence, 159-167; for industrial expansion, 103-116; for market institutional growth, 78-87; for specific variables, 468-477

Davis, Lance E., 8

Deane, Phyllis, 96n

De Janvry, Alain, 9-10, 40; neomarxist model of dependency, 20-21, 31

Demographics, and poverty, 179

Demographic variables, 43-44; net immigration, 232-233, 380-390; rate of population growth, 232, 378-379; total population, 231-232, 367-377

Dependent growth, theories of, 19-20, 219-220; neomarxist, 20-21

Deutsch, Karl W., 47

Development optimists: classical, 5-8; neoclassical, 8-10, 218-219

Development pessimists, 19-22; Adelman and Morris on poverty and income distribution, 21-22; de Janvry's

Cynthia Taft Morris is Charles N. Clark
Professor of Economics at Smith College.
Irma Adelman holds the Thomas Forsyth
Hunt Chair at the University of California,
Berkeley, where she is professor of economics
and agricultural and resource economics.
Morris and Adelman are coauthors of
*Economic Growth and Social Equity in
Developing Countries* and *Society, Politics,
and Economic Development: A Quantitative
Approach.*

Designed by Chris L. Smith.
Composed by Action Comp Co. Inc. in
Times Roman text and display. Printed by
Edwards Brothers, Inc., on 50-lb. Glatfelter
offset, and bound in Joanna's Arrestox A
and stamped in silver.